Thriving in the Workplace
ALL-IN-ONE
FOR
DUMMIES®

by Marty Brounstein, Michael C. Donaldson,
Peter Economy, Allen Elkin, PhD, Sue Fox, Kevin
Johnson, Malcolm Kushner, Susan Manning,
Mark McCormack, Bob Nelson, PhD, Vivian
Scott, Dirk Zeller, and Zig Ziglar

D1314256

WILEY

Wiley Publishing, Inc.

Thriving in the Workplace All-in-One For Dummies®

Published by
Wiley Publishing, Inc.
111 River St.
Hoboken, NJ 07030-5774

www.wiley.com

WILEY

About the Authors

Marty Brounstein is the principal of The Practical Solutions Group, a training and consulting firm that specializes in management and organizational effectiveness. Marty is the author of numerous books, including *Handling the Difficult Employee: Solving Performance Problems; Coaching and Mentoring For Dummies; Managing Teams For Dummies;* and *Communicating Effectively For Dummies.*

Michael C. Donaldson, in his entertainment law practice, represents writers, directors, and producers. In addition to working on films by such industry icons as Oliver Stone, Davis Guggenheim, and Lawrence Bender, Michael serves as General Counsel to Film Independent and the Writers Guild Foundation. He was recently honored with the Amicus Award by The International Documentary Association — an honor bestowed on only two others before him: Steven Spielberg and John Hendricks, the founder of the Discovery Channel. His book *Clearance and Copyright* is used in over 50 film schools and has become the standard industry reference book.

Peter Economy is associate editor of *Leader to Leader*, the Apex award-winning magazine of the Leader to Leader Institute, and author of numerous books, including *Managing For Dummies, The SAIC Solution: How We Built an $8 Billion Employee-Owned Technology Company, The Management Bible, Home-Based Business For Dummies, Lessons from the Edge: Survival Skills for Starting and Growing a Company, Writing Fiction For Dummies,* and many others.

Allen Elkin, PhD, is the director of The Stress Management & Counseling Center in New York City and holds workshops and presentations for professional organizations and corporations, including the American Society of Contemporary Medicine and Surgery, the Drug Enforcement Agency, Morgan Stanley, IBM, PepsiCo, and the New York Stock Exchange.

Sue Fox provides etiquette products, educational material, group training, and private consultations to business professionals, celebrities, corporations, and educational institutions through her company, The Etiquette Survival Group. She has set up many Etiquette Survival consultants throughout the United States and internationally. She is a professional member of the International Association of Protocol Consultants (IAPC).

Kevin Johnson is the CEO of The Cutting Ed, Inc., a consulting company that specializes in helping clients envision education and training for the 21st century. He has more than 20 years' experience working in education and figuring out how to use technology to his advantage.

Malcolm Kushner, America's favorite humor consultant, is an internationally acclaimed expert on humor and communication and a professional speaker. Since 1982, he has trained thousands of managers, executives, and professionals how to gain a competitive edge with humor. His clients include IBM, Hewlett-Packard, AT&T, Chevron, Aetna, Motorola, and Bank of America. Co-creator of a humor exhibit featured at The Ronald Reagan Presidential Library, he also created the annual Cost of Laughing Index.

Susan Manning teaches online courses for the University of Wisconsin-Stout and the University of Illinois' Illinois Online Network in online learning, instructional design, technology tools, the synchronous classroom, and group work online. She has taught hundreds of faculty, including international faculty from Saudi Arabia, Denmark, Vietnam, and Russia. Susan can be heard regularly on The LearningTimes GreenRoom podcast (www.ltgreenroom.org).

Mark McCormack is the founder of International Management Group, a multi-million-dollar worldwide corporation that is a consultant to 50 Fortune 500 companies. His books include *What They Still Don't Teach You at Harvard Business School* and *The World of Professional Golf.*

Bob Nelson, PhD, is president of Nelson Motivation, Inc., a cofounder of Recognition Professionals International, and a multi-million-copy best-selling author of numerous business books including *1001 Ways to Reward Employees, Managing For Dummies,* and his most recent: *Keeping Up in a Down Economy.* For more information or interest in scheduling Dr. Nelson to present for your management group, conference, or association, visit his Web site at www. nelson-motivation.com or contact his company directly at 1-800-575-5521.

Vivian Scott, author of *Conflict Resolution at Work For Dummies,* is a Professional Certified Mediator with a private practice in Snohomish, Washington and a member of the Washington Mediation Association. She also mediates with her collaborating authors at the Dispute Resolution Center of Sno. & Island Counties helping to resolve a variety of disputes. She received the Silver Screen Award from the U.S. International Film and Video Festival for her role as developer and executive producer of the *America at Work* video series, which aired on the USA Network.

Dirk Zeller, CEO of Sales Champions and Real Estate Champions, is one of the world's most published authors on success, time management, sales, and productivity. As a speaker and lecturer he has presented before large audiences on five continents. His tools, systems, and strategies for success are used in more than 97 countries worldwide.

Zig Ziglar, chairman of The Zig Ziglar Corporation, is an internationally known authority on high-level performance. He is considered the icon for motivation and inspiration. A renowned speaker and lecturer, Zig addresses over 300,000 people annually at Get Motivated seminars across the United States. He is the author of 29 books, ten of which are bestsellers, including *See You at the Top, Over the Top,* and *Something to Smile About.*

Publisher's Acknowledgments

We're proud of this book; please send us your comments at http://dummies.custhelp.com. For other comments, please contact our Customer Care Department within the U.S. at 877-762-2974, outside the U.S. at 317-572-3993, or fax 317-572-4002.

Some of the people who helped bring this book to market include the following:

Acquisitions, Editorial, and Media Development

Compilation Editor: Tracy L. Barr

Project Editors: Alissa Schwipps, Sarah Faulkner

Acquisitions Editor: Tracy Boggier

Copy Editor: Caitlin Copple

Assistant Editor: Erin Calligan Mooney

Editorial Program Coordinator: Joe Niesen

Technical Editor: Shweta L. Khare

Editorial Managers: Jennifer Ehrlich, Christine Meloy Beck

Senior Editorial Assistant: David Lutton

Editorial Assistant: Jennette ElNaggar

Art Coordinator: Alicia B. South

Cover Photos: Nicholas Rigg

Cartoons: Rich Tennant (www.the5thwave.com)

Composition Services

Project Coordinator: Patrick Redmond

Layout and Graphics: Christin Swinford, Julie Trippetti

Illustrator: Pam Tanzey

Proofreaders: Laura Albert, Cynthia Fields, John Greenough

Indexer: BIM Indexing & Proofreading

Publishing and Editorial for Consumer Dummies

Diane Graves Steele, Vice President and Publisher, Consumer Dummies

Kristin Ferguson-Wagstaffe, Product Development Director, Consumer Dummies

Ensley Eikenburg, Associate Publisher, Travel

Kelly Regan, Editorial Director, Travel

Publishing for Technology Dummies

Andy Cummings, Vice President and Publisher, Dummies Technology/General User

Composition Services

Debbie Stailey, Director of Composition Services

Contents at a Glance

Table of Contents

Book IV: Get to the @#% Point! Communicating Effectively..................................... 269

Introduction

. . . .

*W*ith the cost of living rising and retirement savings dwindling, millions of older workers are re-entering the workforce, and younger workers are facing more competition than ever. When you consider the additional impact of globalization and the current economic environment on businesses, it's no wonder that workers of all ages are seeking hands-on information, tips, and advice to help them boost their value and increase their job security.

Surviving in today's workforce isn't just about the skills you have, the awards you've won, or the tasks you perform day in and day out. It's also about the qualities, habits, and capabilities you bring to the work environment. *Thriving in the Workplace All-in-One For Dummies* can help you take stock of the skills that make you important to your employer, and it offers strategies to help you use those skills to get ahead in your career and increase the success of your company.

In addition to those concerns, many employees find themselves having to stay at their current jobs, no matter how difficult or unpleasant their environment may be. Working in a toxic environment can damage not only your career but also your health. For those struggling in toxic work environments, *Thriving in the Workplace All-in-One For Dummies* can help you manage your stress, deal with difficult co-workers and employers, and make it through each day with energy and focus. ***Remember:*** Despite the popular saying about teaching old dogs new tricks, you can always make changes that ease your job — and, if you're a manager, the jobs of your employees.

About This Book

Thriving in the Workplace All-in-One For Dummies is the perfect book for employees everywhere. Whether you're new to your office or you're a grizzled veteran, you can find everything you need to know to be successful in today's ever-changing workplace.

The key is to shift perspectives and take a fresh look at what it takes to succeed in the modern workplace. Notice that we use the word *succeed*. While many books and articles focus on just how to hang on in today's marketplace, this book is devoted to sharing strategies and advice to help you thrive. In this book, you find information like

- How to set goals and see them through to fruition
- Ways you can become a key player on any team you're part of
- Why delegating tasks makes you an even more effective employee, and how to do so wisely
- Communication strategies you can use when the message you have to deliver (or hear) is a hard one
- Tactics for dealing effectively with difficult people in the workplace without looking like a heel yourself
- How to resolve conflict in a way that increases the likelihood that all involved can agree on and support the solution
- Stress-management exercises you can use to diffuse tension and make your day more manageable
- Advice on ways to pursue certification and online courses to earn a better performance review, raise, or promotion

The great thing about this book is that *you* decide where to start and what to read. It's a reference you can jump into and out of at will. Just head to the table of contents or the index to find the information you want.

Conventions Used in This Book

To help you navigate through this book, we set up a few conventions:

- *Italic* font is used for emphasis and to highlight new words or terms that are defined.
- **Boldfaced** text is used to indicate the action part of numbered steps.
- Monofont is used for Web addresses.

What You're Not to Read

This book is written so that you can find information easily and quickly understand what you find. And although you may, indeed, want to pore over every last word, this book is designed to make it easy for you to identify material that, although interesting and related to the topic at hand, isn't essential for you to know:

- **Text in sidebars:** Sidebars are the shaded boxes that appear here and there. They share personal stories and observations but aren't necessary reading.

✔ **Anything with a Technical Stuff icon:** This information is interesting, but you can thrive in your workplace without it.

✔ **Anything you don't want to read:** The modular format of this book ensures that every discussion is complete on its own, which means you can simply go to those topics that are of particular interest to you and overlook the rest.

Foolish Assumptions

Every book is written with a particular reader in mind, and this one is no different. Here are a few of the assumptions that have been made about you:

✔ You're currently employed and want strategies you can use right now to help you boost your value and increase your job security.

✔ You are overwhelmed with the amount of work you're expected to do and need information on how to use your time and resources more efficiently.

✔ You want to hone your communications skills at the workplace because you realize that how you say things is an important part of maintaining and building good business relationships.

✔ Your work environment has become, if not toxic, at least stressful, and you're looking for ways to navigate through the political minefields and manage difficult co-workers and bosses.

✔ You don't want to get burned out. If you're already burned out, you want to reclaim some sense of control on the job, as well as a sense of satisfaction.

How This Book Is Organized

Thriving in the Workplace All-in-One For Dummies is divided into seven minibooks, each covering a particular topic related to success on the job. Within each minibook are chapters devoted to that minibook's focus.

Book 1: Key Business Skills to Enhance Your Chance of Success

Most people don't stumble into success (at least not prolonged success). Successful people possess certain characteristics that prime them for achievement in the workforce: They know what kind of success they want, they set goals and are prepared to work diligently to achieve them, and in today's team-oriented workplace, they know how to promote the goals of their teams while standing out as important team members. A few people possess these skills naturally, but anyone can learn and apply them. The chapters in Book I are devoted to these fundamental topics.

Book II: Getting Organized and Managing Your Time: Smart Ways to Preempt Problems

Chances are, because of reductions in force (whether because of layoffs, outsourcing, or any of a variety of other things) or dwindling resources of money and time, you may find yourself with a plate fuller than any one person can comfortably handle. But handle it you must. What's a person with so much work and so little time to do? Get organized and make the most of the time you have.

Fortunately, you can employ a variety of concrete strategies to gain control of seemingly out-of-control situations: Book II provides the details, not only on prioritizing your tasks, managing your time, and getting yourself organized, but also on how to circumvent the biggest challenges you may face from others (in the form of interruptions) and from yourself (in the form of procrastination).

Book III: Taking Charge of What You Can

You may not be able to set your deadlines. You may not be able to get the resources you've asked for. You may not be able to influence who is on your team. But Book III gives you the scoop on things you can and should take charge of when doing so helps you achieve the goals set before you. And just what are these things?

- **Yourself:** Figure out how you can balance your work and personal life and how to make decisions you can live with.

- **Meetings you're in charge of:** Ineffective meetings are the bane of the business world. Don't be one of the (too many) people who run such meetings. Be one of the few people who can run an effective meeting.

- **Your work:** As counterintuitive as it may seem, being in charge of your work doesn't mean you have to do everything yourself. Delegating tasks is a key business skill that, when done wisely, enhances the value of all involved.

Book IV: Get to the @#% Point! Communicating Effectively

Wherever you are on your company's organization chart, your biggest challenges probably come from dealing with others. The quickest way to circumvent problems in this area is to become a skilled communicator, someone who knows how to listen closely and speak positively (even when what you have to say is difficult) in all your interactions, whether they're face-to-face, electronic, or in front of a large crowd. Book IV puts you on the path to being an effective communicator in any situation.

Book V: Can't We All Just Get Along? Navigating Tricky Workplace Relationships and Situations

Interacting with others presents challenges, and these challenges can be heightened in a work environment, where common goals can compete with personal goals, and deadlines can be tight and resources tighter. Book V tells you how to navigate successfully through workplace relationships and situations that require you to understand the role that office politics plays in how things get done, commit to being a positive force among your peers, and learn how to deal with conflict and ethical dilemmas without burning bridges in the process.

Book VI: Managing Stress in Stressful Times

People are experiencing more stress at work than ever before. Long hours made worse by long commutes. Heavier workloads. Impossible-to-please bosses and crushing deadlines. Toxic environments and possible layoffs. While you may not be able to fundamentally change the environment in which you work, you can employ several strategies — both physical and mental — to reduce the stress these situations cause. Book VI tells you how.

Book VII: Going Further to Get Ahead: Certifications and Courses to Enhance Your Value

Although getting more education is generally better for your career, it's more effective if you pursue each course and degree with specific career goals in mind. Book VII explains what options are available for you and how you can use coursework or certification to advance your goals.

Icons Used in This Book

The icons in this book help you find particular kinds of information that may be of use to you:

This icon indicates a suggestion or bit of advice — like how to save time, who to use as a resource, or how to overcome a pesky obstacle — that can help you with the task at hand.

This icon points out important information worth remembering.

This icon serves as your warning to alert you to actions or situations that can undermine your success or even put you in danger of losing your job.

This icon appears beside information that's interesting but not necessary to know.

Where to Go from Here

This book is organized so that you can go wherever you want to find complete information. Want to know how to protect your day from interruptions? Head to Book II, Chapter 4. If you have a presentation coming up and want guidance on how to make it even more effective, go to Book IV, Chapter 5. You can use the table of contents to find broad categories of information or the index to look up more specific subjects. Or just flip through the book and look for a topic that catches your eye. Wherever you go, you'll find info you can use in any work environment.

Book I

Key Business Skills to Enhance Your Chance of Success

The 5th Wave   By Rich Tennant

©RICHTENNANT

"...faster than a speeding bullet...more powerful than a locomotive...these are just a few of your positive attributes."

In this book . . .

Although some people stumble into good fortune, most members of the workforce have to work diligently to achieve it. While the other books in this tome deal with specific topics, this initial book outlines what's at the foundation of on-the-job success, such as displaying characteristics commonly associated with success, establishing and prioritizing goals, and working well in a team while still standing out for your individual accomplishments. These chapters put you on the right track toward thriving in any workplace.

Chapter 1

Recognizing the Hallmarks of Success

Success is made up of numerous characteristics, including conviction and commitment, hard work and persistence, personal character and passion for what you do, and integrity and discipline. A sense of humor helps, too.

You learn and acquire these hallmarks of success over time. No one begins life instantly knowing how to work hard, be disciplined, have a good sense of humor, be persistent, have integrity, and so on. To thrive at work, you need to understand not only what the characteristics of success are, but how to put together a plan to move toward that goal and why you should bother. This chapter explains how the qualities work together and how to put each one to work for you.

The qualities necessary to succeed in *any* area of life are similar in *all* areas of life. A successful businessperson, for example, is effective and hard working. He or she has to duplicate those qualities in marriage and in parenting to be successful in those roles as well. Conversely, a successful parent is patient and consistent — qualities that, when exhibited in the workplace, enhance success there. For that reason, this chapter takes a broader view of success than just what you have to do to get ahead at work.

Recognizing Success

You must achieve some degree of success in each area of life before you can experience the true satisfaction of genuine success. So just what is success?

Obviously, people define success in many different ways. Here are a few signs of success:

- Leaving work at the end of the day with a smile of satisfied contentment crossing your face, knowing that you did a good job and that those who interacted with you had a positive experience

- Looking forward to getting home and seeing the people you love; being mentally and emotionally free to share yourself with them and to be interested in them

- Sitting down to pay the bills and knowing that you have enough money to cover them, this month *and* next month, and knowing that you've taken measures to ensure the financial security of your family in the event of your demise

- Knowing where to turn when your problems overwhelm you

- Having interests or hobbies to call your own, finding joy and peace in things that you personally anticipate doing again and again

- Waking up in the morning and feeling good, knowing that you eat right and exercise regularly and that you do everything you can to ensure continued good health

- Turning out the lights, slipping under the covers, and thinking to yourself, "It just doesn't get much better than this!" before you fall into a deep, restful sleep

And here's what success is *not:*

- Calling home from work for the fourth time this week, apologizing because you're going to miss dinner with the family again

- Hurrying into the house and hiding behind closed doors or the television set because "After the day I've had, I need my space!"

- Having all the riches in the world and still trying to figure out how to have *more* of all the riches in the world

- Crossing your fingers and hoping everything turns out for the best without much effort on your part

- *All* work and no play

- Burning the candle at both ends and living on a diet of food that's delivered via drive-through windows

- Spending mental energy figuring out how to explain why your project isn't going to come in on time, why you have to miss your child's school play, or why you can't pay the bill in full as you promised

In other words, success is directly related to having a balanced life. If any one area is out of sync, all the areas of your life suffer. So to thrive at work, you need to thrive in the other areas of your life as well.

Committing to Success

Success begins with the *desire* to be successful and the *conviction* that you can be successful. Bolstered by this drive and determination, you can make plans to achieve success. But making plans isn't enough. You have to commit to them.

Suppose, for example, you want to give up smoking. Over and over again, you put down the cigarettes just to pick them back up. Until you make a firm decision that you *want* to quit, you won't be able to form a game plan on how to go about it and then set a date to lay down the cigarettes once and for all. When you're committed, however, you can devise a strategy for achieving your goal. Suzan and Julie, two women facing this dilemma, came up with different strategies for finally kicking the habit:

- Suzan sought the help of her physician. She received nicotine gum, a mild tranquilizer, and instructions to see the doctor once a week and call if she felt that she wanted to light up.

- Six weeks in advance of the date she had chosen, Julie started telling everyone she saw that she was quitting smoking. She then sent for literature and started a Nicotine Anonymous group that met once a week in her home. She wrapped silver duct tape around her last pack of cigarettes, wrote "God and I can do this" on the outside, and made a commitment that if she decided to have a cigarette, she *had* to get it out of *that* pack.

Both women were successful because first they were convinced that they needed to quit, then they developed the desire to quit, and, after a lot of trial and error, they made and committed to workable plans to quit. Their plans were as different as Suzan and Julie are, which makes another important point: Your goals have to be set by you, and you're the only one who can make a plan to reach them in a way that's both comfortable and natural for you. No one has ever quit smoking because his partner's, mother's, father's, doctor's, friend's, or child's goal was for him to quit.

Look at the hallmarks of success that both women had to employ to successfully give up the cigarette habit. In addition to committing to their plans, they displayed hard work, integrity, consistency, commitment, discipline, humor, and lots of persistence — both quit *several* times before they were successful.

Regardless of the kind of success you're seeking, the hallmarks of success are essential to attaining it. The following sections describe these hallmarks in more detail.

Hard work

Yes, hard work is necessary. Many people today are somewhat like the fellow who, when asked how long he had been working for his company, responded, "Ever since they threatened to fire me!" Unfortunately, too many people don't take their work seriously until their employment is endangered. The same may be true in your relationships with your mate and your children: Only when you get into trouble do you get serious about working to solve a problem.

Instead of waiting to be chastised for doing subpar work and neglecting your responsibilities, why not apply yourself and remove that feeling of dread or impending doom from the corners of your mind? Set yourself free by giving your best in every situation.

Integrity

Integrity is a hallmark of success that everyone can readily identify. People with integrity do the right thing. When you have integrity, you have nothing to fear because you have nothing to hide. In doing the right thing for the right reason — whether in your personal or business life — you experience no guilt and no fear. With those two albatrosses of fear and guilt removed from around your neck, you can travel farther and faster.

Integrity is transferable. The lessons you learn and use in your personal life transfer to your work, and vice versa. Your integrity influences the kind of person you are and determines the things you do, whether at home, on the job, or in social situations.

Character

Character, like integrity, is another key component of the success formula. You can have millions of dollars and not, by any stretch of the imagination, be considered successful. The reason is simple: You can make millions of dollars without having character. But without character and integrity, the other signs of success mean nothing.

Each of your actions is an indication of your character. When you buy a packaged basket of peaches, tomatoes, or apples, the marketing capability of the merchant is displayed at the top, where you see ripe, flawless fruits. The merchant's *character* is displayed in the product found at the bottom of the basket, hidden until you get it home. When the butcher shows a beautiful side of a steak or roast through clear plastic, but you get home and see that the other side is the one with all the fat and bone, you rightly feel that you have been taken — because you have. Unfortunately, the butcher just lost your trust and, many times, your business. Character really is a hallmark of success.

You can't inherit character, but you can learn it and then demonstrate it. Ultimately, the measure of your character isn't what you inherited from your ancestors, but what you leave to your children and descendants. Character on the job, with your significant other, and in the home is constantly on display, building good relationships. Conversely, lack of character destroys relationships and any chance for real success.

Persistence

Many roads and qualities lead to success, but sheer, dogged persistence is one hallmark that everyone can employ and use. The intriguing thing about persistence is that the longer you persist, the more focused you become on the objective you pursue. Persistence enables you, through various experiences and failures, to uncover talents and develop creativity that first astonishes you, then delights you, and finally brings you material rewards far beyond your initial expectations. If you quit when you encounter the first obstacle, you never develop that creativity or earn the ultimate reward for keeping a commitment and persisting until you reach your objective.

When you encounter intolerable conditions or impossible situations, the very act of persisting forces you to ask yourself these all-important questions:

- Am I missing something or overlooking the obvious?
- What other route can I take?
- Does my mentor have the answer?
- Can I accomplish this objective by taking shorter steps or working harder?
- Will it help me to set time aside for the specific purpose of thinking about this problem and this problem alone?
- Should I literally walk away from it and take a long, quiet walk? (A walk to clear your mind is a great way to approach overcoming obstacles.)
- Should I back away temporarily because, at this precise instant, the timing isn't right?

Asking these questions doesn't mean that you're abandoning your goal; you're simply planning and preparing to reach the objective in a different way. Everyone has worked through this process in one form or another. You work and work on solving a problem with no results. Then, in essence, you forget about it, only to have the solution suddenly pop out, clear as day. Actually, you didn't forget it. All the thought processes and experiences of your lifetime were quietly working in the back of your mind, until one day an event, a word, a thought, or a comment taken out of context suddenly fit directly into the plan and — bingo! — your answer appeared. Why? Because you persisted.

Consistency

Maintaining your character demands that you be consistent in your actions and that they back up your words. Nathaniel Hawthorne expressed well the need for consistency in character when he wrote in *The Scarlet Letter,* "No man, for any considerable period, can wear one face to himself, and another to the multitude, without finally getting bewildered as to which may be the true."

At best, inconsistency can lead others to think you're flighty; at worst, it can give the impression that you're deceitful or hypocritical. If you don't behave in a way that is consistent with the values you claim are important, how will others trust you? The fact is, they won't. That's why, even when doing so may be difficult (admitting to a co-worker that the info you promised is going to be delayed, for example, or tactfully offering an objection to a question-able statement or decision), acting according to your principles is better for you in the long run.

Self-discipline

Another hallmark of success is *self-discipline,* which means bringing your mind under control. Discipline is something you do *for* yourself or others, not something you do *to* yourself or others — that's *punishment.*

Think about that definition for a moment. Isn't it an appropriate guideline for success in business, as well as at home with your partner and kids? Discipline teaches children rules and acquaints them with the importance of following the instructions and leadership of their parents, which they will transfer to their managers or bosses in years to come. And in the workplace, until you know how to manage (that is, discipline) yourself, you can never successfully manage or lead others. In a nutshell, the way to prepare yourself for a profession and get ahead is through discipline.

Playing with passion

Any study of history or current events reveals a multitude of stories about average people whose accomplishments have been extraordinary. You can give passion the credit. Take for example Bill Bates, a special teams player for the Dallas Cowboys. Despite being a good player, Bates was considered too slow and too small to play in the NFL. He wasn't drafted but made the team as a free agent and for many years was an invaluable member of the Cowboys' secondary. He not only gave his all but also inspired the other players to do the same. He brought more than just his ability; he brought a commitment fueled with passion that made him infinitely more valuable.

The same approach to any job, profession, or other endeavor is the difference between survival and genuine success. Check the records: Whether in music, medicine, physics, science, academics, or athletics, the great ones have passion for what they're doing.

When you discipline yourself to do the things you need to do when you need to do them, the day will come when you can do the things you want to do when you want to do them.

Passion, even if you don't love what you do

Passionate people get things done. So how do you develop passion? Try following these steps:

1. **Analyze what you want in life and come up with a plan for reaching those goals.**

   Though passion can come on suddenly, it usually begins with a careful analysis of what you want in life. What is your direction? In short, what are your goals? After you clearly identify your goals (which Chapter 3 in Book I helps you with), develop a plan of action to reach those goals. When the plan makes sense, then and only then do you make the commitment to move ahead.

2. **Take steps toward your goals.**

   As your plans unfold, each step that you take toward your goals has a direct bearing on your excitement, enthusiasm, and confidence. As you enjoy little successes, your imagination (which includes a picture of your future that you paint in your mind) explodes, and passion enters the picture. And when your passion is full-blown, you're unlikely to abandon your objectives.

3. **Use your head to direct the passion that develops.**

   Effective passion is a directed emotion that boosts all your qualities to make a total you who's considerably greater than the sum of all those qualities. Some people identify passion as "heart," because passion can let you accomplish things that go beyond your physical and mental abilities. While your heart may be a dominant force, your head provides the direction, brings the passion into focus, and provides the imagination that makes it happen.

The right connections

Many people are doing a great deal of networking these days. You've no doubt heard people say, "You've got to have the right connections to get ahead," or that a person "had all the doors opened for him — no wonder he's making it big!" Although the right connections can open doors, what happens inside those doors is entirely up to you and your own persuasiveness and abilities.

When making the "right connections," don't limit yourself to the obvious, those who can open doors for you professionally. In fact, you should work hardest to make connections with people you can learn from: Look for people who lead lives of integrity and who know things that you may need to know to accomplish your objectives. While you can get valuable information any time from magazines, newspapers, and books, occasionally you should tap into the experience and wisdom of others.

You know what they say about getting lucky

To reiterate the point that luck is "what happens when preparation meets opportunity," consider these other observations about luck:

- Ralph Waldo Emerson: "Shallow men believe in luck; wise and strong men in cause and effect."

- Calvin Coolidge: "Those who trust to chance must abide by the results of chance."

- Goethe: "Woe to him who would ascribe something like reason to chance."

- Barbara Bush: "You don't just 'luck into' things. You build step by step, whether it's friendships or opportunities."

Book I

Key
Business
Skills to
Enhance
Your
Chance of
Success

A sense of humor

Because winning relationships are hallmarks of your success with your spouse, children, associates at work, and social acquaintances, having a sense of humor is critical. However, you want to be sure to use *nice* humor if you want to build friendly relationships with your peers. Don't use humor that makes anyone look bad.

Learning to take things in stride and choosing to be amused instead of choosing to get angry is to your advantage 100 percent of the time. If you can find the humor in otherwise distressing situations, you can enjoy life more fully and move past obstacles with relative ease.

Luck

Some people observe that the harder they work, the luckier they get. Others spell *luck* with a *p,* because they believe that *pluck* determines your luck. Either way, being at the right place at the right time is better than being the smartest person in town. However, most people appear at the right place at the right time not by luck but by design. They get what appears to be a big break, but in reality, they worked hard to get to where the big breaks come.

Bottom line: Success is determined more by effort than by luck. Consider a salesman who hits the jackpot with a big sale or a large number of sales that come in a flurry. While his colleagues may attribute his success to luck, what the salesman knows is that if he makes a certain number of calls day in and day out, he gets a certain percentage of appointments. Out of those appointments, he gets a certain number of presentations. Out of those presentations, he gets a certain number of sales. Although this formula doesn't play out exactly every day or week, by the end of the month, the salesman can tell just how much business he produced per call, per display, and per sale. His "luck" is actually the direct result of consistent, organized, enthusiastic effort.

Finding the Right Mental Attitude

Many people contend that attitude is everything when it comes to being successful. They believe that a positive attitude is the answer to all their challenges and problems. And attitude, while not the only determiner of success, *is* extremely important.

Positively successful

According to legend, Wilma Rudolph was repeatedly told by her childhood doctors that because of polio, she would never walk. However, her mother told her that she would. Fortunately for sports fans, Wilma chose to believe her mother, and therefore she maintained the right mental attitude. She won three gold medals in track and field events in the 1960 Olympics and set the world record for the women's 100-meter dash in 1961. Wilma Rudolph won the most important race of her life when she decided to compete with herself at each step. The message? Choose to stay optimistic. As Ralph Waldo Emerson said, "A believer...is never disturbed because other persons do not yet see the fact which he sees."

Attitude plays a part in virtually every phase of your life. Your attitude affects many people, from your family to the stranger you smile at on the street corner. It's particularly important in keeping you motivated when you face seemingly hopeless situations. And attitude is a big factor in how successful you are at work. A poor attitude, for example, can impede your progress at work, while a positive attitude can propel you forward.

The following sections explain the hallmarks of positive attitude. Try to cultivate these characteristics.

Choosing optimism over pessimism

You can find at least two ways to look at virtually everything. A pessimist looks for difficulty in the opportunity, whereas an optimist looks for opportunity in the difficulty. Unfortunately, many people look only at the problem and not at the opportunity that lies within the problem. Many employees complain about the difficulty of their jobs, for example, not realizing that if the job were simple, the employer would hire someone with less ability at a lower wage.

Pessimism muddies the water of opportunity. Any time a new innovation comes along promising to make life easier and people more productive, for example, someone always complains that the innovation will put people out of work. At the advent of the computer, folks initially believed that many people would lose their jobs because computers can do certain tasks much faster than humans can. Some people have had to retrain themselves to stay marketable, but almost everyone agrees that computers have created — not deleted — jobs and have improved our capabilities immeasurably. E-commerce, which wouldn't exist without computers, is a great example of how a new innovation has revolutionized the way the world does business. It literally removed boundaries and borders and created countless jobs, not to mention a whole new language.

You can't do anything to change the fact that a problem exists, but you can do a great deal to find the opportunity within that problem. You're guaranteed a better tomorrow by doing your best today and developing a plan of action for the future. Just remember to maintain a positive mental attitude so that as you plan for tomorrow, you're doing so with the sense of expectancy that produces substantially better results.

When you face a problem, take a step back. A small coin can hide even the sun if you hold the coin close enough to your eye. So when you get too close to your problems to think objectively about them, take a step back and look at the situation from a new angle. Look up instead of down.

A positive attitude doesn't guarantee success, but a pessimistic attitude guarantees failure. On the brighter side of life are the idealists — individuals who have the tendency to see the best solution or possibility in any situation. Sow those optimistic seeds, and you raise the optimist hidden inside you.

Regardless of what happens to you, something good can come out of it. Yes, attitude is important. With the right attitude, you may be able to do even more with your life after a tragedy than you would have if the tragedy had never occurred. Consider Christopher Reeve, who, despite suffering a paralyzing accident, gave hope and encouragement to literally millions of people, disabled and not. His optimistic, upbeat approach to life inspired people around the world. Or Michael J. Fox, who has used his diagnosis of Parkinson's disease as an opportunity to become a healthcare advocate. Or any number of people less famous who nonetheless are doing remarkable things in the face of personal tragedy or what look like impossible odds.

Book I

Key Business Skills to Enhance Your Chance of Success

Are you a cynic?

Here's a fun description of a *cynic:* someone who would demand a bacteria count on the milk of human kindness. Cynics still believe that somebody pushed Humpty Dumpty, and they'd vote against starting a Pessimist's Club because they don't believe that such a club can work.

Almost half of American workers fall into the cynic category. Cynics mistrust just about everything — government, big business, the products they purchase, their employers, supervisors, and colleagues. An additional portion of workers is classified as *wary,* with strong cynical leanings.

How many friends and how much peace of mind do cynics have? How well do they get along with their mates, children, and neighbors? Not many, not much, and not very well.

One cause of cynicism may be unrealistic expectations — expecting great things to happen to you with no effort on your part. Having high expectations for yourself is an important part of success, but you must also develop goals and plans to make those expectations a reality. (The next two chapters in this book tell you how.)

Having the happiness attitude

Everyone wants to be happy, yet many people base their happiness on having what they want instead of wanting what they have. Many people, for example, equate wealth with happiness and actually believe that if they win the lottery, they will be happy. Doing so puts your emotions on a roller coaster controlled by what happens in your life.

So what are the keys to happiness? Read on:

- ✔ **Being humble:** One key to happiness is humility. The reason is simple: Humility reduces stress. Humble people don't believe that they have to have all the answers; consequently, they don't have to fake having those answers, which reduces anxiety. When anxiety goes down, happiness goes up. Humility certainly improves your relationships — nobody likes a know-it-all. A humble approach enables you to be genuinely interested in and respectful of other people. And they, in turn, become genuinely interested in you. The number of your friends and positive acquaintances (those people who encourage you and build you up) grows, and your happiness increases.

- ✔ **Accepting the here and now:** Another key to happiness is your willingness to accept that happiness is a "here" and a "now" — you can't wait for it to come to you. If you decide to be happy, you probably will be. Will Rogers said it best: "Most people are about as happy as they make up their minds to be."

- ✔ **Helping others:** Certain activities increase your chances of being happy — for example, when you help someone else for purely altruistic reasons and have nothing to gain except delight in doing a good turn. Committing selfless acts is a major step toward real happiness.

  People who are only out for themselves miss out on the joy that comes from giving. People who do things for others with no personal gain in mind reap great benefits. For example, look at the glow on the faces of volunteers who serve holiday meals to the homeless. The smiling faces of the recipients of the meals are a beautiful sight, but infinitely more beautiful are the even broader smiles of those volunteers.

- ✔ **Looking at every day as a great day:** Each day is an important piece of your life, and your attitude concerning each day makes a difference. If you make today a good day and repeat that process daily, you'll live a lifetime of good days. This approach to life is simple, but it isn't simplistic. Expect today to be a good day, and then do what's necessary to make your expectations come true.

  Ralph Waldo Emerson wrote, "Write it on your heart that every day is the best day in the year. He or she is rich who owns the day and no one owns the day who allows it to be invaded with threat and anxiety. Finish every day and be done with it. You have done what you could. Some blunders and absurdities no doubt crept in. Forget them as soon as you can. Tomorrow is a new day. Begin it well and serenely with too high a spirit to be encumbered with your old nonsense. This new day is too dear, with its hopes and invitations, to waste a moment on the yesterdays."

Choosing success

In a lifetime, you make literally millions of choices. Most choices, after you make them a few times, become ingrained in you. You know from past experience what works for you, so you repeat the process. You only get into trouble when you *don't* get good results but keep doing the same things over and over again anyway. You may find it hard to believe, but many people operate that way.

You literally can opt to be happy or miserable by the choices you make. If you choose to be happy, you need to explore what *makes* you happy. Identify whether happiness is a sense of accomplishment when you earn an A in school, achieve a specific weight-loss goal, close a difficult sale, complete a mini-marathon, win over the sourpuss at the checkout counter, or whatever. Accomplishments make you feel good, and you're happy as a result. After you determine what makes you happy, choose to do those things.

Unhappy people generally are unhappy because they think that other people should be doing things *for* them. From time to time, people say to me, "I want to thank you for making me successful." But I can't accept credit for making anyone successful, nor do I accept responsibility for causing anyone to fail. I'm responsible *to* people but not *for* them. And that credo also applies to you.

People who choose to follow the success procedures I offer get good results. But, to be honest, I give those principles to several hundred thousand people each year, and by no stretch of the imagination do I believe that all of them follow those principles and become successful. I do believe that people of good character who follow these procedures are far more successful than they otherwise would be. However, following or not following my suggestions is their choice, so if they follow the procedures and are successful, they're the ones who did it — not me.

On the other hand, if someone says, "I attended your seminar, read your books, and listened to your tapes, but none of it worked for me," I have to question whether he actually followed the principles carefully, whether he followed those principles believing that they would work, or whether he followed them with the idea that "I'll do it, but I know it's not going to work."

That's one of the reasons I'm careful to emphasize that the right mental attitude needs to go behind each procedure you follow.

Success is a choice in all areas of life — physical, mental, spiritual, financial, personal, family-related, and career-related. As you explore each area of life, concentrate on your area of greatest need and your chances of succeeding in that area go up substantially. Then move on to the next area. In this way, you choose to be successful in every area.

Being, Doing, Having: A Strategy to Get You Heading in the Right Direction

Here's a saying to keep in mind: You've got to be before you can do and do before you can have. In short, you have to be a person of character and do the right things, and then you can have the things you really want. To make the *be, do, have* theory valid, believable, and usable on your part, look at some examples in your own life:

1. **Take a sheet of paper and draw two vertical lines to make three columns.**

2. **At the top of the left column, write** Be; **in the middle column, write** Do; **and over the last column, write** Have.

3. **In the right column, list all the things that you really want in life.**

   Write whatever comes to mind, whether it's an education, good family relationships, a beautiful new home, a fancy luxury car, a trip around the world, better health — you name it.

4. **In the center column, identify the things that you have to *do* in order to have the things listed in the right column.**

   As an example, say that you want a successful marriage. So you write things like "be willing to share my innermost thoughts and concerns with my spouse," "carry more than my share of the workload," "encourage my spouse when he or she is down," "defend my partner against criticism," "remember special occasions," and so on.

5. **In the left column, identify what you have to *be* in order to do the things you listed in the center column.**

   Continuing the example of a successful marriage, you write down things like "be faithful, attentive, loving, caring, helpful, empathetic, encouraging, persistent, committed, kind, thoughtful, considerate, and responsible."

Everybody's list varies, because each of us has unique needs, beliefs, and interests. However, the formula remains the same. Regardless of what you want to have — whether it's more sales, a closer relationships with your children, or a handicap of ten on the golf course — you can use this basic formula. Just look at what you have to do in order to accomplish that objective, and then examine yourself and determine what kind of person you have to *be* in order to *do* so that you can *have.*

Eight benchmarks of success

Following are some other benchmarks for success (from Zig Ziglar's *Over the Top,* reprinted with permission from Thomas Nelson Publishers):

Knowing that a success doesn't make you and a failure doesn't break you: A single event — scoring the winning goal, acing a difficult course, getting a promotion — can catapult you to a more successful future. And, admittedly, failing to reach a coveted objective can negatively impact your future. But you must understand that failure is an *event* and that success is a *process.* The events themselves are important, but don't build your future on a single event or allow your future to be destroyed by a single failure. Instead, acknowledge what happened and give each event the recognition that it deserves. If the event is a success, build on it; if it's a failure, learn from it and go full speed ahead.

Making friends with your past and seeing bright things in your future: To be successful, you must accept that you have to make friends with your past if you're going to live up to your potential. Your past is important because it has brought you to where you are; however, your past is not nearly as important your future. How you see your future determines your thinking today; your thinking today determines your performance today; and your performance today determines your future. Understanding

that connection enables you to learn from your past, which is the best way to make your future even better.

Thinking of your responsibilities rather than your rights: In a society that focuses on getting everything immediately, many people get every little thing they want right now, which prevents them from getting the important things that they really want later in life. Don't worry about "rights." Maturity says, "I can wait for something this insignificant in order to achieve worthwhile objectives later." Choosing to accept and meet your responsibilities now is the best way to have the things that are important to you later.

Standing for what's right: Years ago, Edmund Burke observed that, for evil to succeed, good men simply had to do nothing. When you tolerate brutality, crime, spouse and child abuse, drunk driving, drug dealing, and so on, you're actually contributing to problem, and you yourself may become a victim in time. Your greatest failing occurs when you do nothing.

Gaining love and respect from enemies and friends alike: It's been said that we should be proud of our enemies because we're the ones who made them. Because you made those enemies (in most cases) through your actions and attitudes, you can often make friends of them by reversing those actions and attitudes. Doing

(continued)

(continued)

so not only enables you to deal effectively with your enemies, but in the process, you also earn love and respect from the people who know you best for what you have done.

Forgiving those who have wronged you: Until you forgive someone of wrongdoing, that individual remains in control of your thoughts and actions. Until you extend that hand of forgiveness, you concentrate on the problems of the past. After you extend forgiveness, your burden lightens, and you can move forward with excitement and put yourself in a position to help others.

Being a "servant friend": You may have heard about *servant leadership,* in which the leader,

owner, manager, clerk, and so on see themselves in the role of serving internal or external customers. This approach to customer service makes sense. Extending a helping hand in a "what can I do for you?" manner rather than a "what can you do for me?" manner is a philosophy that really works. It also clearly separates you from a fair-weather friend who is always there when he needs you; as a servant friend, you are there when your friend is in need.

Recognizing and using your talents: Recognizing who you are is a prerequisite to using your qualities and abilities. When you know who you are, your potential for doing great things explodes.

Chapter 2

Gearing Yourself Up to Get Results

In This Chapter
▶ Taking the first steps toward becoming results-oriented
▶ Achieving goals step by step
▶ Increasing your chances of success

The road to getting results begins with realizing that achieving is an ongoing process that evolves over time. Like honing any new skill, you must start slowly, gradually becoming comfortable with each new step in the process. No one can give you a magic potion or fail-proof formula for getting results. A fair amount of your education will be trial and error. Too often people think, "I would love to get better results, but I just don't have the ability in me." These people assume that achieving great results is a talent — a product of good genes and natural ability. Nothing could be farther from the truth.

You don't have to be gifted to get positive results. Getting results is a learned craft, not a talent, and can be taught, practiced, and perfected over time. Anyone willing and committed can become better at getting results. Whether you need to clean out your closet, manage a complicated project, or complete the 12 tasks of Hercules, the process is the same for everyone. First and foremost, you have to believe that you can get great results, and you have to take control of your life and your surroundings. This chapter helps you understand where you are right now (always a vital exercise when you want to change directions, either literally or figuratively) and how to use a results-oriented approach to get things done.

Getting Ready to Get Results

Everyone wants to get better results. Who hasn't heard (or said), "Gee, I wish I could . . ." or "Why can't I . . . "? For most people, chaos and confusion permeate everyday life, creating a great deal of stress and a lot of unnecessary anxiety. Taking control seems daunting. The classic response is, "I wish I could get more done, but there are just so many things going on, and I'm pulled in so many different directions by so many different people that my schedule is out of my control." If you've ever uttered those words or thought that way, take heart. You can begin to take control and accomplish all of your personal and business goals. The first steps are nurturing the right mind-set, figuring out where you are, and determining where you want to go.

Adopting a can-do mind-set

Your journey toward success will flow more smoothly if you ride the "right" attitude all the way to the top. "I think I can" beats "I can't" every time. A can-do outlook on life helps you achieve goals in record time and make friends and lifelong business associates along the way. Everyone enjoys being around someone who's a solution-finder and who looks for the good instead of the bad in everything.

A can-do mind-set doesn't mean, however, that you should set unrealistic expectations or be blindly optimistic. To avoid these traps (which will keep you stuck where you are), remember these important points:

✔ **You need to have an accepting, open-minded attitude toward your personal growth and education.** The world changes constantly; as they say, "Change is inevitable — except from a vending machine." Unless you change with it, you're destined for mediocrity at best.

   If you don't stay abreast of the knowledge brought about by modern technology, the trends in the marketplace, and new discoveries, you will be left far behind or, at best, will experience only a portion of the progress that you're capable of experiencing. Having the desire to stay familiar with these changes and being open-minded about them ensures your continued success well into later life.

✔ **You need to have a positive yet cautiously realistic attitude toward your own abilities.** Knowing your capabilities and being realistic about your possibilities are starting places for success. For example, your chances of being a rocket scientist are slim if you flunked fifth-grade math twice, so spending several years in college taking every course you need to be a rocket scientist but avoiding the math classes until the last semester is the same as planning to fail. Unrealistic expectations are the seedbed of depression.

   Having said that, you also need to strive to be far more positive than negative in your outlook. You can undermine your success by setting your sights too low. If you set out to lose one pound a month, for example, the slow pace will eventually cause you to lose hope, interest, and enthusiasm.

Book I

Key
Business
Skills to
Enhance
Your
Chance of
Success

Counselors and mentors are an important part of the mix that makes the success formula work. Everyone needs help in setting realistic goals, especially in areas where they've previously suffered setbacks. Then they need encouragement and motivation to hang in there until they reach those goals. Book V, Chapter 1 provides more information on working with a mentor.

✔ **You must have a sensible attitude toward positive thinking.** You've no doubt heard the saying that "Attitude is everything" or that "With positive thinking, you can do anything." Careful analysis forces you to realize that this idea is simply not true. You may be an upbeat, optimistic, enthusiastic, highly motivated positive thinker, but if you're 5 feet 4 inches tall, weigh 130 pounds, and lack physical coordination, those mental assets will do you absolutely no good if you decide you want to become a defensive lineman for the Green Bay Packers.

Blind optimism can make you a target for victimization. Some people take the concept of "being positive" out of context and try to apply it when it simply doesn't fit. If your car breaks down, for example, taking the positive approach and assuming that the individual who stops to help you has only good intentions is foolhardy in this day and age. To believe everything that everybody says and to think that everybody's motives are honest is taking naiveté to the absurd. Unfortunately, this world includes charlatans who see a person with a warm, positive, open attitude as an easier mark than a person who is cautious.

The "right" attitude — positive thinking that's tempered with a dose of realism — really does permit you to use your own abilities. And those abilities are awesome! When you recognize, develop, and use what you have, positive thinking is enormously effective.

Negative thoughts, negative outcomes

Somebody once said that you become what you think about, and that saying certainly has an element of truth. Understand that your thinking determines your actions, and your actions determine your rewards. When you don't set specific and conscious goals, that which you think about most of the time becomes your goal. And when you fantasize about the negative things in life, you paint mental images that you'll have a tendency to work toward and eventually become.

An employee who fears flubbing a presentation has a better chance of failing than an employee who is confident about giving a presentation. Think about it: Both probably base their feelings on facts. The employee who fears failure probably hasn't done the work that he needed to do, such as gathering all the relevant information or organizing his notes, so he thinks, "What's the use? I'll probably blow it anyway." The confident employee has done all the things mentioned and knows that she has prepared thoroughly enough to give an effective presentation.

Knowing yourself and where you are

Everyone can benefit from a regular checkup from the neck up. Unfortunately, the checkups that most people give themselves are fairly limited, which is one reason why people too often fail to see their true potential. So slow down and make the following checkup as thorough as possible — this evaluation doesn't have a time limit. Whether the checkup takes you five minutes or five hours is of little importance; the results are what you're interested in.

The purpose of this checkup process becomes clearer as you go along: You simply must know where you are if you're going to get where you want to go. You must have a starting place. After you complete the checkup, you can look at the Wheel of Life (see Figure 2-1) and measure whether your life is in balance and whether you're on your way to getting more of the things that money can buy and *all* of the good things that money can't buy.

To perform your checkup from the neck up, follow these steps.

1. **Using the following chart, mark each item with a number 1 through 5, with 1 being an area needing much improvement and 5 being an area needing no improvement.**

   Mark each item carefully and honestly, because these are the key factors in each goal-setting area of your life. If a factor doesn't apply to you, simply write *n/a* (for not applicable) in the space provided. In the space provided for *Other*, list any significant items that apply to you that are not listed. You'll know them automatically. For example, if you have asthma, you can list your condition in the physical section and rate how you take care of yourself in relation to that condition. List your achievements as well as the areas in which you may earn a low score.

Physical

Appearance ___

Regular checkups ___

Energy level ___

Muscle tone ___

Weight control ___

Diet and nutrition ___

Stress control ___

Endurance and strength ___

Regular fitness program ___

Other ___

Financial

Proper priorities ___

Personal budget ___

Impulse purchases ___

Earnings ___

Living within income ___

Charge accounts kept low ___

Book I

Key
Business
Skills to
Enhance
Your
Chance of
Success

Adequate insurance ___

Investments ___

Financial statement or "bottom line" ___

Other ___

Career

Challenged ___

Happy ___

Chance to advance or grow company ___

Growing in career knowledge ___

Continuing education ___

Goals program in place ___

Are where you want to be ___

Other ___

Family

Relationships with parents ___

Relationships with siblings ___

Relationship with mate ___

Relationships with children ___

Relationships with extended family ___

Spend time with family ___

Enjoy time with family ___

Make family a priority ___

Other ___

Personal

Recreation ___

Friendships ___

Community involvement ___

Hobbies ___

Quiet time ___

Growth time ___

Consistent life ___

Other ___

Spiritual

Believe in God or a higher power ___

Involvement at place of worship ___

Share faith with others ___

Prayer ___

Religious study ___

Inner peace ___

Other ___

Mental

Read/listen to motivational material ___

Associate with uplifting people ___

Positive outlook ___

Happy most of the time ___

Stable moods ___

Contentment ___

Other ___

2. **When you've completed the chart, circle every item that you scored 2 or less.**

   Doing so lets you easily see which areas need improvement.

3. **Look at your scores in each area and determine what number is your average.**

   If you're like most people, two numbers will dominate each section; for example, your responses in the *Career* section may be mostly 3s and 4s. To find your average for each section, add up all the scores and then divide by the number of responses.

4. **Keeping the results of this chart in mind, complete the Wheel of Life (see Figure 2-1).**

   Starting with your score on the mental spoke, draw a line clockwise to your score on the spiritual spoke and continue all the way around the Wheel of Life.

5. **Evaluate how balanced your circle is.**

   Is your circle big and round? Lopsided? Extremely small? The visual aid of the wheel tells you instantly how balanced your life is. The closer you are to having a full-sized, rounded circle, the better balanced you are.

What you learn about yourself and your life from the wheel can help you as you complete the procedure for qualifying your goals, listed later in this chapter.

Determining where you want to go

It takes no effort at all to get *somewhere*. Just do nothing, and you're there. (In fact, everywhere you go, there you are!) However, if you want to get somewhere meaningful, you first have to know where you want to go. And after you decide where you want to go, you need to make plans for how to get there. This practice is as true in business as in your everyday life.

For example, suppose that you have a vision of starting up a new sales office in Prague so that you can better service your eastern European accounts. How do you go about achieving this vision? You have three choices:

- ✔ An unplanned, non-goal-oriented approach
- ✔ A planned, goal-oriented approach
- ✔ A hope and a prayer

Book I

Key
Business
Skills to
Enhance
Your
Chance of
Success

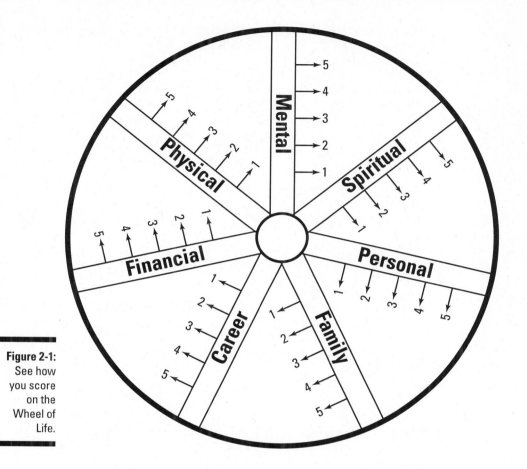

Figure 2-1:
See how
you score
on the
Wheel of
Life.

Which choice do you think is most likely to get you to your goal? Go ahead; take a wild guess! (And if you guess the unplanned, non-goal-oriented approach to reaching your vision, shame on you! Your assignment is to write 500 times, *A goal is a dream with a deadline.*) Obviously, the planned, goal-oriented approach is the right answer.

Direction is important. If you don't know where you want to go, you'll probably end up somewhere you don't want to be. Consider the story of Florence Chadwick, the first woman to swim the English Channel in both directions and the holder of numerous other swimming records of her day. She didn't always succeed on her first try, though. On her first attempt to cross the Catalina Channel off the coast of California, Chadwick encountered rough seas. Fortunately, she had trained in the cold Atlantic Ocean, was in peak condition and prepared for the huge waves and chilling temperature, and had her trainers alongside her in a boat, greasing her body to help provide protection from the cold and giving her hot soup from a thermos. In short, she had many things going for her on her quest. All her planning and training, however, didn't include what to do when a heavy fog set in. As the fog descended, limiting her vision to only a few feet, the water seemed to get colder, the waves seemed to get higher, and she began suffering from cramps in her arms, legs, feet, and hands. Although she was close to shore, she gave up and asked her trainers to take her aboard the boat. Later, reporters asked her why she gave up when she was such a short distance from shore. Her answer? Essentially that she lost sight of her goal, both figuratively and literally.

Doing What Results-Oriented People Do

Every action — planned or unplanned — has a consequence, but unintended consequences are more likely if you don't have a plan. With a well-thought-out plan, you can certainly impact, and often determine, what the final results are. Results-oriented people keep the end result in mind as they decide how to allocate their time, how to interact with others, and what things to focus on.

Identify goals

The first step in organizing your brain is to visualize your objectives. Where do you want to be? In what area do you want to achieve better results? Can you see your goal in your mind? If you can't answer all of these questions, you need to exercise your imagination and come up with some very distinct organizational goals. These goals must be

- ✔ **Written down:** A goal isn't a goal until you write it down. Committing a goal to writing makes it real. The action also requires putting something that could be extremely personal on paper — a tough task for some, but necessary nonetheless. Until you write down the goal, it's nothing more than a fantasy or a wish. After you put down the goal on paper, the pressure is on. Action is required. You're committed to either success or failure — to either reaching your goal or falling short. The second you write down the goal, you place your credibility on the line, if only with yourself.

- ✔ **Specific and detailed:** The more specific your vision, the more likely you are to organize yourself around it. For example, if your goal is "To increase business," you have nothing on which to develop an organizational strategy. The statement is too vague. If, however, you say, "I want to increase my personal contribution to revenues by 30 percent," then you have begun to shape your vision. You have defined clear goals.

✔ **Within your control:** Being able to achieve a goal requires that you have the ability to affect the process. You could set a goal of making the sun burn hotter during the cold winter months, but the temperature of the sun isn't within your control. In the earlier example (increasing your contributions to revenues by 30 percent), for example, you'd determine what elements of revenue are within your control.

✔ **Compatible with your character:** What stirs your soul and gets you excited? What can you wrap your character around and get enthused by? After you answer these questions you can hone your vision even further. A goal you're excited about is one you're more likely to accomplish.

✔ **On a schedule:** Goals need time frames for completion. If the time frame is too open-ended, you may lack the motivation to work toward your goal. With a set schedule for completion, you can evaluate your progress along the way and gain encouragement from the results you see.

Book I

Key Business Skills to Enhance Your Chance of Success

NASA's changing goals

Although an institution, not an individual, NASA provides one of the best examples of both specific and nonspecific goals and the results affected by each. In the 1960s, at the organization's peak, NASA had one very specific goal, articulated by John F. Kennedy: "Put a man on the moon by the end of the decade and return him safely to Earth." This goal was the rallying cry, the vision, and ultimately the mission of thousands of scientists, engineers, administrators, and astronauts. The entire nation latched onto the vision because it was specific, attainable, on a definitive schedule, and soul-stirring. As a result, thousands of people from hundreds of disciplines came together and accomplished one of the greatest feats in history: a man on the moon.

Contrast that achievement with the debacle NASA went through in the 1990s with the Hubble Telescope. Designed to be a giant magnifying glass in Earth's lower orbit, the Hubble Telescope was supposed to provide astronomers with a broader view of deep space.

However, as the Hubble project was gaining momentum, NASA's vision changed. Rather than rallying around a clearly defined goal like the one articulated in the 1960s, NASA's objective in the 1990s became to deploy the Hubble Telescope as cheaply and quickly as possible. Costs were cut, tests were overlooked, and the focus shifted from the mission to the expense ledger. As a result, the Hubble was deployed with an embarrassing and costly flaw. An out-of-focus lens made the orbiting telescope virtually useless. The mistake was like giving a nearsighted man the wrong prescription glasses — but these spectacles cost U.S. taxpayers over a billion dollars.

Ultimately the problems with the Hubble Telescope were corrected, but NASA's credibility could not be repaired. Had the institution that put a man on the moon in 1969 become inept? Not at all. NASA simply lost its vision (quite literally, in this case), which made all other actions irrelevant.

Here's an example of a goal you can sink your teeth into: "My goal is to close three of the ten projects I am currently working on in order to increase my contribution to company revenues by 30 percent in the next 18 months. I also want to contact ten new people in the next year and develop relationships that will lead to long-term future business." You've clearly defined the vision and established a reasonable time frame and end result.

From this point, you can break your goal into manageable bites, focusing on each step needed to close the three deals and establishing a detailed strategy for how to spend your time and resources on each. The organizational process becomes easy because the vision is clearly defined.

Prioritize tasks

Before any organized action can be taken, you must have a list of priorities. You can do this for a day, an hour, or a particular project. Here's how:

1. **On a notecard, list the things you need to accomplish within the time frame you established.**

   If you're like most people, your list includes making a few phone calls, reading some material (hopefully, a few more chapters in this book), perhaps attending a meeting or two, completing some administrative tasks, and maybe blocking some time for recreational or leisure activities.

   No doubt the list is pretty full (probably too full given the block of time allotted).

2. **Go back through your list and put a number by each item to denote order of importance.**

   Number one should be the most important thing that you hope to accomplish during the allotted time, number two the second most important, and so on. This ranking takes a little more time than writing the list, because you may view reading the paper and calling one of your work colleagues as equally important tasks. Still, you should weigh all of the variables and then assign priorities.

3. **Cut the list in half.**

   This is the hard part. You're not going to do everything on your list in the time you've allotted. You aren't going to complete some of the things, or you are going to finish them late. Even worse, you may try to squeeze a task into a time ill-suited for it, and as a result, either perform very poorly or be more concerned with rushing the task than focusing on doing the job well. By cutting the list in half, you not only give yourself plenty of time to accomplish everything that you've set out to do, but you also force yourself to reexamine your priorities and move what's really important to the top of the list.

Put together a plan

Book I

Key
Business
Skills to
Enhance
Your
Chance of
Success

After you establish a goal, you need a plan for achieving it. You've probably heard the maxim, "Plan your work and work your plan." Hackneyed or not, it's good advice. The point: Accomplishing a task or achieving a goal requires that you spend time deciding what needs to be done and organizing your resources and time as needed before you start working it, and then actually following the plan you mapped out. Then your plan, if well thought out, is your path to success.

To plan effectively, remember these rules:

- ✔ Don't insist on 100 percent when 90 percent will do nicely.
- ✔ Always strive for at least 90 percent.
- ✔ Don't get detoured onto the side streets.
- ✔ If you do find yourself on a side street, return to the main path as quickly as possible.

In other words, figure out what the situation requires, don't allow yourself to get distracted, and if you do get distracted, get yourself back on task as quickly as you can. When you eat dinner alone, for example, your plan may consist of going to the refrigerator and throwing together some leftovers. If you're serving a dinner to an important client or customer, on the other hand, you may pull out all the stops, planning everything from the wine that's served to the seating to where the salt and pepper shakers are placed on the table. A business lunch may benefit from arranging to have the meal delivered shortly after the participants receive their drinks. Such subtleties set the pace (the meeting will be swift) and help you avoid distractions.

You can apply the same logic to other planning, as well. Most chief executives, for example, have neither the time nor the inclination to read 50-page proposals, no matter how glossy and expensive they may be. Generally, they need encapsulated information. If you spend thousands of dollars and hundreds of hours developing a flashy proposal, you may find that the money and time were wasted because your proposal is never seen by the decision maker.

Contrary to what you may think, there is no "right" amount of planning when managing an event or working on a project. Of course, you can plan yourself into oblivion and never get around to actually doing anything. Conversely, you can start reacting to whatever is thrown your way without any plan at all. Both strategies achieve the same bad results.

Execute the plan

After you make a plan for your week, for your day, and for the next hour, quickly begin executing that plan to get results.

Tom Peters (a Palo Alto, California, management consultant and author) once said that most American companies would be better off if they adhered to a "ready, fire, aim," strategy instead of the "ready, aim, aim, aim, aim, aim, fire" strategy. In many ways that's an apt assessment, with a little revision: Most people, whether at home or in business, would be better served by a strategy of "ready, fire, aim a little closer, and fire again." The point? Don't be afraid to execute a plan sooner rather than later as long as you're prepared to evaluate your errors, make corrections, and try again.

Your plan may look wonderful on paper, but you have to execute it in the real world. And in the real world, you will always come across distractions and interruptions and events that sometimes require you to modify you plan at a moment's notice. Instead of throwing up your hands and saying "What's the use?" follow the advice in the following sections. It'll help you persevere and adapt in the face of challenges big and small.

Allocating time to get the important stuff done

Any item that tops your priority list deserves to be handled first, unless you have time-constraint reasons for delaying action. You should always take care of the most important items before the ancillary items, even if doing so means changing or disrupting your regular routine.

A key to getting your high-priority tasks done is to make sure you give them the time they need. Of course, time isn't unlimited, which means you have to allocate the time you do have wisely. If you're in a meeting or having a conversation with someone, make sure that you prioritize the important items you want to accomplish during the meeting, and try to get to those items as quickly as possible. Too often you're hoping to pitch an idea or broach a particular subject, but, rather than jumping right into the topic, you ask about the person's family, her golf game, or how her stock portfolio is doing. That's fine if you have plenty of time for the person to recount every shot she hit during last Saturday's round, but few people have that luxury. If you have a one-hour meeting with someone and you have three things to discuss in that one-hour period, you'd better not waste time chatting about unrelated issues.

Compartmentalizing the tasks

Whether you're organizing your desk so items can be easily found or structuring your day so you can focus on the task before you, compartmentalization is key to getting results. *Compartmentalization* means focusing on each individual item without letting any one activity encroach upon the timing and effectiveness of any other.

Compartmentalizing is easier said than done. However, you can take several steps to maximize your compartmentalization:

Book I

Key Business Skills to Enhance Your Chance of Success

✔ **Write down every action you plan to take.** After you've committed your priorities to paper, you can free your mind of worry and anticipation.

Get into the habit of writing down every single activity you need to accomplish in a day, no matter how small or rudimentary the task. In some cases, writing down the task may take longer than the action itself. But writing everything down is one of the only ways to condition yourself to make lists and focus on the tasks you have before you.

✔ **Cross items off your list as you complete them.** You get a feeling of accomplishment when you take the time to mark through a completed item. Whether the outcome of the task, meeting, or call was to your liking, crossing the item off your list lifts a burden from your mind.

At the end of each day, take inventory of the things you accomplished and the things you wanted to do but didn't complete. Then check where both the complete and incomplete items fall on your priority list. You may be surprised by how many high-priority items on your list don't get done, whereas you easily finish items much further down the list.

✔ **Think in terms of the present.** If you can't do anything about a particular matter until hours, days, or even weeks later, cluttering your mind with that item is a monumental waste of space. By focusing on the here and now, you accomplish more by avoiding the distraction of worrying about future events that you can't impact now anyway.

If you find that you're having trouble compartmentalizing your time and activities, transfer the item on your schedule that's currently your priority to a notecard and keep that notecard in sight while you perform the assigned task. If your mind begins to wander, just glance at the notecard to remind yourself of your current focus. Hopefully this snaps you back to the matter at hand and frees your mind of clutter. When you complete the task, rip up the notecard and throw it away. This action is more dramatic than crossing an item off a list. Actually throwing the card away and figuratively tossing out the task with it allows you to move ahead.

You don't just compartmentalize tasks. You also need to compartmentalize your emotions. If you're in an intense meeting in which you have a vocal disagreement with someone, you can't let your feelings carry over into your next meeting or call. That would be unfair to the next person you encounter. Snap at your assistant because your earlier meeting irritated you, and you give her the impression that you're angry or upset about something she's done. Remember, each new person or task you encounter deserves your full attention and effort — not just what's left over from an earlier interaction. If you feel yourself injecting emotions from a previous task into the current one, remind yourself again of your focus by looking at the notecard with your current priority on it. (And for help on dealing effectively with conflict, head to Book V, Chapter 5.)

Adjusting to accommodate a high-priority task

Be prepared to adjust your schedule if a high-priority item comes up while you're in the middle of a lower-priority project. Sometimes adjusting is easy. If you're reading the paper and one of your children comes in with a bloody nose, you put the paper down and attend to the child. The paper may be a morning priority, but your child's health overrides it. Plenty of times, however, your choices aren't so clear.

Imagine that you're on the phone with someone from your office who wants to go over "a few items." You know, however, that doing so will cause you to be late for another call with an important client. What do you do? Unfortunately, most people don't do the right thing. Instead of asking the office colleague to postpone the conversation, most people sit, listen, and even prolong the call by asking for more details — all while an important client is waiting. In this situation, the "few more items" aren't the priority; the customer is. You never want to leave a client wondering why you can't seem to call him on time.

If you have a family emergency, disrupting your routine is simple. A trip to the emergency room always comes before vacuuming the living room carpet. Less urgent items, however, require a little more thought. If you must choose between calling a friend on her birthday or going through your standard routine of sorting the mail and reading the paper, you may consider foregoing your standard way of doing things to pick up the phone (if you value your friend's feelings).

Evaluating whether you're maximizing every moment

To focus on each task, you need to maximize your day and the space around you. The best way to describe maximization is to think of your day as a trip to the grocery store. If you're out of milk, you have several options as part of your trip:

- You can go to the store and just buy milk, getting in and out as quickly as possible.

- You can go to the store to buy milk but, while there, you can walk through every aisle, maybe making a few purchases along the way, and maybe not.

- You can create a list of everything you need and use the opportunity to pick up all the items in one highly productive trip.

Book I

Key
Business
Skills to
Enhance
Your
Chance of
Success

Option three makes the most sense, but people don't often carry that same logic over to their business dealings or other aspects of their lives.

In real estate, maximizing is known as _highest and best use_ — a phrase used to describe the most economically efficient use of a particular piece of land. For example, a gas station situated on beachfront property near Monterey, California, would not be considered the highest and best use of that acreage, nor would a pig farm in a bustling downtown area. The land has more value than the assets currently on it. Time also has a highest and best use. If someone asks Tiger Woods to attend a luncheon a week before the U.S. Open, for example, the answer is most likely no. The highest and best use of Tiger's time during that week is to prepare for a major championship, no matter how important the business luncheon is.

In order to maximize your time and improve your results, you need to constantly ask yourself whether what you are currently undertaking is the highest and best use of your time. If it isn't, stop what you're doing, adjust your priorities, and maximize the time you have left.

Many people often spend their days scurrying from place to place, completing tasks without ever stopping to analyze the cost of the time they're spending. But when you understand that time has value, you're more likely to make wise decisions about how you spend your time. Consider an executive who takes an hour out of the middle of her day to go home and mow her lawn. She could be making calls, conducting meetings, generating business, and probably creating more income than the $20 it would cost her to have a neighborhood kid mow her lawn after school. The highest and best use of her midday hour is in the office, not at home behind a lawn mower.

Put a dollar value on every minute of your day and, before embarking on any activity, ask yourself whether the results you hope to accomplish are worth the amount of time (in dollars) that you have to spend. Check out Book II, Chapter 1 for more advice on managing your time.

You don't have to handle every item that comes your way. Your success and efficiency will improve dramatically if you let go of certain things. What should you let go of? Tasks that either

- No longer require your personal attention
- Take away from higher priority items on your list

Distinguishing between what you must do and what you can delegate to others is a key part of maximizing every moment of your time. See Book III, Chapter 3 for tips on delegation.

Use a surefire strategy for tackling big tasks

Some tasks are — or at least seem to be — overwhelming because they're so big, complex, or time-consuming. Even if you know what you need to do, you may be stumped by how on earth you're ever going to be able to get it done. With the right approach, you can complete even the largest of tasks. Here's how: If a task seems overwhelming, break it down into manageable pieces.

Suppose that you need to clean and organize the messiest room in your home or office. As a first step in that process, shield your eyes with your hands so you can only see the 3 square feet of the room next to the door. You can certainly clean up that small area. Then shift your vision to another 3-foot area. Surely you can clean up that small section, too. Repeat this process as many times as needed until you have completely cleaned the room. Perhaps your manageable bites are bigger than a 3-foot-square area, or maybe they're smaller. Whatever size bite you choose, if you focus solely on that area, you conquer the toughest tasks. You can eat an elephant as long as you take the beast one bite at a time.

You can do the same thing with your time. Every day has 1,440 minutes. Assuming that you need 8 hours (or 480 minutes) of sleep, you're left with 960 minutes in which to complete all the tasks you set for yourself in a given day. Of course, thinking in one-minute increments is difficult for anyone — reading this page has probably taken you more than one minute — but you can divide your day into manageable bites of between 15 and 30 minutes. View a task that's likely to take an hour as consuming four 15-minute time increments. A half-hour task takes two bites.

Eight points a quarter

When Michael Jordan retired the second time from the NBA (in 1999), he did so with an astonishing average of 31.5 points per game — an NBA record. No matter who the opponent or what incarnation of the Chicago Bulls were on the floor, Jordan got his 32 points every night for 13 years. When he was asked how he could maintain that astonishing consistency at such a high level for such an extended period of time, Jordan said that, instead of thinking about scoring 32 points a game, he thought instead about scoring 8 points a quarter — a feat that didn't seem nearly so insurmountable.

When he retired the third time (from the Washington Wizards in 2003), his stats were still impressive: averaging 30.1 points per game. In addition to being an incredible testament to Jordan's skill as a basketball superstar, these numbers are great indicators of his mental drive and determination.

Maximizing Your Chances of Success

Book I

Key
Business
Skills to
Enhance
Your
Chance of
Success

Contrary to what some people believe, achievers aren't born organized and prompt. It isn't genetic, nor is it a divinely inspired talent. Organization and time management are learned traits, habits that can become just as natural as tying your shoes or brushing your teeth. There are no magic formulas, no pills or drugs to take, and no hypnosis or meditations. You can, however, adopt a few simple principles to increase your chances for success. The following sections tell you how.

Get mentally organized

Disorganization, missed opportunities, missed appointments, chronic lateness, and feelings of being overwhelmed are all symptoms of the same affliction: a lack of mental organization and discipline. Mental organization is not to be confused with IQ or brainpower. You don't have to be smart or even well educated to get results. You do, however, have to harness your thoughts.

Mental organization goes well beyond just conceptualizing and visualizing or having the right attitude — even though those things are important. Waking up in the morning and saying to yourself, "Okay, today I have to make ten phone calls, attend three meetings, and be home for little Johnny's piano recital," does not constitute mental organization. Those appointments should already be committed to paper so you don't have to expend any mental energy on them. Mental organization means focusing on the tasks at hand and trusting that your short-term objectives move you toward your longer-term goals. That means each task you identify must move you closer to achieving your goal. (See the earlier section "Identify goals" for a short introduction to goals and Chapter 3 in Book I for more detailed information).

A goal that's clearly defined and has a reasonable time frame and end result is one that you can break into manageable tasks — tasks that you can focus on and for which you can create a detailed strategy for accomplishing. The organizational process becomes easy because the vision is clearly defined.

Visualize your success

One key to success is seeing yourself achieve. Professional athletes are exceptionally adept at visualization. Arnold Palmer, for example, never tees off in a tournament without first playing the course in his mind. He executes each shot perfectly in his imagination before walking onto the first tee. By the time he reaches the third or fourth hole, he has already played the hole in his mind, so all that's left to do is execute what he has already visualized. This sort of positive reinforcement gives Arnold an advantage before striking the first shot of any tournament. It can work the same way for you.

It ain't a left-brain/right-brain thing, folks

The number of people who assume that being mentally organized requires squashing, or at least stifling, creativity is astonishing. The objection comes down to the old left-brain, right-brain argument: The results-oriented person must be the buttoned-down bean-counter who thrives on structure and who never created anything unique in her life, and the free-spirited artist or genius can't be encumbered by the boundaries of discipline. These stereotypes lead to myths such as the absent-minded professor or the flighty, bohemian artist, and those who strive to be organized at home and at work are classified as "plodding" and "uncreative." These labels are hooey of the highest magnitude.

Getting results is not left-brain or right-brain dominated. In fact, the most successful actors, artists, authors, and musicians are extremely structured people. They understand that in order to excel in their crafts they must structure their surroundings and be organized and disciplined in their thinking and actions. Mental discipline and organization free their minds for more creative pursuits.

Stay focused

Have you ever been so engrossed in reading a book or an article that you completely shut out the world around you? Have you ever been so enthralled with a story that your imagination took over and you forgot you were reading? If your answer is yes (most of us have experienced that suspension of disbelief at some point), then you have experienced the kind of mental focus needed to be an achiever. You must have an extraordinary amount of discipline to go through your day without letting your mind wander. But just as you can't wait to get to the next page of your good book, when you apply this same intense focus to your daily list, you realize an enormous sense of accomplishment after you complete each task.

Other things always attempt to divert your attention away from the tasks that need to be done. But the achiever is able to put those distractions aside. All interruptions are self-inflicted: You either let the interruptions happen or you don't. Following are ways you can keep yourself on-task.

Dealing with common distractions and interruptions

Many managers have open-door policies. They even insist that the doors to their offices literally be open at all times — an admirable stance that shows employees that the boss is accessible. Unfortunately, such a setup also invites interruptions. If everyone believes that you're available at all times, you are.

How you deal with incoming phone calls is another indicator of how much control you have over your own agenda. If you accept every call that comes in, your schedule is at the mercy of anyone in the world who has your phone number. Taking control of when and how you accept phone calls is critical to your time and perhaps to your sanity. Instead of simply taking calls whenever they come in, try returning someone's call or scheduling a call at a predetermined time. Doing so lets you control when a conversation takes place and usually how long it lasts.

Based on the nature of the call, schedule it to occur during a time that's most conducive to the conversation you're anticipating. You may decide to make short calls earlier in the day, for example. If you have to call a client about a highly charged situation that may last half an hour or longer, try to schedule that call toward the end of the day so that, if the conversation runs a little longer than expected, it doesn't throw off the rest of your day.

For ideas on how to keep interruptions and phone calls from waylaying your day, head to Book II, Chapter 4.

Nowadays, e-mail interruptions are another source of potentially endless distractions. Unless you've disabled the alert that lets you know whenever an e-mail arrives, every message that comes in beckons for your attention. You can use a variety of strategies to manage e-mail: Set a particular time of day when you address any messages, use filters to eliminate spam and other unnecessary messages from hitting your inbox, and so on. For more information and suggestions for how to tame the e-mail monster, go to Chapter 7 of Book II.

Timing yourself

Put yourself on a deadline with each task you undertake and keep applying pressure. In the beginning, you may want to purchase a stopwatch (an inexpensive one) and put yourself on the clock as you start each task on your list. Meeting your time limits is challenging at first. You find yourself feeling anxious as conversations with colleagues drag on longer than your allotted time and the stopwatch continues to tick. This pressure heightens your awareness of time wasted each day on unproductive conversations and activities. You also become more creative in cutting conversations short and eliminating distractions from your day.

Rewarding yourself

If you're like most people, you tend to focus on those things that offer the most satisfying rewards. Based on this assumption, employers base bonuses and compensation structures on goals they want to see completed. Unfortunately, a lot of mundane tasks with no immediate rewards must also be tended to on a daily basis. One way to mentally gear yourself up for those tasks is to assign a reward for each task you complete within a specified time frame. For example, if you finish cleaning your office and sorting through all the papers in your inbox by 5 p.m., you allow yourself to go to the golf course or indulge in an after-work social activity you would otherwise skip.

Be careful, though. You don't want to set the bar too low or fudge on the rewards. Doing that just undermines your efforts to become more efficient and productive. If you're one minute past your deadline, you must have enough discipline to deny yourself the reward; otherwise, the exercise is useless. If, however, you're honest enough with yourself to stick to your guns and you set your deadlines realistically high, this drill improves your ability to focus and minimize distractions.

Flush the worry (or at least learn to manage it)

Too much worrying can not only disrupt your concentration and detract from your efficiency, but can also harm your health. High blood pressure and certain heart conditions have been attributed to stress — one of the side effects of worrying.

When worrying becomes a distraction, you need to act on the worry. Too often people allow their worries to encroach into other areas of their lives, which leads to poor performance and the addition of new worries. To reduce the amount of time you spend worrying, or to minimize its effect on the rest of your day, try these strategies:

- ✔ When you receive bad news, try to counterbalance it with good news so that you can come away feeling positive and not carry your worry with you throughout the day.

- ✔ If a situation is so critical that you are consumed with worry, change your schedule in order to deal with the worrisome item. Rearranging your day may disrupt an otherwise carefully orchestrated schedule, but a little reshuffling is better than letting your worries carry over into other unrelated events and activities.

To find out more about dealing with stress, flip to Book VI.

Practice!

Just like everything in life, the more you practice working toward results, the more proficient you become. At first the practice is laborious, and you experience some frustration when you don't see the instant results you had hoped for. But just like the beginning golfer has to hit a seemingly endless stream of practice balls before he feels marginally proficient, you must practice the basic fundamentals of achieving results if you want your project or task to end successfully.

Chapter 3

Goal Setting Made Easy

Ask any group of workers, "What is the primary duty of management?" The answer "setting goals" is likely to be near the top of the list. In most companies, top management sets the overall purpose — the vision — of the organization. Middle managers then have the job of developing goals and plans for achieving the vision set by top management. Managers and employees work together to set goals and develop schedules for attaining them.

If you're a manager, you're probably immersed in goals — not only for yourself but also for your employees, your department, and your organization. This flood of goals can overwhelm you as you try to balance the relative importance of each one. Goals are just as important — and challenging — when you're an employee.

Goals provide direction and purpose. Don't forget: If you can see it, you can achieve it. Goals help you see where you're going and how you can get there. And the *way* that you set goals can impact how motivating they are to others. You may think to yourself, "I've tried that goal-setting stuff before and it didn't work." Most people agree that goals are important; some can even give you a list of their goals. But the majority stop there, never taking action toward those goals or, almost worse, taking action but then abandoning their goals when challenges arise.

In this chapter you find out just how important goals are to your career journey and what characteristics comprise an effective, motivating goal. When you give careful thought and attention to creating the right goals, you'll find that you stick with them instead of drifting back into business as usual. But just in case you need an extra boost, this chapter also gives some advice on how to keep yourself or the people you manage inspired and working hard.

Recognizing the Importance of Goals

Did you realize that Lewis Carroll's classic book *Alice's Adventures in Wonderland* offers lessons that can enhance your business life? Believe it or not, Alice and the Cheshire Cat have an exchange about the importance of setting goals. Consider the following passage from Carroll's book, in which Alice asks the Cheshire Cat for advice on which direction to go.

"Would you tell me please, which way I ought to go from here?"

"That depends a good deal on where you want to get to," said the Cat.

"I don't much care where —" said Alice.

"Then it doesn't matter which way you go," said the Cat.

"— so long as I get *somewhere*," Alice added as an explanation.

"Oh, you're sure to do that," said the Cat, "if you only walk long enough."

Alice doesn't have a goal. The Cheshire Cat points out that she'll arrive somewhere eventually, but how many circles will she walk in before that, and who's to say that she'll like where she ends up? Your life and career are too important for you to waste time with aimless wandering.

Following are the main reasons to set goals whenever you want to accomplish something significant:

✔ **Goals provide direction.** To get something done, you have to set a definite vision — a target to aim for and to guide your efforts (and the efforts of your team or your organization if you're in a management role). You can then translate this vision into goals that take you where you want to go. Without goals, you're doomed to waste countless hours going nowhere meaningful. With goals, you can focus efforts on only the activities that move you toward where you want to go.

✔ **Goals tell you how far you've traveled.** Goals provide milestones along the road to accomplishing your vision. If you determine that you must accomplish several specific milestones to reach your final destination and you complete a few of them, you know exactly how many remain. You can see exactly where you stand and how far you have yet to go.

✔ **Goals help to make the overall vision attainable.** You can't reach your vision in one big step — you need many small steps to get there. Suppose your vision is to open a new sales office in Chicago. You can't expect to proclaim your vision on Friday and walk into a fully staffed and functioning office on Monday. You must accomplish many goals — shopping for office space, hiring and relocating staff, printing stationery and business cards, and so on — before you can attain your vision. Goals enable you

Book I

Key
Business
Skills to
Enhance
Your
Chance of
Success

to achieve your overall vision by dividing your efforts into smaller pieces that, when accomplished individually, add up to big results.

✔ **When your goal requires the help of others, it clarifies everyone's role.** When you discuss your vision with the people you're counting on to help you (your employees if you're a manager, for example, or your team members if you're leading a collaborative project), they may have some idea of where you want to go but no idea of how to go about getting there. As they head off to help you achieve your vision, some may duplicate the efforts of others, some may ignore certain tasks, and some may simply do something else altogether (and hope that you don't notice the difference). Setting goals clarifies what the tasks are, who does which tasks, and what is expected from everyone.

✔ **Goals give people something to strive for.** If you're like most people, you're more motivated when you're challenged to attain a goal that's beyond your normal level of performance — this is what's known as a *stretch goal.* Not only do goals give you a sense of purpose, but they also relieve the boredom that can come from performing a routine job day after day. *Note:* If you're helping your employees set stretch goals, be sure to discuss the goal with them and gain their commitment.

The best goals have these characteristics:

✔ Link directly to the final vision.

✔ Are few in number, specific in purpose.

✔ Are stretch goals — not too easy, not too hard.

✔ Involve others — when you involve others, you get their support because it becomes their goal too, not just yours.

Compelling visions

To stay ahead of the competition or simply to remain in business, organizations create compelling visions. Then management and employees work together to set and achieve the goals to reach those visions. Look over these examples of compelling visions that drive the development of goals at several successful enterprises (which are, perhaps, even more important as they fight to thrive in the face of a depressed economy):

✔ Samsung is a Korean-based manufacturer of electronics, chemicals, and

heavy machinery, as well as a provider of architectural and construction services. Samsung's vision is to lead the digital convergence movement. This vision drives the organization's goals.

✔ A century ago, the chairman of AT&T created this vision for the organization: the dream of good, cheap, and fast worldwide telephone service. AT&T's vision today is "to be the most admired and valuable company in the world."

Creating SMART Goals

You can find all kinds of goals in all types of organizations. Some goals are short-term and specific ("starting next month, I will increase production by two units per hour"), and others are long-term and vague ("within the next five years, we will become a learning organization"). Employees easily understand some goals ("line employees will have no more than 20 rejects per month"), but others can be difficult to fathom and subject to much interpretation ("all employees are expected to show more respect to each other in the next fiscal year"). Still others can be accomplished relatively easily ("I will always answer the phone by the third ring"), but others are virtually impossible to attain ("I will master the five languages that our customers speak before the end of the fiscal year").

How do you know what kind of goals to set? The whole point of setting goals, after all, is to achieve them. You're wasting time if you go to the trouble of calling meetings, hacking through the needs of your organization, and burning up precious time, only to end up with goals that aren't acted on or completed. Unfortunately, this scenario is far too common.

The way to avoid this scenario is to create smart goals — well, actually, *SMART* goals is more like it. The following sections tell you how.

Top goal Web sites

Wondering where to find the best information on the Web about the topics addressed in this chapter? Well, you've come to the right place! Here are some favorites:

- Personal goal setting: www.mindtools.com/page6.html and www.mysuccessbox.com

- Business and personal goals for staying focused: www.strategicacceleration.com and www.humanresources.about.com/library/weekly/aa121000a.htm

- Business and personal goals: www.ziglar.com

- Goal setting with employees: http://managementhelp.org/emp_perf/goal_set/goal_set.htm

- Setting goals for management: www.dummies.com/how-to/content/setting-smart-management-goals.html and www.mygoals.com

Getting SMART

SMART refers to a handy checklist for the five characteristics of well-designed goals:

- ✔ **Specific:** Goals must be clear and unambiguous; broad and fuzzy thinking has no place in goal setting. When goals are specific, they tell employees exactly what's expected, when, and how much.

- ✔ **Measurable:** What good is a goal that you can't measure? If your goals aren't measurable, you never know whether you're making progress toward successful completion. Not only that, you may have a tough time staying motivated to complete the goals when there are no milestones to indicate progress.

- ✔ **Attainable:** Goals must be realistic and attainable. The best goals require you to stretch a bit to achieve them, but they aren't extreme; they're neither out of reach nor merely standard performance. Goals that are set too high or too low become meaningless and eventually ignored.

- ✔ **Relevant:** Goals must be an important tool in the grand scheme of reaching your company's vision and mission. Some believe that 80 percent of workers' productivity comes from only 20 percent of their activities. Relevant goals address the 20 percent of workers' activities that has such a great impact on performance and brings your organization closer to its vision.

  This relationship comes from Italian economist Vilfredo Pareto's *80/20 rule.* This rule, which states that 80 percent of the wealth of most countries is held by only 20 percent of the population, has been applied to many other fields since its discovery.

- ✔ **Time-bound:** Goals must have starting points, ending points, and fixed durations. Commitment to deadlines helps you focus your efforts on completion of the goal on or before the due date. Goals without deadlines or schedules for completion tend to be overtaken by the day-to-day crises that invariably arise in an organization.

No matter what your job or what you hope to accomplish, you can set more meaningful goals in your career and personal life using the SMART principles. And for all you managers, remember that SMART goals make for smart organizations. In our experience, many supervisors and managers neglect to work with their employees to set goals together. And for the ones that do, goals are often unclear, ambiguous, unrealistic, unmeasurable, demotivating, or unrelated to the organization's vision. By developing SMART goals with your employees, you can avoid these traps while ensuring the progress of your organization and its employees.

Considering other factors when setting goals

Although the SMART system of goal setting provides guidelines to help you frame effective goals, you have additional considerations to keep in mind. These considerations (explained in the following list) help ensure that the goals can be easily understood and that group goals can be acted on by anyone in your organization.

- ✔ **Ensure that goals are related to your (or your employees') role in the organization.** Pursuing an organization's goals is far easier when those goals are a regular part of your job or your employees' job. For example, suppose you set a goal for employees who solder circuit boards to "Raise production by 2 percent per quarter." These employees spend almost every working moment pursuing this goal, because the goal is an integral part of their job. If, however, you give the same employees a goal of "Improving the diversity of the organization," what exactly does that have to do with your line employees' role? Nothing. The goal may sound lofty and may be important to your organization, but because your line employees don't make the hiring decisions, you're wasting your time and their time with that particular goal.

- ✔ **Whenever possible, use values to guide behavior.** What is the most important value in your organization? Honesty? Fairness? Respect? Whatever it is, ensure that you model this behavior, and if you're a manager, reward employees who live it.

- ✔ **Simple goals are better goals.** The easier your goals are to understand, the more likely your manager and co-workers are to support you, and the more likely employees affected by the goals are to work toward achieving them. Goals should be no longer than one sentence; make them concise, compelling, and easy to read and understand.

Goals that take more than a sentence to describe are actually multiple goals. When you find multiple-goal statements, break them into single, one-sentence goals. Goals that take a page or more to describe aren't really goals; they are books. File them away and try again.

Don't let all your hard work go for naught. When you go through the trouble of setting goals, keep them to a manageable number that can realistically be followed up on. And when you finish one goal, move on to the next.

Choosing the right goals to pursue

When it comes to goal setting, less is more. The following guidelines can help you select the right goals — and the right number of goals:

- ✔ **Pick two to three goals to focus on.** You can't do everything at once (neither can your employees). A few goals are the most you should attempt to conquer at any one time. Picking too many goals dilutes your efforts and can result in a complete breakdown in the process.

Avoid taking on too many goals in your zeal to get as many things done as quickly as you can. Too many goals can overwhelm you, and they can overwhelm your employees, too. You're far better off if you set a few, significant goals and then concentrate your efforts on attaining them.

- ✔ **Pick the goals with the greatest relevance.** Certain goals take you a lot farther down the road to attaining your vision than do other goals. Because you have only so many hours in your workday, it clearly makes sense to concentrate your efforts on a few goals that have the biggest payoff — rather than on a boatload of goals with relatively less payoff.

- ✔ **Focus on the goals that tie most closely to your organization's mission.** You can be tempted to take on goals that are challenging, interesting, and fun to accomplish but that are far removed from your organization's mission. Don't.

Book I

Key Business Skills to Enhance Your Chance of Success

Revisiting your goals

Periodically revisit the goals and update them as necessary. Business is anything but static, and periodically assessing your goals is important to making sure that they're still relevant to the vision you want to achieve. If so, great — carry on. If not, revise the goals and the schedules for attaining them.

Avoiding Surprises: Taking a Good Look at Your Goals

Before you decide whether a single goal fits into your goals program, take a good look at what it would require, what challenges you're likely to face, what resources would be available to help you, and so on. *Note:* This process can take considerable time — but it can save you much time and frustration later by eliminating goals that are not for you at this point and helping to identify what you need to focus on now. Simply complete these three tasks to get a better grasp on your goals:

- ✔ **List the skills and knowledge required.** How can you know whether a goal is possible until you know what skills and knowledge are necessary to accomplish it? Quite frankly, you don't. That's why determining what resources you need (skill-wise, knowledge-wise, and otherwise) is so important. So make a list of the things you (or others, if you are enlisting others' help) need to have to achieve the goal.

✔ **List the obstacles you face.** You need to identify obstacles you're likely to face so that you can view the project realistically and avoid being surprised. You don't want to be unprepared for how demanding, how time consuming, or how difficult pursuing a particular goal is. Nor do you want to be taken aback by the pitfalls you have to face. Such unpleasant surprises can quickly turn into a self-defeating attitude. Careful planning in advance eliminates much of this disappointment.

Of course, you can't see every roadblock that lies ahead. That's why commitment and attitude are vital to any successful endeavor. Patience is also extremely important. Just remember that by keeping yourself focused on the goal, you can see the benefits and not just the obstacles. Head to Chapter 1 of Book I to find out how important your outlook is to achieving success.

✔ **Seek counsel and guidance.** You may need a counselor of some kind to carefully identify what skills are required to reach your goal. Seeking guidance also helps you along the way because a counselor can help you carefully prepare a plan of action for dealing with obstacles.

In many cases, being able to achieve your objectives depends upon support from your family, friends, co-workers, boss, and your mentor (if you have one). You need to carefully identify friends who can be encouragers — people to whom you are close enough to share your goals and who can check your progress and encourage you. These actions encourage you to maintain your focus and keep your eyes on the goal itself. You'll find that some goals are absolutely impossible without the direct help of friends.

People often fail to reach their goals because they concentrate on the costs rather than the benefits. It's "If I quit smoking, I'll be irritable and gain weight" syndrome — allowing the negatives to discourage you from moving ahead. Instead of concentrating on the negatives, think of the benefits that you're going to enjoy. As you set goals, make a list of the tangible rewards that will be yours when you reach each goal. Each time you begin to ask yourself whether pursuing a goal is worth the effort, simply take out the list of benefits and read them aloud again.

Sharing Your Vision and Goals

As you find out in the preceding sections, a lot of work and thought goes into developing effective goals. And if you're a manager, you have an additional piece of work to do before progress towards those goals can begin: communicating them to you employees. Goals grow out of an organization's vision.

Establishing goals helps you ensure that employees focus on achieving the vision in the desired time frame. You have many possible ways to communicate goals to your employees, but some ways are better than others. In every case, you must communicate goals clearly, the receiver must understand the goals, and the goals must be followed through on.

Sharing the vision

Communicating your organization's vision to employees (as well as clients, customers, and suppliers) is as important as communicating specific goals. Companies usually announce their visions with much pomp and fanfare. The following are different ways that companies commonly announce and communicate their vision:

- ✔ By conducting huge employee rallies where the vision is unveiled in inspirational presentations.

- ✔ By printing their vision on anything possible — business cards, letterhead stationery, massive posters hung in the office, newsletters, employee name tags, and more.

- ✔ By encouraging managers to model and "talk up" the vision in staff meetings or other verbal interactions.

To avoid a cynical _it's-just-a-fad_ reaction from employees who are suspicious of management's motives when unveiling a new initiative, consistently modeling and making casual references to it is much more effective than a huge, impersonal event. In this case, doing less is often better.

Often an organization's vision is pounded out in a series of grueling management meetings that leave the participants (you, the managers!) beaten and tired. By the time the managers reach their final goal of developing a company's vision, they're sick of it and ready to go on to the next challenge. Many organizations drop the ball at this crucial point and are thereby slow to communicate the vision. Also, the further down the org chart an employee is from the level that created the vision, the less energizing its effect, so by the time it filters down to the frontline employees, the vision has become dull and lifeless.

When you communicate vision and goals, do it with energy and with a sense of urgency and importance. If your employees don't think that you care about the vision, why should they? Simply put, they won't.

Sharing the goals

Goals are much more personal than visions, and the methods you use to communicate them must be more formal and direct. The following guidelines can help you out:

- ✔ **Make sure the goals are written down.** Everyone has difficulty defining, measuring, and tracking progress toward attainment of goals when they aren't in writing.

- ✔ **Always conduct one-on-one, face-to-face meetings with your employees to introduce, discuss, and assign goals.** If physical distance or another reason prevents you from conducting a face-to-face meeting, conduct your meeting over the phone. The point is to make sure that your employees receive the goals, understand them, and have the opportunity to ask for clarifications.

- ✔ **Call your team together to introduce team-related goals.** You can assign goals to teams instead of to individuals. If this is the case, get the team together and explain the role of the team and each individual in the successful completion of the goal. Make sure that all team members understand exactly what they're supposed to do. Get them fired up and then let them have at it.

- ✔ **Gain the commitment of your employees, whether individually or on teams, to the successful accomplishment of their goals.** Ask your employees to prepare and present plans and milestone schedules explaining how they can accomplish the assigned goals by the deadlines that you agreed to. After your employees embark on the pursuit of their goals, regularly monitor their progress to ensure that they're on track and meet with them to help them overcome any problems.

Making Your Goals Happen

After you create or are given a wonderful set of goals, how do you make sure that they get done? How do you keep your motivation to follow through or turn your priorities into your employees' priorities? The best goals in the world mean nothing if they aren't achieved. You can choose to leave this critical step in the process to chance, or you can choose to get involved.

Tapping into the primary sources of power

You have the power to make your goals happen. Even though power has gotten a bad rap, nothing is inherently wrong with power — everyone has

Book I

Key
Business
Skills to
Enhance
Your
Chance of
Success

many sources of power within them. And not only do you have power but you also exercise power to control or influence people and events around you on a daily basis. Generally, power is a positive thing.

You can use the positive power within you to your advantage — and to the advantage of the people around you — by tapping into it to help achieve your organization's goals. People and systems often fall into ruts or nonproductive patterns of behavior that are hard to break. Properly applied power can jump-start these people and systems and move them in the right direction — the direction that leads to the accomplishment of goals.

Power can be a negative thing when abused. Manipulation, exploitation, and coercion have no place in the modern workplace.

Everyone has five primary sources of power, and each person has specific strengths and weaknesses related to these sources. As you review the five sources of power that follow, consider your own personal strengths and weaknesses and how they can be used to your advantage.

- ✔ **Personal power:** This is the power that comes from within your character. Your passion for greatness, the strength of your convictions, your ability to communicate and inspire, your personal charisma, and your leadership skills all add up to personal power.

- ✔ **Relationship power:** Everyone has relationships with others at work. These interactions contribute to the relationship power that you wield in your offices. Sources of relationship power include close friendships with top executives, partners, or owners, people who owe you favors, and co-workers who provide you with information and insights that you normally wouldn't get through your formal business relationships.

- ✔ **Knowledge power:** To see knowledge power in action, just see what happens the next time your organization's computer network goes down! Then you'll see who really has the power in an organization (in this case, your computer network administrator). Knowledge power comes from the special expertise and knowledge that you have gained during the course of your career. Knowledge power also comes from obtaining academic degrees (think MBA) or special training.

- ✔ **Task power:** Task power is the power that comes from the job or process that you perform at work. As you have undoubtedly witnessed on many occasions, people can facilitate or impede the efforts of their co-workers and others through the application of task power. For example, when you submit a claim for payment to your insurance company and months pass with no action ("Gee, we don't seem to have your claim in our computer — are you sure you submitted one? Maybe you should send us another one just to be safe!"), you are on the receiving end of task power.

✓ **Position power:** This kind of power derives strictly from your rank or title in the organization and is a function of the authority that you wield to command human and financial resources. Although the position power of the receptionist in your organization is probably quite low, the position power of the president or owner is at the top of the chart. However, the best leaders seldom rely on position power to get things done today.

If you're weak in certain sources of power, you can increase them if you want. For example, work on your weakness in relationship power by making a concerted effort to know your co-workers better and to cultivate relationships with higher ranking managers or executives. Instead of passing on the invitations to get together with your co-workers after work, join them — have fun and strengthen your relationship power at the same time.

Be aware of the sources of your power and use them in a positive way to help you and your employees accomplish the goals of your organization. For getting things done, a little power can go a long way.

Persevering beyond the initial excitement

After you've determined the goals that are important to you and to your organization, you come to the difficult part. How do you maintain the focus of your focus — and the focus of your employees or teammates, for that matter — on achievement of the goals that you've set? Staying focused on goals can be extremely difficult — particularly when you're a busy person and the goals are added on top of your regular responsibilities. Think about situations that fight for your attention during a typical day at work:

✓ How often do you sit down at your desk in the morning to plot out your priorities for the day only to have them pushed aside five minutes later when you get a call from your boss?

✓ How many times has an employee or co-worker come to you with a problem?

✓ Do you remember getting caught in a meeting scheduled for 15 minutes that dragged on for several hours?

In unlimited ways, you or your employees can fall off track and lose the focus that you need to get your organization's goals accomplished.

The process of goal setting often generates a lot of excitement and energy— whether the goals are set in large group meetings or in one-on-one encounters. This excitement and energy can quickly dissipate as soon as everyone gets back to his or her desk. You must ensure that the organization's focus remains centered on the goals and not on other matters (which are less important but momentarily more pressing):

- ✔ **Accountability is everything.** If you're heading up a group effort to achieve a goal, you're responsible for checking on the progress and focus of your group. When everyone realizes you are going to be asking them how they're making progress toward reaching the goal, they'll keep that task in mind and at the top of their priority list.

- ✔ **Program reminders to go out automatically to members of your team.** In these reminders, you can suggest strategies for reaching all goals ahead of schedule.

- ✔ **Set up a short, weekly telephone conference.** Take ten minutes during which everyone explains what progress they've made toward reaching the goal. Hearing how others have made progress will inspire those who may be lagging behind and focus will once again be on reaching the goal.

Avoiding the activity trap

One of the biggest problems is confusing activity with results. Do you know anyone who works incredibly long hours — late into the night and on weekends — but never seems to get anything done? Although this employee always seems to be busy, the problem is that he or she is working on the wrong things. This is called the *activity trap*, and falling into it is easy. "Help, I've fallen and I can't get out!"

As mentioned earlier, 80 percent of workers' productivity comes from 20 percent of their activity. The flip side of this rule is that only 20 percent of workers' productivity comes from 80 percent of their activity. This statistic illustrates the activity trap at work. What do you do in an average day? More important, what do you do with the 80 percent of your time that produces so few results? You can get out of the activity trap and take control of your schedules and priorities. However, you have to be tough and single-minded in pursuit of your goals.

Achieving your goals is all up to you. No one, not even your boss (perhaps especially not your boss), can make it any easier for you to concentrate on achieving your goals. You have to take charge, and you have to take charge now! If you aren't controlling your own schedule, you're simply letting everyone else control your schedule for you.

Following are some tips to help you and your employees get out of the activity trap:

- **Do your number one priority first!** With all the distractions that compete for your attention, with the constant temptation to work on the easy stuff first and save the tough stuff for last, and with people dropping into your office just to chat or to unload their problems on you, concentrating on your number one priority is always a challenge. However, if you don't do your number one priority first, you're almost guaranteed to find yourself in the activity trap, finding the same priorities on your list of tasks to do day after day, week after week, and month after month. If your number one priority is too big, divide it into smaller chunks and focus on the most important one of those. See Book II, Chapter 2 for more on prioritizing your to-do list.

- **Get organized!** Getting organized and managing your time effectively are incredibly important pursuits for anyone in business. If you're organized, you can spend less time trying to figure out what you should be doing and more time doing what you should be doing. Flip to Book II, Chapters 1 and 7 to get detailed tips on organizing.

- **Just say no!** If someone tries to make his problems your problems, just say no! If you're a manager, you probably like nothing more than taking on new challenges and solving problems. The conflict arises when solving somebody else's problems interferes with solving your own. You have to constantly be on guard and fight the temptation to fritter your day away with meaningless activities. Always ask yourself, "How does this help me achieve my goals?" Focus on your own goals and refuse to let others make their problems your own.

Chapter 4

Being an Integral Part of a Team

In This Chapter

▶ Understanding the benefits of teams

▶ Categorizing teams

▶ Increasing the value of teams in the real world

▶ Making team meetings work

Some years ago, a revolution occurred in the business world that touched everyone who works in an organization — from the very top to the very bottom. What was this revolution? Teams. You know, when two or more people work together to achieve a common goal.

Businesses use teams to tap the knowledge and resources of all employees — not just supervisors and managers — to solve the organization's problems. A well-structured team draws together employees from different functions and levels of the organization to help find the best way to approach an issue. Smart companies have discovered that to remain competitive, they can no longer rely solely on management to guide the development of work processes and the accomplishment of organizational goals. The companies need to involve those employees — the frontline workers — who are closer to the problems and to the organization's customers.

Thriving in the workplace means functioning as a fully contributing member of any team you're on. This chapter discusses the major kinds of teams, how they work, and how you, as either manager or employee, can get the most benefit from them.

Identifying Advantages of Teams

More than ever before, businesses worldwide are rewarding employees for cooperating with each other instead of competing against one another. This innovation in today's business environment is truly amazing! Organizations are no longer measuring employees only by their individual contributions, but also by how effective they are as contributing members of their work teams.

Coupled with this shift of authority is a fundamental change in the way that many businesses structure their organizations. They're moving away from a structure of traditional, functional divisions that once separated departments from each other. In their place are *teams* — made up of employees from different departments — whose members work together to perform tasks and achieve common goals. Of course, most businesses still organize their operations by departments, divisions, and so forth, but smart managers now encourage, rather than discourage, their employees to cross formal organizational lines.

Following are benefits that organizations reap from promoting cooperation:

- ✔ **Reducing unproductive competition:** Promoting a cooperative, team-oriented work environment reduces the chance that employees can become overcompetitive.

  If allowed to continue unabated, overcompetitiveness results in the shutdown of communication between employees and, ultimately, reduced organizational effectiveness (as overcompetitive employees build and defend private fiefdoms). Besides, overcompetition between employees invariably leads to the release of incredible amounts of bad karma.

- ✔ **Sharing knowledge:** Knowledge is power. If you're in the know, you have a clear advantage over someone who has been left in the dark — especially if your finger is on the light switch. In a cooperative work environment, team members work together and thereby share their areas of knowledge and expertise.

- ✔ **Fostering communication:** The use of teams helps to break down the walls between an organization's departments, divisions, and other formal structures to foster communication between organizational units.

- ✔ **Achieving common goals:** The development of teams with members from various departments encourages workers from all levels and all parts of a company to work together to achieve common goals. Not only that, but it also gives you someone to hang out with on coffee breaks.

- ✔ **Making better decisions faster:** Because team members are closest to the problems and to one another, a minimal amount of lag time exists due to communication channels or the need to get approvals from others in the organization.

- ✔ **Competing more nimbly:** The rate and scope of change in the global business environment has led to increased competitive pressures on organizations in most every business sector. Large organizations often have a hard time competing in this marketplace against smaller, more nimble competitors. Smaller units within a large organization — such as teams — are better able to compete.

✔ **Increasing innovation and adaptability:** Teams of people with different ideas and perspectives can lead to increased innovation. Teams are also more adaptive to the external environment as it quickly or constantly changes. Thus, a team's size and flexibility give it a distinct advantage over the more traditional organizational structure of competing organizations. In many companies, design, engineering, and manufacturing functions are now closely intertwined in the development of new products — dramatically shortening the time from concept to production.

Book I

Key Business Skills to Enhance Your Chance of Success

Defining the Three Types of Teams You May Find Yourself On

Three major kinds of teams exist: *formal, informal,* and *self-managed.* Each type of team offers advantages and disadvantages depending on the specific situation, timing, and the organization's needs. Think about these things when you consider what type of team to set up or participate in.

Formal teams

A *formal team* is chartered by an organization's management and tasked to achieve specific goals. These goals can range from developing a new product line, determining the system for processing customer invoices, or planning a company picnic. Types of formal teams include

✔ **Task forces:** Formal teams assembled on a temporary basis to address specific problems or issues. For example, a task force may be assembled to determine why the number of rejects for a machined part has risen from 1 in 10,000 to 1 in 1,000. A task force usually has a deadline for solving the issue and reporting the findings to management.

✔ **Committees:** Long-term or permanent teams created to perform an ongoing, specific organizational task. For example, some companies have committees that select employees to receive awards for performance or that make recommendations to management for safety improvements. Although committee membership may change from year to year, the committees continue their work regardless of who belongs to them.

✔ **Command teams:** Made up of a manager or supervisor and all the employees who report directly to him or her. Such teams are by nature hierarchical and represent the traditional way that tasks are communicated from managers to workers. Examples of command teams include company sales teams, management teams, and executive teams.

Formal teams are important to most organizations because much of the communication within an establishment traditionally occurs through the team. News, goals, and information pass from employee to employee via formal teams. And they provide the structure for assigning tasks and soliciting feedback from team members on accomplishments, performance data, and so on.

Informal teams

Informal teams are casual associations of employees that spontaneously develop within an organization's formal structure. Such teams include groups of employees who eat lunch together every day, form bowling teams, or simply like to hang out together — both during and after work. The membership of informal teams is in a constant state of flux as members come and go and friendships and other associations between employees change over time.

Although informal teams have no specific tasks or goals assigned by management, they are very important to organizations for the following reasons:

✔ Informal teams provide a way for employees to get information outside formal, management-sanctioned communications channels.

✔ Informal teams provide a (relatively) safe outlet for employees to let off steam about issues that concern them and to find solutions to problems by discussing them with employees from other parts of the organization — unimpeded by the walls of the formal organization.

Top five teams Web sites

To find the best information on the Web about the topics addressed in this chapter, check out the following five sites:

✔ *The Power of Teamwork* film: `www.powerofteamworkmovie.com`

✔ Teamwork quotes and articles: `http://humanresources.about.com/lr/team_work/89508/1/`

✔ Teambuildinginc.com: `www.teambuildinginc.com/ei_news.htm`

✔ Teams and teamwork: `www.hq.nasa.gov/office/hqlibrary/ppm/ppm5.htm`

✔ Teamwork: `www.fastcompany.com/guides/leadteam.html`

For example, a group of women employees at Verizon Communications' Northeast Bureau created *mentoring circles*. The purpose of these informal teams — developed outside the formal organization — was to fill the void created by a lack of female top-level managers to serve as mentors for other women in the organization. Organized in groups of 8 to 12 employees, the circles provided the kind of career networking, support, and encouragement that mentors normally provide to their charges.

Ad hoc groups are informal teams of employees assembled on an impromptu basis to solve a problem, often (though not always) by regular employees. Such teams could be initiated by an employee who has been given a specific assignment — say, to develop a new worker scheduling system — or by a manager. For example, as a manager you may form an ad hoc team when you select employees from your human resources and accounting departments to solve a problem with the system for tracking and recording pay changes in the company's payroll system. You don't invite participants from shipping to join this informal team because they probably can't provide meaningful input to the problem.

Self-managed teams

Self-managed teams combine the attributes of both formal and informal teams. Generally chartered by management, self-managed teams often quickly take on lives of their own as members take over responsibility for the day-to-day workings of the team. Self-managed teams are usually comprised of employees whose job is to meet together to find solutions to common worker problems. Self-managed teams are also known as *high performance teams, cross-functional teams,* or *superteams.*

To compress time and gain benefits, an organization's self-managing teams must be

- ✔ Made up of people from different parts of the organization.

- ✔ Small, because large groups create communication problems.

- ✔ Self-managing and empowered to act, because referring decisions back up the line wastes time and often leads to worse decisions.

- ✔ Multifunctional, because that's the best — if not the only — way to keep the actual product and its essential delivery system clearly visible and foremost in everyone's mind.

Consider this example of a self-managing team at the Tennessee Valley Authority (TVA). A TVA civil engineering unit had the monthly responsibility of checking the operation of 100 warning sirens at a local nuclear power

Book I

Key Business Skills to Enhance Your Chance of Success

plant. When a second plant opened nearby, this team was given responsibility for checking 105 additional sirens — double their normal workload. On their own initiative, the team put together a work schedule that ensured the work was completed on time, while streamlining reporting requirements. The initiative was a great success: Deadlines were met and the TVA saved the money it would have had to spend on hiring more people to inspect the sirens.

More and more, where management is willing to let go of the reins of absolute authority and turn them over to workers, self-managing teams are rising to the challenge and making major contributions to the success of their firms. Indeed, the future success of many businesses lies in the successful implementation of self-managed teams.

Teaming Up in the Real World

Empowerment is a beautiful thing when it flourishes in an organization. When they are real and not pale imitations, empowered teams typically

- ✔ Make the most of the decisions that influence team success
- ✔ Choose their leaders
- ✔ Add or remove team members
- ✔ Set their goals and commitments
- ✔ Define and perform much of their training
- ✔ Receive rewards as a team

However, real empowerment is still rare, and employee empowerment, for the most part, may be only an illusion. Many plastic substitutes are out there masquerading as empowerment! Although many managers talk a good story about how they empower their employees, few actually do it.

Conducted by management expert Bob Culver, a recent study of managers, team leaders, and team members at nine different companies discovered that real-world teams are more participative than empowered. Basically, top management is still making the real decisions. If you manage a team, use Culver's study results as a basis for applying the following specific recommendations to counter the ineffectiveness of many teams:

Book I

Key
Business
Skills to
Enhance
Your
Chance of
Success

New technology, teams, and the changing role of managers

According to _Fortune_ magazine, the three dominant forces shaping 21st-century organizations are the following:

- A high-involvement workplace with self-managed teams and other devices for empowering employees.

- A new emphasis on managing business processes rather than functional departments.

- The evolution of information technology to the point where knowledge, accountability, and results can be distributed rapidly anywhere in the organization.

The integrating ingredient of these three dominant forces is information. Information technology and the way information is handled are increasingly becoming the keys to an organization's success.

In a team environment, _process management information_ moves precisely to where the team needs it, unfiltered by a hierarchy. Raw numbers go straight to those who need them in their jobs because frontline workers, such as salespeople and machinists, have been trained in how to use that information. By letting information flow wherever the team needs it, a horizontal self-managed company isn't only possible, it's also inevitable. Information technology-enabled team support systems include e-mail, computer conferencing, and videoconferencing that coordinate geographically, as well as across time zones, more easily than ever before. The development and use of computer software to support teams is also growing. An example is the expanding body of software called _groupware._ Groupware consists of computer programs specifically designed to support collaborative work groups and processes.

As organizations make better use of information technology, they don't need middle managers as often to make decisions. The result? The number of management levels and the number of managers can be dramatically reduced. Jobs, careers, and knowledge shift constantly. Typical management career paths are eliminated, and workers advance by learning more skills to be of greater value to the organization.

Those managers who remain need to take on new skills and attitudes to be more of a coach, supporter, and facilitator to the frontline employees. Supervisors and managers no longer have the luxury of spending time trying to control the organization — instead, they change it. Their job is to seek out new customers at the same time as they respond to the latest needs of their established customers. Managers still have considerable authority, but instead of commanding workers, their job is to inspire workers.

- **Make your teams empowered, not merely participative:** Instead of just inviting employees to participate in teams, grant team members the authority and power to make independent decisions.

  - Allow your teams to make long-range and strategic decisions, not just procedural ones.

- Permit the team to choose the team leaders.

- Allow the team to determine its goals and commitments.

- Make sure that all team members have influence by involving them in the decision-making process.

✔ **Remove the source of conflicts:** Despite their attempts to empower employees, managers are often unwilling to live with the results. Be willing to start up a team, and then be prepared to accept the outcome.

- Recognize and work out personality conflicts.

- Fight turf protection and middle-management resistance.

- Work to unify manager and team member views.

- Minimize the stress of downsizing and process improvement tasks.

✔ **Change other significant factors that influence team effectiveness:** Each of these factors indicates that an organization has not yet brought true empowerment to its employees. You have the power to change this situation. Do it!

- Allow the team to discipline poorly performing members.

- Make peer pressure less important in attaining high team performance.

- Train as many team members as you train managers or team leaders.

Although clear examples of companies where management has truly empowered its teams do exist (they're out there somewhere), team empowerment doesn't just happen. Supervisors and managers must make concerted and ongoing efforts to ensure that authority and autonomy pass from management to teams.

Meeting Productively in a Team Structure

Teams are clearly an idea whose time has come. As organizations continue to flatten their hierarchies and empower frontline workers with more responsibility and authority, teams are the visible and often inevitable result. And meetings are the primary forum in which team members conduct business and communicate with one another. Bottom line? Teams can't be effective if your meetings aren't.

Book I

Key
Business
Skills to
Enhance
Your
Chance of
Success

Consider the meetings instituted at General Electric by former chairman Jack Welch. Welch determined that if the company was going to be successful, it had to move away from the old model of autocratic meetings and direction from top management. He instituted the following meetings:

- **Town-hall-like meetings throughout the entire organization.** These meetings, called *work out* meetings, bring workers and managers together in open forums where workers are allowed to ask any question they want and managers are required to respond.

- **Regular meetings of senior executives — each of whom represents one of GE's individual business units.** The purpose of these meetings is to shape the company's core business strategies. In these high-energy meetings, attendees are encouraged to explore every possible avenue and alternative and to be open to new ideas. GE's ventures in Mexico, India, and China are a direct result of these meetings.

- **Employee teams responsible for specific plant functions — shipping, assembly, and so forth.** However, instead of tapping only employees from shipping to be on the shipping team, for example, teams consist of employees from all parts of the plant. This process enables representatives from all affected departments to discuss how suggested changes or improvements may affect their part of the operation. Hourly workers run the meetings on their own, and *advisers* — GE's term for salaried employees — participate in meetings only at the team's request.

The results of the employee team experiment at GE's lightning arrester plant in Bayamón, Puerto Rico produced clear and convincing evidence that General Electric's approach is quite successful. A year after startup, the plant's employees measured 20 percent higher in productivity than their closest counterpart in the mainland United States. And if that wasn't enough, management projected a further 20 percent increase in the following year.

With the proliferation of teams in business today, it pays to master the basic skills of meeting management; the following sections give you the highlights. For an entire chapter devoted to this topic, head to Book III, Chapter 2.

What's wrong with meetings?

Far too many meetings in organizations today are run poorly. Instead of contributing to an organization's efficiency and effectiveness, most meetings actually make employees less efficient and less effective. How many times have you heard someone complain about getting stuck in one more useless meeting? With today's business imperative to get more done with less, making every meeting count is more important than ever.

Meeting experts have determined that approximately 53 percent of all the time spent in meetings — and this means the time that *you* spend in meetings — is unproductive, worthless, and of little consequence. And when you realize that most businesspeople spend at least 25 percent of their working hours in meetings, with upper management spending more than double that time in meetings, you can begin to gain an appreciation for the importance of learning and applying effective meeting skills.

So what's wrong with meetings, anyway? Why do so many meetings go so wrong, and why can't you ever seem to do anything about it? Here are a few of the reasons:

- **Too many meetings take place:** The problem is not just that too many meetings take place; the problem is that many meetings are unnecessary, unproductive, and a waste of your time.

- **Attendees are unprepared:** Some meetings happen prematurely, before a real reason to meet arises. Other times, individuals who have prepared neither themselves nor the participants for the topics to be discussed lead the meeting. What often results is a long period of time where the participants stumble around blindly trying to figure out why the meeting was called in the first place.

- **Certain individuals dominate the proceedings:** You may find one or two in every crowd. You know, the people who think that they know it all and who make sure that their opinion is heard loudly and often during the course of a meeting. These folks may be good for occasional comic relief, if nothing else, but they often intimidate the other participants and stifle their contributions.

- **They last too long:** Yes, yes, yes. Meetings should last only as long as they need to. No less, no more. Most managers let meetings expand to fill the time allotted to them, dragging the meeting on and on rather than letting the participants leave after the business at hand is completed.

- **The meeting has no focus:** Meeting leadership is not a passive occupation. Many pressures work against keeping meetings on track and on topic, and managers often fail to step up to the challenge. The result is the proliferation of personal agendas, digressions, diversions, off-topic tangents, and worse.

The eight keys to great meetings

Despite the numerous meeting pitfalls, you have hope. Although many meetings are a big waste of time, they don't have to be. Your dysfunctional meeting blues have a cure! And good news again: The cure is readily available, inexpensive, and easy to swallow:

Book I

Key
Business
Skills to
Enhance
Your
Chance of
Success

✔ **Be prepared:** You need only a little time to prepare for a meeting, and the payoff is increased meeting effectiveness. Instead of wasting time trying to figure out why you're meeting ("uh, does anyone know why we're here today?"), your preparation gets results as soon as the meeting starts.

✔ **Have an agenda:** An agenda is your road map, your meeting plan. With it, you and the other participants recognize the meeting goals and know what you're going to discuss. If you're running the meeting, distribute the agenda to participants before the meeting to multiply its effectiveness many times over because the participants can prepare for the meeting in advance. If you're a participant, ask the meeting leader for an agenda in advance. Your request may encourage her to write an agenda if she hadn't already been planning to.

✔ **Start on time and end on time (or sooner):** You go to a meeting on time, and the meeting leader, while muttering about an important phone call or visitor, arrives 15 minutes late. Even worse is when the meeting leader ignores the scheduled ending time and lets the meeting go on and on. When you're the meeting leader, respect your participants by starting and ending your meetings on time. You don't want them spending the entire meeting looking at their watches and worrying about how late you're going to keep them. And if you're a participant at the meeting, it should go without saying: Don't be late.

✔ **Have fewer but better meetings:** If you're in charge of calling team meetings, don't abuse the power — call a meeting only when a meeting is absolutely necessary. And when you call a meeting, make the meeting a good one. Do you really have to meet to discuss change in your travel reimbursement policy? Wouldn't an e-mail message to all company travelers do just as well? Or how about the problem you've been having with the financial reports? Instead of calling a meeting, maybe a phone call can do the trick. Whenever you're tempted to call a meeting, make sure that you have a good reason for doing so.

✔ **Think inclusion, not exclusion:** Be selective with whom you invite to your meetings — select only as many participants as needed to get the job done. But don't exclude people who may have the best insight into your issues simply because of their ranks in the organization. If you receive a meeting invitation and know of other people who would be valuable additions, speak to the meeting leader in advance and suggest extending the invitation. She may not have thought of them.

You never know who in your organization is going to provide the best ideas, and you only hurt your chances of getting those great ideas by excluding people for non-performance-related reasons.

✔ **Maintain the focus:** Ruthlessly keep your meetings on topic at all times. Although doing everything but talking about the topic at hand can be a lot of fun, the meeting is being held for a specific reason. Stick to the topic, and if the meeting finishes early, participants who want to stick around to talk about other topics don't have to hold the other participants hostage to do so.

✔ **Capture action items:** Make sure that you have a system for capturing, summarizing, and assigning action items to individual team members. Flip charts — those big pads of paper that you hang from an easel in front of the group — are great for this purpose. Have you ever come out of a meeting wondering why the meeting took place? You may feel that way because the meeting had no purpose, no direction, no assignments or follow-up actions. If you're the meeting leader, make sure that your meetings have purpose and that you assign action items to the appropriate people. If you're a participant, be sure to clarify with the leader what is expected from you when the meeting is over.

✔ **Get feedback:** Feedback can be a great way to measure the effectiveness of the meetings you call. Not only can you find out what you did right, but you also can find out what you did wrong and get ideas on how to make your future meetings more effective. Ask the participants to give you their honest and open feedback — verbally or in writing — and then use it. You can never see yourself as others do unless they show you.

Chapter 5

Negotiating to Get What You Need and Deserve

The skills you need to be a successful negotiator in your everyday life are the same skills powerful businesspeople use during major international and industrial negotiations. Sure, you can refine these skills with additional techniques and strategies, and you enhance them with your own style and personality. But only these six skills are essential:

✔ Thorough preparation

✔ The ability to set limits and goals

✔ Good listening skills

✔ Clarity of communication

✔ Knowing how and when to push your pause button

✔ Knowing how to close a deal

The six basic negotiating skills apply to all areas of life. They can empower you to be happier and more successful in your life by enabling you to gain more respect, reach better agreements with your business partners and family, and maintain more control in your negotiations. They're so important, in fact, that everyone should have them hanging on the wall, just as every chemistry lab displays the periodic table of elements.

This chapter explains these six steps in detail. After you understand how you can use these skills in a negotiation, use them every time you sit down at the negotiating table. As your skills grow, you will take charge of *all* the negotiations you face in your life. Even if your dreams or your paycheck seem to hinge on forces beyond your control, you can create a master plan for your life and achieve your dreams — one negotiation at a time.

Getting Prepared

Preparation is the bedrock of negotiation success. You cannot be overprepared for a negotiation. Whether you're involved in a business or personal negotiation, you must be thoroughly prepared to achieve your goals. Heck, you have to be well prepared just to know what your goals are. In any negotiation, you must prepare in three areas:

- Yourself
- For the other person
- For the market

Each of these aspects deserves your attention. Pay special attention to the first point because you are the most important person in the room. The second item will change as your negotiations change. The third point deserves your lifelong attention.

Prepare yourself

Preparing yourself for a negotiation means knowing yourself and what you want out of life and recognizing your strengths and weaknesses. With adequate preparation, you boost your confidence and improve your performance during a negotiation. To adequately prepare, you need to take time to reflect and plan. Be sure to think through the following items:

- **What you want out of life:** Long-range thinking about your own life provides a context for every negotiation you have. Your negotiations are likely to go astray if you don't prepare your personal, long-range game plan *before* entering the negotiating room. For example, if you're buying ski equipment, you want to know how much you'll be skiing in the next five years because it may be cheaper to rent the equipment. On the job, considering where you want to be in five years might lead you to be more concerned about title and staff allocations than salary.

> ✔ **Strengths and weaknesses:** The better you know your own needs, the more easily you can identify the qualities that may help you in negotiations. For example, are you a good listener, or do you ignore what other people have to say? Are you a morning person? If not, don't let someone schedule a conference call for 7:30 in the morning.

Prepare for the other party

When you find out who will be negotiating with you, whether it's one person or a group, research the participants. Try to determine what's key to the other party: Is it the bottom line, or is quality more important? Knowing what the other party values helps you emphasize that aspect of your proposal. You also want to know the other party's level of authority. If the person or group you're negotiating with has to get approval from folks several rungs up the organizational ladder, you know you'd better provide some written materials or your proposal probably won't be repeated accurately.

One of the most common instances where you should do some research on the other person is before a job interview. Perhaps you and your interviewer share a similar past experience such as attending the same college. When you show that you know a fact or two about the other person from having done your research, you usually score points with the interviewer. It can also help you build rapport. In a negotiation, showing that you've prepared for the other person also serves as an icebreaker before getting down to the nitty-gritty.

Prepare for the field

Research your industry. It's as simple as that. A car dealer knows best about cars. A chemist knows best about chemistry. An art dealer knows best about art. If you're going to negotiate in a world that isn't familiar to you, research it. Know the players, know whom to talk to, study the terminology. Do whatever it takes to be the smartest person in the room.

Be a constant student of the industry or business in which you work. People who have a spent a lifetime with a company bring added value to the company simply because of all the information they have stored in their heads. The more you know about the business environment in general and your company in particular, the better off you are.

Setting Goals for a Negotiation

The only way to achieve anything is to set goals. Even when you make an impulse purchase, your subconscious mind has set a goal: You see something you want, you set your goal to acquire it, your hand goes out, you grab it, and (after paying for it, of course!) it's yours. That's a familiar retail scenario. In a business situation, setting goals is a more serious, labor-intensive process. Chapter 3 in Book I provides general information on how to set goals. When setting goals for a negotiation, you have to go through a winnowing process so that you can ensure that your *key* objectives — and not necessarily *all* your objectives — are addressed. You don't want to overload any single negotiation with all your hopes and dreams for all times. So a key element of goal setting for a negotiation is to pare your list back to a manageable number of goals to work on.

Establishing your goals

Setting goals for yourself, for others, or for your organization is a practical activity that demands preparation and disciplined focus. Setting goals is not wishful thinking. It's not fantasizing. It's not daydreaming. A *goal* is any object or end that you strive to reach. For example, becoming rich and famous may be the result of achieving certain goals, but fame and fortune are not the goals themselves. Deciding to write a best-selling book is not setting a goal; it's daydreaming. Deciding to write a book that is interesting and makes a solid contribution is a goal (an ambitious one, but a goal nonetheless).

Before setting specific goals, you should know what your life goals are. Knowing what you want to achieve in life gives you an overall perspective that shapes your everyday decision-making process. Ask yourself these questions:

- ✔ What level do I want to reach in my career?

- ✔ What kind of knowledge, training, or skills will I need to reach a certain level in my career?

- ✔ How do I want my partner or other members of the team to perceive me?

- ✔ How much money do I want to earn? At what stage in my career do I want to earn this amount?

- ✔ Do I want to achieve any artistic goals in my career? If so, what?

If your life goal is to become an Olympic champion, set all your goals with that ultimate purpose in mind. You must take many steps along the way to becoming a champion of any kind — the training, the dedication, the discipline. Think about your purpose in life, your ultimate goal; your negotiating goals should contribute to that purpose deal by deal.

The easiest and fastest way to keep your goals in mind is to write them down. This helps you visualize them and makes them real. Place them somewhere you see them on a daily basis. Being reminded of your goals each day can help your intuition guide you toward achieving them.

Research shows that individuals who set challenging, specific goals do better than those who don't. The following sections outline a few points to keep in mind when thinking about your goals.

For detailed information on what SMART goals are and how to set goals, refer to Book I, Chapter 3.

Book I

Key Business Skills to Enhance Your Chance of Success

Set your personal goals yourself, before a negotiation begins

Get all the information you can from others about the marketplace and the person with whom you'll be negotiating (refer to the earlier section "Getting Prepared"), but set your own goals. Only you know what your personal dreams are and what will make you happy. Keep a practiced eye on your goals during the course of the negotiation.

Make sure your goals are challenging yet attainable

When setting your goals, shoot high or not at all — you can be sure that the other side will never ask you to raise your goals. But remember, goals that are *too* high for the deal lead to frustration and failed negotiations. For the specific negotiation at hand, consider the marketplace, current values, and your available options.

Don't set your goals too low. Setting very low goals is as detrimental to a negotiation as setting unrealistically high goals. Setting low goals signals weakness and indifference during a negotiation. The other party will see right through you. You should set goals that are slightly out of your grasp, but not so far that you can't achieve them.

Make your goals specific

Your goals shouldn't be so abstract that no one — including you — can tell whether you achieved them. To avoid any ambiguity, quantify your goals as much as possible. If you're selling your home, for example, saying, "I want as much as I can get" isn't a good goal. While probably a true statement, it doesn't help you achieve anything. A well-stated goal for the price portion of the negotiation must include an exact amount, like $325,000. If you can't be that specific, you'd better prepare some more.

Separate long- and short-term goals

Set your goals for any particular negotiation with an eye on your long-range life goals, but keep your feet planted firmly on the ground. You want to accomplish the immediate objective of the current negotiation; you also want each negotiation to advance you toward achieving your ultimate life goals. Your goals in any negotiation should help you march along the life path you've set for yourself.

Choosing the right number of goals

The negotiation itself dictates the number of specific goals you should set. I've been amazed at how many goals some people can squeeze into even a simple negotiation. Recognize that you can't get everything done in one negotiation. If, for example, your priority is to get a raise, don't demand a car allowance, overtime pay, and an assistant all in the same session. By putting too much on the table at one time, you just confuse people. Your boss's eyes will glaze over, and you may not get anything at all.

Be realistic about your goal setting. Setting too many goals in a negotiation can make you look ignorant and naive. To combat this situation, walk into the negotiation with a written schematic of your goals. Stay on course with what is written on the page.

Prioritize your goals

It's a rare negotiation in which you achieve all of your goals. You must know which are the most important. So prioritize them in order from most to least important.

If you find yourself goal setting on a team, you want to achieve 100 percent consensus about the official ranking of your goals. However, be aware that different individuals may hold onto their personal agendas. This is often a tougher negotiation than the one with the other side. If you can't reach a consensus, then a serious question arises as to whether the faction that was outvoted continues on the negotiating team.

Set limits

After you've nailed down your goals, you need to set limits. Setting your limits simply means determining the point at which you're willing to walk away from this deal and close the deal elsewhere. For instance, you set limits when you interview for a job by establishing the lowest salary you'll accept.

Setting limits is a scary thing. It takes practice for some people, but if you don't do it, others will take and take and take as long as you keep giving. At some point, you realize that you have given too much — a line has been crossed — all because you didn't set your limits ahead of time. To help yourself set limits, keep these points in mind:

✔ **Know that you have other choices:** Poor negotiators tend to attach themselves to the notion that they must close every negotiation with a purchase or sale. Good negotiators, on the other hand, often walk away. Walking away from a bad deal is just as important — maybe more important — than closing a good deal.

The worst prison is the one you build around your mind if you decide you don't have choices. So make this phrase your mantra: *There is always another deal around the corner.*

✔ **Know what the other choices are:** Don't develop just one alternative deal in a negotiation. List all the alternatives available to you should the negotiation fail to close on the terms you want. What are your options if you walk away from this deal?

Don't edit your list. You have nothing to lose and everything to gain by listing all your options, even if you don't think they're very valuable or practical. You have plenty of time to edit them down later.

✔ **Know your *or else:*** After you've created the list of alternatives, decide which alternative is most acceptable to you. Pick your personal *or else.* Decide what you want to do if the negotiation doesn't close. Think about that course of action. Play the scenario out in your mind. Knowing what your *or else* is — that is, knowing what your favorite option is if the deal doesn't close — defines your limits for each negotiation.

Becoming a Good Listener

To become successful in the business world and stay successful, you must be a good listener. Here are some examples of the importance of listening effectively while you're on the clock:

✔ Many managers face setbacks in their careers when they prejudge an employee before they hear all sides of the story. If you want to gain respect as a manager, gather all the data from all the parties before you take any action.

✔ When they enter a meeting or a department, new employees need to listen first. Get the lay of the land. Resist that first verbal contribution, which will be everyone's first impression of you, until you know that the contribution is a good one.

✔ Salespeople lose sales when they talk more than they listen. The successful ones use empathetic statements to show they understand what the customer is saying and how he's feeling.

In a negotiation, silence is golden — in fact, it's money in the bank. Remember, you can't listen and talk at the same time (not to yourself or to anyone else). Many a negotiation has been blown — and many a sale lost — because someone kept talking long after discussion was necessary or desirable. Conversely, many an opportunity to gain valuable information has been lost because the listening activity stops too soon.

One of the best ways to control a meeting is to listen to everyone in the room. If a big talker is monopolizing the negotiation, that person probably doesn't even recognize that others want to contribute to the discussion. Stifle your instinct to grab the floor yourself. Instead, point out someone else who looks as though he or she is trying to talk. "Jane, you look like you had a comment on that." Jane appreciates it, others appreciate it, and you suddenly control the meeting even if you're the junior person at the table. Sometimes others can make your point for you. If you find that you still have something to add, the group will probably let you do so. You are now a hero, even to members of the other negotiating team. When you do say something, everyone listens out of appreciation — if not admiration.

The following sections describe several ways you can improve your listening skills right now. (See Book IV, Chapter 2 for more help developing your listening skills.) These techniques are easy to use and bring immediate results.

Restate and rephrase

Whether you're at home, at the office, or on an airplane, start working on your listening skills. In your next conversation, use two active listening tools: restatement and paraphrasing. Both tools involve checking in with the person who's talking to find out whether you're hearing what she's saying.

- ✔ **Restating:** Repeat, word-for-word, a short statement that the other person has just made to you. Even if the next speaker is a flight attendant offering drinks, you can say, "Okay, so my choices are . . ." and rattle off the list. It's harder than you think. You won't use this technique all the time or in every circumstance, but it's a good place to start raising your own awareness level about listening.

- ✔ **Paraphrasing:** Recount, in your own words, the longer statements that the other person has said to you. You can use this technique far more often than restating. Don't be embarrassed if you get it wrong a lot when you first start paraphrasing back. This is a good technique to use when someone is making a dense presentation and you want to be sure that you understand it, every step of the way.

In either case, introduce your efforts with respect and good humor. Try starting with the phrase, "Let me see if I got that right. . . ." (For more tips on communicating effectively, refer to the first three chapters in Book IV.)

Book I

Key
Business
Skills to
Enhance
Your
Chance of
Success

Clear away the clutter

To be a good listener, you have to clear out the clutter. This isn't just a question of good manners; it's an absolute necessity if you want to focus on the person speaking to you. Noise clutter, desk clutter, and even mind clutter all interfere with good listening. It also keeps others from listening to you.

Think about the worst listener you've encountered in your life. If you have a teenager, you probably don't have to look too far. Consider the all-too-typical teen's life: an MP3 player plugged into both ears, cellphone in hand, television set blaring, books and clothes strewn everywhere. No wonder your teenager can't hear you. Your words may temporarily penetrate the chaos, but the full content of your message doesn't get through. It can't get through all the clutter. Why not learn from your teenager's mistakes? Following are ways to maintain complete focus on the person and avoid interruptions and other distractions during the meeting:

- ✔ When you talk to someone, don't just mute the television set, turn it off.

- ✔ If you have something else on your mind, write it down before you enter a conversation. With a note as a reminder, you won't worry about forgetting to address the issue — and your mind is free to concentrate on the conversation.

- ✔ Clear your desk — or whatever is between you and the speaker — so you can focus on what the speaker is saying.

- ✔ Don't accept phone calls while you're talking with someone else. Interrupting a conversation to take a telephone call makes the person in the room with you feel unimportant and makes what you have to say seem unimportant.

When a co-worker comes to your office, don't feel that you need to engage in a discussion right away. If you know that you need to finish a task, you may be better off delaying the conversation. Otherwise, the unfinished task will play gently on your mind and distract you from listening effectively. If the project you're engaged in will only take a moment to complete, try saying, "Just a minute, let me finish this so I can give you my full attention." If it's going to take a while, ask to schedule a meeting for later that day. You may be afraid that the other person will be insulted if you put him off. In fact, the vast majority of people are flattered that you actually want to listen. Your co-workers would rather wait until you can listen than have you tending to other business while they're trying to talk to you.

The same rule holds true for phone conversations. Never try to negotiate on the telephone while you're reading a note from your assistant, catching up on filing, or doing research on the Internet. Trying to do two tasks at once simply doesn't work. True, your ears can be engaged in listening while your eyes are occupied with something else. However, your brain cannot simultaneously process the conflicting information from your eyes and from your ears. Both messages lose out.

A lot of people like to brag about their ability to multi-task, and they're probably safe to do so, if the tasks are not very important or accuracy isn't critical. But if it's anything important, don't multi-task. Don't ever try to con yourself into believing that you can listen effectively while you're doing something else that requires the least little bit of brainpower.

Take notes

Taking notes is a great listening aid. Regardless of whether you ever refer to your notes again, the mere act of writing down the salient points boosts the entire listening process. Writing information down engages other parts of your brain, as well as your eyes and fingers, in the listening process. It's almost impossible for a person to fully absorb an entire conversation of any length without making some written notes.

Making notes is important throughout every step of the negotiating process. Immediately after a negotiating session, review your notes to be sure that you wrote down everything you may want to recall, and that you can read everything you wrote down. (Remember from your student days how confusing old notes can be: strange abbreviations, unintelligible squiggles, large coffee stains!)

When you're comfortable with your notes, consider providing a status report to the other side. A confirming memo is an excellent way to assure that you listened well. Writing down what you think you heard and verifying the material with the other side are positive experiences for both parties. And if the other party agrees, consider recording the meeting.

Ask good questions

How you ask questions during a negotiation is very important because questions open the door to knowledge — knowledge about the other party and knowledge about the negotiation at hand. Questions are the keys to the kingdom. No one ever wasted time asking a smart question.

Guidelines for better questions

Asking a good question is a learned skill requiring years of training. The foundation of good question asking is knowing what information you want to obtain. The following list offers several handy guidelines for asking better questions — questions that are likely to get to the meat of things.

- **Plan your questions in advance.** Prepare what you're going to ask ahead of time. If you plan ahead, you can follow the speaker's train of thought and harvest much more information. Pretty soon, the speaker is comfortably divulging information. The question-and-answer format can act as an aid to good communication rather than a block.

  Don't memorize the exact wording of your question, or you'll sound artificial. A script is too restrictive to flow naturally into the conversation. However, it pays to outline your purpose and a sequence of related questions.

- **Ask with a purpose.** Every question you ask should have one of two basic purposes: to get facts or to get opinions.

- **Tailor your question to your listener.** Relate questions to the listener's frame of reference and background. If the listener is a farmer, use farming examples. If the listener is your teenager, make references to school life, dating, or other areas that will hit home. Be sure to use words and phrases the listener understands. Don't try to dazzle your 5-year-old with your vast vocabulary or slip computer jargon in on your technologically handicapped, unenlightened boss.

- **Follow general questions with more specific ones.** These specific inquiries, called *follow-up questions,* generally get you past the fluff and into the meat-and-potatoes information. This progression is also the way that most people think, so you're leading them down a natural path.

- **Keep questions short and clear — cover only one subject.** If you really want to know two different things, ask two different questions. You're the one who wants the information; you're the one who should do the work. Crafting short questions takes more energy, but the effort is worth it.

- **Make transitions between their answers and your questions.** Listen to the answer to your first question. Use something in the answer to frame your next question. This approach sounds more conversational and therefore less threatening. And even if it takes you off the path for a while, it also leads to rich rewards because of the comfort level it provides to the person you are questioning.

- **Don't interrupt; let the other person answer the question!** You're asking the questions to get answers, so it almost goes without saying that you need to stop talking and listen.

Responding to non-answers

People use certain techniques to avoid providing accurate answers. Do not allow these ploys. When you're alert to these substitutes for honest information, you can demand the real McCoy.

- ✔ **The "dodge":** Sometimes people provide an answer, but it's not an answer to the question you asked. For an example, tune into the Sunday morning shows that feature our elected representatives. If someone asks about the state of public education, the representative may launch into a dissertation about family values. When you're given the dodge, recognize it for what it is and repeat the question, this time insisting on a real answer or an exact time when you can expect an answer.

  When people say that they have to look into something and get back to you, about the only thing you can do (without making a rather obvious and frontal assault on their honesty) is wait. However, you *can* nail them down to a specific date and time that they will "get back to you." If the question is important enough for the other side to delay (or not answer at all), the issue is important enough for you to press forward. Asking, "When can I expect an answer from you?" is a direct way of obtaining that information. Be sure to make a note of the reply.

- ✔ **An assertion that isn't an answer:** A person who doesn't want to answer your question may try instead to emphatically state something close to what you're looking for. This technique is common when you're asking for a commitment that the other party doesn't want to make. For example, you ask whether a company plans to spend $50,000 on advertising in the next year. You receive an emphatic statement that the company has spent $50,000 each year for the past four years, that sales are rising, and that any company would be a fool to cut back now. Don't settle for such assertions — push for an answer. Say something like "Does that mean that your company has made a final commitment to spend $50,000 for advertising this year?"

  Because assertions are sometimes delivered with a great deal of energy or passion, you may feel awkward insisting on the answer to your question. Not persisting with the inquiry can be fatal to your interests.

- ✔ **The wishy-washy "they":** Beware the deadly pronoun: *he, she,* the infamous *they,* and the power-gilded *we.* Pronouns can send you into a quagmire of misunderstanding. During a negotiation, force your counterpart to use specific nouns and proper names. This preventive measure avoids a great deal of miscommunication.

Count to three before you speak

One. Two. Three. Here's an extraordinarily simple device to help you listen more effectively. Just count to three before you speak. This slight delay enables you to absorb and understand the last statement before you respond. The delay also announces that you've given some thought to what you're about to say. It gives oomph to the words that come out of your mouth. As you practice this skill, counting may not be necessary, but the pause always pays off. You absorb the message, and you give the other party one last chance to modify the statement or question. Even if your response is simply that you must consult with your client, spouse, or boss, pausing for three beats helps you better comprehend and remember what the other person said.

Wake yourself up

If you are truly interested in what the other party is saying, look the part. Keep your eyes focused. Acknowledge the other party's words with a nod. However, if you feel yourself getting drowsy or boredom is setting in, don't give in. Sit up straighter. Stand up. Get the blood flowing in whatever way works for you.

Don't think that you can effectively hide flagging interest without changing your physical position. If you're tired, it'll show. And if boredom sets in, don't expect a lively conversation or a good negotiation.

In your very next conversation, assume the most attentive position you can. Observe how this change in behavior improves your listening skills. Follow these tips for enhancing your next conversation:

- ✔ Uncross your arms and legs.
- ✔ Sit straight in the chair.
- ✔ Face the speaker full on.
- ✔ Lean forward.
- ✔ Make as much eye contact as you can.

As you listen to the other party in a negotiation, be alert to the occasional indicators that the other person is not really listening to you. If the other person says something like "uh-huh" or "that's interesting," find out immediately whether this response is an expression of genuine interest, a way of postponing discussion, or — equally fatal to communication — a signal that she's fighting the dreaded doze monster. Those little demons that tug at the eyelids in the middle of the afternoon cause odd, nonspecific utterances to fall from the lips.

Stating Your Points Clearly

In many ways, clear communication is the other side of effective listening. Just as you cannot listen *too* well, there is no such thing as being *too* clear. You can be too blunt, too fast, and too slow. You can't be too clear. When you speak, write, or otherwise communicate clearly, your listener understands your intended message.

Sounds simple enough. Why aren't more people successful at it? Because most people communicate from this point of view: What do *I* want to tell my listener? How am *I* going to appear? What are they going to think of *me?* Not effective. Your point of view must be from the listener's side of the communication. Ask yourself these questions: What does my listener need to know? What information does my listener need in order to make a decision? What is my listener's knowledge of the subject?

First, you must be clear with yourself about what information you're trying to get across. Then you must know who the listener is, what filters are in place, and how to get through those filters so you can be understood.

Organizing your thoughts

Before you can organize your thoughts, assess what your listener needs and then find out how experienced he is with the subject matter. When you know that, you can figure out how much of your presentation needs to focus on general education — bringing the other person up-to-speed, as they say.

After you find out that background information, spend some time organizing the thoughts and information that will go into your presentation. Here are three favorite ways to organize a presentation.

P.R.E.P. for a presentation

The first way to get organized is by using the P.R.E.P technique: *point, reason, example, point.* It works because it's so logical; you won't leave anyone in the dust. Here's an example:

- ✔ **My point is:** Exercise is energizing.

- ✔ **The reason is:** It gets your heart rate up.

- ✔ **My example is:** After at least 20 to 30 minutes of increased heart rate, you are more energized when you come out of the gym than when you went in.

- ✔ **So, my point is:** Exercise is energizing.

This formula works with any presentation, from a five-minute informal chat to a thirty-minute formal speech using many examples. The P.R.E.P. approach is a great way to get organized and be clear.

Book I

Key
Business
Skills to
Enhance
Your
Chance of
Success

Outline your points

Another strategy is to list and number your points. The following is an example:

I recommend that you hire the consultant to create a plan that will

1. Increase sales
2. Improve morale
3. Generate productivity

Tell 'em once, tell 'em twice, tell 'em again

This example is a classic standby used by presenters and writers across the country because it drives a point home:

- ✔ Tell 'em what you're gonna tell 'em.
- ✔ Tell 'em.
- ✔ Tell 'em what you told 'em.

Avoiding barriers to clarity

The biggest barriers to clarity are your own fears and lack of concentration. You fear that if you make yourself clearly understood, an adverse reaction will follow — some vague, unspoken, definitely unwanted reaction. Identify those fears and work to make them less of a roadblock.

- ✔ **Fear of rejection:** You may be afraid that if you present your ideas clearly, the listener will reject you or your conclusions. The natural inclination is to avoid rejection by blurring lines, being unclear, and failing to state your case accurately. If it's true that an accurate statement of intent would cause the deal to fall apart, being clear is even more important. When you close a deal without being clear, the parties have different understandings and expectations. You're finalizing a bad deal. In fact, you're closing a deal that can't possibly work.

  If you postpone the inevitable, when the listener eventually understands you, she may very likely reject the concept with the added energy that comes from frustration. "Why didn't you say so?" or "Why did you waste my time?" are the spoken — or unspoken — questions. These are tough questions to answer.

✔ **Fear of hurting someone else:** Often, people avoid hurting the feelings of others not out of compassion, but out of self-protection. If you have bad news to deliver, do so with dignity and respect for the person's feelings. Even if you feel, in every fiber of your being, that the person is overreacting to your news, don't say so. Let the feelings run their course. But don't flinch or amend your statement. Just wait. This, too, shall pass.

✔ **Fatigue:** You may be just plain tired and unable to focus. Pay attention to your body's signals. Sometimes a brisk walk outdoors revives you. Good nutrition and adequate rest are requirements for a master negotiator. If you eat right and get plenty of sleep, you can eliminate the need for cup after cup of coffee to stay alert. But in a pinch, an occasional dose of caffeine works, too.

✔ **Laziness:** You may not have prepared well enough and you're dreading being clear on some facts that are unsubstantiated. If this situation strikes a familiar chord, do your homework.

✔ **Interruptions:** Your listener may be doodling or not making eye contact. The room temperature may be extreme. Noise levels may be too high for you to be heard clearly. Hopefully you're assertive enough to request changes to the situation appropriately.

Pushing the Pause Button

Everyone has a *pause button* — a little device inside your head that helps you maintain emotional distance in a negotiation. Some people use it more than others. Others don't use it all. The pause button is the secret to keeping your emotional distance in a negotiation, and it can help you not to fall in love with the deal.

The pause button can take many forms — it can be a break during a heated negotiation, or it can be a moment of silence when you don't agree with someone's argument. *Pushing the pause button* just means putting the negotiations on hold for a moment or an hour or an evening while you sort things out.

When you push the pause button, you freeze-frame the negotiation — much as you freeze-frame a movie on the television screen with your remote control or on your computer. You step away, physically or psychologically, to review the work you have done up to that point and check over your plan for the rest of the negotiation. You take a break. It may be purely mental; it may be imperceptible to the other side; but you give yourself whatever time it takes to review matters before you continue.

Pushing the pause button gives you the opportunity to review the entire process of negotiating and to make sure that you aren't overlooking anything. It allows you to avoid getting boxed into a corner. By pushing the pause button, you keep your emotions from ruling (and ruining) the negotiation. When you don't use your pause button, you may jump into a deal too quickly because you didn't spend enough time thinking about your words and actions.

When to hit the pause button

Simply put, your pause button is anything you do to create a space so you can think over your next move. The following are times when you want to push the pause button:

- **At each critical moment in the negotiation.** You need some time to review the negotiation or to decide when to close a deal. Definitely use the pause button whenever you are feeling pressured or under stress. Decisions made under artificial pressures — especially time pressures imposed by the other side in a negotiation — are often flawed, simply because the decision maker doesn't have sufficient time to consult that most personal of counselors, the inner voice.

- **At every request for a concession.** A pause, no matter how slight, before making a concession gives you an opportunity to be sure it's the right thing to do in addition to giving the concession some importance. You want to be sure that you always have something left to give up in order to hold onto what is important to you. Plus, your moment of reflection gives the concession some significance; otherwise, you aren't perceived as having made a concession — the other party doesn't realize he's gained anything.

- **When your emotions are getting the upper hand.** Never let your emotions take control of your actions. Figure out in advance what sets you off. Identify your hot buttons. When you know what upsets you, talk about it with others on your team so you and they are ready if this kind of situation arises.

- **If a negotiation looks to be headed south and talks are at a standstill.** Think about the steps that got you to this point. Instead of making outlandish demands or angrily storming out of the negotiating room, take a breather and suggest meeting at a later time.

How to push the pause button

Everyone owns a pause button, so to speak, and everyone pushes it in a different way. Sometimes, how you push pause depends on the situation. Here are some of the more common pause buttons you can use:

> ✔ **Ask for a night to think the negotiation over.** Most people will respect your request to "sleep on it."
>
> ✔ **Excuse yourself to the restroom.** Who's going to refuse *that* request?
>
> ✔ **For a short break, just lean back in your chair and say, "Wait a minute, I have to take that in."** For a dramatic touch, try closing your eyes or rubbing your chin.
>
> ✔ **In a business situation, have someone with whom you have to consult before giving a final answer.** Simply say, "I'll have to run this by my partner (or family or consultants or whomever) and get back to you at 9 tomorrow morning."

One of the best times to pull out your pen for note-taking is when you need to pause. Writing down statements that confuse or upset you is an excellent way to push pause. Rather than blurting out an inappropriate or angry response, tell the speaker to hold on while you write down the statement. Asking the other party to check what you've written to be sure that you got it right can be enormously effective if the words upset you. The process of putting those words to paper almost always causes the other party to backtrack, amend, or better yet, erase the words altogether. You'll find that most people don't want their unreasonable statements on paper for all the world to see.

Closing the Deal

Closing is the culmination of the negotiation process. It's the point where everything comes together, when two parties mutually agree on the terms of the deal. Of course, it's seldom a single moment with crashing cymbals and loud drum rolls. Typically, closing a deal is a process of reaching agreement on one point after another, adjusting back and forth.

Arriving at a win-win solution

A *win-win* solution is a deal that fills your needs and goals while at the same time filling the needs and goals of the other side. Some negotiations are pretty straightforward, and the interests of each party are clear. For instance, when you're buying a car from someone who wants to sell a car, the negotiation is win-win if you find a price that works for each of you (assuming the wheels don't fall off the day after your check clears). In more complicated negotiations, the motivations of the other side aren't always so easy to find, at least not the more subtle factors that are driving the negotiation. Sometimes some head scratching and imagination are required to fully understand their interests.

Before you can have a win-win deal, your counterparts must determine their needs and be sure they are satisfied. You can't play mind reader and divine their needs and then start giving up what you want to make them happy.

Because creative thought is often necessary to arrive at win-win solutions, the best negotiators in a tight spot are also people who enjoy games or riddles — people who enjoy figuring things out. This is not to say that the only good negotiators are those with a Sudoku puzzle lying around the house. But it does help if you enjoy the challenge of figuring out what serves both sides — and the solutions are not always easy.

Your goal is to reach a win-win solution, a deal in which both sides are satisfied that it's a good one. Doing so is difficult, however, if you don't even know when your own team is getting what you want. To avoid this confusion, remember these definitions:

✔ A *good deal* is one that's fair under all circumstances at the time the agreement is made. It provides for various contingencies before problems arise. A good deal is workable in the real world. What is and isn't fair is very subjective, so the parties must decide for themselves whether an agreement is fair based on their own criteria. Make sure that everyone's in agreement. Draw the other side out on this basic point before closing the deal. You don't want to sign a deal with someone who is harboring resentments over some aspect of the agreement. Be sure that the other side agrees that the deal is a good one.

✔ A *bad deal* is not fair under all the circumstances. It allows foreseeable events to create problems in the relationship after the deal is struck. Some aspect of the agreement looks great on paper but simply doesn't work out in the real world — for reasons that were predictable during the deal-making process.

Assessing the deal

Before closing, assess whether the deal is good or bad. You determine whether a deal is good or bad for you; the other party determines whether that same deal is good or bad for him or her. To be sure that you have a good deal and a win-win situation, take a break just before closing and ask yourself the following questions:

✔ Based on all the information, can the other side perform the agreement to my expectations?

✔ Does this agreement further my personal long-range goals? Does the outcome of the negotiation fit into my own vision statement?

✔ Does this agreement fall comfortably within the goals and the limits I set for this particular negotiation?

✔ Are the people on both sides who have to carry out the agreement fully informed and ready to do whatever it takes to make the deal work?

In the ideal situation, the answer to all of these questions is a resounding *yes*. If you're unsure about any one of them, take some extra time and push your pause button. Review the entire situation. Assess how the agreement could be changed to create a *yes* answer to each question. Try your best to make the change needed to get a firm *yes* to each question.

When you have a *yes* response to each of the preceding questions, close the deal. Don't go for any more changes even if you think that the other person wouldn't mind — you never know! As Solomon wrote many years ago: "There is a time to reap and a time to sow." When it's time to close a deal, close it.

Recognizing when to close

The *when* of closing is easy: early and often. Keep the closing in mind as you prepare for your negotiation, as you listen to the other side, and every time you speak. A little piece of your mind should always focus on the closing — on bringing the negotiation to a mutually acceptable solution. You aren't likely to miss an opportunity to close when you view closing as a separate aspect of the negotiation rather than just the lucky result of a negotiation. In fact, the proper moment to make your first effort at closing a deal is when you first sit down.

If you have trouble closing deals, intentionally try to close your next negotiation earlier than you think is possible. You find that no harm is done and that the other side actually becomes sensitized to the need to conclude matters. Make a game of it. Chart your efforts to close. Your rate of successful closings rises as you become more and more aware of closing as a separate skill to bring out early and often.

Many people find it easier to close a deal if they set a deadline to do so. Negotiations tend to fall into place at the last minute. Having a deadline is like having a referee at the bargaining table. Remember, every deal has time constraints, so establishing a deadline can help the negotiation come to a smooth end.

Knowing how to close

The entire country seems to be in a search of the perfect close — the one that won't fail. Here's the big secret: The three ways to make the sale or to successfully close the negotiation are:

Book I

Key
Business
Skills to
Enhance
Your
Chance of
Success

1. Ask
2. Ask
3. Ask

And just what do you ask? Whether your counterpart will agree to the current terms. If you have trouble asking for commitments, address that issue. Being able to clearly state your need helps in every negotiation and in every other aspect of your life. (If you need to practice making yourself clear, refer to the earlier section "Stating Your Points Clearly.") Nothing short of persistent, organized inquiry is going to close a negotiation. It won't happen by itself.

And don't hesitate to confirm your understanding in writing. Even in complicated business negotiations, shooting off a simple e-mail confirming what you understand to be the deal is helpful. Don't wait for the lawyers to do it, although if the lawyers are going to be involved, it doesn't hurt to mention in your e-mail that everything is subject to the legal beagles working out the language and (in some cases) the details.

Overcoming barriers to closing

If you find it difficult to close, the real question is probably not "How do I do this?" but rather "Why do I hesitate instead of going for it?" Merely stating the question helps you to start thinking about the answer. It may just be your own personal, mental blocks to closing a deal. Many people have them. Do your best to deal with your own demons on your own schedule in your own way. But deal with them. Your negotiation skills will improve when you face your fears and refuse to let them get in the way of closing a deal. The most common fears are:

- ✔ **Fear of failure:** Most people have this fear to one extent or another. After all, no one likes to fail. It's not fun. In extreme cases, this fear will keep you from asking for what you want in the negotiation. After all, if you don't ever make your request, you can never fail to get it. The deal you are seeking is a piece of ever-dangling fruit waiting to be plucked.

- ✔ **Fear of rejection:** Everybody wants to be loved. Nobody really likes being cast aside. So the fear of rejection can block a person from asking for agreement. No asking, no rejection. It's as simple as that.

- ✔ **Fear of criticism:** Some people live or work in a situation in which they're likely to be criticized when they get back to what should be their support group. One way to prevent negative words and looks is to never close the deal. Who can criticize a deal while it's still being negotiated?

- ✔ **Fear of making a mistake:** Some people believe that making a mistake is a sin instead of a normal part of life. The mere possibility of doing something that could be deemed a goof dredges up all sorts of uncertainties and self-doubts. So instead of finalizing the deal, these people shy away from closing the negotiation in a timely fashion.

- ✔ **Fear of commitment:** Sometimes closing a deal triggers a short-term commitment like buying a particular car, but the consequences are sure to last for a year or two or five. Sometimes closing a deal results in a commitment that requires participation on both sides for longer than many American marriages last, so it's not surprising that many people get hung up on this idea.

- ✔ **Fear of loss:** Some negotiations last a long time and can be pretty intense. Closing the negotiation means losing that intense relationship.

Be sure to keep in mind that the other party also may have some mental blocks to closing. These blocks are the same fears that you may face, and the other side is unlikely to acknowledge how they affect the negotiation. If you sense that the person you're negotiating with has a fear that is blocking a close, don't play psychologist — unless you are one. Instead, try setting a time frame for the negotiation, mention the folks who want the other side to close the deal, or mention the consequences of not closing the deal.

Book II

Getting Organized and Managing Your Time: Smart Ways to Preempt Problems

The 5th Wave   By Rich Tennant

@RICHTENNANT

"So Frank, what's your secret for saving time?"

In this book . . .

This book should be entitled "Know Thy Enemy" because it focuses on the two most threatening forces out there that can sabotage your efforts to become the go-to person in your organization: disorganization and poor time management. If you think you're safe from these tendencies because you don't forget appointments and you're always busy, you may be surprised by all the ways seemingly essential tasks can actually impede getting the important stuff done. The chapters in this book help you understand where you're letting these forces derail you and how to get organized, efficient, and back on track for success.

Chapter 1

Peas in a Pod: Organization and Time Management

....

In This Chapter

▶ Increasing the value of your time

▶ Setting up a time-management system and anticipating challenges

▶ Getting a little help from your friends and persevering

▶ Recognizing the role organization plays in time management

....

Time is the great equalizer — everyone has the same amount in a day — and though you may not have the power to get yourself more time, you *do* have the power to make the most of it. You can take your 52 weeks a year, 7 days a week, and 1,440 minutes a day and invest them in such a way that you reap a return that fulfills your life and attracts success.

The key? Managing your time. This chapter is about taking control of how you spend your time to make sure you're using it how you really want to. And because being organized is a key component of time management, this chapter covers that, too.

Valuing Time

To manage time more effectively, you need to remember two things:

✔ **Time *is* money, and yours has a value.** In other words, you're always on the clock. Giving away your precious time without a sense of its value is like throwing money on the sidewalk. By knowing what your time is worth, you can prioritize those tasks that yield the greatest return, delegating or eliminating tasks that provide little to no return on your time investment.

✔ **Twenty percent of your efforts produce 80 percent of the results.** After you uncover which efforts produce that return, you can crank up those efforts to increase your results. Most success comes from prioritizing activities that produce results and giving them the focus they warrant, so anything you can do to increase the attention you give those activities serves you well.

You don't have to get everything done, but make sure that you get the *important* things done. By assigning value to your time, you can clearly identify what's important and make conscious, wise choices.

Calculating how much your time is worth

No matter what occupation, everyone sells time for a price; the pricing is just a lot more transparent in some situations than others. Most obvious are individuals who receive a wage or a fee based on the hours they work, including minimum-wage workers and anyone self-employed, such as tutors, baby sitters, and consultants.

Other people advertise their prices on a per-project basis but in reality base that fee on an estimate of hours the job takes. Freelance writers, for instance, may charge $1,500 to write a promotional brochure, but that amount is likely a reflection of the writer's value of his time at a certain figure — say, $75 per hour.

Some businesses and professions charge customers an hourly rate, although workers don't directly receive that per-hour fee. Instead, their salary or compensation is based on the revenue the company can bring in based on those hours. Law firms and plumbers, for example, may charge for their services on an hourly basis and pay their employees a salary or a different per-hour rate.

If you earn a salary, you may not perceive yourself as having an hourly rate, but you do. This hourly income doesn't affect how you're paid, but it puts you in touch with what an hour of your work time brings you. Here's how to calculate it:

1. **Calculate the number of hours you work per week.**

   Work hours/day × days/week + overtime = hours/week

   To be completely accurate, calculate your hourly rate based on the hours you actually work. If you consistently put in more than 40 hours a week (most salaried folks aren't paid overtime for additional hours worked), add those hours to your total. Here's an example:

   8 hours/day × 5 days/week + 2 hours overtime = 42 hours/week

2. **Figure out how many hours you work per year.**

   Work hours/week × weeks/year = hours/year

   Make sure you subtract time off. For instance, if you take three weeks of vacation each year, subtract that from your total number of weeks worked. If your salary is based on a three-week vacation and an average 42-hour work week, here's how many hours you work per year:

   42 hours/week × 49 weeks/year = 2,058 hours/year

3. **Divide your gross salary by the number of hours you work per year.**

   Salary ÷ hours/year = hourly income

   For instance, $80,000 divided by 2,058 hours is $38.87 per hour.

Boosting your hourly value through your work efforts

Money isn't the scarcest and most valuable resource; time is. There are plenty of ways to make more money, but there's no way to add more minutes to an hour. You have a limited amount of this precious commodity, so you want to protect it and spend it as if it's your own personal trust fund.

Most people think that if they work more hours, they'll automatically make more money. That's faulty thinking: You can devote more hours to work, but if you invest the hours in the wrong actions, you gain nothing — and you lose time.

The solution may be to ask more money for your time. However, most people don't have the luxury of raising their income at will. So what's the next best step? Change how you use your time so you get the best return on investment — after all, what you do with your time leads to greater prosperity.

To increase your hourly value, you have to decide whether you'll work toward earning more money or earning more time. Then focus on performing high-value activities to achieve that goal; the process of discovering the really important actions or items you can invest your time in can help you change your hourly rate. The decision of how to increase your hourly value — whether to work toward generating more money in the same amount of time or generating the same amount of money in less time — depends on your circumstances:

✔ If you're in a commission- or bonus-compensation structure, you can increase productivity to earn additional income.

✔ If you're in a salary-based position, you can find ways to be more productive within the 40-hour week and reduce the additional hours you put in.

If, however, your job doesn't enable you to increase your hourly value, whether in terms of money or time, then you have bigger decisions to make. Other changes you can make to directly impact your income are to simply do the following:

✔ Find a similar job at a company that pays a bigger salary or offers more freedom with your work hours.

✔ Improve your performance and earn a raise or a promotion. Know, however, that the success of your efforts toward a raise or promotion is ultimately in the hands of the higher-ups.

When evaluating time-for-money trades, be sure not to limit your definition of *return* to money: Ask yourself whether the exchange improves the quality of your life. Look at how your life outside of work would change if you were to double or triple your hourly rate. If what you're trading for dollars does any of the following, it's a good trade:

✔ Increases your ability and opportunity to earn more money

✔ Increases your amount of family time

✔ Decreases your work hours

✔ Enhances your physical and mental fitness

✔ Provides an opportunity for someone who needs it

✔ Removes something you don't enjoy or don't do well from your life

So that's a simple look at the overall strategy behind improving your return on investment. Chapter 2 of Book II takes you through the specifics, helping you schedule your to-do list each day so you make sure all your efforts align with your goals (refer to Book I, Chapter 3 for information on setting goals).

Creating a Time-Management System You Can Live With

Discovering how to manage your time well is part mental restructuring and part creating a system. Effective time management requires more than good intent and self-knowledge. To keep your time under careful control, you need a framework. In your arsenal of time-management ammunition, you want to stock organizational skills, technology that helps keep you on track, and planning tools that help you keep the reins on your time, hour by hour, day by day, week by week, and so forth.

Establishing a solid system you can replicate is key to succeeding in managing your time. Time-management skills are applicable whether you're the company CEO, a salesperson, a midlevel manager, or an administrative assistant. No matter your work or your work environment, time management is of universal value.

Scheduling your time and creating a routine

Sticking to a time-scheduling system can't guarantee the return of your long-lost vacation days, but by regularly tracking your meetings, appointments, and obligations, you reduce your odds of double-booking and scheduling appointments too close. And by planning ahead, you make sure to make time for all the important things first.

The time-blocking system, covered in Chapter 2 of Book II, ensures that you put your priorities first (starting with routines and then moving to individual tasks/activities) before scheduling in commitments and activities of lesser importance. Such time-management techniques are just as applicable to the other spheres of your life. You should plug in your personal commitments first when filling in your time-blocking schedule because your personal time is worthy of protection, and you can further enhance that time by applying time-management principles.

Book II

Getting Organized and Managing Your Time: Smart Ways to Preempt Problems

A word to free spirits

Many people feel that a time-management system is too restrictive. They think the freedom they seek with their schedules and their lives is contained in a more flexible environment. They're afraid establishing a routine will keep them wrapped in the chains of time. However, most people waste too much time figuring out each individual day on the fly. They react to the day rather than respond. *Reacting* is a reflex action that turns over your agenda to others, and that can't possibly lead to freedom. *Responding* is a disciplined act of planning that determines where and how you invest your time.

If you're a free spirit and this whole idea of scheduling your time and establishing a routine just fried your circuits, start with a small amount of routine. Ask yourself, "Can I establish a daily routine to try it out? What can I do without having it send me into withdrawal?" Then implement a new routine every week. You'll add more than 50 new pieces of structure to your schedule in a normal work year and see a significant improvement in your freedom.

Organizing your surroundings

A good system of time management requires order and organization. Creating order in your world saves time wasted searching for stuff, from important phone numbers to your shoes. But even more, physical order creates mental order and helps you perform more efficiently.

Your workspace should be clean and orderly, with papers and folders arranged in some sort of sequence that makes items easy to find. Your desk should be cleared off, providing space to work. Your important tools — phone, computer, calculator — ought to be within reach. And your day planner, of course, should be at your fingertips. Your briefcase, your meeting planner, even your closet has an impact on your time-management success. (For more on keeping your workspace in order, read Chapter 3 of Book II.)

Of course, you need more than an organized workspace to maximize your use of time. The later section "Being Organized: The Key to Managing Your Time" explains how to assess how organized — or not — you are and how you can put more than your space in order.

Using time-saving technology

Organization extends beyond your work area: Not only should your computer be nearby, but the files, documents, and contact information on that computer should be ordered for quick access. The computer stores your address list, tracks your correspondence, and contains your calendar and upcoming appointments.

But that's just the beginning. Today's teleconferencing and videoconferencing equipment means you can hold weekly meetings with your colleagues who live on the other side of the globe without anyone having to turn in a travel-expense report. Cellphones and PDAs mean you can conduct business anywhere you happen to be without having to find a phone booth.

In fact, technology is advancing at such a rapid pace that keeping up with all the advances is a struggle. Chapter 7 of Book II presents an overview of the many technologies available to help you make the best use of your time.

Overcoming Time-Management Obstacles

Anyone can conquer time management, but it's not always easy. Your obstacles are your own shortcomings (perhaps poor communication skills, procrastination, or the inability to make wise and quick decisions), time-wasting co-workers and bosses, phone and people interruptions, and unproductive meetings. You have to crawl before you can walk, so you need to identify your stumbling blocks before you can improve your time management. The following sections give an overview of some common obstacles you may be facing.

Communicating effectively

Communicating effectively is one of the best ways to maximize your time. One of the biggest time-wasters on company time is, no surprise, talking with co-workers. But what may be a surprise is that the abuse isn't usually a function of weekend catch-up discussions that take place at the water cooler or the gossip circle at the copy machine. Rather, the problem is the banter at the weekly staff status reports, the drawn-out updates of projects that never seem to conclude, the sales presentations that get off-track — all the meetings that could be as brief as ten minutes but somehow take an hour or more.

At your disposal, however, is an amazing weapon for taming these misbehaving encounters: your words. With a few deft remarks, you have the power to bring these meetings to a productive close. In Book IV, you can find information on which types of situations are most appropriate for each of the primary communication methods — face-to-face, verbal only, and written — and plenty of ideas for communicating your message and posing questions strategically, succinctly, and successfully so your communication ends in results, action, and decisions — whether you're leading a meeting or simply attending it.

Circumventing interruptions

Interruptions creep into your workday in all sorts of insidious manners. They come in the form of unproductive meetings, phone calls, hall conversations that drift into your office and distract you, and the pesky co-worker stepping into your office with "Got a sec?" Even e-mail notification systems are a near-constant interruption.

Book II

Getting Organized and Managing Your Time: Smart Ways to Preempt Problems

Additionally, most poor time managers interrupt themselves by trying to do too much at once. Study after study supports that multi-tasking isn't the most effective work style. The constant stops and starts disrupt a project, requiring startup time each time you turn back to the task.

Chapter 4 of Book II explores a number of these interruptions and offers plenty of advice on preempting such disruptions, as well as cutting them short so you can get your train of thought back on track.

Getting procrastination under control

Sometimes, you may be tempted to use interruptions as an excuse to postpone a project or a task. How nice to have someone else to blame for not getting started! And before you know it, you've found so many good reasons not to do something that you've backed yourself into a really tight 11th-hour corner, and the pressure's on.

Procrastination has a lot of causes, but most of the reasons to procrastinate leave you headed for trouble. Book II, Chapter 5 addresses the perils of putting things off and offers secrets to overcoming that all-too-human tendency to postpone until tomorrow what you could've done today.

Making decisions: Just do it

One of the easiest things to put off is making a decision. Even sidestepping the smallest decisions can lead to giant time consumption. Think about it: You scroll through your e-mail and save one to ponder and respond to later. You revisit a few times and still can't bring yourself to a commitment. So you get more e-mail from the sender. To stave off making a decision, you ask a couple of questions, which requires more time and attention. By the time the issue is resolved and put to bed, you may have invested five times more attention than if you'd handled it immediately.

Many factors create the confusion and uncertainty that prevent you from making sound but quick decisions. Often, part of the struggle is having too many options. Most people have a tough enough time choosing between pumpkin and apple pie at the Thanksgiving table. But every day you're forced to make decisions from choices as abundant as a home-style cafeteria line. Having options is usually a good thing, but too much choice is overwhelming, even paralyzing. To find out how to make quick but good decisions, head to Book III, Chapter 1.

Garnering Support While Establishing Your Boundaries

Sometimes your family, friends, and co-workers are your biggest challenge to managing your time successfully. Whose phone calls interrupt your train of thought when you're on a roll? Who expects you home for dinner, despite a pressing proposal deadline? For whose meetings do you have to take a break from your critical research?

Yet despite all the challenges they throw your way, these same folks can also serve as your allies as you pursue the quest of better time use. Getting them on board and perceiving them as comrades in shared goals is a great way to offset the interruptions that they also inevitably bring to the table.

Balancing work and time with family and friends

All work and no play, as they say, means something is askew with your life balance. Recognize that although your job and career are critical components of who you are, they're also a means to support aspects of your life that, I suspect, are more important to you: your personal life, which includes your family, your friends, your community, and your leisure and social activities.

If you find yourself constantly putting in long hours at work for months on end, something's off-kilter: Either you're not managing your time effectively, or something's wrong with your job. No one — not even Wall Street lawyers — should be putting in 70-hour weeks on a regular basis. A 70-hour work week leaves little time for sleep, recreation, family, or relationships.

Still, getting the support of family members is critical for success. If you're like most people, you put your family before your job, but that doesn't mean you can drop work whenever you want. So get your spouse and children on board as your support system and work together to manage your time so that you can have more of it together.

Streamlining interactions with co-workers and customers

Most people find themselves in a work environment in which they regularly interact with others, whether co-workers, business associates, or customers. The workday is rife with opportunities for interruption, distraction, and time wasting. In addition to the phone calls and cubicle pop-ins, you have business appointments, associates who keep you waiting, or meetings that are unfocused and poorly run.

Maintaining control of your time at work requires you to develop some ways to manage meetings, appointments, and other work interactions so they're as efficient and productive as possible. Book III, Chapter 2 explores tactics for planning, setting, leading, or just plain attending such gatherings. Whether you initiate the interaction or you're merely a participant, you can have some control over the meeting.

Trying to keep co-workers from impinging on your productive time is ticklish enough; things get even more sensitive when you have to tell your boss that you don't have time to waste. But your supervisor is often the one who throws the most curveballs your direction when it comes to using your time in the most productive way. How do you deal with the boss who waits until the last minute to drop a big project on your desk that needs to be done yesterday? When trying to keep a rein on a time-wasting boss, you need to be prepared to summon up all your powers of diplomacy. You also need to be more direct from the outset. You may even have to suggest some of the time-management tips and tools from this chapter and others.

Keeping Motivation High

Like most goals, mastering time-management skills isn't something that happens overnight, and you'll occasionally encounter points where you start feeling disappointed, wondering whether your efforts are paying off. Whenever you hit those lows — and you will — remember to give yourself credit for every step you make in the right direction. One way to stay motivated is to link incentive to inducement: In other words, reward yourself. For example, if you complete certain actions that tie to your goals, give yourself Friday afternoon off. Or savor an evening on the couch with a good movie or dinner at a favorite restaurant. Do whatever serves as an enticing reward.

Take motivation to the next level by involving others in the reward. Let your spouse know that an evening out awaits if you fulfill your week's goals before deadline. Tell the kids that if you spend the next couple of evenings at the office, you can all head for the amusement park on Saturday. This strategy is a sure-fire way to supercharge your motivation.

As you work through this difficult but worthy bout of self-improvement, keep your mind on the positive side and remember this simple truth: Work always expands to fill the time you allow for it. No matter how productive you are, whether you have just a couple things to accomplish or a sky-high pile on your desk, and whether you leave work on time or stay late, there's always something that doesn't get done. So don't get hung up on those things you don't accomplish — just keep your eyes on the goal, prioritize accordingly, delegate what you can, and protect your boundaries carefully so that you take on only as much as you know you can handle while still remaining satisfied with all parts of your life. When you start to get frustrated about the never-ending flow of work that comes your way, remind yourself that you're blessed with more opportunities than time — and if you're in pursuit of success, that's better than the alternative.

Being Organized: The Key to Managing Your Time

At some point, everyone has felt the panic that disorganization brings: the racing heartbeat as you sit in traffic while a meeting you're supposed to attend gets underway; the breathless apologies you utter to friends as you arrive late for an engagement; the anger you heap on yourself when you forget a task, a phone call, or even an item at the grocery store. The reactions are natural, even reasonable. They are also unhealthy. Your blood pressure and heart rate go up, your patience goes down, your mind races, and before you know it you're driving faster and more recklessly than normal, you're rude to strangers, and your day is, for all practical purposes, ruined. The dominos begin to fall as you let one disorganized fiasco spill over and contaminate other activities you have planned.

Before you know it, the day is over and you're exhausted. Your schedule has been hectic, but you have little to show for your efforts. You're tired, but you have no sense of closure; no satisfaction that comes from completing your goals. You're anxious, and in some cases you take that open-ended anxiety to bed with you. Sleep is fitful, if it comes at all, and in no time the next day is upon you, and the cycle starts again.

Becoming more organized in your work, your home, and your everyday life not only makes you more efficient and productive, it frees your mind of anxiety and changes your life for the better. Rather than being scattered and overwhelmed, you can be happier and perhaps healthier. Relationships at home and at work will improve as other people notice your promptness, and the control you display over your life will bring you both joy and a sense of accomplishment. The more organized you are, the more manageable your home, your business, and your life become. And who doesn't want that?

There is a tremendous opportunity cost associated with remaining disorganized. Every misplaced message or task left unaccomplished has a cost. Every meeting you're late to or phone call you forget to return sends a signal — one that will cost you greatly in the long run, sometimes in the form of a diminished reputation. Because the disorganized person is constantly reacting to what others are throwing her way, she has very little time to proactively go after more business. She's constantly on the defensive.

If being disorganized has all these associated costs, being organized has a number of benefits: Being organized enables you to handle your schedule in such a way that you have time to make new contacts, develop new relationships, and expand your horizons on all fronts.

How organized are you?

An organized person is

- ✔ Time sensitive and realistic about what he can accomplish in a given block of time
- ✔ Space sensitive, realizing that everything has a place, even if that place is the trash can
- ✔ Aware of the demands on her time and careful not to overpromise
- ✔ Disciplined in sticking to his organizational system, whatever that system might be
- ✔ Confident and focused on her goals
- ✔ Able to leave work-related problems at work because they're written down and assigned a time to be handled in the future

Does this description fit you? If not, you have some work to do.

The organizational continuum

Organization and disorganization are not quantifiable absolutes. For example, you may know someone who keeps her office immaculately organized with not a single scrap of paper out of place. Yet this same person may have trouble getting to meetings on time or promptly returning phone calls. In one respect (the housekeeping of her office), this person is considered organized, but in another (time and task management) she's considered disorganized. Which is she? Certainly the people in the meetings and the ones sitting by their phones waiting for her to call believe one thing, while those who only see this woman in her office have an entirely different opinion.

The truth is that both opinions are accurate. She's both organized and disorganized. Her desk and the space in her office are her priorities; therefore, she keeps those areas organized. Meetings, phone calls, and interaction with others are obviously not as important to her, so she is disorganized (and rude) in those areas.

Think of organization as a continuum. At one end sits the completely disorganized person — the one with piles of paper on his desk and personal belongings strewn about or piled in corners throughout his cluttered home. He's always late, always harried, and has a reputation for being absent-minded. Chances are good that this person hasn't reached his full career potential. The excuses he uses include: "Hey, it's my own special system. I know where everything is." Or, "I don't want to be a neat freak. Those people are weird." Or, even better, "It's not my fault. My boss keeps piling things on me, and I can't seem to catch up." But in fact, this person is the epitome of all things disorganized.

On the other extreme of the organization continuum is the organizational freak — the person who has mapped out every minute of every day for the next year of his life. His surroundings are immaculate. He knows the exact location of everything in his office and home, and nothing is ever out of place. This person has never been late, never missed returning a phone call, never let a pile accumulate on his desk, and never worn unmatched socks. Nothing is ever impetuous with this person. He jealously guards his time and his surroundings, and manages the clock better than an NFL quarterback. He is a classic overachiever who has probably been labeled obsessive at some point in his life. This man has taken organization to an extreme.

Ninety-nine percent of people fall between these two extremes. Unfortunately, too many people relate more to the disorganized example than to the organized one. In order to change your place on the continuum, you have to ask yourself three questions:

- ✔ Where am I on the organizational continuum?
- ✔ Where do I want to be on the continuum?
- ✔ How am I going to get there?

Humans have a marvelous knack for deluding themselves. Everyone believes herself to be organized, because the alternative is to be disorganized and unproductive — no one wants to admit that. To figure out where you are, read through the following sections.

No one intends to overschedule or run late, but the problems that most people experience are based on self-delusion and unintentional dishonesty. So take the time to assign realistic times to the tasks you want to complete. Then you can see whether the schedules you make for yourself are unworkable.

Book II

Getting Organized and Managing Your Time: Smart Ways to Preempt Problems

Place yourself on the organizational continuum

To determine where you are on the organizational continuum, draw a horizontal line on a notecard. On the left end of the line write the traits of the completely disorganized person. At the other end, write a description of the fanatically organized person. Next, place a mark on the line to denote where you think you currently fall in the organizational continuum and list a few of your weakest and strongest organizational traits. Now draw a star at the point on the line where you want to be and list your organizational goals. Keep this card with you as a constant reminder. As you work on your organizational goals, add additional marks on your notecard to denote your progress.

Keep a record

Keep a record of how often you're late for meetings or with deadlines, and jot down the reasons you believe you fell behind schedule. Also, jot down a list of items you've misplaced over the course of the last month. Put both lists aside. Then, in a few weeks, come back to them and try to objectively evaluate whether or not you were being honest with yourself. A little distance can open your eyes to your own organizational shortcomings.

Take this short test

Answer the following questions and score your answers according to the instructions following the test. Questions 1–11 deal with personality; Questions 12–20 deal with organization.

1. Do you know what you'll be doing at 10:37 tomorrow morning?

2. Could you find your car keys inside of one minute?

3. Do you have an organizational tool (a day planner, a legal pad, or a series of notes) at your side at all times?

4. Of the calls you know you will make tomorrow, do you know whom you will call first?

5. Are your most important business and personal phone numbers written down in one place?

6. Do you have meals with your family around a table at least three times a week?

7. Is over half your closet floor visible without moving or removing anything?

8. If you were to be hit by a truck and killed this afternoon, would your family know all the necessary critical information, and could they find all the documentation needed to keep the household running?

9. Do you have a will?

10. Have you scheduled your next physical examination with a doctor?

11. Has your garage been organized in the last six months?

12. Has a bill collector called your home or office in the last two years?

13. Have you ever forgotten a family member's birthday or your anniversary?

14. Are there any unread newspapers or magazines lying around your house or office?

15. Have you been late for a meeting, dinner, or appointment in the last two weeks?

16. Are all the storage spaces in your home full?

17. Have you misplaced or had trouble finding an important document in the past month?

18. Were you interrupted more than twice today?

19. Have you gone to the grocery store without a list more than once in the last month?

20. Have you had a disagreement or discussion with your spouse or a family member in the last month that centered around information you hadn't shared with anyone?

In questions 1–11, give yourself five points for every *yes,* and in questions 12–20, give yourself five points for every *no.*

If you scored:

- ✔ **90 or above:** You are an exceptionally well-organized person who has little trouble completing tasks. In addition to being successful in your chosen field, you're likely to be healthier and happier than many people your age and in your profession.

- ✔ **80 to 90:** You have good organization systems in place, and you adhere to those systems most of the time. A little fine-tuning and you could elevate yourself to new heights in your career and personal life.

- ✔ **70 to 80:** Face it, you're disorganized. Try as you might, circumstances tend to overwhelm you and you're often at the mercy of others. Make a commitment to change your life immediately by applying the systems outlined here.

- ✔ **Under 70:** You need help, and you need it quickly. Life must be a constant struggle, with strained relationships at work and home. The answer to your chaos could start with something as simple as a pen and a notepad, but you must make a personal commitment in order to improve.

Here's an easy, inexpensive, and effective organizational system requiring nothing more than a yellow legal pad and a pen. Each page in the legal pad represents a day. Draw a vertical line down the center of each page. On the left half of the page, write down the names and numbers of people you need to call that particular day. The things you need to do go on the right side of the line. Beside each item, write times during the day when you plan to attend to each task. As you complete each activity, draw a line through it. If the call or activity requires follow-up at a later time, simply turn to the appropriate page and make a follow-up note. Tasks that don't get completed are transferred to the next page (or the next day) in your pad.

What being organized doesn't mean

The idea of *being organized* brings with it all sorts of misconceptions that, if you believe them, may undermine your intentions to become more organized. The following lists the most potent myths and the facts:

✔ **The "uptight personality" myth:** This myth claims that people who are organized are way too uptight or that they can't — or don't — ever stop and smell the roses. Actually, organization relieves tension; therefore, by being more organized you're better equipped to smell the roses than if you're always running late or sorting through the latest mess in your home or office.

✔ **The "chained to your day planner" myth:** Another often-repeated fallacy is that organized people are somehow bound to their schedules like prisoners. The disorganized person who says, "I don't want to be held captive by a predetermined schedule," sums up this myth. The disorganized masses need their freedom — or so they claim. To them, having a written organizational system means the death of flexibility and spontaneity. Nothing could be further from the truth. By writing everything down and setting times in which to accomplish certain tasks, you can easily see where you have time to accommodate unexpected tasks or events that pop up. You also can enjoy leisure activities without worrying about the next meeting or the proposal that's coming up in a few days. You're also in charge of your day and your surroundings.

✔ **The "inflexible ogre" myth:** Despite what seems to be conventional wisdom, organized people are neither mean nor inflexible. They simply understand the value of their time and space, and they do their best to conform to the guidelines they have set for themselves. Some of the nicest and most accommodating people are also the most organized.

✔ **The "obsessive-compulsive" myth:** Obsessive-compulsive disorder is a serious psychological problem that affects millions of people. This disorder is also a label wrongly given to people who are simply meticulous and regimented in their personal organization. Being systematic doesn't make someone obsessive or compulsive.

Chapter 2

Focusing Your Efforts, Prioritizing Tasks, and Blocking Your Time

*W*hat you do with your time is more important than how much time you have. Just as recognizing and understanding your life goals helps you achieve successful time-management skills, the effective use of your time goes a long, *long* way to shortening the journey to those goals. By investing your time with care and consideration, your journey toward your dreams is certain to be a smoother road. In fact, an old time-management adage says that for every minute you invest in planning, you save ten minutes in execution. Spend an hour planning how you're going to accomplish your goals, and you'll free up *ten* hours — to achieve better business results, reduce stress, and add quality time at home.

The best way to achieve your goals is to prioritize them and develop an ordered plan to reach them. A universally recognized method for maximizing productivity called the *80/20 rule* has proven successful time and again for more than 100 years. This chapter explains the general concept and shows you how to apply it — at work, at home, in your relationships, and beyond. And to ensure you're able to act on your priorities in the order that's most important to you, this chapter also helps you match your overall time investment to your goals, prioritize your tasks, and create a schedule to take you safely to your destination.

Focusing Your Energy with the 80/20 Theory of Everything

In 1906, Vilfredo Pareto noted that in his home country of Italy, a small contingency of citizens — about 20 percent — held most of the power, influence, and money — about 80 percent, he figured. That, of course, meant that the other 80 percent of the population held only 20 percent of the financial and political power in the country. Pareto found a similar distribution in other nations. In the 1940s, Joseph M. Juran applied the same 80:20 ratio to quality-control issues, and since then the business world has run with the idea of the "vital few and trivial many."

The basic principle that in all things only a few are vital and many are trivial is known as the *80/20 rule* (also referred to as the *Pareto principle*), and you can apply it to almost any situation. It's been used in the workplace ("20 percent of my staff makes 80 percent of the revenue") and even by investors ("20 percent of my stocks generate 80 percent of my income"). You can also apply the 80/20 rule to time management, as this section explains. ***Note:*** Because you can't thrive at work — at least not in the long run — if your home life is in chaos or if you're always making short shrift of it, this section also explains how to apply the 80/20 rule to your personal life.

Matching time investment to return

Generally speaking, only 20 percent of those things that you spend your time doing produces 80 percent of the results that you want to achieve. This principle applies to virtually every situation in which you have to budget your time in order to get things done — whether at work, at home, or in your relationships.

The goal in using the 80/20 rule to maximize your productivity is to identify the key 20-percent activities that are most effective (producing 80 percent of the results) and make sure you prioritize those activities. Complete those vital tasks above all else and perhaps look for ways to increase the time you spend on them.

This section shows you how to implement the 80/20 rule.

Step 1: Sizing up your current situation

Before you can do any sort of strategizing, you need to take a good, honest look at how you use your time. For people who struggle with time management, the problem, by and large, lies in the crucial steps of assessing and planning. Perform your assessment with these steps:

1. **Observe how you currently use your time.**

   Through the observation process, you can discover behaviors, habits, and skill sets that both negatively and positively affect your productivity. What do you spend most of your day doing? How far down the daily to-do list do you get each day?

2. **Assess your personal productivity trends.**

   During which segments of the day are your energy levels the highest? Which personal habits cause you to adjust your plans for the day?

3. **Take a close look at the interruptions you face on a regular basis.**

   During what segments of the day do you experience the most interruptions? What sort of interruptions do you receive most frequently, and from whom?

Later in this chapter, in "Blocking Off Your Time and Plugging In Your To-Do Items," you find out how to control and plan your time by time blocking your day.

Step 2: Identifying the top tasks that support your goals

Some folks tend to follow the squeeze-it-in philosophy: They cram in everything they possibly can — and then some. These people almost always end up miserable because they try to do so much that they don't take care of their basic needs and end up strung out in every possible way. The quality of what they do, as well as the amount of what they do, suffers as a result of their ever-increasing exhaustion.

To work efficiently, you need to identify your 80 percent — the results you want to achieve. Break out your list of goals (Book I, Chapter 3 explains how to set goals), take a good look at your top 12 goals, and identify the tasks you need to do that align with those goals. If your number-one goal is to provide your kids with an Ivy League education, for example, then your priorities are less likely to center around taking twice-yearly vacations to the Caribbean and more likely to revolve around investing wisely and encouraging your offspring to do well in school (can you say "full-ride scholarship"?).

After you identify what you need to do — your vital few — spend a bit more time in self-reflection to double-check that you've correctly identified your goals and essential tasks. Changing your direction, priorities, objectives, and goals is a big waste of time. Successful people and successful time managers take the direct route from point A to point B.

Here's what to ask yourself about these key tasks:

✔ How much time do you devote to those activities? Twenty percent? Less? More?

Book II

Getting Organized and Managing Your Time: Smart Ways to Preempt Problems

✔ What are you doing with the remainder of your time?

✔ How much return are you getting for the investment on the remainder?

Step 3: Prioritizing your daily objectives

After you identify the tasks and activities you need to accomplish to achieve your goals, assign a value to those goals so you can decide how to order your daily task list. Take the send-your-kids-to-an-Ivy-League-school scenario in the preceding section, and say another of your priorities is to be at home for your kids instead of sending them to daycare. If you value their college education more than the short-term joy of being a stay-at-home parent, you may decide to return to the workforce as you see tuitions skyrocketing. You can make this decision because you have a clear idea about how you rank your priorities. This clarity may help direct you to a job with hours compatible with your kids' schedules.

To personalize how you prioritize your goals at work, do the following:

✔ **Look at your long-term career goals.**

Do you want to advance to a particular career level? How does that align with your goal of, for example, the Ivy League education for your children? Do you want to achieve a particular income? Is that income level high enough to allow you to save for the Ivy League education?

✔ **Review your company's priorities.**

Having a solid understanding of the company's priorities, goals, objectives, and strategic thrusts guides your own prioritization so you can help your company get the edge on its competition. To get a global perspective, review your company's mission statement, review its published corporate values and goals, and see how they pertain to your position. Ask your supervisor for further elaboration on these statements and on her priorities so you can make sure you align yours accordingly.

The vital 20 percent: Figuring out where to focus your energy at work

Used effectively, the 80/20 rule can increase your on-the-job performance. From boardroom to lunchroom, executive suite to mailroom, this time-management principle can help you accomplish the most important tasks in less time and help you advance in your career.

The 20-percent investment in the 80 percent of results remains relatively constant. What's truly important for success changes very little within a given profession. The two global objectives of any successful business are profit and customer retention. What differs among professions is how those global objectives translate to match individual objectives.

The following sections explain how the 80/20 rule factors into some major job categories.

Ownership/executive leadership

As an executive or owner, your most important role is to establish the vision, goals, and benchmarks for the business. What are the core values and core purpose for the business? What are the goals for next quarter? For the year? What are the most pressing problems that need to be solved? What are the strengths, weaknesses, opportunities, and threats the company or marketplace is experiencing? You then have to convey those answers consistently in clear terms for your lieutenants to follow and hold the lieutenants accountable to the standards. These high-level tasks represent the vital 20; they're the ones to which you absolutely must devote time to accomplish.

Sales

For sales professionals, lead generation brings 80 percent of your return. Without new leads and new prospects to sell to, your customer and prospect base remains fixed to your current clients. In sales, because your most important tasks are prospecting and following up on leads, put a priority on securing and conducting sales appointments and building personal relationships. Don't forget your existing client base as well. They usually follow the same 80/20 rule, where 20 percent of them contribute 80 percent of the revenue. Spend your time with this group to increase sales and referrals.

Management

For those in leadership positions, your vital 20 percent is the coaching and development of people. You use coaching strategies to encourage and empower your employees, and you monitor your staff's adherence to the company's strategic plans. In addition, you help your employees acquire the knowledge, skills, attitude, and actions to advance their careers.

Task- or service-based roles

This group of people varies the most because it's the broadest. To identify your vital tasks (the 20 percent that produce 80 percent of the results you want), take a look at your company's objectives, your department's objectives, and your own objectives to get a well-rounded picture of how your role fits into the bigger picture. Then decide which of your job responsibilities increase sales or improve customer retentions.

After that, consider the value of the product or service you offer, and weigh the importance of quality versus speed or quantity — your ultimate goal is to serve your customers better so you retain and grow your relationships with them. (If you're not sure how much weight each element deserves, talk to your supervisor about where you should focus your efforts.)

✔ If quality takes higher priority, ask yourself how you can deliver a better product or service in the amount of time you're given.

Book II

Getting Organized and Managing Your Time: Smart Ways to Preempt Problems

> ✔ If delivery speed or quantity is more important, ask yourself how you can deliver that product more efficiently while maintaining quality.

Administration

To determine what things you need to spend your time on, figure out what tasks have the most impact on helping you achieve your goals. If you're in an administrative role, for example, your goal is to enhance the company's performance, whether you support frontline sales staff or assist the corporate leadership in steering the business toward profit. If you're in sales support, how can you help free up the salespeople to do more selling? Can you fill out reports for the salespeople? Research new market opportunities and get contact information? Can you also help the sales manager by better tracking the salespeople's numbers so the manager can do more coaching and shadowing of the salespeople?

If you're working in customer service, does your department have a recurring customer service problem that needs to be solved? Can you identify it? Can you find at least two solutions to the problem and bring them to your boss for review? You can make yourself an indispensable asset to the company with these actions and save time for yourself and your superiors as well.

Personal essentials: Channeling efforts in your personal life

The 80/20 rule isn't strictly business, so don't lose sight of its influence on your personal life. In fact, the 80/20 rule can have the greatest impact at home. For most, personal and family life is the realm that matters most. But with all the demands of work and the outside world, it often takes the back seat. By categorizing and ordering your personal priorities, you can customize your approach to the people and priorities in your home life and make the most of your time spent on family, hobbies, leisure, and friends.

When factoring in your personal priorities, think of a variety of areas, such as time with loved ones, a worthy cause, your faith, education, and future plans. This section covers the two areas of prioritization that affect most people (for other situations, follow the general process outlined earlier in "Matching time investment to return").

Investing wisely in your personal relationships

One of the great things about the 80/20 rule is that it doesn't apply only to task-oriented items — it's also about the quality of your time and the energy you put into what you choose to do with it. If you have a significant other, for example, consider how 20 percent of all the time you spend with him shapes 80 percent of your relationship with that person.

Outside of work, personal relationships are number one, so always consider them first, before you even start thinking about chores. Evaluate your connection with each of the important people in your life, both family and friends. In this way, you can customize your approach to the people and priorities in your home life instead of lumping everything into the generalized category of *home* and perhaps not giving any individual or activity its due attention. When dealing with people, ask yourself these questions to help you identify the 80/20 balance:

✔ How can I invest my time with this person to create a better relationship?

✔ What's most important to this person, and how can I serve and support these needs?

Many other questions can help get you to the root — or the 20 percent — of actions that produce a bumper crop of love, security, appreciation, and experience that builds meaningful relationships at home. For example, if you're raising children, you may ask yourself these questions as well:

✔ How can I invest my time to nurture this child's developing interests?

✔ How can I show that I value this child in a way that she understands?

✔ What do I need to do each week to teach this child an important life skill?

✔ What shared activities allow me to serve as a positive example?

✔ What can I do to create a positive family memory?

Balancing crucial household tasks with at-home hobbies

Face it: Your days are filled with tasks that really don't bring much return on investment. Whether it's doing the laundry or filling out paperwork, you'll never be able to eliminate those loads of necessary-but-not-monumental duties. And in your personal life, these activities may include housework, home maintenance, or walking the dog.

However, you can apply the 80/20 rule to help balance how you invest your time in chores so it aligns with your hobbies. Which activities bring you the biggest return? For example, do you spend every summer evening and weekend on your back patio, entertaining or simply admiring your backyard and flower garden? Then for you, trimming, mowing, planting, and weeding may be a wise way to invest that vital 20 percent of your time. If, however, you get more enjoyment from traveling to new places, you may allocate that time to budgeting for and planning exciting vacations.

Cooking, cleaning, shopping, laundry, yardwork, bill paying, and other tasks are essential, but that doesn't mean that *you* have to do them — sometimes, the added cost of hiring help is worth the time it frees in your schedule. If you gain no joy or fulfillment whatsoever from cleaning or household maintenance or feel you simply don't have the time or energy to do all this without sacrificing your most important priorities, hire out those responsibilities. Sure, a cost is involved, but you buy back time to spend on the activities that mean the most to you. So send out the laundry if it frees you up to explore new menus in the kitchen or bring in a personal chef if you'd rather be out in the garden planting tomatoes.

If you can hire someone who makes far less money than you do to do something you don't enjoy, hire out the task immediately. If you can work a few more hours and increase your pay or set yourself up for promotion sooner, then work the extra hours and hire the help. In the end, you'll be doing something you enjoy rather than something you despise.

The 80/20 rule doesn't stop there — you can also apply it to the quality of those hobbies or tasks you enjoy and the results they have on your well-being. If you're a gardener, for example, think about the 20 percent of your efforts that bring forth the 80 percent of your pleasure and satisfaction from gardening. For example, maybe you don't need to sculpt a perfectly arranged flower garden to reap the personal benefits — the very act of digging your hands into the earth may give you the greatest sense of joy. So focus on the act of planting more than on the planning and shopping.

Don't forget to include those activities that support and improve your physical, mental, and emotional health. Those activities that keep you sane, happy, and fit may seem insignificant when taken one at a time. But if they start getting squeezed out of the schedule, sanity, happiness, and health may start slipping. Be sure to account for all those little pleasures — reading, study, yoga, your weekly facial — that add texture to your life.

Getting Down to Specifics: Daily Prioritization

After you identify the vital few tasks you need to accomplish to meet your top 12 goals, break the tasks down a bit further into daily to-do items. Then prioritize them to make sure you accomplish the most important tasks first, identifying which ones you must do on a given day. In that way, you progressively work through all the minor tasks that lead to the greater steps that, in time, lead you to achieving your goals. Here's how:

1. **Start with a master list.**

   Write down everything you need to accomplish today. Don't try ranking the items at this point. You merely want to brain-dump all the to-do actions you can think of. You may end up with 20, 30, even 50 items on your list: tasks as mundane as checking e-mail and as critical as presenting a new product marketing plan to the executive board. Or if you want to work on your personal to-do list, the items may range from buying cat food to filing taxes before midnight.

   Remember to account for routine duties that don't have a direct effect on your company's mission or bottom line: turning in business expense reports, typing up and distributing meeting minutes, taking sales calls from prospective printing vendors. Neglecting to schedule the humdrum to-do items creates a destructive domino dynamic that can topple your well-intentioned time-block schedule.

2. **Determine the A-list.**

   Focusing on consequences creates an urgency factor so you can better use your time. Ask yourself, "What, if not done today, will lead to a significant consequence?" Designate these as *A activities*. If you have a scheduled presentation today, then that task definitely hits the A list. Same goes for filing your tax return if the deadline is today. Buying cat food probably doesn't make this list — unless you're totally out or have a particularly vindictive cat.

3. **Categorize the rest of the tasks.**

   Use these categories:

   - **B-level tasks:** Activities that may have a mildly negative consequence if not completed today.

   - **C-level tasks:** Activities that have no penalty if not completed today.

   - **D-level tasks:** D is for *delegate*. These are actions that someone else can take on. Go to Book III, Chapter 3 for more on how and what to hand off to others.

   - **E-level tasks:** Tasks that could be eliminated. Don't even bother writing an E next to them — just mark them out completely.

4. **Rank the tasks within each category.**

   Say you've categorized your list into six A items, four B items, three C items, and two D items. Your six A tasks obviously move to the top of the list, but now you have to rank these six items in order: A-1, A-2, A-3, and so forth.

Book II

Getting Organized and Managing Your Time: Smart Ways to Preempt Problems

If you have trouble ordering several top priorities, start with just two: Weigh them against each other — if you could complete only one task today, which of the two is most critical? Which of the two best serves your 80/20 rule? Then take the winner of that contest and compare it to the next A item, and so on. Then do the same for the B and C items.

As for the D actions? Delegate them to someone else! Everyone likes to think they're indispensable, but for most people, the majority of their duties could be handled by someone else. That's where the *85/10/5 rule* — first cousin to the 80/20 rule — comes into play: You tend to invest 85 percent of your time doing tasks that anyone else could do, and 10 percent of your time is devoted to actions that some people could handle. Just 5 percent of your energy goes to work that only you can accomplish. But whether at home or at work, this doesn't mean you can kick back and leave 95 percent of your responsibilities to someone else. It simply helps you home in on the critical 5 percent, allocate your remaining time to other activities that bring you the greatest satisfaction, and recognize those tasks that are easiest to delegate.

Now you're ready to tackle your to-do list, knowing that the most important tasks will be addressed first.

Rocking out: Putting the A-list tasks in place

Steven Covey, A. Roger Merrill, and Rebecca Merrill illustrated the importance of prioritizing tasks in their book *First Things First* (Simon and Schuster) with an illustrative metaphor: A guest lecturer was speaking to a group of students when he pulled out a 1-gallon, wide-mouthed Mason jar, set it on a table in front of him, and began filling it with about a dozen fist-sized rocks. When the jar was filled to the top and no more rocks would fit inside, he asked the class whether the jar was full, to which they unanimously replied, "Yes."

He then reached under the table and pulled out a bucket of gravel, dumping some of it into the jar and shaking the jar, causing pieces of gravel to work themselves down into the spaces between the big rocks. He asked the group once more whether the jar was full, to which one suspicious student responded, "Probably not."

Under the table he reached again, this time withdrawing a bucket of sand. He started dumping in the sand, which sank into all the spaces left between the rocks and the gravel. Once more, he asked the question "Is the jar full?" "No!" the class shouted. "Good!" he said, grabbing a pitcher of water and pouring it in until the jar was filled to the brim.

He looked up at the class and asked, "What is the point of this illustration?" One eager beaver raised his hand and said, "The point is no matter how full your schedule is, if you try really hard, you can always fit some more things into it!"

"No," the speaker replied. "The truth this illustration teaches us is if you don't put the big rocks in first, you'll never get them in at all."

Don't expect to cross off as many items on your list as you may be used to. Because you're now focused on more important items — which likely take more time — you may not get as many tasks completed. The measure of a great day is whether you wrap up all the A-list items. If you follow this system and consistently complete the As, you can be assured success. Why? Because the B and C items quickly work their way to As — and you always get the most important things done.

Don't assume that you just move the B and C priorities up the next day, though. You need to repeat this process each day. Some of the Bs will move up, but others will stay in the B category. Some of the Cs — due to outside pressure, your boss, or changed deadlines — may leapfrog the Bs and become the highest priority As.

Blocking Off Your Time and Plugging In Your To-Do Items

After you identify and order your priorities (see the preceding sections), you place them into time slots on your weekly calendar, broken into 15-minute segments, in a process called *time blocking*. You'd be hard-pressed to find a better system for managing time on a daily, weekly, monthly, yearly, and lifelong basis.

Like exercise, time blocking can be tricky because it requires a lot of thought and adjustment, both in the initial stage, when you're doing it for the first time, and for a while thereafter, when you're developing the skill. You may know what day two after the beginning of a new fitness program feels like: Stiff joints and sore muscles have you moving like the Tin Man after a rainstorm. At first you may feel like you'll never achieve the goals you've set, but sticking to the daily program eventually brings the results you want.

Figuring out how to best manage your time depends on two things:

✔ **Consistent, diligent practice:** If you want to build those time-blocking muscles, not only do you have to work them regularly, but you also need to increase the weight, stress, and pressure as you progress. Understanding the key to managing your minutes, hours, days, weeks, and so on takes repetition.

Don't panic when you find yourself a little stressed or sore from all your time-blocking exercises. It's simply a sign that your efforts to build up those skills are working.

✔ **A span of time to improve:** Achieving a level of time-blocking mastery takes time — a minimum of 18 months and as much as 24 months. Why so long? Because you're developing a complex skill. A typical day has you switching from refereeing an argument between your kids to making an important presentation to the corporate executives; from putting together your department's annual budget to paying for your groceries in the checkout line. That's a lot to orchestrate, and even Handel didn't write his *Messiah* overnight. If you accept that time-blocking skills require time to develop, you're more likely to remain motivated. Your objective is to make measureable progress in reasonable time.

Implementing time blocking to help organize your schedule takes a bit of time, but you reap huge dividends on that initial investment. This section walks you through a general outline of the process.

People who are most productive have a common trait: They treat everything in life as an appointment. These people value their time and the activities to which they commit, whether business or personal. They lend importance to their duties, commitments, and activities by writing them down and giving them a time slot, whether they're one-time occurrences or regular activities. They even make appointments with themselves.

Step 1: Dividing your day

To start, you need a daily calendar divided into 15-minute increments. Why such small bites of time? Because even 15 minutes can represent a good chunk of productive activity. Losing just two or three of these small blocks each day can diminish your ability to meet your goals, from finishing that project at work to writing your bestselling (you hope) memoir.

On a blank schedule, begin by dividing your day; draw a clear line between personal time and work time. When you take this step, you're creating work-life balance from the start. Don't take it for granted that Saturday and Sunday are time off just because you work a Monday-through-Friday work week. Block it into your schedule, or work activities may creep into your precious downtime. The more you take action on paper, the more concrete the time-block schedule becomes.

Apprehensive about drawing a line between work and personal time because you're wary of having to tell a business associate you can't attend a business function that extends into personal time? Not to worry. You don't have to tell a client that your Tuesday morning workout is more important than a break-fast meeting with her — simply say you're already booked at that time. That's all the explanation you owe; professional colleagues who want to do business with you respect your boundaries.

Step 2: Scheduling your personal activities

Blocking out personal activities first gives weight to these activities and ensures that they won't be overtaken by obligations that have lesser importance in the long run. Personal obligations are almost always the first thing most people trade for work; because of that, hold fast and tight to the personal area so it doesn't get away from you. Another advantage? You help establish a reasonable end to your workday. If you're scheduled to meet at a friend's for Texas Hold 'Em on Thursday nights, you're more motivated to wrap up your project in enough time to cut the deck.

Scheduling personal activities is twofold:

Book II

Getting Organized and Managing Your Time: Smart Ways to Preempt Problems

1. **Schedule routine activities you participate in.**

   Do you have dinner together as a family every night? A weekly date night with your significant other? Do you want to establish family traditions? Don't just assume these activities will happen — give them the weight they deserve and block out the time for each one. Don't forget to include your extracurricular activities here: All those PTA groups, fundraising committees, nonprofit boards, and other volunteer commitments get plugged in as well.

2. **Schedule personal priorities that aren't routine.**

   Put those personal agenda items first before filling in your day with tasks and activities that don't support those priorities.

Step 3: Factoring in your work activities

Begin with the activities that are a regular part of your job and then factor in the priorities that aren't routine. Whether you're a company CEO, a department manager, a sales associate, an administrative assistant, or an entry-level trainee, you're responsible for performing key tasks and activities each day and week. They may include daily or weekly meetings. Or maybe your responsibility is scheduling meetings for others. You likely have to prepare for these appointments. Perhaps you have to write and turn in reports or sales figures on an ongoing basis. You may have to call someone for information routinely. If you report to work daily and always spend the first hour of your day returning phone calls, time-block it into your schedule.

Step 4: Accounting for weekly self-evaluation and planning time

Your goals — whether a one-year business plan or long-range retirement vision — warrant routine checkups. Consider them as rest stops on your journey: Are you still on the right road? Is a detour ahead? Have you discovered a more direct route?

Use weekly strategic planning sessions — ideally for Friday afternoon or the end of the work week — to review your progress toward those near-future business projects as well as your larger career aspirations or personal goals. This is an opportunity to review the previous week and jump-start the upcoming week. Spend 15 to 30 minutes daily and then take 90 to 120 minutes for self-evaluation and planning at the end of the week.

This strategic planning time is probably your most valuable time investment each week. It gives you a tremendous wrap-up for the week and a good start to next week, and it reinforces your vision for long-term success. It also enables you to go home and spend time with your family in the right frame of mind.

Step 5: Building in flex time

Plug segments of time into your schedule every few hours to help you minimize the fallout from unplanned interruptions or problems. About 15 or 30 minutes is enough time to work in at strategic intervals throughout your day. Knowing that you have these free blocks of time can help you adhere to your schedule rather than get off track.

As you begin to build your time-blocking skills, insert 30-minute flex periods into your schedule for every two hours of time-blocked activity. This may seem like a lot of flex time, but if it allows you to maintain the rest of your time-block schedule and maintain or increase your productivity, it's worth the investment. The best time for flex time is after you've put in a couple of hours of your most important work — whether sales calls, report preparation, or meeting a deadline.

Don't schedule flex time right before you go into an important activity time: You're more likely to get distracted and fail to get started with your critical business. Schedule it after the work — then you can use it, if necessary, to resolve any unforeseen problems.

Rarely will you have unused flex time. Murphy's Law, you know: Something always comes up. However, in the event that you're lucky enough to find yourself with free flex time, the best course of action is to select something that you can complete within that period of unused time. Alternatively, if you're *really* caught up, reward yourself with a few minutes of additional break.

Assessing Your Progress and Adjusting Your Plan as Needed

Book II

Getting Organized and Managing Your Time: Smart Ways to Preempt Problems

Becoming comfortable with time blocking takes time, and achieving a glitch-free schedule that you can work with for a stretch may take a half-dozen revisions. Even then, routinely evaluate your time-blocking efforts and adjust them periodically to make sure you're getting the desired results. It's not a huge time investment — you can check yourself with a few minutes a day or use 15 to 30 minutes of your weekly time to review your results. Ask yourself the following:

- ✔ What took me off track this week?
- ✔ What interruptions really affected my success with my time?
- ✔ Is someone sabotaging my time blocking?
- ✔ What shifts would help my efficiency?

This section discusses this review in detail.

Surveying your results

One way to determine your time-blocking effectiveness is to check results. In as little as two weeks from when you launch your time-blocking schedule, you can probably see where you need minor adjustments. The best way to keep tabs on results is to track them on an ongoing basis. Perform both a weekly review that focuses on the past week and a periodic review of where you stand in relation to your overall goals.

The weekly review is a time for you to replay the tape of the week, looking at the highs and lows. You're guaranteed to have days where you want to pull your hair out because you face so many problems and distractions. You'll also have days that are smooth as silk. What were the differences in those days besides the outcome?

As for the periodic review, review your job description, key responsibilities, and the ways in which your performance and success are measured. Then ask yourself these questions:

- ✔ Am I moving closer toward achieving my goals?
- ✔ Can I see measurable progress in reasonable time?
- ✔ Am I monitoring my performance well enough to see improvement?
- ✔ What changes do I need to adopt now to increase my speed toward reaching the goal and reduce the overall amount of time I invest?

Your success in meeting your objectives tells you whether the time blocking is working for you.

Looking at measurable goals

If you can measure your goals in terms of numbers (dollars or sales, for example), then checking your results is a cinch. As a salesperson, for example, you may follow your sales numbers or commissions results over several months in order to get a good understanding of the effectiveness of your time-blocking efforts. Or say you're a magazine editor who's evaluated on consistently meeting weekly publication deadlines; if your goal is to publish three articles per month in national magazines, you can assume that your time-blocking efforts require some tweaking if your review reveals that you're getting only one story in print.

Evaluating qualitative goals

If your goals aren't easily measured in terms of dollars or sales, you may need to get creative in developing your own tally for results. Family and personal goals are difficult to measure, but you can likely gain a good sense of how your efforts are tracking by just paying attention to your daily life and how you feel about it, rating your day on a 1-to-10 scale. Are your kids comfortable in talking and spending time with you? Do they look forward to being with you? Are you on friendly terms with the people in your community activities? Do you and your spouse laugh together more often than you argue?

You can also turn to other measuring sticks, which are especially useful in the workplace:

- ✔ What went well this week? What could you have done better?
- ✔ Did you accomplish what you really needed to do? How many high-priority items did you carry over to the next day or week? (See the earlier section titled "Getting Down to Specifics: Daily Prioritization" for more on prioritizing.)

✔ How would you rate your week on a 1-to-10 scale, with 1 being utterly overwhelmed and dissatisfied, and 10 being completely in control of and happy with how you spend your time?

✔ How do you feel you performed at work? How does your supervisor feel you're performing?

✔ Did you meet your goals at home?

✔ Has what you've accomplished this week positioned you better to achieve your long-range goals?

✔ What are the key improvement areas for you next week?

✔ What adjustments to your long-range plans do you need to make?

✔ What's diverting you from your schedule?

✔ Were you unrealistic in your time estimates for tasks?

✔ What segment of the day or activity is tipping your schedule off track?

As you're reviewing your results, be careful to do so with an open, observant mind, not a judgmental one. Give yourself a couple of weeks before you resolve to change your schedule. Doing so helps you get through a long enough period of time to account for anomalies.

Book II

Getting Organized and Managing Your Time: Smart Ways to Preempt Problems

Tweaking your system

Looking back at your personal behaviors and skills and the interruptions you routinely face, identify two or three steps you need to take to increase your success. Here are a couple of tips to point you in the right direction:

✔ **If you're not completing the most important tasks or working toward the most important efforts each day:** Weed out some of the trivial tasks to make room for the most important ones. (For help on doing that, refer to the "Getting Down to Specifics: Daily Prioritization" section, earlier in this chapter.)

✔ **If your most productive times of day are filled with trivial tasks:** Shift the tasks and the time slots you fit them in. (Your trouble is time blocking; see the earlier "Blocking Off Your Time and Plugging In Your To-Do Items" section for help.)

After you figure out what you need to change, you can adjust your schedule accordingly. Unfortunately, there's no one-size-fits-all set of answers to help you figure out what to change — those decisions depend on your job requirements, your personal strengths and weaknesses, your personal goals and desires, and the amount of control you actually have over those aspects you'd like to improve.

Remember the old adage "Grant me the serenity to accept the things I cannot change, the courage to change the things I can, and the wisdom to know the difference"? You can apply it to the way you manage your time. If you can balance the results you expect to achieve (more productivity, greater efficiency, reduction in time worked, and greater sales) with the results you need to achieve, then you'll be successful.

Following are some examples of quick evaluation questions that can help you make the most effective, results-oriented changes to your schedule:

- **What's the standard?** Do you have a sales quota that needs to be met? Are you getting your boss's priorities done? Going home, how are you feeling about your progress?

- **How accurate does the time-block schedule need to be?** In time blocking, a little goes a long way. The real question is how well you did this week with the most important activities — the vital 20 percent of the 80/20 rule.

- **How much have you improved?** How have you improved since you started time blocking? How large is the improvement? Would you be happy if you improved each week for a year at this level?

- **With additional revision, how much additional productivity would you gain?** Before revising a time-block schedule, look at the anticipated return on investment. Is this change going to bring significant benefits in productivity, efficiency, or personal satisfaction?

- **How good is good enough?** Where is the point where you'll achieve diminishing returns on your effort? At some point, further refining your schedule can lead to reduced results. Where do you think that'll happen?

Perfectionism is a scourge of people who are trying to achieve more with their time. An obsession with revising, redoing, and readjusting one's time-block schedule every few days — or even hours — leads to frustration. In your time blocking, clearly define the line of success so you can achieve your goals without going overboard.

Setting Up and
Productive Wor

· ·

In This Chapter

▶ Designing a productive workspace

▶ Taming your desk and limiting clutter

▶ Keeping comfortable with ergonomics and decoration

▶ Making a home office work

· ·

Suppose you waste an hour each day trying to find papers lost on your desk (at least, that's where you think the papers are lost). That's not so bad, you say. But an hour per day adds up to 250 work hours per year, or more than 31 wasted days per worker annually. Multiply that by the number of executives, professionals, salespeople, and administrative employees in this country, and you're talking a significant loss of work time. (And that doesn't include hours spent at home trying to find misplaced eyeglasses, library books, keys, cellphones, gym shorts, earrings, pacifiers, and so on.) Think how productive you'd be if you spent all that time, well, being productive!

If your work area is a parking lot for everything from C-level "someday" tasks to hotter-than-hot, this-project-can-make-my-career assignments, you're the Titanic heading for an iceberg. Ask yourself the following:

✔ Do you know all the tasks you have to get done, complete with timelines?

✔ Do you have all the materials, documents, and tools you need right now to take each project to completion without putting out an all-points bulletin?

✔ In short, do you have everything you need to do an exceptional job in record time?

If you can answer all these questions with truthful and unequivocal yeses, you can skip this chapter. Everyone else, read on.

mlining Your Workspace

"Don't touch my desk! I know exactly where everything is." Ever heard that line — or used it yourself? You probably have. If you're like many people, most of the time, as you stare at the forest of papers on your desk, you *are* clueless. You may have known where that phone number was yesterday, a few weeks ago, a month ago — or even a few minutes ago — but more stacks have since been added to the mix.

Knowing which chart, report, or snippet of paper is on which pile, whether it's on the left or right side of your desk, or whether it's stashed in the catch-all drawer of your filing cabinet isn't enough. This is your career you're talking about. Get a handle on it!

Make way! Clearing off your desk

Repeat after me: My desk is not a parking lot. If you want to get your desk under control, remember: Less is more. The more pictures, notes, boxes, tools (staplers, paper-clip holders, books), and so on that occupy your desk, the greater your odds of being distracted, and the more cluttered your desk feels.

You also have less room to spread out if you're consulting multiple sources of information, using a laptop in addition to your desktop computer, or studying oversized charts or graphs. What's more, a topsy-turvy desk translates into greater stress and the misleading feeling that you have all the time in the world to complete your projects.

Remove everything that isn't absolutely necessary from your desk. Be brutal. Here are some ideas to get you started:

- Move family photos to your credenza or bookcase, where you can still see them throughout the day (and remember why you're working so hard) without their distracting you.

- If you have other pictures — perhaps of you with mentors or celebrities — hang them on the wall.

- Store extra tools, supplies, and items you use weekly in desk drawers and filing areas.

- Don't allow items you rarely use or haven't looked at since slipping them into a pile to take up desk space. Put those items away in a filing cabinet, storage box, closet, or other less-accessible area.

As for your workspace, ignore your inner Boy Scout telling you to be prepared. It's a recipe for desktop disaster, especially if you're one who likes to prepare for a flood, an earthquake, an alien invasion, and every other conceivable catastrophe. The cleaner and clearer your desk, the better you can use your time.

Assembling essential organizational tools

Having the right tools for the job is really the start of great organization. If you haven't already done so, get all piles off your desk, even if you have to put them temporarily on the floor. Then gather these tools:

- ✔ **A desk organizer:** You need some way to keep the standard office fare — stapler, paper clips, pens, calculator — handy at your fingertips.

- ✔ **Inboxes and outboxes:** You need some type of organizational flow to your work that's based on an in-and-out system. Too often, interruptions happen when someone drops off something you don't need right now or stops by to pick something up. Setting up inboxes and outboxes outside the door of your office or cubicle keeps your desk clear and reduces chitchat.

- ✔ **A quality filing cabinet with space for growth:** You may be surprised at how much filing space you need if you're a piler-turned-filer. You may prefer lateral filing cabinets: They're more costly but can save a lot of time because you can see all the files at once. (Ah! There's that folder for my volunteer project — and the one for my customer service committee.) If you prefer, use stacking, modular filing systems, such as those in many doctors' and dentists' offices.

- ✔ **Colored file folders:** Ban bland manila! Use the rainbow of colored folders available today. Consider a color-coded filing system, such as a stoplight approach with green for new business and other money-generating items, red for problem issues or customers, and so on. You'll likely find that that colors jog your memory when it comes time to find the files.

- ✔ **File folder labels:** Labeling files is paramount to organization, efficiency, and time savings, even if you use colored folders. Labels can also be color-coded to further differentiate one file from another.

For more tools and tips you can use to organize your desk, check out *Organizing For Dummies,* by Eileen Roth and Elizabeth Miles (Wiley).

Setting up a timely filing system

Before you start going through papers, think about how you're most likely to search for the documents you need. You can choose from numerous file-labeling strategies, but here are some possible categories:

- ✔ Customers (alphabetically)
- ✔ Past clients you no longer serve
- ✔ Due dates and project timing
- ✔ Pending projects
- ✔ On-hold projects
- ✔ To-dos, miscellaneous, or a similar catch-all type of label

You can choose to file by subject, client name, importance, or a number of other ways, but if time is of the essence, setting up a tickler filing system may be ideal. *Tickler* or *reminder files* have been around for ages. They make sure you remember to deal with delayed or deferred items at the correct times. Here's how they work:

1. **Establish two complementary tickler files, one labeled *monthly* and the other labeled *daily*.**

   Your monthly tickler can be as simple as a 12-slot expandable folder with the months written on each slot. Your daily tickler can be a 31-slot accordion file folder or even 31 hanging file folders, each labeled with dates 1 through 31.

2. **As you receive new documents, place them in the appropriate slots of your monthly file.**

   If a document you receive in December requires no action until March, place the document in the March slot of your monthly tickler file.

3. **When you enter a new month, move documents from that month's slot into the daily folders.**

   When March rolls around, pull all the papers from your March tickler and place them in the appropriate days of the month in your daily tickler file.

This system is tremendous for both home and office. You can use it, for example, to pay bills: Say you write your bills twice monthly. Place them in your daily tickler file so you can remember when they're due and when to mail them (if a bill is due on July 25, for example, put it in the July 15 slot to be sure you mail it well ahead of its due date). Best of all, you've invested minimum time in keeping track of what's due when.

Note: For many businesspeople, powerful software programs called *customer relationship management* (CRMs) have replaced tickler files. Turn to Chapter 7 of Book II to find out more on CRM software and organizing computer files.

If your filing skills are truly abysmal, have someone who's a natural filer help you develop your filing system. Of course, only you can file some items (confidential personnel reports, salaries, information you want to keep personal, and the like). But as for the rest, use your team's strengths and gifts so you can make better use of yours.

Tackling piles systematically

To de-clutter yourself, you need to remember this simple rule: Put the important things where you can remember where they are and where you can get to them quickly.

Here's how the de-cluttering process breaks down:

1. **Figure out what you can get rid of.**

   Here are a few simple questions to ask yourself:

   - Is there value in saving this item? (If the answer isn't a definitive yes, toss it.)

   - What happens if you don't keep this?

   - What's the worst that could happen if you throw this away?

   Never throw away important documents, such as tax returns and business receipts. The IRS requires you to retain tax records and all supporting material for seven years. Before you toss, think carefully about whether an item has future value and whether copies are filed elsewhere so you can access them if you need to.

2. **Condense the remaining material into smaller piles by selecting items to go into a single master important pile.**

   Many piles are simply files in disguise: documents that haven't been put away where they belong. By collecting the most important items into a single pile, you get an idea of how much time you need to dissolve this pile into nothing.

   At first, you may not be able to do much more than create your master important pile. After all, you still have meetings to attend, e-mails to respond to, and work to finish. However, the master file ensures that you tackle the important stuff first; the smaller, less-important items have to wait.

3. **Schedule an appointment with yourself in the next 48 hours to rid yourself of your master important pile.**

   You don't need to be in tip-top mental form to file. Set your filing appointment toward the end of the week, preferably in late afternoon when your energy level is low. Friday afternoons are a good time to file with comparatively few interruptions. (If you're struggling with interruptions, turn to the next chapter for help.) Don't worry about your other piles yet. Using the filing system you chose (see the preceding section), focus on the master important pile until it disappears.

4. **After making your master important file disappear, go back to your remaining clutter and repeat the process.**

   Start a *second* most-important master file and move all most-important items into that pile; then file them. Then make a third most-important master file. By now, you can probably see the surface of your desk, and you may even have a substantial area cleared.

Taking notes you can track

Note taking is a valuable time-saving tool in the workplace to help you remember details and conversations. If you're like most people, you probably take notes on whatever's handy: sticky notes, slips of paper, cocktail napkins, envelopes, or even important documents. Wrong approach! You can face significant time-loss and embarrassment when you later find out you lost the slip of paper where you took notes.

Whether you're using specially designed and cut pads printed with *From the desk of,* a full 8½-x-11-inch pad that's a color other than the standard white or yellow, or a smaller white or yellow notepad, you need to use something that stands out.

If you know you'll need to file the notes, make sure you go with large paper so you can find it later. When you finish writing, add action items to your priority list for the following day and then drop the notes into the appropriate file for record keeping. If your action items make it to the A level during the next day's priority sort, all you have to do is pull out the file folder and find your notes there as you left them, safe and sound.

 Although sticky notes are great for attaching quick reminders to your computer screen so you don't forget to buy ice cream and pickles for your pregnant wife, they're one of the worst places to jot down information. Here's why:

✔ **They're too small for extensive notes.** You run out of room and have to transfer information to a larger note pad or, worse, to a second (and possibly third) sticky note. Then you have a sticky note stuck to a sticky note stuck to a sticky note, and if you lose one, you lose them all.

✔ **Sticky notes tend to sprout legs, sticking where you don't want them to: to the wrong document headed to the wrong file.** Then you're on a frantic mission to find your all-important sticky notes (and when they've hitched a ride on an unknown document going who-knows-where, your chances of finding them are slim to none).

✔ **Aged sticky notes lose their stick over time.** A sticky note that comes unstuck and flutters into oblivion takes your important information with it.

If you're not sharing a document with others, consider taking notes directly on the document rather than on a sticky note. You can take notes in the margins around the key issues in the document or use the white space at the beginning or end for summaries or more-general points.

Keeping Clutter from Coming Back

Not so long ago, a handshake or verbal agreement sealed the deal. No more. Today, you need paper to confirm an agreement, assure mutual understanding, and even organize tasks. Paper has taken over people's lives.

Whether you're at home or at the office, maximizing your time means that all paper has to quickly find its way to the proper place, even if that place is the recycle bin or shredder. The key to controlling paper before it controls you is to decide quickly where to put it.

The best strategy for maintaining a clutter-free workspace is to avoid creating piles in the first place. You need to be more strategic in your work time to circumvent pile explosion. This section gives you quick starts to avoid the explosive growth of piles on your desk (or credenza, bookshelves, filing cabinets, extra chairs, window ledges, floor, or any other flat surface).

Handling papers once

Those who master paper have mastered *single-handling*. These people touch a paper and take action. They don't pile, table, ponder, check, reconsider, or delay. They get rid of the paper the first time they handle it.

If you want to become a single handler, follow the five Ds: *dump it, delegate it, detour it, do it,* or *depot it.* Otherwise, you confront a less-productive list of Ds: dawdle, daydream, deliberate, and deceive — all of which lead to your demise.

Dump it

The dump-it principle is simple: Do you need it? If you don't, dump it or dispose of it. Say no to all of the following questions, and you can feel comfortable sending it to the shredder or recycling bin:

- ✔ Do you really need to act on this or keep it?
- ✔ Is this new, relevant information you need now or in the future?
- ✔ Does this information benefit a colleague or client?
- ✔ Are there consequences for not keeping it?
- ✔ Will this increase revenue or customer service?

Sort your mail over the recycling bin or waste basket. Everything that swirls into the bin or basket is no longer your problem.

Delegate it

Do you have an inner pack rat that wants to hold onto everything, including every paper that crosses your desk? One way to shut down this impulse is to delegate papers to someone else. Even if you *know* you could complete the task with two hands tied behind your back, that doesn't mean it's the best use of your time. Delegate and give yourself more time to work on high-value tasks while building the skills and confidence of people you delegate to.

Detour it

Handling every sheet of paper once is a fantastic goal, but sometimes it's impossible. Maybe you need more information before you can delegate or dispose of a paper, or perhaps the paper raises significant questions that need to be answered before you act. If you can detour and park the paper for later follow-up, you've saved time deliberating *now.*

Don't park paper permanently! Create a detour file for delayed papers, but be sure you get the information you need and deal with the paper. Don't let your temporary file grow into a pile hidden in a file.

Do it

Do it is the easiest and most straightforward of all the Ds. Take action, either to get the task done quickly or because there's a high level of urgency associated with it:

✔ **Tend to urgent matters.** If the task moves to the top of your priorities list after you read the paper, the best course of action is to do it now. Change your priorities and work until the new priority is completed, even if it takes you the rest of the day.

✔ **Get the task done quickly.** Follow the five-minute rule: If the necessary task, phone call, response, or clarification is something only you can do, and it'll take fewer than five minutes, do it yourself right now. By the time you detour it, pick it up again later, reread it, and refocus, you'll have invested far more time than the five minutes required now.

Depot it

A *depot* is a place where something is deposited or stored. You can find essential tools for filing earlier in this chapter in "Streamlining Your Workspace," so you can establish an effective depot for papers you need to keep (and *only* the papers you need to keep).

Book II

Getting Organized and Managing Your Time: Smart Ways to Preempt Problems

Filing regularly

Because the task of filing is mundane, it's all too easy to allow other tasks, people, and priorities to creep into the time you set aside to deal with your piles and files, and in a few short weeks, the weeds can take over your garden again. Don't let that happen! Daily filing may not be necessary, but waiting a month or six weeks is too long. Make your time spent filing a priority. At the end of filing, your desk is devoid of piles, and you can still keep on top of your paperwork by filing for a short amount of time once a week. Keep up with your filing, and you won't find it so tedious.

 Schedule a weekly filing appointment with yourself and put it on your calendar. As you look ahead to assess your week and see your filing appointment, you begin mentally preparing for it. When you're prepared, you're more likely to keep your appointment with yourself, and when the time arrives, you'll be more efficient. You may find yourself throwing away more marginal items throughout the week and completing the task in less time.

When you're facing a few hours of filing, set a goal or benchmark. If you can't complete the whole project, break it down into a portion you can complete and commit to finishing that part without fail.

Limiting the paper you receive

Many people receive more material via snail mail and e-mail in one day than they can read in year. No one wants to miss news or seem out of it, but few people have time to read, let alone organize, the printed gridlock paralyzing their inboxes and mailboxes.

The question isn't how to handle the information, because you can't. All you can do is decide what's important and try to limit what you receive. You may have an information-overload problem if you

- Have stacks of periodicals around that you intend to read but never do.

- Buy books that sound good, only to get home and find that they're already on your shelf.

- Get frustrated because you haven't read your weekly news magazine in six months.

Here's how to cut down on the paper overload:

- **Cancel subscriptions that you don't read regularly.** Don't immediately renew subscriptions to magazines you read infrequently — take a break for a couple of months and see whether you really need them or miss receiving them. Rest assured the publishers are eager to have you back and may make you a sweeter deal than if you were a regular renewal.

- **Move to Internet-based subscriptions.** Most quality publications now offer Internet-based subscriptions. They save time because you can search issues by topic and you can read only the articles that interest you. You can also search topics by date.

- **Get off mailing lists.** Unsolicited correspondence can easily make up 60 to 80 percent of your daily incoming mail. If you're on one mailing list, your name is bought, sold, and bartered to numerous others before you can say "spring catalog."

  Most reputable firms belong to the Direct Marketing Association (DMA). Write the DMA (1120 Avenue of the Americas, New York, NY 10036) or visit online at www.dmachoice.org and ask the DMA to remove your name from its lists.

- **Take a sabbatical from the news.** The news can be negative, biased, and sensationalized to attract an audience. Don't let that be you. If you're interested in a topic, research it in depth (remember books?). You may find that your news sabbatical turns into a permanent vacation. (If you do need a news fix, look for the online version of your newspaper of choice.)

- **Create a tear file of all the articles or papers you do want to read.** A tear file can save you countless hours because it helps you decide quickly what's worth your time and what isn't. Creating one is simple: Tear out articles you want to read from trade publications, magazines, newspapers, and so on and file them in your tear file. Throw the rest of the publication into the recycle bin. Carry your tear file with you all the time, so whenever you're waiting — in traffic, at the doctor's office, at the car repair shop — you use your time productively. If the same article remains unread in your tear file for more than a couple months, pitch it.

Going paperless

One way to clear your desk is to reduce the amount of paper you handle altogether by increasing your use of electronic files. In today's technology world, you can scan most documents and create a digital version; many computers then allow you to apply optical character recognition (OCR), which changes the scanned image into text that you can edit and search through. You can also have your faxed documents turned into digital documents that can be shared on servers or via e-mail. Electronic versions are especially useful when you need to retrieve files. You can organize the digital or electronic files in multiple places at one time. For instance, you can keep a prospect's information in a *prospect file* as well as in a file under the prospect's name — it's like being two places at the same time. You can also search for files or have your computer do the search while you're working on something else — the only true multi-tasking one can do! To find out more ways your computer can help you go paperless and get organized, check out Book II, Chapter 7.

Accounting for Ergonomics and Aesthetics

Not all time-saving techniques pertaining to your workspace are directly related to organization; elements such as comfort and positive energy also affect your productivity. Two of the most important and often overlooked areas are *ergonomics* (a fancy term for fitting the job tools to the worker, rather than vice versa) and aesthetics (how you decorate your space to make the place where you spend your time enjoyable and uplifting).

An ergonomic workspace increases your productivity, reduces your work hours, and prevents workplace injuries by placing your body at optimal angles and at distances where productivity increases and fatigue decreases. (Many work-related injuries can be traced to poor posture, poor work practices, and badly designed office chairs, desks, workstations, and computer keyboards.)

Likewise, aesthetics plays an important part in time management because it encourages you to be more productive. By surrounding yourself with things that inspire you, you help yourself keep all things in perspective, particularly the balance between your work and personal life so you can make better decisions and — on those days you feel like you're drowning — remember why you're doing what you do.

Book II

Getting Organized and Managing Your Time: Smart Ways to Preempt Problems

Setting up a proper workstation

Although today's desks are more likely to be designed to accommodate PCs, many desks are still manufactured first and foremost for writing, note taking, phone conversations, and getting organized.

The standard desk is a couple of inches too high for comfortable computer use, so if you spend a considerable amount— say, 50 percent — of your time on the computer, a keyboard at desk height can lead to problems with your back, shoulders, and neck. You probably know someone who's had carpal tunnel syndrome — numbness, tingling, and pain — in his or her wrists because of repetitive and incorrect computer use. That's one ailment resulting from nonergonomic work stations.

You probably spend the bulk of your office time sitting. To avoid fatigue and injury, invest in a good, ergonomically sound chair. Features to look for include the following:

✔ Adjustable height and tilt

✔ Adjustable back rests for your lower back

✔ A rotating seat

✔ At least five wheels

Be sure you align your keyboard and monitor, too, instead of letting pieces jut left or right.

Decorating your space

Productive people create workspaces where they enjoy spending time. You spend many hours working, so make your work environment a place where you can focus and be productive for long stretches. You may have a strictly utilitarian view of your work area (it's Spartan but functional — what more do you need?). Or it may be important to you to dress up your space a bit. Whatever your preferences, keep them in mind as you begin planning your work area. Consider the following aspects of your workspace:

✔ **Walls:** Do you work better if your walls are a softer, more comfortable color than the harsh white of most offices? Consider painting or hanging wallpaper or swaths of fabric.

✔ **Images:** Are pictures, art, and photographs important in your surroundings?

✔ **Floor:** Should you buy a rug to add color and form or give your office a warmer feel?

- ✔ **Lighting:** What's the lighting like? Most people work beneath the low hum of fluorescent lighting. To give your area a warmer feel, you may try a desk lamp or even a lamp on your credenza behind you to create better ambience.

- ✔ **Furniture:** Do you need to upgrade your office furniture? Is your boss okay with you adding a couch for afternoon cat naps or creative brainstorming? Do you need a small table for meetings with your team?

Here are a few points to remember as you personalize your space:

- ✔ **Limit the items on your desk to the more utilitarian variety.** The top of your desk is not a decoration zone. Use the walls, floor, and credenza to bring the environmental influence in your workspace.

- ✔ **Pay attention to placement.** If you're someone who toils away so that you can take great vacations during your time off, place that large photo of your last trip to Hawaii where you can look at it during a moment of relaxation and envision what you're doing all the hard work for. If, however, seeing it sends you into (day)dreamland, you probably don't want to place it where it will compete with the work that needs your attention.

- ✔ **Be careful not to add anything that adds to the responsibilities you have to tend to each day.** After all, the point is to increase your productivity, not give you more to do. A mini-aquarium may be beautiful and soothing and draw plenty of attention, but think about how much work time you'll have to spent cleaning it (or how much later after work you'll have to stay to get the job done) — and how you'll be able to persuade your co-workers to feed your fish when you go on vacation!

Book II

Getting Organized and Managing Your Time: Smart Ways to Preempt Problems

Maintaining a Productive Environment in the Home Office

With gas prices skyrocketing and technology booming, the number of people working from home continues to grow. You can cash in on big savings in both time and money if you work from home. Here's how:

- ✔ You can redirect the daily time you used to spend commuting into exercise, hobbies, family time, or even work.

- ✔ Flexible hours give you almost total control over your work schedule. If you need to get up early or stay up until midnight to meet a deadline, it's doable, and you're minutes from bed.

- ✔ You spend less on lunches, dinners, and snacks, not to mention what you save on departmental gifts for holidays, parties, and other special occasions.

✔ You chalk up lower costs for clothing.

✔ Transportation expenses such as gas, car maintenance, tolls, parking, and train or bus fare drop.

On the other hand, beware of perceptions and misperceptions that can cause your productivity at home to fizzle. This section explains how to set up your office away from the office.

Creating an environment that fosters solid focus

When choosing a location for your home office, you want a place that affects your productivity and your ability to manage your time in a positive way. When the space is less than ideal, or when you struggle to focus on work even when your location is ideal, consider trying these tips to nurture your productivity:

✔ **Choose an out-of-the-way locale.** Look for an area that's yours alone, removed from general traffic and noise, where you can shut the door and hang a do-not-disturb sign on the knob. The more out of the way your office is, the better use you'll make of your time.

Setting up your home office in Hub Central — the family center of your home — without physical boundaries is unwise. Today's typical den off the entry doesn't provide enough physical distance. It's right in the middle of the home, so noise from both ends of the house reaches you clearly. Your family walks by numerous times, and in some homes the office doors are glass, providing no visual barrier whatsoever.

✔ **Employ other physical barriers if your office location isn't ideal.** If your home office isn't off in a private area of the house and your doors are glass, your best defense is a shade or visual barrier. When children see you "not working" (that is, thinking), they may figure it's playtime. The other necessary item is a lock on the door, which announces that you're busy and uninterruptible.

✔ **Use white noise to block out other household noises.** You can establish auditory boundaries by blocking household noises with white noise. *White noise* is a constant low-level background sound, such as static or a whirring fan, which your brain quickly tunes out but drowns out other, more disruptive noises.

✔ **Drown out distracting noise with music.** If you go this route, you may want to avoid the radio because of the constantly changing style and tempo of songs, the newscasts, and disk-jockey monologues (though some people claim to work better with this sort of background noise). Opt instead for instrumental music rather than songs with lyrics — words can be distracting. Consider orchestra and symphonic music, such as classical or easy listening.

Establishing boundaries and getting yourself in the work mind-set

Crafting and adhering to a set of rules for you as well as your entire family and friends increases your chance of success when you're working at home. By drawing lines between your work time and your personal time, you allow yourself to be fully present with each — and presence is a key component of productivity.

To establish a solid set of boundaries for yourself, follow these suggestions:

✔ **Treat a day at the home as you would a day in your office.** Start your day the same time you'd begin your commute to home-away-from-home and end it at the same you'd end your work day. Take only a half-hour lunch (but be sure to take that half-hour lunch). Regular start and stop times and set lunch breaks allow everyone to recognize your schedule and abide by it.

✔ **Start early.** If you work at home, you may find, as most office workers have, that you're most productive before others arrive. In the home office world, that's before your household wakes up for the day.

✔ **Dress for success.** Because you don't have to shower, shave, and don office clothes, you lose the empowering feeling you get that makes work seem like work. If you need formal dress to perform better and are negatively affected by staying in sweats or pajamas most of the day, by all means, get up, shower, and get dressed, just as you would if you were heading to the office. If you *feel* successful, you'll be successful, regardless of where you work.

✔ **Set goals for yourself.** Set goals in terms of work completed and reward yourself for achieving them, just as you would at the office.

✔ **Don't answer personal calls during your workday.** Using a home office to increase your productivity is an act of discipline. Others sometimes adopt the attitude that you're not really working; people who wouldn't imagine interrupting you at the office call to chew the fat simply because you're home. Parents are often guilty of this. Be polite but firm: "Mom, I'm sorry. I'd love to talk, but I'm working right now. I'll call you back at five, as soon as I'm finished, okay?"

✔ **Control interruptions from your family members.** Patiently train your family on your work schedule and etiquette. You may want to establish set times when you allow for interruptions.

Setting these boundaries can be challenging, especially if your children are very young, like preschool age. While your work time should be "uninterruptible," you may have to accommodate some interruptions (be warned, though, children have an uncanny ability for selecting the worst possible times to interrupt!) Here's the one exception you may want to make to the come-on-in rule: Absolutely *no* interruptions when you're on the phone. Whatever inviolable rules you settle on, make them few but enforce them rigorously.

Consider bartering for the uninterrupted time you need. For example, if you have to finish something up and your daughter keeps popping in, offer a trade: no more interruptions for the rest of the morning in return for an hour of fishing or playing together. Chances are, your child will let you complete your work (which will take you less to finish than it would've otherwise).

✔ **End on time.** Being available to work extended hours can diminish the quality and quantity of family time. Set boundaries. When the office door closes, let voice mail pick up work calls. Leave the office behind.

✔ **Allow yourself uninterrupted time each day to compress.** A commute allows you time to shift gears. On your way home, you move from CEO, salesperson, manager, assistant, or customer service representative to daddy, mommy, husband, wife, partner, or Fido's master. When you exit the door of your home office, the shift is over, and you're on! So when you're done for the day, take ten minutes to decompress before you walk out the door. You may even want to play some relaxing music so you can leave the troubles of the day behind.

Chapter 4

Defending Your Day from Interruptions

*W*ithin the past two decades, people have embraced communication technology. But in many ways, these miracles of convenience have robbed workers of their ability to control their own time. Multiplying points of access — voice mail, e-mail, instant messaging, phone- and videoconferencing, and of course, the cellphone — can shackle you like a house-arrest ankle bracelet, sentencing you to a life-sentence of perpetual availability. Business colleagues can track you down on vacation, and friends can interrupt an important client presentation. Whether you can call this *progress* or not is a matter of debate, but it's inarguably a fact of modern life.

Consider this: Every one of these interruptions — no matter how small or insignificant — robs you of at least five *additional* minutes of productive time because it takes you some time to clear your mind of the distraction and refocus on what you were doing. Whether your spouse calls and talks to you for 30 seconds or 30 minutes, you can subtract at least five more minutes from your day. Tally up 20 interruptions over the course of your day, and you lose nearly two hours of productivity — and that totals to the loss of 36 hours a month!

Distractionitis is the scourge of time-block adherents; the fastest way to render a time block or even a day useless is to deal with distractions badly (see Chapter 2 in Book II for more on time blocking). So now's the time to gain control of the interruption game, whether you're at risk from wandering bosses and colleagues, demanding clients, or the technological tools that can slice through your best defenses.

The Fortress: Guarding Your Focus from Invasion

Being successful in time management and adhering to your time-block schedule happens through controlling access: You need to limit the frequency of the interruptions you allow. Recognize the use of the word *allow* here. You're the one who controls your time and allows other people and situations to pull you away from your goals, dreams, objectives, and time-blocked schedule. You're in control, and you're the master of your time.

Think of yourself as the castle guard: Your workplace is a fortress, one that must be protected in order for it to remain a happy and productive place. Your best strategy is to establish an impenetrable wall between you and interruptions. In this section, you discover how to protect yourself from invaders on foot and how to disconnect from the electronic devices that can cut through your physical defenses. Finally, you discover how to screen your calls so only the essential information gets through.

Protecting your domain from walk-in intrusions

The biggest interruptions in your workday frequently come from within. Your co-workers pose a great threat to your effective time management. What's doubly scary is that you don't always recognize your colleagues as threats. Hey, these folks are on your team — they're the good guys, they're *there* for you! However, it's important to recognize the signs of danger from time-wasting co-workers. If not, you're at risk of falling to friendly fire.

The modern work environment is often designed on an open-office concept. Few (if any) employees are granted an office with a door, and most workers are parked in open cubicles, often with partitions that do little to block views (and definitely not the noise) of co-workers. The idea is to manifest a more unified effort and team spirit guess. But it doesn't do much to protect you from your teammates' intrusions on your time. Unfortunately, the same open-door philosophy that allows employees to drop in on their supervisors at will is often carried throughout the workplace, so co-workers may stop by to talk about a mutual project — or the office football pool.

Creating virtual barriers

When you have little in the way of a physical barrier, defending your border from invasion becomes a challenge. But it can be done — just because you don't have a door to keep people from entering your space doesn't mean you can't create *virtual* barriers when you're unavailable:

- **Communicate subtly through the posting technique.** Put signs on your office door or cubicle letting others know you're busy.

  The best action you can take is to post a do-not-disturb sign outside your cubicle, perhaps indicating the critical project you're working on. Your co-workers and supervisor may be more sympathetic to your plight if it's a project they're familiar with.

- **Verbally communicate your schedule to others so they know when you're unavailable for interruptions.** For repeat offenders, the posting alone won't work. You have to explain to them verbally and with authority that you don't have an abundance of time. This is called *communicating the standard.*

- **Threaten to put them to work.** If you're in sales, for example, inform the would-be interrupters that you're prospecting and that if they interrupt, they have to come in and make calls with you. That'll usually stop any salespeople from the interruption because they won't want to join you in the prospecting quest.

Set your unavailable time for the hours before 11 a.m. It's uncanny, but the world seems to start delivering problems to your doorstep just before midday. If you set your closed hours prior to 11 a.m., you can get your important stuff done before you start to hear the buzz of trouble brewing outside your cubicle wall.

Scheduling time to manage and interact with your staff

If you're a manager, you walk a fine line: Being available to staff to address issues and offer encouragement is important, but a manager who loses control of the border may discover that the flow of employee communication is akin to a circus parade with a never-ending line of elephants connected by trunks and tails.

Fortunately, you have a few additional ways to keep those elephant invasion forces at bay, preventing in-person interruptions while maintaining your role as a teamwork facilitator and employee go-to resource. Both management techniques center on blocking time in your schedule to interact with staff so you put constraints on the open-door policy. Creating specific time blocks to interact with the staff allows you to shut your door and focus a greater percentage of the day so you follow your schedule more readily. The times before and after lunch — when you're more likely to be between projects — are excellent for open-door hours.

The following sections offer some options on how to approach this scheduled time for interaction.

Making the rounds

A popular preemptive tactic that managers have followed since the first workplace self-help books came out, *management by walking around,* puts the time control back in the manager's domain. It suggests that making the rounds on a scheduled basis allows you to establish your availability and deflect those interruptions that could otherwise come later. Instead of getting snagged on the way to get a cup of coffee, *you* proactively seek out your staff, asking how their projects are going or whether they have any concerns or issues you can help with.

Setting your rounds for the morning is a sound strategy, though it's a good idea to wait until everyone gets settled in at their desks and the caffeine kicks in so they can respond to your "How's that proposal coming?" with some clarity.

Having employees come to you

Establish your scheduled interaction time as open-office time for staff to drop in. Or require employees to make appointments to meet with you during that time.

The danger in setting up specific drop-in hours is that it puts you in a state of waiting. You may not get any takers of your time, but your ability to focus on any other work is more challenged because you're expecting to be interrupted at any moment. To avoid this, implement scheduled-appointment hours in your office. Set aside the same time block to be available to your staff, but insist that they make appointments. They can't just stop in without notice.

You can require whatever advance notice you're comfortable with — 15 minutes or 15 hours. That way, if some of the time goes unbooked, you can schedule something else in that slot. You can choose to limit these appointments in length —15 minutes, a half-hour — and you can require that employees explain what they want to talk about when they schedule so you can be prepared.

Scheduling time offline

Used effectively, the telephone and e-mail can enhance performance, increase productivity, boost profitability, and expedite career growth. But there's a flipside: Because modern communication allows for easier interruptions, it creates a greater loss of production, performance, profitability, and advancement than ever before. And to a certain extent, e-mail has taken many people hostage. Do you feel compelled to open all e-mail immediately? Do you jump on to the next e-mail even before you've responded to or resolved the previous e-mail? Just as with cellphones, the fact that you *can* be reached easily and at any time seems to dictate that you must be available to anyone — all the time.

When you stop to open each and every e-mail as soon as it arrives or answer the phone every time it rings, you are, in essence, *multi-tasking,* trying to perform one or more tasks simultaneously. And as pointed out earlier, multi-tasking is just not time efficient.

To keep your focus, set aside time — daily or several times per week — during which you simply do not take calls, check e-mail, or allow other interruptions. Such prescheduled segments ensure blocks of concentration, a tactic certain to raise productivity and lower frustration. If you're concerned about being unavailable for too long a time, then limit these periods to one or one and a half hours, with time afterward to return messages.

Letting e-mail wait in your inbox

If you have a hard time resisting the temptation to check your e-mail every time your computer tells you a message has arrived, try working offline. During your offline time, turn off your e-mail notice or disconnect from the Internet. Schedule your e-mail time and devote a reasonable time block to take care of it. Then turn off your e-mail program so you don't see the new-mail icon on your computer until your next scheduled e-mail session.

Or compose all your own e-mail correspondence in your word processing program, and when you've completed, reviewed, tweaked, polished, and made sure each message says exactly what you want, you can go online and send those e-mail messages off. If you compose your e-mail in a word processing program, you gain yet another advantage: This tactic serves as a safety precaution — you won't inadvertently shoot off a critical e-mail before you're completely satisfied with it; no more "recalls."

The toughest decision you may face is whether to check your e-mail first thing in the morning when you fire up your computer. Wait and knock out a few priorities first? Or open it up and relieve the suspense — and possibly get waylaid by some marauding issue you feel compelled to pursue? It's your choice — do what works best for you. But by staying offline for the bulk of your workday, you're likely to stay focused on the tasks at hand and get much more accomplished.

Stopping the ringing in your ears

Let your voice mail or assistant take phone messages. Voice mail is your not-so-secret weapon for dodging phone interruptions and taking back your time. If your system has a do-not-disturb button, push it or put your ringer on mute and you won't be tempted to ponder who called. If you're an executive, forward the calls to your assistant for a time or ask the receptionist to let your callers know that you're in an appointment and will call them back.

Additionally, give yourself times when you turn off your cellphone. The most brilliant innovation with these amazing devices? You can turn them off! Without missing a message, you can continue with your conversation, errand, or work without distraction and get back to the call when you're through. Of course, you may already protect yourself against uninvited interruptions by limiting who you give your cell number to. But unless you're awaiting an urgent call from your kids, your boss, or the state lottery commission, you can likely afford a period of off-time while you attend to important tasks that require your full concentration.

Screening interruptions before letting them through

You may need to make sure certain types of information can get through to you, even while your barriers shut out everything else. The solution is to screen your calls using caller ID or to have your assistant screen your calls for you.

Using your assistant to screen calls

If you're the boss, you're the wizard who turns business transactions into gold, and your assistant or receptionist operates the drawbridge, keeping out those who attempt to foil your efforts. Your administrative staff needs to adopt the gatekeeper philosophy. The first step is to set your business up as a fortress, making it hard to get in to see the royalty — *you*.

The administrative staff has total control of the drawbridge that grants access to the fortress. They should have a militant approach to allowing people access to you. You need to clearly identify to your staff who is to be granted access and who is not. Only a few people should pass easily through the gate; the rest should be screened thoroughly to see whether another team member can assist them first.

Arm gatekeepers with the tools necessary to identify and keep out intruders and the knowledge to recognize whom to lower the drawbridge for. Their role in managing access is instrumental to your productivity and that of the department. A properly armed assistant is able to

- Answer most questions from callers and eliminate the need to talk to you.
- Capture enough information so that you're prepared with a response, which means a shorter interaction when you do get back to the individual.
- Schedule an appointment for you.
- Know which issues or requests require your immediate attention.
- Take messages from people who must talk with you.

Taking a message is more than just noting the caller's name, phone number, date, and time of the call. A highly trained assistant finds out the specific reason for the call and tries to handle the question right there on the spot. This is one of the biggest time-saving techniques of all. If unable to handle the situation on the initial call, the assistant finds out the answer and then returns the call.

If it's absolutely necessary for you to speak to the caller, set a specific time when you'll return the call, effectively making a mini-appointment for the return telephone call.

Using technology to screen calls

Those who don't have a loyal staff can turn to technology. What a miraculous invention, caller ID! By glancing at the phone number ID on your receiver, you can determine in a second whether it's a call you want to take. Not only is caller ID helpful for screening out unsolicited telemarketing calls, but you can also use it to determine whether a call is critical to take *now*. And at work, if you're on a roll on that big proposal and you'd only take a call from your boss, your phone helps you make that decision.

If you're working from home, you face some unique challenges in handling phone calls (they don't call it *tele*commuting for nothing!). Not only do you have to contend with more calls from the office (if you were there, you could at least put up a do-not-disturb sign on your door), but you also catch all the solicitation calls you'd miss if you were out of the house during the day. Plus there's a strange phenomenon at work for telecommuters: Both friends and business contacts seem to feel more comfortable interrupting your workday when you work from home.

For the telecommuters, having two separate phone lines, one for work and one for personal calls, proves more effective. That way, you can tell by the ring which is which. When you're "at work," you can choose to disregard the personal line — and if you're sitting down to a family dinner, you can ignore your work line with a clear conscience. A second phone line is a small monthly investment that can help you manage your time and increase your productivity.

Limiting phone interruptions from loved ones

In some cases, family calls are the primary source of telephone interruptions. Have a frank talk with your family members about when it's appropriate to call you at work.

If you have young children, you know how they want to tell you all the cool things that happened during the course of their day, well before family dinnertime. You likely expect and welcome these calls. Certainly you want to set opportunities for them to reach you, but it's good to establish boundaries at the same time. You may, for example, ask your kids to call you and fill you in on their day at a certain time — say, after they get home from school or in the case of preschoolers, after lunchtime. Same goes for your spouse or partner.

Most job environments allow for some personal-call time, but few are tolerant of employees who receive calls throughout the day. That type of phone interruption can undermine your productivity, not to mention your career. At work, you really don't need the kinds of emotional distractions that'll dramatically affect your performance and productivity for the next thirty minutes, an hour, or even the rest of the day. Calls from family can move your mind to home even though your body is still at the office.

Secondary Defenses: Minimizing Damage When Calls Get Through

If you set up the defense mechanisms and blocking techniques covered throughout this chapter, you can avoid more than 90 percent of the interruptions that most people experience each day. But no matter the system or strategy you use to protect yourself, telephone interruptions are certain to penetrate your defenses. When this happens, your best strategy is to accept it and go with the flow. Okay, so an interruption slipped past your perimeter: Instead of expending effort to repel the breach, just deal with it. A negative attitude or reaction is likely to cause more damage and waste more time than simply resolving the matter that made its way to you.

The most effective technique to help you adhere to time blocking is to plan for the distractions that'll undoubtedly come. You may use the preemptive strike technique (described in the preceding sections), which allows you to deal with distractions from others on your terms. In this section, you discover a few plans for handling the unwanted phone calls that make it through to you.

Delegating the responsibility

When the call penetrates your defenses, attempt to delegate the call to someone who can handle it for you. Inform the caller that you're booked, buried, under a deadline, committed, or heading into a meeting — and that you're shifting the responsibility for the call as the fastest way to resolve the problem or challenge. Assure the caller that you're bringing in someone qualified to help.

You also convey a strong reassurance when you explain that the other person is better equipped to resolve the situation. Often, especially if you're the boss, clients and business contacts want to talk to *you*. When you confess that you aren't the best person to fulfill the request, you're more likely to gain the caller's confidence that you have his best interests in mind.

Shortening or condensing the conversation

When a call does sneak past the fortress guard, your best defense is to bring that call to a close as quickly as possible. Your focus has been broken, and it'll require five minutes from the point you wrap up the call to regain your momentum. You want to keep the conversation short so you can get back in the groove.

Inform the caller upfront how much time you can offer. You may, for example, explain that you're in the middle of an important project and have only ten minutes available. You can also plead an appointment — and if you've implemented the time-block schedule (see Chapter 2 in Book II), you've blocked out your day, so your claim is true.

Some people feel uncomfortable about cutting calls short in this way, especially with clients or prospective customers. Giving the caller a time limit feels abrupt. But it doesn't have to. Here's one way your speech may go:

> "I know we can resolve your problem, but I have an appointment in ten minutes that I have to keep. If we can't resolve the problem to your satisfaction in the ten minutes, then we can set a time to talk later today to finish up."

This approach still gets you off the phone in the allotted time but gives you an out. The customer can also feel better that you're offering more time.

Rebooking discussions for a better time

If now's a bad time to handle the call, then reschedule. The caller certainly doesn't know your schedule, and it probably never occurred to the caller that this could be a bad time. Offer a brief explanation — you're in a meeting, on your way to an appointment, or simply tied up at this time. Then without allowing time for a response, offer two options of when you're available:

> "I'm not able to give your situation the full attention it deserves at this moment. Can we schedule a phone meeting for this afternoon after three or first thing tomorrow morning?"

By offering options, you give back some control to the caller. If you've been caught without your day planner, give a general time, such as Wednesday morning or Thursday afternoon. Then don't forget to transfer the call appointment to your planner.

Handling Recurring Interruptions by Co-Workers

Being very clear on your personal boundaries is essential with your co-workers. However, there's a fine balance between being viewed as a hermit, loner, or outcast and conveying your commitment to your job and the deadlines that you've been given, so you have to approach the confrontation with finesse.

Especially if the interruption outbreak is a department-wide epidemic, suggest to your supervisor that the team get together to talk about solutions. By coming together as a department or work group, each individual is more likely to take ownership of the situation. Call a team meeting to discuss workflow, distractions, and interruptions. As a group, you can brainstorm solutions and come up with a strategy that everyone can buy into. Because you're all making a commitment in each other's presence, everyone is more likely to honor it.

Time-wasting co-workers fall into a few categories, each of which can cause you interruptions that are detrimental to your career. You first have to figure out which category the offender falls into so you can respond in a way that'll effectively remedy the specific situation. This section previews four of the most common colleague categories and some signs to watch out for. These individuals may be hard workers, possibly overburdened, and very productive. Unfortunately, they sap a lot of their productivity from their co-workers, often disrupting others in the office to seek assistance, whether it's emotional support or actually trying to pass off specific tasks.

The colleague with nothing to do

Face it: In most companies, the division of labor is rarely parceled out equally — not fair, maybe, but it's a fact of life. For you to survive with your time intact, you need to recognize who's not carrying her share of the work. Why? Because to add insult to injury, these are often the same people who sabotage the efforts of those who do the bulk of the work by interrupting their productivity. These folks often pop into your space, flop into a chair, and strike up a conversation about anything and everything.

If you get interrupted by someone who clearly doesn't have enough to do, ask her what she's working on. What are her priorities and deadlines? Inform her of yours and ask for her help. Asking offenders to help or to work sends most of them the other direction to their own cubicles — voilà!

The colleague who just doesn't want to work

Workers owe the company that pays their salaries and benefits their best efforts for the whole time they're working. The people who lumber along, encourage others to waste time, take two-hour lunches, and generally don't give their best effort have unethical work behavior. The problem is that you can't help these individuals a whole lot. Your boss needs to be the one to lay down the law.

Make sure your own responsibilities aren't at risk. In time-management terms, give a few minutes, and someone will take an hour. That means you can't sugarcoat the issue with co-workers. You have to be direct and firm, noting (with a smile) that you don't have time for frivolity. Better to confront your co-worker than miss a deadline and be viewed as untrustworthy of performance under pressure. Don't allow someone else's agenda to diminish you in the eyes of your boss.

If all else fails, go to your boss for help. If the time waster is influencing your performance, then your boss will want to know. When you do so, be careful not go directly from telling the lazy co-worker he's lazy to talking to your boss about the problematic behavior. Give yourself a few days between each discussion so you reduce the chance of backlash.

The colleague who's wrapped up in her world

Some people are excited about everything in life, especially their family and outside interests. They're constantly talking about their weekends, their dates, their favorite teams, and their families ad nauseam. Their focus is so scattered and their excitement is so high that they're almost like puppies jumping at your feet for attention. The real challenge is that like puppies, they don't get the subtle hints you drop that you're busy. It's as if you have to hold them still, bring your face to theirs, and say, "I am busy!" nose to nose. Be direct. Say something like "I'm afraid I can't chat right now. I'm really busy with this project" or "I'd love to hear about it when I have more time, but right now I need to get back to work."

The colleague who treats work as his sole social outlet

Some people have such a limited life outside of work that they want to know all about yours. They live vicariously through your life experiences, from dating to family to your weekends past or future. Short of being their dating or activity secretary, you need to limit the interaction. The lunch hour is usually a bad option for talking with these people because it can wipe out time before and after lunch as well as lower productivity, but if you want to help them get their life in order after work, go for it.

Dealing with Interruption-Oriented Bosses

In most companies, probably the biggest offenders who interrupt the staff are people in supervisory positions. In some ways, this is understandable. These folks are presumed to have an inside track on corporate priorities and often have to call upon staff to change gears and redirect their efforts. It's no surprise when the director whips into your cubicle, announcing that you've just been tagged to take on the company's latest and greatest new program — and you have to put anything else on the back burner. However, that's a far cry from the boss who sidles into your guest chair and launches an hour rant on executive office demands, reduced budget, and upcoming weekend plans. Or the one who drops in every 15 minutes to ask you how you're coming on that report that's due in three hours.

Most bosses aren't out to find ways to deliberately disrupt their employees' work. More than likely, they're focused on their goals — whether those goals are meeting sales quotas, completing a project on time, reducing costs, or maintaining production. And in their quest to meet those goals, they're often simply not sensitive to others' need for focus.

Enlisting the cooperation of your direct supervisor can be a bit touchier than confronting a co-worker with your interruption issues. It may take some more diplomacy and tact, but it can and must be done. Meeting with your boss to discuss your time-block schedule or to ask your boss to help you with your schedule is a good opening move. Get your boss's commitment to not interrupt you during a certain segment of your day — it can pay large dividends for you both.

The seagull manager

Gaining control of the seagull manager is hard. These types of managers do the aerial attack of interruption by flying over, pooping on everyone, and flying back out. Their bombing run of new ideas, changed priorities, and emergency deadlines is ever-changing because their organization and skills in management are lacking.

This type of manager is generally young and inexperienced in management and motivation. These managers can also be overly aggressive and unrealistic about the results that can be achieved in a specified time frame.

With seagull managers, your best bet is to play up to their desire to achieve. Point out that you understand the importance of having the department pull together to help meet these goals. Confirm with your boss that the work you're currently involved in is in alignment with those goals. (You may uncover that it's not — and that may be the reason for your boss's repeated interruptions.)

If you get an affirmative, however, you then have an opportunity to ask for your boss's help in assuring that you fulfill your role in the process. The talk may go this way:

> "I want to do everything I can to help meet our goal. As I understand your expectations, I need to devote at least X hours of uninterrupted time each day to this work. To make sure I'm investing that time on the right tasks, would you like to meet briefly to go over what I plan to accomplish during that period?"

With a response like this, you establish that you're on board with the boss's agenda and you assume an implied agreement that she believes that your work should be uninterrupted. But by asking for the boss's advice on your approach, you soften your declaration and offer an opportunity for the boss to reaffirm your need for uninterrupted time.

The verbal delegator

The verbal-delegator type of manager can really gum up productivity and performance. With skilled staff members, delegating small projects, small tasks, and deadlines works better through writing. The verbal delegator often delegates because something popped into his head and he wants to move it off his plate because he doesn't want to think about it again. He moves it into some subordinate's world at that moment, regardless of schedule.

Book II

Getting Organized and Managing Your Time: Smart Ways to Preempt Problems

Your best solution is to try to turn the verbal delegator into a nonverbal delegator. To do so, urge your boss to put any work request in writing. This ensures that you get the directions straight and avoids the risk that the boss will double-assign a task. The icing on this cake is that you reduce the number of interruptions. If your supervisor has to put the order in writing, he's sitting at the computer writing up an e-mail rather than buzzing you on the phone or stopping in your cubicle. If you're working with a boss who's still in the information cul-de-sac trying to find his way to the information highway, then use written request forms instead. You can use something as simple as the example in Figure 4-1.

Request Form

Date: _____

Request:

_____
_____
_____
_____
_____
_____
_____
_____
_____
_____

Requested By: _____
Date To Be Completed By: _____
Completed By: _____
Date Completed: _____

Figure 4-1: Written request forms clarify details and reduce interruptions.

Working with Intrusive Clients

Most businesses have customers of some sort — and most embrace a philosophy of placing a high level of value on their customers. From department stores to fast-food drive-throughs, most companies follow some iteration of *the customer is always right*.

That said, you know that to provide the best service to each customer, you have to seek some balance. If the squeaky-wheel clients take up more than their share of your time and resources, you won't be able to give the attention to other deserving customers. Although all customers and clients are important to a growing and thriving business, some *believe* they're more important than others — even if they aren't. Some customers just require more attention, and they often manifest those feelings by being more disruptive. Their interruptions are simply cries for attention — they want to be valued and appreciated.

The truth is that some customers and clients really do have more value than others to the company. Their revenue to the company is larger. They buy products and services that have higher profit margins. They're more influential in the marketplace as your advocates in sending you more business through referrals. To assume that all customers and clients are alike is a naive approach.

When dealing with intrusive clients and investing large amounts of time, make sure they're worth it. If they're high maintenance, they must be also high revenue and high reward. In the following sections, I tell you how to handle customers who want attention.

Giving a bit of attention that goes a long way

Book II

Getting Organized and Managing Your Time: Smart Ways to Preempt Problems

It's amazing how taken for granted customers and clients are in today's business world. Expressing appreciation packs a powerful professional punch. When was the last time you were thanked or told, "I appreciate your business," by your attorney, doctor, dentist, accountant, realtor, dry cleaner, gas station attendant, grocery clerk, barista, or food server? Just that simple act stands out significantly as a positive interruption for clients.

A preemptive strike can reduce the interruptions you may entertain from some of your more high-maintenance clientele. Here are a few strategies for making your customers feel appreciated and — at the same time — reducing interruptions from them:

- ✔ **Send a handwritten thank-you note for their business.** Then send one again any time they upgrade, add to their order, or increase their business with you.

- ✔ **Remember their birthdays.** Send a handwritten card or small token.

    A terrific service for mailing cards is Send Out Cards (www.sendout cards.com). You can program a business follow-up plan for key clients or even your nephew's birthdays for years in advance with a few clicks of the mouse.

- ✔ **Call them on a regular basis.** How frequently you should call depends on the business, the client, and other particulars. But a check-in for no other reason than to make sure everything is going okay racks up a lot of points.

- ✔ **Deliver added value.** Forward articles of personal or professional interest. Alert customers to resources, products, and services that may or may not be related to your business interests. This gesture conveys that you value the relationship beyond business motives. (See Chapter 7 of Book II for tips on keeping client information with a customer relationship management [CRM] program.)

Another technique is calling customers back and telling them that they're so important that you squeezed them into your schedule or that you called them first. This technique is extremely effective when you return a call before the appointed time. If you informed them on voice mail that you'll be calling them back at 11 a.m. and you manage to get your priorities done early and can start calling the high-interruption clients back at 10:30 a.m., they'll think you walk on water.

Setting clients' expectations

Educating customers about your availability is important. Let new customers know your schedule and the best times to reach you as well as how to leave a message when you can't be reached. As part of this education, you also want to establish how quickly they can expect a response from you after they leave a message: Within 24 hours? The same business day?

What you're trying to avoid is the person who calls you five times that day because you were in meetings. With every call, the client gets more frustrated that you haven't called him back. Or worse yet, he reaches you on the fifth call before you're walking into your most important meeting of the day, creating the worst interruption of your life because he unloads on you and ruins your focus.

Creating reasonable expectations is key in good customer relations. Taking 24 hours to return a client's call may be reasonable — but it won't seem that way if the client expects to hear from you within an hour.

As for existing clients and customers, be sure to update them whenever your availability circumstances change. If, for example, your work hours are changing — maybe you're switching to part time or a four-day workweek — notify customers of the schedule revisions and your new availability. Depending on the importance of the client and the immediacy of the situations you deal with, you may even want to let customers know when you're on vacation or on a business trip where you can't be reached.

You can also reinforce wait times through your voice mail message. By leaving your availability and response details as part of your message, callers are more likely to recall and retain. Here's an example:

> "You've reached *[your name]*. I am out of the office today, Tuesday, September second. Please leave a message and I will return your call by end-of-day Wednesday, September third. If you need immediate assistance, please call *[so-and-so]*. Until then, make it a great day!"

This message sets the scenario: The caller shouldn't expect a return call from you today. And in fact, because you'll be returning to an inbox filled with calls, e-mail, and correspondence, you may not be able to get back until the end of the next day. It also offers a back-up plan if the situation is more urgent. This should satisfy virtually anyone who calls.

Don't be tempted to include "If it's an emergency, call me on my cellphone" unless you're prepared for lots of interruptions. After all, isn't *interruption* exactly what you're trying to avoid?

Book II

Getting Organized and Managing Your Time: Smart Ways to Preempt Problems

Chapter 5

Overcoming Procrastination

*Y*our work probably involves long-term, complex, multi-staged projects that require investments of research, development, and time. And you can't afford to get behind. Fortunately, you don't have to — not when you can conquer the tendency to put things off. In this chapter, you find out what procrastination is and how to recognize it. Not all procrastination is bad, however, so this chapter also helps you see the difference between good reasons to postpone action and mere excuses to put something off.

But most importantly, this chapter provides tools and tactics to help you overcome that debilitating paralysis that keeps you from getting started or the attacks that slow you down or stop you midproject. One of the most important principles in overcoming procrastination is to take the first step — so go ahead and get started.

Tomorrow's Another Day! Letting Procrastination Take Hold

Although many people believe that they postpone the unpleasant when they indulge in procrastination, the fact is, putting things off carries a lot of emotional unpleasantness. Boiled down to its purest form, *procrastination* is simply deferring or delaying action. But of course, it's not nearly that simple. Understanding what provokes procrastination and how it affects you is the first step in overcoming the impulses that keep you from moving forward.

Recognizing procrastination isn't always easy, especially when your time of reckoning is a few weeks or months away. You may simply believe you're waiting until the right time to get started. Here are some indications that you may be putting off what you shouldn't.

Calling on short-sighted logic: "I have plenty of time"

Justifying the idea that you don't have to start on a project is easy when its completion date isn't for some time off. Perhaps your tax returns don't have to be submitted until April 15, and it's the middle of January. True, you still have time, so you don't need to put *file taxes* at the top of your priority list at this point. But you should pull your documents together at least 30 days before the deadline. If you use an accountant, you may need even more time to have meetings and research a few deductions to get the proper documentation. Procrastinators, on the other hand, tend to cling to this logic way past the point of manageability. Nine times out of ten, the procrastinator who says "later" in January is scrambling to get in the extension form at 11 p.m. on April 14.

Avoiding the unpleasant: "I don't want to think about it now"

If you just discovered that you hold the winning lottery ticket, you wouldn't delay calling in for your reward. Who feels conflicted about winning money? But putting off tasks that are unpleasant, that are difficult to accomplish, or that you feel conflicted about is human nature. Consider these examples:

- ✔ You delay turning in the expense report for your recent business trip. Tallying up receipts is such a bore.
- ✔ You've ignored keeping up with your quarterly statistics for weeks.
- ✔ You rearrange your office and clean your desk instead of picking up the phone and starting on your sales calls for the day.

When someone faces a situation that requires confrontation with others, the tendency is also to procrastinate. Most humans — talk show hosts excluded — seem hard-wired to avoid disagreements with others. Sometimes, however, what may have been a small confrontation turns into a major confrontation because it builds over time. Say, for instance, Boy meets Girl. Boy and Girl go out. Boy decides he wants to go out with someone else. Boy keeps putting off the talk with Girl because he knows it'll be uncomfortable. But every time Boy postpones until the next date, he has a miserable time with Girl and adds even more guilt and discomfort.

Or take the case of delaying a disciplinary action with an employee. When you avoid that conversation, the employee's behavior may continue or become even worse. In some cases, it can lead to cause for dismissal. But most companies require that certain steps be taken to resolve issues before termination, and documenting disciplinary actions is one of those steps. Because you haven't followed the process, you're in the middle of an unavoidable and ugly conflict that you can't quickly resolve.

Triggering your fears: "What if I screw up?"

Sometimes putting off something stems from more than poor planning or overcommitment. Many procrastinators are unsure of themselves and their abilities. They wait until the last minute to complete projects because that way, if their work isn't well received, they can tell themselves it was because they didn't have enough time to finish the project to their satisfaction.

You can just as easily procrastinate because of fear of success as fear of failure. Fearing success and how it may change your relationships and friends is real. Many people don't reach outside their comfort zones because of what their parents, siblings, and Uncle Ned will say. In some circles, becoming too successful may cause you to leave some people behind.

Paralyzed by perfection: "I'll wait till the time is right"

Sure, you want to do the best job you can. But procrastinators often use their quest for perfection as an excuse to delay. As a close cousin to fear of failure (see the preceding section), the desire for perfection can paralyze you. If you spend too much time checking facts, trying to select the perfect words or phrases, or rewriting a paragraph numerous times, you're probably doing so at the expense of other more important things. Frequently, procrastinators try to avoid and delay challenges, like projects that are mentally taxing or big-picture tasks. They rationalize that they're not in the right frame of mind, are too distracted to give it their best, or are waiting for inspiration to strike. The danger here, of course, is that by procrastinating, you push yourself into a corner and, without adequate time, do a job that's far less than perfect.

A bit of perspective may lead you to the root of the problem, because procrastination is often a symptom of something that's troubling you on a subconscious level. Perhaps consider why you feel the need for things to be perfect. Have you always felt the need for perfection, even as a child? Could you have learned this behavior from circumstances in your childhood? Is your current or previous boss a perfectionist?

The message isn't that you shouldn't try to do an outstanding job. You should absolutely strive to make every task and project a masterpiece — whatever it is. But be careful not to use it as an excuse to postpone taking that first step. Doing your best with the resources you have is truly the goal in life. Use your time, skills, mental capabilities, and actions to help you avoid becoming paralyzed by perfection. Also, keeping the 80/20 rule in mind can help you move on to the next project or goal (turn to Chapter 2 of Book II for more on the 80/20 rule).

Sabotaging at midprocess: "I've earned a break"

Although most people are stricken by procrastination before they take their initial steps, the urge to put off completing a project occurs frequently, too. The more complex and lengthy the task, the greater the odds are of losing momentum, getting distracted, and giving up before you reach the end.

Procrastinating midproject isn't hard to understand. Starting something new revs you up. Maybe you love launching a new idea or working on a new project with a client and therefore dive in with enthusiasm. As the project progresses, though, the excitement and enthusiasm tends to wane, and the tendency to procrastinate appears.

For information on how you can keep moving forward, see the later sections "Motivating yourself with the carrot-or-stick approach" and "Maintaining Your Motivation as You Press Ahead."

Looking for thrills: "I work best under pressure"

Many people who claim to work best under pressure are merely procrastinators in disguise. The first thing to do is to figure out whether you really work well under the pressure of tight deadlines. Most high-dominant behavioral style individuals do work best under pressure. That's only 18 percent of the population, so the chance you fit that category is about one in five.

You can get a rush from having to work in a state of high productivity and hitting the deadline. You feel a sense of accomplishment in knowing that most of your colleagues couldn't have pulled it off. The problem with forcing yourself into those situations is that once in a while, you get burned by not hitting the deadline or by crashing as soon as you cross the finish line.

The best advice? Do some of the planning for your projects when you get them. Invest the time in planning out the steps even if you don't have the time to complete them. One of the benefits is that you'll be sure of the time, resources, materials, and help you'll need to pull off your project. This planning enables you to accurately gauge what you need so you get fewer surprises when you put your whole effort in motion.

And if you still feel you need more deadline-driven excitement in your job, perhaps your boss will reward you with more responsibility — and a raise to go with it.

Knowing Whether to Put It Off

Postponing action isn't productive when it holds you back, costs you time and money, and results in a negative outcome. But sometimes, putting something off is the best course of action. The challenge is knowing when it's right to procrastinate. This section helps you sort that out.

Poor procrastination: Considering the costs

With procrastination, the bottom-line loss of time, money, and productivity is enormous — enormous to you, to your company, to your country, and to the world. A global tally of the cost of procrastination is more than a little overwhelming to take in, but the negative impact is clear in closer-to-home examples, too. Here's what poor procrastination costs you:

- **Money:** Consider the impact when you pay your bills late: You're dinged with a late fee, which can be as much as $25 or more. If you do that half the time, you rack up $150 per year. And that's not factoring in the increased interest (compounded daily) you pay.

  Now crank it up a bit. When you routinely pay your bills late, your credit rating isn't so hot. So when you apply for a mortgage or home equity loan, you don't get the best interest rate. You may not even realize how much that fraction of an interest point can make over your 30-year mortgage. Your habit of procrastinating can cost you as much as $50,000 over the loan's lifetime!

- **Quality:** Putting things off until the last minute means you have less time to do the job than it probably warrants. Some of you can boast pulling an A out of such an experience. But most people, if they're honest, confess that the 11th-hour cram session doesn't bring them their best grades — or a meaningful understanding of the material. So as you try to cram ten days into five doing a job you're not comfortable with in the first place, you lose even more sleep, work even more fatigued, and — surprise — your paper is returned to you for major rework.

✔ **Time:** When you put off a task, you spend a limited amount of time actively choosing not to start your project. And then there's the time that the thing you should've been doing but weren't takes up residence in your mind, even though you're doing other things. It still counts as time invested in the task you're putting off because it's affecting the quality of whatever else you're doing in the moment.

✔ **Your well-being:** The responsibility doesn't go away simply because you put off doing the job, and you end up carrying the guilt of not doing what you know you should. The stress of the work ahead and the not-doing-it causes both emotional anxiety and physical stress, from loss of sleep to stomach problems to depression. In short, procrastination feels lousy.

Wise procrastination: Knowing when to hold 'em

The secret to successful procrastination is to do it deliberately, based on the time that you have and the status of the tasks. Take a look at what's on your plate and choose the tasks that are least time-sensitive and least at-risk, and then postpone them for a bit. In other words, allow yourself to procrastinate — but give yourself a deadline by which to complete those tasks. This section covers tasks you can afford to — and probably should — procrastinate on.

When haste could cause harm

Many tasks or decisions that require action are critical and must be accomplished in a timely manner. But when making the right decision is important, opt for procrastination if haste could result in a damaging outcome. When you feel pressured to make a choice or are forced to take an action you're uncertain of, in most cases, putting it off until you're clear-headed and can think through your decision is a good use of procrastination.

Here's an example: The salesperson offers you a hefty discount on those super-insulating windows — but it's only good at the time of the offer. Defer until tomorrow, and the price goes back up by 20 percent. You're torn. The salesperson assures you that the company is highly rated and the product is the best quality. You know you need new windows, but until the salesperson knocked on your door, you hadn't planned to buy them.

In this case, your instinct to hold off is a good one. The windows and the deal are probably legitimate. But you haven't had a chance to investigate this opportunity as carefully as you should to ensure that you make a wise move. Plus, this is probably not your last opportunity to buy those windows at a special price.

When the timing isn't right

Sometimes, the key to success is timing. You may have an important objective on your to-do list: It may be something that's critical in helping you achieve your goals. But your instinct to put on the brakes may be because the timing isn't right — the time and energy you'd put out is far greater than what you'd get in return.

Maybe you delay putting your house on the market — it's a bad time to sell, so why invest the time and energy when the likelihood of selling at the price you need to is minimal? Or perhaps you need to put in some time in the evening to prepare for a meeting in the morning. But the baby is sick, and even if you ignore his distress or leave your spouse to handle it, you're distracted and worried.

The point is that you can't possibly be as productive or accomplish as much when the timing isn't right. You may end up investing a lot more time and energy — and not get the return you hoped for. So do the best that you can; you need to invest the time necessary so that you're prepared enough for the meeting but also give the necessary assistance to your family. Learn to recognize those times that you're swimming against the current, and then stop and reevaluate your priorities and change direction if needed.

When the task isn't critical

You're loaded down with projects and commitments, all of them important and none of them offloadable. Heck, you're not procrastinating — you're *drowning*. In situations like this, procrastinating can be a survival strategy. You just need to decide which items to put off. Some advice:

- ✔ Be cautious about postponing the growth and big-picture aspects: Even though they tend to be more long-term in scope, if you don't stay on top of these issues, the consequences can be significant.

- ✔ If you have to put off doing something because of time limitations, make it one of the routine day-to-day tasks. These are the low-value, low-reward actions that produce limited results, something you can most likely delegate to someone else.

You can put off less-important to-do items in your personal life, too. For instance, say you have to accomplish the following tasks: Do your taxes by next week, finish an important presentation for work in a week and a half, paint the guest room before your in-laws come next week, and talk with your travel agent about your trip to Bali this summer. You may choose to put off painting the guest room because it's not critical to your in-laws' visit (they'll be just as happy with smoky-blue walls as moss-green ones). Or you can postpone the meeting with the travel agent because you have more time to accomplish that than you have for the taxes and the presentation. To find out more about effectively prioritizing tasks to reduce stress and increase productivity, see Chapter 2 in Book II.

Book II

Getting Organized and Managing Your Time: Smart Ways to Preempt Problems

Breaking the Procrastination Habit

Everyone has three weapons in the arsenal for fighting procrastination. Call upon these formidable forces, unleash their power, and reclaim control of your time:

- ✔ **Decision:** It's important to recognize procrastination when you see it and admit that you're guilty. At that point, you can take action to squelch the urge. Decide to begin the steps to stay on course with your obligation. In short, make a commitment and hold fast.

- ✔ **Determination:** Determination is the push that gets you through the late hours, the long days, and the uncomfortable places that make you want to put off your obligation. It's the commitment to see the task through to completion and on time. Although determination is often an innate sense of responsibility, it's also a habit that you can learn, and constant practice keeps it working.

- ✔ **Discipline:** Just as you use discipline to train yourself in other areas — picking up a sport or taking a class; sticking to a time-management plan and schedule-planning system; going on a diet or undertaking an exercise plan — your vigilant effort to keep on course with your commitments can serve as a major motivator. Approach your procrastination with the same focus: Discipline yourself to get started and stay on course.

The following sections name a few alternate routes to keep you on track so you arrive at your destination — on time.

Motivating yourself with the carrot-or-stick approach

The nature of human beings is to move away from pain and toward pleasure. In setting up a prioritization plan, you can use the carrot-or-stick approach to drive yourself toward accomplishment. When you feel the urge to procrastinate, maybe what you need is a carrot dangling in front of your face — an incentive to keep pressing on. Hey, it worked when you were a kid: "If you clean your room now, you can stay up tonight and watch monster movies." On the other hand, some folks respond better to reminders of consequences — the threat of the stick. For them, the promise of a reward gets no reaction, but avoiding negative consequences scares them into action.

Here's an example: You hate working out — it means you have to get up earlier to get to the gym, work up a sweat when you could be getting another hour of sleep or enjoying a latte and the newspaper. But keep in mind the end result of your choice: the awful feeling of being overweight or out of shape, ill-fitting clothing, high blood pressure, and low stamina. On the flip side is the pleasure of a fit physique, boundless energy, and a stab at a longer, healthier life.

A work-life example is the salesperson who drives herself to put in two hours of prospecting calls each day (instead of just one) by reminding herself that a higher commission check, management recognition, and a grander family vacation are the rewards for the effort. If she neglects this effort, consequences await her: a poor performance evaluation, lower income, more effort to make up for sales shortfall, and perhaps even termination.

Seeking reward

If anticipating the pleasurable consequences of tackling an action you don't really enjoy motivates you to perform it, then focus on those positives. And if rewards help, shower yourself with them. If the vision of a latte and your favorite scone gives you the get-up-and-go to take care of your task, go for it (after you finish the job, of course!). Or if a vacation moves you toward finishing a difficult freelance project, set a date for when you'll book the trip, and follow through when you wrap up the project.

Whenever motivation lags, pause to remind yourself of your incentive upon achieving success. Consider tacking up an enticing photo near your most tempting place of hesitation. The photo can be any number of things: A place you want to go, a person you want to spend time with, someone with qualities you'd like to attain, and so on. If your reward for a freelance writing project is a Caribbean vacation, for example, tack up a photo of a tropical setting or beach along a sparkling blue ocean right by your computer.

Avoiding consequences

If you're more leery of the results of neglect than excited about a reward upon completion, ask yourself about the consequences you'll face if you fail to complete certain steps toward your goal, and remind yourself of them as often as you need to.

If you find that consequences are your surest motivators, make sure you focus on the immediate ones. Unfortunately, when consequences are delayed, the human response is to delay positive action. Skipping your workout today won't give you a heart attack tomorrow — so why not sleep in a little longer? Putting off your prospecting calls today won't reduce your paycheck this week. Because skipping these steps toward your ultimate goal doesn't immediately produce pain, it's easy to (wrongly) convince yourself that there are no consequences.

You can set up new, unpleasant consequences if you have trouble focusing on the long term. You might try something a little unorthodox: Write a $500 check to a political party that you absolutely abhor and would never contribute to. Then give it to a friend, colleague, or your spouse to hold onto, with permission to address and mail the check if you don't break through your procrastination. Chances are the check will never be sent. Your desire to avoid violating your political integrity will ensure your daily move through the valley of procrastination.

Recognizing excuses and shoving them aside

Procrastination is definitely in your control, but some influences in your life certainly seem to affect your inclination to procrastinate. And when that happens, the tendency is to make excuses or blame someone or something else.

Resisting peer pressure

A fact of life is that co-workers, friends, acquaintances, and family all seem to conspire to tempt you away from what you *should* be doing. But on some level, when you want to avoid an obligation, you're looking for those opportunities to postpone, and having someone else or some situation to blame is very convenient.

Say, for example, that your friend tries to talk you into taking the day off to go to the beach. You have a big presentation coming up the next week and you need every minute to prepare beforehand. But it's a painfully tedious process, you're dreading the presentation, and the last thing you want to be doing is writing yourself a speech. Sounds like a great opportunity to procrastinate. But here's where discipline comes in.

When another person encourages you to forsake your work, before you submit to the pressure, acknowledge that you're likely using this person as an excuse. Then remind yourself what you need to do to meet your priorities now. Here's the real question: Is taking time off with your friend bringing you closer to or further away from your goals?

Seeing whether outside forces really do prevent work

Sometimes, you may feel like you're forced to procrastinate due to some external factor beyond your control — weather, traffic jam, power failure. In situations like this, step back and assess the situation. Ask yourself the following:

- Is there another way you can accomplish this task?

- Would the quality of your work be compromised if you were to complete the task under these circumstances?

- Can you at least take some action to stay on track?

Granted, in certain situations, you have no choice but to put off your task. If you're poised to cut the grass and a sudden downpour soaks the lawn, you have to postpone the chore. But be sure that you're not manipulating the situation so that you have an honorable excuse to do what you wanted to do anyway.

You have some options when you really can't make progress on the task at hand:

- Move to the next most important task on your list and come back to the most important one later.

- Trade time off. Take a break this afternoon but plan to work later this week during your previously scheduled afternoon off. Or choose to get up earlier tomorrow to make up for it.

Book II

Getting Organized and Managing Your Time: Smart Ways to Preempt Problems

Give me a break: Putting off procrastination

Sounds counterintuitive, but sometimes putting off procrastination is the proverbial hair of the dog that bit you. That is, a little planned procrastination can solve a larger procrastination problem. As soon as you become aware that you're procrastinating, don't beat yourself up; instead, allow yourself to procrastinate — but just not yet.

Here's how it works: Identify the ways you're likely to put off working on your project. Then, instead of fighting a losing battle with your willpower, tell yourself it's okay to do those activities — after you put in a set amount of work on your project.

Suppose you're trying to get a good head start on a paper for a class, but you've been putting it off for almost anything else that comes along: a lunch date, a shopping errand, even a TV show. You can plan to run that errand — *after* you spend a half-hour getting your notes in order and reviewing your outline. Chances are, by the time you look up at the clock, you'll have spent an hour or longer and have made a lot more progress than you anticipated. You may decide to keep on working, now that you're engrossed in the task. But even if you do break at this point, you'll have gotten more done than had you simply quit earlier. The psychological edge is likely to help motivate you to make even further progress.

When postponing your procrastination, give yourself fairly short time commitments. Tell yourself you'll just spend a half hour or an hour on the project before you allow yourself a break. This is more likely to keep you on task than if you commit yourself to three hours of work. With that time commitment, you may end up procrastinating on your procrastination of procrastinating.

Conquering Dreaded Tasks with Sandwich Tactics

Sometimes what's on your plate seems so big that you can't sink your teeth into any of it. In these cases, taking things apart may be the best way to make progress, stay on track, and put away that project. Here's the breakdown.

The eat-the-crust-first approach: Starting with the tough job

One extremely successful technique to move beyond procrastination is to tackle the toughest job first. Or if you're working on a single, big task, take on the most difficult aspect of it before the rest.

Coordinate this tough-stuff-first effort so that you start it first thing in the morning, a time when most people are at their peak in terms of energy, intensity, and focus. If you conquer the most difficult task first, your day will be a lot more productive.

To ratchet up your results further, start the prep work for the toughest tasks the night before. In Chapter 2 of Book II, you find out how you can set the stage and make quick work of even your most challenging projects. When you prepare well for your effort, you won't spend 30 minutes just getting ready to go.

If you get stuck on the big task, you can regain momentum with the salami approach or Swiss-cheese approach, outlined next.

The Swiss-cheese approach: Poking little holes in the task

When biting into a major or complicated task seems overwhelming, start with the easier pieces — the aspects that you know you can complete quickly and with little effort. In this way, you poke holes in the project, making lighter work of the steps that remain after you polish off the manageable aspects.

For example, suppose you're facing your kitchen after a dinner party: dishes piled to the tops of the cupboards, leftovers cooling in their serving dishes, the sink clogged with kitchen scraps, and the roaster pan caked with burned food and tenacious grease. The job is more than you can fathom at midnight. You're tempted to turn around, go to bed, and hope the kitchen fairies come in the night to transform your kitchen into its former spotless self.

Or you can tell yourself you'll do two simple things before you turn out the lights: maybe put away all the food and scrape the scraps into the compost bin or garbage disposal. And then when you make short work of that, you tell yourself that loading the dishwasher won't take that long. When that's done, you decide you can at least rinse and stack the other dishes. By the time you poke these holes into the project, not too much is left. Even if you give up at this point, the task that awaits you in the morning isn't nearly so formidable.

Book II

Getting Organized and Managing Your Time: Smart Ways to Preempt Problems

The salami approach: Finishing it one slice at a time

The salami approach is a great tactic for those long-term projects in which the deadline seems so far away that you convince yourself you don't need to start yet. So you don't resort to cramming at the 11th hour, take the time immediately to cut up the project into bite-sized pieces. These slices should be small enough that you can schedule them day-by-day or at least week-by-week.

The number of ways you can slice and dice a large task are many, but here's one option for breaking it down:

1. **Set time aside to plan the project completely so you can begin working on it and cut it down to size.**

2. **Create an action order of what needs to be done and when.**

   Creating a timeline helps you segment the task into pieces.

3. **Figure out what materials you need for the task.**

   Collect all the materials and make them ready and available.

The discard-the-garnish approach: Getting it off your plate

Often when you order an entree at a restaurant, the dish may include some sprigs of parsley or an orange slice in addition to a side or two and a drizzle of some fancy sauce. It makes for a pretty presentation, and it's edible, too. But unless you're really hungry, those items are often still on your plate when it's cleared away.

Just as with a restaurant meal, you probably have a few commitments on your plate that aren't really a key part of your responsibilities. Take a look at your schedule and see whether some of these tasks are mere garnishes. You then have choices:

✔ Remove them from your plate.

✔ Give them to someone else.

✔ Save them until you finish everything else.

Maintaining Your Motivation as You Press Ahead

Everyone has struggled with procrastination, and many still do. So if you battle with the temptations of putting off those obligations that seem too big, too hard, or just plain no fun, you're in good company. Recognizing your tendencies is the first step toward recovery. By following the strategies outlined in this chapter, you can make remarkable progress in overcoming the procrastination.

Staying on the right course, however, is a never-ending vigil. Use these maintenance tactics to do so:

✔ **Keep your expectations realistic.** Before you beat yourself up for your woeful procrastinating ways once again, take a look at your schedule and first figure out whether what you're attempting to accomplish is realistic. Have you accepted an assignment you're not qualified to take on, or is too much expected of you? Have you committed to an absurd deadline?

Again, when you begin to feel overwhelmed by your workload, this may be an indicator that you'll slip into postponement mode. So do whatever you can to get over being overwhelmed. It may require some adjustment in expectations — your co-workers', your boss's, or yours.

✔ **Handle the big stuff and delegate the rest.** When you find that too many obligations and projects are demanding your attention to the point that you're putting off making headway on any of them, it's time to lighten your load.

After you examine your workload and identify what's really important to your job or your career goals, you know what to attend to first. But instead of putting those smaller or less-important tasks on the back burner, see whether someone else can take over for you.

✔ **Prevent clutter overload.** Another sign that your procrastinating proclivities may soon raise their ugly head — or already have: Your office or home is cluttered with a confusion of papers and files, your e-mail inbox contains more than a week's worth of unread mail, and you've lost control of your schedule.

You can't maintain control of your time or stay on top of your obligations if your life has become so disorganized that you can't keep on top of your work and home. It's no wonder you're procrastinating — if you have a project in all that mess, you don't even know where to start.

You may be on overload. You may have too many projects at once. At any rate, it's time to clear your head and your desk. Take a day or a few hours once a month to purge, file, respond, and clean up. (See Chapter 3 of Book II for tips on clearing your workspace.)

✔ **Focus on maintaining a healthy balance.** Both your work life and your personal life are important to your well-being. Keep an eye on the scale to be sure that these different areas are in balance. If you become weighted down at the office, you lose energy and perspective, and procrastination — both at home and at work — creeps in. If family issues take over, you risk your performance at work. When one aspect of your life gets out of whack, do everything you can to regain balance.

Chapter 6

Putting an End to the Perils of Paperwork and Data

In This Chapter

▶ Finding out what paper to touch and when to touch it

▶ Deciding whether to act on, file, delegate, or toss paper

▶ Sorting through the clutter at home and at work

▶ Exploring ways to keep useless data at bay

*O*ne of the most perilous aspects of getting organized is figuring out what to do with all the paper and data that comes into your life. Even for the most organized and efficient individuals, the sheer volume of paper and information — from junk mail to memos, personal letters to newspapers — can be overwhelming. Because paper and data tend to accumulate, you must have a system in place to attack this information, and you must be diligent in sticking to that system if you are ever to dig out from under your personal mountain of pulp.

In this chapter, you find ways to get those accumulated piles of data organized and deal with the constant daily barrage. When you know how to prioritize incoming info that you can't avoid, weed out unnecessary items you already have, and avoid getting more than you ask for, paperwork and data don't seem so perilous after all. And if you need to get your electronic data organized as well, flip to Chapter 7, Book II for more information.

Accepting the Most Important Lesson: You Can't Read Everything

Suppose that you love golf (or knitting or bird watching, or any of a variety of other pursuits): You play regularly, attend matches or watch them on TV whenever you can, subscribe to a variety of golfing magazines, and enjoy reading books about golf technique and biographies of golf's greats. Even as much as you love golf, chances are you wouldn't be able to read every golf-related item that catches your eye or ends up in your mailbox, let alone the hundreds of golf publications circulated on a daily, weekly, or monthly basis. Even if you gave up everything else in your life, you still wouldn't have enough time.

So the first lesson in managing paperwork and data is to acknowledge that you just don't have the time to read everything that passes your desk, even if you want to. You have to be selective. With the golf example, you'd narrow your reading to a few prominent magazines and books that deal with those areas of golf in which you have a particular interest.

In the workplace, someone needs to read and attend to everything, but the trick is knowing that it doesn't have to be you. If you have so much material passing your desk that you're sure you could fill the Superdome in a year, you need to learn how to prioritize, skim, and delegate. The following tips can help you tackle your paper pileup:

- ✔ **Prioritize:** Figure out what items fall into your *must read* pile. These are the key documents that relate to important tasks and projects you're responsible for and must handle yourself.

  If even your *must read* list is out of hand and you have the luxury of an assistant or secretary, have that person prepare summaries of these documents, highlighting the key points, important supporting details, and any action items and deadlines. Sure, all these papers will still make for a pretty healthy dose of reading material, but nothing compared to the volume of paper that goes across your desk every day.

- ✔ **Skim:** For most of the documents you receive, you don't need to pore over every word or punctuation mark. Doing so just makes getting through the document that much more time-consuming. So learn to skim. In most types of correspondence, the key points are highlighted in some way (such as in a bulleted list) or they appear as the opening or concluding sentences in paragraphs (the stuff in between is primarily supporting detail). As you skim, look for important terms, action items, and deadlines.

- ✔ **Delegate:** Decide which papers you have to see and which documents can be handled by others. Then delegate! Yes, letting go is tough, but you really don't have a choice — not if you want to be able to accomplish the important things that move you toward your goals and retain your sanity at the same time.

Unless an item fits into your schedule and moves you closer to your goal, don't force yourself to read it. As you narrow your own reading list, make sure to keep — and read — the important items.

Processing Your Paperwork

When a piece of paper or bit of data comes into your possession, you have four options: You can act on it, file it away to be acted on later, delegate it to others for action, or toss it.

Designate one spot in your home or office for handling paper, and only deal with mail and other documents when you are physically in that spot. Setting aside this special area keeps your paperwork from encroaching on other activities and other areas of your life.

Dividing your mail into discrete piles

When your mail arrives, go through the stack and make four distinct piles:

- ✔ **Pile 1: Items to delegate:** Into the first pile, place the items you can delegate to others. Attach a self-adhesive note to each document with instructions on how and to whom the letter or document is to be delegated.

- ✔ **Pile 2: Items to act on now:** Places all the items that need your immediate attention into this pile. Arrange this pile so that the most important documents are on top and the least pressing items are at the bottom of the stack.

- ✔ **Pile 3: Items to file away for later action:** These are items that need your attention but don't need it immediately.

- ✔ **Pile 4: Items to toss:** This pile, which really isn't a pile at all, includes the useless bits of information that cross your desk or fill your inbox every day. During your first pass through the mail, keep a trash can within easy reach and then simply toss these items into the can as you sort your mail. (Make sure to shred papers with sensitive information such as Social Security numbers or account information.)

The boldest move you can make when you sort through paper is to increase the number of items you pitch into the trash or recycling. In other words, be honest with yourself about what you can and will make time for and throw out everything else.

Although the preceding relates specifically to paperwork that crosses your desk, the same principle applies to e-mail and other electronic messages and data you receive.

Dealing with the items in each pile

After this first pass (which will take less time to do that it does to read about), attack each pile with one mission in mind: To touch the mail as few times as possible and handle each item as quickly and efficiently as you can. Ideally, your objective is to handle each piece of mail *one* time. Sometimes doing so is impossible, but by setting the *one touch* goal as your ultimate objective, you enter the process with a get-in-and-get-out mind-set.

Consider these examples:

- ✔ You receive a letter from one of your oldest and dearest friends, and you want to answer it as promptly as you can. That doesn't mean that you drop everything and write a letter on the spot. Instead, make a note to write a follow-up letter at a predetermined time in the future. Then you can file the letter away or toss it. Either way, you've acted on this piece of mail, even though your action has been to defer follow-up until a later time.

- ✔ You receive a notice from your boss requesting key information for a meeting scheduled later in the day much differently. In that case, you would most likely stop everything and attend to the letter immediately.

- ✔ You receive a thank-you note from one of your clients or customers and no follow-up is required (immediately or in the future). If you want to keep the letter, you'd file it away in an "incoming correspondence" or other such file. This action eliminates it from your list of things to touch, but places the letter where you can find it again if needed.

Keep files in alphabetical order and segregated between business and personal, and make sure that your files are convenient, but not out in the open or strewn about. See Chapter 3 in Book II for more tips on setting up an efficient filing system.

Using this procedure, you can handle every item in an efficient manner, touching each piece of mail as few times as possible to achieve maximum results.

If you can't touch a paper only once, at least make sure that you never touch it more than twice. If you touch a paper more than twice, it had better be one of the most important documents in your possession. Otherwise, you're wasting your time and being ruled by a paper tiger.

Storing or Pitching: More Advice for Dealing with Your Stuff

If you're like most people, you could literally throw away half of the items you currently have stored in your home and office and never miss any of them. Throwing away half the items you currently have tucked away in storage takes courage, self-discipline, and at least two (if not more) tries. Whether the area you want to tidy up includes a closet you haven't cleaned out in months, an attic, a basement, a file drawer, a desk, a cabinet, or a garage, you should make your goal to throw away half the items you have in storage within the next 30 days.

The rules of pitching

To determine whether an item should be kept in storage or pitched, whether at home or in your office, ask yourself a series of questions:

- ✔ **Have I touched this item in the last year?** A *yes* doesn't automatically mean that the item is worth keeping, but if you haven't touched it in a year, the item should probably go.

- ✔ **If I haven't touched it in a year, does it have sentimental value?** Be strong in your definition of sentimental. If the item is a family heirloom, why isn't it on display, or why haven't you touched it in a year? Is it only sentimental the moment you find it? Is it something you would pass down in your will to your heirs? If you can't provide unqualified answers to all of these questions, get rid of it.

- ✔ **If it doesn't have sentimental value, should I still keep it just in case I need it someday?** Absolutely not! Even if your first impulse is to put the item back in storage because "You just never know when something like that might come in handy," get it out of your sight immediately. Throw it away or, if it's still in good condition, donate it. Disposing of the item is the only way to break your cluttering habits.

A primer for storing efficiency

If you're looking for a perfect example of both good and bad storage practices, open your closet to find a consolidated microcosm of every storage area in your home, office, car, and other personal space. The closet is a frequently used storage area, a place to store items you need every day. But the closet is also a hideaway for things such as the Halloween costume from three years ago or the shoes that you meant to get repaired last December. The closet has shelves, space for hanging items, and room on the floor — all of which have become jumbled masses of shoes, dry cleaning bags, empty luggage, hats, sweaters, ties, and items you couldn't put anywhere else. The closet is a combination desk drawer and dungeon, a convenient spot for your most needed items and a final resting place for things you will probably never touch again.

If you want to find out how to organize all your storage areas, start with your closet, and take copious notes.

1. **Pull everything out.**

   The only way to properly organize storage is to start from scratch. Pull out every item so that you're forced to touch it at least twice, once when pulling it out and once when putting it back or disposing of it.

2. **Make four distinct piles.**

   • Things you touch every day

   • Things you touch at least once a week

   • Things you have touched in the last month

   • Things that you haven't touched in more than a month

3. **Start with the things you haven't touched in more than a month and make subpiles.**

   • Seasonal items you'll need next spring, summer, fall, or winter

   • Items with no seasonal distinction that have been put in the closet and forgotten

4. **Place the "Items with no seasonal distinction that have been put in the closet and forgotten" into two large containers (plastic bags or large plastic containers work well).**

   Label one container *Give away* and the other *Throw away*. If you think that an item in the pile has value and you just can't bring yourself to throw it away, give it to charity. If you're embarrassed to give an item away, throw it out — obviously, the time is well past for the item to go.

5. **Examine the remaining "Seasonal items" subpile and determine whether the closet is the best place to store your sweaters, swimsuits, ski caps, sandals, or other items you aren't likely to touch for several more months.**

   If you have a large closet with plenty of room for these items, the closet may well be the proper storage area. If you're strapped for closet space, however, box those items up and put them in the attic, garage, basement, or other out-of-the-way place until they are needed.

6. **Go through the "Items you have touched in the last month" pile and put a portion of those items in the Give away and Throw away bins.**

   This step is tough. If you've touched an item in the last month, you might have a legitimate use for it, but the likelihood of needing every item you have touched in the last month is extremely small. Some things you currently handle need to be removed from your life. How many sweaters, for example, do you really need? Is having a candy jar in every room really a necessity (or for that matter, healthy)? Take this opportunity to throw them out or give them away.

7. **Place the remaining items from the "Items you have touched in the last month," pile back into the closet first.**

   Stack or hang these items in the back of the closet or in the areas that are most difficult to reach and work your way toward the door. Never pile or throw an item into the closet. If you need to retrieve it every month, you need to be able to reach it, so be conscious of accessibility to each item.

8. **Fill in the closet with the remaining items you touch every week, constantly remaining mindful of the Give away and Throw away bins.**

   No matter how often you touch that 10-year-old paint-stained running suit, the time has come to give it up.

9. **Put the items you touch every day in the closet last and keep them front and center.**

   The items you need the most should always be within easy reach.

10. **Repeat this process every six months.**

    After reorganizing your storage area, the number of items you thought you couldn't live without but that you haven't touched in six months will shock you. In reality, you didn't need them as desperately as you thought. You also need to make room for the new items you acquired since you last went through this exercise. Your stuff may change, but if you're diligent about what you keep and how you keep it, your storage areas will always remain orderly and manageable.

Book II

Getting Organized and Managing Your Time: Smart Ways to Preempt Problems

Applying the principles to the office

A closet was used to illustrate the ten-step program in the preceding section, but the fundamentals are the same whether you're cleaning out a barn or a billion-dollar factory. Keeping these principles at the forefront of your organizational agenda helps you get the results you need from the areas where you store your belongings. Consider these examples:

- ✔ **Notes from long-ago meetings:** All those notes you took at the corporate retreat last year (the ones you were sure would change your career the second you got back to the office) are, for the most part, worthless and should be thrown out. If you acted on those notes, they're now a part of your organizational system, and you have incorporated them into your to-do lists and long-term goals. If you haven't acted on them, the time to do so is now: Wad up the notes, throw them into the recycling bin, and forget about them. If they weren't important enough to cause you to act quickly, keeping them now only prolongs your disorganization.

- ✔ **Ancient computer files:** Even though computer files don't take up space in the same way as the mountain of junk piled inside a cluttered closet, the old information stored in your hard drive takes up valuable memory space and should be purged from your system on a regular basis. The best rule for deciding when to delete a file from your computer is the hard-copy rule: If the file or document only existed in hard copy (a physical paper file) would you still keep it? If so, where and why? If you can't legitimately answer the question, or if your answer is, "Well, you never know when it might come in handy," point, click, drag the file into the trash icon, and delete it forever.

- ✔ **Files that have outlived the project they dealt with:** Strongly consider throwing them out. Unless a file contains compelling procedures or notes that are applicable in the here and now, keeping it around "just in case" doesn't make a lot of sense. Historical relevance is the biggest excuse used for keeping old files, but unless the information in those files is being accessed, they serve very little purpose. A permanent record of a memo for an event that no longer exists isn't as significant as you may think.

- ✔ **Files that have outlasted the tenure of their primary author:** Examine why you are keeping them. Sometimes good, solid reasons exist, many of which deal with legal protection for employees and employers against potential future claims. You do not, however, have to keep everything ever written by a former employee. If a file has outlived its usefulness in your office and no long-term legal reasons exist for keeping it, throw the file out. If there are legal reasons for keeping the file, transfer it to a safe place (perhaps the legal department or an independent attorney's office), but don't keep it stashed away in a closet or file drawer in your office.

Delegate or eliminate. If you don't touch a certain item in your office on a daily or weekly basis, either hand it off to someone else or throw it away. A file, document, letter, or memo that has been sitting around your office in the "Oh, I've been meaning to get to that" pile needs to move on out. You have already demonstrated that you probably won't get to the item, so delegate it to someone else or take the plunge and trash it.

As you work out a storage system for the files you want to keep, organize the materials you use regularly as well. If you frequently use a dictionary, thesaurus, or phone book, keep those items on a shelf or in a drawer within easy reach. They should be stored, but in a spot where you don't have to search for them when you need them. The same principle holds true for other materials you use regularly. Keeping them on your desk or piled on top of a filing cabinet only adds to the clutter, but storing regularly used reference materials in a place where you can easily reach them is a critical part of effective storage.

Storage solutions for sensitive documents

Certain documents need special attention, whether or not you touch them regularly. Some companies have archiving or storage procedures for sensitive documents or those that need to be stored long term that you can (and should) use. If your company doesn't have an established storage procedure for these types of documents, following are some ideas to help you keep sensitive documents safe (but make sure to follow your company's rules regarding taking material off-site or copying company documents):

- Put sensitive documents in a locking file cabinet.
- Store key information off-site (if your company allows it).
- Make duplicates and store the documents in multiple places.
- For permanent or long-term storage, place the materials in storage boxes that you can warehouse off-site.

Create a detailed cover sheet of the box contents to help identify the contents further down the road. You can also create a number system for the boxes and log this information into a system to help you track archived information in the future.

Storing important personal documents

Your homeowner's insurance policy isn't something you're likely to keep by your nightstand, but you should keep it stored in a convenient and safe place for easy access. The same holds true for your life insurance policy, deeds or titles to any property you own, your will, important legal documents, and sensitive financial information. You might not touch these items for years, but you must keep them safely stored.

To ensure your safety and the protection of your most sensitive documents, consider the following storage options:

✔ Purchase a fireproof safe or filing cabinet. These are expensive, but the protection they provide is well worth the price.

✔ Lease a safety deposit box from a local bank. You can't put an entire file cabinet into it, but for your most sensitive and valuable items nothing beats a dual-key safety deposit box.

✔ Duplicate important documents and keep copies in several locations. This option may be a little more complicated than simply sticking an original document in a fireproof safe, but having back-up copies in several different places is certainly a viable alternative.

Tell someone you trust where your documents have been stored. It would be awful if someone passed away unexpectedly without his or her family knowing where to find all the important documents they would need.

Solving storage dilemmas with technology

Even if you diligently weed through your documents and regularly save only a few very important ones, you'll still eventually face a shortage of storage. This is especially true if you tend to save paper versions. Fortunately, technology can come to your aid. Here are some suggestions to relieve you from paper overload:

✔ Use a wireless reading device, such as Kindle, to read books and periodicals.

✔ Scan documents or articles so that you can store them electronically.

✔ Look into online storage services offered by numerous companies, including Amazon, Iomega, Microsoft, Yahoo! and Google.

A word about shredding

You don't have to work in a high-security government installation to need a paper shredder. In fact, if you aren't shredding the credit card applications and other sensitive financial mailings you receive, you're leaving yourself open to a huge risk. Millions of dollars are swindled each year, and thousands of innocent citizens have faced long-term credit nightmares because of identity theft. With a Social Security number and an address (both of which can be found in your garbage if you aren't careful), criminals can wreak havoc with your life, sometimes putting you on a credit blacklist that takes years to clear up.

Shredding documents doesn't completely protect you from the perils of fraud, but doing so is certainly a good start. Shredding also protects others with whom you correspond. A friend might feel more comfortable sending a personal letter if he's aware of your vigorous shredding practices.

The only disadvantage to shredding is that, once shredded, a document is gone forever — but that's not a bad thing if your goal is to de-clutter your life and eliminate your problems with paper.

Book II

Getting Organized and Managing Your Time: Smart Ways to Preempt Problems

Avoiding Data Overload: Getting Only the Info You Really Need

Decisions today aren't hampered by a lack of data, but rather by an overabundance of data — some good, but mostly useless — that floods your home, television, phone, and computer screen on an almost daily basis. This excess fuels disorganization and hampers decision making.

Data overload plagues most businesses (and homes, for that matter). So what can you do? How can you cut through the clutter and obtain the data you need without wasting a great deal of time and energy?

When you need information, your first task is to determine how much data you want or need. That task isn't always as easy as it initially sounds. If, for example, you want to know how much money your company spends on long-distance telephone service, the way you make your request for information impacts how much and what kind of information you get back. You could get one number (the total amount spent on long distance calls from all phones in all offices around the world) or you could get 1,000 or more lines of detail complete with methodologies, trends, and breakdowns by office, country, city, department, or individual. If you're not specific in your request, you may even receive a comparative analysis of long-distance charges between departments with historical references to show how much more or less you're spending on long distance this year over last. In fact, one simple question — "Hey, how much are we spending on long distance?" — could result in a 50-page glossy report, complete with color charts and graphs.

As ridiculous as this scenario sounds, it shows how access to too much data can get out of hand. The sections that follow give examples of the best ways to avoid this data overload.

Ask better (more specific) questions

The first way to tackle data overload is to make sure you ask the right questions — that is, questions with answers that actually give the information you need. The key is to ask specific questions. Ask a vague question, or one without the salient details, and the answer can come back in a number of forms, most less than helpful. Ask specific questions, though, and you're likely to find out what you need to know with minimal extraneous detail.

Consider the following examples. The first question in each set is well meaning but vague, followed by the result such a question could conceivably produce. The second question in each set is more specific and therefore more likely to result in the answer you need.

Wrong way:

> Q: "What is our company's current payroll burden?"

> A: A 92-page listing of all full-time, part-time, and independent contract employees, along with the income of each, the highest and lowest salaries, the benefit packages offered, a summary from the payroll registry, and a pie chart showing payroll as a percentage of total expenditures.

Right way:

> Q: "I'm examining some new tax laws, and I need to know the average monthly amount we're paying in pretax salaries (no benefits) in all our U.S. operations. I don't need a breakdown right now, just one number."

> A: One number.

Wrong way:

> Q: "Where should I go to buy a computer?"

> A: 1,000 pages of reference and advertising material listing everything from system mainframes to pocket PCs.

Right way:

> Q: "What local stores have the best prices and most reliable service for desktop PCs with 500-gig hard drives, high-def monitors, DVD±RW drives, and state-of-the-art processors?"

> A: A list of six to twelve retailers in close proximity to your home or office.

Wrong way:

Q: "If I relocate to Orlando, where should I live?"

A: Over 30,000 residential listings in the greater Orlando metropolitan area ranging from a $30,000 mobile home to a $16 million estate with frequent updates from hundreds of real estate agents interested in making you their customer.

Right way:

Q: "I'm considering a move to the greater Orlando area. Because I have small children, I need to live near the best schools, in a low-crime area with easy access to shopping and dining. My price range is the low $300,000s and I would prefer a quiet cul-de-sac in a planned residential community. What properties meet these requirements?"

A: A healthy but manageable 100 or so listings.

Wrong way:

Q: "How should I invest my money?"

A: Over 10,000 books and over 41,000,000 Web sites willing to answer (and help you by taking your money away).

Right way:

Q: "I have $350,000 in employee stock options that are going to roll over in six months when I retire. My investment goals are conservative, and I want low capital risk. What is the largest and most reputable financial planning institution that specializes in small to midsized retirement plans?"

A: A list of 20 to 50 reputable investment firms.

Identify the purpose of the data

Data falls into three distinct categories: need to know, nice to know, and useless. One of the primary flaws of disorganized people is their inability to differentiate between the three types of data. The disorganized person confuses nice-to-know information with need-to-know information, for example, and spends entirely too much time sorting through and humming over useless information. The following sections explain the three types of data and how you can discipline yourself to focus on the most important kind: the need to know.

Distinguishing among the three types of data

Obviously, *need-to-know data* is the most important. This is the information you must have in order to make informed choices and take intelligent action. It may be the income projection you need before committing yourself to a project or the flight information you need before departing on a trip. Sometimes the data is right at your fingertips, and other times it's frustratingly illusive, but regardless of how easy or how difficult it is to find, need-to-know data is the information you need most.

Nice-to-know data can range from the baseball box scores to the five-day weather forecast. Not finding this data won't kill you, but you may feel better about life if you have it at your disposal.

Useless data is just that: useless. It doesn't help you make short- or long-term decisions, nor do you find it particularly interesting. Unfortunately, this is the data that often seems most prevalent in today's media-rich communications environment. As more sources for information become available, the pitfall of this information age is that those outlets are filled with trite, trivial, and ultimately useless information that has no redeeming social value. You might win a Trivial Pursuit game by knowing who styles Tom Hanks's hair or how far it is from the Earth to the sun (in kilometers), but the data primarily causes confusion and clutter.

Categorizing data with questions

In order to avoid the data trap and use data as part of your overall organizational plan, you need to discipline yourself in determining which data you review. Whenever you come into contact with data, ask yourself the following questions:

- **Does this information deal with my most immediate concerns?** If your answer is yes, then the data falls into the need-to-know category. If the data deals with an issue that you may eventually address but one that isn't on your short-term agenda, it falls into the nice-to-know category, and if you couldn't care less, it's useless.

- **Will I be better equipped to make a decision because of this data?** Again, if the answer is yes, then it is information that you need to know. If the answer is no, then determine whether the information is nice-to-know data that you should file away for future reference or a worthless waste of your time.

- **Will I save time or waste time with this data?** If you'll be able to take decisive action as a result of knowing the data, then you're obviously saving time and future anxiety. If you won't be able to do much after you examine the data and it doesn't interest you, then it's a waste of your precious time.

✔ **Will the information lead me to future positive action?** Sometimes a nugget of data may come your way that has no immediate use but steers you in a positive direction for the future. In that case, the data is definitely need to know, even though you don't act on it the day you receive it. These tidbits are rare, but they're always worth pursuing.

✔ **Did I ask for this information?** The best way to judge certain data is by whether or not you asked for it. Obviously, if one of your children has been in an altercation at school, that's information you need to know (even if you haven't explicitly asked for it). As for other information, however, the "Did I ask for this?" test is a fairly good measure of the priority you should place on data.

As with most decisions you have to make in your newly organized life, the amount of data you receive and the way you respond to it evolves over time. If you're constantly mindful of the pitfalls and diligently do your best to keep the process simple, you stand a better-than-average chance of using data effectively. Without that mind-set, however, the information monster may consume you, and the rest of your organizational efforts will have been for naught.

Gather data with a surefire strategy

One way to gather the information you need without inviting a glut of unnecessary (and sometimes just plain useless) information is to use the back-end first strategy, in which you start with the bottom line (or the back end) of the data and work your way back through the details as you need them.

To use this strategy, limit the initial data you receive (or request) to no more than one page of information. For example, if you want to know how much your department spends each year on courier services, start at the back end with one number. From there you can get a summary of how much is being spent in each office, or how the number is broken down by work group or by month. By knowing the bottom line first, you can control how much detail you choose to pursue. It may be none, and it may be several pages of spreadsheet information. Either way, you control the data, because you start at the back end and work your way forward.

Taking a hard look at software

Most computers these days come with a standard business software package already installed or ready to install, and for most small businesses and households, that package (along with an Internet connection) is sufficient for 90 percent of the things they need. Many office computers, in addition to any special applications required for that particular job, also include the standard package.

When you select software, whether for your office or home, be mindful of one rule: If the application saves you time and moves you closer to your goals, buy it. If it distracts you from your goals and wastes your time, trash it. Same with the preinstalled applications and games. If you find yourself playing game after game of Spider Solitaire, consider disabling that program. And don't install games (despite the wow factor of the graphics) on computers that you use for work. Games, CD-making software, flight simulators, and other novelty software probably won't make you more organized, nor will they save you time or improve your efficiency.

Saying no to games and novelty software is easy. It's a little harder when a program you need includes features you don't. A household budgeting program, for example, which helps balance family checkbooks, store receipts, and keep track of grocery lists, could also include a general ledger, a spreadsheet function, and a depreciation calculator. Maybe you need a depreciation schedule on your living room suite of furniture, but probably not. Chances are this feature is overkill — and a monumental waste of time and computer memory. Here are a couple of suggestions: Choose programs that provide only the functionality you need. If pared-down versions aren't available, you may be able to select which features to install. If so, install only those you plan to use.

Chapter 7

Fine-Tuning Organization Skills with Technology

. . . .

In This Chapter

▶ Scheduling success using high-tech tools

▶ Streamlining your computer's performance

▶ Managing your e-mail

▶ Pegging your customers with CRM software

. . . .

*P*icture this: You're getting ready to go on vacation when a critical client asks you to make a sales presentation to one of the largest sales networks in the country. For a moment, you panic — the event is scheduled immediately after you return from vacation. If you're going to be prepared, you'll have to disappoint your family and cancel your getaway. But then you remember — you have a similar version of that presentation wrapped up on a PowerPoint program. A few tweaks and some minor revisions, and you'll have a new and customized presentation in a couple of hours. You put in some research time, modify your PowerPoint, and head out for a week of fun and sun.

If you've been in a situation like this, you probably love what technology can do for your and your business. Computers are the lifeblood of many organizations, from communication and data storage to organizing projects to dealing with clients, suppliers, and prospects.

This chapter explains how you can use electronic scheduling and a personal digital assistant (PDA) to become more efficient. It also helps you eliminate excess baggage on your computer, organize and name the files you save so you can access them quickly, and archive files you may need to refer to in the future in a way that minimizes the time you spend searching for them. It also shows you how a customer relationship management (CRM) program can help you organize your client information and increase business. Read on.

Plugging into Electronic Scheduling

Electronic tools can help keep your time and schedule under control. A quality PDA, for example, acts as your electronic assistant on the road or in your office. It's an easily writable, very compact computer that takes only seconds, not minutes, to boot. This section outlines your options for electronic planners, whether you're looking to use calendar software on a desktop computer or to pull out your smartphone when you're on the go. It also discusses the pros and cons of PDAs and considerations to keep in mind before deciding which one to use.

The calendar-sharing benefits of electronic scheduling tools

One of the biggest benefits of using electronic scheduling tools is that you and your co-workers have access to each others' schedules *without* making a phone call or pestering administrative assistants. This slashes the time you need to set up a meeting because the software also informs you where others are, what they're doing, and when they're available. Electronic scheduling saves time on the recipient's end, too — because others can see your schedule, you receive meeting invitations only at times you're available and you don't have to consult your schedule to see whether you can attend.

Say, for example, you've been trying to reach Bob Smith for two days. Every time you call him, he's in a meeting, and every time he calls you back, you're out in the field. You cut through the time-wasting telephone tag, check into your network scheduling system, and schedule a time for you and Bob to talk. You can see that he's in the office but free of meetings between 2 and 3 p.m.

Scheduling systems, such as Microsoft Outlook, are great for setting up meetings for the convenience of the majority. For example, suppose you need to set a meeting next week for the ten people on your budget task force: Your attendance, as well as those of three department heads, is required. By using Outlook to schedule the meeting, you can see others' schedules before you even send a meeting invitation. You can search through the week to find the best time for the most people, ensuring your numbers and the attendance of those critical to the meeting.

And when you're not available? Don't worry: No one knows that you're actually getting a haircut at 3 p.m. Thursday — they just know you're not available to meet.

The utility of portable planners

Portable planners have an incredibly wide variety of uses. A PDA allows you to carry your calendar — and every one of your client and prospect contacts — in one hand. You can even put your time-block schedule, which shows what you're doing at each moment of each day and keeps you on track, into your electronic planner (see Chapter 2 of Book II for in-depth guidance on that crucial time-management tool). In most programs, you can copy your time block for years into the future with a few keystrokes. And when you want to share your schedule with others, you can quickly and easily upload it to your computer network.

A PDA also serves as your multimedia center: It can function as an MP3 player, portable flash drive, electronic photo album, or video player. You have instant Internet access for stock quotes, news, sports, and so on.

The last ten years have brought an explosion of options in this area: You can choose from Palm smartphones, Apple iPhones, and BlackBerries (not to mention numerous other "berries"). Your cellphone carrier may influence which make and model you select because the make and model can affect coverage, service, and reception.

Most PDA companies partner with cellphone companies, so when you get your first PDA or upgrade an existing one, keep an eye on what your cellular provider recommends as well as any specials the company may be running.

Where you use your PDA influences your choice as well. Many PDAs offer global coverage. You can use BlackBerries, for example, in more than 90 countries, so when you land in Hong Kong, London, Sydney, or Los Angeles, you can send and receive e-mail. However, if you travel nationally or internationally, some PDAs are more effective than others. If you find yourself the keynote speaker at a conference in Australia, you'll be in trouble if your PDA doesn't work Down Under.

Beware: Some PDAs don't work with some brands of CRM software (see the later section "Managing Contact Info with a CRM Program"). Be sure to check whether your PDA is compatible with your CRM program before investing in either. Also check whether you can sync from remote locations or whether you need to physically be in your office to sync. In addition, some PDAs, as well as some CRM software, won't sync if you're connected remotely. This means e-mail you send and receive, calls you make, notes from those calls, and appointments booked by your staff won't show up in your PDA — or in the server containing your CRM program — resulting in missed appointments, duplications, wasted time, and lost revenue.

Despite all their benefits, PDAs do have drawbacks: You become married to the technology; you can be too accessible; if you lose the PDA, it's as if you lost your whole life and database. Although most of the world has embraced the PDA revolution, at times you may want to be *less* accessible.

When deciding whether a PDA will save or cost you time overall, consider your job and the level of concentration that you need to perform well. Do you really need to be accessible at a moment's notice? Are you the type of person who can turn it off or put it down? Do you answer all the calls that come to your home? If you're unable to screen calls at home, you may have a hard time screening your PDA. For suggestions on how to avoid interruptions and reclaim control of an out-of-control schedule, refer to Chapter 4 in this book.

De-Cluttering Your Computer (And Keeping It That Way)

Is your computer a junk drawer, collecting everything you don't have time to deal with? Your computer has limited space, and sooner or later, you'll be forced to clean it or find another drawer (and computers are far more expensive than drawers!). The more junk on your computer, the harder it is to find what you're looking for. And just as an overflowing drawer gets harder to open and close, an overstuffed computer also works less efficiently.

The best way to tackle an overburdened computer is to sort its inventory and then purge what you can from it, whether you back up files to a disc and delete them from your computer or simply delete them once and for all.

Naming files and organizing them with an electronic tree

Start by creating categories for your electronic files, with one folder for each of your major areas of responsibility. Typical categories include *sales, marketing, human resources, promotion,* and *current projects,* as well as categories based on your products and services. You may also include folders for key customers. Again, just as you create subfolders under these headings in your file cabinets, create electronic subfolders for smaller, more specific categories.

Build your *filing tree* — an outline of major folders and the subfolders to go beneath them — in your computer before you begin to file individual documents. Don't start filing and *then* try to organize your files. Seeing all your files at once on a computer is difficult, so that strategy rarely works. Having at least a rough outline of the files and folders on your PC (and perhaps even on paper) before you begin eliminates a lot of copying, cutting, and pasting. Result: greater efficiency and significantly less frustration.

The most challenging part of organizing, whether physical or electronic, is developing a system. The key to being able to retrieve information without wasting time is to file it correctly in the first place. The following subsections present some questions to help you devise a system that works for you.

How do you usually need to access information?

Do you need to retrieve information by date? Subject matter? Company? Project name? Everyone has different priorities based on the type of business, job description within that business, and personal preferences. If you're the keeper or primary resource of spreadsheets, reports, correspondence, or contracts, you may have to be able to pull up files quickly for others or communicate or share this information. In that case, you may need to tailor your filing system to what works best for someone else. Think about how your boss or colleague asks you for a document. Does she usually remember the name of the contact she was working with, the location she travelled to, or the time of year that she was working on the project?

If your projects are very large, break them into smaller, more easily accessed files. Here are a couple of basic breakdowns for your filing system:

- ✔ **If you do the same set of projects for several different clients, you may want to file under client names.** If you're going to file by name, decide whether to file by last name, first name, or the name of the company that person represents. (Does your client Mike Wallace of ABC Company go under *m, w,* or *a?*) Whatever you decide, stick with the system for all your files so they're grouped together and easy to retrieve.

- ✔ **If you're prone to look for files by date or if your files are continually evolving with newer versions each time they're used, structure your system so that the date information is always part of the file or folder name.** If you primarily access information based on when it was created, regardless of the client or project, the date it was created is the most important item in your document or folder title. If due date is more important, make that part of the filename.

Inconsistency and even spelling or punctuation errors can send your folders and files to unintended locations, which can make them difficult if not impossible to find later. Your computer organizes files in alphabetical and numerical order, so set some guidelines for how you plan to name your files before you start. For instance, regardless of where you place a date in your document or folder name, you need to create your date the same way each time. July 29, 2008 ends up in a different location than a document titled with 7-29-2008 or even 072908. Also be consistent in whether your date comes at the end of the filename or the beginning.

Because of all the information you want to include in the filename, your documents may have names that create a file path that is too long. An overly long file path can also prevent you from moving the document to another location, or in some cases even e-mailing the file. Abbreviations can help, but be sure to be consistent. If you abbreviate Joe's Coffee Shop as JCS on one project and Joe's CS on another, they won't show up next to each other in your computer.

If you work in a fast-paced environment, set aside a blocked-out period of time each month to go through your current files and make sure they're correctly labeled and filed. As time passes, it's easy to forget which file belongs to whom and where it should go. Files can easily become lost, creating a huge time loss when you launch into a long search or end up having to re-create a file from scratch. (Of course, you can always use the search function on your computer to look through a single document, subfolder, file folder, or your entire computer. After you find your missing document, check to see why it was misfiled in the first place and then correct the error.)

How far back must you keep files?

Depending on your business, you may have years' worth of files you need to keep on your computer for a long-standing client or project. How often do you call up archived or nonactive information? If you keep data and detail for a long time, you can set up a system that gives you quick access to "closed" files without cluttering your screen.

You may want to try keeping the current year or the last two years in your everyday files; when the time comes that you need to look up those files only occasionally, create a subfolder where you can combine information for each past year — then put that folder in a different area. You may even be able to move this seldom-used information out of your personal files and into your company's main folders on the server, which can keep your current computer files less cluttered and save you time.

How do you create new documents?

Do you work regularly with documents based off a template? For example, do you send out client contracts? Put together a weekly status report? Submit expense reports or check requests? Generate form responses? Think about the best system for pulling up the appropriate templates and revising them accurately and efficiently — and storing them so you can find them quickly.

If you create documents from scratch regularly, look for a way to create templates for frequently created formats to avoid reentering the same information for each version you produce.

Do you work on projects that generate multiple versions of documents? For example, do you have proposals that are reviewed, edited, and revised by numerous people? If so, you want to incorporate a system that allows you to easily track the history of changes and pull up what's been done in the past. For instance, when people save new, updated versions of a document, you may have them alter the filename by adding their initials, adding an abbreviation to indicate a certain stage of a project, or dating everything so you don't end up searching through proposals that are old and outdated. Make sure everyone knows the naming system.

Are most of the new documents you create specific to one issue or one client? When you spend time producing documents for specific clients, your organization method should make it easy to call up a client and identify everything related to that client.

If you're constantly creating new documents, the job of organizing is more challenging. Your document load is heavy and constantly increasing. Consider setting up your organizational system by client or having an archive file where you store master contracts, proposals, letters, templates, checklists, and other regularly used items. You can also set up folders so these frequently used master files are easy to access.

Offloading excess by archiving or deleting

The more files your computer has on its hard drive to search, the more slowly it works. As with paper files, a key part of organizing your computer is removing what you don't need to keep, including duplicate files. Electronic clutter is hard to see because unlike the physical stacks piling up on your desk, it tends to be invisible — until your computer slows or balks. Chances are, you've found numerous copies of the same programs on your computer because you forgot that you installed earlier versions.

You know you need to archive when the icons proliferate on your desktop until it looks like the parking lot at a busy superstore. *Archiving* files doesn't mean deleting those old files; it means backing them up to a CD, DVD, external hard drive, or other storage device. Archiving frees up hard-drive space and speeds up your computer's performance. To weed out excess, follow these steps:

1. **Search your computer to make sure that the programs installed are ones you need and that you're using the most recent versions.**

   Save the data in the old versions onto a CD or DVD, or update the program and transfer it to the new version. Then send the old versions to your computer's recycle bin or uninstall them.

2. **Create a permanent archive directory or folder and get in the habit of archiving any files you don't use regularly but want to keep.**

Always label your CDs or DVDs. Don't just throw them into storage in anonymous jewel cases. If nothing else, print a hard-copy list of the disc's contents, fold the paper to the size of the case, and secure the package with a rubber band. That way, if you come back to it five years from now, you'll know what the disc contains.

Be sure to keep CDs and other backups in a safe place. Buy a fire safe that's rated for electronic storage (read the label before you buy because not every safe protects CDs, zip or flash drives, or floppy disks from damaging temperatures). Store particularly important records, such as periodic complete system backups, in a safe deposit box. Also use multiple backups so you're well-covered for a catastrophe — if one disc is corrupt, you don't want to lose all your data. Consider mirrored servers. With *mirrored servers*, you always have a backup — if one server goes down, you can be up in minutes on the other server without losing data.

Cleaning up a hand-me-down computer

You may inherit hand-me-down computers filled with old files. If and when that happens, check organization dates or last-edit dates. Often, files have been passed on for generations of employees. Instead of sending the files out to be carbon-dated, do the following:

1. Store the file in an out-of-the-way interim file so you can research what or who it pertains to when you have time.

2. If after examining the file you can't tell whether it's still needed, print out a hard copy and ask your boss or the computer's previous owner whether you should save it for yourself or someone else.

3. If co-workers need it, save the file for them on a CD, zip or flash drive, or floppy disk, and purge the file from your computer.

After you've purged the excess files, periodically defragment your computer. This process helps increase the speed of your computer by compressing and organizing the data in a manner that the computer can easily navigate.

Saving new files strategically

The Save As feature on your computer is one of technology's greatest functions — for personalization, for producing numerous letters with only minimal changes, or for tailoring presentations to specific groups without losing your original documents. When you save without Save As, you replace one file with another, losing potentially valuable information that could save you time later should you need that info for a similar situation in the future.

For all its benefits, the Save As option can be your hard drive's demise if you don't use it judiciously —creating (and storing) numerous documents that are almost identical. For example, if you have a master file of a letter to customers, Save As makes it easy to personalize the letter from your master file. But do you need to keep copies of all your personalized letters? You may want to save the letter into the appropriate customer file, but you probably don't need to keep a copy of every personalized letter in the master letter file.

Handling E-Mail Correspondence

If all the e-mail correspondence you've ever received, sent, saved, responded to, forwarded, and deleted were turned into paper mail, your output alone could probably fill a U.S. Postal Office. Of course, you don't keep it all, but if you're like me, you let your e-mail accumulate at times, perhaps until your system notifies you that your mailbox has exceeded its limit.

A good tool is only as good as the person wielding it. If you know how to use e-mail properly, it makes your productivity hum. If not, you can end up sabotaging your efforts to get things done. This section helps you rein in the all-too-often unwieldy paperless communication system.

Filtering what comes in

Even militant time masters can lose hours of productive time to e-mail — and much of that e-mail isn't even work-related. Sometimes it's not even something you *want* to receive, yet you still have to dig through the sludge.

Spam is only one factor that adds to the deluge of e-mail you find in your inbox on a daily basis. If you're like most people, you probably authorized or even requested most of the promotional e-mail you receive. Here are some tips to slow the flow of spam and other incoming e-mail that only clutter your inbox:

- **Unsubscribe from newsletters or mailing lists that you no longer read.** When you were starting your organic garden last spring, a weekly e-mail about composting tips seemed like a great idea. Now you find that you almost always delete without opening. Time to put that idea to bed.

- **Think twice before signing on for new mailing lists.** You may appreciate a monthly newsletter about one of your hobbies. But instead of bulking up your inbox, why not add the Web site to your Favorites list and visit when it's convenient for you?

- **When ordering online, seek out the checked box that confirms your agreement to receiving e-mail — and _un_check it.** Called the _negative option_ response, many merchants include a box on the order form that indicates, "Yes, I want to receive regular notices about your company's special offers." That box is already checked off for your "convenience." In order to get _nothing_, however, you have to take action and get rid of that mark.

- **When visiting or leaving personal or contact information on a Web site, always check the privacy policy to confirm that your information won't be sold.** You can usually find a link to the privacy notice at the bottom of the Web page or next to where you enter your information.

- **Install spam-filtering software on your computer.** Remember, though, that these programs typically don't remove the spam; they simply filter it to your junk folder so you can review or simply delete.

Don't ever respond to spam. You may hope that your polite request to remove you from the mailing list will stop the mailings, but most often the opposite happens. Your reply confirms that your e-mail address is a valid one. You may start getting even more e-mail, and your address may be sold to other annoying spam-senders. Clicking on an opt-out link can also put you at risk if the e-mail is spam, so let your spam software do its job and leave it at that.

Employing an e-mail response system

If you've ever seen an episode of the TV show _M*A*S*H,_ you may remember that, when wounded soldiers would come into the medical unit, the doctors would perform _triage_, the process that determined patient priority. Does this wound need medical attention now? Will this soldier die without immediate care? Will this one die even if he receives attention? In this way, the medical team could most efficiently prioritize their work in a situation of chaos.

Well, performing triage is an excellent way to approach your e-mail responses. Some mail you get is dead on arrival, other messages are of interest to you but not critical to address immediately, and others need your attention right now. Those of you who can turn on your computer to find as many as 100 new messages need the critical care of a good e-mail management system.

Try this approach: When you open up your mailbox, resort to the three Ds: *delete, do it,* or *defer*. Every e-mail fits into one of these categories.

Press Delete

Although your computer doesn't take up any more space if you have 10 e-mail or 10,000, the clutter of useless, obsolete, irrelevant correspondence in your inbox can *seem* like a mile-high stack of stuff you have to carry with you.

Book II

Getting Organized and Managing Your Time: Smart Ways to Preempt Problems

Keep your inbox clean by discarding any e-mail that's unimportant or long-obsolete. As for the advertisements, forwarded jokes or urban myths; and the string of thanks, you're-welcome, have-a-good-day, see-you-after-work correspondence, read 'em (or don't) and delete immediately.

Also delete without opening any e-mail with a subject line that seems too good to be true or seems like a marketing pitch from an unknown sender. How realistic is it to think that some company has sought *you* out to offer you an opportunity to make millions? And if a deal is really so incredible, would the advertiser really need to tell you that? Probably not. Beware any e-mail with subject lines containing misspelled words or words with symbols in place of letters (such as *Fr** Mon!y*).

Knowing how to delete helps everyone in your company. When employees share a network, the server fills up when everyone retains all e-mail, which can stop the flow of inbound e-mail for the whole company. Most networks establish a limit to the size of individual inboxes and send notices when you get close to the limit. Then you're in for some major housecleaning. Better to keep up with the cleaning rather than let it build up.

Just do it

The shoe company Nike may have had athletics in mind when they coined the phrase *Just do it,* but that's not bad advice for e-mail management, either. Of course, this *do it* response is critical if the matter is urgent or must be done today, but it's also a sound strategy for most other e-mail, too. If a message warrants a response, do it. Now. Answer the question. Forward the message. Transfer the to-do to your task list or schedule. Send a response. If you can respond, file, or forward it in five minutes or less, then don't waste time by keeping it for later.

Just as with mail or papers in your inbox, the best strategy is to handle it once (see Chapter 3 in Book II) and then get it off your plate.

Defer until later

For those e-mail messages that aren't critical-care matters, it may make sense to set them aside to address after you pass through all your correspondence. So you *don't* forget and leave them buried in your inbox to be remembered too late, immediately place these e-mail messages in an appropriate folder so they'll pop up later for your attention. Messages that fall into this category may include personal e-mail that you want to read carefully and to which you want to take time to craft a response. They can also include flexible-timeline projects that don't have to be done today or even this week.

Another D that falls in the defer category is *delegate*. Although you can simply click the Forward command and send the message along with instructions for carrying out the requested action, the reliability of e-mail is suspect enough that you want to remind yourself to follow up if you hear nothing back from the delegate.

Automating your responses

The ability to plan ahead with e-mail communication saves you loads of time. If you regularly field the same FAQs numerous times during the week or day, it may make sense to craft template e-mails of standard responses. Place these templates in a folder where you can easily access them and you're ready to cut and paste your reply, using the form language and making the personal tweaks as necessary. For example, if you get queries from clients about the status of their projects, you can put together a standard response informing them that you're attending to their project and will get in touch with them by such-and-such a date.

Don't forget about the automated message function when you're out of the office. Set up a message with the pertinent details: when you'll return, whether you'll be checking e-mail, when people can expect to hear from you, and who they can contact if they need immediate assistance.

Organizing and storing e-mail

Managing, organizing, categorizing, and filing your e-mail is a practice that can serve you as well as maintaining a well-organized paper filing system does. Many of your e-mail messages are probably important to you as reference, especially business correspondence. And you have probably searched in vain for that important e-mail you know you received, oh, maybe eight months ago.

Fortunately, you don't have to print every e-mail and stick it in a filing cabinet. Your e-mail program includes valuable tools that help you keep information as close as a click of the mouse. Most e-mail programs include various folder and filing systems that serve, in a way, as a virtual lateral file cabinet — but searching and finding what you want is a lot easier, with just a little experience. You can sort and store e-mail by a number of categories, grouping them by sender, date, project, importance, or subject. Here are just some ways you can use the features your e-mail software provides:

- Set it up so that certain messages — periodic newsletters, for example — automatically route to a specific folder. (This tool works on the same concept as spam blockers, except these items go in a folder you actually want to see.) With the help of filtering software, you can flag specific e-mail addresses and automatically send them to a folder — or even delete them — before they hit your inbox. If you're like most people, you use only a small portion of what the filtering features in your e-mail software can do. Take a few minutes to explore your options — filtering takes very little time to set up.

- Create a new-arrivals folder, defining *new* as a day, a week, or whatever you determine.

- Establish a *dump* folder that you clean out once a month or as often as you choose.

Don't look at all the e-mail in the dump folder before you dump them. That takes too much time. You've filtered them enough to be able to let them go.

- Make specific project folders where you can save relevant e-mail, providing a record of all conversations for the future. When you no longer need the file because the project is long-complete, you can delete it. This setup also presents a great backup system.

- Employ the search function to track down any correspondence about a certain topic. For example, if you're looking for an e-mail outlining details for a trip to the Bahamas, you can type "Bahamas" in the search field and all inbox e-mail with *Bahamas* somewhere within the body or subject line will come up.

Managing Contact Info with a CRM Program

If you're in business, you already know the profit to be tapped from existing customers. They're already yours! In countless customer-service studies published in the last 20 years, one conclusion stands out over and over: It takes many times more effort, energy, and time to acquire a new customer than it does to retain an existing one.

No matter what your business, the ability to contact existing customers easily and frequently — with the inside knowledge of someone who knows them well as customers — is invaluable. Add the ability to send customers personalized communications at the exact time they're in the market for your product or service, and you're in business: *profitable* business. Even if customers won't need to replace your product for many years, you may be able to offer them related items or garner a referral to their friends.

One of the most valuable tools in business is a customer relationship management (CRM) program. CRM helps you maximize the service, communication, sales, and relationship-building with prospects and existing clients — the lifeblood of any business — by providing quick access to critical customer information, whether you're selling, serving, or invoicing.

Additionally, CRM enables your office practices to become nearly paperless, especially if you have compatible software that changes faxes into electronic documents. You can even enter notes into your CRM software while you're on the phone with prospects and customers, allowing you to keep records of discussions in one centralized place, banishing sticky notes and random slips of paper. This automation saves time and money and provides practically unfettered access to documents and client files from anywhere in the world. What's more, it's kind to trees.

Looking at software and services

Most computers come with simple CRM systems. In Microsoft, it's Outlook. However, Outlook isn't powerful or customizable enough to keep more than basic client and prospect data. Two alternatives are ACT! (www.act.com) and GoldMine (www.goldmine.com). These two programs are affordable (around $500 for a single user) and readily available, and they've stood the test of time as high-quality CRM programs, so they're reasonable tools for businesses big or small. They offer powerful abilities to customize your business data, and they also help segment your customers and clients so you can tailor your communication, service, and sales strategies to particular groups. (For information on using the program features, check out *ACT! by Sage For Dummies,* 9th Edition or *GoldMine 8 For Dummies* [Wiley].)

If you need multiple users, then you'll need to establish a network for the CRM programs to run on so all people in your company have access. Another option is the *SaaS* (software as a service) model, in which you access the program online. In this case, a separate company houses the data and software, charging you a monthly service fee per user for their CRM program and all the servicing. Programs that operate that way include Salesforce (www.salesforce.com) and SugarCRM (www.sugarcrm.com). You have some options in what you use, but as a businessperson, not having a CRM program shouldn't be an option at all.

CRM software programs change frequently, with new and better features being introduced practically every year. Before investing in any particular program, be sure to check out your options and ask others in businesses similar to yours for recommendations.

Unleashing the capabilities of a CRM program

A well-utilized CRM program can do the following:

- Enable you to provide better, personalized service to categories of customers, leading to higher customer satisfaction, more referrals, and perhaps more sales

- Allow you to efficiently target a specific group of clients with information that will be of interest

- Automate recurring contact with existing customers, ensuring they aren't neglected and freeing up valuable time for you to do other things

- Share information and assignments with your co-workers so that your team stays organized and on schedule

This section covers some of the ways you can use the program to make it happen.

Categorizing clients

You can use a CRM program to segment your clients, which is a tremendous strategy. All customers are important, but some are more important than others. Your most important customers

- Do more (and more profitable) business with you

- Send more of their friends, neighbors, business contacts, family members, and associates your way

- Hold strategic positions in companies or organizations you'd like to do business with, meaning they can send even more business your way

You can use CRM to reach out to clients based on their relationship with you. You can, for example, segment your customers and clients into three distinctive categories:

- **Platinum clients:** These are your best customers. They're delighted with your service, are likely to send you referrals regularly, and wouldn't think of going anywhere else. CRM helps you stay in touch with them through newsletters, phone calls, or special correspondence on a regular basis.

✔ **Gold customers:** These people may not be as excited about you and your company as the platinum people, but they continue to do business with you, even if you get raves and referrals only when you ask. CRM helps identify gold-level clients and reminds you to communicate frequently — with the goal of raising them to platinum level.

✔ **Bronze customers:** These are folks who may only sporadically do business with you, switching to other sources from time to time; or they're individuals and businesses who haven't called you for a long time. You can use CRM to help you make a more concerted effort to build a stronger relationship with them.

In addition to current customers, you can also segment prospects and customize your communication with them. A strategic CRM program helps you categorize and organize your prospects as well as separate them from suspects. (*Suspects* have a less than 50 percent chance of using your products or services. *Prospects* offer you a better than 50 percent chance of creating a new business relationship.) Using the technology of a CRM program effectively, you can increase the frequency and effectiveness of contact and move the prospects up the *loyalty ladder* more quickly.

Contacting target groups all at once

When you group your prospects, customers, and clients, you can communicate with them with a few keystrokes or clicks of a mouse. If deliveries of your pressure washers are back-ordered, for example, you can easily notify all your pressure-washer customers. Or if you're changing the pricing on the half-page ads in your magazine, you can contact all your customers and let them know. You may tell them that, beginning at month-end, ad prices go from $4,000 to $5,000 (but as valued customers, they can lock in the lower price by signing a one-year contract now).

Most CRM programs can merge information, including inserting customer and company names in both greetings and bodies of letters. This allows you to craft a generic e-mail or business letter, but use customer and company names in strategic spots so the letter is more personalized. It also saves you from writing 20, 50, or even 300 separate customer letters.

Putting customer contact on autopilot

After you categorize your customers and clients, you can take the final step to saving time with a CRM program: automating customer contact. The companies and people who use CRM most effectively automate *everything*. They have documents, communications, letters and systems, troubleshooting communications, and so on in the CRM program. This allows you to find the document, write the letter or e-mail, attach the document in a PDF file, and keep it in the current client record — all electronically and automatically. After you design the automated process (who, what, where, when, and why), the CRM program does the rest. You can even set up some software, such as ACT! and GoldMine, to dial the phone for you.

CRM programs let you set up long-term communication systems delivered through automation. After your customers receive their 5,000 tongue depressors, an automated thank-you note goes out. The following week, you (automatically) offer a special on gauze. The week after that, you may (automatically) send a customer-satisfaction survey. You can set this system up in advance for customers, clients, prospects, and suspects in platinum, gold, and bronze groups (see the earlier "Categorizing clients" section for more on these groupings).

Keeping your co-workers in the loop and on track

The CRM program can also integrate the notification for calls from different people in your company or department as well as e-mail and faxes. You can establish a system in which each person gets his or her marching orders from the CRM program. For instance, you can tell Sue in accounting to send the invoice and tell Bob in sales to make a follow-up call at 3 days, 7 days, and 14 days after the delivery; and the CRM software will also generate a thank-you letter that Sally in administration can send out tomorrow. And finally, Mike in customer service gets the notice to make a call in five days to check in on any training needs the customer has with the new product.

Book II

Getting Organized and Managing Your Time: Smart Ways to Preempt Problems

Creating effective client profiles

The building blocks of a profitable customer file are standard: name, address, phone number(s), e-mail address, and (if applicable) administrative assistant's contact info. These five or six bytes of information provide you with the start of a great customer record. To take customer communication to the highest level, however, you need more information.

The more you know about your customers, the easier it is to prevent defections — times a client chooses to do business with someone else or refers business to another company or agency. That's a killer for your business: You invested an enormous amount of time in getting and keeping your customers, just to let them slip away! When you know more about your customers, you can anticipate their needs and be better positioned to offer what they want.

Figure 7-1 shows a chart you can use to increase your knowledge of your customers and create more personal connections with them. You can program this information into your CRM program by customizing the fields.

Say you've collected this information about your customers over time and you've entered it into your CRM program. The next time you come across a couple of extra tickets to the golf tournament in town, you search your CRM information for customers who are golf fanatics and give them the tickets. Of course, it doesn't hurt your relationship that the tickets came from you!

Date: _____

Customer Profile

1) Customer Name _____
   Nickname _____
2) Company Name _____
3) Company Address _____
   Home Address _____
4) Telephone Numbers _____
   Business _____
   Home _____
5) Date of Birth _____
   Place of Birth _____
   Hometown _____

Education

6) High School _____
   Year Graduated _____
   College _____
   Year Graduated _____
   College Fraternity/Sorority _____
7) _____
8) Sports _____
   _____

Family

9) Spouse name and occupation _____
10) Spouse education _____
11) Spouse's interests _____
12) Anniversary _____
13) Children _____
    names/ages _____
    _____
14) Children's education levels _____
    _____
15) Children's interests (hobbies, problems) _____
    _____

Special Interests

16) Clubs, fraternal associations, service clubs _____
    _____
17) Community activities _____
    _____

Lifestyle

Figure 7-1:
A sample
customer
profile.

18) Favorite place for lunch _____
    Favorite place for dinner _____
19) Favorite spectator sports _____
    Favorite sports teams _____

Another example: You see a great article about the University of Alabama. You search for University of Alabama alumni on your customer list and e-mail them the article. What have you invested? A few minutes of *really* listening to your customers (and you do that anyway, right?) and a few minutes of data entry. What have you achieved? You've brought your relationship with this customer to a new level and spent minimal time doing it.

If you really want to impress a customer, take great notes in your CRM program and start the next call with something like the following:

✔ "How did (the wedding, your party, the conference) go?"

✔ "How was Bobby's soccer game last week? Did his team win?"

✔ "What did you do with X? Last time we spoke, you said Y."

Take a few moments of your time to note nuggets of information in your CRM program, use that information to make your prospect or customer feel valued and unique, and watch your customer relationship grow and solidify.

Putting a CRM program on a server to maximize accessibility and backup

Everyone in the company must be able to access public information in real time at all times. All employees who serve or sell to customers need access to client documents and information. This is true for all departments: sales, marketing, administration, accounting, and so on. And you can set up a CRM program so all employees can tap into the data. Putting CRM on a server has security advantages as well.

Not only does having company data spread around on various computers create an organizational nightmare, but it also represents a security flaw — you can lose valuable customers in a keystroke. For example, if you have a salesperson who has given notice or, worse, one you've terminated, that person may have 200 customers — and all their customer information — saved on his or her computer. Before leaving, that person can easily delete every customer file in the computer.

Ouch! You just lost the history and possibly the contact information for 200 customers. You also lost potential customers that current salespeople were hoping to close a deal with in the next 30, 60, or 90 days. Now you have to try to reconstruct which customers the salesperson sold to, what he or she sold to them, and what the customer-salesperson relationships were like. And you're back figuring out how you can increase sales and service to these customers in the future.

If you have multiple independent computers with company data stored on each, connect your company's computers in a network run by a server. Server-accessible CRM data ensures that your business can avoid data-loss nightmares. With the CRM program, you can immediately lock an ex-employee out of the system and have system backups to reconstruct data as needed.

Some companies may be reticent to open access to this information because of client confidentiality or simply the risk of corrupting or deleting important data. If you want to protect accounting, personnel, and other private information, you can do that — no problem. The programs offer password protection so that only certain employees can access the most confidential information. You can also set it up so employees can *see* the data but not delete or modify it in any way.

Book III
Taking Charge of
What You Can

The 5th Wave   By Rich Tennant

©RICHTENNANT

DO-IT-YOURSELF PUBLISHING CO.

PLUMBING

CARPENTRY

UPHOLSTERY

AUTO

ROBERT KROWSKI FOUNDER

"His only drawback as a manager was his inability to delegate."

In this book . . .

*W*hen so much seems outside your control, take comfort in knowing that there are still some things you can take charge of. Obviously, the first thing is to make sure you take care of yourself, and not in an every-man-for-himself kind of way but in a what-do-I-need-to-be-happy-and-healthy-(or-at-least-not-clinically-depressed)-at-work kind of way. Beyond that, you may find yourself in situations that call for decisive intervention — ever been to a meeting that meanders into a several-hour marathon or been charged with tasks that don't require your exper-tise? This book tells you what to do when you need to intervene but don't want to look like you're taking over.

Chapter 1

Managing Yourself: Taking Care of No. 1

. . . .

In This Chapter

▶ Balancing work and personal time

▶ Improving your situation when you can, and coming to terms with it when you can't

▶ Making decisions that are good for you

. . . .

*1*n all the hustle and bustle of a typical day at the office — proposals due yesterday, another rush order to get out, meetings stacked up one right after another, the latest crisis du jour — you can easily get caught up in work. Nothing is wrong with getting caught up in your work, but when work begins to intrude into your personal life — a bit too far and a bit too often — then you have a problem.

The problem is that work becomes your number one priority, and everything and everyone else — including yourself — are automatically required to take a back seat. And what results from this shift in priorities? You have poorer health because of all the junk food lunches caught on the run and infrequent exercise. You have increased stress because of your endless workdays and nights and your inability to take vacations or tear yourself away from your work. You also have a trail of ruined relationships as friends and family begin to tire of waiting for you to make room in your life for them.

No matter where you are in the organization, how important your job is, or how much you're getting paid, you have to take care of yourself first. You have to be your number one priority. When you take care of yourself, you're in top form, and you're a more valuable asset to your organization, your customers, your employees, and your boss. And you also have a much better chance of surviving to retirement and having an opportunity to enjoy the fruits of all your hard work. Doesn't that sound nice? This chapter explains how to balance your personal life with your professional life and make decisions that reflect forethought and integrity.

Dealing with the Work-Life Dilemma

Finding the correct balance between your work life and your personal life is important. Employees whose work and personal lives are in balance are happier, healthier, more productive, and a lot easier to work with. In addition, they provide better customer service. But when employees allow their jobs to take over their lives, the results can be devastating.

Who benefits when your work life and personal life are balanced? You do, and your company, co-workers, partner, family, and loved ones do, as well. Here are some of the positive outcomes:

- Employees have improved self-esteem and health, are happier, and feel more valued by their employers.
- Employees have more control over their working lives.
- Employees are more motivated, efficient, and effective.
- Employees feel more loyalty and commitment to their jobs.
- Relationships between workers and managers improve.
- Absenteeism goes down.
- The number of worker's compensation and disability claims decreases.
- The organization transforms into an employer of choice, attracting talented and motivated job candidates.
- The organization enjoys increased employee retention rates.

Take a look at yourself. Are you in charge of your life, or is your job in charge? Are your relationships falling apart? Are you a stranger to your family and friends? Do you feel like you're constantly under stress? Does your work performance suffer because you're just too overwhelmed to take care of all the loose ends?

If you're a manager, ask these same questions about your employees. Are they in the same boat as you? If so, you have to do something about these issues — the sooner the better.

Achieving balance when work becomes more demanding

When economic conditions are difficult, many employers find it necessary to lay off employees — leaving the remaining employees to shoulder the extra burden. In cases like this, there may be no avoiding the fact that your work-life balance is going to necessarily tip in the direction of work. So what can you do?

✔ **Take your breaks:** Taking the breaks that are due you, including lunch, is more important than ever. If you're working harder — and longer — you need these breaks to clear your head.

✔ **Get away — on the job:** When you take your breaks, find a quiet room or other space, perhaps a vacant conference room, where you can relax without interruption. If you stay at your desk, you'll find it hard to keep others from drawing you back into work.

✔ **Volunteer for special assignments:** As your regular tasks become more demanding and drudgery sets in, volunteering for special assignments can help make your job more interesting, providing you with a break of sorts from your normal duties.

✔ **Have fun:** While work can be a very serious enterprise, there's no law against having fun on the job. Indeed, it can provide you with the balance you need to get through a strenuous work schedule.

Finding balance in your life is up to you — you can't rely on someone else to do it for you. Constantly seek opportunities to inject some life back into your workday and to remember that there's more to life than getting a paycheck every other week.

Working toward a more flexible workplace

Book III

Taking
Charge
of What
You Can

If you're a manager, not only do you have to watch out for yourself, but you also have to keep a close eye on your employees to ensure that they aren't showing the symptoms of overwork and burnout. Although managers have always had certain tools available to help their employees balance work and personal time — hiring them on a part-time basis or granting employees an unexpected day off with pay — you can lead the way by investigating and testing some of these popular alternatives:

✔ **Flextime:** Allowing employees to set their own work start and end times within a band of time approved by management

✔ **Compressed workweek:** Working a full-time, 40-hour-a-week schedule in fewer than five workdays each week (for example, four 10-hour days a week)

✔ **Shift swapping:** Allowing employees to trade shifts as desired among themselves

✔ **Self-rostering:** Allowing employees to sign up for their own work schedules each week or month

✔ **Job sharing:** Sharing a full-time job with another employee, with each person usually working 20 hours a week

✔ **Telecommuting:** Working from home or from a remote office, sometimes a day or two a week, sometimes on a full-time basis

TECHNICAL STUFF

Who works most?

Workers in the United States put in more time on the job than workers in most other countries. Although American workers today toil on average 1,978 hours a year, Australian, Canadian, Japanese, and Mexican workers get by with about 100 hours — or two and a half weeks — less each year, and British workers about 200 hours less. German workers work 500 fewer hours (or about 12 weeks) than their American counterparts. Only South Koreans (who put in 500 hours more a year) and Czechs (who put in 100 hours more a year) work more hours than workers in the U.S. Not surprisingly, most Americans feel tremendous pressure to spend more time on the job, to take work home, and even to work while on vacation, ill, or otherwise indisposed.

The following sections outline the steps to take to convince the powers that be that, first, this idea is good to implement and, second, that company policies should be modified to make it happen.

Step 1: Identify core business needs

Does your organization truly need to adopt alternative work arrangements? Why or why not? Survey employees to find out what they think. Identify the core needs of your business and then determine what kinds of alternative work arrangements may be appropriate. Consult with management (and with labor unions, if necessary) to determine what kinds of arrangements may be acceptable and what kinds aren't. Quantify the benefits of making the desired change — and the costs — to the organization. Present your findings and your specific ideas to management for approval.

Step 2: Develop policies and procedures

Don't reinvent the wheel. By doing a search on the Internet, you can find plenty of policies that you can model yours after. (See the sidebar "Top five work/life Web sites" for a start.)

REMEMBER

For alternative work arrangements to be successful — and to ensure that all employees are treated fairly — develop and implement clear and complete policies and procedures before any new program is rolled out.

Step 3: Have a trial period

When making a change that's as significant as this change will be, first run a pilot program before you finalize your alternative work arrangements. Communicate your new policies widely, and make sure that employees understand them. Invite employees to participate, and then start your program. After a month or two, gather results and evaluate them. Are they positive or negative?

Step 4: Go final

Make changes to your program as determined in Step 3, and then create your final policies and procedures. Inaugurate your new program with much fanfare and celebration. You're on your way!

Avoiding workaholics 'R' us

When overwork becomes more than an occasional event and you often push everything that isn't related to your job out of the picture, then you have a classic case of *workaholism*. And workaholism isn't good. Not only can workaholism lead you to neglect your family and social life, but it can also actually make you less productive and less efficient. Although you may think you're getting more done with all the extra time you put into your job, chances are, you're actually getting less done.

So, how can you tell whether or not you're a workaholic? Here are the seven deadly warning signs of workaholism. How many do you have?

✔ When you go to parties, you talk mostly about work.

✔ You dream about work.

✔ You rarely miss a day of work or go on vacations.

✔ On the rare days that you do take a vacation, you take work with you and regularly call in to check your voice-mail messages.

✔ You work more than 45 hours a week.

✔ You eat lunch at your desk or skip lunch altogether because you don't have time to take a break.

✔ You're absolutely convinced that you're not a workaholic, even though you exhibit some or all of the preceding symptoms.

If you find that several of these descriptors apply to you, make the time now to take positive steps to cure yourself. Some suggestions:

✔ Work fewer hours. Commit to a 40-hour-a-week schedule and stick to it.

✔ Clearly separate your work life from your personal life. Leave your work at the office when you go home every day and spend more time with friends and family.

✔ Slow down! Take vacations (and don't bring your work with you or check in with the office before your vacation is over).

✔ Set up a regular exercise schedule and stick to it.

✔ Take time for lunch and get out of the office as often as possible to eat it.

Book III

Taking Charge of What You Can

Top five work/life Web sites

Here are five good Web sites that provide more info about the topics addressed in this chapter:

✔ Work & Family Connection:
www.workfamily.com

✔ Work Options:
www.workoptions.com/
articles.htm

✔ Work-Life Balance in Canadian Workplaces:
http://labour-travail.
hrdc-drhc.gc.ca/worklife

✔ BlueSuitMom.com:
www.bluesuitmom.com

✔ Families and Work Institute:
www.familiesandwork.org

Improving your attitude and interactions

In the business world, relationships are an integral part of success or failure. They play a major role in the security and productivity of every individual involved, as well as in the growth and success of the company. Your work relationships also play a major factor in how you feel about life even when you're outside of work.

The following sections outline ways you can enhance your work relationships, not only to engender goodwill and burnish your value among co-workers and managers alike, but also to improve your life overall. If you have a good attitude at work and experience positive interactions there, the good feelings and positive effects will stick with you even when you go home for the day.

Go the extra mile

Don't do only enough to get by. Make it a point to be available when someone comes to you seeking information or inquiring about techniques or procedures at which you excel. Patiently and cheerfully share information.

Be the person who gets along well with other employees, buys into the company's mission, and is excited about what you do. Make an effort to know and understand the roles that others play in the company and to cement relationships with people above and around you, developing team spirit.

Managers, help develop your employees

Leadership in any company with a future is always looking for managers who develop dedicated, motivated, and happy employees. Following are a few key principles that you as a manager can use to help your employees become better workers and happier people:

✔ Understand what your people's talents are and provide an environment in which they can succeed.

✔ Have defined and reachable goals for the individuals who work for you. Where do you want them to be in six months, one year, and so on? Let them know your expectations.

✔ Commit time and effort to all projects and be a cheerleader for everyone you come in contact with.

✔ Talk up the positives. Recognize and correct the negatives, but don't dwell on them.

Manage your frustration

Don't let your anger and frustration negatively impact the people around you. When you're feeling angry or frustrated, make it a point to do absolutely nothing. Sit down, take a deep breath, pause for a moment, recognize that you're upset, and ask yourself, "What can I do to turn my anger into a positive by doing something constructive instead of destructive?"

Good communication reduces your frustration and makes it easier to build and maintain the kind of relationships that build profitable businesses.

Get along (or make friends) with your boss

Your employer keeps you on the payroll because of your productivity, but your relationship with your employer also affects your promotability. Some key points:

✔ **Even a bad boss can teach you good lessons.** Working with or around a rotten boss teaches you how to set priorities, neutralize potentially explosive situations, and choose your moments. In fact, a bad boss can be a good teacher. How? By helping you acquire patience and learn how to deal with conflicts constructively — in essence, by inspiring you to be better than they are.

✔ **Never forget that your boss is your boss.** Your job is to do the work the way the boss wants it done. Your objective should be to do your job in a way that makes the boss's job easier. You're there to remove obstacles for the boss, not to *be* the obstacle. Your job security and opportunity for promotion often rest on your effectiveness in this function. Management frequently judges you by how well you get along with the boss, and that judgment can affect your progress.

Treat everyone like VIPs

Why not treat everybody like Very Important People? Would it make a difference in your relationships with them? Would it improve your business and make you a lot of friends? The answers are obvious, aren't they?

Book III

Taking
Charge
of What
You Can

Consider the story of a young woman who worked for a large hotel chain. One day, she heard that the head of the chain was going to be a guest in the hotel. Neither she nor the other clerks had ever seen him, and she was really concerned that she might foul up if she checked him in. To play it safe, all day long she treated every man who checked in as if he were the boss. That evening, she got a call from the head of the chain, who said, "When I checked in this afternoon, you were so professional, so gracious and friendly; I am delighted to have you as a member of the staff." She hadn't known which man he was, but by treating everyone like a VIP, she was successful.

Recognizing and managing the symptoms of stress

No matter how hard you try to prevent it, some amount of stress in the workplace is inevitable. Organizational changes, quarreling co-workers, challenging projects, or a boss who doesn't understand you can create a lot of work stress for you, which gets added to all the stresses from your life outside of work.

Have you ever wondered why so many organizations make such a big deal about stress management training? Organizations must deal with stress because when employees allow stress to overcome them, they lose their effectiveness. And when employees lose their effectiveness, the organization loses its edge.

So how do you know whether you're stressed out? The list of stress indicators in Table 1-1 can help you identify the extent of stress in your business and personal lives. Because one affects the other, determining and dealing with the source of stress is important. If you experience more than a couple of these symptoms, take a serious look at what creates the stress in your life. Quick! Do something about stress before it's too late!

Table 1-1	Symptoms of Stress
The Symptom	*Yes, I Have It!*
Aggression	❏
Hostility	❏
Headaches	❏
Indigestion	❏
Sleep disorders	❏
Defensiveness	❏
Poor judgment	❏
Nervousness	❏

The Symptom	Yes, I Have It!
High blood pressure	❏
Ulcers	❏
Fatigue	❏
Anxiety	❏
Depression	❏
Memory loss	❏
Inability to concentrate	❏
Mood swings	❏

Any one of these symptoms can indicate a stress problem, but the longer your list of symptoms, the greater the damage being done to your mind and body. Fortunately, you can figure out how to manage your stress. Although you can't always prevent stress from entering your life, you can take definite steps to reduce the negative effects.

You can't wait for someone else to do something to reduce your stress. You have to do it yourself, but fortunately, managing stress isn't as hard as you may think. Effective stress management boils down to this: Change the things that you can change and accept the things that you can't change. The following section provides a quick overview. For even more stress-management techniques, head to Book VI, which is devoted to this topic.

Book III

Taking Charge of What You Can

Changing the things that you can change

You can take several steps right now to change your work environment and decrease your stress:

- ✔ **Get healthy:** Regular, vigorous exercise is one of the best ways to work off tons of frustration and stress. And when you're under stress, your body quickly becomes depleted of certain vitamins and minerals, so be sure to eat right, too.

- ✔ **Have fun:** If you're not having fun, why bother? You're going to spend roughly a fourth to a third of your adult life at work. Sure, you need the money, and you need the psychological satisfaction that doing a good job brings with it, but don't ever take work so seriously that you can't have fun with your job and your co-workers.

- ✔ **Find out how to say no:** Recognize that you can't do everything. And when you try to do everything, the result is that nothing gets done well. When you already have a full plate of work to do and someone tries to give you more, say no.

- ✔ **Relax:** Relaxation is an extremely important part of any program of stress management. When you relax, you give your brain a break, and you provide yourself with the needed opportunity to recharge your batteries and eliminate tension before going back into overdrive.

- ✔ **Manage your schedule:** If you don't manage your own schedule, it will quickly find a way to manage you. Get a personal planner, desk calendar, or PDA, and take charge of the meetings you attend and the appointments you keep. Book II offers strategies for managing your time.

- ✔ **Streamline:** Simplify, shorten, and condense. Fewer steps in a process translates into your workforce expending less effort, fewer problems going wrong, and, ultimately, less stress for you to endure.

- ✔ **Look for silver linings:** Be an optimist. Look for the good in everything you do and everyone you meet. You'll be amazed by how much better you feel about your job, your co-workers, and yourself.

Accepting the things that you can't change

You just can't change certain things, no matter how hard you try. When you can't change the unchangeable, you have one choice left: Change yourself.

- ✔ **Surrender:** Stop fighting change; become one with it. Instead of trying to row against the swift currents of change, let go and drift with them. After you stop fighting change, you can concentrate on making it work for you and for your organization (see Book V, Chapter 8 for more on dealing with change).

- ✔ **Adjust your attitude:** After you've worked at a job for a few years, you can begin to get visions of grandeur. "How would this place survive without me?" Before long, you become resentful when your opinion isn't given the widespread respect that you feel it deserves, and you begin to dislike performing the mundane tasks that are a part of your job.

  As you get hot under the collar about your current status, remember that many people are only a couple of paychecks away from bankruptcy. How long could you survive if you lost your job? And don't be so sure that your organization will never have a layoff or reduction in force. Who do you think would be let go first: Employees who willingly do whatever they can to get the job done or employees who think that they're above all that? If you picked the former, you may be due for a major attitude adjustment. Adjust your own attitude before someone adjusts it for you!

- ✔ **Don't be a victim:** Don't give up and unplug yourself from the organization. Refuse to be a victim of change and, instead, become its biggest fan. And, if you absolutely can't stand your organization any longer, then find another one.

- ✔ **Control your anger:** Getting mad when your job doesn't go your way may be expressive, but showing anger isn't a productive use of your time and energy.

- ✔ **Don't sweat the small stuff:** Most of what you do is small stuff. If you're going to worry, at least save it for something that's really important!

Making Decisions You Can Live With

Each choice that you make takes you toward or away from what you want in life. Each choice has an impact, however slight, upon your path. A series of bad decisions can derail you from your big-picture goals, and finding happiness and balance in your life (not to mention success) will be nearly impossible if you find yourself miles from where you hoped to be. When you understand that every choice has an end result, you place yourself in a position to become successful, especially when those decisions are in the context of the workplace.

Too little thought is given to making decisions. How they are made, why they are made, and when they are made are often taken for granted. People expect to think seriously about decisions like accepting a job offer that moves them hundreds of miles or getting married, but they give little thought to the actual process of decision making. Taking too much time to make a decision can be as harmful as never making the decision. Making decisions too hurriedly can also cause years of regret.

The following sections explain several points that you need to keep in mind as you make little decisions, such as who you ask to read over your report before you submit it, as well as life-changing decisions, such as whether you ask now for a promotion. They can help you identify whether your choices in the workplace take you on- or off-course and help to get you heading down the path toward your goals if you aren't there already.

Thinking it through

If you allow yourself time to think decisions through to their possible conclusions, you ultimately make better decisions. Ask yourself the following questions:

- ✔ How would I feel if this decision appeared in tomorrow's paper?
- ✔ What impact will this decision have on my family?
- ✔ Am I compromising my integrity with this particular decision?
- ✔ Is this decision consistent with my personal, family, corporate, or team goals?
- ✔ Will this decision take me closer to or further from my major objective in life?
- ✔ Am I making this decision under the influence of people who have a great deal to gain if I say yes (or no)?
- ✔ Are the people who are influencing my decision looking after my best interests or their own?

Answering those questions makes your decision a little clearer and more certain.

Don't make significant decisions at home or in the workplace (except in emergencies) when you're really tired. If someone is pressing you to decide something "right now," unless an immediate decision is critical, say, "If I have to decide now, the answer is no. After I have had a chance to catch my breath and review the facts, there's the possibility it could be yes." Then put the ball back in the other person's court and ask, "Do you want my decision now, or should we wait?" Because he or she usually receives some benefit from your yes, chances are that the person will agree that waiting is best.

Taking your side — and others' sides — into account

The position you occupy — whether in a company, in a family, or in any other relationship — has a direct bearing on the decisions you make. If you work in your company's marketing department, for example, you're probably gung-ho about any legitimate method of getting your product and/or business in front of the people who are in a position to buy. You may not be quite as cost-oriented in making decisions as the head of the accounting department is. That individual probably regards direct-mail advertising as an expense, whereas in marketing you regard it as an opportunity to generate income.

When you're confronted with a choice that affects not only you but also other people, the decision-making process becomes more complicated. Before making any decision that involves more than one person, get input from all sides.

When a decision impacts a number of people who are part of your team, remember that decisions are more likely to be implemented effectively and enthusiastically when everyone feels like an important part of that team. When possible, include the others in the process. If involving them is either impossible or impractical, understand that their acceptance of your decision depends on your credibility. If you have a track record of using mature judgment and doing what's right, your decision is more likely to be well received. For more on working well in a team, refer to Book I, Chapter 4.

One decision you should make right up front is to be open-minded and empathetic to other people's needs and desires. That decision enables you to get along better with other people, bring balance to the process, and maintain harmony, which are important for achieving maximum effectiveness.

Deciding in advance when possible

Many decisions can and should be made in advance. By establishing parameters about what you are and aren't willing to do, you can avoid a lot of confusion and ensure that your efforts are going to the things that truly matter.

Consider the story of a company that, over time, began offering products that weren't directly related to its primary mission of teaching, training, encouraging, and inspiring. Because of these tangential products, the company's inventory expanded (requiring more warehousing), and its message became diluted. Eventually, the board made the decision to eliminate all products and services that did not directly relate to the company's work and mission. In so doing, it also established the fundamental principle that, going forward, choices for new products and/or services would depend strictly on how those products or services fit into and advanced the company's mission. Now, when proposals come the company's way for involvements that do not support and improve its mission, the company doesn't waste time in even reviewing those proposals.

Although you may not be in charge of your company's product line or have a say in what alliances it builds, you can incorporate this same strategy in your own professional life. When you establish parameters ahead of time, you're facilitating decision making. The result is better decisions that allow you to concentrate your time and expertise on advancing your goals.

Making principle-based decisions

Someone once said, "When one bases his life on principle, 99 percent of his decisions are already made." Make sure that a decision fits your long-term objectives. Today's marketplace is replete with opportunities, and it can be easy to become distracted by offers that seem promising. Losing focus can be costly, not just from a monetary standpoint but in terms of time and effort as well.

Most big decisions require a tradeoff. Making a principle-based decision means knowing what's most important to you, figuring out how the decision you're contemplating will impact the different areas of your life, and then moving forward in a way that keeps your principles intact and your conscience clear. Ask yourself, "How will this decision affect all the areas of my life — personal, family, career, financial, physical, mental, and spiritual?" Obviously, not all decisions affect all areas, but it can still help you assess where the biggest impact is and whether the tradeoff (what you have to give up versus what you have to gain) is worth it.

Book III

Taking Charge of What You Can

Listening carefully to advice you ask for

For significant business-related decisions, run your decisions past people you know (and trust) who have a considerable amount of knowledge, experience, and wisdom relating to the topic at hand. All these attributes are musts in the decision-making process. After you get their advice, chances are that following their recommendations will give you good results.

Most people ask for advice on occasion and, even as they are being advised, start the picking and choosing process about what parts of the advice they'll take and what parts they'll leave behind. You don't have to take advice just because someone gave it to you, but understand that you're on your own when you choose to heed only portions of the advice you're given. If you see a road sign that indicates an S-shaped curve ahead and has the speed limit listed at 15 miles per hour, and you decide to slow to 15 but drive in a straight line, you're in big trouble. Don't blame the advisor if you use only bits and pieces of the advice and it doesn't work for you.

Weighing the benefits versus risks of decisions

When you're making decisions, one factor should always be paramount in your mind: What do you have to gain and what do you have to lose by saying yes?

Obviously, all choices and all decisions that come your way are not clear-cut and easily defined. This is where the evaluation process can be so critical. Try the following:

1. **Draw a line from top to bottom on a piece of paper.**

2. **On one side, list the "whys" and on the other side list the "why nots;" then begin to fill in the columns.**

   Commit as much time as you need to thinking through the pros and cons of the question at hand. Invite key personnel, those directly involved whether you go with yes or no, to contribute opinions based on their experience and interest. Include those involved with the financing of the project, as well as any other key players you feel are important to the proposed project.

3. **Looking at your list, determine your maximum benefit of a decision.**

   In other words, what would you gain if everything went your way?

4. **Now determine the maximum exposure.**

   Ask yourself, "Suppose nothing goes my way? Suppose this doesn't develop and materialize as I expect it to? What would I lose?"

5. **After you've weighed both sides, follow this simple rule: If you can handle the worst and the potential gains are significant, take the risk. If you can't accept the worst and the potential gains are insignificant, don't give your okay.**

Listening to your feelings

Many times, you simply don't know what to do. You consider every angle, weigh all the facts, consult with experts, and maybe even pray about the decision, and still no distinct answer comes. That's when you need to take a quiet walk and listen to your instincts. Many times, you instinctively know the right decision to make, particularly when making major decisions. Act on those hunches.

Frank Capra once said, "A hunch is creativity trying to tell you something." Hunches, also known as intuition, are only recognized by those folks who listen to their feelings.

A clue that a decision is unwise is that uncomfortable feeling that lodges just below your breastbone — you know, that uneasy, nagging sensation that occurs whenever you think about the decision you're leaning toward. Use this feeling to change course toward a better decision, one that gives you peace of mind.

Doing the best you can with a decision you're stuck with

Sometimes you don't have a choice: A decision has been made, and you must live with it. For example, say that you're promoted to manager at your company, and the previous manager had committed to constructing a new four-story office building. You ascertain that the building should be at least six stories tall, but the foundation is already in place, and construction for the first floor is complete. At this point, you can't add two floors because the foundation can't support them. In this situation, you have a choice:

✔ Complain and grouse about the poor planning and throw up your hands at the untenable situation.

✔ Make the best of the situation and maximize the use of the four stories.

Either way, you end up with four stories.

In situations like this, the key is to accept, as graciously as possible, what you can't change.

Book III

Taking Charge of What You Can

The important thing is not to follow one poor decision with another. Many times, people do exactly that: They deny the original mistake or try to cover it up, even to the extent of lying about it. That strategy isn't wise; it simply leads to a series of bad decisions. Integrity demands that you do the right thing so that you have fewer things to apologize for, explain away, or regret. Whether the mistake is one you made or inherited, cut your losses as quickly as possible. Think through the situation and then make good choices, followed by any necessary corrective action. In other words, make the new decision based on where you are at this moment in an effort to solve the problems that the poor decision brought about.

Chapter 2

Managing Meetings

*I*f you regard meetings as a massive waste of time, then read on. You're in good company if meeting invitations cause your stomach to tie up in knots and your blood pressure to climb a little higher. That feeling may arise because you know you'll walk out with more projects on your already over-flowing plate. Or because your day is so packed with to-dos that squeezing in one more commitment is certain to push you over the edge. Or because you know from experience that you'll find yourself a prisoner of the Meeting That Wouldn't Die.

Meetings with colleagues and corporate minions — as well as appointments with clients, customers, vendors, and so on — are an important part of business life. Meetings aid in the communication of critical issues, stimulate needed action, and help measure and maintain progress. But far too often, the meeting is overused, confused, and abused, leading to gross inefficiencies and wasted time. While the information in this chapter can't help you make meetings go away, it does offer strategies to tame them from wild time-predators into a manageable and even productive part of your job.

Your meetings may be ones that you set and manage, or they may be appointments that someone else is eager to arrange with you. The initiator starts out with a little more control of the situation simply because he's set-ting the appointment, but just because you're the invitee doesn't mean you have to relinquish control or time. Regardless of whether you're leading the meeting or simply participating in it, this chapter gives you valuable strate-gies and tactics that you can use before, during, and after meetings to make them more valuable and less time-consuming.

Devising Objectives, Listing Attendees, and Crafting an Agenda

When you're the one calling a meeting, adhere to this strategy: Invest twice the time in preparation as the length of the meeting. If the meeting is scheduled for an hour, put in approximately two hours of prep time. This section explains how you can best fill that time.

Clarifying the purpose of the meeting

Before you schedule a meeting, get your arms around the big picture and consider all the specifics. Begin your preparations by starting with the goal and working backward. What outcome do you desire for this meeting? How are you most likely to arrive at that outcome?

At first consideration, you may think that if you're the one asking for the meeting, you automatically have a good handle on why you need to meet. Sure, you may know that you want to get to the bottom of the service problems you're having with your office supplies vendor, but chances are you have a ways to go before you've crystallized the situation and know how you can resolve it.

So give the purpose of the meeting careful thought. Start with the motivating factor for the action. Is it to get to the bottom of the service problems with your vendor? Really? Do you just want to understand the problems, or would you rather clear up the problems at the conclusion of the meeting?

 Be clear with yourself about what you want to walk away with. Put it into as precise a framework as possible, identifying the action you seek and when you want it accomplished. The questions you ask yourself before the meeting really increase its effectiveness and efficiency. Here's the need-to-know info:

- ✔ What's the problem or goal?
- ✔ How do you want it resolved or accomplished?
- ✔ What do the parties involved have to do to make that happen?
- ✔ When should this action be accomplished?

Meeting overload in the United States

Is the United States a nation on a fast track to meeting meltdown? Have meetings overtaken the world of business like some invasive corporate kudzu? Consider these findings:

✔ The average professional employee spends approximately 1.7 hours per day in meetings, according to 3M Meetings Management Institute.

✔ In a survey by Microsoft, participants felt that 71 percent of the meetings they attended were unproductive.

✔ In a survey conducted by MCI Conferencing, 91 percent of the participants admitted to daydreaming in meetings, and 39 percent had actually dozed off during a meeting.

✔ The same survey showed that 73 percent had brought other work to a meeting.

Look at the difference between the following two statements of purpose; the second includes the proper amount of detail:

> "Hi, Mary. I'd like to meet with you to discuss the problems we've been having with your service department."

> "Hi, Mary. We've been having some issues with prompt service calls from your department for the past three months. I'd like to meet with you so we can clear up any barriers that may be causing this problem and get back on track with on-time response within the next two weeks."

Often, while working through the process of clarifying the purpose of the meeting, you may discover other ways to address the issue you want to meet about. This exercise may help you realize that a phone call or other action can resolve the situation — without holding a meeting at all.

Creating a guest list

For the most effective meetings, keep the size to as few people as necessary to accomplish the goal of the gathering. Numerous studies show that five to eight is the ideal number of participants for a productive meeting. Of course, the subject matter often dictates the number of people who attend a meeting, but as soon as the number of attendees climbs above eight or ten, the return on time investment begins to decline rapidly. In addition to taking more people away from their primary duties, the larger number increases unproductive discussion.

The individuals invited should be able to represent others and assume the responsibility of communicating the results of the meeting to those people. Don't invite someone just because she would be offended not to be included.

Given a limited number of meeting participants, you want to make sure that everyone who *must* be at the meeting is invited. Depending on the purpose and topic of your meeting, consider these criteria when making out the guest list:

- ✔ Have you included people who have information about or answers to critical questions?

- ✔ Did you invite those in a position to authorize decisions required to move ahead?

- ✔ Have you considered representatives from each of the departments or areas that will be affected or play a role in the outcome of the meeting?

- ✔ Did you include someone who can take notes and communicate the details of the meeting to attendees and others who aren't part of the meeting?

Official *minutes* — a detailed chronological record of everything that happened during the meeting — may not be necessary, especially if meetings involve few participants. But at the very least, you should invite someone you can assign to take notes. Here's what the notes should capture:

- • Key discussion points

- • Significant concerns or unresolved questions

- • The action items and all details surrounding them

Give the note-taking responsibility to someone other than the host so that the host can focus on shepherding the meeting to its productive conclusion.

While considering the right people to invite, give some thought to the *wrong* people as well. Don't weigh down the invite list with *redundants* — people representing the same area or interest. When you have a choice of two people, consider their communication styles and which candidate may be more compatible to the meeting environment: the co-worker who likes to hold forth with filibuster-length pronouncements or the colleague whose contributions add value to the discussion.

Holding informal, preliminary mini-meetings

Setting up a meeting to discuss a meeting? Okay, before you declare this suggestion certifiably insane from meeting overload, consider this: Prep work is all about keeping the meeting as short and focused as possible. The better you prepare, the more you accomplish in less time. So yes, if a quick mini-meeting improves the outcome of the big meeting (such as if the project you're working on is complex or if you'll have multiple presenters at the meeting), it's worth the effort.

Here's how it works: Say you've set a meeting with eight co-workers to talk about a project that involves multiple departments. You anticipate some of the attendees may resist the proposals you plan to present. Instead of walking into the meeting and spending some or all of it defending your program or deflecting criticism, meet informally with just a couple of the participants at a time. Share with them a preview of your intent for the meeting and ask for their feedback — even proactively ask them to play devil's advocate and point out what they think some of the challenges may be. That 15 minutes or so that you spend with each key person helps you identify the curveballs that may be thrown your way during the meeting — you can now prepare a response to them. And believe it or not, you've gained support from those attendees. Because you sought them out for their input, they're more likely to support your plan, particularly if you take their concerns into account.

Mini-meetings are best set for a week in advance. This allows you to adjust the agenda for the larger meeting, revise your presentation, and be better prepared for reactions. Face-to-face mini-meetings are advisable when possible, though they aren't always practical, so use your best judgment. You don't have to schedule a formal meeting; stand-up conversations or quick sit-downs in your office or theirs work well.

Putting together the agenda

A tailor-made agenda allows you to proceed in the most direct path with the fewest distractions. Here's the process you follow to ensure that your agenda provides all the pertinent details:

1. **Create a detailed outline for the meeting.**

   Although the purpose of the meeting determines the agenda, all agendas contain some consistent elements:

   - An agenda begins with greeting and introducing all the participants as well as reviewing housekeeping issues, such as the length of the meeting and who's taking notes.

   - An agenda reviews the goals, ensuring that everyone understands the purpose of the meeting and what the expected outcome is.

   - At the conclusion of the meeting, the *action items* cover any follow-up activity expected of the participants.

Components of the agenda need to be specific. Don't just have an agenda that has "old business" and "new business." List the projects and discussion points as well as any interim decisions that need to be made. Be sure to use a format that identifies main topics, subtopics, and then action points in outline format. Providing detail helps spark ideas and conveys to the attendees that to get through everything, the conversation has to keep moving.

Try to keep the agenda to a single page. Like a résumé, you want to communicate that there's substance but not overwhelm the readers with so much detail that their eyes glaze over.

2. **Clarify which items on the agenda are reports or presentations and which are discussions.**

   Make these notes in the margin of the document for all to see.

3. **Assign a time limit for each agenda item.**

   Printing it on the agenda helps participants adhere to the times. Again, you can place this info in the margin so all attendees know the expected time you're granting to this issue.

Say you're discussing the launch of a company-wide environmental initiative. A solid agenda may look like the example in Figure 2-1.

Sample Meeting Agenda

I) Greeting and Introduction (5 minutes)

II) Overview of meeting (5 minutes)
   a. Length of meeting
   b. Roles of participants

III) Summary of what is to be covered and review of the goals (10 minutes)

IV) First Item (15 minutes)
   a. The problem or goal
   b. Possible solutions
   c. Who needs to be involved?
   d. What do they need to do to make that happen?
   e. When should it be accomplished?

V) Second Item (15 minutes)
   a. The problem or goal
   b. Possible solutions
   c. Who needs to be involved?
   d. What do they need to do to make that happen?
   e. When should it be accomplished?

VI) Closing/Q & A/Action Plans (10 minutes)

Figure 2-1:
A meeting agenda outline to follow (adapt time slots according to your needs).

Send out the agenda a few days before the meeting, giving invitees at least a day to review it. This allows them to request that you add to or change the agenda based on information you may not have had. It also gives you a heads-up if any items have sparked a bit of controversy — you're better prepared to head off problems if you're aware ahead of time.

If you're the invitee, ask whether you can have an agenda in advance so you can better prepare. Review the agenda in advance, and based on the topics and subtopics of the meeting, determine what relates directly to your job, customers, and department. If you're not leading the meeting, you still have responsibilities before, during, and after the meeting. If everyone comes prepared, the value of the meeting increases while the time you spend at the meeting decreases. Here are some general questions to review and even craft responses for:

✔ What are the most important agenda items as they relate to your job?

✔ Have you found specific solutions to the issues that'll be presented?

✔ What do you have to share to help the department, your company, and your co-workers for each agenda item?

✔ Are you or your department having problems that relate to the issues on the agenda?

✔ Can you take on projects that'll help out and advance your career? Which projects?

Scheduling the Meeting Time and Place

Smart scheduling can go a long way toward maximizing time effectiveness when setting up business meetings. Issues such as *where* and *when* to meet can determine whether a meeting takes a huge chomp or a small nibble out of your day.

How far in advance of the meeting you send out the invitations depends on the type of meeting that you're holding. If this is a once-per-year, all-company meeting, then six months in advance may be necessary. If this is a two-person check-up meeting, 24 hours to two days may be enough. If other people are presenting and you need to allow more lead time so they can prepare, you may need a week. As with all decisions, use your best judgment.

Finding a good time slot

For internal meetings, the best time to schedule them is before lunch or before the end of the day; with lunch or home on the horizon, people tend to be a bit more efficient and less likely to drag down a meeting with wandering discussions, lengthy oratories, and micro-debate. Be careful, though, *how far* before or after lunch you hold the meeting. Here's some advice:

- ✔ **Schedule meetings for midmorning or close to lunch, not first thing in the morning.** The most productive time for most people is early in the morning. That's when most people have the highest level of energy and focus. In general, most internal meetings in a company don't require that level of focus. Employees need that time to tackle the priorities for the day.

- ✔ **Schedule meetings midafternoon or near the end of the workday, not right after lunch.** Many people suffer from a little lethargy in the early afternoon after the midday meal. After the body is fed, the brain is more focused on digestion than discussion. Better your attendees spend this slow time answering e-mail or dealing with paperwork than dozing off in the middle of your meeting.

For meetings, don't make the mistake of doing a pitch-in — pitch-ins tend to drift into recipe discussions. You may also want to avoid having lunch brought in. Why? Somehow in these situations, the food seems to take over. There's always someone who didn't get what they requested and others' orders are mixed up.

If your guest list is small, you're meeting with an outside vendor or a client with a service problem, or you need to be off-site with other managers or employees of your company, you may find that a business lunch is best. Lunch meetings at a restaurant or coffee shop can be very productive. The meeting leader can introduce the topics, present reports, or provide updates while the rest of the attendees are attending to their pastrami and potato salad. No one's distracted by hunger, and the eating part is usually fairly short before the lunch stuff is cleared away and everyone gives the meeting undivided attention. Also, being off-site has its advantages in lowering the distraction factor — office emergencies tend not to find you as easily. One caveat of lunch meetings: The more relaxed environment may lead to a longer meeting, so be sure to weigh your priorities before scheduling.

Considering the location

If all the attendees are in one place, your choice about location is simple: Meet wherever you have the space and resources you need. Most companies have a few conference rooms of varying sizes, so meeting space is rarely a problem. Choose a location that's large enough for your group, and make sure any equipment you need is available.

You don't have to hold a meeting in a traditional location if other options are available. For instance, if you're meeting about problems on the production line, you may meet in the plant for a walk-through before sequestering yourselves in a quieter spot. Do choose such a location with care, though — the location you choose needs to foster a good environment for achieving the objectives of the meeting. Your goal is to schedule and run a meeting that's as efficient and short as possible. If the logistics get complicated, you defeat your purpose.

Running the Meeting Well on the Day Of

The secret to holding a productive meeting that eats up the least amount of time is half in the planning and half in the organization and facilitation. If you're the meeting initiator, it's up to you to grab the old bull by the horns and stay in control at the same time. If you're not the one in charge, help the meeting stay on track by only bringing up issues that align with the agenda. If an open dialogue time is part of the meeting, save your off-the-agenda problem for then. You may even go to the meeting initiator in advance to see whether your item can be placed on the agenda.

Being on time, prepared, and engaged is the best help that any attendee can give to the meeting leader. If the meeting has openings for discussion on issues, then chime in with something of value. The best advice? Be brief, bright, and concise. You win more points and respect if you're prepared and on point rather than rambling. If someone else uses the meeting to talk about nothing, help the leader guide that person back in the fold, perhaps by pointing out that time is short and that the meeting is running over. The more you can support the leader, the better the meeting will flow and the less time it'll take.

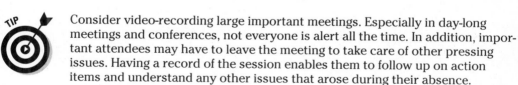

Consider video-recording large important meetings. Especially in day-long meetings and conferences, not everyone is alert all the time. In addition, important attendees may have to leave the meeting to take care of other pressing issues. Having a record of the session enables them to follow up on action items and understand any other issues that arose during their absence.

| Book III |
| Taking Charge of What You Can |

Arriving early for setup

Everyone's suffered through this scenario: The meeting host starts his presentation and the PowerPoint won't work. There's a problem with the laptop connection. The videoconferencing equipment is down. So you wait while someone runs to get the tech people to fix it. The minutes tick off and you're ticked off at the host for wasting your valuable time.

Here are some ways to make sure your meeting's ready to go:

- ✔ **Get to the meeting room early to test out all the equipment.** If something's not working, you still have time to get the tech people in to work out the bugs. You may be able to delegate this testing, but that depends on the competency level of the staff. Try to arrive between 60 to 90 minutes early so you can test all the audio-visual equipment personally.

  If the meeting is off-site, are people available to help you set up? If you've used the venue before, did the staff previously handle the logistics capably?

- ✔ **Be sure to have the needed charts, graphs, handouts, and any other material critical to your presentation.** Bring extra copies of handouts or other items that attendees may forget.

- ✔ **You may want to check the heating or air-conditioning system.** That way you can be sure participants won't be leaving the room for their sweaters or opening the door to get a breeze.

Launching the meeting

No matter the meeting's length or formality, the most important rule to launching your meeting off right is to start on time. Even if some of the folks haven't yet arrived. Even if your boss hasn't arrived. If your office environment is one in which start times aren't respected and attendees walk in 10 or 15 minutes late, resolve to do your part to reeducate your people.

How you launch the meeting has a lot to do with your success in maintaining control. If the meeting is with a customer, client, or prospect, you may want to allow for a little more small talk, but otherwise dispense with the chitchat before the meeting begins. Suggest that if people want to catch up, they should come early.

Begin by taking five minutes to establish the ground rules:

- ✔ Define the main purpose and objectives quickly.

- ✔ Make sure an agenda is visible to all attendees. When attendees can follow the flow, you have fewer distractions and interruptions.

- ✔ Tell the group what you want to have accomplished by the time you end the meeting at the appointed time.

- ✔ Explain whether attendees should hold questions until a certain point on the agenda.

✔ If you have a large number of attendees and are concerned that some members will hold the floor, advise the group of discussion guidelines. For example, you may want to explain that everyone will have an opportunity to speak, but each person can hold the floor for only three minutes at a time before someone else gets to speak.

✔ If your meeting is scheduled for longer than an hour, plan for a break and let the attendees know about it. If everyone knows they'll get a bio-break at a given point on the agenda, it'll help reduce walkouts that disrupt the meeting as people leave one by one. Be sure to tell them how long the break will be. (Five minutes? Ten minutes?) Then reconvene when you say you will.

✔ Ban cellphones and BlackBerries! It's bad enough when meeting attendees keep their cellphones on ring and then actually carry on hushed conversations as the meeting is conducted around them. It's even worse when they're busy checking messages on their BlackBerries and text-messaging — who knows whether it's business or personal?

As part of your meeting preamble, tell the folks to turn off their cellphones and PDAs or whatever electronic devices they have and put them away. You may even tell them that if a phone rings during the meeting, discussion will halt until the phone is turned off and the interruption is concluded. This usually shames people enough so that they're willing to adhere to the rules.

Dealing with habitual latecomers

If attendees typically arrive at meetings late, deal with the problem head-on: Talk with the culprits individually. Visit habitual latecomers before the meeting to make sure they arrive on time, or chat with them after the meeting and ask for their cooperation in arranging their schedule so they can arrive on time in the future. If that doesn't work, you may have to resort to stronger action:

✔ Reward early attendees. Give the on-time people single gifts of company logo wear, coffee cups, movie tickets, or coffee shop gift cards.

✔ Hand out the most desirable projects or assignments in the first five minutes, leaving the tougher or less desirable assignments to the tardy people.

✔ Create a late-meeting fund. Latecomers have to kick in some cash to the kitty. Make the late fee enough to cause a bit of pain but not a financial hardship. Asking people to pay up can be touchy, but if you have a relatively informal environment, you can establish that late funds go to the company's charity of choice or have the money go toward coffee and doughnuts for the department.

✔ When the appointed time for the meeting arrives, lock the door. This suggestion isn't for the fainthearted — you're sending the message loud and clear, preventing latecomers from slipping in under the radar. Latecomers either have to knock and ask to be let in or must return to their offices and miss the meeting.

Keeping the meeting moving

As for smooth-running meetings, the agenda is your best friend. There's a reason you come up with one: to make sure you accomplish what you set out to do when you scheduled the meeting. Sticking to the time parameters also establishes you as a person of your word and sets a positive precedent for future meetings, so follow the plan.

Your skill as a facilitator can also influence the movement of a meeting. Here are some tips for staying on track:

- ✓ **Get input from participants as you go along.** Your ability to ask questions and involve each participant keeps everyone engaged and the momentum going forward. You shouldn't have to backtrack, because attendees contribute to the conversation before you move on to the next major topic.

- ✓ **Don't adjust the time given to each topic as you work through the agenda.** This virtually guarantees that you'll get behind and either meet longer than scheduled or simply not get through all the items. And you know what that means: another meeting!

If something doesn't look like it'll be resolved in time, you may want to create a smaller group to meet and discuss solutions so you can come back to the larger group at an appointed time. Put that separate meeting on your action list and set it up at the end of the current meeting.

- ✓ **Remind attendees of the agenda.** The agenda serves as your enforcer when someone gets off-track or goes on a little too long. For instance, you can say something like the following:

  - "Joe, you make some good points, but I promised we'd end the meeting at 2 p.m., and if we're going to get everything done, we have to stick to the agenda. I'll make a note of your concerns to follow up after the meeting."

  - "That's an important point — can we add it to the end of the agenda and discuss it if we have time left?"

- ✓ **Never rehash, backtrack, or review to catch up late arrivals.** Set the standard that they need to bring themselves up-to-speed after the conclusion of the meeting. Rehashing the past ten minutes because of someone else's lack of regard is a monumental waste of everyone's time.

- ✓ **Give attendees a ten-minute warning before the end of the meeting.** Just as the last two minutes are critical in a football game, the last ten minutes of a meeting carry that level of importance. If attendees have been out of the game mentally, you can now grab their attention. If they've been with you the whole time, they're alerted that it's time to wrap up and focus on the conclusion.

Assigning action items

As the meeting leader, your job is to make sure that action items are agreed upon and assigned with specific instructions. After you identify an action item, record it and either assign it then and there or wait until the discussion has concluded and assign all the action items at once. Be sure to clarify the following:

✔ Who's responsible for seeing that the action is fulfilled

✔ What exactly needs to be done

✔ When the action item must be started and completed

✔ Where the chokepoints of the project are

✔ What the interim timelines are for each phase of the project

✔ Who is to be notified of progress and at what points of the process

✔ What the expected outcome is

Failing to assign action items can turn a meeting from a productive collaboration into a colossal waste of time. Especially when the situation is time-sensitive, you can put a project at great risk if no one puts the action items into action. Don't neglect this critical step in the meeting process. Without it, you may find yourself in yet another meeting revisiting the same issue — and discovering that because of delay, the project is at risk.

If you want career advancement and an increase in income, make sure that as a meeting participant, you're stepping up to volunteer for action items that benefit the company and group. The people who are engaged are the people who earn more income.

Book III

Taking Charge of What You Can

Summarizing and concluding the meeting

Work in time at the end of the agenda — at least five minutes — to review the meeting. Your job as the meeting leader is to make sure that all attendees understand and accept the outcome and follow-up action from the meeting. In your summation, be sure to touch on these points:

✔ Key highlights of presentations and discussions

✔ All action items and to whom they're assigned

✔ Unresolved issues and how they'll be addressed

✔ Any follow-up activity, including setting the next meeting

Take this opportunity to ask whether people have questions, concerns, or issues they feel are unresolved. Your primary objective is to make sure everyone understands what's been decided upon and to ensure that anyone with action items on his or her plate is aware and has taken ownership of that responsibility.

If the questions are very specific and don't pertain to the whole group, or if they're more complex and require more time than is left in the meeting, simply make note of any comments and commit to addressing them after the meeting — this isn't the time for continued or protracted discussion. You don't want to waste the group's time if you need a lengthy discussion with one person. A quick judgment at this stage allows you to avoid boring others and wasting their time.

Don't extend the meeting, even if you didn't complete everything you'd hoped. Agree to set another meeting, or if a couple of people can address and resolve the other agenda items, suggest that those folks stay after to tie things up.

Following Up for Maximum Productivity

Most people forget a large chunk of what happened at a meeting. They leave the meeting and walk back into their office with tasks that have piled up in the last hour. Their minds move to those even before you've left the meeting room. That's why you should usually plan to spend at least an hour following up on your meeting to ensure an effective outcome. Follow-ups should be twofold: Communicate the results of the meeting and periodically review the status of action items.

Distributing meeting notes

Within 24 hours, distribute the meeting notes to all attendees. Send out an e-mail that summarizes the same points you made at the end of the meeting regarding decisions you agreed to and responsibility for action. By putting your understanding in writing — and requesting confirmation from the recipients — you further clarify what happens next. This way, no one can drop the ball and later on claim that that's not the way he or she understood it. Be sure to give notes to any other employees who weren't invited but may be affected or involved in the action items.

Checking in periodically regarding action items

Keep an eye on the list of action items covered in the meeting and check in with each associated individual regularly to see how he or she is progressing. Also make sure that you continue to remind that person of the timeline of completion that was arranged at the meeting. Then make sure that you hold him or her to the timeline.

No, you're not responsible if an employee doesn't follow through. And no, it shouldn't be your job to hover over all the meeting attendees who were assigned action items. But in terms of protecting the time you've invested in the project, it's well worth a few minutes to shoot off a reminder or a quick status request by e-mail.

To help you stay on track with the check-ins, keep the notes visible so you're reminded of them throughout the day. Or add notes to your day-planner to remind you to check on an employee's status. For example, if one attendee was asked to send out an announcement in the company newsletter by Friday, list on your to-do notes to check in with the individual on Wednesday.

Preparing for Virtual Meetings: Phone-, Web-, and Videoconferences

As business is increasingly conducted on a global basis, face-to-face meetings are rapidly becoming the exception rather than the rule. And that's a good thing. It reduces the expense and time of travel, not to mention the heavy carbon footprint on the environment.

Although nothing can replicate a face-to-face encounter, video, telephone, and Internet conferencing technology continue to improve so that a meeting with colleagues scattered around the world is literally as easy as pressing a button.

Your meetings can run off schedule or be ineffective if you aren't focused on a few key rules. The following sections offer specific strategies you can use to keep these meetings productive and within the given timeframe.

Keep it short and sweet

Too many meeting planners and meeting leaders try to do too much with today's technology. Unless you invest a small fortune to achieve true video-conferencing, you lack a visual component with much of the technology. And when you can't see the other attendees, you need to be more careful of the length of your meetings.

When meeting attendees aren't accountable to a visual check-in, the value of a phone- or Webconferencing meeting starts to dramatically reduce after an hour. As the meeting leader in this setting, you don't get the visual feedback you do with a face-to-face meeting. It's harder to know if the participants are bored, engaged, understanding your point, or even physically present! Unlike a live meeting, they could be focused on something else during the meeting, like their PDA, computer, e-mails, or another task.

Create interactivity at least every 10–15 minutes

These technologies become less effective when the meeting leader overuses "lecture mode." You won't see the eyeballs rolling back in the participants' heads as they start thinking, "Here he goes again." Protect yourself by designing in pauses for interactivity between the participants. By designing in advance, you improve your odds the meeting will be interactive and engaging.

Be sure to draw out people who are normally in the background as well. A few people are always willing to actively participate. You don't have to worry about these people; it's the quiet ones that may be checking out during the meeting.

Be careful about how you craft your questions to create interactivity. Using a yes or no question, like the ambiguous "Does anyone have any questions about _____?" is close to worthless. Yes or no questions don't lead to interactivity, and few people will raise their hand or voice to say "No, I'm stupid. I didn't get what you just spent the last 30 minutes explaining." Questions that are open-ended, like the following, with who, what, where, how, and why, engage the participants in dialogue:

- ✔ "What additional ideas on this project do you want to share?"
- ✔ "I don't have all the answers; who else has potential solutions?"
- ✔ "How do we decrease costs another 10 percent?"
- ✔ "Why do you feel that sales are down 15 percent?"

Know (and target) thy audience

The participants or audience will dictate the meeting style, agenda, and depth of information you can deliver in this technology medium. Frequently, this technology is used to deliver highly technical or in-depth information to a nontechnical group — a recipe for disaster.

For example, if you're mixing technical staff, administrative staff, and sales staff in one meeting on a problem you're having with your widgets in manufacturing, you're asking for an ineffective meeting. The technical staff can talk all day about the problems, issues, and potential solutions. The sales staff just wants a great widget to sell to their customers. The administration staff just wants fewer problems to deal with after the sale.

You're better off having three separate meetings to deliver the information and get feedback. Don't create oil-and-water meetings due to the broadness of your audience.

Choosing a teleconferencing company

A number of teleconferencing companies, such as Sparks Communications and Excel Conferencing, facilitate global exchanges. Services vary from company to company in quality, security, recording, and a host of other features. When choosing a teleconferencing service, think about features such as these:

✔ Digital recording, so you can capture the conversation and share it with others; some providers offer that service for a nominal fee

✔ Multiple codes, so you can conduct more than one conference at a time using a universally known company-wide phone number

✔ A security feature to announce all attendees before they're placed in conference, keeping out uninvited guests and preventing eavesdropping on proprietary calls

Another way to expand your capabilities is with an online conference service such as GoToMeeting (www.gotomeeting.com) or WebEx (webex.com). These services enable you to operate a PowerPoint presentation from a centralized location and control a slide show on hundreds of computers around the world. Many of these services offer Voice over Internet Protocol (VoIP) connections so the audio can be delivered over your computer connection. You can even combine these Web-based tools with your business conference line to control who can be heard and allow only the meeting leader to see or hear questions and comments from participants.

Book III

Taking Charge of What You Can

Chapter 3

The Fine Art of Delegating

The power of getting things done comes not from your efforts alone (sorry to burst your bubble) but from the sum of all the efforts of your work group. If you're responsible for only a few employees, with extraordinary effort, you perhaps can do the work of your entire group if you so desired (if you want to be a complete stranger to your friends and family). However, when you're responsible for a much larger organization, you simply can't be an effective manager by trying to do your entire group's work.

Managers assign the responsibility for completing tasks through *delegation*. But as we explain in this chapter, simply assigning tasks and then walking away is not enough. For delegation to be effective, managers must also give authority to their employees and ensure that employees have the resources necessary to complete tasks effectively. Finally, managers who delegate like experts can monitor the progress of their employees toward meeting their assigned goals.

No matter what your position is in your organization — manager, supervisor, frontline employee, or part-time help — you can benefit from the power of delegation. Although the sections that follow primarily refer to managers doing the delegating, the techniques addressed also apply — and are just as effective — to nonmanagement employees. In addition, the last section in this chapter addresses issues specifically relevant to delegating when you're not the boss or have no formal authority over those whose help you're seeking.

Delegating: A Key to Improved Efficiency and Effectiveness

If you're a manager, you're required to develop skills in many areas. Not only do you need good technical, analytical, and organizational skills, but most important, you also must have good people skills. Of all the people skills, the one that can make the greatest difference in your effectiveness is the ability to delegate well. Delegating is a manager's number one management tool, and the inability to delegate well is the leading cause of management failure.

Yet people have such a hard time delegating. Why? A variety of reasons exist:

- ✔ You're too busy and just don't have enough time to figure out who should do what.

- ✔ You don't trust others (your employees or your peers) to complete their assignments correctly or on time.

- ✔ You don't know how to delegate effectively.

Or perhaps you're still not convinced that you need to delegate at all. If you're a member of this large group of reluctant delegators *(Hey! You there in the back! Yeah, you know who you are!),* then the following list is why you must let go of your preconceptions and inhibitions and start delegating today:

- ✔ **Your success as a manager depends on it!** Managers who can successfully manage team members — each of whom has specific responsibilities for a different aspect of the team's performance — prove that they're ready for bigger and better challenges. Bigger and better challenges are often accompanied by bigger and better titles and paychecks and the other niceties of business life, such as offices with windows and computers that actually work on occasion.

- ✔ **You can't do it all.** No matter how great a manager you are, carrying the entire burden of achieving your organization's goals by yourself isn't in your interest unless you want to work yourself into an early grave. Besides, wouldn't it be nice to see what life is like outside the four walls of your office?

- ✔ **Your job is to concentrate your efforts on the things that you can do and your staff can't.** They pay you the big bucks to be a manager — not a super programmer, accounting clerk, or customer service representative. Do your job, and let your employees do theirs.

- ✔ **Delegation gets workers in the organization more involved.** When you give responsibility and authority to employees to carry out tasks — whether individually or in teams — they respond by becoming more involved in the day-to-day operations of the organization. Instead of being drones with no responsibility or authority, they're vital to the success of the work unit and the entire organization. And if your employees succeed, you succeed, too!

✔ **Delegation gives you the chance to develop your employees.** If you make all the decisions and come up with all the ideas, your employees never learn how to take initiative and be responsible for seeing tasks through to successful completion. And if they don't learn, guess who's going to get stuck doing everything forever? (*Hint:* Take a look in the mirror.) In addition, keep in mind that learning and development opportunities are increasingly reported as one of the top motivators by today's employees.

As a manager, you're ultimately responsible for all your department's responsibilities. However, for most managers, personally executing all the tasks necessary for your department to fulfill its responsibilities and for you to achieve your organizational goals is neither practical nor desirable. Say, for example, that you're the manager of the accounting department for a software development firm. When the firm had only five employees and sales of $500,000 a year, it was no problem for you to personally bill all your customers, cut checks to vendors, run payroll, and take care of the company's taxes every April. However, now that employment has grown to 150 employees and sales are at $50 million a year, you can't even pretend to do it all — you don't have enough hours in the day. Now you have specialized employees who take care of accounts payable, accounts receivable, and payroll, and you have farmed out the income tax work to a CPA.

Each employee that you've assigned to a specific work function has specialized knowledge and skills in his or her area of expertise. Sure, you could personally generate payroll if you had to, but if you've hired someone to do that job, why would you want to? And, by the way, your payroll clerk is probably a lot better and quicker at it than you are.

On the other hand, you're uniquely qualified to perform numerous responsibilities in your organization. These responsibilities may include developing and monitoring your operations budget, conducting performance appraisals, helping to plan the overall direction of your company's acquisitions, and selecting the flavor of the coffee that your department stocks. You can find out more about your managerial responsibilities in the later section "Reviewing What to Delegate and What to Do Yourself."

Explaining the Myths about Delegation

Admit it: You rationalize to yourself why you can't delegate work to your employees. Unfortunately, the reasons you tell yourself you can't delegate are guaranteed to get in the way of your ability to be an effective manager. Do any of the following myths sound familiar to you?

Book III

Taking Charge of What You Can

Myth: You can't trust your employees to be responsible

If you can't trust your employees, whom can you trust? Assume that you're responsible for hiring at least a portion of your staff. Now, forgetting for the moment the ones who you didn't personally hire, you likely went through quite an involved process to recruit your employees. Remember the mountain of résumés that you had to sift through and then divide into winners, potential winners, and losers? After hours of sorting and then hours of interviews, you selected the best candidates — the ones with the best skills, qualifications, and experience for the job.

You selected your employees because you thought that they were talented people deserving of your trust. Now your job is to give them your trust without strings attached.

You usually reap what you sow. Your staff members are ready, willing, and able to be responsible employees; you just have to give them a chance. Sure, not every employee is going to be able to handle every task that you assign. If that's the case, find out why. Does he need more training? More time? More practice? Maybe you need to find a task that is better suited to his experience or disposition. Or perhaps you simply hired the wrong person for the job. If that's the case, face up to the fact and fire or reassign the employee before you lose even more time and money. To get responsible employees, you have to give responsibility.

Myth: When you delegate, you lose control of a task and its outcome

If you delegate correctly, you don't lose control of the task or its outcome. What you lose control of is the way that the outcome is reached. Picture a map of the world. How many different ways can a person get from San Francisco to Paris? One? One million? Some ways are quicker than others. Some are more scenic, and others require a substantial resource commitment. Do the differences in these ways make any of them inherently wrong? No.

In business, you have countless ways to get a task done. Even for tasks that are spelled out in highly defined steps or have previously been done a certain way, you can always leave room for new ways to make a process better. Why should your way be the only way to get the task done? "Because I'm the boss!" Sorry, wrong answer. Your job is to describe to your employees the outcomes that you want and then to let them decide how to accomplish the tasks. Of course, you need to be available to coach and counsel them so that they can learn from your past experience if they want, but you need to let go of controlling the how and instead focus on the what and the when.

Myth: You're the only one who has all the answers

If you think that you alone have all the answers, have you got a thing or two to learn! As talented as you may be, unless you're the company's only employee, you can't possibly have the only answer to every question in your organization.

No one in the organization can know everything, yet a certain group of people knows enough to deal with an amazing array of situations every day. The group may talk to your customers, your suppliers, and each other — day in and day out. Some members of the group have been working for the company far longer than you, and many of them will be there long after you're gone. Who are these people? They are your employees.

Your employees are a wealth of experience and knowledge about your business contacts and the intimate, day-to-day workings of the organization. They are often closer to the customers and problems of the company than you are. To ignore their suggestions and advice is not only disrespectful but also shortsighted and foolish. Don't ignore this resource. You're already paying for it — whether you use it or not!

Myth: You can do the work faster by yourself

You may think that you're completing tasks faster when you do them than when you assign them to others, but this belief is merely an illusion. Yes, discussing and assigning a task to one of your employees may require slightly more time when you first delegate that task, but if you delegate well, the second through nth times take substantially less time. Not only does doing the task yourself actually cost you more time, but it also robs your employees of a golden opportunity to develop their work skills.

When you do the task yourself instead of delegating it, you're forever doomed to doing the task — again and again and again. When you teach someone else to do the task and then assign her responsibility for completing it, you may never have to do it again. Not only that, but your employee may come to do it faster than you can. Who knows, she may even improve the way that you've always done it.

Myth: Delegation dilutes your authority

Assigning a task to an employee instead of doing it yourself actually extends your authority. You're only one person, and you can do only so much. Imagine all 10, 20, or 100 members of your team working toward your common goals. You still set the goals and the timetables for reaching them, but each employee chooses his own way of getting there.

Do you have less authority because you delegate a task and transfer authority to an employee to carry out the task? No. What do you lose in this transaction? Nothing. Your authority is extended, not diminished. The more authority you give to employees, the more authority your entire work unit has, and the better able your employees are to do the jobs you hired them to do.

 As you grant others authority, you gain an efficient and effective workforce — employees who are truly empowered, engaged in their jobs, and working as team players — and the ability to concentrate on the issues that deserve your undivided attention.

Myth: The company recognizes your employees for doing a good job and not you

One of the biggest difficulties in the transition from being a doer to being a manager of doers is letting go of the belief that your good work will be overlooked. When you're a doer, you're rewarded for writing a great report, developing an incredible market analysis, or programming an amazing piece of computer code. When you're a manager, the focus of your job shifts from your performance in completing individual tasks to your performance in reaching an overall organizational or project goal through the efforts of others. Although you may have been the best darn marketing analyst in the world, suddenly, that talent doesn't matter anymore. Now you're expected to develop and lead the best darn team of marketing analysts in the world. The skills required are quite different, and your success is a result of the indirect efforts of others and your behind-the-scenes support.

 Wise managers know that when their employees shine, they shine, too. The more you delegate, the more opportunities you give your employees to shine. Give your workers the opportunity to do important work and to do it well. And when they do well, make sure that you tell everyone about it. Give your employees credit for their successes publicly and often, and they will be more likely to want to do a good job for you on future assignments. Don't forget: When you're a manager, you're being primarily measured on your team's performance — not so much what you're personally able to accomplish.

Myth: Delegation decreases your flexibility

When you do everything yourself, you have complete control over the progress and completion of tasks, right? Wrong! How can you when you're balancing multiple priorities at the same time and dealing with the inevitable crisis of the day? Being flexible is pretty tough when you're doing everything yourself. Concentrating on more than one task at a time is impossible. While you're concentrating on that one task, you put all your other tasks on hold. You can't be flexible when you're bogged down in unnecessary work.

The more people you delegate to, the more flexible you can be. As your employees take care of the day-to-day tasks necessary to keep your business running, you're free to deal with those surprise problems and opportunities that always seem to pop up at the last minute.

Myth: Your employees are too busy

What exactly are your employees doing that they don't have the time to learn something new — something that can make your job easier and boost the performance of your work unit at the same time?

Think about yourself for a moment. What about your job makes you want to return day after day? For most, it's not the paycheck or the lunch truck. It's the satisfaction you feel when you take on a new challenge, meet it, and succeed.

Now consider your employees — their job satisfaction is no different from yours. They want to test themselves against new challenges and succeed, too. But how can they if you don't delegate new tasks to them? Too many managers have lost good employees because they failed to meet employees' needs to stretch and to grow in their jobs. And too many employees have become mindless drones because their managers refuse to encourage their creativity and natural yearning to learn. Don't learn this lesson the hard way!

Myth: Your workers don't see the big picture

Well, actually, your workers really may not see the big picture, but only because you keep them from doing so. How can your employees see it if you don't share it with them? Your employees are often specialists in their jobs or fields of expertise. They naturally develop severe cases of tunnel vision as they pursue the answers to their assignments or process their routine transactions. Your job is to provide your employees with a vision of where you

Book III

Taking Charge of What You Can

want to go and the priorities of what needs to be achieved and then allow them to find the best way to attain those goals.

 Unfortunately, many managers withhold vital information from their employees — information that can make them much more effective in their jobs — in hopes that by doing so, they can maintain a close rein on their behavior and stay in control. By keeping their employees in the dark, these managers don't create the better outcomes that they hope for. Instead, they cripple their organization and their employees' ability to learn, grow, and become a real part of the organization.

Taking the Six Steps to Delegate

Delegation doesn't just happen. Just like any other task that you perform as a manager, you have to work at it. The six steps to effective delegation are the following:

1. **Communicate the task.**

   Describe exactly what you want done, when you want it done, and what end results you expect. Ask for any questions.

2. **Furnish context for the task.**

   Explain why the task needs to be done, its importance in the overall scheme of things, and possible complications that may arise during its performance.

3. **Determine standards.**

   Agree on the standards that you plan to use to measure the success of a task's completion. Make these standards realistic and attainable.

4. **Grant authority.**

   You must grant employees the authority necessary to complete the task without constant roadblocks or standoffs with other employees.

5. **Provide support.**

   Determine the resources necessary for your employee to complete the task and then provide them. Successfully completing a task may require money, training, or the ability to check with you about progress or obstacles as they arise.

6. **Get commitment.**

   Make sure that your employee has accepted the assignment. Confirm your expectations, your employee's understanding of the task, and her commitment to completing it.

Clearly, delegation benefits both workers and managers alike when you do it correctly. So why aren't you delegating more work to your employees? It's not too late to start!

Delegation can be scary, at least at first. When you delegate, you're putting your trust in another individual. If that individual fails, then you're ultimately responsible — regardless of whom you give the task to. But like anything else, the more you do it, the less scary it gets. Here are some pointers to make delegating a success:

- ✔ **Begin with simple tasks that don't substantially impact the firm if they aren't completed on time or within budget.** As your employees gain confidence and experience, delegate higher-level tasks. You probably aren't, for example, going to delegate a huge task to someone who has been on the job for only a few months.

- ✔ **Make sure you understand each of your employees' strengths and weaknesses.** Carefully assess the level of your employees' expertise, and assign tasks that meet or slightly exceed that level.

- ✔ **Set schedules for completion and then monitor your employees' performance against them.** This will allow you to avert disaster if it becomes clear that the employee's performance is inadequate. And if he's ahead of schedule, it may indicate that he isn't being challenged enough or is bored.

After you get the hang of it, you find that you really have nothing to be afraid of when you delegate.

Reviewing What to Delegate and What to Do Yourself

Theoretically, you can delegate anything to your employees. Of course, if you delegate all your duties, then why is your company bothering to pay you? Clearly, you have tasks that should be delegated to your employees and tasks that you should retain for yourself.

Tasks to always delegate

Certain tasks naturally lend themselves to being delegated. As a manager, you can take every possible opportunity to delegate the following kinds of work to your employees.

Book III

Taking Charge of What You Can

Detail work

As a manager, you have no greater time-waster than getting caught up in details — you know, tasks such as double-checking pages, troubleshooting a block of computer code, or personally auditing your employees' timesheets. You can no doubt run circles around those detailed technical tasks that have to be done by someone in your department. But your higher-ups selected you to be a manager, not a specialist.

Now that you're a manager, you're being paid to orchestrate the workings of an entire team of workers toward a common goal — not just to perform an individual task. Leave the detail to your employees, but hold them accountable for the results. Concentrate your efforts on tasks that have the greatest payoff and that allow you to most effectively leverage the work of all your employees.

Information gathering

Browsing the Web for information about your competitors, spending hours poring over issues of *Fortune* magazine, or moving into your local library's reference stacks for weeks on end isn't an effective use of your time. Despite that fact, many managers get sucked into the trap. Not only is reading through newspapers, reports, books, magazines, and the like fun, but it also provides managers with an easy way to postpone their more difficult tasks. You're being paid to look at the big picture — to gather a variety of inputs and make sense of them. You can work so much more efficiently when someone else gathers needed information, which frees you to take the time you need to analyze the input and to devise solutions to your problems.

Repetitive assignments

What a great way to get routine tasks done: Assign them to your employees. Many of the jobs in your organization occur again and again; drafting your weekly production report, reviewing your biweekly report of expenditures versus budget, and approving your monthly phone bill are just a few examples. Your time is much too important to waste on routine tasks that you mastered years ago.

If you find yourself involved in repetitive assignments, first take a close look at their particulars. How often do the assignments recur? Can you anticipate the assignments in sufficient time to allow an employee to be successful in completing them? What do you have to do to train your employees in completing the tasks? After you figure all this out, develop a schedule and make assignments to your employees.

Surrogate roles

Do you feel that you have to be everywhere all the time? Not only can't you be everywhere all the time, but you *shouldn't* be everywhere all the time. Every day, your employees have numerous opportunities to fill in for you. Presentations, conference calls, client visits, and meetings are just a few examples. In some cases, such as in budget presentations to top management, you may be required to attend. However, in many other cases, whether you attend personally or send someone to take your place may not really matter.

The next time someone calls a meeting and requests your attendance, send one of your employees to attend in your place. You gain an extra hour or two in your schedule, and your employee can present you with only the important outcomes of the meeting. This surrogate arrangement benefits you in several different ways. You have the opportunity to spend the time you need on your more important tasks, and your employee has the opportunity to take on some new responsibilities. Not only that, but your employee may discover something new in the process.

Future duties

As a manager, you can always be on the lookout for opportunities to train your staff in their future job responsibilities. For example, one of your key duties may be to develop your department's annual budget. By allowing one or more of your employees to assist you — perhaps in gathering basic market or research data — you can give your employees a taste of what goes into putting together a budget.

Don't fall into the trap of believing that the only way to train your employees is to sign them up for an expensive class taught by someone with a slick color brochure who knows nothing about your business. Opportunities to train your employees abound within your own business. An estimated 90 percent of all development occurs on the job. This training is free, and by assigning your employees to progressively more important tasks, you build their self-confidence and help to pave their way to progress in the organization.

Responsibilities to avoid delegating

Some tasks are part and parcel of the job of being a manager. By delegating the following work, you fail to perform your basic management duties.

Long-term vision and goals

As a manager, you're in a unique position. Your position at the top provides you with a unique perspective on the organization's needs — the higher up you are in an organization, the broader your perspective. One of the key functions of management is vision. Although employees at any level of a company can help provide you with input and make suggestions that help to shape your perspectives, developing an organization's long-term vision and goals is up to you. Simply, every employee can't decide which direction the organization should move. An organization is much more effective when everyone moves together in the same direction.

Book III

Taking Charge of What You Can

Positive performance feedback

Rewarding and recognizing employees when they do good work is an important job for every manager. If this task is delegated to lower-level employees, however, the workers who receive it won't value the recognition as much as if it came from their manager. The impact of the recognition is therefore significantly lessened (assuming it gets done at all!).

Performance appraisals, discipline, and counseling

In the modern workplace, a strong relationship between manager and employee is often hard to come by. Most managers are probably lucky to get off a quick "good morning" or "good night" between the hustle and bustle of a typical workday. Given everyone's hectic schedules, you may have times when you don't talk to one or more of your employees for days at a time.

However, sometimes you absolutely have to set time aside for your employees. When you discipline and counsel your employees, you're giving them the kind of input that only you can provide. You set the goals for your employees, and you set the standards by which you measure their progress. Inevitably, you decide whether your employees have reached the marks you've set or whether they have fallen short. You can't delegate away this task effectively — everyone loses as a result.

Politically sensitive situations

Some situations are too politically sensitive to assign to your employees. Say, for example, that you're in charge of auditing travel expenses for your organization. The results of your review show that a member of the corporation's executive team made several personal trips on company funds. Do you assign the responsibility for reporting this explosive situation to a worker? "Gee, Susan, I was hoping that you could present this information to the board — I don't think I want to be around when the news hits." No!

Politically sensitive situations demand your utmost attention and expertise, and placing your employee in the middle of the line of fire in this potentially explosive situation is unfair. Being a manager may be tough sometimes, but you're paid to make the difficult decisions and to take the political heat that your work generates.

Personal assignments

Occasionally, your boss assigns a specific task to you with the intention that you personally perform it. She may have very good reasons for doing so: You may have a unique perspective that no one else in your organization has, or you may have a unique skill that needs to be brought to bear to complete the assignment quickly and accurately. Whatever the situation, if a task is assigned to you with the expectation that you and only you carry it out, then you can't delegate it to your staff. You may decide to involve your staff in gathering input, but you must retain the ultimate responsibility for the final execution of the task.

Stepping in when delegation goes wrong

Sometimes delegation goes wrong — way wrong. How can you identify the danger signs before it's too late, and what can you do to save the day? You can monitor the performance of your workers in several ways:

✔ **Personal follow-up:** Supplement your formal tracking system with an informal system of visiting your workers and checking their progress on a regular basis.

✔ **Sampling:** Take periodic samples of your employees' work and check to make sure that the work meets the standards you agreed to.

✔ **Progress reports:** Regular progress reporting from employees to you can give you advance notice of problems and successes.

✔ **A formalized tracking system:** Use a formal system to track assignments and due dates. The system can be manual (think: big chart pinned to your wall) or computerized.

If you discover that your employees are in trouble, you have several options for getting everything back on track:

✔ **Increased monitoring:** Spend more time monitoring employees who are in trouble, keeping closer track of their performance.

✔ **Counseling:** Discuss the problems with your employees and agree on a plan to correct them.

✔ **Rescinding authority:** If problems continue despite your efforts to resolve them through counseling, you can rescind your employees' authority to complete the tasks independently. (They still work on the task, but under your close guidance and authority.)

✔ **Reassigning activities:** The ultimate solution when delegation goes wrong. If your employees can't do their assigned tasks, give the tasks to workers who are better suited to perform them successfully.

Confidential or sensitive circumstances

As a manager, you're likely privy to information, such as wage and salary figures, proprietary data, and personnel assessments, that your staff isn't. Release of this information to the wrong individuals can be damaging to an organization. Salary information should be kept confidential, for example. Similarly, if your competitors get their hands on some secret process that your company has spent countless hours and money to develop, the impact on your organization and employees can be devastating. Unless your staff has a compelling need to know, you should retain assignments involving these types of information yourself.

Checking Up Instead of Checking Out

Now delegation gets tough. Assume that you've already worked through the initial hurdles of delegation — you assigned a task to your employee — and you're anxiously waiting to see how he performs. You defined the scope of the task and gave your employee the adequate training and resources to get it done. Not only that, but also you told him what results you expect and exactly when you expect to see them. What do you do next?

Here's one option: An hour or two after you make the assignment, you check on its progress. In a couple more hours, you check again. As the deadline rapidly approaches, you increase the frequency of your checking until finally, your employee spends more time answering your questions about the progress he has made than he spends actually completing the task. Not only that, but every time you press him for details about his progress, he gets a little more distracted from his task and a little more frustrated with your seeming lack of confidence in his abilities. When the appointed hour arrives, he submits the result on time, but the report is inaccurate and incomplete.

Here's another option: After you make the assignment to your employee, you do nothing. Instead of checking on your employee's progress and offering your support, you assign the task and move on to other concerns. When the appointed hour arrives, you're surprised to discover that the task is not completed. When you ask your employee why he didn't meet the goal that you had mutually agreed upon, he tells you that he had trouble obtaining some information and, rather than bother you with this problem, he decided to try to construct it for himself. Unfortunately, this slight diversion required an additional two days of research before he found the correct set of numbers.

Clearly, neither extreme is a productive way to monitor the delegation process. However, in between lies the answer to how to approach this delicate but essential task. Depending on the situation, this may mean daily or weekly progress updates from your employee.

Each person in an organization is unique. One style of monitoring may work with one person but not work with another. New or inexperienced employees naturally require more attention and hand-holding than employees who are seasoned at their jobs — whether they realize it or not. Veteran employees don't need the kind of day-to-day attention that less-experienced employees need. In fact, they may resent your attempts to closely manage the way in which they carry out their duties.

Effective monitoring of delegation requires the following:

- ✔ **Tailor your approach to the employee.** If your employee performs her job with minimal supervision on your part, then establish a system of monitoring with only a few, critical checkpoints along the way. If your employee needs more attention, create a system (formally, in writing, or informally, verbally) that incorporates several checkpoints along the way to goal completion.

- ✔ **Diligently use a written or computer-based system for tracking the tasks that you assign to your employees.** Use a daily planner, PDA, or project management software program to keep track of the what, who, and when of task assignments. Making a commitment to get organized is important. Do it!

✔ **Keep the lines of communication open.** Make sure that your employees know that you want them to let you know if they can't surmount a problem. This, of course, means making time for your employees when they come by to ask you for help. Find out whether they need more training or better resources. Finding out too early — when you can still do something about it — is better than finding out too late.

✔ **Follow through on the agreements that you make with your employees.** If a report is late, then hold your employees accountable. Despite the temptation to let these failures slip ("Gee, he's had a rough time at home lately"), ignoring them does both you and your employees a disservice. Make sure that your employees understand the importance of taking personal responsibility for their work and that the ability of your group to achieve its goals depends on their meeting commitments. Be compassionate if your employee has indeed gone through a tough personal challenge (mother died, spouse diagnosed with cancer, and so on) — you may need to assign someone else to cover his duties for a short period of time. If, however, an employee consistently misses goals and shows no hope of improvement, then perhaps he is in the wrong job.

✔ **Reward performance that meets or exceeds your expectations, and counsel performance that falls below your expectations.** If you don't let your employees know when they fail to meet your expectations, then they may continue to fail to meet your expectations. Do your employees, your organization, and yourself a big favor and bring attention to both the good things and the bad things that your employees do. Remember the old saying (which happens to be an accurate one), *praise in public and criticize in private.*

Delegating When You're Not the Boss

As we mention at the beginning of this chapter, the delegation techniques described in the preceding sections apply both to management and nonmanagement employees. While you can't really share responsibility for completion of a task or duty that's been assigned to you — you always remain responsible for that — you can share the burden.

Of course, there are a few things to consider if you're not the boss:

✔ **You're not the boss.** Although managers are usually granted the authority to delegate work to others — requiring them to follow orders by way of their positional power in the organizational hierarchy — that is unlikely to be the case if you're a regular employee. As a result, you need to find other ways to convince your co-workers to accept delegation from you. One of the best ways of doing this is to show the other parties what's in it for them — specifically, how they will benefit.

✔ **Get help if you need it.** You may find yourself over your head in certain situations. If you encounter a problem that could have a significant and negative impact on your work unit or company, then don't hesitate to notify your manager and ask for help. Allowing a problem to spin out of control is not the right way to delegate.

✔ **You may need to get permission first.** If you want to delegate tasks to co-workers — especially co-workers in other departments or organizational units — you may first need to get the permission of your manager and the managers of the other employees' departments. Ignore this important step and you may wind up in hot water.

Delegation is a powerful thing. Anyone can do it, no matter what your place in the organization. Give it a try and see how it works for you.

Book IV

Get to the @#% Point! Communicating Effectively

The 5th Wave

By Rich Tennant

"Get ready, I think they're starting to drift."

In this book . . .

As you probably know, success in your work comes from more than just having expertise in your field or discipline. It also comes from being able to express that expertise so that others can understand it, hearing what others need so you apply that expertise to serve them, and working with others in ways that build, not damage, relationships — especially when you're in a leadership role.

For many people, the biggest challenges they face in their jobs deal with communicating with others. From co-workers and direct reports to your boss and other members of management, from customers to vendors, you have to communicate with people to get your job done. This book deals with every angle of effective communication, whether speaking or hearing, writing or presenting.

Chapter 1

Telling It Like It Is: The Fundamentals of Communication

*W*ho needs to communicate effectively with others to be successful at work? In today's often fast-paced and ever-changing world of work, the far more enlightened question is: Who doesn't? You probably need to interact in the workplace with bosses and low-level employees, superiors and underlings, managers and the managed — co-workers in some way, shape, or form — to be successful at your job. Meeting that challenge begins here. This chapter explains why effective communication is so important and outlines each of the four approaches that people use to express themselves. It also helps you understand what makes assertiveness the best approach and gives suggestions for how you can adopt that approach in your own communications.

Why Communication Is Key to Success

You'd be hard-pressed to find any job function or field of employment where communicating effectively with people isn't vital. Regardless of your job title or the type of organization or industry you work for, if you're like most people, the greatest challenges you face lean less toward the technical side of your job (your area of expertise) than they do toward interacting with other people. Why? Because you have to be able to communicate well with multiple categories of people. Many organizations, in the public as well as private sectors, stress that all workers have customers that they must serve. The two basic types of customers are external customers and internal customers:

✔ **External customers:** These are people outside your organization who need the products and services that your business provides. In the broadest sense, external customers are people outside the workplace with whom you need to build good working relationships for success on the job. That includes a variety of folks ranging from suppliers to investors.

✔ **Internal customers:** These are your fellow employees, inside and outside the department where you work, to whom you provide services or assistance.

In addition to communicating with both types of customers, you also have to communicate with co-workers. You likely do your job in cooperative, team-like situations for part or most of the workdays. And if you work in management, most of the demands placed on your job require you to effectively interact with others — staff, peers, and bosses.

Your interactions with all these people in the workplace can be stressful and challenging when communication goes awry. What those stressful and challenging situations are, how often they occur, and with whom they occur vary greatly from individual to individual. One person's stressful encounter can be a no-big-deal situation to someone else. For some people, the workday is filled with constant stress, while for others, the day is peaceful and friendly. You are half the equation in any communication situation, though, and your approach to interacting with others greatly influences how stressful and challenging your work situations have been and will be.

Having the Right Mind-Set to Avoid a Tug-of-War

Ever play tug-of-war? The two teams on opposing ends of a rope try to pull each other across a dividing center line — sometimes into a hole filled with water and mud. It's a really dirty competition.

Interactions between people at work can be like tug-of-war. The rope serves as a metaphor for the bond or connection between two people as they interact. If the two parties yank on it, tension is higher, and conversations are less productive. The tug-of-war creates stress and strain that block effective communication. Alternatively, when neither party makes an effort to hold onto the rope, the bond breaks. In either case, you have scenarios that block effective communications: one where the participants are at cross purposes; the other where they aren't engaged at all.

The goal of successful communications is to share the rope so that it's strongly held but no one gets dirty — a big challenge but key to the success of communicating on the job.

Understanding where the tug-of-war comes from

As a human being, you have two versions of communication at your disposal: speaking and listening, and writing and reading. With the increased use of electronic communications, such as e-mail and text messaging, some people in their jobs use reading and writing as their main channel of communication. Yet the live, person-to-person form of communication, listening and speaking (which includes both the verbal and nonverbal messages), is still involved in nearly every job and, for many people, remains a big part of the communication time spent in doing their work.

You were probably taught the traditional three Rs (reading, 'riting, and 'rithmetic) from elementary through high school, but you probably didn't receive any formal instruction about how to listen effectively and express yourself constructively while interacting with others. Yet these are the very skills required to understand each other, work together, and solve problems with one another. Critical skills, yet seldom taught — whoa!

In addition to the lack of practical instruction on how to communicate effectively, elements like stress, differences of opinion, or demanding customers make it easier to get caught up in that tug-of-war feeling, which can lead to adversarial communications. These situations can range from waging verbal war against the other person to appeasing that person just to get past a difficult situation to using a subtle but negative *get-even* approach. Adversarial ways of communicating, represented by the tug-of-war, block people from working out their differences and interacting respectfully.

Achieving the main objective: Mutual understanding

Communication involves senders and receivers. A *sender* is the speaker, expressing his or her message to other parties. A *receiver,* on the other hand, is a person who listens. In a good conversation, participants take turns being senders and receivers. When participants in a conversation try to be senders at the same time, the tug-of-war rope stretches taut. Or if one participant is a receiver but tunes out the sender, shows little interest in the conversation, or passes judgment on nearly every point that the sender makes, the tension mounts as the tug-of-war goes on.

The goal of the communication process is mutual understanding. When this goal is achieved, participants hear each other out and understand where everyone is coming from. They don't battle as adversaries or competitors. Instead, they communicate in a collaborative fashion — a conversation characterized by respect and sincerity. They may have their differences, but

Book IV

Get to the @#% Point! Communicating Effectively

differences aren't an excuse to have a tug-of-war; rather, differences are issues to work through to reach the desired outcome.

The following sections of this chapter provide guidelines and information that can lay the groundwork for better communication in the future. For complete details on improving your listening skills, see Chapter 2 of Book IV.

Watching Out for Assumptions

To listen actively and speak assertively, you must first become aware of and perhaps even change the pattern of your *assumptions* when interacting with others. That is no easy feat.

Understanding the good and bad things about assumptions

An *assumption* is a belief that something is true without proof or demonstration or that a person is going to behave a certain way before that person has a chance to act. Assumptions are part of the human condition. You've probably been making them (and have had them made about you, too) all your life. But not all assumptions are negative. The following list describes some ways that positive assumptions can help you:

- **Processing stimuli:** Assumptions help you gather the information and stimuli to make sense of the world around you. When you're driving, for example, assumptions help keep you alert and aware of what other drivers may do so that you stay safe.

- **Anticipating problem situations:** Assumptions can help you prepare for problems and plan how to respond appropriately if challenges arise.

- **Trying new things:** Assumptions can help you make educated guesses about new people or situations. They can aid you in drawing upon past experiences and determining how to apply them in future situations — in essence, allowing you to take risks and do something new and different.

 The problem with assumptions is that they can lead to mistakes, misunderstandings, and strained relationships when they're acted upon as absolute facts. The following is a list of common assumptions that people make that can undermine effective communications at work (and elsewhere):

✔ **Jumping to conclusions:** In this scenario, you *know* what someone is going to say or whether something can work before you get the whole story. This assumption usually manifests itself in several annoying ways, including

- Finishing people's sentences for them

- Interrupting before a message has been fully stated

- Tuning out as soon as a person whom you find unfavorable starts talking

- Dismissing a new idea before hearing the rationale for it

Although jumping to conclusions can be useful if you're playing *Name That Tune,* it tends to have little benefit in work situations.

✔ **Focusing on intentions:** People have intentions and they have actions, and you can only see the actions. Yet people often make assumptions on what they perceive are someone else's intentions — and quite often assume the worst about those intentions. Focusing on intentions instead of actions sometimes causes you to interpret well-meant actions as destructive or of ill will. If a colleague asks you to do the most challenging part of a group presentation, you may think she's trying to set you up to fail, when in fact she simply respects you and thinks you'll do a better job than she could. When you focus on someone's intentions, you often approach people with undue suspicion.

✔ **Thinking you know best:** When you think you know best, you're already taking actions or making decisions for someone else without first checking with the person who is affected directly by what you do. These actions range from making commitments to initiating changes. Quite often, the person most affected doesn't find out about these changes until after they're made. Save such surprises for birthdays.

✔ **Stereotyping:** The term *stereotyping* means assuming that anyone who is from a different group than you — whether in race, ethnicity, gender, religion, sexual orientation, occupation, or other grouping — behaves and thinks in the same way as the group. Engineers all do one thing, men are all like that, all women do that, and so on. Stereotypical remarks often offend others and do nothing more than show your ignorance and biases.

You've no doubt heard that old saying that goes something like this:

"When you assume, you make an A S S out of U and M E."

When you make negative assumptions, you make a donkey out of yourself, but you also affect others and make them look or feel pretty silly, too. Worst of all, by acting on your assumptions, you've probably hurt someone else. Jumping to conclusions, focusing on intentions, thinking you know best, and stereotyping are mistakes.

Becoming aware of your own assumptions

Although assumptions are a normal part of the human thought process, you need to become aware of your own assumptions to have effective interactions. Here are a few tips to help:

- **Deal with each person as an individual.** Don't assume you know what people are like based on the categories they fall into. Get to know each person you work with or each customer you serve as an individual. The more you understand others, the better you can communicate with them.

- **Listen first.** Hear people out. Ask questions and check your understanding after you've heard the message so that you know what someone really means. When something sounds contrary to your thoughts, avoid reacting quickly with a negative comment or disagreement. Instead, ask the person the rationale or benefits of the idea or proposal at hand. Get the facts first.

- **Avoid generalizations.** Generalizations about people often come off as stereotypical remarks. By taking a few experiences with a limited number of people and attempting to make those experiences sound like absolute facts, you ignore profound individual differences. Rather than talking in generalizations, phrase the comments you make about groups of people or situations in terms of your own experiences and be sure the comment is relevant to the conversation.

- **Communicate first; act second.** Because so much of work requires cooperating and coordinating efforts with others, check with the people involved first, making sure that everyone is on the same page before you take action. No matter how well intentioned you are or how brilliant an idea you have, when you don't consult important people first, they're often upset, and as a result, may even reject a legitimate action or idea.

- **Make the safest assumption of them all.** The safest assumption to make when working with others is to assume that the other person means well. Put all conspiracy theories aside. (What a relief!) This assumption allows you to see and deal with the actions and ideas of others at face value.

Four Approaches to Communicating

People express themselves in four ways: aggressively, nonassertively, passive-aggressively, and assertively. This section discusses each of the four patterns of communication in detail so that you can recognize each pattern and begin to move your own way of speaking toward assertiveness.

REMEMBER

If you're like most people, you've used all four speaking approaches at various times. But you may find that when you deal with certain people or encounter certain situations — especially challenging and stressful ones — you often fall into one of the less-productive patterns of expressing yourself (aggressive, nonassertive, or passive-aggressive). If you do, join the club known as the human race. You become a successful communicator by dealing with these situations assertively, the most positive and respectful way of resolving issues with others.

The first aspect of good interactions relates to the tone and approach you use with other people, which the following sections go into detail. The other aspects — listening and the content of your message — are covered in Chapters 2 and 3 of Book IV.

My way or the highway: The aggressive approach

Aggressive speaking is a hard-charging approach that's often hostile and comes across as controlling or dominating. Here are some common messages you may hear when someone speaks aggressively:

- ✔ "You must . . ."
- ✔ "Because I said so."
- ✔ "You idiot!"
- ✔ "You always/never . . ."
- ✔ "Who screwed this up?"

The aggressive approach is never subtle. The following are common behaviors that an aggressive speaker displays:

- ✔ **Blaming, accusing:** In problem situations, an aggressive speaker is quick to find fault and focus on the wrongs that the other person supposedly committed.

- ✔ **Intimidating body language:** An aggressive speaker sometimes uses threatening or intimidating body language, such as demonstrative finger pointing, moving closer to you, getting in your face to argue a point, or pounding on a table with his fist.

- ✔ **Demanding, ordering:** The aggressive approach to getting something from another person is to demand it or give orders. An aggressive speaker tells you what you must do.

- **Raised voice:** As you may have guessed, when someone is making a point aggressively, her voice gets louder and the tone becomes sharper.

- **Harsh, personal language:** An aggressive speaker focuses more on the person than on the issue. The language is often filled with a lot of *you* insults and, at times, with profanity. Tact or diplomacy is tossed aside.

- **Verbal browbeating:** When you have a difference of opinion with an aggressive speaker who feels strongly about a point, or when something isn't going the way that person desires, the conversation turns into a competition — a battle to be won. He tries to *win* by interrupting, talking louder, arguing, and verbally attacking you. He forgets about listening.

The appeasing way: The nonassertive approach

Nonassertive speaking comes off as the softest of the four approaches. A nonassertive speaker is passive and allows others to dominate the conversation. Here are some common messages you hear when someone speaks in a nonassertive manner:

- "Uh . . . if that's the way you want to do it . . . um, that's fine with me."

- "I don't know if I could do that."

- "I'll talk to him soon about that problem; I've just been really busy."

- "I'm sorry to ask you."

- "I hate to bother you."

- "Maybe that's a good idea."

The nonassertive approach isn't strong or certain. Instead, nonassertive speakers often display the following behaviors:

- **Soft voice:** In nonassertive speaking, the volume in the speaker's voice is often low and sometimes hard to hear, especially in group settings. The tone also may come across as meek.

- **Overly agreeable, no point of view expressed:** A nonassertive speaker agrees with you in order to go along and keep everything nice. A nonassertive speaker also seldom expresses her point of view and certainly doesn't express an opinion that's contrary to yours.

- **Avoidance:** The nonassertive way to deal with a concern is to avoid dealing with it: Avoid talking to the person, let the problem linger, and try to put off dealing with the situation for as long as possible. The more uncomfortable the matter is, the more effort a nonassertive person puts into avoiding it.

✔ **Withdrawn body language:** A nonassertive speaker doesn't make direct eye contact with other people, stays at a distance, and may slump or cower. Nothing confident comes across in the speaker's physical effort to communicate the message.

✔ **Sounding uncertain:** When someone speaks nonassertively, he hesitates and sounds unsure. A nonassertive speaker may use qualifier language such as *perhaps, maybe,* or *hopefully,* or may start sentences with comments like, "I don't know if this idea will help."

✔ **Beating around the bush:** Nonassertive speakers express critical or sensitive points by talking around the issue and rambling, leaving the point — at best — implied. The speaker never states the point clearly and directly.

✔ **Sounding hopeless or helpless:** Another common nonassertive speaking characteristic is language of despair or inaction, sometimes with a whining tone included. A typically resigned or hopeless message, such as, "I tried that once, but it didn't work, so what can you do?" is common. You may hear a lot of *I can'ts* and *I don't knows* such that no plan of action or possible solution is introduced.

Subtle but aggravating: The passive-aggressive approach

Passive-aggressive speaking is an approach in which a person comes off as subtle and indirect, but whose underlying tone may hurt or manipulate others. Take a look at some messages you hear when someone speaks in a passive-aggressive manner:

✔ "I knew that wouldn't work."

✔ "If that's the way you want it . . ."

✔ "How could you even think that?"

✔ "When was the last time you helped me?"

✔ "The problem with Joe is . . ."

The subtleties of the passive-aggressive approach are not pleasant. Someone speaking passive-aggressively often displays the following behaviors:

✔ **Appears to agree but really doesn't agree:** One of the common behaviors of passive-aggressiveness is that the speaker sounds as though she's going along with or agreeing to something, but her actions that follow don't show support or commitment. Instead, the passive-aggressive speaker claims that any agreement was actually a misunderstanding, or the speaker carries out actions that are contrary to the supposed commitment.

Book IV

Get to the @#% Point! Communicating Effectively

✔ **Tells others but not the source of the concern:** A passive-aggressive person doesn't deal directly with concerns about others. Complaining about that person to other people — behind that person's back — is a common way to handle concerns. Generally, such behavior stirs up gossip and divisiveness.

✔ **Makes subtle digs and sarcastic remarks:** Heard the old line that many a truth is said in jest? This line summarizes one behavior of passive-aggressive speakers: Put-downs are concealed with sarcasm. When the speaker uses no sarcasm, his tone may be condescending and hurtful to the person hearing it. Sometimes a passive-aggressive speaker expresses displeasure not through words but through nonverbal means, such as rolling the eyes, shaking the head, or making sighs of disgust.

✔ **Keeps score, sets conditions:** In the passive-aggressive approach, cooperation comes with limitations or conditions. Ask a passive-aggressive speaker for support and you'll likely meet reluctance. Memories are long and forgiveness is short. Sometimes a passive-aggressive speaker comes off sounding like a martyr: "For all the work I've done for you, this is the appreciation I get!"

A passive-aggressive speaker also may try to settle the score by giving you the silent treatment, not showing up when help is needed, sabotaging your efforts behind the scenes, and sending harsh messages via e-mail and copying others on them (see Chapter 4 of this book for more on communicating via e-mail).

✔ **Nonverbal message contradicts the verbal message:** In passive-aggressive behavior, stated words sound positive, but body language or tone of voice gives the words the opposite meaning. *Everything is fine* said with a scowl means that something *is* wrong, *Nothing is bothering me* muttered without eye contact means that something *is* bothering me. *That's a good idea* with a not-so-hidden roll of the eyes means that it *isn't,* and so on.

✔ **Holds back expressing concerns or providing assistance:** A passive-aggressive speaker may withhold information or other forms of support when others can use it to get a job done. In addition, she holds emotions in, although you may get a sense of them in her body language, such as pouting, stern looks, or looking away rather than giving direct eye contact. But nothing is said directly, and when asked about a concern or issue, the passive-aggressive speaker often responds to the inquiry by saying "Never mind" or "No big deal."

✔ **Criticizes after the fact:** This behavior is sometimes referred to as *second-guessing* or *armchair quarterbacking.* After an event or action has taken place, a passive-aggressive communicator responds with what you should have done or what you did wrong — sometimes even when you requested input beforehand and he gave none. A passive-aggressive speaker is quick to pass judgment.

Straight and positive: The assertive approach

Assertive speaking involves expressing yourself in a positive, confident, and respectful way and allowing and encouraging others to do the same. This pattern of speaking requires the most skill and effort, for unlike the other three approaches, it requires you to think before you speak. Here are some common messages you hear from assertive speakers:

- ✔ "Yes, that was my mistake."
- ✔ "As I understand your point, . . ."
- ✔ "Let me explain why I see that point differently."
- ✔ "Let's define the issue and then explore some options to help resolve it."
- ✔ "Please hear me out and then work with me to resolve my concern."

The following are some of the behaviors that someone who speaks in an assertive fashion displays:

- ✔ **Takes responsibility:** The assertive approach says that each individual is responsible for her own actions — no excuses, no woe-is-me language, no blaming others for problems. The speaker accepts what has happened and focuses on what needs to be done next.

- ✔ **Takes initiative:** An assertive speaker doesn't play games. If something needs to happen, he takes the initiative to get the process rolling — no waiting for others to say what to do and when to act. The assertive approach is action-oriented.

- ✔ **Listens actively:** Assertiveness allows for two-way conversation. Assertive speakers show a willingness to hear the other person out and understand his or her point of view.

- ✔ **Speaks up, is direct and constructive:** If a point needs to be made or a thought needs to be expressed, an assertive communicator speaks up. She states the point directly without beating around the bush. Assertive speakers use language *constructively;* that is, they communicate the message in the best way possible and make the point clearly. The language focuses on the issue at hand.

- ✔ **Shows sincerity:** When you express yourself sincerely, you say what you mean and mean what you say — and do so with respect for others. This is heard in both the tone and language used.

- ✔ **Is solutions-focused:** In problem situations, an assertive speaker takes a problem-solving approach. He examines the problem, not to blame or find fault with anyone but to understand the issue and move toward developing a solution. Creating the solution becomes the main focus in working with others.

✔ **Assumes a confident voice and body language:** The voice of an assertive speaker sounds strong, certain, and firm when needed. The speaker's posture, gestures, and facial expressions support her message. She sounds and looks alive when speaking, coming across nonverbally as positive and enthusiastic to an appropriate degree.

✔ **Addresses concerns directly to the source:** An assertive speaker addresses issues directly to the source as opposed to telling others about the problems. At the same time, the speaker states the problem constructively and places the emphasis on collaborating with the other person to work out a resolution. No browbeating or blaming occurs.

✔ **Requests needs:** Whereas an aggressive speaker demands or orders to get what's needed, an assertive speaker *asks for* or *requests* what's needed. The message makes the sense of importance clear so that the request and any rationale for it are understood.

Contrasting the four approaches

Say you just received an important assignment with a tight deadline. You know that you need assistance from Sue, a co-worker, to get it done. Using each approach, how would you communicate this need? Take your thoughts and compare them to the following samples:

✔ **Aggressive approach:** "Sue, look, I'm in a jam right now. You need to help me get this critical project done right away! I don't have time to hear that you're busy with something else. That excuse just won't fly. So come on, sit down, and let me show you what I need you to do."

✔ **Nonassertive approach:** "Hi, Sue. I hate to bother you. I know you're probably busy with a lot of other issues right now. I have one of those tough assignments. If you have a chance, maybe you could lend me a hand for a little bit. But, uh, it's okay if you don't want to."

✔ **Passive-aggressive approach:** "Sue, I know you're the type who doesn't want to put yourself out too much. Hey, I'm just kidding. But look, when you were in a pinch last week, who helped you out? That's right — me. So look, I'm in the same boat now. Don't worry, I won't have you do most of the work anyway."

✔ **Assertive approach:** "Sue, I was just assigned a critical project that needs to be done in a week. I would appreciate it if you could lend some assistance. The project involves an area in which your experience will really come in handy. What I'd like to do is take a few minutes with you now or this afternoon to determine what time and support you can lend and to fill you in on the needs of the project. Does that work for you, and if so, what time can we meet?"

Don't confuse aggressive with assertive

People sometimes confuse the words *aggressive* and *assertive*. What they share in common is that the speaker is willing to share his or her viewpoint and is willing to take action to deal with issues. But after that, the two approaches are quite different:

Aggressive	Assertive
Blunt	Direct
In conflict situations, harsh in tone	In conflict situations, firm in tone

Aggressive	Assertive
In problem situations, blames and browbeats the other person	In problem situations, collaborates on solutions
Pushes own way	Speaks up, yet hears what the other person has to say
One-way conversation flow	Two-way conversation flow

As you see in this example, the same message can be communicated in four different ways. Only an assertive speaker is able to directly and positively request Sue's help and communicate the importance of the situation. The aggressive message comes on as a strong demand, the nonassertive approach leaves you wondering whether anything is being asked at all, and the passive-aggressive message tinges with sarcasm and you-owe-me conditions — all of which are turnoffs to most fellow team members.

Becoming an Assertive Speaker

If you're like many people, you can see yourself in each of the other approaches — and probably see people you've encountered in both your professional and personal lives in each approach, too. But as the preceding sections make clear, the assertive approach is the most effective for achieving success on the job.

Speaking assertively is the toughest approach — not in terms of difficulty but in terms of effort. It requires more effort than the aggressive, nonassertive, and passive-aggressive approaches because you have to be aware of your own behavior and be considerate of the other person. You also may have noticed that you have to listen effectively to speak assertively. The better you understand where the other person is coming from — you do so through active listening — the better you can tailor your message so that the other person understands it well (which is a great definition for assertive speaking). See Chapter 2 in Book IV for more on active listening.

Book IV

Get to the @#% Point! Communicating Effectively

To change your pattern of behavior so that you become an assertive speaker, apply the following principles:

- **Collaboration:** Conversations work best when they're two-way — that is, where both parties contribute and work to understand each other.

- **Flexibility:** Not everyone you interact with is the same; however, being direct, positive, confident, and willing to listen is a good place to start with everyone. From there, you can adjust to the individual after you get to know the person. For example, with some people, the less you say, the better. With others, you have to be firm to be taken seriously. And with still others, you have to be patient in order to work effectively with them.

- **Self-control:** The toughest person to manage in any interaction is yourself. Assertive speakers are in control of their emotions. Aggressive, nonassertive, and passive-aggressive speakers allow their emotions to control them.

- **Continuous respect:** Assertive speakers take a long-term view to working relationships. People you deal with today will remember you tomorrow. If you treat everyone with unconditional respect, you build more partners and allies for the future. (You may not like everyone you encounter in your job, but you don't have to take them home with you.)

Don't respond to disrespectful actions directed toward you with disrespectful actions in return; otherwise, you go down the aggressive or passive-aggressive tracks for tug-of-war relationships. You can take actions to deal with situations you don't like (Book V deals with difficult situations), but always do so with respect for the other person.

- **Fix problems, not blame:** Problems are inevitable in any work situation, and many involve other people. When speaking assertively, your focus is on problem solving versus problem dwelling — on creating solutions together versus blaming one another.

Chapter 2

Listening Actively

Although you spend much of your communication time giving an ear to what other people say, are you really *listening* to them or just *hearing* them? Most people are never given any sort of real instruction in the difference between those two actions. *Hearing* is simply the physical effort of taking in the speaker's message, but *listening* is the process of receiving a message from a speaker, processing that message to make sense of it, and then responding to it in ways that show understanding of what the speaker means. After reading those definitions, you won't be surprised to know that good communication at work requires listening.

This chapter walks you through the process of listening, shows you the ways that people commonly engage in listening, and helps you understand the most effective way to listen (called *active listening* and sometimes referred to as *reflective listening* or *responsive listening*). It also explains what not to do when listening.

Recognizing the Impact — Good and Bad — Your Listening Skills Have

You can gain a lot when you listen effectively; you can lose a lot when you don't. You've probably experienced both the benefits of good listening and the costs of poor listening. Recognizing both the benefits and the costs can motivate you to improve your own listening.

Chances are, when someone really listens to you, you come away from the experience feeling

✔ Respected

✔ Cared for

✔ That you've established rapport

✔ Rewarded

✔ Satisfied

✔ A sense of achievement

When the people you interact with — from co-workers to customers — walk away from interactions with you with these kinds of positive feelings, chances are the impact on your job will be positive, as well: increased productivity, better quality of work, greater customer satisfaction, greater cooperation and teamwork, and more.

Listening well can increase your effectiveness on the job. People often overlook or take for granted the power (*power,* in this case, meaning *positive influence*) of listening. When you become aware of the power that active listening gives you, you're ready to develop and use listening tools and begin to have a positive impact on others.

In simple terms, poor listening can be quite costly, resulting in negative impacts, such as:

✔ Strained working relationships

✔ Messed-up customer orders

✔ Loss of current or potential business

✔ Dissatisfied customers

✔ Little problems escalating into big ones

✔ Increased errors and the need for rework

✔ Greater inefficiency

You can't afford to be a poor listener. The key is to recognize the impact of effective listening and work hard to gain the benefits that come from it. Taking the time and effort to listen actively makes your job easier, not harder.

Identifying What Kind of Listener You Are

Listening occurs in three stages:

✔ **Stage 1 — Receiving:** In this first stage, you take in the speaker's message through your senses, most notably through hearing and seeing. In fact, you listen as much with your sense of sight as you do with your sense of hearing. Your eyes help you read the nonverbal cues that play a part in how the speaker expresses his message. (The exception is when you're talking to someone over the telephone.)

✔ **Stage 2 — Processing:** After you take in the speaker's message with your senses, the internal processing begins. This activity takes place in your mind and involves analyzing, evaluating, and synthesizing. Your goal is to make sense out of the speaker's message; that is, to help you figure out the answer to the question, "What does the speaker mean?" Because all this processing is internal, the speaker doesn't yet see any visible reaction from you, the listener.

✔ **Stage 3 — Responding:** This third stage in the listening process is the one in which the speaker sees and hears what the listener does. In this stage, the listener verbally and nonverbally acknowledges that she has received and understood the message.

People engage in listening in the following ways, with the first two being the most common:

✔ Passive listening

✔ Selective listening

✔ Attentive listening

✔ Active listening

People tend to use a single approach as a regular practice — whether in stressful or nonstressful situations. You may see yourself, plus others in your life, in the approaches described in the following sections.

Is anybody really home? The passive listener

Passive listening is a common way that people listen to others. In this approach, the listener is present nonverbally but verbally provides little feedback to the speaker. Here are some common behaviors exhibited by someone who is listening passively:

✔ Gives some eye contact with the speaker

✔ Shows a fairly expressionless look on the face

✔ Nods the head occasionally

✔ Provides occasional verbal acknowledgments, such as, "Uh huh," especially on the telephone

✔ Sits quietly and says little in response to the speaker's message

A passive listener is present but adds little to stimulate the flow of conversation. He lets the speaker talk and speaks up only when the speaker is done and if he has something to say. The result is a one-way conversation with little effort to connect to the other person's message.

Getting what you want, not what you need: The selective listener

Selective listening, which is nearly as common as passive listening, is usually defined as hearing what you want to hear. When you hear the message you want to hear, you may function as a more engaged and understanding listener. But when you don't want to hear about the particular message being delivered, you tend to either tune out or become reactive to the speaker. In other words, you're consistently inconsistent in your listening efforts when you function as a selective listener.

Someone who is listening in a selective manner to a message that she doesn't want to hear displays these behaviors:

✔ Gives looks of disinterest

✔ Looks away at other things — a watch, papers, and so on

✔ Shakes the head in disapproval

✔ Reacts with high degrees of emotion, such as being defensive or debating every point

✔ Jumps in before the speaker has finished and takes over the conversation as a speaker

✔ Changes the subject

✔ Asks a question about a point of self-interest, sometimes in an interrogating manner, that doesn't fit with the speaker's current message

People are selective not just based on what they hear — the subject matter — but also on who is speaking and how the message is presented. For example, your department vice president comes into your office to make a request of you. You're fully attentive and receive the message well. A few minutes later, a co-worker stops by, one who annoys you because of his verbose nature. What do you do when he starts talking? Tune him right out. That's selective listening.

Grabbing the facts: The attentive listener

Functioning as an *attentive listener* is more productive than functioning as a passive or a selective listener. When you function as an attentive listener, you're more engaged and less judgmental, both nonverbally and verbally. You seek the facts and information that the speaker wants to relay to you in your conversation. An attentive listener displays these behaviors:

- Gives steady eye contact to the speaker
- Shows interested looks and sincere facial expressions
- Nods to indicate understanding
- Provides simple verbal acknowledgments ("I see," "Okay," "Yes," and so on) to encourage the speaker to express her message
- Raises questions to begin to draw out the message
- Asks questions that seek greater detail

When the message is mostly factual, you do well. When the message involves much emotion, you tend not to deal with it or acknowledge it directly. This is where attentive listeners fall short. They don't capture the entire message to get the full meaning — both the facts *and* the feelings.

Capturing and confirming the message: The active listener

Active listening, sometimes referred to as *responsive listening* or *reflective listening,* is the most powerful way in which people engage in the effort of listening. An active listener receives a speaker's message with care and respect and then works to verify his understanding of that message — as the speaker meant it to be.

When you function as an active listener, you capture the speaker's whole message — the facts *and* the feelings. Among the behaviors displayed by an active listener are the positive ones listed in the section "Grabbing the facts: The attentive listener," plus the following:

- Shows patience
- Gives verbal feedback to summarize understanding of the message

> ✔ Acknowledges and addresses the reasons for the emotions being expressed when they are significant to the overall message
>
> ✔ Speaks up when something is unclear or confusing

Active listeners do talk. But what they talk about and where their attention goes is the speaker's message — not their own message or their commentary on the speaker's message. The later section, "Making Active Listening Work: Capturing the Whole Message," provides you with the strategies to listen actively.

Using the Keys to Active Listening

If you're like most people, at some point in a conversation, you've been turned off by your listener. You've wanted someone to listen to exactly what you were saying, but your listener was either inattentive, distracted, or reacting in ways that showed displeasure with what you had to say. You've also probably been in the listener's shoes in a situation where you passively or selectively listened.

Both experiences emphasize that effective communication goes beyond the actual words spoken. As a listener, you can invite a speaker to go forward with a message or block the expression of that message. As a listener in the workplace, you need to tune into and read the speaker to gain a full understanding of her meaning. Your *radar* — your openness and attentiveness to the speaker — has a powerful effect on the flow of the conversation. Are you open to listening, or are you coming off as judgmental; are you tuned in, or are you tuned out?

This section shows you how the most effective form of listening, active listening, really works. It emphasizes the cues you need to listen for and how to situate yourself to receive and process the speaker's message accurately.

Identifying the three components of every message

If you only hear the words, you won't understand the message. Every message you listen to is expressed by verbal and nonverbal means, and quite often, the nonverbal aspects have more to do with the meaning of the message than the verbal aspects do. An important part of listening effectively is knowing what to listen for as the speaker talks. A speaker's message contains three components:

✔ **Words:** The verbal component of the message; that is, *what* the speaker is saying.

✔ **Tone of voice:** Different from volume, which is how loudly or quietly you speak, tone involves the inflection and the level of sincerity of the speaker's voice as he speaks.

✔ **Body language:** A nonverbal component that further describes *how* the speaker's message is being conveyed. Body language includes all the things you do with your body, including the use of gestures, eye contact, facial expressions, and posture, to express your message.

A speaker's message contains the facts or content (the words) and the feelings or emotions (demonstrated by both the tone of voice and body language). Together, they comprise the meaning of the speaker's message. This concept is fundamental to results-oriented communication:

Content + Emotion = The meaning of the message

This formula represents the substance you want to listen for when you listen.

Recognizing the feelings behind the facts

Body language and tone of voice greatly impact the overall meaning of a speaker's message. In many cases, they carry the vast majority of the meaning. If you tune in to only the words, you don't fully know what the speaker truly means. To recognize the impact of tone and facial expression on the meaning of a message, do the following:

1. **Say the following sentence with a smile on your face: "Today is a beautiful day."**

2. **Now repeat the same sentence with a frown on your face.**

   What happened to your message from the first time to the second time it was said? When your facial expression changed, your message's meaning changed from a positive outlook to a negative one.

3. **Say the following sentence in a calm and sincere tone: "Today is a beautiful day."**

4. **Now repeat the same sentence with a sarcastic tone in your voice.**

   What happened to your message from the first time to the second time it was said? When your tone of voice changed, your message's meaning changed from one of patient truthfulness to one of annoyed deceit.

To truly understand what the speaker means, you need to tune in to the feelings being expressed behind the facts. Simply saying, "I am angry with you," is clear, yet quite often people show their emotions instead of stating them. A speaker who is angry, for example, may develop a flushed face, or use a sarcastic or harsh tone, or pound her fist on the table. Sometimes the signs are more subtle, like a clenched jaw or silence and looking away.

When emotion carries much of a message's overall meaning, double-check that you understand it. In listening terms, this means acknowledging the emotion or reflecting the feelings. The section "Capturing the emotions: Reflecting feelings" gives more detail about reflecting feelings, an important active-listening skill.

More pointers for improving your listening skills

To prepare you for active listening, here are a few tips:

- **Hold off on the assumptions.** Don't assume you know what someone is saying before he states the entire message. (Chapter 1 of Book IV covers the problems with making assumptions.) Hear the message all the way through and ask questions and check your understanding if you need to.

- **Don't be quick to offer advice.** Remember the old adage, "Advice is best received when asked for." Sometimes what sounds like a problem is merely the other person sharing the day's trials and tribulations — no more, no less. Your desire to be helpful may have you giving advice freely, without knowing whether it's really wanted. Unwanted advice may make the recipient feel dictated to or imposed upon — major turn-offs for most people.

- **Exercise patience.** People have different communication styles, some of which may please you and others of which may be difficult to deal with. For active listening to work, you need to take control of your emotions so that you can deal with the variety of people who come your way.

- **Eliminate distractions and physical barriers.** Within the environment in which you're working, create the best possible conditions to allow for a comfortable conversation. Keep your cellphone off and turn down the volume on your pager. Don't run to answer your desk phone simply because you hear it ring. Instead of sitting across from someone at a distance because of a huge desk between you, arrange your chair so that you can sit facing each other without a physical barrier in between.

- **Be continuously respectful.** When your actions or reactions come across as judgmental, you add tension to the relationship. When you come across as respectful, you build confidence and trust. Regardless of your intentions, people see only your actions. Without consistent efforts to show respect, active listening won't work.

✔ **Shift attention.** If, as you attempt to listen, your mind's attention is focused more on what's going on around you or on what your next word back to the speaker is going to be, you're not really listening. Active listening puts attention on the speaker and her message, not on yourself.

Making Active Listening Work: Capturing the Whole Message

This section provides you with eight skills that help you listen actively and effectively. Four of them are devoted to drawing out the speaker's message, and four help you verify your understanding of the message. Quite simply, to get more of the speaker's message — anywhere throughout the beginning, middle, or conclusion of a conversation — apply these listening skills.

Drawing out the speaker's message

Active listeners rely on the four tools covered in this section to help draw out and focus a message. This first set of tools aid and stimulate the speaker to express the message freely. By using these four skills, the listener is better equipped to help the speaker express the content of the message and, as needed, explain the basis of the feelings being heard in the message.

Letting the speaker in: Door openers

Door openers are signals listeners use to encourage speakers to express and elaborate upon their messages. They tell speakers to proceed without caution in presenting their messages. Door openers can be nonverbal or verbal expressions by the listener; however, nonverbal door openers are especially helpful because they can be given while the speaker is talking without being interpreted as interruptions.

Nonverbal door openers

Nonverbal door openers communicate to the speaker that you're attending to him and that you're really tuned in and want to hear what he has to say. The following list describes nonverbal door openers:

✔ Turning and facing the speaker

✔ Leaning in slightly toward the speaker

✔ Offering steady eye contact

✔ Nodding your head to acknowledge that you're following the message

✔ Showing a look of interest

Book IV

Get to the @#% Point! Communicating Effectively

✔ Giving a sincere smile for an upbeat message

✔ Showing a look of concern for a serious message

✔ Providing a patient look with silence

Providing a patient look with silence is one of the more powerful and sophisticated nonverbal door openers. Use it when someone indicates she wants to express concerns or other important information.

When a speaker has something serious to say, she often expresses the message in a manner that's more deliberate than normal. Unless the speaker is extremely eloquent, such messages usually come out a piece at a time with noticeable pauses along the way. You can tell by the look on the speaker's face and the tone in her voice — these are called *nonverbal* cues — that the message is important and serious. When poor listeners don't tune into these nonverbal cues, they become impatient and jump in after the speaker's first pause. They become speakers themselves, never allowing the original speaker to complete her message. Active listeners who use the silent, patient-look door opener signal the speaker to take the time necessary to tell the entire story. Without interruptions, the depth of the speaker's message comes out.

Sincerity is key to the effectiveness of nonverbal door openers. Facial expressions showing insincerity often close rather than open the door. If you're smiling when your speaker is saying something serious, the behavior may come off as a smirk, a major turnoff to the speaker. In fact, the exact opposites of these nonverbal door openers are detractors or barriers to a good flowing conversation as covered in the section "Avoiding Barriers to Listening."

Verbal door openers

Verbal door openers are one or two spoken words that have the same effect as their nonverbal counterparts. Because you say these while the speaker is talking, they're not seen as interruptions. Use any of the following door openers to communicate to your speaker that you're following along and want him to tell you more.

Uh-huh	Really
Mm-hmm	Neat
Right	Oh
I see	Okay
Yeah	Wow
Yes	

The tone of your verbal door openers is critical. It needs to be nonjudgmental — in a range that allows for curious, interested, and patient sounds. A judgmental tone creates a barrier to the conversation and will probably block the speaker from communicating the full message.

Say again: Echoing

The second tool in this first set of active-listening skills is called *echoing*. Echoing is repeating a key word or phrase of the speaker's message as a way to draw out more of the message and gain a clearer picture of it. Echoing involves two steps:

1. **Repeat the key word (or two) from the speaker's message (use the speaker's words, not your own).**

   That's the echo. Your voice inflection punctuates what you say with a question-mark sound. In echoing, you want the pitch to go higher at the end of your remark. The inquisitive sound invites a response from the speaker without your having to ask a direct question. It creates a smooth, comfortable environment.

2. **After making your echo response, wait patiently.**

   Sometimes the speaker responds right away to the stimulus of the echoing and explains what the word or term means. Other times, the response doesn't come as readily, especially when strong emotion lurks behind the words. Waiting patiently and allowing for silence acts as a door opener to encourage the speaker to take her time. When you wait patiently (as opposed to anxiously) in a matter of seconds, the speaker starts to express what's going on.

To echo correctly, you need to know when to use the technique. Three situations work best:

- **When the statements are vague or general:** Vague, general statements tell you little and may mean a variety of things. For example, the person says to you, "That was a really interesting meeting yesterday." Who knows what that means? The statement is unclear. You, as the listener, should echo, "Interesting meeting?"

- **When the statements are vague yet loaded:** Vague yet loaded statements give you little substance or clarity, but by the tone of voice or body language, you can tell emotionally that a strong message lies beneath the surface. For example, you ask a co-worker how a meeting went, and you get a response with a very sharp tone: "Fine. Just fine!" What happened is vague, but the emotion is strong — in essence, loaded. You should echo, "Fine?"

- **When an unfamiliar word or term is used:** Often this happens when a speaker uses various forms of technical jargon or an acronym that not everyone knows. If, for example, the speaker says, "We got a new MRP system that I'm not sure will help us" (and you don't know what an MRP is), you would echo, "MRP system?"

Book IV

Get to the @#% Point! Communicating Effectively

In all three cases, echoing encourages the speaker to open up to you and explain his point. Using an inquisitive tone encourages the speaker to tell you more information about the message without having to work hard to get it.

Digging deeper: Probing

Probing is third tool in this first set. It is asking questions to gain more information and get below the surface of the message. Probing relies on *open-ended questions,* questions that seek to elicit information, explanation, and expressions of thoughts and feelings that can't be conveyed in a mere word or two. Here are a couple of examples:

- ✔ "What are your ideas for solving this problem?"
- ✔ "How would you go about implementing that new program?"

Unlike open-ended questions, *closed-ended questions* solicit short definitive answers that more often can be said in a word or two. The question "Did you get that report done?" is a closed-ended question because it can be answered with a simple yes or no. "When is the meeting?" is another closed-ended question because the answer doesn't need more than a word or two to be complete.

To probe effectively, consider these tips:

- ✔ **Use the keywords *what, how, why, explain, describe, elaborate, give,* and *tell* to ask questions in an open-ended way.** For example:
  - "What happened at the meeting yesterday?"
  - "Please give me an example of what you mean."
  - "Tell me more about that."

  Don't overload the speaker; go with one question at a time, and, in most cases, keep your question to one sentence, too.

- ✔ **Give the speaker some space:** Make sure your questions provide the speaker with the freedom to express what's on her mind in response to the question. Avoid *leading-the-witness* type of questions such as "Do you really think that idea is going to help the team?" or "Don't you think my idea is really the best?" Questions like these make clear what the answer *should* be. The speaker is being influenced to answer a certain way as opposed to having the space to express her own thoughts. Instead, ask the following in a probing manner:
  - "Please explain how that can help the team."
  - "What do you think of my idea?"

- ✔ **Use a nonjudgmental and inquisitive tone:** This means inviting the speaker to feel comfortable expressing thoughts, providing information, and exploring issues on a deeper level.

Exercise caution when asking *why* questions. Why? Although why is a good first word to shape open-ended questions, it often carries a more judgmental tone, and why questions can have an accusatory or critical tone that can put a speaker on the defensive rather than inviting that person to speak freely ("Why did you do that?" for example). If you tend to use why questions, make sure you manage your tone carefully so that you sound inquisitive rather than accusatory, or rephrase the question ("Please explain your thinking on the handling of this issue").

Making sure you're following along: Checking the subject

Checking the subject is the fourth active-listening tool in this first set for drawing out the speaker's message. It involves clarifying a detail of the speaker's topic or subject so you can follow the flow of the speaker's message without becoming sidetracked or confused. Checking the subject is beneficial when the topic of the speaker's message starts to become unclear or fuzzy or it goes off on a tangent.

Instead of sitting back passively when the topic becomes unclear in these situations, implement the tool by using following steps:

1. **As soon as the speaker takes a breath, jump in.**

   Don't let the speaker continue. Interject the moment that the subject becomes unclear.

2. **In an inquisitive tone, state the subject you think the speaker means.**

   Sometimes you can use starter phrases like the following:

   - "You're referring to . . . (then say what you think the subject is)?"
   - "You're talking about . . . ?"
   - "You mean . . . ?"

Checking the subject by this two-step process invites an immediate response before the speaker has a chance to proceed with more of the message. Use this strategy in the scenarios explained in the following sections.

- ✔ **When the speaker's message starts to become unclear or fuzzy:** Here's an example:

  - **Speaker:** "John and Bill finally got together and met yesterday. He came up with quite a creative idea." (*He* is the subject but who is he? Is he John or Bill? The subject has gotten fuzzy.)
  - **Listener:** "You're talking about Bill?" (Note: Sometimes you can skip the starter phrase and just say, inquisitively, "Bill?")
  - **Speaker:** (In return) "Yes." Or, "No, I meant John."

- ✔ **When the speaker goes off on a tangent:** Every speaker occasionally announces a topic but then diverts herself and takes a different path.

Book IV

Get to the @#% Point! Communicating Effectively

You can check the subject to get the speaker back to the main topic. For example:

- **Speaker:** "I want to go over the proposal for executing this project. Projects like these can be very involved. I've been on a few that got way too complicated, like one just a few months ago."

- **Listener:** (Spotting an unrelated tangent starting to divert attention from the main subject) "Now you wanted to review that proposal with me, right?"

- **Speaker:** (Responding — as so often happens) "Oh, yeah. Let me get to it."

Checking the subject does more than clarify the point or get the speaker back on track. It also reassures the speaker that you're following along with the message. Speakers like to know they have receptive and attentive listeners.

To check the subject effectively, you need to know the difference between *interjecting* and *interrupting* in a conversation. In both instances, you jump into the conversation before the speaker has finished his message. People generally don't like to be interrupted, because the conversation gets taken away, and the interrupter takes over and becomes the speaker. When you talk before the other person feels heard, you're interrupting, and more often than not, you're turning off the other person. When you interject, on the other hand, you keep your comments brief and focus on the speaker's message, not away from it. As a result, many speakers don't even notice this little clarifying effort by you. Instead, they end up benefiting from it.

Verifying your understanding of the message

People often walk away from conversations *thinking* they understood what the other person meant. You should walk away *knowing* exactly what the other person meant and knowing that the person feels understood. That's how productivity increases and working relationships strengthen. The following sections present the second set of four active listening tools that help you verify this understanding.

Capturing the emotions: Reflecting feelings

Reflecting feelings is checking your perception of the speaker's feelings in the message to understand the emotional meaning being expressed. You want to use this technique when the feelings being expressed represent a great deal of the message's meaning. In doing so, you act like a mirror, reflecting the emotional meaning you hear from the speaker. Here are some tips:

✔ State the emotion you perceive being expressed.

✔ Use the word *you* because the message is from the speaker, not from you.

✔ Keep the statement to no more than one sentence.

✔ Because you're checking, your voice inflection should pick up at the end of your statement to make it sound like a question. If you can't do that clearly with your voice, you can add a question to your reflecting statement, such as: "Is that right?"

The following are a few examples of reflecting feelings, based on what has been heard from the speaker:

✔ "Sounds like you're excited by that opportunity. Is that right?"

✔ "That was a frustrating experience for you?"

✔ "I sense you're irritated with Don. Is that correct?"

In each case, the emotion being expressed — excitement, frustration, irritation — is the main emphasis of the speaker's statement. It reflects the significance in the speaker's message.

Avoid saying (even with good intentions), "I understand how you feel." This statement can rub people the wrong way and is sometimes met with an emphatic, "No you don't!" (Don't try this at home either.) Why is saying "I understand how you feel" a turnoff? Sometimes it's perceived as patronizing or it can come across as an assumption. (As Chapter 1 in Book IV explains, assumptions can annoy people and can add tension to an interaction.)

When you reflect feelings, you're acknowledging what you're hearing. You're not trying to play therapist, nor are you judging the emotion being expressed as good or bad. Not acknowledging the emotion when it is a strong negative one may keep the speaker on edge and the tension in the interaction brewing. Not acknowledging the emotion when it is a positive one also serves to deflate the speaker. In both cases, not tuning in and reflecting the feeling that's so much a part of the speaker's meaning sends that person a message that is the opposite of your intentions: "I don't really care what's going on for you." Keep your tone sincere when you use the tool and your actions will match your intentions.

Book IV

Get to the @#% Point! Communicating Effectively

Capturing the content: Paraphrasing

Paraphrasing is the second tool in this set to check understanding. You use this tool by restating the main idea of the speaker's message in your own words to verify or clarify your understanding of the facts or content of that message. Paraphrasing is similar to reflecting feelings except that its purpose is to establish understanding of the content side of the message rather than the emotional side.

In most cases, do your paraphrase in one sentence. You're looking to capture the essence of the speaker's message, not all the details. Quite often, you can set up the paraphrase with starter phrases that cue the speaker that you want to check your understanding. Here are some common starter phrases to use:

- ✔ "What you're saying is . . ." (then comes the paraphrase)
- ✔ "In other words . . ."
- ✔ "What you mean is . . ."
- ✔ "What you're telling me is . . ."
- ✔ "If I understand your point correctly . . ."
- ✔ "What I'm hearing you say is . . ."
- ✔ "Sounds like you're saying . . ."

Like reflecting feelings, with paraphrasing you're checking your understanding, not assuming that you know what the speaker means. So you want to have that inquisitive inflection in your voice at the end of the paraphrase statement or add "Is that right?" so that you clearly sound like you're checking and asking for confirmation in return.

Utilizing the combo version: Reflective paraphrasing

Sometimes, messages you hear have meanings that factor in both facts and feelings. In those cases, try the third active listening tool for verifying understanding, *reflective paraphrasing*. This tool is a combination of reflecting feelings and paraphrasing (explained in the preceding two sections). In short, you identify the emotion in the meaning of the message and summarize in your own words the content that serves as the explanation for the emotion. In most cases, you can check the meaning with just one sentence. For example, "You're feeling frustrated because your proposal has gotten little response so far from management. Is that right?"

Relating when it counts: Sharing a relevant example

Sharing a relevant example is the last tool in this second set of active listening skills. You provide an example of a situation that relates to the point the speaker is making to show an understanding of where that person is coming from. This tool is used for special circumstances, and when done right, it can be powerful in a positive way.

You must meet a couple of prerequisites before you can decide to share a related event:

- ✔ You've heard the whole story from the speaker.
- ✔ You have an example from your experience that you see as relevant and believe will help show the speaker that you understand her circumstance.

Contrasting listener talk with speaker talk

Speakers talk. Because people commonly don't understand what listening involves, they often don't realize that effective listening involves talking, too. Active or responsive listeners talk when they listen. But speaker talk differs from listener talk as follows:

✔ ***You*-focused versus *me*-focused:** Active listeners maintain the focus on the speaker and the speaker's message, not on themselves. With speaker talk, the focus is on the speaker saying what's on his mind.

✔ **Drawing out, reflecting back on the message versus telling, reporting:** Active listeners help the speaker to get her facts and feelings across and to reflect back the listener's understanding of that message. Speakers tell what's on their minds or report their information.

✔ **Receive and stay nonjudgmental versus expressing opinions, feelings, ideas, and information:** Active listeners receive; speakers give. Active listeners stay neutral and respectful; speakers, if they so desire, take a stand and give their opinions, ideas, or feelings.

✔ **Less said versus more said:** Active listeners talk, but they usually say much less than speakers in conversations. Using active listening tools is generally accomplished in a few words or a sentence or two. Speakers say that much and usually a whole lot more.

✔ **A difference in emphasis:** Active listeners work to gain an understanding of what speakers' messages mean. Speakers emphasize getting their messages across.

In truly productive conversations, people take turns being listeners and then being speakers — a nice ebb and flow takes place. When they're active listeners, they create an opportunity for issues to be heard and addressed and for speakers to walk away knowing that results were achieved and respect was maintained.

If those prerequisites have not been met, don't share your example. You want to avoid giving your speaker a feeling of what's called *one-upmanship* — "If you think that's bad, you ought to hear what happened to me!" Your role is to keep the focus with the speaker, not take it away. That's why you want to use this strategy only under special circumstances.

When the prerequisites have been met, you follow one of two processes in using this tool. In either case, you may paraphrase or reflectively paraphrase first to check that you do understand your speaker's situation.

In one process, you give a brief, usually one-sentence, relevant example. For example, "So the struggles you've encountered with this client are much like what Joe went through last year when he was assigned this client, right?"

The second way is a three-step process that's good to use when you have an example from your own experience that you want to share. Here are the three steps:

Book IV

Get to the @#% Point! Communicating Effectively

1. **Make a connecting statement from the speaker to you.**

   "Your situation sounds like something similar to what I went through."

2. **Tell your related story briefly, briefly, briefly.**

   Get to the point. Just because you heard a detailed story doesn't mean you offer one in return. Yours should be the concise highlights version that you're only sharing to show relevance to the speaker's situation.

3. **Make a connecting statement back to the speaker.**

   "Much like you've experienced, right?"

Checking by asking, "Right?" at the end of the statement lets the speaker know he still is the focus of the conversation. You, on the other hand, merely shared something to add value to what you heard and to show that you understood where the speaker was coming from. Speakers greatly appreciate that.

Avoiding Barriers to Listening

Sometimes as a listener you may knowingly or unknowingly create barriers that hinder the flow of meaningful, nonjudgmental conversation. These barriers can be verbal or nonverbal.

Part of listening effectively involves being aware of what not to do in your listening behaviors. Sometimes you need to know which old habits to curb so that new ones can kick in and work for you.

What follows are six nonverbal behavior categories, each with its respective habits that you — as a listener — should avoid. These habits or pitfalls create barriers that turn off your speaker and prevent the speaker's message from being communicated. If you're like most people, many of the behaviors on this list will be familiar to you, either as a listener or a speaker.

Poor eye contact

Eye contact is one of the more influential behaviors that affect the flow of conversations. Steady eye contact with your speaker enhances the flow, while these behaviors hinder it:

> ✔ **Looking away:** The occasional glance away is not a barrier, but when eye contact often breaks away, the speaker feels that your attention is drifting elsewhere.

✔ **Locking in:** This is the glare or stare that creates a great deal of discomfort for the speaker — even more so when your eyes are looking below the speaker's face level. Steady eye contact is a relaxed look, not an intense stare down.

✔ **Rolling your eyes:** This is one of the most judgmental looks you can ever give a speaker while he's talking. It communicates sarcasm and displeasure with the message being heard and sometimes even stops a speaker right in his tracks — a conversation barrier at its worst.

Unfavorable facial expressions

Without a mirror, you can't see your face. But your speaker sees it and often reacts to the unfavorable messages it may be sending. Here are a few of these barrier makers:

✔ **Giving a frown or scowl:** A frown or a scowl is a look of disapproval and dismissal. These looks sometimes are accompanied by a shaking of the head from side to side and often communicate to the speaker, regardless of intention, that you don't like the person and/or the message being heard.

✔ **Flashing a smirk:** The smirk is that half-smile that often comes out when the speaker is talking about something serious. Again, regardless of intent, it has a mocking effect on the speaker, as if his serious message is a big joke to you — a major turnoff when someone is talking to you.

✔ **Raising one eyebrow:** Similar to the scowl, this behavior comes across as a stern, disapproving, or questioning facial expression. Unlike a curious look in which the forehead scrunches a bit and both eyebrows go up slightly, this is a look in which one eyebrow goes up the moment something unpleasant is said. It's often a conversation stopper.

✔ **Displaying a blank look:** This is a passive, expressionless look. It leaves the speaker wondering what, if anything, is getting through to you. Is anyone home? Does anyone care? In many cases, this behavior is the most unnerving to speakers — they get the feeling that they're talking to a wall.

Unwelcoming posture

Posture is how you sit or stand as you receive a speaker's message. Here are some postures that can create barriers:

✔ **Slouching:** Slouching is sitting back in your chair almost to the point at times where your feet are nearly as high as your head. You may like to relax in your chairs — especially the big cushy ones. But instead of sitting up alertly to take in the speaker's message, slouching communicates a disinterest and inattentiveness to the speaker.

Book IV

Get to the @#% Point! Communicating Effectively

✔ **Being closed:** In this case, the listener's arms are tightly folded such that the entire body looks stiff, too. This behavior is often accompanied with a scowl or stern look. It gives the message to the speaker that you're not open and that you're sitting in judgment of what you're hearing. That's a conversation stopper.

Too much movement

The listener occasionally uses gestures while checking her understanding of the speaker's message. Otherwise, the expectation is for the receiver to sit still and hear the message all the way through. Of course, sometimes that isn't what's happening with the listener. Avoid the following distracting behaviors:

✔ **Fidgeting:** With this behavior, the hands are in frequent motion, such as playing with paper clips, pens, pencils, or whatever else you can get your hands on. When your hands are on display while someone is talking to you, they create a sense that your attention is elsewhere or that you are too nervous to tune in and fully understand the message.

✔ **Squirming:** Squirming is the habit of shifting around a lot in your seat. It lends the appearance that you just can't sit still, like having ants in your pants. This restless body movement becomes an annoyance to someone who is trying to express a message to you.

✔ **Grooming yourself:** This is a habit in which, as you attempt to listen, your hands are occupied with something on your body. You're twirling a necklace, playing with a ring, constantly pulling on a tie, making a curl out of your hair, or rubbing your beard. The list goes on and can get downright personal. People often are unaware of these habits, but they nevertheless create a great distraction — if not a turnoff — for the speaker.

Ineffective placement

This nonverbal behavior — where and how you place yourself to receive a speaker's message — is subtle yet powerful in its effect on the speaker. When you place yourself at a comfortable yet fairly close distance, without major physical barriers and in a face-to-face manner, the influence on the conversation flow is positive. However, communications barriers go up when you do the following:

✔ **Remain distant:** This habit commonly shows itself in a couple of ways: Standing a good distance across the room instead of coming up close to easily hear the speaker or sitting behind a large desk instead of coming from behind the desk to sit side by side. While no one wants you to get up in his face — a habit more common to speakers than listeners — nonetheless, when you're too distant, you have the effect of discouraging the message from being openly received.

✔ **Facing away:** With this habit, you're turned away from the speaker. Sometimes, your back is turned while the person is talking to you, or you're staying shoulder to shoulder while listening rather than turning and directly facing the speaker. These behaviors often are discomforting to the speaker because they communicate that, as the listener, you aren't comfortable engaging in conversation.

✔ **Being preoccupied with something else:** Holding onto reading material, working away at your computer, focusing on your PDA (personal data assistant), or even engaging in a telephone call while someone is talking to you are common ways to display this barrier-creating behavior. Even in your fast-paced work life, doing two things at once often slows you down and hinders your productivity because you're blocking the speaker and, as a result, not getting the entire message the first time.

Attempting to attend to a speaker when you aren't ready to do so doesn't work. Giving subtle hints such as looking at your watch or continuing to work at what you're doing doesn't always help the person understand that now is not a good time for you to listen. The key to managing interruptions — so as not to miss important messages you need to hear and not to turn off your speaker — is to be direct and courteous. Head to Book II, Chapter 4 for ways to deal with interruptions in a positive way.

Uninviting tone of voice

As a listener, you may speak or make sounds in response to the speaker's message, and that makes your tone of voice important. A slight change of your tone from sounding receptive to becoming irritated or displeased can disrupt the flow of a conversation. Here are some tone-of-voice habits that may create a communications barrier:

✔ **Using harsh, reactive tones:** You hear an explanation from the other person and respond with, "You did what!" Sharpness in tone of voice has the effect of putting the speaker on the defensive. Often used before the speaker has even finished the message, this tone — usually fueled by emotions of anger or displeasure — comes out strongly and harshly in response to the message heard.

Book IV

Get to the @#% Point! Communicating Effectively

✔ **Biting with sarcasm:** This behavior is usually a reaction to what the speaker has said. In this case, it is tinged with subtle put-downs and just-kidding humor, neither of which are funny to the person getting it in return, such as "Yeah, great idea, Joe," or "Sounds like you're giving your best effort." These comments, while sounding positive in words, are negated by the sarcastic tones that communicate the opposite meaning and pass degrading judgment on the speaker and the message heard.

✔ **Being monotone:** This is the tone in response to a speaker that comes across as bored or disinterested. It's that dull and lifeless sounding, "Oh, that's nice," when the speaker has enthusiastically discussed, for example, an exciting experience. A monotone response can quickly deflate a speaker.

Tune in to your own behavior when listening. Stay aware and put your *concentration* on the speaker. Simply defined, concentration is focused mental energy. It involves giving your full attention to the matter at hand and being truly present in the conversation — actions that speakers most appreciate.

Chapter 3

Speaking Assertively

In This Chapter

▶ Understanding positive language and using it to show service and commitment

▶ Using your voice and body language to support your point

▶ Engaging your listener: Getting the best out of your voice

▶ Mapping out your speaking strategy for difficult situations

*S*ticks and stones can break your bones but words can never hurt you. You probably heard this old nursery rhyme when you were a child growing up. Unfortunately, it isn't true. Words that you say to someone else can be damaging. In fact, you've probably met a few people in your life who can remember the stupid things you said, sometimes years ago. (These people are usually called "family.")

How you use language greatly influences how people receive and understand your verbal and written messages. In the workplace it's vitally important that you communicate clearly without hurting your co-workers' feelings, damaging your reputation, or causing problems through misunderstandings. The idea, then, is to *speak assertively*. This phrase summarizes the package of positive, effective tools you can use in your interactions. In brief, it's about saying your messages the best way possible — the very topic of this chapter.

Being Powerfully Positive: The Can-Do and Will-Do Uses of Language

Chances are that co-workers, superiors, subordinates, and customers are making requests of you all the time. They want you to provide answers to their questions. They want you to perform certain duties or functions. They want to know when you're going to get something done. The list of requests and inquiries you get goes on and on. Much of how you manage and then meet these expectations ties into how you communicate about them with others. The first set of tools of speaking assertively helps you use language in its most powerful and positive form to respond effectively to these requests and inquiries.

Emphasizing what you can do instead of what you can't

Emphasize what you *can* do far more than what you *can't,* especially in response to requests and inquiries. When you emphasize what you can do first and foremost, you lead with a positive rather than a negative statement and come across as honest, clear, and helpful, which evokes a positive feeling in return. Take a look at the following examples to see how leading with the positive strikes a more helpful chord than leading with the negative:

- **Positive:** "Based on a few other matters I need to handle now, I can take care of your issue by the end of today."

  Negative: "I can't do that right now."

- **Positive:** "I can give you an update in two days. I'll know more about where that issue stands then."

  Negative: "I won't know for at least two days."

Emphasizing what you will do

Suppose you tell someone in another department that you can provide the information that person needs. She then asks you, "When can you get that information to me?" Which of the following two replies to that request would you respond to more favorably?

- "I'll have that information to you by the end of this week."
- "I'll try to have that information to you by the end of this week."

Most people respond more favorably to the first reply. The second reply sounds less certain; you're just going to *try* and may not actually do it. The first reply says that you *will* get the job done. It communicates a clear commitment — and that evokes a positive feeling in the requester.

Actions that match expectations are key to building credibility in your communications. The old customer-service maxim *underpromise and overdeliver* is a good one to remember and practice. When you underpromise and over-deliver, you pick a deadline that you can meet or beat. Therefore, when you say, "I'll have that information to you by the end of this week," and you get the job done by Friday at the latest, then your actions have matched your words and you have managed others' expectations of you.

On those occasions when what the other person wants you to do simply cannot be done, offer alternatives or options for the person to consider instead. If that isn't possible, say no to the request and briefly explain why it can't be done. This response makes you sound firm and reasonable as opposed to unyielding and hostile, the latter of which are aggressive characteristics as described in Chapter 1 of Book IV.

Avoiding false positives

Speaking positively helps you make an important point in the best way possible, and it requires combining tact and clarity. Sometimes, however, people think they're speaking positively (but actually aren't) when they sugarcoat or put a falsely positive spin on their words. Avoid using these tactics:

- **Sugarcoating:** When you *sugarcoat,* you try to sweeten a bad message in an effort to make tough news not sound so bad. It often involves saying something nice even though that nice point isn't necessarily relevant to the main issue at hand.

- **Putting a positive spin on the message:** When you put a *positive spin* on your message, you make something sound better than it is. When you put a positive spin on difficult news, few of your listeners will buy your message because it doesn't address the real issues (their concern, for example) and they may even view your message as condescending. At the very least, it undermines your sincerity.

Say What? Communicating Your Messages with Clarity

By making your message short and sweet and avoiding jargon, you make your meaning clear — a key aspect of speaking assertively. Quite simply, the clearer your message, the more the listener tunes in to receive it. The more the message is tuned in to, the more the listener understands it the way you intended it to be understood.

Keeping it short and sweet

Sometimes people get in the way of their own messages. They say too much or keep talking too long, and, as a result, lose the interest of their listeners or convince their listeners not to support their proposal or idea. This is the opposite of what you want to achieve in your interactions. Concentrate on three efforts with every message you express to others:

Book IV

Get to the @#% Point! Communicating Effectively

✔ **Be direct.** This means _get to the point._ Get there as quickly as you can so that your main idea doesn't get lost on the way, but do so with tact and respect.

Don't confuse being direct ("You have a spot on your shirt right by the pocket") with being blunt ("Look at your shirt. Ever heard of napkins?"). Being blunt doesn't take the other person into consideration, is often hurtful, and is less clear.

✔ **Be as concise as possible.** Fewer words are better than too many words when making an important point. As the old saying goes, "When I ask you what time it is, please don't tell me how the watch works."

✔ **Focus on main ideas.** Make sure to get your important points out when you speak and then use the necessary details to support them. Don't focus on too many ideas. Having only a few main ideas or just one main point keeps your message short and sweet.

By focusing on those three efforts, you can avoid the following traps that people often fall into when talking to others:

✔ **Beating around the bush:** Don't talk around a point (a tendency that occurs more often when sensitive issues are being discussed).

✔ **Rambling and being verbose:** _Rambling_ is talking on and on and on, often on tangential subjects. _Being verbose_ is using too many words when fewer make the point just fine. Either way, the main point usually is lost.

✔ **Overloading on details:** Details have their place and importance, but when you overload on details, the listener is left with the job of figuring out how all these details fit together, if they do at all.

Speaking in terms your audience understands

Jargon is special terminology, usually technical in nature, that only those closely associated with a job or field of study really understand. Because many people are uncomfortable admitting they don't understand what some terminology means, they tend to nod and smile and then walk away baffled. Therefore, be sure to speak in terms you know your audience understands.

Be aware of who you're addressing and use language familiar to your audience so that audience members can easily understand your message. Here are some key points to keep in mind:

✔ Speak in technical terms only when your audience understands the technical language of your job nearly as well as you do.

✔ When giving statistics or other supporting data, state the information in ways that can be commonly understood and that are familiar to those outside your area of expertise.

✔ Use acronyms correctly and translate them first for listeners who may not know the terms. This is especially helpful to new employees on the job.

✔ Avoid figures of speech, idioms, and metaphors around people for whom English is a second language and is relatively new.

Using language that focuses on solutions

Problems are a part of almost every job. In fact, developing solutions to problems is what many employees get paid to do. How you talk about problems and the language you use when you talk about them are important tools in speaking positively.

When you speak positively about problem situations, you use terms and statements that encourage dialogue and focus attention on developing solutions. When you use the language of solutions, you talk about problems long enough to understand them, analyze them as needed, and then spend more time talking with others about the actions to take to fix them. The following list provides some techniques that facilitate solutions-based language:

✔ **Lead your statements with an *I, me,* or *my* focus as opposed to a *you* focus:**

  • "As I see the problem . . ."

  • "What I've noticed is . . ."

  • "From my experience, the problem deals with . . ."

  • "To me, what's happening is . . ."

✔ **Describe what you have seen or know about the situation.** Avoid speculating or offering opinions without factual basis.

✔ **Invite dialogue with questions.** Problems are best defined, analyzed, and resolved as collaborations. The best way to get someone else to join in such discussions is to ask questions that truly request constructive input:

  • "Describe what you've seen happening here with this problem."

  • "What do you see as possible causes for this problem situation?"

  • "Brainstorm with me some ideas to help improve this situation."

  • "How would you propose implementing that idea?"

Remember to avoid accusatory *why* questions.

Book IV

Get to the @#% Point! Communicating Effectively

✔ **Focus on solution terms.** Use these terms to start people thinking about solving problems versus dwelling on them:

- *Option:* "Let's explore some options for resolving this situation."

- *Idea:* "I have an idea that can help solve this problem."

- *Recommendation:* "Here's what I recommend we do."

- *Suggestion:* "May I offer you a suggestion or two on handling that challenge?"

- *Solution:* "Let's take a look at some possible solutions that can help us."

- *Proposal:* "I have a proposal that can help resolve this issue."

✔ **Be constructive, even when you have a problem or disagreement:** Be as objective as possible with the words you say and make your point clearly and respectfully. Keep your tone sincere and emphasize in your language what you disagree with and not merely the fact that you disagree. Compare the following constructive and destructive uses of language:

- *Constructive:* "I had a chance to review the marketing plan that you submitted yesterday. It's going to need revision to meet our needs. Let's review what's needed and strategize on the corrections to be made."

- *Destructive:* "That marketing plan you did just isn't going to cut it. If this is the best you can do, you've got major problems."

Before you state your disagreements, hear the other person's idea all the way through and ask questions to draw out the thinking behind the idea so that you fully understand her point of view. In many cases, you may be able to dwell on parts you agree with most and not on parts you disagree about — a positive approach.

Avoiding language that hinders your message

Most of this chapter focuses on how to use language to get your points across in the most positive way possible — being honest, direct, and constructive. This section aids that effort by reminding you of language that people often use that does the opposite of what is intended. You may think some of this language is harmless, but it all ends up muddying your message:

✔ **Gender-specific nouns:** Saying *policeman* instead of *police officer, foreman* instead of *supervisor,* or *mailman* instead of *postal carrier* shows little consideration for women today. Before bemoaning political correctness, remember that inclusive terminology can show respect to everyone with whom you interact on the job.

✔ **Loaded language:** These are words or comments that offend, insult, hurt, anger — or all of them together — or otherwise trigger a negative emotional reaction regardless of your intention. *Idiot* and *stupid* are some common examples.

✔ **Accusatory language:** These are words that seek to blame or find fault, commonly said with a sharp tone of voice, too. Sentences with such language often start with the pronoun *you,* which gives them the feel of a personal attack. Then comments are made like the following: "That's your fault," or "You screwed up!" Such comments only add to the blaming feel of the message and are not received well. As mentioned in the previous section, stick to using the language that focuses on solutions when addressing problems and concerns with others.

✔ **Mixed messages:** Mixed messages are statements of contradiction in the same sentence. They usually contain the words *but, however,* or *although* in the middle of the sentence. When you use a word such as *but* in the middle of your thought, it communicates to your receiver that what you said before it didn't really count (consider "Joe, I know you've been working hard lately, but . . .").

✔ **Qualifier statements that negate your message:** These are statements at the beginning of the message that prepare your listener to tune out the message that follows — the opposite of what you're trying to achieve. For example: "Now don't take this personally . . ." or "This probably isn't a good idea . . ."

✔ **Profanity and vulgarity:** An occasional cuss word among close associates is seldom a big deal. Frequent use of swearing soils a good message and calls into question your intelligence and education.

✔ **Sexualized language:** When you comment in the workplace about someone's anatomy or sexual activity, you're certain to offend that person (or friends of that person) without even trying. Harassment laws aside, language of a sexual behavior is unwelcome and offensive in the workplace.

✔ **Stereotypical and derogatory remarks:** When you make comments that refer to people's characteristics — their color, ethnicity, religion, age, weight/stature, sexual orientation — with sweeping generalizations or other pointed comments, you're certain to offend and anger people around you, even if they aren't who you're targeting.

✔ **Trigger words and phrases:** Trigger words aren't negative by definition but they often trigger negative reactions from listeners. Here are some common examples of trigger words:

- *Always, never,* and *constantly:* These words are the language of absolutes and imply that no exceptions exist.

- *Should, must,* and *need to:* These are often used to order others around.

- *Try, maybe, perhaps,* and *may:* These words communicate doubt and uncertainty and no sense of commitment.

Book IV

Get to the @#% Point! Communicating Effectively

- *Policy:* "I'm just following company policy." In this context, the word *policy* makes you sound inflexible and gives the impression that you're hiding behind a rule that you really don't understand.

- *Promise:* As the saying goes, promises are meant to be broken. Sometimes when you promise you'll do something, doubt and uncertainty are communicated instead. (If you'd just do what you say, you wouldn't need to promise it.)

Similar to trigger words, trigger phrases like *to be honest with you* or *trust me on this one* are unnecessary, add no real meaning to your message, and sometimes disengage your listener from hearing your message in a positive light.

Tactfully requesting what you need

The trigger words listed in the preceding section make you sound like you're demanding to get what you need from others; for example, "You need to give me that information right away" or "You must be there at the meeting tomorrow." Assertive speaking says be clear and tactful by *requesting what you need.* Here are some requesting examples:

- "Can you provide me that information this week?"
- "Please look into that issue and let me know what happened."
- "Would you be willing to attend that meeting with me tomorrow?"

Sometimes providing rationale for your need is important because it helps the receiver of your request understand why his assistance is desired. Do so first in your message and keep the explanation relatively brief, followed directly by your request:

> "Sam, your financial expertise would be very helpful in responding to one of our key customer's concerns about our service. That customer is here for a meeting tomorrow afternoon. Would you be willing to attend that meeting with me?"

The words of common courtesy, especially *please* and *thank you,* are also a big part of how to assertively request and appreciate assistance from others. They add a professional tone to your message when spoken sincerely, and they positively reinforce cooperation others provide. Don't leave home without them.

Showing that you take responsibility

In addition, assertive speaking means you use language that shows you *take responsibility for your actions*. Acknowledging oversights or mistakes you made in a straightforward manner is quite alright to do. Sometimes adding sincere words of apology helps the message as well. And if the situation is fixable, follow the acknowledgment of responsibility by stating the corrective measures you will take.

> ✔ "Sue, you're right. That data I gave you yesterday does have a few errors in it. My apologies for that."

> ✔ "Sue, please let me recheck those figures and get the errors fixed. I can have the corrected data back to you within a day."

Everybody makes mistakes at times. Reacting defensively, blaming others, denying anything is wrong, or looking to cover up a mistake only tends to build tension and break down trust. Unless you keep repeating your mistakes, most people respond favorably when you sincerely admit them and take responsibility for correcting them.

Sending the Same Message with Your Body Language and Tone

Assertive speaking is about delivering your message in a positive, direct, and confident manner while maintaining respect for the person or people to whom you're expressing that message. When your audience feels respected, you'll be effective in your interactions at work (or anywhere, for that matter). When you speak assertively, you need to take care with more than just your words. What you convey nonverbally can greatly impact how your message is expressed and received by others. The following sections help you get the most out of your style so that others receive your messages the way that you intend for them to be heard.

You don't have to use any particular communication style to be effective at assertive speaking. You can be anything from reserved to highly expressive in your style, as long as you're assertive.

The eyes have it

Your eyes lend credibility to your spoken messages. They give the message much of its meaning and affect whether the listener believes and trusts your message. To use your eyes assertively, do the following:

316

Book IV: Get to the @#% Point! Communicating Effectively

✔ **Make steady eye contact.** Look at people when you talk to them. Steady eye contact is the key. Steady does not, however, mean constant. Blinking and occasional glances away are expected and normal.

People often ask how long you should continue eye contact. In general, eye contact can range comfortably from 6 to 20 seconds in one-on-one interactions, while in group situations, the time is less per individual — 3 to 6 seconds — because you want to address everybody in the group.

✔ **Look in the right places.** Look directly at your listener's face, near the eyes. Looking above and below the face captures less of the listener's attention and can make the listener uncomfortable.

You no doubt already know to avoid staring and glaring, darting glances, letting your eyes wander all over the place, letting them glaze over, and other obvious no-nos. In group settings, focusing on one person to the exclusion of others is also a problem. Addressing someone who has asked you a question is one thing. However, when your eye contact stays with only one person, providing little eye contact to the rest of your audience, the other listeners feel isolated and left out, which usually creates resentment and keeps them from truly hearing your message. The person you're focusing on begins to feel uncomfortable, too.

Putting the oomph in your voice

Your voice is a powerful tool for delivering your message in an assertive manner. When used wisely, it makes others pay attention to what you have to say. Follow these suggestions:

✔ **Project your voice appropriately for the situation.** The idea is to be heard easily and clearly by whoever your audience is. Vary your volume for the situation. Go a little louder in group situation, and then turn it down slightly for one-on-one interactions. Always keep it at a volume that makes your voice easy to be heard.

When people have trouble hearing what you're saying, you increase the likelihood that no one is listening to you. If you can't speak up to be heard, you come across as lacking confidence in your own message.

✔ **Inflect your voice.** Inflection deals with pitch. A high-pitched voice comes across as shrill, which nobody wants to hear. A one-pitch, monotone voice, especially a rather flat one, sounds dull. The key is to modulate your pitch. Doing so conveys energy in your message.

Use variation in either volume or inflection to highlight an important point. You'll come across as confident and positively engage the attention of others.

✔ **Display sincerity in your tone.** Sincerity certainly is impacted by the words you say, but it's more affected by the tone of your voice. In fact, a tone of sincerity basically says to the other person, "I mean what I say, I say what I mean, and I do so with respect toward you." When your tone communicates this kind of message, you're in control and can have a positive influence in your interactions and assertively make your point — productivity at its best.

Your voice can often be your greatest tool for communicating your message positively and effectively to others. However, when it isn't used assertively, it can be a great hindrance to being understood. Here is a list of pitfalls that make you sound less than assertive:

✔ **Being too loud:** When you speak too loudly, you come across as over-powering, potentially intimidating — especially when dealing with problem situations — and sometimes out of control. If you have to shout to be heard, generally no one wants to listen.

✔ **Dropping your voice at the end of a sentence:** When you do this, your sentences sound incomplete and give the impression that you lack the energy to complete your thoughts.

✔ **Mumbling:** Because people can't make out clearly what you say when you mumble, some make the assumption that you're saying something negative under your breath. Others just get the impression that you're unsure about what you're talking about.

✔ **Putting people down with your tone:** Tones that sound arrogant, scornful, or condescending are quickly heard as disrespectful — regardless of your intentions.

✔ **Sounding harsh:** When negative situations happen (welcome to the world of work!) and associated emotions enter into your message without any self-control, people may interpret your meaning as something worse than you intended. For example, your frustration sounds like whining; your feeling down sounds as though you're defeated.

✔ **Sounding uncertain:** When your voice sounds shaky or hesitant, you sound unsure about what you're saying and no one will have confidence in you or in what you say.

Putting your body into it

Body language includes facial expressions, posture, and gestures. The idea with assertive speaking is to get these myriad expressions and cues involved in your message. Use your face and body to positively engage others and come across as confident, animated, and relaxed. No one wants to listen to an uncertain, stiff, and uptight person for long. Here's how you use body-language to your advantage:

- **Posture:** Most important interactions take place while you're seated. Sit up and face your listener. When you sit up straight, you're more alert. Sitting up also helps put strength in your voice. And facing your listener straight on enables you to positively engage her. Leaning forward a bit is also sometimes helpful.

- **Facial expressions:** You want your facial expressions to match your verbal message. Doing so gives your message confidence and sincerity — a double dose that positively engages people. So keep that chin up and get that face of yours to come alive when you express your message.

- **Gestures:** Use gestures, or hand movements, to help your message flow properly and punctuate or emphasize key points.

You want your posture, facial expressions, and gestures to come across as confident, animated, and relaxed. Certain behaviors, however, make you less than assertive and create a negative response to your message:

- **Exhibiting distracting habits:** Don't pick, scratch, twirl your hair, or pull on jewelry when you're talking to someone else. These habits distract your listener from hearing the message and bring attention to you rather than what you have to say.

- **Folding your arms:** Folding your arms when speaking is different from folding them as you listen. When you're listening, as long as you don't look closed off, folding your arms helps you appear relaxed and receptive to hearing someone else's message. When you're speaking, however, folding your arms makes you come across as stiffer and less interested in your own message — signals that are the opposite of what you want to convey.

- **Invading space:** You're invading others' space when you get too close for comfort to the other person. If that person is leaning away from you, that's a sure sign you've crossed the comfort zone of physical space.

- **Looking blank:** Keeping your face expressionless conveys a lack of feeling, one way or another, for your own message. If you look disinterested, others will come to feel that way fast.

- **Looking stern:** Furrowed eyebrows and a near frown or scowl are uninviting, if not intimidating, and cause your listener to want to disengage. A stern demeanor can also increase or exaggerate the sharpness in your tone of voice.

- **Making threatening gestures:** Gestures like demonstrative finger pointing at someone else or pounding a fist on the table are often part of strong messages and make you sound aggressive instead of assertive.

- **Not using gestures at all:** Some people tuck their hands in their pockets when speaking. Others keep them under the table. Some keep them folded tightly together or pasted tightly to their legs. When your hands look cut off and are nowhere in sight as you express your message, you appear stiff or timid.

> ✔ **Slouching:** When you slouch, you come across as too relaxed. Less energy gets behind your voice as well. Slouching is no good if you want to be taken seriously by others.
>
> ✔ **Standing over the listener:** When you have important matters to discuss, have a seat with the person you're speaking to. When both parties are seated, it gives a sense of ease to the conversation. In a chair, it no longer matters how tall each of you is; you're physically equal and more comfortable talking with each other.

Helping Your Listener Stay Involved

Getting your listener's attention requires you to express your message in a positive and confident manner. If you don't show interest and certainty in your own message, how can you expect others to want to hear it? You want your listener *engaged* (that is, tuned in and interested) with your message. When your listeners are engaged, the likelihood of being understood and coming across well increases. Similarly, when your listener is engaged, you have the opportunity to influence him to action when needed.

When people are disengaged from you and your message, your communication with them is troubled. Listeners become disengaged for many reasons, but mostly from what they sense in you — disinterest, disgust, disrespect, or disillusionment. You can minimize disengaged reactions and maximize engaged reactions by helping listeners to sense your enthusiasm, enlightenment, and interest.

Adding meaning to your message

To make your message more appealing and easier to follow, follow these suggestions:

> ✔ **Show what you mean:** Seeing is believing. More important, seeing helps your listeners understand your topic. Take the person to the scene of the event to explain what you mean. To describe how the equipment works, put the other person in front of it. To explain the features of a product, demonstrate it as you talk.
>
> ✔ **Tell stories and anecdotes:** When you tell stories or anecdotes that clearly support the point you're making, your messages are much more interesting to listen to and easier to understand. Make sure to tie your stories into the point rather than have the story be isolated from it.

The longer the story you tell, the less effective it is for illustrating your points. Likewise, the less organized the flow of your story, the less your listeners can make sense of it.

Book IV

Get to the @#% Point! Communicating Effectively

✔ **Use visual aids:** Visual aids can help others see or read your message. They come in various forms — graphs and charts, handouts, articles, drawings and diagrams, slide presentations, and so on.

When you're expressing an important message, visuals provide data — pictorial or written — that support your key points. These aids help provide a clearer understanding of your message. If, however, they become the focus of the receiver's attention, they can distract and diminish the clarity of your message.

Avoid reading to your listeners, especially when your visual aids contain written information. Reading what people can read for themselves has two major drawbacks. First, it insults people's intelligence. Second, reading information to others doesn't come across as well as telling people about the information, because reading generally results in less eye contact with your receivers and often puts you into a monotone voice — a boring look and sound that cause most people to tune out.

Adding good sense to your humor

Humor often adds a nice touch to important messages. When done well, humor eases tension and relaxes people. Humor builds rapport with the audience when:

✔ Your receivers laugh *with* you and not *at* you, and they don't feel as though you're laughing at them either.

✔ Making light of a situation relaxes your receivers but doesn't distract them from the seriousness of your message.

✔ Your receivers relate to your situation and laugh if they feel like it was fun, and not because they're expected to laugh at any certain point.

Stories often work best when you want to include humor in your message. They recount life's experiences that others can relate to in different ways and cause people to laugh because they find familiarity in what they hear to be funny — the best way for humor to happen.

When you include humor, however, make sure you completely avoid any of the following:

✔ **Off-color jokes:** These are jokes of a sexual nature or about people's personal background such as race, ethnicity, religion, and sexual orientation. While some people laugh, others are greatly offended. Off-color humor doesn't fit into the workplace; in fact, it can get you fired.

✔ **Ridicule:** Ridicule is kidding that goes too far. Ridicule makes people feel that they're being laughed at and that they're the butts of your jokes.

✔ **Sarcasm:** Sarcasm is the biting remark said in so-called jest that people more often take personally as a put-down.

Getting your listener to respond

As a speaker, you can invite your listeners to participate more actively in your conversation and thus help your message be heard and understood the way you want. You do this by requesting feedback, encouraging questions and then answering them, answering questions with questions, checking for understanding, and tuning in to how your message is being received.

Requesting feedback

When you get a passive, no-feedback response to your message, avoid repeating yourself. Finish your point and then ask open-ended questions such as the following:

- "What do you think?"

- "What do you see as the pros and cons of what I expressed?"

- "Tell me your view of the issue I've described."

- "Give me your evaluation of the recommendation I'm making here."

Open-ended questions, covered in Chapter 2 of Book IV, solicit responses that require the expression of thoughts, ideas, or feelings. They can't be answered in a word or two the way closed-ended questions can. When you're talking to a passive listener, open-ended questions work well by allowing you to switch from the role of speaker to that of listener in the conversation.

Encouraging questions and answering them

When your listeners ask questions about your message, your job of expressing it clearly gets much easier. Questions from listeners provide you the opportunity to clarify key points, address concerns, and persuade people to see another point of view. In simple terms, questions help you greatly. Therefore, you have to take actions to encourage questions from your receivers. Here are a few ways that help:

- When you have a fairly long message, tell listeners upfront that they're welcome to ask questions at any time.

- When you get a question, provide positive reinforcement, "That's a good question," or "Thanks for asking."

- When you finish expressing a point of considerable length, say, "What questions can I answer for you?"

- Answer the questions clearly and positively.

To effectively answer questions from your receivers, be direct and concise. In more-involved conversations, use this three-step approach to handling questions:

1. **Open your response with a positive or an affirmative.**

   "Yes, I'm glad you raised that issue."

   If you're not fully certain of the question that was asked, paraphrase first to make sure you're clear. This effort also helps give you time to think of a response.

2. **Give your explanation in answer to the question.**

   Provide examples or anecdotes as needed to make your response specific.

3. **Close with a brief recap of your answer.**

   Make this recap a one-sentence summary.

To effectively answer questions from your listeners, avoid comments that express disagreement, sound like an excuse, or suggest the other person is wrong right from the start. These all cause receivers to disengage.

Answering a question with a question

You occasionally can answer a question initially with a question. This tip is best to use when you're asked a challenging question and you want to gain more insight into the questioner's thinking. Here are a couple of examples:

- ✔ "Sandy, I hear a concern about something in your question. What is that concern about?"
- ✔ "Bob, please help me understand; what prompted your question?"

As these examples point out, you're switching from a speaker to a listener in the conversation. Your purpose is to gain a better understanding of where the other party in your conversation is coming from. You may even want to paraphrase or reflectively paraphrase (see Chapter 2 of Book IV) the explanation behind the question you hear. Thus, when you respond to the issue raised, you're more likely to address the real core of it, rather than give information that may not be the focus of the other person's need or concern. Therefore, even when you need to speak, listening first sometimes is the better strategy with which to start.

Checking for understanding

Sometimes a better way to find out if your message was clearly received is to ask your listeners to explain their understanding of your message. Slightly different than requesting feedback, here you're going after understanding alone, not after what the other person thinks about your message. To check for understanding after you've expressed a lengthy message, use an open-ended question that lets your listeners know you're checking in. You can ask something such as the following:

"To make sure I'm clear, what's your understanding of what my message was all about?"

When you periodically check for understanding, you help avoid misunderstandings and encourage your listeners to speak up, letting you know when something isn't clear.

Tuning in to how your messages are being received

Pay attention to the nonverbal messages that your listeners sometimes express when they hear your message: their tone of voice, body language, and facial expressions. When you identify looks such as concern or confusion, instead of proceeding with your message, respond to what you see. Sometimes you can do this by adjusting your vocabulary or pace to better connect to your listener. Even better, you can be direct and reflect back what you think you're seeing:

"You look confused by what I'm saying. Please tell me about it."

Such reflections invite your listeners to share what's going on in their minds and provide you opportunities to make adjustments or address concerns. They turn the nonverbally responsive person into a verbally responsive one, which makes the job of getting your message across clearly, concisely, and positively a whole lot easier.

Dealing with Sensitive Subjects

From time to time you may encounter situations in your job in which you need to deal with sensitive issues or important matters. You want these critical interactions to go well. Mapping out your strategy prepares you for these challenging situations and develops your communication plan of action for how you want a serious meeting to go. When you have a plan, you'll likely achieve the positive results you're aiming for much more often than when you don't have a plan.

Mapping out a plan of communication is beneficial for special occasions; that is, critical situations in which important or sensitive issues need to be addressed, where being organized and careful in what you say are crucial for influencing positive outcomes. For example:

- ✔ Addressing conflicts or concerns with others
- ✔ Delivering important presentations
- ✔ Handling client meetings

✔ Leading group meetings

✔ Making proposals to managers above you

✔ Persuading others to support your major idea

✔ Reporting important news to others

The aim of mapping out your plan is to organize your communication effort for when you speak face to face with others. To map out your communication plan, you prepare the written outline, supporting documents, and visual aids that you need to have with you at these meetings. The following sections outline key tips to follow when mapping out your communication plan to increase the likelihood of good results in your important interactions. (For more general advice on planning meetings, turn to Book III, Chapter 2.)

Doing your homework first

Know what research you do need to do, what data you need to gather, and what issues you need to understand better. Nothing is worse than communicating something important to a decision maker and leaving out vital information or not having all your facts in order to back you up.

Sometimes you do your homework by reading reports, articles, or other records of information; sometimes you do it by talking to others and getting answers from them. Other times you do both. When needed, homework also involves developing visual aids and supporting documents to help make your case.

People often are quite impressed when you come to an important meeting and show that you've done your homework. The way you make your presentation shows preparation and thoroughness — efforts that increase the likelihood of your message being received in desirable ways.

Considering your audience in your plans

How you develop your plan depends on who's going to hear your message. Here are some factors to take into account:

✔ Who is your target audience and what's important to them?

✔ What are your audience's hot buttons (critical points you need to address and sensitive points you want to stay away from)?

✔ What's their level of understanding of your issue and what's the best language to use to discuss the issue with them?

✔ When is the best timing to discuss your issue and where is the best location to do so?

✔ What possible objections or negative reactions are you likely to encounter, and what's the best way to address those concerns, if they come up?

Considering these factors should always be part of the homework you do prior to preparing your plan. If you tailor your message to your audience, you increase the likelihood of getting favorable responses in return.

Putting your plan in writing

With homework complete and audience factors considered, you're ready to map out your plan in writing. You want your outline to follow these steps:

1. **Set the opening.**

   • Set your topic and provide context as needed.

   • State your purpose; that is, say what you're trying to accomplish in this meeting. Know and state the positive outcome you're seeking.

   • Tell your listeners what you want them to do so they best receive your message.

2. **Organize the key points.**

   • Determine the key points and the order in which you want to make them.

   • Determine what stories and anecdotes will help illustrate your points and when to tell them.

   • Determine whether you're using visual aids and when best to present them.

   • Determine when you're going to provide the positive punch to your message by showing your audience the benefits or positive gains from what you're proposing, the recommended solution for the problem you have defined, or the idea for change that makes the improvements desired.

3. **Get the listener's response.**

   • Determine when you want your listeners to respond: at a certain time, like at the end of the presentation, or at any time.

   • Prepare a few questions to invite feedback.

   • Prepare responses in anticipation of possible concerns you expect to hear.

4. **Bring the meeting to closure.**

   From a recap of important points to a confirmation of an agreement or an outline of the next steps, set how you want your closure to go.

Chapter 4

You've Got Mail: Communicating Electronically

*E*veryone makes real efforts to get messages across to family, friends, colleagues, business associates, and supervisors. But many of those messages fail because they're unclear, inaccurate, or too long. And for every message that doesn't succeed, you waste time: repeating, redoing, reworking, and reorganizing. In this chapter, you discover how to head off those problems by choosing your medium and using it effectively, keeping your message direct, and asking the right questions.

Most offices in the United States today have e-mail and Internet access as standard features. With these tools, not only can you talk electronically to everyone within your company, but you can also communicate online with people outside your organization. Although technology has provided new means for person-to-person communication, it's not without pitfalls, and it has created many challenges for people as they do their jobs. This chapter can help you understand how best to use e-mail and how best *not* to use it when communicating on the job.

Note: Documents and reports that can be sent via e-mail as attachments aren't the focus here; they are work products in and of themselves. Rather, the focus of this chapter is on direct communication through e-mail. If you want to find out about managing documents and electronic files you create and receive, check out Chapters 3 and 6 in Book II.

Choosing the Right Electronic Medium for Your Message

Whether you realize it or not, you communicate in three main ways: words, tone of voice, and body language. When you communicate with someone face-to-face, you can employ all three forms of communication, dramatically increasing your effectiveness and speeding your way to the desired outcome. When you communicate over the phone, you use two, and when you do so over e-mail, you're down to one. So despite e-mail's speed and efficiency, sometimes a face-to-face meeting or a phone call is the best way to address and resolve a situation.

How you decide which medium is most appropriate for the information or for your topic of discussion depends largely on the complexity of the information you're sharing as well as on the nature of the topic of discussion. When you have to communicate by e-mail or telephone rather than in person, you need to make these channels work for you as much as possible.

To E-Mail or Not to E-Mail: That Is the Question

You may be one of the many people who literally can spend their entire workday reading and responding to e-mail. Even for people who don't use e-mail to that extent, receiving and sending messages can take one or two hours a day. E-mail has become a standard part of communication in today's workplace. Like any form of communication, you need to use skill and judgment to maximize e-mail's value. As with all seismic tech changes, e-mail has its infinite blessings — and its bitter curses. E-mail can help you get more work done, but it can also distract you from working.

Indeed, the e-mail explosion has been one of the most significant advances in the world of work in the twenty-first century. The speed with which e-mail communicates, the breadth of its reach, the efficiency in the ability to store, respond, forward, copy, follow up, and conduct business online is beyond momentous. But for all its advantages, e-mail is often misused in ways that result in inefficiencies, misunderstandings, and lost time.

Knowing when to use e-mail

One of the major factors that has led to the popularity of e-mail is its speed and ease of use. Just type away on your keyboard, and in no time, you can send a short message to someone — a message that person receives soon after you send it. Using e-mail is much easier than writing a letter and putting it in the regular mail (or *snail mail*). As a result, e-mail can be a tool for many useful communication purposes, such as the following:

- **Sending interoffice memos:** Written communication in the office is nothing new. Many workplaces used to live and die by the interoffice memo. Today, you can send memos giving news and announcements about business, personnel, and policy matters via e-mail. Type the message and click the Send button, and you can reach as many people in the organization as you want, at one time — a much more efficient process for distributing the news than the old interoffice memo method.

- **Making requests:** E-mail works well for making requests. Perhaps you need assistance on a project or you want to set up a meeting. People often respond quickly to these kinds of requests.

- **Making inquiries:** Sometimes, the quickest and easiest way to find an answer to a question is to ask in an e-mail. If the inquiry isn't overly involved and doesn't require a great deal of explanation, e-mail is a handy communications vehicle for getting an answer.

- **Keeping in touch:** Letters and cards aren't going away; they make for a nice personal touch in communications. On the other hand, e-mail enables you to drop quick notes to clients, staff in other departments, and other business associates. A simple here's-what's-been-happening-with-me, how-goes-it-with-you communication lets key businesspeople who you may not see often know that you care about how they're doing.

- **Conducting routine business transactions:** Some business relationships, such as customer-vendor ones, run under established processes. In such cases, e-mail helps transactions run efficiently. For example, you (the customer) need so many parts from your vendor. The vendor tells you the price and when he can ship them, you confirm, and away you both go. When transactions and negotiations require little discussion, e-mail helps you exchange information and get the deal done.

- **Providing status and news:** If you're a manager who, for example, has salespeople in different locations or who oversees the work of field-service technicians — employees you don't have the opportunity to see very often — you can use e-mail to find out the status of their work efforts. If you want to keep your boss in the loop on your latest project or on what happened with that important customer issue you tackled today, e-mail is a great option for passing on the news and highlights. These kinds of updates and status communications help keep fellow staff informed and can usually be handled via e-mail.

- **Recapping agreements and discussions:** One of the best uses of e-mail is to reinforce verbal interactions, especially when decisions or agreements are made or when action items are established. Instead of leaving what you worked out in a meeting to your memory, you can recap these important points in an e-mail to team members. When minutes of

Book IV

Get to the @#% Point! Communicating Effectively

meetings — the absolute essentials, such as decisions and agreements — need to be recorded, e-mail works well. By not leaving these important items to memory, you enhance productivity.

✔ **Communicating when time differences are an issue:** If you have clients in the Middle East and Asia, for example, while you're busy working, they're either done with their workday or sound asleep. E-mail allows you to keep your business deals flowing without getting up really early or staying up late. Just send off your queries and get the replies the next morning.

✔ **Seeking ideas:** E-mail can be useful for generating ideas. Maybe you're working on an assignment or planning an event for which you need assistance in brainstorming ideas. Using e-mail to solicit this input, which often doesn't require a thorough discussion or a meeting, enables you to save time.

✔ **Giving simple feedback on others' work:** *Simple feedback* means that the comments you write aren't long, aren't controversial, and have been requested. Many an occasion arises in which people want your feedback or thoughts on their plans, proposals, or other work. If that feedback doesn't require a great deal of explanation, e-mail can be a quick and easy way to pass along your comments.

E-mail can be an effective vehicle for sending and receiving various forms of news and information when live interaction isn't really needed. As the preceding list shows, it's best in straightforward situations that require simple and direct responses.

Recognizing when not to use e-mail

Many of the problems connected with e-mail communication result from people using e-mail when they should be talking — and listening. Remember that e-mail is one-way communication and isn't usually live. You have less opportunity with written messages to be understood clearly than with live conversation because you can't use your tone of voice and body language to convey sincerity. In fact, on sensitive (or even some not-so-sensitive) matters, people often interpret your e-mail messages in a far worse light than you ever meant. Relying on e-mail when engaging in live conversation is more appropriate tends to increase the tug-of-war in working relationships.

In short, some subjects are better handled by phone or face-to-face, where you can gauge responses as you're delivering the message and add information through tone of voice and/or body language. To keep working relationships on a constructive level and to enhance productivity, the following sections outline those situations in which you shouldn't use e-mail.

When you need to give constructive feedback on performance

There are two types of constructive feedback: positive feedback for good performance and negative feedback for performance that needs improvement. Although positive feedback given in an e-mail message may be well received, it still has less impact and seems less sincere than feedback given in person.

The recipient of negative feedback often interprets e-mailed feedback as far worse than was ever intended and may stew about what was written. When the feedback is given via e-mail, the receiver doesn't have the opportunity to discuss the matter and work out solutions. Giving verbal, face-to-face feedback allows you to explain your messages, helps the other person understand them as they were intended, and lets you listen to and understand the recipient's perspective.

The nature of giving constructive feedback — positive and negative — is verbal and informal. It works best when it's part of a two-way conversation.

After your previous e-mail messages get little or no response

You may encounter situations in which your inquiries made by e-mail get no response or your questions are met with partial answers. You may send follow-up messages, but you still get little or no response. The reasons for this lack of response vary: disinterest in your issue, too many e-mails to pay attention to yours, poor follow-through skills. Just because you write the message clearly doesn't guarantee that the receiver thoroughly reads and acts on it.

Continuing to send follow-up e-mails after a couple of tries may turn you into an irritating pest and give those who want to ignore your messages even more reason to do so. Instead, talk to the person to find out what has happened and determine when you can get an answer to your inquiry. Although reaching the person, either by phone or in person, may take a few attempts, it's well worth the effort. The truth of the matter is that only live conversation can get an unresponsive person to respond.

When you address sensitive issues

Suppose you have a co-worker who wants to act on an idea that you know from experience will lead to problems, you have reservations about your boss's proposal for a business change, or you've received a message from a customer who is unhappy about service. In these kinds of circumstances, attempting to share your feedback, thoughts, or feelings via e-mail often exacerbates an already touchy situation.

With e-mail, you don't have a chance to listen to what the other person is thinking. When you choose one-way communication to communicate about sensitive matters, you increase the risk of misunderstanding and tension, which is the opposite of what you're trying to achieve.

Book IV

Get to the @#% Point! Communicating Effectively

E-mail can be particularly dangerous in situations where your response is strong or emotional. Who hasn't received an e-mail or voice message that riled them up to the point of pounding out a ferocious e-mail response? In most cases, this situation only ends badly. The blessings of e-mail can also be its curse: Its immediacy gives little time to reflect and process. *Never* send an e-mail when you're still angry, whether to your colleague, vendor, boss, or political representative. Give yourself adequate time to completely calm down before shooting off an emotional message.

That said, the process of writing an e-mail can help you work through anger. The exercise helps you work off some of that emotional energy and serves to clear your head so you can think through your reaction and response. But don't actually send the message! Go ahead and write your e-mail response — do it offline so you don't inadvertently send it — and then park it in your draft folder until you cool down some. If you reread it the next day and still feel justified, go ahead and send. But if you review and blush at your vitriol, you're saved the embarrassment of having to apologize for your outburst.

When you want to elicit support and understanding for important changes and initiatives

Organizations are going through so much change that, in many companies, change is the only constant you can count on. Written communications can help reinforce announcements and updates about changes or new initiatives, but as the sole communications for these matters, e-mail messages can create anxiety.

Only live and ongoing face-to-face communication about significant changes helps get people on board. The chance to explain the company's rationale, answer employees' questions, seek input and involvement, and address concerns is lost when this kind of communication is handled by e-mail. Rumor and innuendo — key ingredients in resistance to change — often fill the voids that are created.

When you need to resolve concerns and conflicts

Want to aggravate a conflict? Attempt to address it in an e-mail message. Trying to resolve conflict via e-mail is one of the major abuses of e-mail communications.

New terms from this technology have entered into the communications arena — *flaming e-mails* and *nasty grams*. A flaming e-mail or nasty gram is an attempt by one party to voice a concern to another party through an e-mail message that's harsh in language and tone. What often results is that the other party, hurt by the nasty gram, shoots one back through e-mail. Then, as the terminology goes, the *flame war* is on as the warring parties send negative e-mails back and forth — sometimes copying others on them as well. All this negative communication escalates tensions and brings no resolution to the conflict.

Voicing concerns and expressing disagreements involving strong opinions — which is what conflict is — through e-mail tend to cause worse interpretations than you intended. Attempts to address conflicts in this way come across as hiding behind e-mail — a passive-aggressive communication approach, which is covered in Chapter 1 of Book IV. The only tried-and-true method for resolving concerns and conflicts is live, person-to-person interaction — face-to-face or by telephone when you and the other person are in different locations. Technology can't do it for you.

If you find yourself getting worked up or rewriting much of what you want to say when you're drafting an e-mail, you shouldn't send that message. If you have an important issue or problem that involves a high degree of emotion, go directly to the source to talk and listen — the assertive approach that's introduced in Chapter 1 of Book IV.

Writing Effective E-Mails

The advent of e-mail has forced everyone to focus on keeping communications brief, if only because so many people dislike writing and typing. That's all good. But as short and straightforward as e-mail messages seem to be, they're also dangerously deceptive and easy to misinterpret. Studies indicate that more than 50 percent of those who use e-mail say their business correspondence is misunderstood.

There's no getting around it: E-mail often leads to misunderstandings. For instance, a message from your boss may translate as curt or even displeased to you, when in reality she was simply rushed. A remark that would pass as playful humor in person can come across as an insult in writing.

The following sections explain how to write a clear, effective e-mail that minimizes the potential for misinterpretation.

Applying basic communication skills to e-mail messages

Your high school English teacher was right when he told you that length and quality aren't necessarily synonymous. Similarly, just because someone's lips move and sound emerges doesn't mean communication is taking place. The same idea applies to e-mail communications. To ensure that your audience fully receives your message, invest time upfront crafting your correspondence. For impact, build your message with as few words as possible while still getting your meaning across. Keep the message short, sweet, and to the point. This section tells you how.

Book IV

Get to the @#% Point! Communicating Effectively

Cut out the clutter in your language

Many people are uncomfortable about following a direct approach, so they fluff out their communications with superfluous information or wrap the salient points in a veil of irrelevant niceties. The problem with this fluff is that, at best, it delays getting to the key information, and at worst, it obscures your message. You don't have to do away with social pleasantries — in fact, you shouldn't — but remember what you're trying to accomplish: Communicate a key point as efficiently and effectively as possible.

Being direct doesn't mean being curt, cold, or negatively opinionated — it means that you're clear, concise, and professional; that you convey a constructive and supportive tone, not a confrontational one. The distinction sounds subtle, but it matters greatly when you're aiming for the most time-effective response.

Don't try to impress others with your use of obscure words, phrases, and unnecessary technical jargon — it only blocks communication and wastes time. The result is confusion, hesitation, misunderstandings, and alienation from the receiver. Using simple and straightforward language to communicate your ideas will make you look smarter and more gracious every time.

Include only the essential stuff

To maximize your time (and everyone else's), shoot for a succinct message but don't sacrifice crucial information in the interest of brevity. Ask yourself two questions as you craft your message: Who are you giving information to? What is important for this person to know? Then answer those questions — and don't be afraid to ask others whether you've missed anything. When you communicate directly, you let people know

- What situation you're facing
- What you want or need
- What you expect the receiver to do and what the standards of measurement are
- What the timeline is

Notice how the following statements improve by adding this specific information:

- **Weak:** "As a company, it looks like we need to do a little better."

  Improved: "Our goal is to improve corporate results by 6 percent by the end of the third quarter."

- **Weak:** "You all know what you have to do, so go out and do it!"

  Improved: "Let's work together to cut travel expenses in each of our areas by 2 percent by year-end."

> ✔ **Weak:** "There's a lot to be said for making our goal."
>
> **Improved:** "We outdid ourselves this year. We exceeded our goal by 7 percent! Let's see if we can exceed our goal by 9 percent next year. If we do, you'll all earn a 3 percent bonus!" (Now, *that's* communicating!)

Get to the point and say what you need to say as briefly as possible. Give the highlights (not all the details) and make the point relatively simple (rather than rambling). Go with the main point first and give supporting information next as needed. Verbosity in writing creates more confusion and less interest than in face-to-face conversation, where at least you have the chance to adjust your message and help your listener understand it.

If you write more than a page, nobody wants to read it. In other words, the shorter your message, the more likely people will read and comprehend it. If you find your e-mail exceeding a page in length and you can't edit it to be much shorter, paste the information into its own document, attach the document to your e-mail, and use your e-mail message to briefly introduce the information in the attachment and highlight the key points. Attaching the more-detailed version makes the information easy for the recipient to download and ensures that that at least the key items are front and center. In most cases, you want to stick to short e-mail messages.

Keep your language constructive

Say — or rather, write — your messages in the best way possible. Keep the words respectful rather than harsh. Avoid anything that sounds blaming or threatening: "You didn't do what you said you would do" or "If you don't do this, I won't do that for you." Also avoid words that can trigger negative reactions, such as *always, never,* and the not-words *(don't, won't,* and *can't).* Here are a few examples of what *not* to write:

- ✔ "You always forget to follow the procedure."
- ✔ "You never help out when I request your assistance."
- ✔ "That idea won't work."
- ✔ "We can't do that on such short notice."

In many cases, you can rephrase your message to be more constructive. And in some instances, you may be better off talking to the other person rather than sending an e-mail. The idea is to keep your language straightforward and to focus on the issue rather than on the person. Say what you mean while sounding matter-of-fact and positive. (See Chapter 3 in Book IV for more on how to use language to have a positive impact.)

When people use all caps for some or all of an e-mail message, others interpret it as shouting at them. Stick to the standard practice of using capital letters only where they belong.

Book IV

Get to the @#% Point! Communicating Effectively

Watch the humor

Having a sense of humor is a great attribute, especially in the workplace. Displaying that humor is much harder to do in writing than it is in person-to-person interactions, where you can gauge how the other person is reacting to what you're saying. The receiver of an e-mail may interpret your attempts at clever wit as biting sarcasm.

If you can add an occasional lighthearted touch to your e-mail messages, great. The key is to focus on the content rather than the tone.

Off-color jokes and ridicule are offensive to readers of your e-mail. Even if you think the other person wants to read the risqué joke you're forwarding, such messages can be forwarded to others who could be offended. Sending off-color or demeaning e-mails — even in jest — generally invites more trouble than fun.

Write for your audience

As you do when speaking, consider who you're addressing when sending an e-mail. Understand who your audience is. If they respond best to brief highlights, keep the message short and sweet. If they like detail, give them explanations. If they speak in technical terms, use the jargon they understand. Vice versa — keep the language in lay terms when your audience doesn't know the jargon. Keeping your audience in mind helps you keep your messages clear, understandable, and respectful.

Crafting a clear and targeted subject line

Your Aunt Edna, of course, always opens your e-mails, with or without a subject line. But a potential customer or business contact is flooded with messages from advertisers and with other highly expendable e-mail. You have between 25 and 35 characters to persuade the recipient to move your correspondence from the B pile to the A pile. Make your e-mail a keeper by tagging it with a standout subject line after you write the body of the e-mail. Pull out a phrase or series of words that sums up the message.

As you decide what to write in the subject line, keep in mind that this line has two purposes:

✔ To tell the recipient the purpose of your e-mail

✔ To pique the receiver's interest enough to command attention from the slew of e-mail she's sifting through

In sales and marketing, use a *page-turner* subject line: an unfinished thought that can be completed when the recipient opens the e-mail:

- ✔ "Just one week until . . ."
- ✔ "Our clients have increased sales by 84%"
- ✔ "Don't miss this tremendous . . ."

Spam software programs identify some key words and phrases and may block any e-mail containing those words in the subject line. Steer clear of the following words and phrases (and their relatives):

- ✔ Incredible
- ✔ Free
- ✔ Limited time only
- ✔ Money
- ✔ A friend gave me your e-mail address

Looking at structure and length

E-mails are most effective when they're short and to the point. If recipients have to scroll, the odds increase that they'll miss some of the information toward the end or feel so overwhelmed that reading your missive is a task they shift to the back burner. That's why many experts suggest that e-mail messages should be about four paragraphs long or less — definitely no longer than a screen full. If you find you have more to say than will fit on the screen, consider these alternatives:

- ✔ Use another mode of communication.
- ✔ Send the message as an attachment, including a paragraph of explanation within the e-mail.

If you know for certain that you must include all information in the body of an e-mail and that you need more than four paragraphs to house it all, remember that the first and last paragraphs carry the most punch. To make effective use of your presentation, do the following:

- ✔ Be sure that the most important information is in the top part of the e-mail.
- ✔ Include a call to action earlier in the e-mail rather than at the end, where it typically goes. The reader may not make it to the last paragraph.
- ✔ When you receive an e-mail that warrants forwarding — or one that you want to copy someone else on — delete the trailing chain of discussion so only the issue at hand remains.
- ✔ Use bullet points rather than narrative to call out the critical points for the reader.

What if you're on the receiving end of a litany of questions in e-mail form? Simple: Click Reply (with history) and craft a short paragraph that explains that your responses are found below. Then respond right after each individual question — within the original message — in a professional but standout color so the original sender clearly and easily sees your responses. I frequently use red, blue, or black for my color — and if need be, green. This setup helps senders avoid scrolling up and down from their question to your responses.

Maintaining a professional level of formality

Because of their immediate nature, e-mail tends toward the informal. Between friends and family, dispensing with punctuation, salutations, and even correct spelling may be acceptable. But in the world of business, it's a huge no-no.

Although you may have congenial enough relationships with co-workers and even some clients, my advice is to keep *all* business correspondence formal. These messages reflect on your professionalism and may end up printed out and passed around or forwarded to other businesspeople. Just like dressing for a job interview, it never hurts to keep it formal.

Treat an e-mail the same as you would a paper letter, and follow these tips to maintain your professional appearance:

- Use conventional salutations and closings: *Dear* ____, *Hello* ____ and *Best regards, Sincerely,* or the like.

- Don't assume your recipient knows lingo or abbreviations common in text messages and online chats — leave them out. Abbreviations, single letters, and misspelled characters may only confuse recipients to the point they ignore the message.

- Steer clear of *emoticons,* those sideways facial expressions created from punctuation keys :-P.

- Keep vernacular and slang out of the e-mail.

- Don't use all capital letters. In e-mail vernacular, capital letters indicate shouting. True, the recipient doesn't hear you shout, but it's difficult to read long tracts of copy in uppercase.

- Always close with your name, as if you were actually signing a letter.

- Run the spell-checker.

Reviewing your writing

E-mail produces copies of your writing that you usually can't retrieve after you send it into cyberspace, so make sure everything you write is exactly as it should be. To ensure that you don't accidentally overlook any errors or omissions and that you'll get the response you're seeking (if any), follow these bits of advice:

- ✔ **Allow yourself time to put written communication aside; then come back to it to see it as a first-time reader would.** Time spent upfront, honing your communications, can save you more "expensive" time later in the project. As for your own e-mail messages, try putting them in the draft box and come back to them later. This can help you catch any language that comes off as snippy, short, abrupt, or offensive.

    If you're in a rush to get out a lot of correspondence, go ahead and whip through them all at once. But stick them the draft box and return to each with fresh eyes before launching them.

- ✔ **Have a co-worker look over your memos and e-mail.** If possible, choose someone not involved with the project. Are there unanswered questions?

- ✔ **Proofread your e-mail for spelling and grammar errors by using spell-checker *and* reading through your e-mail one last time before sending it.** Making typos and grammatical errors is common in e-mail, primarily because the communication is so fast and immediate. Again, in a business environment, you want your correspondence to reflect your high level of professionalism. Although you may not get a pay cut for misspelling a few words, others may note your lack of attention.

Preparing for the send-off

Before you click that Send button, review your recipients and give your sending options one last review:

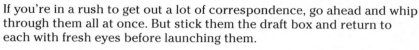

- ✔ **Give the urgent-message flag a rest.** Avoid the boy-who-cried-wolf syndrome: When every single message you send is marked *urgent,* well, you know what happens. Don't use the flag unless you need a response in 24 hours or less.

- ✔ **Don't overuse the carbon copy (cc) function.** If you need to include others, terrific, but keep the list of carbon copies only to the people who really need to know. If someone has only peripheral interest in the discussion, leave that person off.

    People sometimes copy others in conflict situations, which can stir up negative energy around the office. Upper-level managers often receive too many e-mail messages as it is and don't need more messages about matters in which their involvement isn't really needed. In addition, the other party in your discussion becomes aggravated by the move to notify others who aren't involved in the matter — sometimes this is also viewed as a violation of confidentiality. And when other people are copied on the news, they may get involved (sometimes referred to as *butting in*) and make the situation worse. If you see the need to copy others on an e-mail message that contains potentially sensitive information, make sure the other party or parties you dealt with on the issue agree that the need exists. Very simply, you should avoid other people's time and attention with unnecessary e-mail.

✔ **Use the blind carbon copy (bcc) for large e-mail sends.** The advantage of bcc is that you're not sharing your list of contacts. With the explosion of spam, everyone needs to protect privacy, and people who have your address have that obligation as well. By using the bcc feature, no one other than you knows who has received your correspondence.

✔ **Mark it *private*.** With most corporate e-mail systems in companies, you're able to send an e-mail privately. If the message is confidential or sensitive, be sure to make it *private* — for the recipient's eyes and your eyes only. Ask the IT department in your company how you can send private e-mail throughout your division or department.

✔ **Double-check the recipient:** Before sending the e-mail, make sure you're sending it to the intended person. At best, inadvertently sending information to the wrong person is an annoyance; at worst — if the information is confidential or proprietary, for example — it could land you in big trouble.

A Message about Voice Mail

Voice mail is another form of technology that has become a big part of people's daily communication on the job. *Voice mail,* the verbal message you leave when someone doesn't answer the telephone, is often a much more efficient way to leave someone a phone message than to relay it to a receptionist, a secretary, or any other live person. You can say what you want without wondering whether the other person wrote down your message, let alone your name, correctly.

Using voice mail is like using e-mail. It works best when its purpose is to make a request, briefly share news, or pass on basic information. It doesn't work for raising concerns or addressing issues of a sensitive nature. Venting on voice mail, for example, tends not to increase understanding or excite others to help you. Voice mail can be used to request a discussion, but don't use it to present details about an issue.

Like e-mail, voice mail is one-way communication and doesn't work when two-way interactions are needed. Also like e-mail, the shorter your voice mail messages, the better. Briefly tell the other person the nature of your call and what you want the individual to do, such as call you back, and then make sure that you slowly enunciate your name and phone number. Repeating your name and phone number helps the person you're calling write down and double-check your information. The faster you say your number, the less likely the recipient will understand it and return your call.

Be sure, too, to be responsive. When people leave you voice mail messages asking you to call them back, do so on a timely basis. When you are responsive and follow through, you build credibility. Credibility enhances your ability to communicate effectively so that others respond to you in the ways you want.

Avoiding Problems with Other Media

Other forms of electronic communication — such as instant messaging, texting, and tweeting — are increasingly used these days. They have become part of many people's social interactions. In many cases, they're best left to social communication rather than active use in business settings. If you attempt to use these forms of communication in the workplace, then keep these tips in mind:

✔ **Keep the language businesslike:** Make your messages clear and constructive. Stay away from abbreviations and terms your friends may understand but may confuse your business associates. Use plain English and spell out normal words, just as you do in your e-mail communications. Use language appropriate for a professional setting. Avoid anything that can be viewed as off-color comments, from profanity to sexual innuendo, remarks that may be funny to those near and dear to you socially but offensive to many in a business environment.

✔ **Use when you're in a private setting:** These forms of communication work best when you're alone, such as at your desk. If you, for instance, attempt to text a message or respond to one while you are in conversation with a colleague or customer or are attending a business meeting, you come across as disinterested, rude, and self-absorbed. Though that's not your intention, actions always speak louder than intentions. So stay attentive, courteous, and engaged with the people you're with and save the use of these communication devices for when you can be alone.

✔ **Alert others to the need for use when not alone:** Certainly there are times in business situations where you need real-time, quick answers to questions — one of the advantages of instant messaging. So when you're with others, let them know what you are doing and why so they don't feel put off or ignored. For example, when you need to answer a call while meeting with someone in your office, giving the brief explanation first before picking up the phone shows a professional level of courtesy. Do the same if the need to text or instant message can't wait until a later time.

Chapter 5

Taking Advantage of the Spotlight: Giving Effective Presentations

In This Chapter

▶ Understanding the art of audience analysis

▶ Keeping control of your topic

▶ Winning over your audience with a winning delivery

▶ Engaging difficult audiences in your presentations

How well do you perform when you need to give an impromptu talk about your strategy to customers, an answer that defuses a hostile question at a business meeting, or a pep talk to your morale-deprived co-workers? Success or failure in these situations, as well as in formal presentations, depends on how well you present. This chapter gives a new meaning to the term *influence peddling*. No, it doesn't show you anything illegal, but it does help you figure out how to use basic presentation skills to influence your boss, co-workers, customers, vendors, butcher, baker, candlestick maker, and anyone else who matters in your career. In this chapter you can discover everything from how to develop and deliver a presentation to how to think on your feet. An old philosopher once said, "Every time you open your mouth, your mind is on parade." This chapter ensures that your parade looks sharp, sounds smart, and dazzles your audience.

Gathering the Basic Info You Need for Any Presentation

Getting started is always the toughest part of any activity, particularly when you're preparing to make a presentation — and especially if you don't want to give one in the first place! But don't worry. Presentations don't have to be torture. They can even be fun. (Well, more fun than getting poked in the eye with a sharp stick, anyway.) That said, getting started is probably the hardest aspect of developing a presentation, or doing anything else. To ease you into the task, this section explains the kind of information — the who, what, when, where, and why — you need upfront about your audience and situation.

Asking for essential information

No matter what type of presentation you've been invited to deliver, certain information is basic and essential to shaping your talk. You must first know the name of your contact person. Armed with that knowledge, you can ask your contact to provide the rest of the information that you need. Even if you're presenting within your own company, you may not be familiar with the department or division where you're scheduled to talk. The person who arranged your presentation should help prepare you.

The following lists go over some of the questions you want answered:

- What's the purpose of the meeting?
- Is it a regularly scheduled meeting or a special event?
- Is it a formal or an informal event?
- What's the atmosphere — very serious or light?
- Is my presentation the main attraction?

Ask these questions about the format:

- What's the agenda for the day?
- What's the format for my presentation? (A general session? A breakout session? A panel discussion? Before, during, or after a meal?)
- What time do I begin presenting and how long am I expected to present?
- Will there be other presenters, and if so, when will they be presenting and what will their presentations be about?
- What occurs before and after my presentation?

Ask these questions about the location:

- Where will I present? (In my own office building? At another company's headquarters? In an out-of-town convention center?)
- What type of room will I present in? (A meeting room? An auditorium?)
- How will the room be set up?
- What equipment will be available to me?

Analyzing your audience

To relate effectively to an audience, start by discovering as much about the people in the audience as possible. Who are they? What do they believe in? Why are they listening to you? This process is known as *audience analysis*.

The more information you possess, the more you can target your remarks to reflect an audience's interests. By targeting your audience's interests, you increase the likelihood that members of the audience are listening to you. Audience analysis also helps you shape your message. What types of arguments should you make? What will be the most effective examples? How complex can you make your explanations? What authorities should you quote? The answers to these and similar questions should determine much of the structure and content of your presentation.

So how do you find the answers you need? First, if you're presenting at a particular company or organization, read its Web site. That should provide a lot of information about the people who work at the organization. Second, talk to the people who arranged your presentation. Ask them to tell you about your audience and to provide other sources of information. Use all your sources to find out more about the topics listed in the next few sections.

Audience size

Will you be presenting to 10 people, 100 people, or 1,000 people? The size of the audience determines many aspects of the presentation. For example, a large audience eliminates the use of certain types of visual aids and requires the use of a microphone. A smaller audience is often less formal. Certain gimmicks that work with a large group will seem silly with a small one. ("Turn around and shake hands with the person behind you" just doesn't cut it when the entire audience is seated in one row.)

The general nature of the audience

What's the relationship of the audience members to one another? Do they all come from the same organization? Do they share a common interest? You use this information to shape your message at a very basic level.

Pertinent demographic information

What's their age range? What kind of schooling have they had? Here's a list of standard demographic items:

- Age
- Sex
- Education level
- Economic status

✔ Religion

✔ Occupation

✔ Racial/ethnic makeup

✔ Politics

You can collect a lot more demographic info than you'll ever use. You can tailor your presentation to reflect every last characteristic of your audience, but in reality, you probably won't have the time or inclination to do that. In fact, being adept at selecting only the most important demographics may give you a more successful presentation. For example, say you work for a drug manufacturer and you have to present a company overview to prospective investors. You may decide that the key characteristics for shaping your presentation are the audience's occupations and educational backgrounds.

Are some of the prospective investors doctors? (They may know more about drugs than you do.) Are they professional investment advisors or wealthy individuals without a clue about corporate finance? (How sophisticated should you make your analysis of the numbers?) You get the idea. Instead of wasting a lot of time impersonating a census taker, zero in on the audience characteristics that make a real difference to your presentation.

Their attitudes, values, and beliefs

The beliefs, attitudes, and values of your audience members color their interpretation of every aspect of your presentation. What exactly do you need to know? In essence, you want to know where they're coming from. Here are some of the questions you want to answer; the answers help determine your approach to the subject:

✔ What is the audience's attitude about the subject of my presentation?

✔ What is the audience's attitude toward me as the presenter?

✔ What stereotypes will the audience apply to me?

✔ Will anyone have a hidden agenda?

✔ What values does the audience find important?

✔ Does the audience share a common value system?

✔ How strongly held are its beliefs and attitudes?

✔ What companies and departments within an organization do audience members work for?

✔ Will the audience include any of my rivals within the organization?

✔ Will the audience include anyone who can reward or punish me? (My boss, top management, stockholders?)

Although presenters tend to focus on audience census data, they tend to overlook audience beliefs, attitudes, and values. The reason is simple. It's difficult to develop this information. You can easily find out how many audience members are male or female, but you have a much tougher time if you want to know what they're thinking. To get this information, talk to the person who arranged your presentation. Or ask someone who is part of, or familiar with, the audience.

How much they know

Want to start at the beginning with your audience? Then you'd better find out how much it already knows. Two of the biggest mistakes presenters make are talking over the heads of their audiences and talking at a level that's too elementary. Once again, the answers to the following questions play a major role in how you construct your presentation. What your audience already knows determines how much background you need to provide, the sophistication of the language you can use, and the examples you include. Ponder these questions before you make your presentation:

- How sophisticated are the audience members about the material I'm presenting?
- Will any experts on the topic be in the audience?
- Have the audience members heard other presentations about my idea?
- Why are they interested? Am I presenting something that will change the way they work or change their corporate relationships?
- If different departments are included, will they understand the background and the jargon related to my topic?
- Do they already know the basic concepts of my topic?
- Do they think they know a lot about my topic?
- How did they get the information that they already have about my topic?
- Are they familiar with my approach and attitude toward the topic?

Their expectations

You should never have to wonder what your audience members expect. Find out why they're attending your presentation by finding answers to the following questions:

- Are they interested in my topic?
- Were they ordered to attend?
- What do they expect to learn or see or hear?
- What do they expect me to say or do?
- Are they open to surprises?

Getting Your Presentation Together

The key to success with presentations — as with so much else in life — is preparation. After you find all the background info you need (described in the preceding section), you have to find material to wow your audience: attention-grabbing quotes, stories, and statistics. Adding humor can also help. And you definitely want stunning visual aids. But all that's not even enough. You've got to choose your words wisely. They have to convey your message with impact — especially your introduction and conclusion. In this section, you find out how to create a presentation that your audience will never forget.

Setting specific presentation goals

There are three types of presenters: those who make things happen, those who watch things happen, and those who wonder what happened. If you don't want to wonder what happened, you'd better know what you want to make happen. The traditional functions of a presentation are to inform, persuade, or entertain. A more useful way to look at it is in terms of motivation — your motivation for making the presentation and the audience's motivation for listening. What do you want to accomplish? What does your audience want (or expect) to get out of attending the presentation? Your answers to those question are central to every decision you make about your presentation.

You want to know why you're giving this presentation and what you hope the result will be. And you want to build your presentation around that purpose. Therefore, make sure your answers are specific. Do you want your audience to agree with your position? Do you want them to learn something? Write down your goals and refer to them as you develop your presentation. This helps you make decisions about what to include. Anything that doesn't further a goal should be rejected.

Picking material that makes your point

Before you can organize your presentation, you must choose your material. The most difficult task is deciding what *not* to use, because no matter what your topic, you can always find more material than you have time to discuss. And, more important, audiences have a limit to how much material they can absorb. So, find a lot more information than you need and pick out the best stuff, keeping these guidelines in mind:

✔ **Select a variety of material.** A variety of material makes your presentation more interesting. It also increases the chance that each member of your business audience will find something appealing in your presentation. Use anecdotes, statistics, examples, quotes, and so on.

✔ **Keep your audience in mind.** Choose material that your audience will understand and find interesting. In order to make your presentation a success, don't ask what *you* know about the topic: Instead, ask yourself what your audience needs to know. (For more on audience considerations, check out the earlier section "Analyzing your audience.")

✔ **Keep some material in reserve.** You never know when you'll need an extra example, statistic, or anecdote. They come in handy when someone doesn't understand or believe a point that you've made. You can also find them useful when answering questions after your presentation.

Organizing your message

Here's the standard advice for organizing a presentation: Tell the audience what you're going to say, then tell them, and tell them what you've told them. Many consultants offer this bromide, but you need more help to really use it as a planning tool. Alone, it's like informing someone that you build a ship by assembling a bunch of material so that it will float while you're in it. Okay, great. But how do you do that? In order to "tell them" in a presentation, you pick an organizing pattern.

Patterns play a critical role in how people assign meaning and how they interpret messages. You could read a lot of perceptual-psychology theory to figure out this stuff, but suffice it to say that human beings have a natural tendency to organize phenomena into patterns. The way people shape those patterns determines much of the outcome of their communications with each other — especially how easily people understand each other.

Although patterns are infinite in variety, certain ones appear over and over again. Take a look at a few of the most common patterns you can use to give shape to presentations:

✔ **Catch phrase:** "What you see is what you get. What I see today is a research and development department that's overworked, underbudgeted, and less innovative than it used to be. Let's take a look at these problems."

✔ **Cause/effect:** Scientific discussions are a logical place to use this pattern, but it also works well for explaining outcomes. "The company instituted new procedures, bought new expense-reporting software, and made a commitment to innovative sales methods. As a result, its gross sales increased by 50 percent, and its margins grew 10 percent."

✔ **Chronological:** Will you be making a presentation about a series of events (like the increasingly important role of product development at your company over the last five years)? Organizing your presentation in a past/present/future pattern makes it easy to follow.

✔ **Divide a word:** "Today, I'm going to talk about *SUCCESS*. *S* stands for sales. Sales are critical to our success because . . ." You can also use this strategy with a quote. For example, "In *The Art of War,* Sun Tzu states that 'All warfare is based on deception.' What does this really mean? Let's start with warfare. Is it limited to physical altercations? Or can it apply to a modern marketing campaign?"

✔ **Numerical list:** You can use this technique to organize your entire presentation: "Ten Ways to Improve Profits," for example. Or you can use it for individual segments: "We've talked about the importance of advertising and public relations. Now let's talk about six simple ways to get a higher response rate from direct mail." When you use this organizing pattern, don't go overboard. If you make the list too long, you can actually lose the audience.

✔ **Physical location:** You may want to use this one if you're talking about things that occur at various locations. Are you giving the company orientation presentation to new employees? You can divide the talk by floors (first floor, second floor, third floor), buildings (Buildings A, B, and C), or other physical areas (North American operations, European operations, Asian operations).

✔ **Problem/solution:** State a problem, and offer a solution. What you emphasize depends on what the audience members already know. Do you need to make them aware of the problem, or do they already know about it? Are there competing solutions? And so on.

✔ **Theory/practice:** You can use this one for talking about something that didn't turn out as planned (the big gap between theory and practice). "Last year, our company announced a bold new corporate ethics program. It sounded good in theory. But last week, our CEO was arrested for financial irregularities."

✔ **Topic pattern:** This is a free-form pattern. You divide your topic into logical segments based on your own instinct, judgment, and common sense. For example, the three topics in a presentation on appropriate office humor could be: why humor is a powerful business tool, how to make a business point with humor, and simple types of nonjoke humor any executive can use.

If you have to put together a presentation quickly, and you want to be sure it's reasonably well organized, you're in luck. PowerPoint will do the work for you. Use PowerPoint templates for common business presentations. These templates offer outlines for presenting a business plan, conducting an employee orientation, presenting a technical report, and more. Although the PowerPoint outlines may not be the most original ways to organize your presentation, they do provide a solid organization if you stick to them.

An outline is a blueprint for your presentation. It lets you see what points you're making, how they're related to one another, and whether they're arranged in proper order. A good outline shows you how to construct a good presentation. And like a blueprint for a building, an outline for a talk can take many shapes and forms. Don't limit yourself to the traditional method emphasized in high school — the Roman-numeral outline in which main topics are noted with capital Roman numerals, first level subtopics are represented by capital letters, and so on. The key is to choose a method that works for you. As long as your method lets you break the talk into parts and see the relationship among the parts, you're fine.

Making notes for your presentation

After you organize your ideas, you need to organize your presentation notes. Two of the most common formats are index cards and word-for-word scripts. This section gives you the lowdown on each method.

Putting your presentation on cards

Index cards are probably the most popular format for organizing presentation notes. They're easy to handle and easy to carry in your pocket, and they make it easy for you to restructure a presentation in a hurry. (You just shuffle the deck.) What do you put on the cards? Take a look at a few ideas:

- **Roman-numeral outlines:** If you use a traditional Roman-numeral outline to develop your talk, just put the outline on cards. Even if you develop your presentation using other methods, you can still take the finished talk and reduce it to a Roman-numeral outline.

- **Key words:** Some presenters just write a series of key words on their cards. This allows you to glance at your notes and minimize the time spent looking away from the audience. But if you forget what ideas the key words represent, you're in trouble.

  In the desire to reduce the number of cards you're using, you can easily get carried away devising key words and abbreviations. Don't take chances. Use abbreviations with which you're familiar. Use a key phrase rather than a key word if you think that you may forget what the word represents.

- **Key sentences:** Some presenters write out key sentences. This practice overcomes the problem of forgetting what a key word represents. Its disadvantage is that it encourages reading from the cards like a script.

  You may find it helpful to highlight your notes to indicate different parts of your talk: main points, subpoints, quotes, and so on. If you use a color system to highlight your notes, don't go wild and use so many colors that you forget what they mean.

Following is some advice for putting your notes on cards:

- ✔ **Use only one side of the card.** The exception is if you can fit all your notes for an entire presentation on both sides of a single card.

- ✔ **Number each card.** If you drop them, you'll be able to put them back in order.

- ✔ **Code your cards for cutting.** Mark your cards so that you can easily shorten your presentation if you need to. You can mark certain cards or sections of cards as nonessential. For example, anything written in black is important, but anything written in blue can be cut.

- ✔ **Format each card for easy reading.** Leave lots of white space, and make sure that your writing is large enough to read under actual presentation conditions. That means that your cards should be readable if you have only dim light (a common problem).

Working from a script

Most presentations are more effective without a script. Why? Well, unless you're a professional actor, when you read a script word for word, it sounds like . . . you're reading a script word for word. You want to sound like you're having a conversation with your audience. So avoid working from a script.

Of course, exceptions abound. Are you presenting at a trade show or convention where the text of your presentation is released in advance? Are you giving detailed technical information to scientists or engineers? Have you been directed to read a prepared statement to the press? These types of situations require scripts.

If you do require a script, make sure that it's easy to read. Use a large font size, double- or triple-space the text, leave a lot of white space in the page margins, use only one side of the paper, and number each page.

Wowing the Audience with Your Delivery

You have much more to think about when it comes to giving a presentation than your topic. You must decide whether you should use a lectern, what gestures you should use, how fast you should speak, and how you should handle the audience and their questions. And these are just a few issues involved in transforming your written message into a masterful oral performance. This section shows you how to deliver a presentation that wows your audience. These simple, proven techniques guarantee success even if you're nervous, shy, or disorganized. So don't worry; you'll be great.

Sending suitable nonverbal signals

Body language refers to the messages you send through facial expression, posture, and gesture. You don't need a course to learn this language. You already use it every day. Make sure your body language reinforces your message and engages your listeners. Following are some specific pointers for presenters (refer to Chapter 3 of Book IV for more info on body language):

TIP

- ✔ **Use your face to accentuate key points.** Act out what you're saying. Are you incredulous about a statistic you've just cited? Raise your eyebrows in disbelief. Are you briefing the audience on a business strategy that you disagree with? Frown. Are you telling a group of kindergarten students that they'll be getting more homework in first grade? Stick your tongue out at them. (Just kidding.)

  And don't forget to smile! A smile is the single most important facial expression, and it creates instant rapport with an audience.

- ✔ **Stand up straight with your feet slightly apart and your arms ready to gesture.** This is the basic, preferred posture for any presentation. Don't stand with your arms folded across your chest (you'll look like a goon from a gangster movie), your arms behind your back (it makes you look like you've been handcuffed and arrested), or in the fig-leaf position (you'll look like you're posing for a Renaissance-style painting of blushing modesty). You also want to avoid standing with your hands on your hips (you'll come across as a bossy gym teacher) or in your pockets (people will wonder what they're doing down there).

- ✔ **Lean slightly toward the audience.** Leaning forward shows that you're actively engaged with audience members. Leaning back signals retreat. Leaning on the lectern is also problematic. Once in a while for effect is okay. But planting yourself on the lectern makes you look weak.

- ✔ **Don't sway back and forth.** Unless you're giving a presentation about how to use a metronome or discussing the finer points of seasickness, no one wants to watch you sway back and forth.

- ✔ **Make your gestures fit the space.** A common mistake presenters make is transferring gestures used in small, intimate settings to large, formal settings. For example, people at a cocktail party gesture by moving their arms from the elbow to the end of the hand. But if you're presenting to a large audience in a large space, you must adjust your gestures. Are you going to emphasize a point? Move your arms from the *shoulders* to the ends of your hands instead of from the elbows.

- ✔ **Vary your gestures.** If you make the same gestures over and over, you start to look like a robot. And the predictability lowers audience attention levels. Don't let your gestures fall into a pattern. Variation keeps audiences watching. You also look like a robot if you've memorized your gestures. Keep the audience guessing.

Book IV

Get to the @#% Point! Communicating Effectively

✔ **Look at individuals.** As you gaze around the room, make eye contact with as many individuals as possible. A common recommendation is that you should pick out one friendly face and look at it. Don't. This poor person wonders why you're staring at him, and so does the rest of the audience. But you also don't want your head to look like a machine gun pivoting back and forth as it sprays eye contact at the crowd; look around the room in a natural manner.

As you look around the room, don't look out the window. If you look out the window, so does your audience. This applies to looking at the ceiling, the walls, or the floor. The audience plays follow the leader, and you're the leader. Look at them so they'll look at you.

✔ **Don't look over the heads of the audience.** A big myth is that gazing over the heads of your audience is okay. They won't know the difference. Wrong. People can tell if you're speaking to the clock on the back wall. And the smaller the audience, the more obvious this technique is. So what should you do if you're too nervous to look in their eyes? Look at the tips of their noses.

Gestures to avoid

Don't let your gestures turn you into any of these types of presenters:

✔ **The banker:** These presenters keep rattling coins in their pockets. They sound like a change machine.

✔ **The beggar:** These presenters clasp their hands together and thrust them toward the audience as if they're begging for something.

✔ **The bug collector:** These presenters keep pulling at the hair on the backs of their necks or their heads. Yes, the audience knows it's just a nervous habit, but they still wonder when you last washed your hair.

✔ **The hygienist:** These presenters keep rubbing their hands together like they're washing them. It looks weird for a few reasons. There's no soap. No water. No sink. And a bunch of people called an audience are watching.

✔ **The jeweler:** These presenters fiddle with their jewelry. Necklaces are a big attraction

for female presenters in this category. And you'll find ring twisters from both sexes.

✔ **The lonely lover:** These presenters hug themselves. It looks really weird. They stand up in front of the audience and hug themselves while they speak. They lose a lot of credibility.

✔ **The optician:** These presenters constantly adjust their glasses. They're on. They're off. They're slipping down their noses.

✔ **The tailor:** These presenters fiddle with their clothing. The tie is a big object of affection for male presenters in this category. They twist it. And pinch it. And rub it. No one listens to the presentation. Everyone is waiting to see if the presenter will choke himself.

✔ **The toy maker:** These presenters love to play with their little toys: pens, markers, pointers, whatever happens to be around. They turn them in their hands. They squeeze them. And they distract the audience.

Mastering physical positioning and movement

Where do you stand? Rather than asking about your position on an issue, this question is intended to get you thinking about your position on stage or in the presentation area. Where, literally, do you stand? How do you get there? And how do you move from there? The answers to all of these questions have important consequences for your presentation.

Assuming the power position

Divide the stage into a nine-square grid: back left, back center, back right, center left, center center, center right, front left, front center, front right. The power position is front center. But don't just stand there. Move into different squares as you give your presentation. If you want a mechanical formula, find cues in your presentation that suggest moves. "I was in a cattle store looking at bulls. And over on the right, I saw [move to a square on the right] a beautiful set of china teacups. I took one to the proprietor [move into another square], and I said, 'Is this the famous china in a bull shop?'" Now you'd better move to a rear square, because with puns like that, the audience may start throwing things.

This process of moving from square to square is called *making an active stage picture*. It ensures that you don't just stand in one place, and it makes you more interesting for the audience to watch. Just remember to return frequently to the power square. Combine your movements naturally with logical gestures.

Working from a lectern

Here are some tips for using the lectern.

- **Look at your notes while you're moving behind the lectern.** Want to disguise your reliance on notes? Look at your notes whenever you move. When you make a gesture, shift position, or turn your head, take a quick peek at your notes. The audience focuses on your movement rather than the fact that you're reading.

- **Use a lectern to "hide" when appropriate.** Even if you don't like to stay behind a lectern, sometimes you may need to draw audience attention to something other than yourself. Are you using slides, overheads, or a volunteer from the audience? Standing behind a lectern makes perfect sense for these situations, especially if it's placed off to the side.

- **Don't press or grip the lectern.** Go ahead and use a lectern — but not as a crutch. Clutching the lectern distracts your audience, because it's an obvious indication of stage fright.

Putting your voice to work

People judge you by the words you use and how you use them. Do you say the words loudly? Rapidly? Monotonously? Do you have an accent? Do you mispronounce them? All these factors — *how* you say things, not *what* you say — are known as *paralanguage*. Following are some tips for using your voice to good effect:

- **Warm up your voice.** Go into the bathroom before you give your presentation, and do some vocal exercises. Hum. Talk to yourself. Get your voice going.

- **Use inflection and vary your pace.** Monotony refers to more than just tone of voice. Yes, a monotonous voice may be the result of speaking in one tone. But it may also result from speaking at one rate of speed, in one volume, or in one pitch. If you're monotonous in any of those ways, you have a problem. If you're monotonous in all of those ways, your audience will fall asleep. The cure is vocal variety.

- **Use your voice for emphasis.** You can completely alter the meaning of a sentence simply by changing the words you emphasize. Say the following line aloud, and emphasize the word in italics. "Are you talking to *me?*" "Are *you* talking to me?" and "Are you *talking* to me?" All right, enough with the Robert De Niro impressions. You get the idea. Use vocal emphasis to reinforce the meanings you want to communicate.

- **Slow down for flubs.** Inevitably, you will mispronounce a word or stumble through a tongue-twisting phrase. The natural instinct is to speed up when you make a mistake. Don't. It highlights your error and increases your chances for making additional errors. Just slow down.

- **Don't discount volume.** Volume is a powerful tool that's easy to manipulate. It may be tough to change your pitch or tone, but anyone can speak more loudly or softly.

- **Don't be afraid to pause.** A common mistake inexperienced (and nervous) presenters make is speaking without pauses. The pause is a vital part of the communication process.

If you have to use a microphone, familiarize yourself with the sound system well in advance of your presentation. Find out how the mike turns on and off and how far you can hold it from your mouth and still be heard. Sometimes the switch is on but the mike doesn't work, so test to make sure the sound system and mike are actually on.

Making your audience comfortable

Most people are cautious in an unfamiliar situation. If they're interacting with a stranger, they assume a conservative demeanor. They don't let their guards down and kick back until they're sure that it's a safe behavior. Audiences react in much the same way. If Robin Williams steps up to a lectern, the audience knows that laughing is okay. If someone the audience doesn't know steps up to the lectern, people in the audience don't know how they're expected to behave. You have to tell them.

What kind of permissions must audiences receive? It depends on what you want to accomplish and how you want the audience to react. The following list shows you three of the more important permissions you can bestow on your listeners:

- ✔ **Permission to laugh:** Do you want to use humor successfully in your talk? One of the most important permissions you can give your audience is permission to laugh.

- ✔ **Permission to learn:** Tell the audience what points and topics are important, what they should remember. By sharing your view of what's important, you enable the audience to better follow your presentation. They know what to look for and they learn more. That gives your presentation more impact.

- ✔ **Permission to write:** One of the most important permissions that you can give your audience is the permission to take notes. Tell them that your presentation contains important information that they'll want to remember. Suggest they have a sheet of paper and a pen ready.

Timing your presentation just right

Timing refers to how much time it takes to deliver a presentation and how to make the presentation fit the time you've been given.

So how long should a presentation be? Abraham Lincoln's response was, "Like a man's pants — long enough to cover the subject." Take a look at a few additional guidelines:

- ✔ **Don't feel obligated to fill your entire time slot.** Just because you've been given 30 minutes doesn't mean you have to present for 30 minutes. Give your presentation in 20 or 25 minutes if you can.

- ✔ **Being a little too short is better than a little too long.** If you conclude five minutes early, people in the audience are thrilled. If you conclude five minutes late, they're impatient and possibly angry. Your audience members are busy. They have people to see and places to go. They expect you to be done on time. Don't disappoint them.

Book IV

Get to the @#% Point! Communicating Effectively

✔ **Twenty minutes is a good length.** If you can choose the length of your presentation, pick 20 minutes. It's long enough to cover a lot of information thoroughly, let the audience get to know you, and make a good impression. And it's short enough to do all that before the audience's attention span reaches its outer limit.

Einstein's theory of relativity may say that time and distance are identical, but many presenters apparently disagree. They just can't go the distance in the time they've been allotted. Want to avoid that problem in your next presentation? The following list gives a few tips and tricks to ensure that you and your audience finish at the same time:

✔ **Estimate the time from the length of the script:** Here's an accurate script-to-speech ratio: One double-spaced page of 10-point type equals two minutes of speaking time. So preparing a standard 20-minute presentation is like writing a 10-page essay. (Keep that in mind when the person inviting you to give a presentation says it will be easy to do.)

✔ **Convert practice time into a realistic estimate:** Many people practice their presentation aloud to get an idea of how long it takes to deliver. But when you practice alone, your presentation will be shorter than when you present in front of people. Why? They laugh and applaud. Plus, you slow down to wait for their reactions. If you're talking to a large audience (several hundred people or more), the length of your presentation may increase by up to 50 percent. As a general rule, figure that your presentation will lengthen about 30 percent in front of an audience.

✔ **Be prepared to cut:** If you're told in advance that your time has been shortened, cut from the body of your talk. Eliminate some examples or even a main point if necessary. What if you need to cut while you're giving a presentation and you're rapidly running out of time? Find a logical place to stop and sum up what you've already said. Even better, have a conclusion that you can go into from any point in your talk.

Don't cut the conclusion. Your presentation is like the flight of a plane, and the passengers are your audience. When you forgo the conclusion, you're attempting a crash landing. And don't try to solve the problem by talking faster. It doesn't work (although that's what many people try) and it's a big mistake. You come across as hyperactive, and the audience comes away with nothing — except a bad impression of you.

Audiences have been burned over and over again by presenters. You can ease their fears by making occasional references to indicate that you know how much time has passed (and how much more time will pass until you're done). This strategy is as simple as saying things like: "I can't teach you everything there is to know about outsourcing in 20 minutes, but in our time together today . . .", "For the next five minutes, I'd like to discuss . . .", "Now we've arrived at the second half of my presentation, and I'd like to shift gears to . . .", or "And in conclusion, I'd like to spend the next three minutes summarizing what we've just discussed. . . ."

Dealing with Difficult or Non-responsive Audiences

Not every audience you ever address will be an absolute delight. When you face a tough crowd, you have some choices. You can figure out the problem and handle it, or you can wait for a standing ovation — on your chest. You can pick up subtle clues that tell you when you're not clicking with an audience. (People don't nod in agreement, but they do nod off.) If you want to save your speech, you have to take charge.

Reading your audience for signs of life

You can have the world's greatest speech, but that may not mean very much if you have the world's worst audience. An audience is like a thorny, long-stemmed rose. Handled properly, it's a thing of beauty that can blossom as you speak. Handled improperly, it will prick you severely. The key is to be able to read your audience and adjust your presentation to overcome any barriers you see. What follows are a few ways to gauge their reactions and how to reengage a tough audience.

Observing its energy level

One of the easiest ways to read an audience is by observing its energy level. Are people talking and laughing as they wait for the event to begin? That's a high-energy audience, and that's what you hope for. This type of audience is much more receptive to your speech. A high-energy audience is basically yours to lose. If you have a high-energy audience, you don't have to be high-energy yourself (although it doesn't hurt).

A low-energy audience is just the opposite. No one's talking, and the mood is blah. (This mood often correlates to specific times of the day and week. For example, Monday night audiences are typically low energy.) This audience is tough. You have to be high-energy. You have to ignite the audience.

Noticing body language

The nonverbal behavior of your audience can tell you about the effectiveness of your speech. Are people nodding at what you say? Are they looking up at you? Are they leaning forward? Are they smiling? Or are they squirming in their seats, nudging each other, looking at their watches, and staring out the windows? (You don't need a PhD to interpret these signals.)

Don't judge the entire audience by the reactions of a single person. This tip sounds obvious, but speakers do it all the time. You may see one sourpuss who won't crack a smile. You'll become obsessed with this person and make all your speaking decisions based on his or her reaction. That's usually a mistake, because nothing you do will work with the sourpuss. You'll get nervous, feel you're bombing, and screw up. If you look at the other 99 percent of the audience members, you'll see that they're enjoying your talk — at least until you screw it up by focusing on the sourpuss.

Head to Chapter 2 of Book IV for detailed information on the key characteristics of engaged listeners.

Asking questions to gauge the audience

If you don't know whether people in an audience agree with you, disagree with you, or even understand what you're saying, ask them. That's the direct method of reading audience reaction. ("How many of you are familiar with the large oil spill that I was just talking about?" "How many of you disagree with what I just said?" "How many of you have never heard any of these arguments before?")

Softening up tough audiences

Easy audiences are all alike, but every tough audience is tough in its own way. Here are some of the varieties you may encounter and some tips for handling each of them.

- ✔ **Offbeat audience:** An offbeat audience responds in ways that you don't anticipate. The audience members laugh or applaud when you don't expect it, and they're silent when you expect applause. That's why they're tough — they throw off your rhythm. You can't do anything except go with the flow. Just don't cue the audience members that you find their responses unusual. Pause for their applause when you get it and keep speaking when you don't.

- ✔ **Captive audience:** The captive audience is tough because it's not there by choice. Attendance at your speech has been forced upon these people for one reason or another, and they resent it. So they're in a foul mood before you even begin. It's not your fault. It has nothing to do with you, but you have to bear the brunt of their anger. What can you do? Acknowledge the situation upfront and appeal to their sense of fairness. Tell them what benefits they can expect to receive if they simply take the chips off their shoulders and give you a fair chance.

- ✔ **More-educated- or more-experienced-than-you audience:** What can you do when your audience knows more about your subject than you do? You can reframe your entire talk as a review of the basics. As an alternative, you may decide to make the talk intensely personal. The speech becomes a description of *your* feelings, ideas, and reactions regarding the subject matter. Or you can elevate the discussion to a higher, big-picture level. ("I'm not here to talk about floods today. Obviously Mr. Noah knows a lot more about them than I do. My comments today will examine the basic relationship between man and nature and how mankind responds to adverse circumstances. Into each life a little rain must fall. . . .")

✔ **Hostile-to-your-position audience:** You're speaking pro or con about a controversial issue — gun control, abortion, whether dogs are better pets than cats, whatever. Your audience holds an opinion that's the opposite of yours. The best approach is to try to disarm the audience members immediately. Begin by acknowledging that you have a difference of opinion. (And don't apologize for your opinion; you're entitled to it.) Then appeal to the traditional values of fairness, free speech, and dialogue. Let them know that they'll have a chance to air their views after you're finished speaking.

✔ **Didn't-come-to-see-you audience:** This audience comes to see the keynote speaker but has to sit through a few other speakers before it gets to hear the guru. Unfortunately, *you* are one of the speakers that must precede the guru. These audiences are tough because they want you to be finished before you've even started. You can't do much about it, but you may find some relief by referring to the guru in your remarks as often as possible. That may be the only thing you can say to get a positive response from the audience. Is this pandering to the audience? You bet it is. Do you have any other choice? Yes. You can give your speech as planned to the accompaniment of hoots and jeers. It's up to you.

✔ **The-current-event-distracted-them audience:** You're speaking to a group of fundraisers about new techniques to increase donations, and you're an expert on the topic. It's a perfect match between speaker, topic, and audience. Your audience members should pay undivided attention and take notes, but they don't. They seem distracted; they're definitely not listening. What's the problem? Some major event has usurped the consciousness of the audience, and everything else — especially your speech — seems unimportant by comparison. Two hours before you started speaking, the space shuttle Challenger exploded, or the Oklahoma City Federal Building was bombed, or the company your audience works has just announced quarterly losses and indicates that massive layoffs will be forthcoming. If you're scheduled to speak on the day that a distracting event has occurred, try to get your speech canceled or changed to another time. If neither is possible, be prepared to talk about the distracting event because that may be the only subject that interests your audience.

✔ **Reverse-image audience:** You're the only male at a female event or vice versa. You're the only African American at a Caucasian event or vice versa. You're the only Jew at a Christian event or vice versa. You get the idea. You're the reverse image of your audience. Audience members are tough if they assume that you can't possibly understand their point of

Book IV

Get to the @#% Point! Communicating Effectively

view. After all, you're different from them. Start by breaking the tension. Acknowledge your difference. If appropriate, poke fun at it. Then establish your common ground. You're speaking to this audience for a reason. Members of the audience can receive some benefit from listening to you. Let them know what it is — fast.

- **Angry-at-previous-speaker audience:** The speaker before you has really riled up the audience members. In fact, they're downright mad. Maybe the speaker was controversial. Maybe he was insulting. Maybe he was offensive. Whatever the case, the audience members are in a vile mood, and they want to take it out on you. The most important thing you can do in this situation is *be aware of it.* You need to know that the audience is angry at the prior speaker, not you. Failure to recognize this situation can jeopardize your entire speech. You'll assume that you are the problem and adjust your performance accordingly. That doesn't work because you're not the problem. It's imperative to know what any previous speakers said to your audience. Attend their talks if possible. If not, find out what happened. If a problem occurred, you can address it immediately in the opening of your talk.

- **Already-heard-it audience:** The speakers before you made acceptable speeches. They left the audience in decent shape for your talk. The audience isn't angry or upset about anything. But that can change rapidly if you get up and repeat what the previous speakers have already said. If you find yourself in this situation, don't just do your speech as if the audience members haven't already heard the same thing. You'll lose them instantly. You need to adapt. At a minimum, acknowledge that you'll be saying things that they've already heard. A much more effective strategy is to abandon your prepared remarks entirely. Just wing it. Think of a different angle and speak about it on an impromptu basis. Comment on what the previous speakers have already said. Or solicit participation from the audience.

- **Sick audience:** The sick audience is literally ill. Numerous members of this audience cough and sneeze loudly throughout your speech. It's quite a distraction, but there's not much you can do about it. You can try using humor to deal with the situation. ("Please hold your applause and coughing till the end.") If that doesn't work, you're out of luck.

Reviving a nonresponsive audience

An audience first-aid kit includes a variety of devices for reviving interest in your talk. Like the contents of a real first-aid kit, these devices range in strength from bandages to adrenaline shots. You have to know how to use the appropriate device for the audience in front of you. You can diagnose a dying audience by sorting it into one of three categories, referred to as levels.

Level one: You still have audience members' attention, but they look bored or puzzled

The people in the audience are watching you speak, but you can sense that you're not connecting. They're fidgeting. They're not responding. What can you do? You must break out of the pattern you're in. Talk directly to the audience like it's a real conversation. Ask whether they understand what you're talking about. Ask if they'd like you to give another example. Or tell them that what you're about to say is very important. Emphasize a key benefit that really puts them in the picture. ("Now I'd like to tell you the only guaranteed way to prevent yourself from being laid off in the next two years.")

Or you can say something that you feel is guaranteed to get applause. (The energy of their hands clapping helps prevent the onset of lethargy.) What if you're waiting for applause and you don't get it? Say something like, "Oh, I guess you didn't think that was as important as I did." If they laugh, you've connected with them. If they don't, you're not any worse off.

Level two: Audience attention is waning

The audience is starting to drift off. People are staring at the ceiling, out the windows, and at their watches. The only thing they're not looking at is you. One of the simplest things you can do to revive this audience is also one of the most effective — just ask the audience members to stand up. Say something like, "You've been sitting down for awhile now. And I think we could all use a short stretch. Everyone stand up. . . . Okay, sit back down. Feel better?" It's amazing how a stretch can transform the energy level in the room. (That's why they have a seventh inning stretch at baseball games.)

A word of caution: The effect is temporary. When the audience members retake their seats, they pay attention for a minute or two. That's your opening. It's your chance to get your talk back on track with some exciting, dynamic stuff. If you don't, you'll lose the audience again.

Level three: Code blue — they're about to become comatose

The audience is falling asleep or in a trancelike state or just plain dazed. You don't have time to ask them to stand up or applaud. You need to do something immediately that will jar audience members out of their stupor. It must be loud or dramatic or both. Consider these tips:

- ✔ Pound your fist on the lectern
- ✔ Beat your chest like a gorilla
- ✔ Move the mike toward a sound-system speaker to cause loud feedback
- ✔ Wave a $20 bill in the air and then rip it up
- ✔ Throw your notes on the floor
- ✔ Light the lectern on fire

Any of these should wake up the audience. But you need to tie these actions into your speech so that they make a point. Otherwise, it looks like you were just trying to wake up the audience members. (You can't admit that your goal was to wake them up. They would resent that. It has to appear that you were just giving your talk and part of it happened to revive them.)

For example, you pound your fist on the lectern. (Do it near the mike so it really makes a loud noise.) Then you tie it into whatever you're talking about. "That's the sound of people beating their head against a wall because they're frustrated with government regulations." "That's the sound of your heart beating when you go on a job interview." "That's the sound your car makes after you try to save $150 by going to the lowball mechanic."

One of the best ways to coax a response out of an audience is to put people in the audience into your act. It's an ego thing — they identify with the audience member who stands before them. Suddenly your talk becomes a lot more personal. Meeting members of your audience before you speak helps you get a volunteer. Whenever you have to beg for a volunteer, chances are the person who eventually volunteers will be someone you've spoken with earlier. Why does this happen? Maybe some kind of bonding takes place. The person now feels like you're friends and feels obligated to help out.

Book V

Can't We All Just Get Along? Navigating Tricky Workplace Relationships and Situations

The 5th Wave — By Rich Tennant

"Or, we could just agree to disagree."

In this book . . .

*E*very day in offices, retail stores, factories, and any number of other workplaces, people are having conflicts with co-workers and challenges with customers. Whether you work for a nonprofit organization, a small family business, a Fortune 100 company, or a fledgling upstart, if you work with at least one other person, you undoubtedly have disagreements and face difficulties at times. It's normal, natural, and nothing to fear.

Contrary to what you may believe, conflict isn't inherently all bad. When handled properly, conflict can actually create positive changes and new opportunities in your organization. But how do you go about finding positive outcomes in what on the surface looks like a negative situation? You have to become skilled at calming the infernos, and the chapters in this book tell you just how to do that. You also find out how to lessen the number of conflicts around you by being a positive part of the workplace.

Chapter 1

Understanding Office Politics

• •

In This Chapter

▶ Assessing the political environment of your workplace

▶ Identifying the real side of communication

▶ Playing by the rules that no one talks about

▶ Defending your personal interests

• •

*A*t its best, *office politics* means the relationships that you develop with your co-workers — both up and down the chain of command — that allow you to get tasks done, to be informed about the latest goings-on in the business, and to form a personal network of business associates for support throughout your career. Office politics help to ensure that everyone works in the best interests of the organization and their co-workers. At its worst, office politics can degenerate into a competition, where employees concentrate their efforts on trying to increase their personal power at the expense of other employees — and their organizations.

This chapter is about determining the nature and boundaries of your political environment, understanding the unspoken side of office communication, unearthing the unwritten rules of your organization, and, in the worst-case scenario, becoming adept at defending yourself against political attack.

Evaluating Your Political Environment

How political is your office or workplace? Having your finger on the political pulse of the organization is particularly important. Otherwise, the next time you're in a meeting, you may blurt out, "Why is it so difficult to get an employment requisition through human resources? You'd think it was their money!" only to find out that the owner's daughter-in-law heads the human resources department.

With just a little bit of advance information and forethought, you can approach issues like this much more tactfully. Getting in touch with your political environment can help you be more effective, and it can help your department and your employees (if you're a manager) have a greater impact within the organization.

Assessing your organization's political environment

Asking insightful questions of your co-workers is one of the best ways to assess your organization's political environment. Such questions show you to be the polite, mature, and ambitious employee that you are, and the questions are a sure sign of your well-developed political instincts. Answers to questions like the following can reveal useful information about procedures and people at your workplace:

- ✔ "What's the best way to get a nonbudget item approved?"

- ✔ "How can I get a product from the warehouse that my client needs today when I don't have time to do the paperwork?"

- ✔ "Can I do anything else for you before I go home for the day?"

 Although asking politically savvy questions gives you an initial indication of the political lay of the land in your organization, you can do more to assess the political environment. Watch out for the following signs while you're getting a sense for how your organization really works:

- ✔ **Find out how others who seem to be effective get tasks done.** How much time do they spend preparing before sending through a formal request for a budget increase? Which items do they delegate and to whose subordinates? When you find people who are particularly effective at getting tasks done in your organization's political environment, model their behavior.

- ✔ **Observe how others are rewarded for the jobs they do.** Does management swiftly and enthusiastically give warm and personal rewards in a sincere manner to make it clear what behavior is considered important? Is credit given to everyone who helped make a project successful, or does only the manager get her picture in the company newsletter? By observing your company's rewards, you can tell what behavior is expected of employees in your organization. Practice this behavior.

- ✔ **Observe how others are disciplined for the jobs they do.** Does your management come down hard on employees for relatively small mistakes? Are employees criticized in public or in front of co-workers? Is everyone held accountable for decisions, actions, and mistakes even if they had no prior involvement? Such behavior on the part of management indicates that they don't encourage risk taking. If your management doesn't encourage risk taking, make your political style outwardly reserved as you work behind the scenes.

- ✔ **Consider how formal the people in the organization are.** When you're in a staff meeting, for example, do your peers speak casually? For example, "That idea's never gonna work. Can anybody come up with a realistic option?" Or do they buffer and finesse their opinions like so:

"That's an interesting possibility. Could we explore the pros and cons of implementing such a possibility?" The degree of formality you find in your company indicates how you need to act to conform to the expectations of others.

Identifying key players

So now that you've discovered that you work in a political environment (did you really have any doubt in your mind?), you need to determine who the key players are. Why? Because they are the individuals who can help make your department more effective and who can provide positive role models.

Knowing the key players

Key players are those politically astute individuals who make things happen in an organization. You can identify them by their tendency to make instant decisions without having to refer people "upstairs," their use of the latest corporate slang, and their affinity for always speaking up in meetings if only to ask, "What's our objective here?"

All the following factors are indicators that can help you identify the key players in your organization:

- ✔ Which employees are sought for advice in your organization?
- ✔ Which employees are considered by others to be indispensable?
- ✔ Whose office is located closest to those of the organization's top management and whose are located miles away?
- ✔ Who eats lunch with the president, the vice presidents, and other members of the upper management team?

Sometimes influential people don't hold influential positions. For example, Jack, as the department head's assistant, may initially appear to be nothing more than a gofer. However, you may later find out that Jack is responsible for scheduling all his boss's appointments, setting agendas for department meetings, and vetoing actions on his own authority. Jack is an informal leader in the organization and, because you can't get to your boss without going through Jack, you know that Jack has much more power in the organization than his title may indicate.

Working with key players

As you figure out who the key players in your organization are, you start to notice that they have different office personalities. Use the following categories to help you figure out how to work with the different personality types of your organization's key players. Do you recognize any of these players in your organization?

✔ **Movers and shakers:** These individuals usually far exceed the boundaries of their office positions. For example, you may find a mover and shaker who is in charge of purchasing helping to negotiate a merger. Someone in charge of the physical plant may have the power to designate a wing of the building to the group of her choosing. Nonpolitical individuals, on the other hand, tend to be bogged down by responsibilities — such as getting their own work done.

✔ **Corporate citizens:** These employees are diligent, hardworking, and company-loving, seeking slow but steady, long-term advancement through dedication and hard work. Corporate citizens are great resources for getting information and advice about the organization. You can count on them for help and support, especially if your ideas seem to be in the best interest of the organization.

✔ **The town gossips:** These employees always seem to know what's going on in the organization — usually before those individuals who are actually affected by the news know it. Assume that anything you say to these individuals will get back to the person about whom you say it. Therefore, always speak well of your bosses and co-workers when you are in the presence of town gossips.

✔ **The firefighters:** These are the individuals who relish stepping into a potential problem with great fanfare at the last conceivable moment to save a project, client, deadline, or whatever. Keep a firefighter well informed of your activities so that he doesn't interpret or intimate to others that the lack of information is an indication that the project's in trouble and his help is needed.

✔ **The vetoer:** This person in your organization has the authority to kill your best ideas and ambitions with a simple comment such as, "We tried that and it didn't work." In response to any new ideas that you may have, the favorite line of a vetoer is, "If your idea is so good, then why aren't we already doing it?" The best way to deal with vetoers is to keep them out of your decision loop. Try to find other individuals who can get your ideas approved or rework the idea until you hit upon an approach that satisfies the vetoer.

✔ **Techies:** Every organization has technically competent workers who legitimately have a high value of their own opinions. Experts can take charge of a situation without taking over. Get to know your experts well — you can trust their judgments and opinions.

✔ **Whiners:** A few employees are never satisfied with whatever is done for them. Associating with them inevitably leads to a pessimistic outlook, which is not easily turned around. Or worse, your boss may think that you're a whiner, too. In addition, pessimistic people tend to be promoted less often than optimists. Be an optimist: Your optimism makes a big difference in your career and in your life.

Redrawing your organization chart

Your company's organization chart may be useful for determining who's who in the formal organization, but it really has no bearing on who's who in the informal political organization. What you need is the real organization chart. Figure 1-1 illustrates a typical official organization chart.

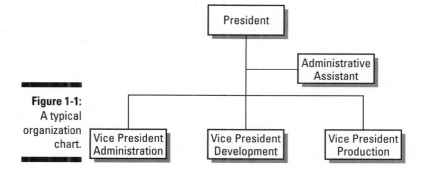

Figure 1-1: A typical organization chart.

Start by finding your organization's official organization chart — the one that looks like a big pyramid. Throw it away. Now, from your impressions and observations, start outlining the real relationships in your organization in your mind. (You don't want someone to find your handiwork lying around in your office or in the recycling bin!) Begin with the key players whom you've already identified. Indicate their relative power by level and relationships by approximation. Use the following questions as a guideline:

- **With whom do these influential people associate?** Draw the associations on your chart and connect them with solid lines. Also connect friends and relatives.

- **Who makes up the office cliques?** Be sure that all members are connected, because talking to one is like talking to them all.

- **Who are the office gossips?** Use dotted lines to represent communication without influence and solid lines for communication with influence.

- **Who's your competition?** Circle those employees likely to be considered for the next promotion. Pay close attention to their work habits and relationships with others.

- **Who's left off the chart?** Don't forget about these individuals. The way that today's organizations seem to change every other day, someone who is off the chart on Friday may be on the chart on Monday. Always maintain positive relationships with all your co-workers and never burn bridges between you and others within and throughout the company. Otherwise, you may find yourself left off the chart some day.

The result of this exercise is a chart of who really has political power in your organization and who doesn't. Figure 1-2 shows how the organization really works. Update your organization chart as you find out more information about people. Take note of any behavior that gives away a relationship — such as your boss cutting off a co-worker in midsentence — and factor the observation into your overall political analysis. Of course, understand that you may be wrong. You can't possibly know the inner power relationships of every department. Sometimes individuals who seem to have power may have far less of it than people who know how to exhibit their power more quietly.

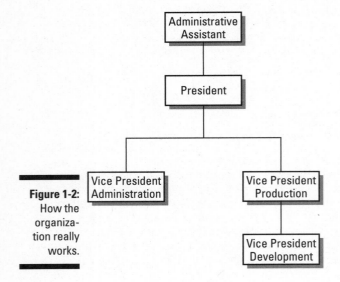

Figure 1-2: How the organization really works.

Scrutinizing Communication: What's Real and What's Not?

One of the best ways to determine how well you fit into an organization is to see how well you communicate. But deciphering the real meaning of communication in an organization takes some practice. So how do you determine the real meaning of words in your organization? You can best get to the underlying meanings by observing behavior, reading between the lines, and, when necessary, knowing how to obtain sensitive information.

Believing actions, not words

One way to decipher the real meaning of communication is to pay close attention to the corresponding behavior of the communicator. The values and priorities (that is, the ethics) of others tend to come through more clearly in what they do rather than in what they say.

If, for example, your manager repeatedly says he is trying to get approval for a raise for you, look at what actions he has taken toward that end. Did he make a call to his boss or hold a meeting? Did he submit the necessary paperwork or establish a deadline to accomplish this goal? If the answers to these questions are no, or if he is continually waiting to hear, the action is probably going nowhere fast. To counter this situation, try to get higher up on your boss's list of priorities by suggesting actions that he can take to get you your raise. You may find that you need to do some or all of the footwork yourself. Alternatively, your manager's actions may indicate that your boss is not a power player in the organization. If that's the case, then make a point to attract the attention of the power players in your organization who can help you get the raise you deserve.

Reading between the lines

In business, don't take the written word at face value. Probe to find out the real reasons behind what is written. For example, here's a typical notice in a company newsletter announcing the reorganization of several departments:

> With the departure of J. R. McNeil, the Marketing Support and Customer Service department will now be a part of the Sales and Administration division under Elizabeth Olsen, acting vice president. The unit will eventually be moved under the direct supervision of the sales director, Tom Hutton.

Such an announcement in the company newsletter may seem to be straightforward on the surface, but if you read between the lines, you may be able to conclude:

> J. R. McNeil, who never did seem to get along with the director of sales, finally did something bad enough to justify getting fired. Tom Hutton apparently made a successful bid with the board of directors to add the area to his empire, probably because his sales were up 30 percent from last year. Elizabeth Olsen will be assigned as acting vice president for an interim period to do some of Tom's dirty work by clearing out some of the deadwood. Tom will thus start with a clean slate, 20 percent lower expenses, and an almost guaranteed increase in profits for his first year in the job. This all fits very nicely with Tom's personal strategy for advancement. *(P.S.: A nice congratulatory call to Tom may be in order.)*

Announcements like these have been reworked dozens of times by so many people that they appear to be logical and valid when you initially read them. By reading between the lines, however, you can often determine what is really going on. Of course, you have to be careful not to jump to the wrong conclusions. J. R. may have simply gone on to better opportunities and the company has taken advantage of that event to reorganize. Make sure to validate your conclusions with others in the company to get the real story.

Probing for information

In general, you can get ongoing information about your organization by being a trusted listener to as many people as possible. Show sincere interest in the affairs of others, and they'll talk about themselves openly. After they begin talking, you can shift the topic to work, work problems, and eventually more sensitive topics. Ask encouraging questions and volunteer information as necessary to keep the exchange equitable.

Even after you've developed such trusted relationships, you need to know how to probe to uncover the facts about rumors, decisions, and hidden agendas. Start by adhering to the following guidelines:

- ✔ Have at least three ways of obtaining the information.
- ✔ Check the information through two sources.
- ✔ Promise anonymity whenever possible.
- ✔ Generally know the answers to the questions you ask.
- ✔ Be casual and nonthreatening in your approach.
- ✔ Assume that the initial answer is superficial.
- ✔ Ask the same question different ways.
- ✔ Be receptive to whatever information you're given.

One more thing: If you find yourself in an organization rife with political intrigue, where you're always looking over your shoulder and are worried when the next rumor is going to be about you, seriously consider changing jobs! Although every organization has its share of politics, spending too much time worrying about it is certainly counterproductive, and it can't be good for your well-being.

Uncovering the Unwritten Rules of Organizational Politics

Every organization has rules that are never written down and seldom discussed. Such unwritten rules pertaining to the expectations and behavior of employees in the organization can play a major role in your success or failure. Because unwritten rules aren't explicit, you have to piece them together by observation, insightful questioning, or simply through trial and error.

Never underestimate the power of the unwritten rules of organizational politics. In many companies, the unwritten rules carry just as much importance, if not more, than the written rules contained in the company's policy manuals.

Be friendly with all

The more individuals you have as friends in an organization, the better off you are. If you haven't already done so, start cultivating friends in your immediate work group and then extend your efforts to making contacts and developing friendships in other parts of the organization. The more favorably your co-workers view you, the greater your chances of becoming their manager in the future. Cultivate their support by seeking advice or by offering assistance.

You never know to whom you'll be reporting in the future. As the saying goes, "Be nice to people on the way up because you may meet them on the way down."

Build a network by routinely helping new employees who enter your organization. As they join, be the person who takes them aside to explain how the organization really works. As the new employees establish themselves and move on to other jobs in other parts of the organization, you have a well-entrenched network for obtaining information and assistance.

Knowing others throughout the organization can be invaluable for clarifying rumors, obtaining information, and indirectly feeding information back to others. An astute employee maintains a large number of diverse contacts throughout the organization, all on friendly terms. The following are excellent ways to enlarge your network:

✔ **Walk around:** Those who walk the halls tend to be better known than those who don't. Return telephone and e-mail messages in person whenever possible. Not only do you have the opportunity for one-on-one communication with the individual who left you the message, but you also can stop in to see everyone else you know along the way.

✔ **Play company sports or games:** You can meet employees from a wide range of functions and locations by joining a company sports league. Whether bowling, golf, or softball is your cup of tea, other employees undoubtedly enjoy the same activities, so start a team if one isn't in place. If you prefer, start or join a lunchtime bridge or chess group.

✔ **Join committees:** Whether the committee has been formed to address employee security or simply to determine who cleans out the refrigerator in the employee lounge, take part. You get to meet new people in an informal and relaxed setting.

Help others get what they want

A fundamental, unwritten rule of office politics is this: Getting what you want is easier when you give others what they want. Win the assistance of others by showing them what they stand to gain by helping you. When a benefit isn't readily apparent, create or allude to one that may occur if they offer to help. Such benefits can include:

- ✔ **A favor returned in kind:** Surely you can provide some kind of favor to your counterparts in exchange for their assistance. Lunch or the temporary loan of an employee is always a popular option.

- ✔ **Information:** Don't forget: Information is power. You may find that many of your co-workers crave the latest and greatest information in an organization. Perhaps you can be the one to give it to them.

- ✔ **Money:** Perhaps you have a little extra money in your equipment budget that you can allocate to someone's project in exchange for that person's help.

- ✔ **A recommendation:** The higher-ups trust your judgment. Your willingness to recommend a co-worker for promotion to a higher position or for recognition for extraordinary performance is a valuable commodity. The right words to the right people can make all the difference to someone's success in an organization.

These ideas are not suggesting that you do anything unethical or illegal. When you provide these kinds of benefits to others in your organization, make sure that you are within your company's rules and policies. And, as a side benefit, you may actually find satisfaction in giving. Don't violate your personal set of ethics or company policy to get ahead.

Don't party at company parties

Social affairs are a serious time for those employees seeking to advance within a company. Social events offer one of the few times when everyone in the company is supposed to be on equal footing. Don't believe it. Although social functions provide managers at the top a chance to show that they're regular people and give those employees below a chance to ask questions and laugh at their bosses' jokes, they are also a time to be extremely cautious.

Beware of whom you talk to and, of course, what you say. Don't sink your career with an injudicious comment or make a fool of yourself just because you're at a social function like a holiday party or company picnic. Managing most social encounters involves art and skill, especially those encounters that involve co-workers. Proper poise begins with proper mingling techniques. Use these techniques at your next company party:

✔ Use the middle of the room to intercept individuals that you especially want to speak to. As an alternative strategy for getting their attention, watch the hors d'oeuvres table or the punch bowl. Go for refills when the person you are seeking does so.

✔ Keep discussion loose and light and avoid discussing work topics with anyone other than your boss. Try to move on before the person you're speaking to runs out of topics to discuss and is overcome with a blank expression. Don't fawn or brown-nose; these behaviors are more likely to lose respect for you than to gain it.

✔ Leave the social function only after the departure of the highest-ranking company official. If you're forced to leave before, let him or her know why.

Manage your manager

The idea is to encourage your manager to do what most directly benefits you, the team you're on, and, if you're a manager, your staff. The following tried-and-true techniques for manager management have evolved through the ages:

✔ **Keep your manager informed of your successes:** "That last sale puts me over quota for the month."

✔ **Support your manager in meetings:** "Antonio is right on this. We really do have to consider the implications of this change for our customers."

✔ **Praise your manager publicly:** "Ms. Lee is probably the best manager I have ever worked for."

Although a well-controlled relationship with your manager is important, you need connections to those above your manager, too. A key relationship to develop is with your manager's manager — an individual who is likely to have a very big influence on your future career.

Volunteer for an assignment that happens to be a pet project of your manager's boss. If you do a good job, you'll more than likely be asked to do another project. If you don't have an opportunity like a pet project, try to find an area of common interest with your manager's boss. Bring up the topic in casual conversation and agree to meet later to discuss it in more detail. But be careful not to appear overeager or anxious.

Move ahead with your mentors

Having a *mentor* is almost essential for ensuring any long-term success within an organization. A mentor is an individual — usually higher up in the organization — who provides advice and helps to guide your progress. Mentors are necessary because they can offer you important career advice, as well as become your advocate in higher levels of the organization — the levels that you don't have direct access to.

Make sure the person whom you select as your mentor (or who selects you, as is more often the case) has organizational clout and is vocal about touting your merits. If possible, get the support of several powerful people throughout the organization. *Sponsorships* (your relationships with your mentors) develop informally over an extended period of time.

Seek out a mentor by finding an occasion to ask for advice. If you find the advice helpful, frequently seek more advice from the same person. Initially, ask for advice related to your work, but as time goes on, you can ask for advice about business in general and your career advancement specifically. Proceed slowly, or your intentions may be suspect. Always display tact and discretion in your approach to your mentor.

Be trustworthy

Similar to having a mentor is being a loyal follower of an exceptional performer within the organization. Finding good people to trust can be difficult, so if you're trustworthy, you're likely to become a valued associate of a bright peer. As that person rises quickly through the organization, she can bring you along. However, whenever possible, hitch your wagon to more than one star: You never know when a star may fall and leave you all alone in the stardust.

Protecting Yourself

Inevitably, you may find yourself on the receiving end of someone else's political aspirations. Astute workers take precautions to protect themselves — and for managers, their employees, too — against the political maneuverings of others. These precautions can also help if your own strategies go wrong. What can you do to protect yourself?

Document for protection

Document the progress of your department's projects and activities, especially when expected changes in plans or temporary setbacks affect your projects. Documenting the changes or setbacks gives you an accurate record of your projects' history and ensures that individuals who don't have your best interest at heart don't forget what really happened (or inappropriately use setbacks against you). The form of the documentation can vary, but the following are most common:

- ✔ Confirmation memos
- ✔ Activity reports
- ✔ Project folders
- ✔ Correspondence files
- ✔ Notes

Don't make promises you can't keep

Avoid making promises or firm commitments when you don't want to or can't follow through. Don't offer a deadline, final price, or guarantee of action or quality unless you're sure you can meet it. When you make promises that you can't fulfill, you risk injuring your own reputation when deliveries are late or costs are higher than expected.

If you find yourself forced to make promises when you aren't certain you can meet them, consider taking one of the following actions:

- ✔ **Hedge:** If forced to make a firm commitment to an action that you're not sure you can meet, hedge your promise as much as possible by building in extra time, staff, money, or other qualifier.

- ✔ **Buffer time estimates:** If you're forced to make a time commitment that may be unrealistic, buffer the estimate (add extra time to what you think you really need) to give yourself room to maneuver. If you deliver early, you'll be a hero.

- ✔ **Extend deadlines:** As deadlines approach, bring any problems you (or your staff) encounter — even the most basic ones — to the attention of the person who requested that you do the project. Keeping people informed prevents them from being surprised if you need to extend your deadlines.

Be visible

To get the maximum credit for your efforts (and if you're a manager, for your staff's efforts), be sure to publicize your successes. To ensure that credit is given where credit is due, the following tips are helpful:

- ✔ **Advertise your department's successes.** If you're a manager, routinely send copies of successfully completed projects and letters of praise for every member of your staff to your manager and to your manager's boss.

✓ **Use surrogates.** Call on your friends in the organization and the folks who've been positively impacted by your work to help publicize your achievements. Be generous in highlighting the achievements of those who've helped you. If you highlight your own achievements at the expense of your hard-working peers (or employees), you appear tactless and boastful.

✓ **Be visible.** Make a name for yourself in the organization. The best way to do that is to perform at a level that separates you from the rest of the pack. Work harder, work smarter, and respond better to the needs of the organization and your customers, and you'll be noticed!

Chapter 2

Preventing Problems with Business Etiquette

A successful career doesn't come only to those who have worked the longest or the hardest, or to those who have the most impressive résumés. These days, many corporations are unwilling to send someone to the front lines unless she has a little polish, style, and finesse. Behaving properly is the new competitive edge.

Of course, a key component of proper business behavior is treating all the people you come into contact with — colleagues, customers, and clients — with respect and dignity. That means avoiding the obvious no-nos like ridiculing, demeaning, or insulting anyone because of real or perceived differences, as well as the not-so-obvious traps such as making assumptions about people based on stereotypes. By following the advice you find in this chapter, you'll know what it takes to be a gracious and generous colleague.

Developing Good Relationships with Your Colleagues

Everyone knows people who are easy to work with and people who aren't. Whether you're just starting a new job or have been with the same company for years, you're likely to ask yourself at some point just why some people are so much harder to work with than others. Psychological explanations may help you understand, but they don't always help you work with difficult individuals. For that, you need patience, respect, and consideration. In short, you need good manners.

The prime directive in basic work etiquette is treating each person with courtesy and respect. Having good manners in the workplace means cooperating with others so that you're a positive part of the work environment, even when the environment is stressful, even when others aren't being helpful, and even when some people are being out-and-out rude.

The following sections explain how to foster happy, well-mannered work relationships with your colleagues. For information on how to interact with you staff and superiors, head to the later sections "Developing good relations with your staff" and "Developing good relations with superiors."

Understanding personality types

A work environment has lots of personality types. A polite person is sensitive to differences in personality types and interacts with each type accordingly. Watch for the behaviors that each personality type exhibits, and appreciate the diversity. People's quirks are inherently interesting, and acknowledging them can help increase harmony.

The idea behind looking at personality types is not to pigeonhole people, but to recognize certain strengths and weaknesses. One of the keys to etiquette is paying enough attention to others to be able to modify your behavior to accommodate them. Appropriate responses to particular personality types are helpful for anyone who wants to be an effective colleague. The following sections describe different personality types and offer suggestions on what kinds of behaviors and interactions work best with them.

Most people are combinations of these basic types, and each of these personality types is helpful in particular situations. Need a quick decision? Go to the steamroller. Need to put a team together for a project? Make sure that you include a consensus-builder. Need someone to sift through a long report? The obsessive worker is your choice.

The control freak

The control freak wants to do it all himself. He doesn't easily trust others but will do a great deal of work. You can identify a control freak by his impatience with others on tactical and strategic decisions and by his constant desire for more challenges. If you work with a control freak, find opportunities to introduce the idea of delegating. Identify simple tasks that need to be completed and suggest other team members who can tackle them. Once the tasks are completed, point out to the control freak the successes and ask whether the process was helpful or freed up additional time for more immediate tasks. For more information on how — and what — to delegate, head to Book III, Chapter 3.

The appreciation fan

This person wants to be recognized by others. You can identify her by her self-promotion and her promotion of her team. She gets sulky if her hard work isn't recognized publicly on a regular basis. Fast-paced, frenetic workplaces, however, aren't conducive to providing constant affirmation. What you can do is send an occasional letter or e-mail of appreciation, noting specific examples of how she has done a great job. Verbally mentioning her accomplishments in one-on-one settings is also helpful. Although you don't want to (and shouldn't) shower this person with accolades for simply doing her job, periodically expressing appreciation can help her eventually understand that she won't always receive acknowledgement.

The obsessive worker

This person wants to get things right. He's an information junkie and may be a loner. You can identify this person by the way he devours information — the more, the better! He'll do outrageous amounts of work, but he doesn't like to make decisions because he's afraid that the decision he makes may be wrong. He also generally functions as the watchdog for the company, being the first to point out that the company or employees aren't following policies or labor laws. Working with the obsessive personality takes a lot of patience. In most cases, the best response is a polite "thank you" when offered advice or suggestions, but don't try to absorb or understand everything that is being said. Try not to feel this person is trying to outsmart you, accept what is factual, and attempt to disregard all the superfluous overlays.

The consensus-builder

This person wants everyone to get along. Not given to making quick decisions — how could there be such a thing when everyone has to agree? — the consensus-builder is inclusive and compassionate. She enjoys working with others but gets nervous when asked to take the initiative by herself. Encourage the consensus-builder to take the reins from time to time, and try to convince her that being able to communicate her points to those who may not agree with her will be beneficial for future success. After all, decisions have to be made, and not everyone may agree on them.

The socialite

The socialite wants everyone to have a good time. You can identify him by his preference for chatting and having fun while others are around. At times the socialite can have a valuable and positive effect, especially if the employee morale is low. However, if the chatting is excessive, his boss should counsel or coach him for the appropriate times for chatting. Help this person understand that most people require quiet and solitude in order to get work done. If he talks excessively in meetings, say something along the lines of, "That's a good point, James, but I'd also like to hear from some individuals who haven't offered their opinions." You may also suggest a time limit for individual comments.

Book V

Navigating Tricky Workplace Relationships and Situations

The steamroller

This person wants to get things done now. You can identify her by her willingness to make decisions, even when information is incomplete. On a team, the steamroller keeps the group moving at full speed and doesn't tolerate seemingly meaningless discussions. You don't need to modify your own behavior to get along with a steamroller: Eventually she'll steamroll herself. You can offer a gentle reminder to her that her teammates also have input on decisions made. Try to compliment her talent and motivation for getting things done, but remind her that it won't add any value if it doesn't have a team consensus or if the project is incomplete. In order for her to succeed, she'll want to be more open to working with a team.

Using the right office manners

All the personality types have to work together in a small space, of course. Keep the following tips in mind for surviving life in the workplace.

Everyone knows that outrageous behavior — such as temper tantrums, yelling matches, crude displays of power, and harassment of any kind — simply shouldn't be tolerated by anyone. But small slights, swearing, peevishness, and forced smiles have a way of getting under everyone's skin and can escalate to bad feelings over time. Problems that start small can become big if you let them go on very long. For tips on handling difficult or uncomfortable situations, head to Book V, Chapter 4.

Dress in a manner consistent with company culture

Like it or not, most people believe that what you see is what you get. What they usually see first is your clothes. Clothes are a nonverbal code of communication. What you wear signals your image to others. What signals do you want to send? Make sure that your clothes are always work-appropriate and clean.

While many companies have an official dress code, the dress code in others is unstated. In these cases, watch the people around you, especially your boss. Whether your boss is a man or a woman, notice the style. How formal is it? Plan your wardrobe in a similar style. If your boss always wears suits, buy a suit or two. While you don't have to match exactly, your style should still conform to company standards, whether they're stated or not.

Remember that cubicles don't have doors or ceilings

The cubicle is a curious invention, giving the illusion of privacy without actually providing privacy. Although you can't see your co-workers, you can certainly hear them. Engrain that fact in your mind. Keep chatting to a minimum, or, if possible, make your personal calls away from your cubicle while you're on a break or at lunch or make them while the people around you are in meetings. Similarly, keep confidential business conversations at a minimum volume. You don't want to spill the beans prematurely about some important deal.

Here are other ways to avoid disturbing your office mates in a cubicle environment:

- ✔ Don't bring odorous food to the office.
- ✔ Keep music low so as not to disturb others.
- ✔ Don't wear heavy perfume or cologne.

Respect others' time

Don't interrupt others unnecessarily or visit their offices or cubicles while they're working. Not sure if your presence is welcome or a distraction? Pay attention to the other person's body language. Does he give you his full attention, or does he look away and begin working again? If he doesn't fully engage you, take it as a hint that he's too busy and say something like, "I'll touch base later when you're free."

Greet people in a friendly way

Being able to introduce people and explain who they are makes everyone feel comfortable in a new situation and is one of the most useful skills you can acquire in the business world. The ability to introduce yourself or others confidently demonstrates that you are at ease and in control — and by extension, you set others at ease too.

When making introductions, keep these rules in mind:

- ✔ In formal business situations, your host (generally, the most senior executive from the company that planned the event) meets, greets, and introduces you to other guests. If your company is hosting the event, and you're the only or most senior representative of your company in a group, your job is to assume the role of host and make introductions.

- ✔ In less-formal situations, you don the role of host for your immediate circle (whoever is standing with you at the time) and facilitate introductions.

- ✔ If you enter a group in which introductions have already been made, introducing yourself is always appropriate and in most instances expected.

Branch out to others

At work, extend your professional network beyond your department. An easy, nonthreatening way to do that is to mingle with people in other departments. Believe it or not, mingling is a vitally important business skill. Mingling well demonstrates that you're a friendly, open, and engaged person who is interested in other people. Mingling poorly shows others that you're either unsure of yourself or so egotistical that you can't listen to others.

You can mingle with people in other departments during your breaks, when you're in the lunch or break room, during the few minutes prior to a company-wide meeting, and so on. One of the best places to mingle, however, is during company parties and business events.

During these occasions when you're making small talk with a new group of people, the worst thing you can do is keep glancing around for someone better to engage in conversation. You can't find a faster way to make someone feel unimportant. When you're speaking with someone, she should receive your full attention — no wandering eyes!

Developing good relations with your staff

Your staff helps you do your work. They're not your slaves, and they're not drones; they're people who deserve your respect. Praise them when their work is excellent. Comment on their work — in private — when it needs improvement. Above all, acknowledge their existence and their hard work, and treat them with courtesy. Without them, you wouldn't get your work done. The following sections show you how to work well with your staff.

Remembering the right names

Learn other people's names and how they prefer to be addressed. Memorizing names is hard for some people and easy for others. If it's hard for you, admit it upfront. If you make a mistake and call someone by the wrong name, apologize and blame yourself. Say something like "I'm terribly sorry, Juan. I'm so bad with names sometimes. I'll get it right from now on." Then make an effort to get it right.

To make sure you remember someone's name, repeat it to yourself as soon as possible; then find a pen and write *Juan in Information Technology* 30 or 40 times. This trick works!

As far as your own name goes, let your staff know how you prefer to be addressed. Say your name slowly and clearly when you meet new employees so that others will understand the proper pronunciation. Spell your name if you think it will help.

Acting calm, collected, and respectful

An oppressive boss is a nightmare. Someone who thinks her employees need to be blamed for her mistakes or who thinks her assistants should understand that her violent temper is simply part of her creativity is a notorious figure. Follow these guidelines for harmonious working relations with your staff:

✔ Treat employees with respect and hold yourself to the same standards.

✔ Keep an even tone in your voice. Yelling at people — even people who deserve it — is rarely effective.

✔ Correct errors privately, politely, and precisely.

✔ Give precise and clear instructions. Vague and ambiguous instructions are stressful for anyone who's trying to fulfill them. Refer to Book IV, Chapter 3 for in-depth information on how to state your needs and expectations clearly.

✔ Apologize when you make a mistake. After all, no one's perfect.

Book V

Navigating Tricky Workplace Relationships and Situations

Developing good relations with superiors

Business culture is based on rank. Most businesses have a defined hierarchy; even businesses that don't appear to have a formalized hierarchy still tend to give more status to some members than others. With a hierarchy comes competition for the top spots, and with competition come rivalries and the need to cope with them. Some companies reward intra-office competition; others work to defuse it through team building.

To develop good relations with those who have more clout than you do, follow these suggestions:

✔ **Find ways to be a good team player and also stand out from the group.** Take pride and care in your job. Build consensus when you need to, make decisions when you have to, and offer to help others who could benefit from your expertise or experience. A good boss notices not only how you treat him or her, but also how you work with your colleagues.

✔ **When you have a problem you have to share with your boss, identify the problem and offer a solution.** For example, if the copying machine suffers frequent breakdowns, you can suggest the purchase of a new machine and include an estimate of the cost. Supervisors love it when they can quickly respond "Okay" on an e-mail.

✔ **Show your loyalty to your boss.** Loyalty is a valued commodity in the business world. Many employers list it as the most important virtue that an employee can have.

Navigating through the "friend" dilemma

Newcomers at a company often believe that they can establish themselves in a company's culture by being unfailingly outgoing and friendly. The trouble is, friendliness, even if well intentioned, is sometimes at odds with rank. Your primary function at work is to do your job. Too much friendliness can actually hurt your effectiveness. One way that friendliness can be unproductive is in your relations with your superiors. Slapping them on the back and assuming that they're interested in your latest adventure may get you nowhere fast. And talking to them as though you're their equal may be seen not as friendly, but as bumptious and pushy. So curb your chumminess and check your sense of humor enough to avoid humiliation.

Interacting with superiors requires that you be aware of certain subtleties. Although your company may have a friendly "backyard barbecue" culture, let your boss be the person to introduce more-personal subjects. If you're in a social situation with your boss, general small-talk topics are permissible until your boss takes the lead and introduces other topics.

Getting some face time with the boss

Part of the reason you were hired is because your boss liked your personality and thought you'd fit in and become a valuable addition to the team. Keeping cordial relations with your boss is important, as is conveying that you enjoy his company as a person as well as your superior, so stop by for some friendly small talk. Initiate chitchat when it's clear he's not in the middle of something and has some downtime. In the break room over the coffee machine, as he's getting back from lunch and hasn't resumed work yet, and when you find yourself sharing an elevator are all good times for small talk.

If your boss's door is closed, or if he's working quietly in his office, he's likely trying hard to get some serious work done and won't welcome a frivolous interruption. Likewise, if your boss is on the phone or has a scowl on his face, you should probably wait for another time.

Giving sincere compliments

Compliment others when they've done exceptional work, when they've done more than you've asked them to do, and when they've done you a favor. Don't cheapen compliments by offering them willy-nilly, like a kindergarten teacher. Give compliments when people deserve them.

Giving compliments should be easy, but surprisingly, most people need practice to do it right. Always compliment in the following ways:

- **Politely:** Be sincere. Insincere or snarling compliments are pointless.
- **Precisely:** Be precise and detailed. Say something like "Jane, you did an excellent job on the Millman project. It was accurate and extremely well written, and I really appreciated receiving it before the deadline. Thank you for such a great effort."

- ✔ **Promptly:** Be timely. No one wants to hear "Oh, by the way, Ralph, the work you did on that contract for what's-his-name last year was good."

- ✔ **Publicly:** Usually, it's best to praise in public. Be aware, however, that shy people and those with cultural prohibitions against public praise are best praised in private.

Receiving compliments is even easier but is done poorly even more frequently. There is one — and only one — rule for receiving a compliment. When getting a compliment, always say, "Thank you." That's it! No other comments or qualifiers need to be added. Certainly don't apologize or belittle your accomplishment (which makes the person giving the compliment think you're fishing for something more), and don't amplify the compliment by adding your own self-praise (you'll appear to be an arrogant so-and-so who doesn't deserve compliments at all!).

Offering (and receiving) constructive criticism

Giving and receiving criticism are difficult. They're also necessary parts of working. Criticism won't be such a bitter pill for you or your co-workers if you use the tips in the following sections.

On the giving end

The *only* reason to give criticism is to improve performance. Criticizing is not complaining, and it's not attacking. Criticize in the following manner:

- ✔ **Privately:** Make comments only to those who need to be criticized, and do so away from others. Nobody else needs to hear what you have to say.

- ✔ **Politely:** Assume that the other person has feelings that will be hurt when she hears your criticism. Focus your comments on the problematic work and not the person.

- ✔ **Precisely:** Criticism should be specific and constructive. Identify the problem and look for a solution. Say something like "Chris, last week's order for Arete Systems was shipped in error to Hexis World instead. This is the third time this month that one of their orders has gone astray. Let's discuss what happened and figure out how to prevent this problem in the future."

- ✔ **Promptly:** Hand out criticism as soon as possible. If you're mad, take a few deep breaths and count to ten. Repeat as necessary! If you need time to formulate your criticism, take it. But procrastinating only increases the chance that the problem will be repeated and makes you feel worse. Deal with it now.

On the receiving end

Being criticized is difficult. When someone is criticizing you, follow the four cardinal rules, always taking criticism

- ✔ **Professionally:** If the criticism is appropriate, accept responsibility. Avoid excuses or blaming others. Apologize, assure the other person that the mistake won't happen again, and then live up to your word.

- ✔ **Politely:** Assume that the other person doesn't mean to insult you when she gives criticism. If she calls you names or is rude, redirect the discussion to the work itself. Avoid retaliating in like manner; you'll almost always make the situation worse.

- ✔ **Positively:** Assume that the other person has something helpful to say. Listen. Try to understand the issue. If you're too mad to understand, count to ten. Repeat as necessary! Ask for clarification. Ask for assistance.

- ✔ **Appropriately:** If the criticism is unfair or misplaced, say so — politely and privately.

Respecting Physical Differences

The United States is home to more than 54 million people with disabilities, and more than half of all Americans say they're a bit unsure around people with disabilities. Pretty clearly, life at work can be tough if you're among the 54 million, and getting over your uncertainty about people with disabilities is a matter of urgent importance if you're one of the others. The following sections help you work more comfortably with colleagues or clients who have disabilities. If you have a disability, take the initiative by giving your co-workers, employees, or boss some guidelines for working with you.

Starting with a few general guidelines

When you work with someone who has a disability, you may think that he should be treated differently. This thought is a mistake, for the most part. People are people first and disabled or nondisabled second. The following sections provide a few simple but helpful general guidelines for working with people who have disabilities.

Making reasonable accommodations

Federal law requires that employers make reasonable accommodations for those with disabilities. Any employer who hires someone with a disability is expected to accommodate the disability unless undue hardship is the result.

These accommodations include providing auxiliary aids for those with vision or hearing disabilities and making sure that physical barriers are removed if possible. If barriers cannot be removed, employers must provide alternatives.

 The National Organization on Disability (NOD) is a great place to start if you want to find out more about disability issues. On its Web site (www.nod.org) you can find frequently asked questions, a summary of the Americans with Disabilities Act (ADA), findings of the NOD/Harris Survey on Americans with Disabilities, links to other sites, and more. Or contact the organization for information: National Organization on Disability, 888 Sixteenth St. NW, Ste. 800, Washington, DC 20006.

Really, these legal requirements are no more than what common courtesy dictates. If you hire someone who uses a wheelchair but have no way for that person to enter and exit the building, you haven't considered her comfort.

Using considerate language

A good place to start treating those with disabilities with respect is with the language you use. Your choice of words and the way you say them have an enormous impact on the way you interact with others. Many disability groups consider terms such as *physically challenged* patronizing.

- ✔ **Avoid using words such as *handicapped, crippled,* and *invalid* to refer to those with disabilities.** When it's relevant to mention at all, indicate the specific disability.

- ✔ **Avoid using words such as *healthy* and *normal* to refer to those without disabilities.** Many people with disabilities are in excellent health.

- ✔ **Don't refer to someone as *wheelchair-bound* or *confined to a wheelchair.*** The chair, in fact, is a freedom machine, affording independence and mobility.

- ✔ **Use people-first terminology.** A general rule is to acknowledge the disability but always place the person first (*person with a disability* rather than *disabled person,* for example).

- ✔ **Talk to everyone in a medium tone of voice.** Don't speak more loudly to someone with a disability.

- ✔ **Avoid getting overly concerned about figures of speech in the presence of people with disabilities.** You can say "I see what you mean!" to someone who has a visual impairment, for example, and you can invite someone who uses a wheelchair to go for a walk.

Acting properly

If you are interviewing or employing a person with a disability, certain rules of etiquette can help you deal with that person appropriately:

- ✔ **As an employer, train your staff to anticipate and accommodate those with disabilities:** Know where the accessible parking facilities, elevators, restrooms, and drinking fountains are in your building. Be prepared to give clear directions to those with visual impairments.

- ✔ **Educate yourself about the assistive technologies people with disabilities are using:** These devices include wheelchairs, hearing aids, enhanced and auditory computer screens, transcription devices, walking aids, and guide animals. Find out about the assistive technologies that your co-workers with disabilities use, and adapt your presentations and communications to accommodate them.

- ✔ **Offer to shake hands when you meet someone with a disability for the first time:** If the other person extends the left hand, shake the left hand using your right hand, not your left. If shaking hands isn't possible, a nod of the head is fine. In the United States, a light touch on the shoulder or forearm to acknowledge the person is also appropriate.

- ✔ **Avoid staring at someone with a disability or averting your gaze:** Staring and averting your gaze are equally hurtful to a person with a disability. The proper reaction? Look everyone in the eye.

- ✔ **"Helping" someone who has a disability is discouraged unless the person has given you permission to do so:** People with disabilities are offended by patronizing offers of assistance. Refraining from helping someone can be painful sometimes. As painful as watching someone struggle may be, however, you must respect a decision to decline your assistance. If you're asked to help, ask for specific instructions, and follow them carefully. Otherwise, assume that the person is no less able to care for himself than you are.

Dealing with specific disabilities

Some rules of disability etiquette are firm; others aren't. You should never feed a guide animal, for example, but whether you should help those who have visual impairments cross the street depends on their interest in having your assistance. The following sections explain how to interact with folks who have hearing, visual, and mobility impairments.

Hearing impairments

Hearing disabilities range from mild to severe; they're usually hidden and often hard to detect. If you have difficulty getting a response from someone you speak to, she may have a hearing disability. She probably isn't being rude.

If someone is hearing-impaired, the best way to get his attention is to move so that he can see you or to touch him lightly on the shoulder or forearm.

If the person with a hearing disability would like to use American Sign Language (ASL), and you know it, by all means use it. If you don't know how to sign, admit it; then either find someone who does know or use writing. If the person has an interpreter, here are a few tips:

- ✔ **The interpreter sits or stands next to you, facing the person with the hearing disability:** An interpreter doesn't say and use every word you say; he often explains and paraphrases the meaning of your words. He may fall behind, so pause occasionally to allow him to catch up.

- ✔ **Always talk to the person, not to the interpreter:** In a business situation, never consult the interpreter. The interpreter's job is to facilitate conversation, not to make business decisions. If there are specific industry words the interpreter should learn, make every effort to provide the interpreter with a list or hold a brief meeting ahead of time.

Although interpreters are common in some workplace circles, particularly political and diplomatic ones, they're not universal. Those with hearing impairments often use sign language or read lips. If the person you're talking to can read lips, here are some tips:

- ✔ **Face your conversation partner:** Don't walk around.

- ✔ **Speak clearly and slowly, but naturally:** Exaggerating your lip movement only makes lip-reading harder.

- ✔ **Don't eat or smoke while talking, and don't talk with your hands near your mouth:** These activities may make it difficult for the person who's trying to read your lips.

Avoid these embarrassing mistakes at all costs:

- ✔ **Never shout:** Shouting won't do any good, even if the person has only partial hearing loss.

- ✔ **Never simplify what you say:** You're talking to an adult, not a child.

Visual impairments

Like hearing impairment, vision impairment has many varieties and degrees. Visual impairments include tunnel vision, in which you see only a small, central part of the visual field; partial vision, in which you see a portion of the visual field, usually one side; and total vision impairment, in which you see nothing.

Always use words with someone who has a visual impairment. Here are some tips to keep in mind:

- ✔ Announce yourself and whoever is with you to the person with a visual disability. Say something like this: "Hi, Juan; it's Sally. I have Wanda Lee with me as well."

- ✔ Say "Hello" and "Goodbye," and tell the person when you're moving around the room.

- ✔ In meetings, use names during exchanges between people to help the person with the visual impairment follow the conversation: "Valerie? John here. Can you give us the latest on the Lohman account?"

- ✔ Offer to read instructions or other printed material aloud.

- ✔ Where danger looms, voice your concerns politely. Say, for example, "Ben, there's a chair directly in front of you. Would you like me to move it?"

You can really inconvenience or harm someone if you make the following blunders:

- ✔ Never touch or move anything in the office of a person with a visual impairment.

- ✔ Never move furniture without informing anyone with a visual impairment.

People with visual impairments often use a variety of technologies to navigate through the world. Some carry canes, and some are accompanied by guide dogs. Offering assistance to someone with a visual impairment is always appropriate, but if she refuses the offer, accept it politely. Keep the following pointers in mind:

- ✔ **If you're asked to guide, offer your elbow.** Describe your route, announcing upcoming transitions and changes. When you reach your destination, avoid leaving the person in empty space. Find a chair, table, or a wall. Place the person's hand on the back of the chair, on the table, or on the wall for orientation.

- ✔ **At meals, describe the location of the food on the plate by using clock time, such as "Shrimp at seven o'clock; peas at three."** Offer to help cut food.

- ✔ **When exchanging money, place bills in separate stacks, and present each stack.** Say, for example, "Your change is $47.54. Here are two twenties, one five, and two ones. And here are the 54 cents."

- ✔ **When signing documents, offer to guide the person's hand to the correct position, and offer a straight edge (such as a ruler) for alignment.**

Never touch a guide or service animal unless the handler gives you permission, and never call out a guide animal's name. Committing these faux pas is dangerous, not only to the animal and its handler, but also potentially to you. If you touch a guide animal, you may inadvertently be giving it a signal to do something that its handler doesn't want it to do. Also, calling out a guide animal's name can divert its attention from assisting its handler.

Mobility impairments

Mobility impairments vary from walking with difficulty to walking with a cane to using a wheelchair. As always, treat people with mobility impairments with respect.

People with mobility impairments often cannot go where people without those impairments can. Be gracious in picking out routes to destinations, taking the impairment into account.

If someone uses a motorized wheelchair, wait until the wheelchair is powered down to shake hands. When having a conversation with someone in a wheelchair, move so that the two of you are at the same eye level.

Mobility aids are part of the personal space of the person with the mobility impairment. Don't let yourself make the following gaffes:

- ✔ While you put a client's coat in the closet, never move mobility aids out of reach.
- ✔ Never try out another person's mobility aids.
- ✔ Never push a person in a wheelchair without permission.
- ✔ Never lean or hang on a person's wheelchair.

Dealing with Racial, Ethnic, and Other Differences

Stereotyping, ridiculing, demeaning, or insulting other people is always a mistake. At work, this behavior can be disastrous. You should not assume that the women in the room are secretaries or nurses, or that the men are bosses or investors. Neither should you assume that the person on the other end of the phone shares your ethnicity. The man using the wheelchair may be the CEO, and your potential client may be gay.

These differences shouldn't be the subject of comment. Even when the story behind the difference may be interesting, remember that prying is rude. Regardless of individual particulars, you have a job to do that brings you together. Focus on the job, and treat other people as important. In other words, treat them with respect.

In this section, you find out how to be a respectful colleague to people who are physically, ethnically, and culturally different from you. You also are introduced to some straightforward principles regarding gender and sexual differences in the workplace.

Inadvertently insulting someone with a racial or ethnic slur is one of the fastest ways to embarrass yourself and hurt others. As a well-mannered person, you should have no problem avoiding this pitfall, because you're alert to your co-workers' sensitivities and needs! As people from different ethnic, cultural, religious, and national origins unite, you need a tolerant and inclusive attitude, which means watching your language and your actions. Here are some guidelines:

- ✔ **Learn the currently accepted terms for the ethnic groups, religions, and nationalities of those with whom you work.** Get rid of all those slang terms that you may have heard in the past.

- ✔ **Don't identify or refer to others by race or ethnic identity.** People are people.

- ✔ **Use names and titles, and avoid other labels.** Sexist terms are strictly taboo. A person is a sales representative, not a salesman or saleslady. An administrative assistant is not a secretary, and an information-systems specialist is not a computer jockey.

- ✔ **Be alert to a person's special needs.** If one of your colleagues must be absent for a religious observance, offer to cover his responsibilities for the day.

- ✔ **Always make a conscious effort to speak inclusively.** Don't let sexist terms creep into your vocabulary, and listen to the words that slip out of your mouth.

Respecting racial and ethnic differences

Along with the cultural diversity inherent in the global marketplace comes confusion about how to behave. People don't always know how to interact with others from different ethnic and racial backgrounds. In fact, people don't even know whether their behavior should be different.

Race and ethnicity are less important than your beliefs and attitudes about these things. Don't typecast or stereotype because of physical or cultural features. The paramount rule of etiquette — respect for others — rules out such behavior. Nevertheless, differences do exist, and you need to know how to respect them. You also need to know the etiquette of particular situations and how to adjust your verbal and nonverbal behavior for those situations. In addition, be careful when you use humor with those from another culture; different cultures have different ideas about what is appropriate humor, and yours may not be that welcome. Also, until you know what the cultural rules are regarding personal contact, keep your hands to yourself.

Over time, a standard code has emerged to allow people to get along with one another in business and to know what to expect from each other. Standard American English is the international language of business, and standard Western manners are the official protocol in the United States.

If you don't speak or behave according to these standards, you immediately set yourself up for criticism. But by the same token, if you don't recognize and respect those who follow other traditions, you may get yourself in a jam.

Knowing more than one language helps almost everyone in the business world. Learning even a few words and phrases can be a real plus. In certain businesses — the music industry, for example — slang and jargon are useful. But in almost all other situations, speaking and writing clearly and grammatically are paramount.

Now that you can communicate, how do you behave? Respect dictates that you take it upon yourself to learn about other cultures. If your business regularly takes you to other parts of the world, take a course in protocol or read about those parts of the world.

Respecting gender and sexual differences

Dealing with gender and sex in the workplace can be a mess. In the same way that business is colorblind, it is sex blind.

The way to get along is to assume that everyone has a sex life — and then forget about it! That doesn't mean that everyone has to act the same way or that you can't express your individuality. But what people do in their private lives is exactly that: private. Don't assume that everyone is heterosexual; don't assume that everyone is gay. Assume that other people are interested in love and sex but that the details are none of your business. Never make jokes or snide remarks about gender or sexual preference.

In addition to being colorblind and sex blind, business should also be gender blind. What matters are rank and status, not gender. When gender isn't the key factor, you may be unsure about things like who opens the door for whom or who pays the bill for a lunch. Use the following common-sense tips as a guide to intergender relations in business:

✔ The first person to the door opens the door for everyone else, regardless of gender. Full arms exempt you from door duty, however. Like all good rules, this one has an exception: You always open the door for your client or customer.

Offer to help an overburdened colleague, regardless of gender. If your colleague has an armful of books and papers, for example, offer to take some of them.

✔ The host pays for a business lunch, regardless of gender.

✔ Help others if they're having a difficult time with a coat, regardless of gender.

✔ Men and women stand to greet someone, regardless of the other person's gender.

✔ Women shake hands in business, as men do.

Chapter 3

Staying Cool When Conflicts Arise

• •

• •

Conflicts are a part of life. Simply defined, a conflict is a problem where a disagreement exists between two or more people. Not surprisingly, the workplace is an environment rife with conflict, and it generally involves two issues — business concerns and working relationships (and sometimes both mixed together). But all conflict situations involve people, which means that interpersonal communications, from listening to speaking, play a major role in the course that conflicts take and how they end up resolved (or not).

Conflict doesn't have to be all bad. Your approach to conflict situations is the key. Successfully resolving conflicts at work starts with taking a constructive approach to them. In particular, you want to take actions that are assertive: Go to the source, listen, focus on the issue, state your views directly and sincerely, and collaboratively come up with solutions.

This chapter discusses behaviors and ways of communicating that greatly improve conflict situations on the job. It also presents an assertive approach applicable not only to conflict situations but also to working relationships on a day-to-day basis and explains two problem-solving models that help you bring conflicts to satisfactory resolution.

Taking the High Road to Resolve Conflict: The Assertive Approach

Conflicts are a normal part of most workplaces. Whether the outcome of a conflict is positive or negative is largely determined by the approach you take. When your approach sends you down a destructive path, the likelihood of arriving at a good resolution is slim to none. When your approach sends you on a constructive path, you increase the likelihood of achieving positive results. You're the driver; it's up to you what road you want to take.

Being assertive takes the most constructive stance in dealing with conflict. Being *assertive* in conflict situations is about expressing your views in a positive and confident manner and enabling others to do the same with the intent and effort to work out resolutions. If you need to address an issue, you tackle it respectfully so that you promote two-way communication.

Assertive behaviors that help resolve conflicts

The assertive approach is the most effective approach for tackling conflict situations. When you use the assertive approach, you're willing to deal with conflict situations regardless of the comfort level you feel. Emphasis is placed on working through the issue with the other person, treating him or her with respect, and problem solving to find a solution. When using the assertive approach in a conflict, here are the common actions you can take:

Go to the source

No invention can ever take the place of face-to-face interactions for resolving disputes. E-mail can't do it; neither can voice mail. Telling others but not the source doesn't do the trick either. People need to meet directly with one another and use conversation to settle their differences. In the assertive approach, you go to the other person with whom you have your difference to open up dialogue, one-on-one and in private. That old-fashioned, tried-and-true method works best for constructively resolving conflicts.

You must know what you're trying to accomplish before having the discussion with the other party. Until you recognize the positive outcome you seek to achieve, you're not yet ready to address the conflict. Figuring out this answer first puts you on a constructive track.

Stay in control

The toughest person you have to manage in interactions, especially challenging ones, is yourself. When you're in control of your own emotions — versus them being in control of you — you're better able to influence the direction of a conversation toward achieving a positive outcome.

You don't control others, but you do greatly influence them. When you take control of your emotions, you have the greatest opportunity to assert positive influence with others. In conflict situations, using your positive influence is the secret to being constructive and achieving the outcomes you desire.

The destructive dozen

Being aware of what *not* to do is an integral part of figuring out how best to resolve conflicts. The behaviors in the following list put you on the destructive track; they make conflicts much more difficult to deal with and resolve. If you're like most people, you've probably had some experience with these behaviors; both doing and receiving them. Consider them the *destructive dozen*:

- ✔ **Yelling:** Yelling intimidates some, angers others, and begets yelling in return.

- ✔ **Blaming:** Ironically, when you cast blame, you discourage — not encourage — people from taking responsibility for their own actions and working with you to come up with solutions.

- ✔ **Reacting defensively:** This behavior is marked by interrupting, getting louder, and reacting with counterattacks, actions that erect a wall between the people involved in the conflict.

- ✔ **Focusing on perceived intentions:** Assumptions prevent you from seeing people's actions, prejudice you into thinking the worst about those actions, and take the focus away from solutions.

- ✔ **Not dealing with the situation:** The situation won't change on its own. Quite often, the problem gets worse because the person you have an issue with is unaware of your concern and, therefore, unlikely to recognize a reason to change anything.

- ✔ **Making subtle digs, sarcastic remarks, or personal insults:** The touch of supposed humor that sometimes comes with these remarks or loaded language that's insulting only heightens the tension in conflict situations.

- ✔ **Complaining constantly about the situation:** Continuously complaining can quickly morph from venting into chronic whining — nothing anyone wants to listen to.

- ✔ **Broadcasting that you think a solution is unlikely:** Pessimism can undermine efforts to find a workable solution. Not only do you end up sounding like a naysayer, but your discouraging tone can cast a pall over the entire workplace.

- ✔ **Issuing ultimatums:** Ultimatums push power, not reason, as the way to work out differences. With customers, they cause business to suffer and even discontinue. With co-workers and staff, they create animosity and defiance.

- ✔ **Pushing harder and harder for your way:** Generally, the harder you push for your way, with little consideration for the other person's view, the less persuasive you become.

- ✔ **Sending flaming e-mail messages:** When you use e-mail to voice concerns to others — especially if you copy additional people on the matter — you fan the flame of tension; you don't spark solutions. In fact, what you'll probably get are harsh messages flaming back. (Head to Book IV, Chapter 4 to find out how to avoid misusing e-mail.)

- ✔ **Going to others rather than the source:** Telling others about your concern rather than the person the issue directly involves is great for stimulating gossip and rumors and stirring plenty of negative energy.

Stay focused on issues

Regardless of whether the issues at the core of the conflict deal with the behavior of others, different styles, or differences of opinion about how to do a job, the key is to focus on the issues and not on the other person in your discussions. When you stay issue-focused, you find it easier to keep your language and tone constructive.

Not surprisingly, conflict frequently evokes feelings of discomfort. Give yourself permission to feel uncomfortable, because otherwise you may simply avoid the problem. Then focus your attention not on your comfort level but rather on how best to resolve the issue with the other party. When you take this step, you can face these challenges and increase your chances of having a positive outcome.

In conflict situations, your ability to listen and understand where the other person is coming from is critical in achieving positive outcomes. Don't get caught up in suspecting the other person's intentions. Assume he or she means well so that you deal with the actions and the issues themselves and focus on solutions. (Go to Book IV, Chapter 2 for information on how to listen actively.)

Be direct, constructive, and sincere

Assertive people don't shy away from acknowledging problems and describing them as they see them. But language and tone are to the point, constructive, and focused on the issue — the *actions* of the other person, not the *person*. The message is expressed with a sense of importance, with sincerity, and in the best way possible to clearly make the point — even if it's a hard one for the other person to hear.

People sometimes worry so much about being nice to others that they can't be clear and honest when they attempt to address their concerns. Conflict situations aren't about being nice or mean; they're about working out issues and differences to make positive results. Save being nice for social situations.

Go for solutions and problem-solve collaboratively

When you deal with problems or conflicts, your whole emphasis must be on working out a solution with the other people involved. You want to be *solutions-oriented* so that your end result creates an improvement, corrects an error, or makes things better than they previously were.

You also want the conflict to be resolved collaboratively so that you can work out a mutually beneficial solution — an agreement you both can support. The problem is stated, but the emphasis from that point forward is on finding solutions (not dwelling on problems) and on working through the issues together as partners (not adversaries).

Stay firm yet willing to compromise

Being firm means being strong in your convictions and confident in your manner, but not harsh in your tone or language. In this assertive behavior, you get your concerns and ideas across but also show an openness to hearing the other person's input. People compromise as needed because it's good for the solution. Don't appease the other person just to get an uncomfortable discussion over with quickly. But also be flexible so that other possible options can be considered.

Now or later? When to deal with the problem

Here are the three choices of assertiveness and descriptions of when they work best in conflict situations:

- ✔ **Dealing with the matter now:** Sometimes, as the expression goes, there's no time like the present. The concern is upon you, and addressing it right away with the other party is better for turning the problem around and preventing it from building up and becoming a bigger problem. You feel in control of yourself and ready to speak up and know your emphasis is on resolving the conflict. You're also in a setting, or can create one right away, in which you and the other party can talk privately.

- ✔ **Dealing with the matter at a later time soon:** You know you have a problem you need to address, but now isn't the best time to do so. Emotions may be too high — yours, the other person's, or both. Trying to resolve conflicts in the heat of the moment is often the worst of timing. You may not be ready. You may not have a plan thought out to express your concerns. You may be in a public setting void of any opportunity to talk privately. Sometimes, the present time simply isn't the right time to work on a conflict.

  If you can't address a conflict right away, set a time to meet with the other party while the issue is still fresh. When the matter is important enough not to let go, delaying for a brief time can be helpful, because you have time to prepare before you meet to resolve the problem. Putting off an issue that you know you need to address (procrastination at its worst) doesn't help and only makes issues harder to handle.

- ✔ **Leaving the matter alone:** This third option works only when the matter at hand isn't really that important — emotionally, you can let go of it and not be troubled. Assertiveness isn't about addressing everything that bothers you. It's about picking and choosing your issues. Some matters are small in nature and are easy enough to tolerate and let go. Showing tolerance for the little issues and focusing on the big ones usually results in other people taking you more seriously.

Getting Started on the Right Foot

In conflict situations, you definitely want to put your best foot forward — whichever one it happens to be — and you don't want to put your foot in your mouth at the same time.

Anatomy aside, you need to start your discussions on a positive track when you address conflicts or concerns with others. Introductions are important for managing discussions involving conflicts, especially when emotions run high. Regretfully, people quite often skip this critical step. You may have even done it yourself. You get up the nerve to sit down with the source of your conflict, and then you dive right into your issue. Unfortunately, the other person (the source of your conflict) becomes confused or reacts defensively to what you're saying. What you intended to happen and where you wanted to go with the discussion weren't made known to the other person, and as a result, you find yourself getting off track.

The following sections focus on how to begin communicating when you're addressing conflict situations, concentrating on setting the right tone and structure to promote constructive dialogue.

Setting an agenda

You want to establish a structure (organization) for the meeting so that it doesn't wander aimlessly. Conflict discussions that have no structure are less likely to reach a resolution. To set a good structure when you initiate a conflict resolution meeting, do the following:

✔ **State that you have an issue.** The point of the issue statement is to let the other person know you have a serious and important matter to address. Do this right at the start in a general statement that either names the overall subject you want to discuss ("Amy, I want to discuss some challenges I see happening with our ABC project") or simply states that you have an issue of concern that you want to address with the other person ("Anthony, something's been bothering me, and I'd like to talk it over with you").

Limit this opening line to one sentence and keep it general in nature. You want to avoid getting into the specifics at the start. Otherwise, you pull the other person's attention into details, making it much harder for you to have an organized flow to your discussion.

✔ **State your positive intention.** Make sure your listener knows that you mean well by stating your own positive intention, by stating the positive intention of the other person, or by stating both. This statement of one to a few sentences at most serves to create a positive tone for the meeting. (See the next section for more on positive intentions.)

Book V

**Navigating
Tricky
Workplace
Relation-
ships and
Situations**

✔ **Outline your agenda.** As a general rule, the more sensitive the issue and the more its potential for strong reactions, the more you want to verbalize an agenda in your introduction. The agenda outlines the flow of your meeting. When you do it right, it describes the problem-solving process you're going to use to guide the discussion. It's a list of headings, as opposed to specific topics of discussion. For example:

"Jen, in our meeting today, I want to first share with you my concerns about what's been happening recently and then hear your point of view. From there, I want us to brainstorm ideas of how we can make things work better, evaluate which of those ideas will be mutually beneficial, and then close by finalizing our plan and even setting a follow-up time to review our progress."

This agenda overview gives your receiver a verbal outline of what's intended to happen at the meeting. It sounds like bullet points you'd actually see on a written agenda and moves from discussing problems to working out solutions — a logical, focused, and positive flow.

By having a set track to follow for your discussion, you and the other party know what to expect. If, during the course of the discussion, you and the other person veer off track, you can use the agenda to steer the other person back on course. The agenda also reinforces your positive intention by letting the other person know that working out a solution is your aim.

No matter what problem-solving process you choose to follow (see the later section "Bringing Conflicts to Resolution" for a couple of models), this is the kind of introduction you want to have for initiating conflict-resolution discussions. It gives you an organized flow with a constructive tone — a winning combination for getting started on the right foot.

Making your positive intentions known

When you address concerns with others, you want to express a *positive intention* as part of a strong opening statement before you get into the specifics of your issue. A positive intention is one of the most important tools to have in resolving conflicts.

A *positive intention* is a statement that indicates you mean well. It tells the other person in your conversation that the discussion and actions that follow are meant to be good. Such statements hold you accountable to actually match your actions with your intentions as the discussion ensues and help the other party refrain from making any negative assumptions about your intentions.

Stating such an intention as part of your opening for a conflict discussion sets the positive tone you seek for the discussion. To make a good statement of positive intention, follow these criteria:

✔ Say it in one to two sentences in most cases. Rambling messages tend to lose their impact.

✔ Express it in a sincere tone. Without sincerity, your statement has negative intentions!

✔ State it in positive language, and avoid mixed-message words such as *but* and trigger words such as *must*. (See Chapter 3 in Book IV for more about trigger words.)

✔ Define the positive outcome you're seeking.

Here's an example of a statement of positive intention:

> "George, as we address this issue today, I want you to know my whole focus here is on helping us clear the air and getting back on track toward having a working relationship in which we support one another."

Try arguing with that statement! The statement of positive intention often helps to put the other person at ease and sets the tone for a constructive dialogue to follow, which, in turn, increases the likelihood that you can steer the discussion toward achieving a mutually beneficial outcome.

In your introduction to a conflict resolution discussion, you can use one of two types of positive intentions, or you may even want to use both. One type of positive intention is your own; the other type is the one you state for the other person.

Your own positive intention

As you can see in the *my* emphasis of the following type of positive intention, you *own* the statement. Words like *I, me, my,* or *mine* show you have possession of the message. It is coming from your perspective:

Example: "Beth, my emphasis with you today is on working out solutions that help us do our jobs well."

A positive intention you give to the other party

Here the emphasis is on the other person. Its intent is to communicate your respect for the other person and acknowledge your understanding of his good intentions.

Example: "Luke, one thing I want you to know is that I greatly appreciate the passion you bring to your work, and regardless of what we come up with, I want to see that continue for you."

When you provide someone with a positive intention as your introduction to addressing a conflict situation, make sure you use positive and sincere language, limit the statement to one sentence in most cases, and ensure that it's relevant to the issue being discussed. This last point is important because you want to avoid saying something about the other person just to be nice. Doing so without any relevance to the matter at hand causes you to lose all sincerity and sets the opposite tone of what you want.

Sometimes, of course, you can't think of anything positive about the other person. Don't force it! If that's the case, then just stick to stating your own positive intention. You won't go wrong by doing that.

 After you state the positive intentions, especially your own, you may be able to repeat similar comments during the discussion to help diffuse tension and keep the other person on a constructive track with you. Occasional reminders that you mean well and want to achieve positive outcomes often help in keeping people focused and working with you to reach resolutions.

Applying Helpful Tools in Conflict Situations

Although people sometimes make the right effort in conflict situations, they often run into trouble because they don't know the right tools to apply. They go to the person who is the source of the conflict and attempt to work something out, but as soon as they speak, they rub the source the wrong way and end up in a heated debate that goes nowhere. After one bad experience like that, many people become leery of addressing their conflicts with others. However, avoiding the issue (the nonassertive approach) doesn't help, nor does venting your frustrations behind the scenes to others (the passive-aggressive approach). And trying to win an argument with the other person (the aggressive approach) doesn't resolve conflicts at all and usually aggravates working relationships.

Taking an assertive approach works best for resolving conflicts; therefore, assertive communication tools are what must be applied. This section reinforces the active listening and assertive speaking tools discussed in Chapters 2 and 3 of Book IV and explains how to apply them in conflict situations. It also adds a few more tools to your kit that help keep conflicts on the constructive track.

Showing understanding

Being an active listener isn't always easy because conflict situations can spark a high degree of emotion. The tool that helps you listen actively is the *shift-and-show-understanding* tool.

When a conflict situation generates an especially high degree of emotion, both parties spend a lot of energy trying to outtalk each other. As the great debate ensues, you end up with two or more people sometimes vehemently talking and no one really listening. The more the tension rises, the further you get from reaching any kind of solution. The *shift-and-show-understanding* tool places an emphasis on active listening that includes two main efforts:

- ✔ **Shift your attention from your own message to the other person's message.** This shift of attention away from yourself brings your emotions under control. When you're in control of your own emotions, you increase the likelihood of influencing the other person to control hers.

- ✔ **Respond by showing understanding of the other person's message before continuing any efforts to express your own views.** Responding with verbal feedback to show understanding of a point, regardless of whether you agree with it, lets the other person feel heard.

When you get yourself under control and verbally show that you're listening to the other person's message, you often diffuse the tension in an interaction. Tensions don't escalate when people are listening to understand each other: Someone has to start the process, so you can take the lead by shifting and showing understanding.

To make shifting and showing understanding work, follow these key steps:

1. **Mentally focus your attention on the speaker.**

   Stop speaking and put your attention into capturing what the other person is saying. (Try mentally saying the word *shift* to yourself just as a reminder to listen.) Then focus on seeking out the meaning of the person's message.

2. **Paraphrase or reflectively paraphrase to give verbal feedback to show understanding.**

   In *paraphrasing,* you summarize the content of the message you've heard: "So your point, Jerry, is that doing further research is only going to slow us down, and it's time for us to move ahead and finish the project. Is that right?"

   In *reflective paraphrasing,* you capture and reflect back to the speaker the emotional meaning that you hear and the content that supports it:

"Audrey, you're feeling frustrated because the research has taken longer than expected and you don't see how spending more time on it is going to help us get this project done. Is that correct?"

Go to Book IV, Chapter 2 for more on paraphrasing and reflective paraphrasing.

3. Gain confirmation or clarification of your verbal feedback.

You want to invite a direct response from the other person to find out if you're hearing the message correctly. To make sure your speaker knows that you need a response, you can either raise your sentence-ending tone to make your feedback message sound like a question or simply ask, "Is that correct?"

4. Ask questions when you need more information to understand the message.

After you've given feedback and gained confirmation, you may need to get more information to further understand why the person thinks or feels the way he does. When you find that you need more information or background, ask for it. Go to Book IV, Chapter 2 to find out how to ask highly effective, open-ended questions.

Your role is to understand the other person's message as that person meant it. Avoid interpreting and adding your own spin to the message. People become aggravated, especially in conflict situations, if they think you're putting words in their mouths. Likewise, avoid judging the speaker's view as right or wrong. The other person's view is merely *different* than yours, which is why you're having a conflict. You don't have to agree with it — just understand it. Occasionally, you may actually find out that the other person's viewpoint is quite similar to your own. Perhaps no one was listening before, so neither of you realized it.

5. State your view, if needed; if not, simply move on to the solution stage.

When you state your view on an issue, do so only to provide background and information. Don't dwell on the fact that you disagree with the other person. In fact, avoid saying that you disagree, because that can trigger an escalation of tension in a conflict situation. Instead, start your message by saying something like the following: "Mario, let me give you another view to consider on this issue." Then you can state your view with constructive language and a matter-of-fact tone. See the later section "Stating thoughts" for more on how to constructively express your views.

In conflict situations, agreeing on the problem isn't as important as agreeing on the solution. The best direction for any discussion is toward working out solutions. If you already made your point, rehashing it will probably take both of you off track. In that situation, simply move on. Adding more to your point may cause the two of you to dwell only on your differences, which usually is pointless. Keep your focus on a far more positive endeavor: gaining agreements around solutions.

Describing the problem

An important skill for expressing the concerns you have about what someone else is doing is *describing,* or reporting behaviors that someone displays in observable and objective terms. It's telling what you see, not giving your opinions about what you see; telling what someone has done, not stating your assumptions about the person's motives. In conflict situations, describing is much better than general criticism. To clearly understand what describing means, keep the following points in mind:

- **Behavior, not attitude:** Describing focuses on behaviors but not on attitudes. Behavior involves someone's actions. You can see them and hear them. Attitude, on the other hand, is how someone thinks or feels about something. You can't see it; it's locked away in the individual's mind. Attitudes influence behavior, yet they aren't the same as behavior. In fact, a person can have a lousy attitude about an issue but still manage to keep it in check by displaying respectful behaviors in an interaction.

- **Substance, not generalities:** Describing, sometimes referred to as *constructive feedback,* gives you a clear, specific, and concrete picture of the events that took place as if you were watching them again on a recording. For example: "As I facilitated today's team meeting, I was concerned about the behaviors you displayed that were different from your usual positive participation. On three occasions, I noticed you interrupted other team members before they were done expressing their points. On one of those occasions, I heard your voice get loud and you told Joe that his idea to solve the shipping delays was 'a waste of time.' As the exchange between you and Joe started to escalate, I asked you to stop. What I saw happen for the rest of the meeting was that you sat quietly, had your arms folded, kept your chin down, and gave no response when asked for your thoughts to help on other ideas."

Stating thoughts

Sometimes in the course of a conflict-resolution discussion, you need to offer an opinion. This primarily happens in the course of examining the problem situation but also can occur during dialogue about the solution. So as not to come across as opinionated, use the *stating-thoughts* tool.

When stating thoughts, you indicate your views about a situation in one of two key ways:

- You tell how the situation is impacting you.

- You respond to the person through comments with constructive feedback.

In either case, this tool provides perspective and clarity for the other person in the conversation and enhances the issue's importance.

When stating thoughts, you can usually use up to a few sentences. Don't be long-winded or you'll sound opinionated, but be sure to place your emphasis on being constructive and providing views supported by factual reasons. Here are some guidelines:

✔ **When defining impact, clarify the effect the problem is having on you.** Give facts to support your views or conclusions. Usually this form of stating thoughts is done right after you've used the tool of describing to state observations about your concern. For example: "Based on the concern I just described to you, not getting the information I was expecting at the agreed-upon milestone dates has caused delays for me on this project and is affecting my ability to meet the final target date for the project."

✔ **When responding with feedback, focus on issues and behaviors.** Explain, as needed, the basis of your feedback in response to the other party's thoughts. Focus your explanations on observations and facts, avoiding interpretations or analysis of other people's perceived intentions. For example: "I'm having difficulty understanding your explanation of the circumstances. Your dates and events aren't coming across in a clear or sequential fashion to me."

Stating feelings

Conflict situations evoke emotions. To act as though no emotions exist isn't realistic. The key is to express your emotions in words rather than show them, and this is where the *stating-feelings* tool comes into play. With this tool, you say the emotion that you feel about a situation in a direct and sincere manner to increase awareness and understanding for the other person and to lend importance to your concern or issue within the conflict.

Stating your feelings isn't intended to make others feel guilty or sorry or to blame anyone for a problem. Pushing guilt or blame on others creates negative energy in a discussion and usually stimulates adversarial reactions, both of which greatly diminish the likelihood of reaching a satisfactory resolution. Don't go after confessions or expect grand apologies in return for telling someone that you feel hurt. People are more willing to accept responsibility for their actions than they are for taking on blame or being humiliated. By stating feelings, you're looking for understanding and dialogue that can lead to a solution.

The stating-feelings tool often is used right after you use the tool of describing (see "Describing the problem" earlier in this chapter). Describing outlines your concern or problem, after which you can state feelings in a few sentences that let the other person know how the situation has made you feel. Here are some guidelines:

- **Name the feeling you have.** Directly identify the emotion you feel from the experience.

- **Give constructive reasons to explain the basis of your feelings.** Keep your explanations brief and focus on issues and behaviors you've seen. Avoid giving interpretations or making assumptions about the other person's perceived intentions. Spare them the psychoanalysis. Stick with what has happened as you've experienced it, and don't guess about the meaning behind it.

Bringing Conflicts to Resolution

This section provides two problem-solving models that help you resolve larger-scale conflicts, when patterns have formed and incidents have built up enough over time to cause the tension that now impedes your work. The *resolving-concerns model* helps you work through conflicts that deal with clashes in working relationships. The *needs-based model* helps you work through differences over business issues such as differing ideas on methods and strategies. As you develop your problem-solving skills, you can mix and match with these two models or even add pieces from other strategies that have worked for you in the past.

Using the resolving-concerns model

The *resolving-concerns model* provides a problem-solving plan to use in situations in which the working relationship, for one reason or another, isn't functioning as well as needed. The following sections walk you through each step and explain how the model works.

Step 1: Introduce the meeting

Before you dive into the details of an issue, you first want to give your meeting a solid opening. Your introduction sets a positive tone and organizes the structure for the meeting. In particular, you want to state your positive intentions, that is, a statement that says the actions that follow are meant to be good. You can also state a positive intention for the other person to indicate that you know she means well, too.

The following are the key points to express in your introduction to the meeting:

1. **State a one-sentence general purpose for the meeting.**

   For example, "Jack, as you know, I called this meeting to address an issue with you that has been affecting our working relationship."

2. **State a positive intention, either your own or one the other person can have, along with your own.**

   For example, "I want you to know my focus in this meeting is about working out ways to determine how to get the job done well when we work together. I also know and appreciate that you want to have good results when you take on a job."

3. **Announce your agenda or plan for the meeting.**

   Keep it brief and tie it to the steps you intend to follow in the conflict-resolution model. This focuses attention and lets the other person know where you intend to go in this discussion. For example, "In this meeting, I first want to briefly cover the concerns that I have as I see them and the impact they've had, and then get your take on the situation. I then want to spend the majority of time exploring solutions with you about how to strengthen our working relationship and then close by confirming an agreement to follow through on what we decide."

Step 2: Describe the concern

Your purpose in this crucial step is to let the person see what you view as the problem in a constructive manner. This is where the communication tool called describing (covered in the earlier section "Describing the problem") comes into play.

At this point, you state your observations, not interpretations — actions you've seen, not your characterizations or assumptions about the actions. You also summarize the pattern of behavior you have seen that has caused you concern. For example: "Jack, one concern I've had deals with your responsiveness to my requests for information. The pattern I have noticed over the last month is that usually two or three reminders are given on my part before I hear an answer from you about my requests." As needed, use a representative example or two to illustrate your points clearly, but avoid using too much detail. Be specific yet as concise as possible.

Quite often, you can communicate the problem coherently by organizing the concerns you've experienced into topics or categories that you'll explain one at a time. For example: "I have three main concerns that I want to share with you." This tells the other party what to expect and allows you to provide the necessary specifics to make each of the three points (in this case) clear.

Step 3: Express your feelings or explain the impact (optional)

This step is optional, and you either express your feelings or explain the impact (explained in the earlier sections "Stating feelings" and "Stating thoughts"). This step heightens awareness, which helps you gain a sense of importance for your issue of concern. For example:

"Jack this responsiveness challenge I've described creates much frustration for me in trying to get my end of the job done on time." (Express your feelings.)

Or:

"Jack, because of the reminders involved in getting answers from you, my work gets delayed because the information I need doesn't arrive when I need it." (Explain the impact.)

If you don't think you can do this step constructively and with sincerity, skip it. When you use Step 3, you do so to help the other person see where you're coming from.

Step 4: Let the other person respond

For some people, this is the toughest step. You almost never describe the concern so well (as constructively as possible) that the other person hugs you and apologizes profusely. As concretely and constructively as you've stated the problem, people still need to process what they've heard and respond to it. That starts you down the road to having two-way conversations. That's why you want to cover Steps 1, 2, and 3 quickly.

Your role in this step is to let the other person have his or her say for a bit. You, therefore, want to listen and not debate what you hear. Employ the active listening tool of probing (discussed in Book IV, Chapter 2) to have the person explain the specifics of his or her thoughts or concerns. Employ the effort called shift and show understanding (highlighted in the earlier section "Showing understanding"), providing verbal feedback with the active listening tools of paraphrasing or reflective paraphrasing to demonstrate your understanding of the individual's messages.

Keep in mind that you both don't have to see the problem situation the same way. You're working toward an agreement on a solution, not on anything else. You both want to be aware of each other's concerns so that you can take them into consideration when you collaboratively work out the solution. If you show an openness to hearing the other party's concerns, you increase the likelihood that your concerns also will be heard. And by showing an understanding of those expressed concerns, you can thereby ask the other person in return to give you feedback showing an understanding of your concerns. When you have two people receptively listening to one another, you manage tension and resolve conflicts.

Step 5: Work out the solution

This is the step with which you want to take the most time. The two of you crafting a solution is the key to success with conflicts. In this meeting, as in others, stay focused on solutions and don't dwell on problems.

Three main steps highlight the solution stage. When applying these three steps, you often need a transition from the problem-discussion phase to the solutions-discussion phase of the meeting. The best transition is a one- or two-sentence statement of positive intention that tells the other person where you want to go in the meeting at this time. For example: "Jack, as mentioned at the beginning, my intent here is to develop solutions that help us work productively together. How about we move ahead now and focus on doing just that?" From there, follow through on the three key steps for working out the solution.

1. **Establish the desired goal.**

   Make this a one-sentence, positive statement that defines the picture you want to see for the working relationship when it is functioning well. Offer the goal statement as *your* recommendation and let the other person then respond to it. For example: "Jack, how about this as the goal to shoot for in our working relationship: Establish a working relationship where we work together in a cooperative, respectful, and responsive manner. What do you think?"

   Hold firm to the idea of the goal but be open to how it is worded. The goal statement defines the *what;* that is, what the target for the relationship should be. It doesn't define how to reach the target. That comes next. When you define this goal in a clear and positive sentence, you seldom find disagreement. Some kind of positive working relationship is what both parties usually want. If the other person has a better way to state this goal, by all means, go with it.

2. **Develop ideas to meet the goal.**

   This step defines the *how;* that is, how you two are going to reach the goal. It defines the actions both parties will take to achieve the goal of the working relationship. This can be accomplished with any of three methods:

   - Recommend your ideas and ask for any other ideas the person may have.

   - Solicit ideas first from the other person and add yours into the mix.

   - Brainstorm in turn.

   Whichever of the three methods you use to develop ideas to meet the goal, be prepared to come up with specific actions for the other person, as well as an idea of what you're willing to do. Both parties must contribute and make commitments if the conflict is to truly be resolved. Be sure to discuss all potential ideas before beginning to evaluate them. Setting ground rules upfront before starting on the next element in the problem-solving process — such as, "Let's share ideas first and then evaluate after all ideas have been stated" — helps bring out all the possibilities so the discussion about a solution isn't bogged down.

3. **Evaluate the ideas and reach consensus.**

   Evaluate the ideas together, trying to determine which will best meet the stated goal. Go after ideas first that have more in common so that consensus can easily be reached. With *consensus,* you're asking the question, "Can we both support this option or idea?" Although people don't generally agree to every idea, they're often willing to support something for the good of the cause.

   Starting out with the ideas you have in common builds momentum toward reaching an overall agreement. For ideas in which differences exist, explore the rationale behind the thinking, listening to one another's points of view and explaining the benefits — that's how you get constructive two-way dialogue. If necessary, propose alternatives to work through the differences by continuing the emphasis on problem solving as you develop the solution.

Step 6: Close

After all of the ideas are evaluated and consensus is reached on the ones you both plan to move forward with, you're ready to bring the meeting to a close. Here are the steps to take in this final stage:

1. **Confirm the plan and all the actions agreed upon by both of you.**

2. **Clarify which steps need to happen for implementation of the solution.**

3. **Close on a positive note, thanking the person for working with you to craft this solution.**

Here are a couple of other tips to cement a strong close for this meeting.

✔ **Commit to typing up the agreed-upon plan and providing a copy to the other person.** Sometimes people are nervous about writing something down. Writing the agreement down as it's formed helps clarify it for both parties and gives your solutions discussion a focus. Otherwise, you may go around in circles. Writing down the plan also helps you both avoid having to rely on memories when honoring your commitments.

✔ **Set a date for the two of you to get back together in the near future, perhaps in a month, to review your progress with the plan.** This effort builds accountability for you and the other person and increases the likelihood that the agreement will stick. Sometimes, doing a second progress-review meeting down the road maintains the good efforts you both have started.

The needs-based model

This second model is adapted from work originally done in the Harvard Negotiation Project by the folks who wrote the series of books that included *Getting To Yes, Getting Past No,* and *Getting Together* — William Ury, Roger Fisher, Scott Brown, and other authors. The following sections take you through the five steps of the needs-based conflict-resolution model.

Step 1: Introduce the meeting

This first step has the following three parts:

1. **State your general purpose for the meeting.**

2. **Provide a positive intention to set the tone for the discussion.**

3. **Briefly outline your agenda for the meeting to give it a logical and organized structure.**

Step 2: Define the problem

In this step, you want to do two main things with the other person:

- ✔ **Develop the problem statement.** This is a one-sentence statement that identifies the issue to be resolved. It's stated as what currently is going on rather than what needs to be in the future. Also, it isn't the conflict you're having but rather the issue over which the conflict stems.

- ✔ **Clarify the source of the conflict and briefly analyze where the differences are coming from.** Differences on business issues often are around such areas as the following:

    - • Ways or methods to get a job done

    - • Ideas or views on how to solve a problem or what strategy to follow

    - • Values or styles in how you approach work

    - • Goals or expectations

    - • Understandings or information about a situation

 To keep the discussion constructive as you define the problem and the source of the conflict, you must recognize that differences aren't right or wrong. The differences help identify why the conflict exists. Understanding the source of those differences often starts to help both of you focus on issues rather than on people alone.

For example: Deb and Pat are managers whose groups have to work closely together to fulfill customer orders. Currently, a fairly high number of orders, approximately 25 percent, go out incomplete or with the wrong items in them. This, of course, leads to the orders being returned for correction and a great amount of rework that slows everybody down. Deb has proposed that work should be done to streamline the order-fulfillment process to make it simpler and more efficient. Pat has proposed implementing a formalized training program for all employees because many tend to just learn on the job. Because they disagree on which approach to take, they have a conflict. They can define the problem this way:

- ✔ **Problem statement:** Approximately 25 percent of customer orders aren't being fulfilled accurately on a consistent basis.

- ✔ **Source of the conflict:** Different ideas and views on how to solve this problem.

Step 3: Identify the needs of the stakeholders

Needs are what drive people; they're your important interests and motivations as related to the business relationship. *Stakeholders* are the key parties affected by the business relationship and by what gets worked out in the conflict resolution. Usually this involves more than just the two people having the conflict: Customers, vendors, investors, other internal groups, your team, the other person's team, management above, or the company or organization as a whole can be affected.

In this step, you want to identify, along with the other person, the key stakeholders and then list the most critical needs each one has in the business relationship. Prepare the list together. For example, in the conflict over the order-fulfillment problems in Step 2, Deb and Pat list the key stakeholders in this issue and their main needs:

Stakeholder	Needs
Deb's team	Have accurate customer orders delivered consistently
	Maintain high levels of customer satisfaction
	Maintain cooperative working relationships with Pat's team
Pat's team	Have accurate customer orders delivered consistently
	Maintain high levels of customer satisfaction
	Maintain cooperative working relationships with Deb's team
The company	Maintain high levels of customer satisfaction
	Ensure long-term relationships with customers
	Provide customers with value for what they buy
	Maintain an efficient operation
Customers	Consistently receive on-time and accurate shipments of product
	Have vendor relationships marked by reliability and high-quality service
	Pay a reasonable price and get value in return

You're looking at their needs, not at their positions on the issue. Focusing on positions, such as your way versus my way, perpetuates a situation trapping you both in the conflict. Looking at needs helps both of you take a broader perspective to see what's really important.

By identifying key needs, you begin moving the conflict away from two people and their own positions on an issue toward a broader view of the big picture — who is really affected by this issue and what's really important to them. This is the key. Avoid focusing on positions and shift toward looking at everyone's needs or interests.

Step 4: Work out the solution

Now the problem-solving effort kicks into high gear. The following are the three main elements to work through in the solution stage:

1. **Brainstorm ideas to meet the needs.**

2. **Evaluate the ideas against the needs.**

   This is the beauty of identifying the needs first. It establishes the criteria for evaluating your ideas. Therefore, the discussion no longer needs to dwell on your position versus the other person's position, or whether your idea or his idea is good or no good. You evaluate the ideas together based on how well they meet any and all of the needs of the stakeholders you've listed.

3. **Reach consensus on what is most mutually beneficial.**

   Part 2 often rolls right into Part 3. You're looking to reach an agreement on which ideas best meet the needs of all of the stakeholders involved in or affected by the conflict.

Step 5: Close

After you reach agreement on the ideas to act upon, confirm this understanding with the other party and clarify what needs to happen to implement the solution — who's going to do what and when.

Setting a follow-up date to review progress often is a good idea. Doing so means that both of you are serious about making the agreement work. You're reinforcing accountability. Consider scheduling the follow-up meeting about four to six weeks in the future. You want to give the solution time to be implemented, but at the same time, you don't want to go so far out that you forget about the agreement. Sometimes, doing a second follow-up a little further into the future, when progress is going well, maintains the positive momentum you're building.

Chapter 4

Dealing with Difficult Bosses and Co-Workers

*O*ffice environments tend to breed weird social dynamics. Most people can relate to the off-the-wall antics that take place in the *Dilbert* comic strip or a television show set in the workplace precisely because those behaviors happen in real life. This chapter offers tips on controlling yourself when someone drives you crazy, working with passive-aggressive co-workers and other personality types (even your own!) that can cause problems, and dealing with offensive behavior — the stuff that makes day-to-day office life fun (or at least exciting). Each of us has a certain kind of individual that riles us up. You know the types — people who have the potential to get your dander up and throw a meeting off course. This chapter also presents guidelines for handling such people.

Controlling the Only Person You Can: Yourself

Here's the most important point to take away from this chapter: The most effective things you can do involve you — not the person who is driving you crazy.

Because your reaction to negative behavior acts like a reward to the offending party, your best bet, if you can pull it off, is not to reinforce negative behavior with a direct reaction. This tactic is, admittedly, hard. In movies, the hero comes up with an instantaneous zinger that puts the other person in his or her place with such deftness that it changes the entire story line. That's the movies, not real life.

The best way to maintain emotional distance that allows you to avoid a direct reaction is through a technique called *pushing the pause button*. Basically, pushing the pause button just means taking a break for a moment or an hour or an evening while you sort things out. The break may be purely mental; it may be imperceptible to the other person, but it gives you time to review matters before you continue.

Knowing when and how to push the pause button not only endows you with an aura of composure and confidence, but also gives you a certain amount of control over a situation. (For more information on pushing the pause button, go to Book I, Chapter 4.)

Everyone owns a pause button, so to speak, and everyone pushes it in a different way. Think about all the situations you've found yourself in and the various pause buttons you've used. On a piece of paper, write down as many as you can think of. Your list may include these popular pause buttons:

- Taking a drink break or a bathroom break
- Telling a joke or story
- Opening a window
- Stretching
- Checking with another team member
- Asking for clarification on some topic that is being discussed

In order to know when to push the pause button to preserve your emotional distance, you need to understand what sets you off and, more importantly, why it sets you off. Think about what makes your blood pressure rise or when you're most likely to get upset at the office. Acknowledging clearly and unequivocally what upsets you is a big step toward avoiding that situation. You recognize your own demons. You won't get rid of your hot buttons, but you'll know to push your pause button as soon as the other party exhibits a certain behavior. Does yelling bother you? If you are aware of that, you can push your pause button at the first sound of a raised voice.

No matter what your pause button is, you are way ahead by understanding this concept and knowing how to use it.

Dealing with Difficult Personality Types

Certain types of people always seem to get what they want and leave a destructive wake of bad feelings behind them. When you work with such people, you feel that the only thing that would get through to them is a sharp jab to the chin. You walk away feeling angry and inadequate. This is the kind of person who makes you say horrible things like, "I coulda killed 'em."

You possess the tools to deal with difficult people. Unfortunately, in the heat of the moment, forgetting that fact is easy. This is exactly when you most need your pause button. Review all the material in the preceding section about the pause button. The following sections offer some helpful tips on how to handle difficult personalities.

The passive-aggressive

Meet the passive-aggressive personality: *passive* because these people don't speak out directly or act openly, but *aggressive* because they are focused on getting what they want, even if it's at the expense of others. Passive-aggressive people can be hostile, and the anger eventually surfaces somehow. They get even in ways that are so indirect that it's difficult to pin these people down. For example, they may leave work half-finished, do it late, or do it inaccurately. Some common excuses are "I forgot," "I didn't know it was due *then,*" "I didn't know it included *all* of this."

If an instruction can be interpreted two ways, the passive-aggressive worker will almost always interpret the directive in the way that allows him to resist fully meeting expectations or fulfilling the request. When the mistake is pointed out, this person will rely on an intensely literal reading of the instruction to justify his actions, saying, "But you said . . ." Always be very clear with this type of person.

Passive-aggressive people seem to be cooperative, are often calm and willing to help, and may never complain. But somehow the work you counted on or the task they promised to do doesn't get done. Aggressive behavior can surface in other ways with these people. Being pleasant to your face, but talking negatively behind your back is classic passive-aggressive behavior.

How can you handle these people? Follow these two general rules when dealing with passive-aggressive people:

✔ **Don't rely on such a person to do anything critical.** You never know how this person will take out his emotions on you, and you frequently don't even know what those emotions are. These people aren't straight with you. And they can end up making you as angry as they are.

✔ **Take your personal feelings out of the equation.** Don't overreact to this person's tactics — accept that this is how passive-aggressive people treat everyone. That is who they are, and you can figure out how to work around them.

If you must work with a passive-aggressive individual, follow these guidelines for remaining cool and objective:

1. **Put it in black and white.**

   Have the person write down all your expectations — or, better yet, write them down yourself and keep a copy. Be very specific in your notes. Then the person can't say, "I didn't know."

2. **Clearly state the consequences if certain actions aren't performed — and have the individual write these consequences down.**

   Even if you are not this person's boss, you can still point out consequences — there should always be consequences if the person doesn't meet expectations. For example, you may say, "I'll keep your boss posted on your progress and the deadline."

3. **Follow up.**

   Don't let a long time go by before checking up on this person. Keep documenting all conversations by writing down what you said and the response. You just make matters worse by not staying on top of things.

4. **Give the person the benefit of the doubt.**

   Be positive. Watch out for any temptation to get nasty. Keep your cool.

The bully

A *bully* is anybody who tries to intimidate someone who is perceived as weaker. Bullies come in all sizes, shapes, and colors. They use a variety of techniques, such as screaming, needling, and making their counterparts the butt of a joke. You may remember such a person from the schoolyard.

Being around a bully is never going to be a pleasant experience. Whatever you do, don't try to outbully a bully. Instead, rely on some basic skills to deal with this person:

✔ **Realize that inside every bully is an insecure person who can't bear the thought of anyone finding out about his weakness.** The bullies of the world don't have any confidence in their inner strength or their true stature, so they create false strength by bullying people. Remember how scared everyone was of the Wizard of Oz and his booming voice. Finally, Dorothy pulls back the curtain and finds this little guy with a huge megaphone. It certainly changes her relationship with the Wizard because she realizes he's only insecure.

Book V

Navigating
Tricky
Workplace
Relation-
ships and
Situations

✔ **Know everything you can know about this person before you take her on.** Particularly, try to find out about the fears and goals of the person. That isn't easy, because bullies have taken great steps to cover up their inner workings. You'll probably have to go out after work one day if you want to have any chance of finding out who this person really is. When you do have an opportunity to relax with this person, be a really good listener. Go to Book IV, Chapter 2 for pointers on listening.

You must work hard to listen to a bully. First, bullies mask their message in a mélange of language that is hurtful or intimidating in some way to someone. Second, your own animosity has probably been building, so empathetic listening is virtually impossible.

✔ **Communicate clearly.** This is very important. Don't speak often, but when you do speak, make it count. With as little emotion as possible, let the bully know exactly what your position is.

✔ **Try telling her that you feel bullied.** This may not do any good, but sometimes a bit of candor can diffuse a situation. Yelling back at a bully does no good, but telling the bully that the behavior is having the intended result may just change that behavior. It's crazy but true: Even bullies don't want to be known as bullies. Your simple, unemotional assessment of the situation will go a long way toward turning things around — especially if other people are around when you make your statement. Use nonaccusatory words and "I" phrases, such as "I really feel beaten up when you talk like that."

Frequently, bullies act from a perceived threat to their position of power. A landlord may be a bully, but a landlord is sharply restricted in every jurisdiction by strict laws governing the rights of the tenants. The same is true of people to whom you may owe money. Harassing tactics used to be stock in trade for creditors. No more. Consumer protection laws exist in every state in the union. If you face off with a bully, find out what your legal rights are. Then speak softly and carry a big stick.

The more bluster you hear, the more frightened and scared the bully is. This knowledge isn't all that comforting when you're being yelled at, but step away from the situation, figure out your next move, and then present it calmly. Sometimes talking about the other person's fears can be very helpful. The other person generally denies any fear but often settles down because you have made fearful feelings acceptable. After that mask is removed, you can get on to the substance of the conversation.

The screamer

The *screamer,* a variation on the bully, is anybody who does a great deal of yelling or screaming. Three distinct types of screamers exist. Each type requires a very different response:

> ✔ **The screaming bully:** If the person is just trying to bully you, read the preceding section and act accordingly. You don't have to accept this behavior.
>
> ✔ **The habitual screamer:** Like Old Faithful in Yellowstone National Park, this person just pops off every now and again. These types are annoying, but harmless — if you know you're dealing with such a person, just don't respond.
>
> ✔ **The truly angry, upset, or scared screamer:** Keep reading to find out how to deal with this subspecies.

The worst thing you can do is sink to the level of someone else's negative behavior pattern. If you are not normally a screamer, don't start just because the person sitting across from you starts screaming.

A chilly "Are you through?" works well in the movies but isn't as effective in most real life situations. A better, if more difficult, approach is to be sympathetic. Empathizing with someone who is yelling at you runs against every instinct in your body, but it may be the best way to take the fire out of an angry screamer. The next time someone is yelling at you, try one of these phrases:

> ✔ "I hear from your voice that you're upset."
>
> ✔ "Let me be sure that I understand you . . ."
>
> ✔ "Tell me more about that."

All these phrases are surprisingly calming. You're not agreeing with the screamer, but you're using empathy, telling her that you want to understand what she's saying and feeling. Let the screamer know that you're not upset by her hysterics and then deal with the behavior independently of the substance of the conversation.

The emotional blast and the content are two different things. If you're able to draw a distinction between the two in your mind, the other person may also be able to establish the distinction. If the blast is more than a style — if it is born out of true emotional outrage — take a break. A situation is seldom so urgent that you can't take a breather and come back at a later time. Even a short break is helpful to clear the air after an outburst.

If your boss is a screamer, the result can be very damaging to your health and your mood, particularly if the screaming is personally insulting, blaming, or shaming. This person's anger is probably an emotional problem that isn't confined to the office, but unless you're a psychologist on the side, don't attempt to treat it. You can attempt to modify the behavior toward you in several ways. When the screaming begins, use an "I" phrase such as, "I feel belittled when you raise your voice this way. Can you speak more calmly?" If the boss yells back and refuses, say, "I can't listen to this. I'll be back in a few minutes," and leave the room. If the screamer isn't calmed down when you come back, it may be time to dust off the old résumé.

The star or top dog

Everybody is awestruck by someone. Trying to accomplish a piece of business with anybody in whose presence you feel helplessly speechless is difficult at best. Having to speak to your boss's boss's boss can give you that same sort of feeling. But you have to go forth. What can you do?

Prepare yourself. Make sure you know what you want, why you want it, and what the justification is for your request. Also, find out about the human under the image. Inside every famous, powerful, or wealthy person is a person. Is he or she married or single? Are there children? What hobbies interest the person? The best way to diffuse the situation is to gather information. If you talk to the real human being rather than the image on the pedestal, you make good progress. Otherwise, things are pretty hopeless.

The biased co-worker

Sometimes, you may suspect that your problems at work are simply because you belong to a particular group — ethnic, religious, gender, and so on. Not fair. Not right. Yet it happens. And dealing with bias is particularly difficult because this subtle discrimination is seldom verbalized.

If you feel sure that bias exists against you, facing it head-on is best, in a matter-of-fact manner, calmly and with dignity. For example, imagine you overhear a colleague who has been known to make offensive jokes about a group you belong to say he'd rather work on a big project alone than on a team with you. A well-rehearsed phrase, delivered without accusation or emotion, is very helpful. "Are you open to working on this project with a woman?", ". . . with an African American man?", ". . . with a Chinese paraplegic?" You almost always receive a torrent of assurances. This is the 21st century, and basing decisions on anything but merit is unacceptable, especially in the business community.

Accepting those assurances is in your best interest, whether the sentiments are true or not. The mere fact that the assurance was offered benefits your position, even if it doesn't change societal behavior in general. But after you acknowledge and accept the assurance, don't drop the matter too quickly. Ask this important follow-up question: "Exactly what are your criteria for an acceptable teammate?" And keep pressing gently and firmly. For instance, if the answer is dedication, ask, "How much time do you want me to devote to this project each day?"

Take good notes about the person's responses and his subsequent behavior. If you devote yourself adequately to the project but he manufactures complaints about you still not working hard enough, you may be able to confront him again. And if you document enough cases of obvious bias, you may be able to file a complaint with your human resources department.

You must be vigilant not to jump too quickly to the conclusion that bias is the basis for a particular result. In the workplace, discouraged workers often complain about their boss and sometimes jump to the conclusion that they're being picked on because of race, gender, religion, or sexual preference. Actually, a large number of supervisors are equal-opportunity oppressors. They savage any underlings who happen along, regardless of what groups they fall into.

What to do when you could be the problem

No matter how hard to face and admit, consider the possibility that the difficult personality in the room may be your own. What a revelation. No one likes to think this, but if you hear people yell often, you may have a style that is particularly frustrating.

If your relationships at work seem unnecessarily contentious, consider what *you* can do to change that pattern. Next time you feel like you're being rubbed with sandpaper, push your pause button and listen twice as much as you usually listen. This gives you an opportunity to observe yourself. Take a hard look at yourself to see what you could do differently to smooth things out.

For example, might you be a passive-aggressive individual at times? How do you know if you are? Answer these questions with a yes or no:

- ✔ Do you utter "tsk" and sigh loudly so someone else can hear?

- ✔ Do you mutter under your breath just loudly enough so someone asks, "What did you say?" and you reply, "Nothing"?

- ✔ Do you find you forget to do things you really don't *want* to do?

- ✔ Can you think of at least three things you recently did above and beyond the call of duty for which you *should* have but didn't receive notice or thanks?

- ✔ Do you judge people as thick if they can't read your mind?

If you answered yes to at least three out of five of these questions, you exhibit passive-aggressive tendencies. Cut it out! Start using direct "I" statements, such as "I want . . ." and "I need. . . ." Why? People most often ignore nonassertive signals — they tend to respond to direct communication. The more your signals are ignored, the more frustrated and unhappy you become.

If two different people got upset with you in two of your last three internal meetings at work, chances are very good that the fault lies with you. No matter how strong a case you can make that the situation wasn't your fault, it probably was. Your version of the facts isn't relevant; the only important fact is that people frequently get upset with you. Try to figure out what element of your style of presentation makes dealing with you frustrating, upsetting, or annoying. Ask someone who loves you point-blank. Don't defend yourself. Sit quietly and listen to the whole awful truth. Then try to fix whatever is wrong.

Responding to Offensive Behavior

Some people don't seem to care if they hurt someone else or tell a joke at someone else's expense. When you're the target of such behavior, you may be shocked that you're being treated unprofessionally, and remembering that the perpetrator is almost always acting out of insecurity is difficult. Take a deep breath and remember the following:

✔ You're probably not the only one being treated this way. So look around the room and see who the other victims are.

✔ Even though your reactions to offensive behavior are typically (and understandably) anger and resentment, you need to continue to behave professionally. And while you may wish you could ignore the situation, more often than not, you need this person's help or input in some part of your job.

The following sections list tactics to keep in mind so you can respond appropriately on the spot to deflect the offensive person and stay in control.

None of the following methods are easy and none of them automatically lead to a healthy work environment. If you use these techniques to show you're not a victim, the office monster usually decides to pick on someone else. That's not the ideal result, but it's better than you being picked on. Then you can become the office hero by helping the new victim go through the same channels to address the offensive behavior, and eventually the offensive person will run out of victims.

Whatever you do, beware of constantly complaining about the situation. Constant complaining can earn you the title of "office whiner." Others in the office may wonder why you're unable to solve your own problems, even if their tolerance of the situation is part of the problem. If you're involved in a constant conflict, fingers may start pointing at you for other problems that arise in the office.

Don't resist the person's remarks

Instead of defending yourself against offensive comments, validate them. For example, if someone says, "You keep forgetting that price over and over again. Have you lost your mind?" you say, "It must seem like that to you, doesn't it?" Refusing to strike back eventually bores your attacker. When there's no fuel for the fire, there *is* no fire.

Admittedly, this is very unnatural. To pull it off you must come from a position of strength. With this tactic, you can appear to be a wimp or a giant, depending on how you handle the situation. So, if you can't respond without rancor or hurt while looking the other person right in the eye, you may be better off trying a different approach.

Acknowledge the truth

The comments that hurt most are those that have an element of truth in them. For example, if you know you're not the most prompt person in returning phone calls, you'll be especially sensitive when someone accuses you of that neglect: "Jan's so 'busy' she can't be bothered to return a simple phone call."

The more you know yourself and your flaws, the better prepared you are when someone points them out to you. You can then make it easier to acknowledge the kernel of truth without agreeing with the way it was said. You can say, "Yes, sometimes I don't return calls as fast as I would like to." You must then determine which attacks deserve an apology or explanation from you and which don't.

Show the person off

If someone makes a disparaging remark to you in front of a group of people, call the group's attention to that person. Say something like, "Well, that didn't sound very nice to everybody, did it?" or "Gee, these people aren't going to get a good impression of you." Then pause and let peer pressure take over. Someone in the group is sure to say, "Hey, yeah Joe, cut it out."

When you do this, make sure you don't sink to the person's level. As bad as the person may be, don't engage in a dysfunctional approach to deal with him. For instance, don't start a trail of e-mails gossiping about the person or bad-mouth him to others. Be professional. If you must have a single confidant, select that person with care. Make sure you have known the person for a long time, and preferably, choose someone far from the workplace.

Take concrete action

After you're fully aware that someone is directing offensive behavior at you, don't simply decide to live with the situation. It won't improve unless you do something about it. In fact, left unaddressed, the situation usually gets worse.

Quietly, professionally, and privately let the person know that you will have to report her difficult behavior. Some advice:

- ✔ **Keep it private.** Keep your conversations with the other person about her behavior private. Never lose your temper at work or engage in a confrontation in front of others in the office.

- ✔ **Make the first move.** Approach a difficult person with the belief that she is as eager as you are to restore rapport, and start your conversation with statements such as "I'm sorry for what I may have done to make you angry" or "I could be wrong."

Make sure to take action swiftly. If you don't, you may eventually become so angry that your efforts to address the situation could become irrational. Tackle the problem while you can maintain some objectivity and emotional control. Consider the case of a film editor, who after working long hours in the tight quarters of an editing bay with a woman who was constantly berating him, picked up an empty soft drink can and hurled it in her general direction. The woman filed a complaint against the company, and — in spite of the provocations — had a very strong case. The editor had suffered in silence much longer than was good for him, his company, or his professional future. Don't let these situations fester. Deal with them well before you feel like hurling something at the person who is bugging you.

Go up the ladder for help

You've done everything right, but nothing has changed. You're frustrated and tempted to take the problem upstairs. While your urge to report other person is natural, first make sure that doing so is the best course of action. Can you answer yes to both of the following questions?

- ✔ **Is this a matter that should be settled by the company?** Some types of problems — like personal annoyances and personality conflicts that don't rise anywhere near the level of abuse or harassment — don't require company involvement. If the problem is persistent and affecting your work or the person is intentionally targeting you, you may want to consider asking for help.

If the conduct is a matter of personal taste or preference, be very careful that you don't come off as a whiner, a difficult loner, or worse. Very few managers have much patience for those who fall into these categories. Of course, if you're one of those types, you probably don't see yourself that way. So check in with a friend to get an objective assessment of the situation. And let the friend know exactly why you are asking so that you get an honest answer instead of the kind of blind support that many people give to their friends when nothing is at stake.

✔ **Is the problem significant enough to warrant consideration by the management level above you?** If the conduct is a breach of company policy, the law, or good business practices, by all means use the internal reporting system to alert upper management to the problem.

Once you determine that "reporting up" is the best course of action, follow protocol, do not be emotional, and point out the importance to the company (as opposed to you personally) in getting the matter resolved. And don't expect anything to change quickly. Managers usually like to mull things over and handle situations in a methodical manner.

Staying in Control during a Meeting

Intense meetings can get pretty emotional for everyone. However, if you don't keep your own and everyone else's emotions in check by curbing inflammatory behavior, you won't get anything accomplished. The following are four types of people who can throw your meeting off course unless you stay in control. (Flip to Book III, Chapter 2 for more tips on running a productive meeting.)

Dealing with dominators

Dominators are people who disrupt your meeting because they need to dominate the conversation. Often these people have strong control issues, and this is how they express them. You need to be strong and firm in dealing with these people. Try stopping a dominator with the first step in the following list, and continue to Step 3 if necessary:

1. **Credit the speaker's knowledge of the subject and constructive contributions.**

   "Daniel, thanks for sharing. You've had a lot of experience in this area, and your input is helpful."

2. **State the need for opinions from other participants.**

   After the speaker has spoken two or three times, look right at him and say, "I need to hear from someone who hasn't spoken yet."

3. **Ask the group or another individual for views or reactions.**

   Be sure to really encourage others to participate. Sometimes the dominant person is filling a vacuum. More often, the rest of the group has become somewhat beaten down, thinking, *Why bother?* Encourage them by saying, "To solve this problem we're going to need everyone to work together. I know there are some valuable, unspoken thoughts out there. Nicole, what's your opinion of the situation?"

Restraining the ramblers

Ramblers are people who go off on tangents and bore the other participants. Usually, these folks just need attention. You need to take control and not sacrifice the attention of many to accommodate the needs of one person. Try these techniques:

✔ Ferret out the final point or question. In this situation, wait until it's clear to most of the people in the room that this person's statements are wandering badly. Then slowly ask, "And your question (or point) is?" Drawing the question out is key because the person has to stop and actually hear that her time is up. The person realizes that she needs to state the question or point.

✔ Confirm your understanding of the point of the story.

✔ Restate the urgency of the objectives and the time constraints.

✔ Direct a question to another participant or to the entire group and refocus on the objectives.

Curtailing the competing conversers

Sometimes people have side conversations while you're trying to move through the meeting agenda. That creates several problems. You lose the attention of the people in the competing conversation. The people right next to the conversation have a hard time hearing. You lose control of the meeting, and side conversations tend to multiply. You need to nip that distraction in the bud and take control. These ideas may work:

✔ Pause and look directly at the conversers.

✔ Ask the conversers to share their ideas with the group.

✔ Restate the importance of the objectives and state that the group will accomplish more if one person speaks at a time.

Addressing the arguers

Some people feel a need to argue with whatever is being presented. It doesn't matter what subject is being discussed; up goes their hand and out comes a slightly contrary view of the matter. Be aware of those people and use the following guidelines:

✔ Address the person who is presenting the argument. Use *paraphrasing* (restating someone else's ideas in your own words) to express your understanding of the remarks he has made. If more than one person is involved, do this for each person. And then give them your position.

Often these people will want to continue their fruitless discussion. In this situation, call on the next person before you answer the arguer again. Say something like, "Okay, let me answer your question, and then I'll take the questions from Melissa and Dale." This makes it very difficult for the arguer to keep up the dialogue. You have cut 'em off at the pass.

✔ Restate the agreed-upon agenda in order to move the discussion back toward your desired outcome. Summarize points of agreement to reestablish a positive tone.

Chapter 5

Handling Conflict Constructively

In This Chapter

▶ Gathering key info and insights before addressing a conflict

▶ Planning your approach and a time and place to meet

▶ Following an effective conflict-resolution strategy

▶ Addressing conflict with subordinates, peers, and bosses

You find yourself in a conflict that takes up way too much of your energy. People are starting to talk, the conflict is affecting work, and when you think about your long-term career goals, you know that maintaining the bad feelings and tension isn't a good idea, regardless of the other person's position in the company.

Whether you're a manager, team member, or the head of an entire department, as a party to a current conflict, you may not know what to do. Perhaps you've tried a few tactics that you thought would fix the problem, like going over the other person's head, addressing the issue directly, or ignoring the conflict altogether. Yet the problem remains unresolved. You're now at a point where you want this whole thing behind you, and you need a plan.

This chapter helps you gain a better understanding of the real issues in the conflict and explains how you can build a winning strategy to address the current situation, as well as how to tackle future conflicts.

Exploring Both Sides of the Conflict on Your Own

Before you rattle off a list of issues you want the other person to address, take some time to fill out the worksheet in Figure 5-1. Doing so helps you take a broader perspective and consider both sides of your conflict. The worksheet has no right or wrong answers. You can work your way down while only considering yourself before turning your attention to the other person, or you can answer each section for both of you as you consider each topic. The following sections walk you through each category.

	You	The Other Person
Issues What are the surface issues?		
Values What are you really trying to satisfy?		
Hot Buttons What words, phrases, or references might cause an emotional response?		
Strengths What does each of you bring to the team?		
Common Ground Where do we agree?		
Proposals What solutions would work for both of us?		

Figure 5-1: Use this worksheet to help you identify what you and your co-worker want.

Issues

Start by filling out the *Issues* section of the worksheet for yourself. In the left-hand box, write as many issues as you can think of that apply to the conflict from your perspective. Don't think too deeply at this point; just write what comes to mind. As an example, suppose you're having a conflict with a store employee about being late to meetings. Perhaps you make entries like these:

1. Shows up late

2. Doesn't apologize

3. Disrupts work flow

4. Doesn't know what's going on

5. Ignores requests to be on time

Note every aspect of the conflict you can recall and put your perspective in the column you've designated for yourself.

In the right-hand box, under the heading *The Other Person,* write what you think the other person would consider to be the issues. Would he say that you spend too much time watching the clock, or perhaps that you micromanage group meetings?

Values

After you've had a chance to identify the issues, think about *why* those issues have impacted you. Take a look at what you've jotted down and spend some time evaluating the deeper reasons that these things have had an impact on you. Underneath the surface issues, what are you trying to satisfy? Are you looking for respect, cooperation, autonomy, or teamwork? Really consider what may be most important to the other person, realizing that his values may differ from your own. After you've done some speculating and evaluating, jot down that information on both sides of the worksheet.

Resist placing your own values on the other person. If you carry around the expectation that others should behave according to your value system, you'll be frustrated and disappointed. When you recognize that you may not share the same values as a colleague, you can go into future situations without being let down by his behavior.

Figuring out your core values

Be aware: What you *think* you want and what you *really* want likely aren't the same — and to figure out the difference, you need to get in touch with your values. Sometimes they're called interests or motivators, but basically, your *core values* are what drive you and influence the way you think about and respond to different situations.

People often describe what they want as an action or an outcome instead of the value that inspires that desire. For example, if someone asks you what you want out of your retirement, you may respond that you want a million dollars in the bank. If you consider what that money allows you to do in retirement, you're getting closer to understanding values. You want to travel (freedom), you want a cottage on the beach (peace and quiet), and you want to care for your family (security). This example demonstrates how looking at desired outcomes helps you discover the underlying values you find most important.

Reflect on your current conflict, jot down a few words or phrases that explain what's happening, and see if you can match them to one or two core values. For instance, if you say you're irritated by your boss's micromanagement, you may discover that one of your core values is autonomy, or maybe respect. If you're a manager and you want error-free reports turned in on time, the value you're addressing is likely competence or responsibility.

What dirty dishes can tell you about core values

Values and interests can pop up in even the simplest situations. Consider the following example: Seven employees share a common kitchen area that often has cluttered counters and a sink full of dirty dishes. Employees frequently discuss the messy site at staff meetings. A few of the team members say they don't give it a second thought and wonder why it keeps getting brought up. One employee says it's embarrassing to bring clients past the area, another suggests a chore schedule, and yet another is irritated that grown adults have to be told to clean up after themselves. The issue is the same for everyone — a dirty kitchen — but the values are different for everyone involved. Those who aren't bothered by it may feel that peaceful coexistence is more important than angry discussions about the dishes. Respect may be important to the individual who says he's embarrassed, cooperation may be an interest of the person requesting the chore schedule, and accountability is likely essential to the person who displays irritation. A manager in this situation may have the team brainstorm a solution that takes into consideration the stated values as a means to ending the conflict and getting on with other business.

Identifying the other person's values

The other person in the conflict also has core values that aren't being met, respected, or honored. He's probably ready for the problem to be resolved and is eager for someone to consider his perspective. Assuming that your co-worker has never explicitly told you what his values are, you have to do some guesswork to fill in the worksheet. You may be able to assume from someone's behavior and language that he values respect or autonomy, but many of his values will remain a mystery to you.

Consider what you know about your co-worker. Be honest but kind. What does his job demand of him? What stress could he be under? Think about what you've noticed when he's most upset. Be clear about what you really know and separate out secondhand information you may have added to strengthen your initial point of view. Can you tie his words or actions to values? Take the time to jot down a few words that describe his needs from his perspective.

When trying to discover the other person's values and what he wants, you may fall into the trap of answering questions with dramatic responses like, "He wants to control everything and take my job, that's what he wants!" Instead, put the theatrics aside and follow these guidelines:

✓ **Spend time putting yourself in his shoes.** If someone continues a conflict even after you've tried to address it, chances are his behavior is a symptom of his values not being met. Thinking objectively about the other person's needs can be difficult, but if it can provide you with tools to manage future conflicts, it's worth it.

  ✔ **Stop thinking in terms of *always* and *never*.** These definitive words tend to create more drama than they resolve. They cement you in place rather than help you look at the situation from a new perspective, so put them aside and use language that more clearly states the situation.

Start a list of what you think may be important to the other person and have it with you when you meet. Let him know you've given his needs some thought and ask to hear from him whether your list is correct. Demonstrating curiosity shows a willingness to listen, creates the possibility for commonality, and can open doors that may surprise you.

Hot buttons

Hot buttons are points that you're most sensitive about. Identify the kind of statements (or actions) that can make you want to scream or blow your top. Your hot buttons are closely tied to your values because anything that can make you that angry is probably something you care deeply about. In the hot buttons area, fill in the aspects of the conflict that bother you most. Here you should enter phrases like, "Thinks an apology isn't warranted," or, "Ignores me when I try to bring it up." Identify topics or conversations you've had in the past that have raised the tension in the room. Which specific words or phrases pushed you past a calm demeanor?

Knowing that you're likely to go off if a co-worker touches on one of your hot buttons allows you to prepare a response that doesn't include turning red and slamming your fist down on the table. Instead, you may answer, "You know, it may not really be control I'm after, but I can see where you might think that. I've discovered that respect is really important to me, and I can understand where trying to earn respect might come across as controlling." This kind of answer is sure to deflate the drama balloon!

As you're creating your list and responses, include potential hot buttons you may inadvertently push with the other person. If you've been tiptoeing around subjects or certain phrases to avoid an emotional response on his part, those subjects or issues are his hot buttons. Complete both sides of the worksheet.

Strengths

Consider the strengths each of you brings to the workplace. The individual who has a difficult time focusing during staff meetings may be the most creative person on the team. The guy who points out the errors in his co-workers' daily receipts may be the person who catches disasters before they happen. Think about what each of you brings to the work group that's unique, valuable, and important. Be generous but realistic.

Every core value has two sides. In one light, a value has the potential to get in the way of a cohesive team, and in another it can reveal itself as a great asset. If you value control, for example, you may hear others complain about micro-management, but that same value may be the very thing that gets you promoted! If you value independence, you may bristle at the idea of being paired with a co-worker on a project, but you may also be more likely to be viewed as a self-starter. And if one of your core values is accomplishment, your co-workers may have assigned you the unflattering title of *taskmaster,* but your boss sees it as doing what it takes to get the job done right and on time.

Common ground

As you prepare to complete the *Common Ground* section of Figure 5-1, remember that both of you would like improved working conditions and for the problem to go away. At least you agree on something! Beyond those things, you may both be interested in improving a process, fostering teamwork, or bringing success to the job site; you may just be working on these issues differently. Be open to the possibility that you may share goals with the other person and make note of these goals on the worksheet. The goals are great starting points for ideas and for your conversation in general.

Before you ask to meet with the other person, take a minute and recognize that he isn't *against you,* he's merely *for himself.* As you prepare for a new conversation and begin to consider his point of view, you'll see him less as an enemy and more as a potential ally in solving the difficulty.

Proposals

When you have the bigger picture in mind, generate some proposals. Now that you have a better understanding of where the two of you stand, think about what you want to ask for and what you can offer the other person. Be creative!

This is a time to be specific about what you'd like to see and what you want to stop. If the other person talks too much in meetings, rather than asking him not to talk, consider proposing he take notes, prioritize his top three issues prior to the meetings, or send suggested agenda items in advance. Remember, these are just proposals, and you can't know if they'll work until you have an open conversation with the other person. Give the ideas some thought but don't get too emotionally attached to them until you've had a chance to brainstorm with your co-worker because he is likely to have a few ideas of his own.

Ask yourself:

- ✔ What has already been tried?
- ✔ What has worked in the past?
- ✔ How can we be more creative?
- ✔ What can we do differently?
- ✔ What solutions or ideas work for both of us?
- ✔ Who else might help us develop a solution?
- ✔ What is within our power to change?
- ✔ Are my proposals realistic and possible? Have I considered all the details?
- ✔ Do I need all the answers right now?
- ✔ What am I willing to give to resolve the conflict?
- ✔ What are my intentions for proposing these ideas?
- ✔ What would an ideal working relationship look like?

Planning to Discuss the Matter

The purpose of filling in the worksheet in the preceding section (refer to Figure 5-1) is to prepare for a discussion with the person you're in conflict with. This worksheet helps you consider what's most important to you, think about what may be most important to the other person, and is an opportunity for you to begin thinking about proposals that can resolve the problem. With all this info in hand, you're ready to ask for the meeting.

Everyone has a different level of comfort with conflict. Some people don't worry about it and some people obsess over the smallest upset. Keep this in mind as you prepare to approach the person with whom you're having a conflict. Be aware of his stress level as well as your own. If previous attempts at resolution haven't gone well, realize that the other person may see you and want to run the other way. Just because you've decided you'd like to give it another try doesn't mean he'll immediately embrace the idea. Be mindful in the way you introduce the request for a meeting so it'll be easier for him to say yes to you. And remember: Conflict can be a good thing! Do a little self-talk to ready yourself for a good approach and use this opportunity to enact meaningful change.

Considering the time and location of your approach

Before you attempt to resolve your conflict, consider when and where to approach the other person. Start by deciding what day of the week or time of day will get you the most receptive response. Before your co-worker has had his morning coffee or right at the busiest point in his workday aren't good options. Look for a moment of relative quiet, when the two of you have the ability to focus on your conversation. For example, early afternoon after lunch may give him some time to have settled into his routine while leaving enough time in the day to give you a few minutes to talk.

Additionally, pay attention to where you both are in the emotional cycle. The best time to talk about a conflict is when both parties have had time to compose themselves. If either of you is likely to raise your voice, completely shut down, or walk away, then by all means let the situation settle down a bit before asking for a meeting.

Next, where should you approach the person? Where would he be most comfortable? Consider your location and what resources are available to you. Approaching the person in the hallway in front of someone else and telling him, "It's about time we figured this mess out" will certainly get his attention, but it probably won't set the tone for a productive meeting. It may catch him off guard, embarrass him, or instantly make him defensive. Instead, choose a private location or politely approach him in his own workspace.

The best option is to make a meeting request in person, but if logistics aren't in your favor and you have to make the request via phone or e-mail, take care to choose your words carefully and speak in a sincere manner (see the later section "Selecting the best mode of communication").

Choosing your words wisely

When you address the person to set up a meeting, use language that's respectful, hopeful, and genuine. Your invitation needs to actually be *inviting*. To demonstrate your desire to sincerely resolve the difficulties, what you say should communicate the following:

- ✓ **Confidentiality:** Communicate that this request and any subsequent conversations will be kept in confidence, just between the two of you. Of course, you should also be open to your co-worker's request that another person be made aware of a meeting.

- ✔ **Optimism:** Show that you're hopeful that the two of you can find a solution. Keep your language future-focused and constructive.

- ✔ **Sincerity:** Make sure your co-worker knows that you genuinely want to hear what he has to say. Use language that demonstrates your interest in hearing his perspective as well as sharing your own.

- ✔ **Safety:** Don't try to intimidate or bully the person. Address your desire to see the situation resolved in a way that's mutually satisfying. This shows your co-worker that you don't want to corner or trap him but rather you want to have a real dialogue.

Here's an example of an optimistic and inviting verbal meeting invitation: "I'd like to meet with you to talk confidentially about the challenge we're having and to find a way to resolve it that would work for both of us. I think if we work together, we can find a solution. Are you willing?" With this invitation your co-worker will have a hard time saying he's *not* willing, because who wants to be accused of being unwilling to work toward a solution? This approach lets him know that you're thinking about all sides, not just your own.

Selecting the best mode of communication

Think about what mode of communication will garner the best response. Communicating in person, on the phone, or in writing are all options.

- ✔ **In person:** Asking for a meeting in person is always your best chance for a positive response. Privately and politely letting the other person see the authenticity on your face, hear your friendly tone of voice, and witness your open body language speaks volumes about your sincere desire to work things out. If you're on his turf and demonstrating how you'll behave in the discussion, your co-worker will find it difficult to rebuff your efforts at mending fences.

- ✔ **On the phone:** If you're not able to approach your co-worker in person or if it would be unsettling for you to show up in a workspace you never visit, the telephone can be an effective tool for requesting a meeting. Before you dial, take a deep breath, make a few notes about what you'd like to say, and above all else, speak with a friendly and approachable tone of voice. Make an effort to speak with the other person directly; leaving a voice mail should be a last resort.

- ✔ **In writing:** If you think you may stumble over your words in person or forget what it is you want to suggest, or if geography prevents you from making your request in person and it's impossible to get your co-worker on the phone, a well-crafted e-mail could be in order. Discuss your awareness of the difficulty and your interest in hearing his perspective, and ask if he's willing to chat with you in person so the two of you can find a solution that works for both of you.

Be careful not to write more than is necessary. Keep it simple and honest, and include your intentions for a positive, productive meeting. Craft a document, set it aside for a while, and then review it before you send it. And have a trusted friend look the note over before you send it, because the tone and intent of written documents can easily be misinterpreted. Finally, allow the other person enough time to respond before taking further action. (For more on using e-mail effectively, see Book IV, Chapter 4.)

Preparing for resistance

In a perfect world, asking someone to meet to discuss a conflict is met with an enthusiastic, "Sure, yes, you betcha!" every time. But because workplace difficulties are often fraught with conflicting emotions and deep issues, a request to talk can be unsuccessful. Therefore, think ahead to how you'll respond if the other person uses one of a handful of common refusals, which are described in the following sections.

Responding to push-back tactics

A person who uses *push-back tactics* acknowledges the problem but reacts defensively. He may see the responsibility for the problem falling predominantly on your shoulders or he may throw out a variety of roadblocks or preconditions to a meeting. Be ready to let the person know that you understand how frustrating the situation has been for him. Try sharing some areas of common ground such as, "It's clear we're both interested in the final outcome of the project, so I'd like us to find a way to work together that would work for both of us."

Someone who pushes back may want to start the conversation right then and there. Be flexible but proactive, and explain that scheduling a private meeting for another time would be beneficial because it would give you both time to think of possible solutions.

Getting past denial

Your co-worker may not admit that there's a problem. Perhaps he's genuinely oblivious to what's happening around him. Maybe the conflict simply isn't a problem for him — he's fine with calling your ideas stupid in the middle of a staff meeting. Or maybe it's a classic case of *denial:* He doesn't want there to be a problem so he's convinced himself that there isn't one.

To combat denial, gently point out inconsistencies — words versus actions. For instance, you can reply with, "I hear you saying that you don't think there's a problem, yet I've noticed that whenever I ask about the project, I see you roll your eyes. Help me understand." Replying in this way allows the person to respond to your observations and acknowledge that something may be going on.

Book V

Navigating
Tricky
Workplace
Relation-
ships and
Situations

Addressing avoidance

Some people are masters at avoiding difficult situations. They'll often freely admit that there's a problem, but doing nothing about it feels better to them than having a conversation about it. They may also hope that the problem goes away on its own or think that it's not serious enough to deal with.

The first step in a response strategy for avoiders is to create safety. Be flexible and focus on language that's open and inviting. Acknowledge his excuse ("I understand that you're very busy"), find a benefit for him ("I think if we can work through this, we'll free up more of our time in the future"), and make sure he knows that he's being *invited* into a conversation, not ordered ("Are you willing to talk with me? Are you interested in resolving this?").

Finding hope in hopelessness

Some employees may have experienced disappointments that have led them to think there's no hope, the ship's sinking, and there's nothing but rough waters as far as they can see. If this isn't the first time the two of you have tried to fix things, for example, let him know that you're interested in change by saying, "I'm hoping we can have a new kind of conversation this time." Address additional concerns and confidentiality issues and invite him to set the boundaries — time, place, length of meeting, topics to discuss, and potential participants — in hopes of making him more comfortable moving ahead with a meeting.

Setting a Time and a Place for a Productive Discussion

The devil is in the details when it comes to making sound agreements, and the same is true for choosing a time and place for a meeting. Spending time upfront to think through what will make both of you equally comfortable demonstrates your sincere desire to resolve this conflict.

Time considerations

Pick a time when both of you can focus on the conversation. Uninterrupted time is a key element to a successful conversation, so choosing to meet right before the staff meeting — when phones are ringing, last minute e-mails are coming in, and co-workers are knocking on the door — isn't the best move. Ten minutes isn't really enough time to discuss the issues and proposals for solutions, so schedule at least an hour, and make room in the calendar for the meeting to run over so that you don't end up cutting off the other person to get to your next appointment. Politely ask the other person to do the same.

People at the height of emotion have the lowest ability to reason. If you're calm and think you can handle the conversation soon, that's only half of the equation — consider that the other person may not be emotionally ready. Let yourself *and* others calm down before attempting to work through a problem.

Geography matters

Think about where to meet before you ask for a conversation. Be prepared to suggest a meeting place that demonstrates you've thought about privacy, safety, and the impact on the team. Impartiality is important to many people, so plan to meet in a space that screams neutral. Take into consideration titles, power, and the desire for a balanced conversation (the later section "Tailoring Your Approach: The Org Chart Matters" tells you more about the importance of the organization chart when resolving conflict).

Approach the other person with a few options for locations in mind, but don't forget to ask him to provide input on a location that works for him. Asking him to suggest a setting shows that you're open to his opinions and that you won't be making all the decisions. Be prepared for him to suggest his own office or workspace. Consider whether you're comfortable meeting there and have an alternative to suggest if you're not.

Working toward a Solution, One Step at a Time

Use your own words and be yourself during the meeting to discuss the conflict between you and your colleague. Have a plan, or the meeting probably won't result in the outcome you had hoped for. The following sections outline a proven mediation process that professional mediators use. Follow it, keeping in mind that you need to balance your needs with the needs of your co-worker.

Step 1: Begin with an opening statement

In the opener, you sincerely greet the other person and briefly acknowledge the conflict and the impact it has had on you. Consider adding a few words to your opening statement that capture some or all of the following ideas:

✔ **A sincere thank you:** A quick (but authentic) thank you to the other person for being willing to sit down and talk goes a long way toward kicking off your meeting with the right kind of attitude.

✔ **A recognition that it has been difficult:** Feel free to share that the conflict has been tough on you. Saying that you've had enough is in no way a sign of weakness. In fact, it may be exactly what the other person needs to hear so he can acknowledge that he's been struggling, too.

✔ **An awareness that others are watching:** If you've seen this conflict radiating outwards, say so. If you know that camps are forming or morale is dipping, share that you want to see the problem resolved before it goes any further.

Don't speak on behalf of others or attempt to interpret how the conflict is affecting them. Instead, speak about this only in an objective manner:

- *Good:* "I notice that there are whispers about how the two of us are interacting, and it would benefit both of us to work this out."

- *Not so good:* "I know for a fact that the accounting department is having a hard time getting anything done, and they want this to stop."

✔ **Your desire to resolve the situation:** Let the other person know that you're committed to resolving the tension between you. Speak about how both of you will benefit from resolving your differences — you'll have less stress, you'll be more productive, and you'll have greater peace of mind.

✔ **A new approach:** If you've tried to have this conversation before but the results have been unsatisfactory, share how this time will be different. What did (or didn't) you do last time that you won't (or will) do this time? Speak about the approach in a hopeful and positive way — a little optimism goes a long way.

Step 2: Explain the process and your goals

Explain that you'll be following a mediation process because you think the method will help you both focus but that you're just as much a participant as he is. At the start of your meeting, briefly go over what will happen when, sharing just enough about each step so your colleague isn't surprised when you call for a break or transition from one phase to another.

You can decide how much of the process you want to share with the other party. Coming to the table and announcing, "So, I read this chapter in a book about conflict resolution at work and I'm going to play mediator" may put off a co-worker who's already upset with you. A brief explanation that you'd like the two of you to follow a proven mediation method in which you take turns speaking, listen to understand each other, and brainstorm solutions that benefit you both is likely to be viewed positively by the other person.

Also explain that your goal is to have a positive, respectful meeting, and that you both should consider this a time to confidentially present your views. Explain what you want to get out of the meeting and what the other person can expect from you. Saying that this is a new and different approach isn't sufficient unless you describe *how* it will be different. Here are some talking points to cover:

- ✓ **Look for answers:** Emphasize that this conversation isn't meant to be a gripe session or a chance for the two of you to hammer away at each other's flaws and prove who's right or wrong. Unite yourselves around idea generation instead of being chained together by negativity.

- ✓ **Be mindful of this opportunity:** Speak about this conversation as an opportunity to build the kind of relationship the two of you want to have and to paint the kind of picture you want to see in the workplace. Suggest that you'll do this by focusing on the things you *can* change rather than those you can't.

- ✓ **Communicate respectfully:** Because this meeting is a step toward changing how you work together, it's important that you speak in a manner that's respectful, professional, and appropriate — and that goes for both of you, of course.

Step 3: Share your experiences and perspective

In this step, you both will have an opportunity to speak about what you've been experiencing, to hear what each other has to say, and to understand how each other sees the issues at hand. So as you begin this step, both of you should consider what you want to know and how you want to present your point of view. When you speak about the conflict:

1. **Describe specific actions, statements, and events.**

2. **Then describe how they affected you.**

3. **Then make any requests you'd like regarding future incidents, keeping your language focused on what you want rather than what you don't want.**

When listening to your co-worker's perspective about the conflict, keep track of any questions you'd like to ask in order to understand better. You'll both have time to clarify and investigate when you get to the brainstorming part of the conversation, but when you're initially sharing your perspectives, all you want to do is be sure that each of you has heard and understood the other.

The following sections show you how to decide who gets to share his perspective first, how to listen for understanding, and how to explain your point of view constructively.

Deciding who will begin

Although each of you will get an opportunity to speak and respond to each other, you have to start *somewhere*. Your specific situation will help determine who goes first.

- ✔ **When you should go first:** If the other person is unaware of your reason for calling the meeting, asking him to start may be unproductive. Also, if you have some insight or information that may be helpful to the exchange, offering to begin isn't a bad thing. Bear in mind, though, that rumors, conjecture, and assumptions are *not* insights or new information. Be sure that the information is pertinent and helpful to your conversation.

  Another time when you may offer to begin the perspective-sharing phase is when you sense that the other person is resistant or hesitant, and you believe his attitude is related to distrust — either of you or of the mediation meeting in general. Choose appropriate and constructive language that demonstrates your sincerity in resolving the problem and shows that this meeting will be different from what has happened before.

- ✔ **When the other person should go first:** If you're both fully aware of the reasons that you're having this meeting, it can benefit you to offer the other person the opportunity to begin. Doing so demonstrates openness and a willingness to hear what he has to say, and it allows you the opportunity to demonstrate how to summarize and highlight what he values before sharing your own point of view.

In a sense, you've *already* gone first. By setting up the meeting and creating an opening statement, you've already shared to some extent what you're hoping to accomplish and briefly touched on how the conflict has affected you. By giving the other person an opportunity to describe his own experience, you're modeling good behavior by sharing the spotlight with him.

Listening closely

As concerns about the conflict are shared, listen closely to how he describes the situation. How each of you interprets the events gives you insight into how the conflict developed, what's keeping it going, and what approaches you can collectively take that will lead you to solutions.

Bear in mind that even though both of you likely experienced the same incidents, he'll probably describe the impact differently than you do. This isn't a time to question who's right and who's wrong, because both accounts are true. They're two different ways of viewing the same situation and are merely reflective of both of your experiences, perspectives, values and emotions. Keep in mind that you don't need to agree in order to understand.

Show the other person that you're listening by using the active listening behaviors explained in Book IV, Chapter 2.

Don't expect your colleague to know what he's looking for when he first begins to tell you his point of view. He may say that he wants *x*, *y*, or *z*. He may say that he sees the problem in the simplest of terms and can't understand why you don't see it that way as well. Just let him talk. The more he shares, the more information about values and emotions you'll have when it's time to respond and you can demonstrate then that you understand where he's coming from.

Summarizing what you've heard

Before launching into a response to your colleague's initial remarks, take a moment and contemplate what to say and how to say it. You've been listening for the values and emotions that are important to him; now you want to reflect his emotions and reframe his statements into what he *does want* instead of what he *doesn't want*. Repeating "you want me to stop talking at staff meetings" gets the point across, but reframing the statement to "you'd like me to find a more effective way to communicate my ideas" gives the two of you something to work with when you get to the brainstorming phase. Plus, it frames the conflict as an opportunity to *do* something!

You don't have to agree with the points you're summarizing — you just need to show that you understand what he said. When you reflect and reframe a co-worker's point in neutral words, you reinforce that you're open and receptive, but you don't sell short your own take. This technique buys you a lot of credibility as the process continues.

Speaking to be understood

When it comes time to chronicle your side of the story, speak in a way that's constructive and clear, modeling the kind of conversation you want to have. Following are some suggestions (head to Book IV, Chapter 3 for more on information on communicating positively):

> ✔ **Describe the incident and then the impact:** If you have particular concerns, address them specifically. What was the event that you experienced, and how did it affect you? You can think of this in terms of the *incident* and the *impact*. Consider this example:

At our last meeting, many of the other employees were unable to share their concerns. **(Incident)** It's important to me that all employees have time to talk about their programs. **(Impact)**

✔ **Use *I*-messages:** When sharing your perspective, only speak to your own experience. Keep your comments focused on how you perceived an event and how it affected you. Use *I* language to take the sting out of a tough message. Talking about hurt feelings is better when you deliver the information by saying, "I was confused when my phone calls weren't returned," even though you may want to say, "What's up with not returning my phone calls?"

Simply starting a sentence with *I* doesn't ensure a positive reaction. If you say, "I'm not the only one who thinks you should return phone calls!" the opportunity to state your perspective in such a way that your co-worker can understand your point of view and not react with defensiveness is lost.

✔ **Be brief and clear:** Keep your message short and sweet. Get right to the point. Repeating the same information multiple times doesn't benefit anybody. Enough said.

Step 4: Build an agenda

After you've each told your side of the story, create an agenda for the rest of the meeting. You may be wondering why you'd create an agenda midway through the meeting. Well, an *agenda* in mediation is *not* a pregenerated list of issues, nor is it a schedule of events and activities for your dialogue. Instead, it's a list of topics the two of you want to talk about that you build together. By generating the list together, you're more likely to see each topic as belonging to both of you.

Use the agenda creation process to clarify and name issues. You can be formal and write them on a whiteboard or easel, or the two of you can create an informal document at the table. The agenda reminds you of the topics you want to discuss, and as you check items off the list, it becomes a visual indicator of your progress.

Step 5: Brainstorm win-win solutions

After you share your perspectives and build an agenda (the topics of the preceding two sections), you're ready to get creative brainstorming possible solutions based on the values you've identified and what you've learned from each other. The following sections can help you arrive at a solution.

Spend a few minutes considering (and explaining) that mediating a conflict between the two of you is different from other negotiations. This part of the meeting isn't about making sure you both get two scoops of ice cream or bartering for the best price at the local flea market. It's about both of you walking away having addressed the values that matter the most and both of you feeling that you've won because you moved beyond the surface issues and understood what's really behind your conflict.

Proposing positive alternatives

You may be really good at telling others what you *don't* like. But in telling your co-worker what you don't want, you haven't offered any alternatives. Alternatives help him understand what he could be doing. Consider these contrasting statements:

- ✔ "You're always late to meetings" versus "It's important to me that you arrive at our meetings on time because I want to make sure there's enough time for everyone to provide updates on their projects."

- ✔ "You never bother to proofread your reports" versus "I need to make sure that your reports are accurate and error-free because I take a lot of pride in the team's reputation with other departments."

- ✔ "Your workspace is a disaster!" versus "I'd like our shared workspaces to be organized and tidy so I can find things quickly when asked."

You may already know what you'd like to see based on filling out the worksheet in Figure 5-1, or you may need to tailor your request based on what you discover in this meeting. Either way, speak to what each of you wants in order to prevent confusion and increase the likelihood that you'll both follow through with requests.

Keeping the conversation on track

Even in the most structured of conversations, sometimes things start to go haywire. Work through the tough spots first by using the agenda and choosing another item that may be easier to discuss. Then be sure to

- ✔ **Spotlight shared interests:** Look for things that unite you. For instance, although you may not agree on the best way to build morale on a team, you both recognize that having a satisfied staff is important.

- ✔ **Underscore progress:** Stay positive. It may be a challenge to look for the silver lining when the two of you seem to be at each other's throat, but remember that changing relationships and building trust takes time. Build on the small victories — they add up in the end.

- ✔ **Focus on what you *can* control:** You can acknowledge if much of the conflict is out of your hands, but don't dwell on it. You won't be able to change some things, but you *can* change plenty of other things. Although you may not be able to control gossip in the workplace, for instance, you can certainly control whether you participate in it.

Book V

Navigating
Tricky
Workplace
Relation-
ships and
Situations

✔ **Remain future-oriented:** After you both share the events that led to the conflict, you gain very little by revisiting and staying invested in the past. Your answers and solutions will come from a more future-focused conversation about what's possible instead of what didn't work.

✔ **Allow for saving face:** This conversation may create vulnerabilities in your co-worker; *never* take advantage of that fact. Don't hold him hostage to the process or use information he shares against him. Instead, allow him the opportunity to test and explore ideas in a safe place. You can point out inconsistencies you hear, but do so from a position of curiosity and inquiry rather than as a means to rub it in his face.

✔ **Take breaks:** Exhaustion is the enemy of constructive dialogue. Take a few minutes to stretch and refocus. And reaching a satisfying outcome may take multiple sessions, so allow some time between meetings to gather information, to test proposals, or just to see how things go.

Step 6: Make decisions

Look at the ideas and proposals you have on the table and turn them into specific actions that will give you the best outcomes and will likely hold up over time. Consider asking some of the following questions as you both test the boundaries of the proposals:

✔ **Does this solution fully address the problem?** Make sure that your agreement speaks to the root of the conflict.

✔ **Are these agreements realistic?** It does you no good to craft an agreement that the two of you are happy with if it violates company policy, doesn't account for time restrictions, costs more money than is available, or (gasp!) is illegal.

✔ **Can we both support the decisions?** Is your agreement likely to hold up because both of you can get behind the outcome? If your decisions are imbalanced or unsatisfying, one party may end up feeling shortchanged and abandon the agreement.

✔ **Are our agreements specific?** Make sure that both of you are clear about expectations and the terms of your agreements.

✔ **Do our agreements have the potential to improve our working relationship?** If your agreements are designed with the preceding points in mind, your relationship with your co-worker is much more likely to improve over the long term.

Step 7: Conclude the discussion

At the end of your discussion, summarize what you've accomplished and what you intend to do next. If you've reached agreements, be specific about follow-through. (Who will do what? By when? And for how long?) If you're at an impasse, consider what both of you can do before coming back together or what you will do in lieu of another meeting. Either way, end your conversation highlighting the progress the two of you made, and be open to continuing the dialogue if necessary. At a minimum, keep in mind that the fact that you both were willing to talk is progress. Good for you!

As hard as you try, you simply may not be able to reach any agreements. Perhaps it's because the dispute is so complex that keeping track of where you are is difficult. Or maybe you've recognized that the two of you are just so far apart in your positions and expectations that you can't see the light at the end of the tunnel. Whatever the cause, you can do some things to end on a constructive note:

- ✔ **Summarize where you are.** Have a quick discussion about your attempt to resolve the situation. Acknowledge that you've hit a rough spot but that you need to discuss what your next steps are.

- ✔ **Agree to return to the conversation after a period of time.** Though you may not have been successful in this conversation, don't close the door on the possibility of another. After some time has passed and each of you has had a chance to reconsider the situation, you may both find some benefit in returning to the discussion for another shot at it.

- ✔ **Bring in a third person.** You may need some assistance in having this discussion. A neutral third party may be able to shed new light on the situation.

Tailoring Your Approach: The Org Chart Matters

Resolving a conflict in which you're one of the players may be at the top of your to-do list, but having to actually sit down and address it is probably causing a certain amount of anxiety, especially if the person you're in conflict with is a peer on equal footing or an individual higher up than you on the corporate ladder. Before you jump in with both feet, take into consideration who the other person is in the organization, what title she holds, and what power she has to affect your future. (**_Hint:_** Everyone has power!)

Resolving issues with someone you supervise

Confronting someone you supervise because the two of you are butting heads is never fun. Yet it's a necessary part of being a manager — and when the subordinate is causing more grief than good, you have no other choice.

Creating a dialogue

If the employee you're approaching has admitted to an egregious action and you're bound by law or company policy to act according to the letter, then do that. But in other cases, you can turn the need for a disciplinary conversation into an opportunity for a new working relationship.

Punitive meetings are usually a *monologue* in which there's no room to negotiate — the boss talks and the employee listens. Facilitating your own conflict discussion should be a *dialogue* in which you and the employee both talk and listen to understand the issues and then work together to bring about change. Being part of a productive dialogue gives your staff member the opportunity to rise to the occasion, maybe even beyond your expectations, instead of operating out of fear or anger.

Keep her focused on what you'd like her to do rather than what she needs to *stop* doing to get out of trouble.

Proactively adapting your approach

When you're having a meeting about a conflict you're directly involved in and that meeting is with one of your subordinates, you need to adapt your approach. Here's how:

- ✔ Keep in mind that even though the person you're addressing is below you on the organizational chart and you may not want to give her concerns credence, the two of you are in this conflict together.

- ✔ Put yourself in your employee's shoes and think about how you'd want your boss to approach you about your communication style or your integrity.

- ✔ Set a goal for the discussion that allows the employee to get back on track and motivated to reach her goals.

- ✔ Think about your part in the trouble (such as the fact that you may have ignored it or let it go on for too long).

Creating a positive environment

Because you're the boss, you have to be a little more mindful of the environment you ask a subordinate into — especially given that the topic of conversation is about the conflict between the two of you. Work to put her at ease.

Follow the general process for a one-on-one conflict meeting (refer to the earlier section "Working toward a Solution, One Step at a Time") and weave these suggestions in as you go:

- Open the meeting by acknowledging the tension or difficulties between the two of you.

- Explain, if relevant, where your work responsibilities may be getting in the way of the relationship.

- Own up to your share of the frustrating dynamics in your work relationship.

- Commit to a new approach.

- Be open to her suggestions for a different relationship; just because the information is coming from an underling doesn't mean it's of no value to you.

- Apologize when and if necessary.

- Ask for the changes you'd like to see between the two of you.

If you think a conflict conversation with a subordinate may be especially difficult because of the nature of the tension or the fact that it's been going on for quite some time, prepare for the meeting by talking it through with a trusted source, such as a supportive supervisor or a human resources representative.

Keep your power in check. Because you're in a position of power over your employee, you have the muscle to intimidate, push, and demand that she do what you say. You also have the ability to frame your conversation as a productive learning experience for both of you. Do the latter. Sit in a way that you can see eye to eye, let the employee know that you're in this together (at least for now) and you're open to finding a long-term solution. If appropriate, suggest that there will be no negative consequences when you both come clean about the situation.

Addressing conflict with a peer

On the surface, it may seem easy enough to treat an equal like an equal, but when you're angry or frustrated, not building armies or creating competitive situations around personal conflicts with a peer can be tough. For the good of your own career aspirations, resist the urge to one-up the other person or compete for the limelight; instead, work to keep a level playing field as much as possible.

How you approach a colleague about an ongoing conflict depends on a number of factors. Take into consideration how well you know her, how often you interact, and how important the working relationship is to you. Use the steps for a one-on-one conflict discussion in the earlier section "Working toward a Solution, One Step at a Time" and adapt your conversation with the following information.

- ✔ **Respect a peer's position:** Take into account how the top brass may value her unique skill set — even if her talent isn't quite evident in your eyes! Respect her priorities, the pressures of her job, and any deadlines she may have looming, and carve out an adequate amount of time to address fully whatever problems you're having.

- ✔ **Be sensitive to location:** Both you and your peer want to retain the respect of your respective staffs and the company at large, so meet in a private place, especially if your disagreements have been public up to this point.

- ✔ **Preserve the working relationship:** If you know your peer well, the issues may be easy to address and the two of you can get back on track, keeping your professional relationship undamaged before anyone is the wiser. Having a discussion with someone you consider a friend may actually be tougher — but rest assured that addressing conflict and keeping friendships aren't mutually exclusive. The level of respect you're willing to give her, the amount of interest you show in her proposed solutions, and your combined abilities to tackle the problem without personally destroying each other will serve as an excellent example for your respective teams.

Having one-on-one conversations with your boss

Just as you would with a subordinate or a peer, if your boss has committed an egregious act that requires you to report it, do that. And, if you feel her behavior is so out of control that her superiors must be notified and you're willing to take the risk, you may have to go over her head. Beyond those special circumstances, how you attempt to resolve a conflict with your manager may depend on both short-term and long-term goals, though you should think more long term than short. Even if you know in your heart of hearts you're just here for the short term, burning a bridge with your boss is never a good idea. Leaving with dignity and knowing that you gave it your best shot will keep you from being an outsider if you ever cross paths again.

Figuring out when to ask for a meeting and when not to

A productive meeting with your boss can be a relief and can motivate you to be the best you can be. But there are times when you may want to consider waiting to ask for a meeting to talk about your difficulties. How do you know the difference? Let the following table be your guide:

Times to Ask	Times to Hold Off
You're determined to stay with the organization.	Tempers are ratcheted up.
One or both of you are relatively new to the position, and you got off to a bad start.	All the relevant issues and players have yet to be revealed.
You're concerned about your reputation.	You're showboating.
Values such as respect and dignity have been violated.	The situation is in flux.
The situation is impossible to overlook and can no longer be ignored.	You want to deliver a diatribe and aren't ready to hear her out.

Making the most of your time

Like you, your boss is busy, so use the time you have with her wisely by following these tips:

- **Let her calendar trump yours and ask for a block of time that will allow for an in-depth conversation with few distractions.**

- **Have a specific goal in mind for the meeting.** Do you want to address a particular incident or are you more interested in speaking in general terms about your working relationship? Either way, come prepared with specific examples.

- **Write down and prioritize what you want your boss to know before you start the meeting.** If you're especially anxious about the conversation, you could forget and miss a great opportunity to talk about what's most important to you.

- **For every complaint or issue you bring up, suggest at least three (yes, three) solutions.** Coming in with nothing makes you sound like a whiner, coming in with only one solution may be misinterpreted as an all-or-nothing ultimatum, and having only two solutions doesn't show the range of your capabilities. Presenting three solutions opens the door for her to add more, and then the two of you can work together to refine the proposals.

✔ **Be the first to apologize if you've erred.** Get your mistakes out in the open, on the table, and out of the way.

✔ **Strategically admit your limitations so she can no longer use them against you.** If you're constantly defending yourself, you miss the opportunity to look at a behavior and choose whether to change it. You also miss the chance to build your résumé with educational opportunities.

✔ **Graciously accept any apology she makes, and don't hold her to an impossible standard.** She may be above you in rank, but she's still human, and admitting mistakes is tough. Give her some credit if she's able to say she's sorry.

Book V

Navigating Tricky Workplace Relationships and Situations

Chapter 6

Serving Your Customers and Hurdling Challenges

*P*roviding quality service and sales to customers is quite a challenge in many jobs. Customers can be demanding and, at times, even unreasonable. Also, problems sometimes affect your customers, many of whom let you know their dissatisfaction when they're unhappy. Yet without customers to serve and sell to, you have no job and no business. Like them or not, you need satisfied customers. Therefore, knowing how to handle the challenges of customer service and sales is the focus of this chapter.

Sales isn't just the responsibility of sales representatives and account executives. Many people who don't carry traditional sales-related titles still perform sales-related functions in their jobs. If you work in a service business such as a law firm, a construction business, or a staffing services agency, for example, part of your work is to help bring in business. That's sales. Likewise, customer service is a responsibility for more than just the people who work in customer-service departments. In a broad sense, *customer service* is work performed that is of help, use, or benefit to someone else. In fact, whether you work in the private sector or the public sector, customer service is a part of your job — and everyone else's — to some degree.

You're Selling, but Are They Buying?

Many people think that the key to success in sales is how well you can persuade a potential customer to buy your product or service. They imagine the stereotypical image of a used-car salesperson — pushy and talkative — and think that's the way successful sales are made. It isn't. This section explores how to uncover customer needs and how to negotiate a business deal. In the following sections, you see how active listening and assertive speaking (which we cover in Chapters 2 and 3 of Book IV) become great selling and service aids for you.

Your ability to listen effectively is as critical, if not more so, than your ability to talk. When you listen effectively, you discover what's important to the customer so that when you talk, you say what the customer needs to hear.

Identifying needs and selling to meet them

One of the common mistakes that people make in sales situations is focusing on the product or service they have to sell. Doing so leads them to talk more than they listen and to say things that the prospective customer may not be interested in hearing. They overlook two important aspects of why people buy:

- People buy to fulfill a need.
- Buying is often an emotional decision first; a rational decision (to justify the purchase) comes second.

If you don't know or understand a customer's need, or if you don't make the buying experience satisfying for them, the likelihood of your persuading the customer to buy anything is slim.

Regardless of what you're selling, the following tips can help you identify customer needs and build a positive relationship that enables you to meet those needs. Keep in mind that all of the following tips can be summed up as *listen first, talk second.*

Probing to uncover customer needs

Because customers often don't express their needs upfront, you want to probe to find out what those needs are. You also may find that what customers say they want isn't what they really need. To get at what they really want, you have to ask probing questions (head to Book IV, Chapter 2 for more details on digging deeper with probing). Here are a few open-ended questions that you can adapt to your sales situations to help uncover these needs:

✔ What are you looking for?

✔ What are the reasons for what you're asking to have done?

✔ What issues or challenges are you facing?

✔ What led you to want to explore the product or service I have to offer?

✔ What questions can I answer about the product or service I have to offer?

✔ What's been your experience with this type of product or service?

✔ With what you're looking for, what would you like to see happen?

✔ What does your business do?

✔ In a business relationship with a vendor or service provider, what's important to you?

Confirming that you understand what the needs are

Probing for specifics draws out your client's or customer's needs. After you get a picture of what these needs are, give feedback to check your understanding of what you've heard. Use the active listening tools of paraphrasing or reflective paraphrasing to do so: In one sentence, they help you check your understanding of the client's main idea in the message (paraphrasing) or the content and emotional meaning heard in the message (reflective paraphrasing). See Book IV, Chapter 2 for more information on these two tools.

When you paraphrase, try to capture in one sentence the essence of the message you heard and end with a question (example: "So you've been frustrated by a lack of reliable service, and if that service is backed in actions, not just words, that's what you really need. Is that right?") to invite the speaker to confirm or clarify.

Understanding objections before you attempt to address them

Sometimes you hear concerns or objections from a customer about what you're offering — from the price to the quality. If, when an objection comes up, you react by speaking first without fully understanding what the concern is all about, you risk alienating the customer. Instead, shift and show your understanding of the customer's concerns first (see Book V, Chapter 3). This effort involves using paraphrasing or reflective paraphrasing in a situation of potential conflict to check your understanding, and may also involve probing first to gather background on what the client's issues are. You may say, for example, "Please tell me what your concerns are with what I've been explaining to you." Ask questions to get specifics and then give verbal feedback to check your understanding. Sometimes what customers say on the surface doesn't reveal the full extent of their concerns and issues. Asking customers for suggestions on what would help them overcome their objections can provide useful input, too.

Emphasizing what you can do to meet the needs or address the concerns

When you understand first what customers' needs are and any objections or concerns they have, you're in a good position to address those needs or concerns when you speak. Focus on what you *can* do as opposed to what you *can't* do. In particular, tell how what you have to offer directly benefits the customer and helps alleviate the customer's concern. For example, if a customer has concerns about your price, explain how your product or service can help solve problems, increase efficiency, or provide some other benefit to meet the person's needs. By doing so, you help the client see value in the money spent.

Keeping your messages concise and clear

You must speak in terms your audience will understand. Avoid being verbose, overloading on details, and using the latest buzzwords and jargon. Get to the point and use language that means something to your clients. Translate terms you need to use so that your client understands your points. You build credibility and rapport when you speak on your client's level.

Speaking with sincerity and confidence

Being sincere and confident engages your client and helps you build a sales relationship. When you listen to gain an understanding of a customer's needs and you speak directly and clearly about how you can help meet those needs, you couple persuasion with credibility without being pushy — and that's the key to success in sales. For information on how to project sincerity and confidence, head to Book IV, Chapter 3.

Sounding sincere and confident means first doing your homework and knowing your products and services well enough to explain their important features and key benefits to customers. You don't have to know the product as well as, say, the engineers who designed it, but you at least need to know how the product works and how it can help meet a customer's needs.

Closing conversations

Check the customer's interest level. Asking for feedback as simple as, "What do you think?" helps you gauge whether you have a potential business deal and also helps you draw out any concerns or objections.

End every sales-related conversation by knowing what's going to happen next. Because many sales situations require further discussion, finish by outlining the next steps with the customer. Determine what needs to happen and when you will talk again. Use questions like, "When should we talk next to explore these matters further?" Also, remember to check your understanding of any agreements reached so far. In this case, you recap and ask for confirmation.

If the time is right, ask for the order: "How about I make you a proposal and we talk next week to finalize it. Will that work for you?"

Sealing the deal

Sooner or later in any sales-type situation, you have to talk money. The customer wants to know how much your product or service is going to cost. In many cases, however, especially in business-to-business sales, one price doesn't fit all situations. Volume of business, complexity of an order, and the time involved to fulfill the order are just some of the factors that come into play in how much a product or service will cost the client. Nonetheless, you have to talk dollars for the deal to close. No customer says, "Charge me whatever you like and I'll gladly pay it."

An assertive approach works best in negotiating deals. What this means is the following:

✔ Business negotiations are treated as a collaborative discussion rather than a game or a battle of wills.

✔ Business deals are worked out to benefit both sides to the greatest extent possible.

✔ The focus of discussions is on meeting needs, not solely on money.

✔ You conduct negotiations so that you build relationships for the future, not just the present.

As these points demonstrate, an assertive negotiator follows the principle of being consistently respectful. The emphasis is not only to make the deal now but also to lay the foundation for future business should opportunities arise again.

When you need to talk money in a sales situation, avoid the approaches of nonassertive negotiators and aggressive negotiators. Don't sound hesitant or apologetic when explaining how much something will cost and don't be too quick to lower the price. These behaviors make you sound uncertain and, as a result, decrease the value of what you have to offer. On the other hand, don't come on too strong or show little willingness to compromise. These behaviors make you appear overbearing and, as a result, convince the other party to avoid doing business with you.

Here are the key steps to follow to negotiate sales deals assertively:

1. **Know the customer's needs before making your offer.**

   As much as you can, find out what the customer's needs are before you offer a quote or begin the actual negotiations.

2. **State your offer firmly and confidently.**

   Don't hesitate. Know that you're giving a fair price for the value of your services and products, and sound that way. As needed, give the business reasoning on which your offer is based — the time involved, the complexity of the work, or the volume requested, for example. Keep your explanations brief.

3. **After making your offer, wait patiently.**

   Let silence be your ally. Sometimes customers go through the *hemming and hawing phase* as they ponder an offer. Stay out of the way. The more you talk at this time, the more you get in the way of their thinking, and the more doubt you create in their minds.

4. **If the client expresses concern with your offer, explore the reasons for it.**

   Listen first, speak second. Probe to find out the reasons for the concern and then confirm your understanding. Avoid talking and making any effort to address the concern until you gain this information definitively.

5. **Address concerns on the basis of worth and benefits.**

   People need to see they're getting value for what they buy. You may be able to persuade a customer to accept your original offer by emphasizing the worth of what you're offering — not your wants or demands — and by explaining its benefits to the customer.

6. **If the concern about price still exists, explore other options.**

   You don't want to provide a lesser offer before this point, but sticking to your original offer now makes you look stubborn and aggressive. Explore options together for mutual gain. Options may include adjusting the quantity of the order, the timing of the order, the amount of features in the product or service, or doing something now and supplying something more at a later time. Discussing these or other options to fit a price that can work for the client is often a good step to take before you consider lowering your price for the original order offered.

   Ultimately, if the client demands a price that isn't reasonable for your business, say, "No, thank you." You're out to make deals that meet the needs of both parties. Thanking the client and saying no firmly and politely leaves the door open should the client reconsider and, more importantly, you leave the relationship on a respectful level.

7. **Confirm the agreement.**

   After both you and the customer agree to the deal, recap and confirm the understanding you reached. Then talk about the next steps for implementation and get the order rolling.

Providing Quality Customer Service

You've probably seen statistics that say the cost of attracting and gaining new customers is far greater than the cost of keeping them. But if you don't provide customers with quality service, they may not come back for more.

For this discussion, *quality customer service* means adding value to the product or service a business offers, especially people value. This people value occurs most often at the points of contact, the interactions during which a customer seeks service. If the customer finds the help at those points of contact to be consistently respectful, responsive, accurate, efficient, and reliable, quality service is achieved — the people value shows, and customer satisfaction is gained. The following sections provide you with the thinking and communication actions that help you deliver quality customer service consistently.

If customers get good service only some of the time, the service isn't good at all. When customers can count on every interaction being positive, you have quality service working well.

Following the golden rule

The tools of active listening and assertive speaking play a major role in delivering quality customer service. You begin the effort by thinking like a customer. Actually, doing so shouldn't be hard because you've been a customer for many years yourself. When you remember what you've experienced when receiving good service and use this thinking in your job, you increase the likelihood of your using the *golden rule* — do unto others as you would have them to do unto you.

Part of thinking like a customer and making the golden rule work for you is putting the focus of your *points of contact* (live interactions with customers, whether in person or on the phone) on understanding and satisfying customer needs. Here are seven common needs that customers bring to business interactions:

✔ **Receive courtesy and respect.** From your nonverbal demeanor to the words you speak, what customers need from you in every interaction is to be treated with care and consideration.

✔ **Receive attention and responsiveness.** Customers are looking for listening and understanding — someone who acknowledges their presence and their issue.

✔ **Get prompt action and timely service.** Customers need to avoid unnecessary delays. Act as quickly as possible in providing the service.

✔ **Have commitments met.** This need is about doing what you stand for and doing what you said you would do.

✔ **Get assistance.** Customers come to you because they need some form of assistance from you. They need that help so that matters are handled properly and efficiently.

✔ **Be given accurate information.** Customers want you to know your stuff and provide information to help them make decisions, complete transactions, and get answers that make sense.

✔ **Resolve problems.** Sometimes this need arises when the other needs aren't met. Customers need you to fix problems, not place blame; to take responsibility, not make excuses.

Customer needs often come in clusters. In one interaction, three or four needs may come into play. The neat part of this is that sometimes one or two actions on your part can satisfy a whole cluster of needs.

Communicating with impact to deliver quality service

A critical element that helps you satisfy these customer needs comes down to how you communicate. This section gives you seven communication tips that lead to quality customer service.

Identify the customer's needs

What is the customer looking for; why is your service being sought? Probing helps you discover the answers to these questions. Often, the effort starts with a simple question asked in a courteous manner, such as, "How can I help you?" Follow this question with further probes that provide you with the specifics of the customer's situation, and then use the active listening tool of paraphrasing to confirm your understanding.

Sound definitive

In terms of your language, speak positively, as covered in Book IV, Chapter 3. In particular, emphasize what you can and will do in response to customer requests and inquiries. Avoid the trigger words such as *try, maybe,* and *perhaps* in your messages. They communicate doubt and uncertainty about whether you can help.

To sound definitive, speak clearly and loud enough to be easily heard. Avoid the hesitation that comes from using nonwords like *um, uh,* and *you know.* Use pauses to help you breathe, and think before you speak so that you sound certain. If you're face to face with the customer, make direct and steady eye contact.

If you do need to say no, briefly give the reasons. Wherever possible, offer alternatives on what you or the customer can do or where the customer can find help. Doing so keeps you positive and helpful in both words and actions.

Avoid using the word *policy* as your primary reason for saying no. Quoting company policy makes you sound like a rigid rule enforcer, not a helpful service provider. Explain the policy in lay terms, how it works, and why it's needed.

Be genuine and sincere

Sound sincere and match your tone to that of the customer speaking to you. Consider using two ranges of voice tone based on what you hear coming from the customer:

- ✔ Customer sounds neutral to lively — you sound upbeat.
- ✔ Customer sounds worried, angry, or upset — you sound concerned.

No one wants to hear a bubbly, happy-go-lucky voice when they're greatly bothered by a problem.

When in doubt, check it out

One of the least useful initial responses to a customer request or inquiry is "I don't know." Saying "I'm new here" is no help either. These trigger phrases make you sound incompetent and unable to help. Of course, making something up when you don't know the right answer is even worse.

Instead, if you don't know the answer to a customer's question, give a response such as, "Let me check that out." Then indicate when you'll follow up with an answer and do so. This kind of response makes you sound resourceful. No one expects you to have all the answers; when you communicate that you'll find out the answers, you're meeting important customer needs — especially for accurate information.

Translate: Stick to lay terms

Talk to customers in plain and simple terms. Hold the technical jargon, keep the acronyms out, avoid citing regulations, and stay away from sounding like a policy manual. Customers don't need to be experts in your field — that's why they come to you. Let your language make them feel welcome by communicating in terms that make sense to them or by explaining the terminology they need to find out in clear, understandable language.

Underpromise and overdeliver

Make time commitments that you can meet, if not beat. Sometimes you're asked when something can be done or when you'll have an answer to a question. Giving a vague answer doesn't help, nor does saying a date that isn't likely to be met just to give an answer. When you underpromise and overdeliver, you first estimate how long fulfilling the request will take you and factor in a cushion of time to be on the safe side. Then you say in definitive language when you will be done.

Handle problems with the language of solutions

Problem situations are a real test of the quality of your customer service, because they're a big part of why customers seek your assistance. How do you deal with such challenges? If you use the assertive speaking tool of the language of solutions (see Book IV, Chapter 3), you communicate the steps that you will take to resolve the problem. For example, you explore options and ideas with the customer. Your language focuses on actions that can be taken to rectify the situation — efforts that greatly relieve customer anxiety when problems come up.

Getting Irate Customers Back on Your Side

Probably the greatest challenge in providing customer service is dealing with a difficult or irate customer. A *difficult customer* is a person to whom you're providing service who is emotionally charged and very concerned about an issue. Anger, frustration, and distraught feelings are the strong emotions that the customer may display — and these aren't easy emotions to deal with.

Reasons vary as to why the strong emotions exist, but from the customer's point of view, they exist because there's a big problem. Don't rely only on volume as an indicator of these kinds of hard feelings; look at tone and body language to tune into emotions. For example, someone seething at you may speak at a low volume, but you may hear a sharp tone coupled with a wicked stare.

The following sections provide a problem-solving model to guide your communications through these difficult customer situations. They also give you a few other key tips to help you manage yourself so that you're in control and you can best help the customer.

Problem solving with difficult customers

When everything is running smoothly, service can look good. But what happens when you have a problem that has created a difficult customer situation? How you handle these situations is the true test of how good your service is. Handle these challenging situations effectively, and you can win a customer for the long-term.

The key to handling difficult or irate customer situations is to look at them as problem-solving challenges. Therefore, you need to have a problem-solving model to follow and at the same time emphasize that you care at each step along the way. Here is a useful model to follow:

Step 1: Show empathy

In simple terms, listen with care and respect and show that you understand what you're hearing from the customer. Because interactions with difficult customers often begin with strong emotions, don't be afraid to acknowledge the emotions you're hearing. This effort involves using the active-listening tools of reflecting feelings or reflective paraphrasing (see Book IV, Chapter 2). For example:

> "Sounds like everything so far has been one frustration after another for you. Is that right?" *(reflecting feelings)*

> "You're feeling inconvenienced because of a process that has not gone as quickly as expected?" *(reflective paraphrasing)*

If you get a strong response in return, such as, "Darn right, this has been frustrating," don't be alarmed; you're actually making progress. The emotion has been identified and verbalized and is less likely to keep grinding and getting in the way in the conversation. As the customer goes on, continue to provide empathetic responses throughout the conversation.

Avoid making the common mistake of passively listening in these situations and letting the customer vent endlessly. Eventually, the person may run out of steam and stop venting, but the customer won't feel understood. The likelihood of that customer feeling that he or she has gotten a satisfactory resolution from you greatly lessens when genuine care seems lacking.

Your emphasis as you start out in a difficult customer interaction is to show empathy, not sympathy. Customers don't need you to feel sorry for them (which is sympathy). Some people view sympathy as condescending; others see it as misleading (you agree with everything they say and will do anything they want, even though it may not be what's best for your company). You want to show understanding of where the customer is coming from in a respectful manner. That's empathy, and that's the best way to begin to handle this challenging situation.

Step 2: Gain an understanding of the problem

Gather information from the customer about the problem at hand. Probe for an explanation of what has happened, and then paraphrase to verify that you understand the problem as the customer sees it. For example:

> "What you're telling me is that no follow-through has occurred to get this damaged product repaired or replaced, despite your repeated efforts?" (*paraphrasing*)

Sometimes, you'll need to diagnose further to get a full picture of what has happened. This means probing with the customer to explore further the circumstances or causes of the problem. If you have worked in a technical support role, you know that this may mean walking the customer through different steps of a computer application to determine exactly where the problem is in a system.

Step 3: Develop alternatives for a resolution

After you gain a full understanding of the problem, you're able to work out a solution. Don't move ahead to do so until then.

Wherever you can, develop the options for the solution with the customer. You can ask something like, "What would you like to see happen here?" Sometimes, what a customer wants for a resolution is far less than what you had in mind. On the occasions that the customer answers with something beyond what can be done, simply say, "We'll need to look at some other options that are more feasible." Remember to focus on what *can* be done; don't dwell on what *can't* be done.

Step 4: Decide on the best resolution

After exploring all the options, bring the discussion to a close by recapping what you decided or the best way to go under the circumstances. Clearly outline the steps you will take and when. When action needs to be taken, under-promise and overdeliver as to when it will happen.

Step 5: Follow through

When action is needed to implement the solution, follow through and get it done by the time you set. As an extra touch that can go a long way in enhancing customer satisfaction, check back with the customer to ensure that everything worked out fine. This proactive move puts you in a position to fix any problems that still exist.

Dealing with irate customers

Following the problem-solving model described in the preceding section gives you an organized approach to work through these challenging situations. This section provides you with eight tips to help increase the likelihood that you can work out satisfactory resolutions when dealing with angry customers.

- ✔ **Stay in control.** When a customer has strong emotions, getting defensive in return is easy to do — and is not helpful for either you or the customer. Your defensiveness will serve as a spark to escalate tensions. Instead, shift your attention from how you're feeling to what the customer is feeling and saying. (See Book V, Chapter 3 for information on how to show understanding.) With this focus, you increase your ability to listen effectively, and when you do so, you eliminate the reactive need to become defensive.

- ✔ **Listen for facts and feelings, not delivery and manner.** Focus on what you really need to listen for and understand — the content of the customer's message and the emotions being expressed. If you get stuck on how the message is being delivered, you're certain to lose what the message really means. Make your objective in the conversation to show understanding of the whole message you're hearing — that is, the facts and the feelings.

- ✔ **Be collaborative, not adversarial.** Sometimes in difficult customer situations, the service provider sees the customer as the problem and therefore shows little understanding or care for the customer's problem. Such a view tends to promote adversarial interactions — you against the customer. Instead, look at the situation with this focus: You and the customer against the problem. With this focus, you work *with* the customer to solve a problem — a far more collaborative, positive approach.

- ✔ **Follow problem-solving guidelines and be flexible with them.** Follow the problem-solving model outlined in the preceding section. Recognize that the problem-solving steps follow a general order, but adapt to the situation. More important, you often repeat Step 1 (providing empathetic responses) throughout the conversation based on how the customer is coming across.

- ✔ **Personalize the interaction.** Get the customer's name and use it periodically in your interaction. Give your name too. Now you have two people who know each other by name working on a problem together, as opposed to two relative strangers stuck in an emotionally charged situation. This personal touch goes a long way in helping diffuse the tension and in creating a comfortable atmosphere for discussion.

✔ **If you need help, ask for it.** Don't put undue pressure on yourself if you're not sure how best to resolve the customer's problem. You don't want to make the wrong commitments — then you'll really upset the customer. On the other hand, you don't want to be an obstacle who can't help solve a problem because you're saying no when you don't know what to do. Let the customer know that you need to check things out or get help and set a time to call back. Then seek the support you need so that the best possible resolution is worked out for the customer.

✔ **Apologize for others' mistakes, but don't criticize them.** When the cause of a customer's upset feelings is another staff member's mistake, sincerely apologize as if you were the one who made the mistake. Then focus your attention on initiating the most positive and corrective action you can as soon as possible.

Avoid criticizing another staff member or department for what went wrong. To the external customer, you represent your whole organization. If you're heard as critical of your own organization or people in it, you convince the customer to avoid doing business with your company again. Keep your focus on getting the problem resolved instead.

✔ **Utilize positive self-talk.** If you're like most people, you talk to yourself. In stressful, challenging situations, the self-talk racing in your mind may be full of negative messages: "Oh, what a pain to deal with" or "Why does this customer have to bother me today!" Many other, more colorful messages may also run through your mind in such situations. With positive self-talk, you give yourself messages that help you stay on a positive track in the interaction. You have to find your own messages — such as "Stay focused" and "Listen" — and make them positive. These kinds of messages help you to be more in control and more ready to help work on a solution — keys to resolving difficult customer problems.

Remembering Your Internal Customers

Internal customers are the people inside your organization to whom you provide some form of service or from whom you need support. If you're in human resources, information systems, office services, finance and accounting, and other administrative support functions, your primary customers are internal. To serve them well, you often need them to carry out certain responsibilities or provide you with support — from filling out forms to following established processes and policies.

Even if your main focus in your job is on dealing with *external customers* (those outside your organization whom you serve), you still may need support from internal staff in order to serve external recipients well. Sometimes, getting other staff people to cooperate with you and trying to satisfy them with the services you provide can be quite a challenge. The key to gaining the support and cooperation you need from employees and managers in other groups is to see them as important customers to whom you provide quality service. This means that you communicate and act in much the same way as you would with your external customers:

✔ Identify customer needs.

✔ Focus on how you can help meet the needs.

✔ Speak in lay terms.

✔ Handle problems with the language of solutions.

✔ Underpromise and overdeliver — that is, communicate your commitments and meet or beat them.

In addition to treating your internal customers the same as your external, to make your internal customer service effective, build working relationships on the principle of being consistently respectful. In working relationships, you give respect without conditions attached and build a track record as someone others can count on to deliver when your services are needed. In terms of applying the tools of active listening and assertive speaking to deliver this quality internal customer service, here a few tips:

✔ **Take initiative.** Assert yourself and be the one to take the first step to make something positive happen. Make that call, set up that meeting, go talk to that internal customer with whom you need to work something out. Don't wait for others to act first. As the expression goes, get the ball rolling.

✔ **Educate your customers so that they understand what to do.** Quite often, internal service providers want their fellow employees to follow certain processes or policies so that they give them the right services. But sometimes these processes or policies aren't followed very well, and the service providers feel frustrated. Prevent the frustration through face-to-face communication in which — and this is key — you show the internal customers what they can do to receive service from you. In other words, let them know how they benefit from taking the right actions that help you deliver quality service to them. Don't assume that they already know what these actions are.

✔ **Listen to concerns and feedback.** When your internal customers have issues or concerns with the service you provide, or they just want to give you some feedback, listen first. Avoid reacting defensively. Probe to get them to explain their messages and paraphrase or reflective paraphrase to check your understanding. You may even get a few good points that you can use to improve the service you provide. At the least, when you show that you can listen to someone else's issues, you increase the likelihood that they will listen to yours — the way to build positive give-and-take dialogue in a working relationship.

✔ **Share what you know.** You have expertise, experience, sometimes-helpful insider tips, and knowledge of useful resources — all forms of information that internal customers need to do their jobs well. Respond to requests for such information and openly share it without being asked when the need is apparent. Gaining accurate, timely, and useful information is a critical need that all types of customers have.

✔ **Ask for what you need.** Sometimes you need your internal customers to do something, or you need help from them for yourself. In such cases, make your request assertively. Don't demand it, because employees in other groups generally don't respond well to orders, but don't shy away from asking, either. Instead, confidently, sincerely, directly, and with a sense of importance ask for what you need with a brief explanation as to why.

Working relationships involve expectations, usually unstated, of give-and-take cooperation. The expectations are that if I help you with what you need, in time you will help me with what I need in some equivalent fashion. When you work to identify and meet the needs of your internal customers as a regular practice, you have a positive influence on others. To then ask these customers to respond to a need you have — assertively so — greatly increases your chances of getting that need met.

✔ **Express appreciation.** The practice of saying thank you to external customers when they receive or buy your service is common. No reason you can't do the same thing when you serve your internal customers. Especially when they do something that shows support for your efforts, thank them profusely. Even put in a good word with someone's boss for special occasions of assistance to you. Displaying common courtesy, with a touch of gratitude mixed in, makes for a very nice dose of quality customer service.

Chapter 7

Managing Ethical Dilemmas at Work

In This Chapter

▶ Understanding why loyalty, confidentiality, and security are important at work

▶ Mixing your personal life and your professional life

▶ Being honest with expense reports

▶ Standing your ground against unethical requests

*E*thics is the framework of values that employees use to guide their behavior. You've seen the devastation that poor ethical standards can lead to — witness the string of business failures attributed to less-than-sterling ethics in more than a few large, seemingly upstanding businesses. Today more than ever, employees — managers and nonmanagers alike — are expected to behave ethically, and, if you're a manager, to purge the organization of employees who refuse to align their own standards with that of their employer.

No one is immune from ethical dilemmas at work. If the company you work for is well organized and has a clear set of policies, ethical dilemmas can be minimized, but they can no more be eliminated than can the pleasure you get from doing a good job. Ethical dilemmas are part of life, so they are part of your professional life as well.

No single chapter in any book can capture every nuance of the ethical issues that emerge in the workplace, but this chapter offers some suggestions about some of the most common ethical issues arising at work and introduces some of the ethical issues that come from your role as an employee.

Doing the Right Thing: Ethics and You

With an endless parade of business scandals — overstated revenues, mistaken earnings, and misplaced decimals — hitting the daily news, rocking the stock market, and shaking the foundations of the global economic system, you often wonder whether anyone in charge knows the difference between right and wrong. Or, if they do know the difference, whether they really care.

Of course, the reality is that many business leaders do know the difference between right and wrong, despite appearances to the contrary. Now more than ever, businesses and the leaders who run them are trying to do the right thing, not just because the right thing is politically correct, but also because it's good for the bottom line.

Ethics are in. And that's good for all of us.

Defining ethics

Ethics are standards of beliefs and values that guide conduct, behavior, and activities — in other words, a way of thinking that provides boundaries for our actions. In short, ethics means simply doing the right thing. And not just talking about doing the right thing; really doing it!

Although each of you comes to a job with your own sense of ethical values based on your upbringing and life experiences, organizations and leaders for which you work are responsible for setting clear ethical standards.

When you have high ethical standards on the job, you generally exhibit some or all of the following personal qualities and behaviors:

- ✔ Honesty
- ✔ Integrity
- ✔ Impartiality
- ✔ Fairness
- ✔ Loyalty
- ✔ Dedication
- ✔ Responsibility
- ✔ Accountability

Ethical behavior starts with you. When you behave ethically, others follow your example and behave ethically, too. And, if you practice ethical conduct, it also reinforces and perhaps improves your own ethical standards.

If you're a manager, remember you're a leader in your organization and you set an example — both for other managers and for the many workers who are watching your every move. When others see you behaving unethically, you're sending the message loud and clear that ethics don't matter. The result? Ethics won't matter to them, either.

Characteristics of a code of ethics

Although most people have a pretty good idea about what kinds of behavior are ethical and what kinds of behavior aren't, ethics are — to some degree — subjective, and a matter of interpretation to the individual employee. One worker may, for example, think that making unlimited personal phone calls from the office is okay, while another worker may consider that to be inappropriate. So, what's the solution to ethics that vary from person to person in an organization? A code of ethics.

A code of ethics spells out for all employees — from the very top to the very bottom — your organization's ethical expectations, clearly and unambiguously. A code of ethics isn't a substitute for company policies and procedures; the code complements them. Instead of leaving employees' definition of ethics on the job to chance — or someone's upbringing — a code of ethics clearly spells out that stealing, sharing trade secrets, sexually harassing a co-worker, and other unethical behavior is unacceptable and may be grounds for dismissal.

Four key areas form the foundation of a good code of ethics:

- ✔ Compliance with internal policies and procedures
- ✔ Compliance with external laws and regulations
- ✔ Direction from organizational values
- ✔ Direction from individual values

Of course, a code of ethics isn't worth the paper it's printed on if it doesn't address some very specific issues, as well as the more generic ones listed previously. The following are some of the most common issues addressed by typical codes of ethics:

- ✔ Equal opportunity
- ✔ Sexual harassment
- ✔ Diversity
- ✔ Privacy and confidentiality
- ✔ Conflicts of interest
- ✔ Gifts and gratuities
- ✔ Employee health and safety

In addition to working within an organization, a well-crafted code of ethics can be a powerful tool for publicizing your company's standards and values to people outside your organization, including vendors, clients, customers, investors, potential job applicants, the media, and the public at large. The code of ethics tells others that your company values ethical behavior and that it guides the way it and its employees do business.

Of course, simply having a code of ethics isn't enough. You must also live it. Even the world's best code of ethics does you no good if you file it away and never use it.

Making ethical choices

You may have a code of ethics, but if you never behave ethically in all your day-to-day business transactions and relationships, what's the purpose of having a code in the first place? Ethical challenges abound in business — some are spelled out in your company's code of ethics or policies and procedures, and some aren't. What, for example, would you do if:

- One of your favorite employees gives you tickets to a baseball game?

- An employee asks you not to write her up for a moderate infraction of company policies?

- You sold a product to a client that you later found out to be faulty, but your boss wants you to forget about it?

- Your department's financial results are actually lower than what appears in your boss's presentation to the board of directors?

- You find out that your star employee actually didn't graduate from college as he claimed in his job application?

- You know that a product you sell doesn't actually do everything your company claims it does?

We all make ethical choices on the job every day — how do you make yours? Consider the following six keys to make better ethical choices:

- **E — Evaluate** circumstances through the appropriate filters (filters include culture, laws, policies, circumstances, relationships, politics, perception, emotions, values, bias, and religion).

- **T — Treat** people and issues fairly within the established boundaries. Fair doesn't always mean equal.

- **H — Hesitate** before making critical decisions.

   ✔ **I — Inform** those affected of the standard/decision that has been set/made.

   ✔ **C — Create** an environment of consistency for yourself and your working group.

   ✔ **S — Seek** counsel when you have any doubt (but from those who are honest and who you respect).

Understanding Loyalty

Typically, you work for someone else who pays you a salary. That relationship establishes the expectation that you owe your professional loyalty to the company or person you work for. It almost certainly means that you'll learn things that, if disclosed, would damage others or the company. But what are you supposed to do when, in the name of loyalty, you're asked to do something wrong?

Loyalty is a valued commodity in the business world. Many employers list it as the most important virtue that an employee can have, because employees who look to promote the business's interests and defend it against competition are essential for a successful company.

When the company's values overlap with your own, being loyal to the company is easy. Trouble arises when either a colleague or a boss asks you to do something you know is wrong and invokes your loyalty in making the request. This kind of request or demand can come camouflaged in many ways and may never be explicit. But the implication is always clear: You're expected to do something that you know is wrong in order to demonstrate your loyalty to your colleague, your boss, or that amorphous entity, the company.

People in positions of authority shouldn't ask their subordinates to lie for them. If you're a manager, and you're doing something on company time that you shouldn't be doing, just tell your assistant that you're unavailable. Don't try to take advantage of someone else's loyalty to you or to the company.

Likewise, subordinates shouldn't agree to lie for their bosses. Loyalty is one thing; lying in the name of loyalty is something else entirely. If your boss asks you to lie for her, try this to give her an opportunity to retract the request:

1. **Politely ask her to confirm the request.**

   For example, ask, "You want me to tell the owner you're in Denver arranging financing when in fact you're in Pebble Beach?"

2. **If your boss doesn't back down from her request that you lie, ask an even more pointed question.**

   For example: "You want me to lie?"

3. **If your boss doesn't get the hint that you're unwilling to comply by now, tell her politely that as much as you respect her and enjoy working with her, you won't lie for her.**

   Be prepared for the worst. Some bosses will take your refusal in stride; others won't. If your boss does, you've established a ground floor, and she'll respect you for it. If the boss is angered by your refusal, you can expect anything from a grunt of disapproval to a campaign of discrimination.

   When your boss goes after you because you won't do something wrong, the following tips may help:

   ✔ Keep a record of all incidents and your responses when your boss asks you to do something unethical.

   ✔ Keep your records at home. Don't keep them at work, where they could be stolen.

   ✔ Follow the instructions in the company's policies and procedures documents (if your company has them) for combating unethical behavior.

   ✔ Direct your concerns to the human resources department, if your company has one.

   ✔ Look for a new job.

Mum's the Word: Confidentiality

As an employee, you know things that, were they to be disclosed, might hurt you, your colleagues, your bosses, or your company. Many companies have nondisclosure and confidentiality agreements written into employment contracts. Many others discuss confidentiality in their employee guidelines. Take confidentiality seriously!

Generally speaking, two kinds of confidential information exist: proprietary company information and information about people.

Company information

Every business has proprietary information — about jobs, layoffs, and performance reviews; about patents and contracts; about sales and earnings; about product developments. The list goes on and on. What should you do, as an employee, to avoid disclosing confidential business information?

If your boss is on the ball, she'll inform you about confidential information. She'll give you answers to the following questions:

- ✔ Which documents are confidential? Are there degrees of confidentiality? If so, what are they?

- ✔ Are you and your boss the only people who can look at these documents? If not, who else can look at them?

- ✔ Do you have the authority to open packages marked "Personal" or "Confidential"? If not, does anyone other than the addressee have that authority?

- ✔ Should you clear with your boss all requests for confidential materials? If not, under what conditions can you exercise your own judgment? If so, what should you do if your boss is unavailable?

- ✔ Does anyone have permission to remove things from your boss's office? If so, who? If not, how should you handle such requests?

Having this kind of blunt discussion with your boss shows her that you care about confidentiality and are willing to work to protect it.

If you're privy to confidential proprietary information, you bear a duty not to disclose it. This duty requires, among other things, that you learn how to live with secrets. Learning to live with secrets in turn requires that you be alert to what you say in the company of others and that you be alert to others' attempts to get information from you. Don't take these duties lightly! Your job depends on doing them well.

These guidelines can help you:

- ✔ Know who's authorized to discuss confidential matters and discuss confidential matters only with that person.

- ✔ Practice self-control by being the model of discretion in all situations.

    Being the model of discretion *in all situations* means just that. Don't kid yourself that you can safely bad mouth company policies or disclose company- or personnel-related information on a blog or social networking site. Quite a few company policies now include a code of ethics on such Web disclosures that might lead to termination.

- ✔ In public, speak softly so that others don't overhear you.

- ✔ When you're asked for confidential information, reply that because it's confidential, you can't divulge it. If the other person persists, politely point out that he's out of line. If that doesn't work, try a blank stare.

✔ Don't allow others to read your computer screen or peruse your desktop. Put confidential documents face down or in a locked drawer when you're not looking at them.

✔ Don't tell your significant other or friends all the details, even if you're tempted to do so.

Personal information

The other kind of confidential information that you can gain is personal information of an embarrassing sort. Everyone knows that administrative assistants sometimes learn things they would really rather not know about their bosses, and that bosses sometimes ask employees to report things about colleagues that are really none of the boss's business.

These kinds of breaches are entirely avoidable, but only by those who are responsible for committing them. Whenever someone else — through what he says or what he does — discloses something that you would rather not know, you're placed in a coercive position, in which you either keep the secret or snitch. Both options are unpleasant.

To keep this kind of situation from happening to you, the first line of defense is to stop someone from saying something before she reveals more than you want to know. You can do this in two ways:

✔ Distinguish between friendly exchanges of benign information and malignant exchanges of harmful information.

✔ Ask whether, given your professional relationship, the other person really wants to give you the information. Most of the time, this tactic prevents the conversation from going somewhere both of you will regret. Having avoided the issue, make sure that it never comes up again.

Sometimes, of course, preventive measures don't work. A colleague may just blurt something out, or you may stumble onto something you shouldn't see, or you find yourself overhearing something you shouldn't hear. In these kinds of cases, you're stuck. Through no fault of your own, you know something about someone that you shouldn't know. The best general advice is to act as though you never had that bit of knowledge in the first place. This method isn't always easy and won't always succeed, but at least you'll have tried to not act on something you shouldn't know.

Here's more advice that can help:

✔ Ask yourself, "Do I want what I'm about to do to be recorded?" If the answer is no, don't do it.

✔ If someone discloses confidential information about clients or patients to you, your best recourse is to keep quiet. If the disclosure continues, you could consider approaching the other person's supervisor with the breach of confidentiality. Correcting the problem is the supervisor's responsibility, not yours.

Secure electronic information

A key part of observing confidentiality rules is to know how to keep both hard copy and electronic documents, including e-mail messages, secure.

Luckily, you can take some straightforward steps to keep confidential hard-copy documents confidential:

✔ Don't leave confidential documents unattended on your desk. At a minimum, turn them face down when you leave. Better still, put them in a locked drawer.

✔ If you have confidential documents at a meeting, keep them under wraps until they're needed. Return them to your briefcase or portfolio as soon as they're no longer needed.

✔ When you're transporting confidential documents anywhere, put them in an envelope or folder. If you leave the office with them, put them in a locked briefcase.

✔ When you mail confidential documents, place them in an envelope marked "Confidential," and place that sealed envelope in another envelope also marked "Confidential." That way, no one can pretend that he didn't see the warning.

✔ Never throw confidential documents away. Shred them.

Your computer support team will no doubt develop security measures to protect sensitive electronic documents. Various encryption codes, password procedures, and clearance procedures may already be in place. Follow those procedures and use the codes consistently.

Here are some ways to protect confidentiality while using computers:

✔ Remove printouts from shared printers as soon as possible.

✔ Store discs containing documents and programs in a locked drawer.

✔ Turn your computer off at night.

✔ Don't share discs.

> ✔ Don't send confidential documents by e-mail unless you're certain that your system is secure.
>
> ✔ Protect your laptop from theft during travel. In addition to personal diligence, laptop security devices (locks and cables, for example, that are similar to bike locks) are available that can deter theft.

You can also take or recommend additional measures if you think that electronic security is lax. Ask your manager for suggestions. Information security is, after all, her responsibility. Talk to the resident information technology officer about what he does to protect documents and then recommend that everyone follow his example.

Mixing Personal Business and Work

In many businesses, the workday is much less structured than it used to be. Flextime, personal days, home offices, and the conveniences of electronic devices have worked together to make the 9-to-5 workday a thing of the past in some companies. Even companies that have rigid structures offer much more flexibility than before.

Additional flexibility in the workday is a huge change and a real boon. But the flexible workday has introduced some new problems into the business environment and exacerbated some existing ones.

For employees, the line between work time and private time has blurred, and the desire and need to take care of personal business during the workday has become acute in some cases. If you have a lot of autonomy in structuring your day and if you act in a professional manner, mixing private and professional activities isn't likely to cause problems. If you don't have much autonomy or if you allow your personal business to interfere with your real business, you'll end up in a bad situation.

Doing personal business on company time

Many employers allow, and even encourage, employees to take enough time to do short personal errands during the day, so long as they complete their work. If you're the manager, you're responsible for making company policy clear. Some companies offer electronic concierge services that perform personal errands for their employees or arrange for dry cleaning to be picked up at the office or home. These services are a real boon to employees.

The difficulties introduced by children call for sympathetic managers and understanding colleagues. If your colleague leaves work early every Wednesday to take his son to violin practice, that doesn't mean he's getting a perk that you're not. He may have to compensate by working on the Saturday that you spend ballooning in New Mexico. This kind of rearranged workweek is a common feature of the contemporary economic landscape.

The following sections explain how to handle a few personal tasks on company time.

Personal calls

Abusing phone privileges is a recurring employer complaint. Spending two minutes talking to your daughter about her pet mouse is fine; spending half an hour talking to your best friend about your latest round of golf while a deadline is looming isn't. Keep personal conversations short and to the point, especially if you're in a cubicle. Avoid having screaming arguments with your spouse.

E-mails

Your work e-mail account is for work-related e-mails. If you want to join chat rooms or dating services, do so from some other computer (such as the one you have at home). Also, refrain from sending racy or highly critical (or flaming) e-mails on your business computer.

Your e-mail is company property and may be monitored. If your boss finds questionable e-mail, she may have grounds to discipline or dismiss you.

Computer games

Some people are addicted to computer games. This includes some professional adults, and this fondness can impinge on work. Don't let yourself get bug-eyed and irritable when you realize that you've been playing for two hours and that the Webding report is due this afternoon. Remove the games from your work computer and put them where they belong — at home.

Web browsing

In the past ten years, employers have lost untold work hours to employees' Web browsing. No doubt, looking at the Himalayan Adventure Outfitters Web site will get you stoked for your next climb in Nepal, but this site probably can wait until you get home.

At work, confine your Web browsing to the personal time that you're given. Managers bear responsibility for letting employees know the expectations. If it's okay with you for an employee to watch a Sam Donaldson Webcast on his break, by all means say so. But also say that when break time is over, he needs to get back to work.

Stay away from porn sites while you're at work, regardless of whether you're on personal time (lunch or coffee break, for example). If you get caught looking at them, you'll be in big trouble, and chances are increasingly good that you will be caught. Employers everywhere are installing software that tracks the Web sites visited by employees. Is getting a cheap thrill really worth a dressing-down from your boss? Is it worth your job? Probably not.

Separating personal space and business space

One consequence of the additional flexibility in the workday is that the line between personal space and professional space is fuzzier now than it has ever been. There's no doubt about it — the new casualness has caused more than a few privacy problems.

Keeping your personal life personal

Taking care of too much personal business on company time is a bad idea. You also have to be careful about involving your business colleagues in your personal life.

No specific rule governs how much of your personal life to reveal to your colleagues and your employer. You can divulge it all if you're comfortable doing so. But remember that some people would rather not know about your latest Atlantic City escapade. Most people are better off not knowing how much you hate your ex-wife. Also, what you divulge today could come back to haunt you tomorrow.

Keep in mind that your lifestyle can become relevant to your employer if that lifestyle has a negative impact on your performance. If you publicize your long tradition of leaving work and getting drunk every Friday while you're still in uniform, you could be called into your boss's office to hear a lecture on the virtues of sobriety and the importance of being a good company representative at all times.

Some personal issues probably are best kept from colleagues and supervisors. Your family's health history, for example, is nobody's business at the office. If you are rash enough to tell someone that the men in your family have a history of prostate cancer, you shouldn't be surprised when the human resources person asks you about it one day while she's filling out an insurance questionnaire. And if you're vain enough to tell your supervisor that your uncle is Bill Gates, you shouldn't be shocked when he tells you that he has a great idea for Microsoft; he just needs your help setting up a quick interview with your uncle.

Keeping your professional life professional

Just as keeping some of your private life away from the office is wise, keeping some of your professional life away from your private life is also wise. Your romantic partner doesn't need to know everything about petty office politics to know that you're stressed in your job. And if you have business information that you can tell your friends or your romantic partner only by violating client confidentiality or company policy, you're obligated not to tell.

Not telling your closest friends or your romantic partner something can be very hard. Psychiatrists, physicians, and lawyers face this dilemma on a regular basis. A sympathetic friend or romantic partner will acknowledge the difficulties entailed by professional codes of conduct and won't pry. Pressing for personal information from someone who's bound to professional confidentiality may cause the end of the relationship.

Violating client confidentiality is grounds for dismissal in some professions and grounds for expulsion from some professional organizations.

Drawing the line between the personal and the professional

Not only are there things about you that your colleagues don't need to know, but there also are some things about you that no one at your workplace has any right to know. Your political views, for example, are irrelevant in the vast majority of business situations. So are your religious beliefs, your ethnic background, your family's lifestyle, your sexual orientation, and your hobbies. And although your moral values may be pertinent, try to keep the dogmatic elements out of your workday environment.

Here's some advice to keep in mind:

- ✔ No one at work is entitled to know everything about you. If someone asks you to reveal a private matter, just say, "I prefer to keep my private life private, thank you."

- ✔ If someone persists in asking impertinent questions despite your repeated refusal to answer them, report the matter to a supervisor.

- ✔ If your supervisor is the one who won't let up on the impertinent questions, report the matter to her supervisor.

Billing the Company for Expenses

Your company may ask you to travel. You may incur expenses while doing the company's work on your travels, of course, and you may ask the company to compensate you for those expenses.

If you're a manager, you're responsible for educating yourself about your company's expense-report policies. If your company doesn't allow gifts or alcohol charges as expenses, for example, inform your employees of that rule before they travel. If exceptions arise, employees need to know what those exceptions are. Suppose that one of your sales representatives stays at a friend's apartment when she travels to New York for a convention, saving the company $280 a night for five nights. Can she claim as an expense the $20 bottle of wine that she gave her hosts? How about the cost of the taxi rides between her friend's apartment and the convention site, the taxi ride back from the Broadway play to which she took a client, or the ticket for that play? Make the rules clear.

When you're doing the company's work and spending money as an employee, you may ask the company to reimburse you, but when you're not doing the company's work or not spending money as an employee, you may not ask to be reimbursed. Always confirm with your boss and CFO what will and won't be allowable expenses before the trip. Keep these tips in mind:

✔ Clarify acceptable and unacceptable expenses before going on your trip.

✔ Most companies appreciate any reasonable ways to cut costs.

✔ Keep expense-report receipts safely together. Use a credit card rather than cash so you have an additional record on your credit card statement.

✔ When you fill out your expense report, attach all the receipts for money spent while you were on company time.

If you host a business dinner while traveling, you usually can include that in your expense report. If you work for a company that doesn't compensate for alcohol, not even wine at dinner, try to separate the alcohol portion of the bill from the meal portion. If you can't do that, compute the amount spent for the meal and the proportion of the tip that went to the waiter for the meal, and submit only that expense.

Don't pad your expense reports. If you rent a car for a business trip and add three days to the trip for a little sightseeing, you aren't entitled to charge the company for those three days. If you buy your daughter a gift at the airport gift shop, you aren't entitled to charge the company for it. Smart accountants have seen most of these tricks before, and you're unlikely to get away with them. But the heart of the matter is that padding your expense report is unfair to the company. Even if the company isn't always fair to you, ethics do not allow you to be unfair in return.

Saying "No" and Keeping Your Job

Some ethical dilemmas come not from your taking advantage of your employer, but from your employer taking advantage of you. These problems are tough because you're no longer in control. If you routinely browse the Web while you're at work, you can change that situation. But if the owner of the company asks you to falsify employee records to avoid paying Social Security taxes, you're no longer in control. Not only is the request unethical, but it's also combined with the implicit threat that if you won't do it, you won't have a job.

This situation is a classic professional dilemma. Millions of workers face variations on it every year. Your success or failure in dealing with situations like this depends more on your tact, diplomacy, and good manners than on anything else.

First, try to defuse the situation by giving the other person the option of retracting the request or demand. Try one of the following methods:

- ✔ Repeat the request. Say, "Let me make sure that I heard you correctly. You would like me to misreport our earnings this quarter. Is that correct?"
- ✔ Give the other person a blank stare.
- ✔ Say nothing.
- ✔ Say, "I'm not sure I heard that."
- ✔ Say, "I'm sorry. Let's look for another solution."
- ✔ Say, "Excuse me a minute. I'm going to go for a drink of water. When I get back, we can start over."

The aim of all these maneuvers is to get the person who's making the improper request to think twice and retract that request.

These techniques won't always work. You may face a choice: Go along with the unethical request and compromise yourself in the process or refuse to go along with it and face the consequences.

Refusing an unethical request from another employee is almost always in your self-interest and in the interest of your company.

If you stand by your refusal, no doubt you will face some criticism and some discrimination from the person who made the request or demand. He may brand you as being disloyal or not a team player. Let him do so. Others will notice when you're being persecuted for no apparent reason, and more often than not, they'll guess what happened.

Continuing your ethics education

You could face lots of other ethical dilemmas at work that aren't covered in this chapter. A few excellent resources are available for understanding the difficulties you face in your job:

✔ *The Bully at Work,* by Gary Namie, PhD, and Ruth Namie, PhD (Sourcebooks)

✔ *Ethics at Work,* by Alice Darnell Lattal, PhD, and Ralph W. Clark, PhD (Performance Management Publications)

✔ *Honest Work: A Business Ethics Reader,* by Joanne B. Ciulla, Clancy Martin, and Robert C. Solomon (Oxford University Press, USA)

✔ *How Good People Make Tough Choices: Resolving the Dilemmas of Ethical Living,* by Rushworth M. Kidder (Harper Paperbacks)

You may lose your job. That outcome is unlikely, but it does happen. Most of the time, the only result will be that the other person tries to get someone else to go along. Maybe he'll find a co-conspirator; maybe he won't. But you won't be going along for the long tumble out of the company that he's likely to take when his shenanigans are discovered — as they probably will be.

Chapter 8

When Worlds Collide: Managing Change on the Job

*N*othing stays the same, in business or in life. Change is all around us — it always has been, and it always will be. But though many people consider change something to be feared and avoided at any cost, the reality is that change brings with it excitement, new opportunities, and growth.

So what does change mean to you? The world of business is constantly changing, and the pressures to perform are greater than they've ever been before. Companies are downsizing, rebadging, outsourcing, offshoring, getting bought out — or simply shutting down. And change isn't just impacting you; it's impacting your friends, family, and colleagues. Business change brings with it plenty of stress because you never know when it will happen or who will be affected.

The words *business* and *change* are quickly becoming synonymous. And the more things change, the more everyone in an organization is affected. This chapter is about handling and thriving on change, and, if you're a manager, about helping your employees find ways to take advantage of this change (instead of change taking advantage of them!).

Handling Urgency (As You Must) and Avoiding Crises (When You Can)

What's your typical business day like? You get into the office, grab a cup of coffee, and scan your calendar. Looks like a light day for meetings. Maybe you can finally get a chance to work on the budget goal you've been meaning to complete for the past few months. Next, you check your voice mail. Of the 25 messages that have stacked up since you last checked, 15 are about problems in the new procedure for filing expense reports, and 10 are urgent. When you check your e-mail, you find much the same ratio.

As you begin to think how you can respond to these urgent messages, an employee arrives with his own crisis that needs your immediate attention — the new computer network has broken down, and until someone fixes it, the entire corporate financial system is on the fritz. While you're talking to your employee, your boss calls to tell you to drop everything because you've been selected to write a status report for the president that absolutely has to be done by the close of business today. You begin to panic. You don't even understand the new procedures or network yourself; how can you be expected to handle all this? And so much for working on your budget goal — you're *never* going to get to it!

The frenetic pace of change in the world today trickles down into your day-to-day life in the form of large-scale adjustments (when your company installs a new network and you must rely on a correctly operating system to get work done) and small-scale alterations (when your regular work takes a back burner to the president's report, which he needs immediately to keep ahead of the competition). Constant change means that new tasks and new problems are part of the workplace, and dealing with them quickly is crucial. However, you need to make sure that you're handling scenarios appropriately, not succumbing to panic when something new and unexpected crops up.

Choosing between legitimate urgency and crisis management

Urgency has its place in an organization. The rate of change in the global business environment demands it. The revolutions in computer use, telecommunications systems, and information technology demand it. Customers' higher standards demand it. In these urgent times, companies that provide the best solutions faster than anyone else are the winners. The losers are the companies that wonder what happened as they watch their competitors streak by.

However, an organization has a real problem when its managers fall into the behavior of managing by crisis and the trap of reacting to change instead of leading change. When every problem in an organization becomes a drop-everything-else-that-you-are-doing crisis, the organization isn't showing signs of responsiveness to its business environment. Instead, the business is showing signs of poor planning and lousy execution. Someone (perhaps a manager?) isn't doing his or her job.

Recognizing and dealing with crises

Sometimes outside forces beyond your control cause crises. For example, suppose that a vital customer requests that all project designs be submitted by this Friday instead of next Friday. Or perhaps the city sends a notice that a maintenance crew plans to cut off the power to your plant for three days while the crew performs maintenance on switching equipment. Or a snowstorm in the Northeast cuts off all flights, in and out, for the rest of the week.

On the other hand, many crises occur because someone in your organization drops the ball, and you have to repair the damage. The following are avoidable crisis situations:

- ✔ Hoping that the problem will go away, you avoid making a necessary decision. Surprise! The problem didn't go away, and now you have a crisis to deal with.

- ✔ Someone forgets to relay an important message from your customer, and you're about to lose the account as a result. Another crisis.

- ✔ A co-worker decides that informing you about a major change to a manufacturing process isn't important. Because of your experience, you would have quickly seen that the change would lead to quality problems in the finished product. When manufacturing grinds to a halt, you come in after the fact to clean up the mess. One more crisis to add to your list.

You have to be prepared to deal with externally generated crises. You have to be flexible, you have to work smart, and you have to work hard. But your organization can't afford to become a slave to internally generated crises. Managing by crisis forgoes one of the most important elements in business management: *planning*.

You establish plans and goals for a reason — to make your company as successful as possible. However, if you continually set your plans and goals on a back burner because of today's crisis, why waste your time making the plans? And where does your organization go then? (See Book I, Chapter 3 for a discussion on the importance of having plans and goals.)

Changing bosses

It has long been known that the one person who has the most impact and influence on an employee is his or her supervisor or manager. This relationship is a very important one in any organization, and it can take months or even years for a strong relationship and trust to develop. So what happens when your boss changes? This chapter discusses change that occurs in organizations for a variety of different reasons, and probably the most frequent change that employees come across is when the managers or bosses change. You may be assigned to a new department or promoted into a new position, or your boss may be replaced with someone new. Regardless of the reason for the change, the outcome can be disconcerting and stressful.

If your supervisor or boss changes, consider doing the following things to help ease the transition:

✔ **Be open to the change.** You may not be happy that your boss has changed, but being unhappy about it isn't going to benefit you in any way. The best course of action is to quickly accept that the change has happened and move forward instead of looking back.

✔ **Build a relationship.** Business is all about relationships, and the relationship you build with your supervisor or manager is the most important one in your workplace. While you don't want to go overboard and push yourself on your new boss, you should do what you can to move the relationship forward at a consistent but natural pace.

✔ **Be patient.** It may have taken you years to build a good relationship with your previous boss, and it make take you months or even years to build a good relationship with your new boss. Be patient, and allow yourselves time for a relationship to develop and strengthen.

✔ **Take initiative.** If you want your boss to notice you and to value your contributions to the organization, offer to do special projects for your boss, and then deliver great results — ahead of schedule if possible. The more you can offer your boss, the more he or she will come to depend on you.

When you, as a manager, allow everything to become a crisis through your own inaction or failure to anticipate change, not only do you sap the energy of your employees, but you also eventually rob them of the ability to recognize when a real crisis is upon them. Remember the old fable about the boy who cried "Wolf"? After the boy issued several false alarms in jest, the villagers didn't bother to respond to his cries when some wolves really appeared to attack his sheep. After responding to several manufactured crises, your employees begin to see the crises as routine, and they may not be there for you when you really need them.

Embracing the Inevitable: Change Happens

Change happens, and you can't do anything about it. You can try to ignore it, but does that stop change? No, you only blind yourself to what is really happening in your organization. You can try to stop it, but does that keep change from happening? No, you're only fooling yourself if you think that you can stop change — even for a moment. You can try to insulate yourself from the effects of change, but can you really afford to ignore it? No, to ignore change is to sign a death warrant for your organization and, quite possibly, for your career.

Unfortunately, most people seem to spend their entire careers trying to fight change — to predict, control, and harness change and its effects on the orga- nization. But why? Change is what allows organizations to progress, products to get better, and people to advance — both personally and in their careers.

Identifying the four stages of change

Change is not a picnic. Despite the excitement that change can bring to your working life — both good and bad — you've probably had just about all the change you can handle right about now, thank you. But as change continues, you go through four distinct phases in response to change:

1. **Deny change.** When change happens, the first response you have (if you're like most people) is one of immediate denial. "Whose dumb idea was that? That idea is never going to work here. Don't worry, they'll see their mistake and go back to the old way of doing things!" Operating with this attitude is like an ostrich sticking its head in the sand: If you can't see it, it'll go away. Right? You wish!

2. **Resist change.** At some point, you realize that the change isn't just a clerical error; however, this realization doesn't mean that you have to accept the change lying down! "Nope, I'm sticking with the old way of doing that job. If that way was good enough then, why isn't it good enough now?" Resistance is a normal response to change — everyone goes through it. The key isn't to let your resistance get you stuck. The quicker you get with the program, the better for your organization and the better for your career.

3. **Explore change.** By now, you know that further resistance is futile and the new way just may have some pluses. "Well, maybe that change actu- ally does make sense. I'll see what opportunities can make the change work for me instead of against me." During this stage, you examine both the good and bad that come from the change, and you decide on a strat- egy for managing the change.

4. **Accept change.** The final stage of change is acceptance. At this point, you have successfully integrated the change into your routine. "Wow, this new system works well. It beats the heck out of the old way of doing things!" Now, the change that you so vigorously denied and resisted is part of your everyday routine; the change is now the status quo.

At the end of your change responses, you come full circle, and you're ready to face your next change.

Are you fighting change?

You may be fighting change and not even know it. Besides watching the number of gray hairs on your head multiply, how can you tell? Look out for the following seven deadly warning signs of resistance to change. If you notice any of these warning signs— in yourself or in your co-workers — you can do something about it. As long as you're willing to embrace change instead of fight it, you hold incredible value for your organization, and you can take advantage of change rather than fall victim to it. Make responsiveness to change your personal mission: Be a leader of change, not a follower of resistance.

You're still using the old rules to play a new game

Sorry to be the ones to bring you this bad news, but the old game is gone, kaput. The pressures of global competition have created a brand new game with a brand new set of rules. For example, if you're one of those increasingly rare employees who refuses to find out how to use a computer (don't laugh, they do exist!), you're playing by the old rules. Computer literacy and information proficiency is the new rule. If you're not playing with the new rules, not only is this a warning sign that you're resisting change, but you can bet on being left behind as the rest of your organization moves along the path to the future.

You're ducking new assignments

Usually, two basic reasons cause you to avoid new assignments. First, you may be overwhelmed with your current job and can't imagine taking on any more duties. If you're in this situation, try to remember that new ways often make your work more efficient or even wipe out many things that you do. Second, you may be uneasy with the unknown, and so you resist change.

Ducking new assignments to resist change is a definite no-no. Not only are you interfering with the progress of the organization, but you're also effectively putting your own career on hold.

You're trying to slow things down

Trying to slow down is a normal reaction for most people. When something new comes along — a new way of doing business, a new assignment, or a new wrinkle in the marketplace — most people tend to want to slow down, to take

Book V

Navigating
Tricky
Workplace
Relation-
ships and
Situations

the time to examine, analyze, and then decide how to react. The problem is that the newer something gets, the slower some people go.

If you want to remain competitive in the future, you don't have the luxury of slowing down every time something new comes along. From now on, the amount of new that you have to deal with is going to greatly outweigh the old. Instead of resisting the new by slowing down (and risking an uncompetitive and obsolete organization), you need to keep up your pace. How? When you're forced to do more with less, focus on less.

You're working hard to control the uncontrollable

Have you ever tried to keep the sun from rising in the morning? Or tried to stop the weather during a storm, or the waves in the ocean? Or tried to stay 29 years old forever? Face it: You just can't control many things in life — you waste your time when you try.

Are you resisting change by trying to control the uncontrollable at work? Perhaps you want to try to head off a planned corporate reorganization or stop your foreign competitors from having access to your domestic markets or delay the acquisition of your firm by a much larger company. You have a choice: You can continue to resist change by pretending that you're controlling it (which is a futile effort), or you can concentrate your efforts on figuring out how to most effectively respond to change to leverage it to your advantage.

You're playing the role of victim

Oh, woe is me! This response is the ultimate cop-out. Instead of accepting change and finding out how to respond to it (and using it to the advantage of your organization and yourself), you choose to become a victim of it. Playing the role of victim and hoping that your co-workers feel sorry for you is easy to do. ("Poor Samantha, she has a brand-new crop of upstart competitors to handle. I wonder how she can bring herself to come to work every morning!")

Today's successful businesses can't afford to waste their time or money employing victims. If you're not giving 110 percent each day that you go to work, your organization will find someone who can.

You're hoping someone else can make things better for you

In the old-style hierarchical organization, top management almost always took responsibility for making the decisions that made things better (or worse) for workers. News flash: The old-style organization is changing, and the new-style organization taking its place has empowered every employee to take responsibility for decision making.

The pressures of global competition and the coming of the Information Age require that decisions be made quicker than ever. In other words, the employees closest to the issues must make the decisions; a manager who is seven layers up from the front line and 3,000 miles away can't do it. You hold the keys to your future. You have the power to make things better for yourself. If you wait until someone else makes things better for you, then you're going to be waiting an awfully long time.

You're absolutely paralyzed, like a deer in the headlights

This condition is the ultimate sign of resistance to change and is almost always terminal. Sometimes change seems so overwhelming that the only choice is to give up. When change paralyzes you, not only do you fail to respond to change, but you also can no longer perform your current duties. In today's organization, such resistance is certain death.

Instead of allowing change to paralyze you, become a leader of change. Here are some ideas how:

- ✔ Embrace the change. Become its friend and its biggest cheerleader.
- ✔ Be flexible and be responsive to the changes that swirl all around you and through your organization.
- ✔ Be a model to those around you who continue to resist change. Show them that they can make change work for them instead of against them.
- ✔ Focus on what you can do — not what you can't do.
- ✔ If you're a manager, recognize and reward employees who have accepted the change and succeeded as a result.

Helping Your Employees Manage Change

Managers, when your organization finds itself in the midst of change — whether because of fast-moving markets, changing technology, rapidly shifting customer needs, or some other reason — you need to remember that change affects everyone. And although some of your employees can cope with these changes with nary a hiccup, others may have a very difficult time adjusting to their new environment and the expectations that come along with it. Be on the alert for employees who are resisting or having a hard time dealing with change and then help them transition through the process.

Opening up the lines of communication

The following tips on communicating and interacting with your employees can help them cope with change on the job:

- ✔ **Show that you care.** Managers are very busy people, but never be too busy to show your employees that you care — especially when they're having difficulties on the job. Take a personal interest in your employees and offer to help them in any way you can.

Book V

Navigating
Tricky
Workplace
Relation-
ships and
Situations

✔ **Widely communicate the potential for change.** Nothing is more disconcerting to employees than being surprised by changes that they didn't
expect. As much as possible, give your employees a heads-up on potential changes in the business environment and keep them up-to-date on
the status of the changes as time goes on.

✔ **Seek feedback.** Let your employees know that you want their feedback
and suggestions on how to deal with potential problems resulting from
change or how to capitalize on any opportunities that may result.

✔ **Be a good listener.** When your employees are in a stressful situation,
they naturally are going to want to talk about it — this part of the process helps them cope with change. Set aside time to chat informally
with employees, and encourage them to voice their concerns about the
changes that they and the organization are going through. For information on listening effectively, refer to Book IV, Chapter 2.

✔ **Don't give false assurances.** Although you don't want to needlessly
frighten your employees with tales of impending doom and gloom, also
avoid sugarcoating the truth. Be frank and honest with your employees
and treat them like the adults they are. Book IV, Chapter 3 offers pointers on sharing not-so-pleasant news.

✔ **Involve employees.** Involve employees in planning for upcoming
changes and delegate the responsibility and authority for making decisions to them whenever practicable.

✔ **Look to the future.** Paint a vision for your employees that emphasizes
the many ways that the organization will be a better place as everyone
adapts to change and begins to use it to their benefit.

Change can be traumatic for those people who go through it. Stay alert to the
impact of change on your employees and help them work their way through
it. Your employees will appreciate your support — and show their appreciation with loyalty to you and your organization — and their morale will
improve, resulting in more productive employees.

Encouraging employee initiative

One of the most effective ways to help employees make it through the change
process in one piece is to give them permission to take charge of their own
work. You can encourage your employees to take the initiative to come up
with ideas to improve the way they do their work, and then to implement
those ideas.

The most successful organizations are the ones that actively encourage
employees to take initiative, and the least successful ones are those organizations that stifle initiative.

Consider how these companies reward employee initiative:

- Federal Express, based in Memphis, Tennessee, awards the Golden Falcon to employees who go above and beyond to serve their customers. For example, one winner took the initiative to order new shipping forms for a regular customer after noticing that the customer had not thought to change his area code on a return address.

- At least one All-Star is chosen monthly at each D'Agostino supermarket location. The chain, based in Larchmont, New York, chooses winners based on employees who go "beyond the call of duty" to help co-workers or customers.

- At El Torito Restaurants, based in Irvine, California, employees receive a "Be a Star" award for going above and beyond their job description. Winners receive Star Bucks, which are entered for a monthly drawing for up to $1,000 worth of merchandise.

As a manager, you need to make your employees safe to take initiative in their jobs. Not only will your employees better weather the change that swirls all around them, but they also will create a more effective organization and provide better service to customers in the process. Ask your employees to take the following suggestions and put them to use:

- Look for ways to make improvements to the status quo and follow through with an action plan.

- Focus suggestions on areas that have the greatest impact on the organization.

- Follow up suggestions with action. Volunteer to help implement your suggestions.

- Step outside of your box. Look for areas of improvement throughout the organization, not just within your department or business unit.

- Don't make frivolous suggestions. They degrade your credibility and distract you from more important areas of improvement.

Keeping spirits high

When a company is downsizing or going through other dramatic changes, employee morale may plummet. Not only is there much uncertainty in the air, but employees may be required to pick up the slack when employees are laid off or reassigned — getting paid the same amount of money (or less) to do more work. Keeping employee morale and loyalty high is critically important during times of change. Here are a few tips for doing just that.

✔ **Have fun.** Don't allow your office to become a morgue, with everyone walking around like zombies. Have a costume contest with employee judges or sponsor an impromptu ice cream social. Telecommunications giant Sprint once turned a regular workday into Beach Day at their Kansas City headquarters. The parking lot was turned into a beach — sand was trucked in, and sunglasses, plastic leis, and live music were provided to the "vacationing" employees.

✔ **Be honest.** Don't sugarcoat the truth — employees don't like it, and they'll lose respect for those who aren't giving them the straight scoop. If a change in your business is going to impact them — whether in a good or a bad way — tell them sooner rather than later.

✔ **Put people first.** Don't forget that it's your *employees* who make your business what it is. When you make employees number one on your list of priorities, they will pay you back many times over in increased loyalty, perseverance, and quality of work. Show your employees that they're important by always putting them and their concerns at the top of your list.

✔ **Set a good example.** When you set a positive example for your employees, then they will naturally follow. Don't wait for others to make the first move — be a leader of change and inspire your employees to give their all to the cause, whatever it may be.

Exploring Alternatives When All Else Fails

If you've done everything you can to deal with change at work and take control of your business life but you're still feeling lost, you may be facing a much deeper issue that's not readily apparent on the surface.

Pursuing your dream

When you read a book, do you ever wish that you had written it? When you go to a seminar, do you ever think that you could teach it? Have you ever wondered what owning your own business is like — being your own boss, completely responsible for your company's profits or losses?

If you answered yes to any of these questions, you may not be truly happy until you pursue your dream. Maybe you want to start a new career or move to a new company. Or perhaps you have an opportunity with your current employer to make a job change that can take you to your dream. Maybe you want to go back to school to pursue an advanced degree. Or maybe you just want to take a vacation or short leave of absence. It may very well be that all the change you need to make is within yourself.

Looking for employment elsewhere

If you do decide that a new job or career is the change that you need, then by all means start looking for a new job — or perhaps even start your own business. But as you do so, be sure to keep the following advice in mind:

- **Remain professional at your current job while you look for another.** Your employer is still paying you an honest day's wages (we hope!), so you should still provide an honest day's work. Do not — repeat, do not — use your office as a personal placement center for your next job. Keep your focus on your current employer, not your next employer.

- **Don't burn bridges.** You may be frustrated. You may be mad. You may be hurt. Even so, do not destroy your work relationships, thinking it won't matter once you leave. It *does* matter. Not only do you need good references from your current employer, but you never know when you might do business again — and need their help. The more people in your personal network the better.

- **Be careful what you say and to whom you say it.** Keep your mouth shut when it comes to sharing your new job plans with others at work. Once you've told one person, you can probably assume that everyone is going to find out about your plans — including your boss. Sometimes, when managers get wind that an employee is about to leave, they will fire him or make his work life miserable. Why should they keep someone around who isn't loyal and dedicated to the company, after all?

Regardless, if you need to go, then you need to go. Just focus on your goal, keep giving the best work you can to your current employer, and don't hesitate to grab the gold ring when it's within your reach.

Book VI
Managing Stress in Stressful Times

The 5th Wave   By Rich Tennant

IN ATTEMPTING TO MEET QUARTERLY PROJECTIONS, MANY COMPANIES USE THE LAMAZE METHOD OF ACCOUNTING

© RICHTENNANT

Breathe, Morris, breathe!

In this book . . .

Are you feeling more tired at work lately than you used to? Is your fuse a little shorter than normal? Are you worrying more about your job? Enjoying life less? If you feel more stress in your life these days, you aren't alone. Count yourself among the ranks of the over-stressed. Your stress may come from your job, your personal life, or simply from not having enough time to do everything you have to do — or want to do — but no matter the source, it negatively affects your performance in the workplace if you don't take care of it.

Thankfully, with a little guidance you can eliminate or certainly minimize much of the stress in your life and manage the stress that remains. This book helps you get started in the right direction. These chapters walk you through some de-stressing exercises for the body and mind and help you find ways to keep negative thoughts at bay, no matter what stress surrounds you.

Chapter 1

De-Stress at Work (And Still Keep Your Job)

· ·

In This Chapter

▶ Recognizing your work stress

▶ Building stress-management into your workday

▶ Creating a stress-resistant workspace

▶ Coming home more relaxed

· ·

*I*f you feel that your job is stressful, don't think you're alone. Ask a variety of people where most of their stress comes from; chances are that the answer will be "my job." The specific source of work stress can be impossible clients, a terrible boss, dreadful co-workers, ridiculous deadlines, nasty office gossip, or not having seen daylight or your firstborn child in the last two months. So before you do something you may regret later, like scream at a customer who can't be satisfied or blow off steam in a nasty letter to your CEO, read this chapter to find out how to regroup, get a grip, and minimize your stress at work.

Identifying Work-Related Stressors

Some people thrive on the adrenaline rush they get from diving into the challenges they face at work. But if you're not stimulated and feel that you're drowning instead, then work stress may be the problem. Recognizing that work is causing you stress and pinpointing the cause are the first two steps toward easing that mental burden.

Stress stats

If you're stressed out at work, you're in good company. Consider these findings of a 2004 survey by the American Psychological Association:

✔ 62 percent of Americans say work has a significant impact on stress levels.

✔ A majority of workers (52 percent) are more stressed because of work than home.

✔ 54 percent of workers are concerned about health problems caused by stress.

✔ 45 percent workers list job insecurity as a significant impact on work stress levels.

✔ 61 percent of workers list heavy workloads as a significant impact on work stress levels.

✔ Executives and managers tend to have the most stressful jobs, while self-employed workers are the least stressed.

✔ One in four workers has taken a mental health day off from work to cope with stress.

Recognize signs that you're stressed at work

See if you recognize the signs of work stress — check off the symptoms that describe you while you're at work:

____ You're often irritable.

____ You have trouble concentrating.

____ You're tired.

____ You've lost much of your sense of humor.

____ You get into more arguments than you used to.

____ You get less done.

____ You get sick more often.

____ You care less about your work.

____ Getting out of bed on a workday morning is a major effort.

____ You have less interest in your life outside of work.

Any one or two of these symptoms by themselves may not mean that you're overly stressed. However, if several of these signs or symptoms are present and they last for longer than a day or two, excessive stress may be the cause.

Know what's triggering your work stress

All right, so you're stressed at work. One of the key steps in managing your work stress is knowing where the stress comes from. Check off any of the items below that you feel are a major source of your stress:

_____ Work overload (too much to do)

_____ Work underload (too little to do)

_____ Too much responsibility

_____ Too little responsibility

_____ Dissatisfaction with current role or duties

_____ Poor work environment (noise, isolation, danger, and so on)

_____ Long hours

_____ Lack of positive feedback or recognition

_____ Fear of your job being outsourced

_____ Fear of cutbacks and job loss

_____ A doubled workload because of layoffs

_____ Lousy pay

_____ Excessive travel

_____ Limited chances for promotion

_____ Prejudice because of sex, race, or religion

_____ Problems with the boss or management

_____ Problems with clients

_____ Problems with co-workers or staff

_____ Office politics

_____ A grueling commute

You have others? Jot them down:

_____

_____

_____

Researcher Robert Karasek and his colleagues at the University of Southern California found that the two most stressful aspects of a job are

- **Lots of pressure to perform.** Tight deadlines, limited resources, productions quotas, severe consequences for failing to meet management's goals — any or all of these can result in a highly pressured work environment.

- **A lack of control over the work process.** Stress often results when you have little or no input regarding how your job should be done.

Pinpoint your stress triggers at work and then ask yourself to what extent you can remove or at least reduce the impact of that stress. In some cases, you don't have the ability to eliminate some of the sources of stress at work: Getting the boss transferred may take some doing, and asking for a raise the day after the company announces downsizing plans may not be in your best interest. What you can change, however, is *you*. You can manage your stress and reduce its consequences by applying some of the ideas in the following sections.

Starting Your Day Unstressed: What You Can Do before Work

Getting to your job in reasonable condition is half the battle against workplace stress. You don't want to feel as if you've already fought and lost several of life's minor skirmishes by the time you walk in the door. Get a leg up on your work stress. Hit the ground running. The following sections tell you how.

Change your bedtime habits

Not getting enough sleep the night before can be a real stress-producer. Your stress threshold is lowered. You find that you're more irritable and find it much harder to concentrate. People and situations that normally wouldn't get to you now do. Arriving at work tired is a guarantee that this isn't going to be one of your better stress days.

Similarly, getting out of bed even a few minutes earlier in the morning can give you enough of a safety net that you don't find yourself rushing, looking for something at the last minute, and racing out the door with a powdered donut in your hand.

Stop feeding your stress

Are you an emotional eater? If so, you may eat whenever you are anxious, upset, nervous, or depressed. Although emotional eaters can still put it away when they're happy, delighted, non-anxious, and nondepressed (and yes, during those rare times when they're actually hungry), most emotional eaters eat when they feel they need to feed their stress.

When you feed your stress, a destructive cycle begins. You feel stressed, so your food choices are not always the best. For some reason of cruel fate, foods that tend to make you feel good are usually the foods that are not so good for your body. Chocolate, ice cream, pizza, cake, donuts, and cookies may make you feel terrific — but, unfortunately, only for about 17 seconds. Then, of course, your stress returns (plus a ton of guilt) and you feel the need for another bout of eating. The cycle then repeats itself.

Don't skip breakfast

To manage your stress, getting off on the right nutritional foot is important. When you wake up in the morning, as many as 11 or 12 hours have passed since you last ate. Your body needs to refuel. You may feel fine skipping breakfast, but studies show that people who don't eat a reasonable breakfast more often report feelings of fatigue and more stress later in the day.

Following are some specific food guidelines that can help you choose foods to lower your stress as well as help your body cope with all the stress in your life. Keep these tips in mind as you think about what to have for breakfast:

- **Include some complex carbohydrates in every meal.** _Complex carbohydrates,_ such as pasta, cereals, potatoes, and brown rice, can enhance your performance when under stress. Foods rich in carbohydrates can increase the levels of serotonin in the brain, making you feel better.

- **Reduce your intake of simple carbohydrates.** _Simple carbohydrates_ like soda and candy can make you feel better in the short run but feel worse in the long run.

- **Eat adequate amounts of protein.** This means eating more fish, chicken, and other lean meats. Foods high in protein enhance mental functioning and supply essential amino acids that can help repair damage to your body's cells.

- **Eat your vegetables.** Beans, peppers, carrots, squash, and dark-green leafy veggies, whether cooked or raw, provide your body with the vitamins and nutrients it needs to resist the negative effects of stress.

- **Get plenty of potassium.** Milk (especially the low-fat variety), whole grains, wheat germ, and nuts all can provide your body with potassium, a mineral that can help your muscles relax. Bananas are also a good source of potassium.

Get some physical exercise

If you can manage it, getting some physical exercise before your workday starts can put you ahead of the game. Hitting the stationary bike, working the stair climber, or even walking briskly around the block can throw you into gear and get you ready for your day. Studies show that even short periods of exercise can speed up your heart rate, increase the amount of oxygen to your brain, and release endorphins, which can exert a calming effect. You're ready for anything your job might throw at you.

Calm your commute

Far from fun, commuting can be a major stressor. Following are some tips to help you reduce the stress of coming from and going to work:

- **Practice some "auto" relaxation.** Try this simple technique while you are caught in traffic or even while stopped for a red light: Using both hands, squeeze the steering wheel with a medium-tight grip. At the same time, tense the muscles in your arms and shoulders, scrunching up your shoulders as if you were trying to have them touch your ears. Hold that tension for about three or four seconds. Release all tension, letting go of any muscle tightness anywhere in your body. Let this feeling of relaxation spread slowly throughout your entire body. Wait a few minutes and do it again.

- **Beat the crowd.** Often, leaving a little earlier or a little later can make a big difference in the quality of your commute. You may get a seat or find that the traffic is less congested, and you may find that what was horrific yesterday becomes a lot more endurable.

- **Amuse yourself.** Commuting can seem like a joyless endeavor. You can, however, make your time in your car (or on the subway, bus, or train) productive, entertaining, or at least pleasant.

A good selection of music can soothe your travel (refer to Chapter 3 of Book VI for musical selections that can be relaxing). Or you can pick and choose from an ever-growing variety of audiobooks that includes most popular novels, poetry, self-help recordings, or collections of short stories. You can even learn another language should you be so inclined.

If you're on public transportation, try daydreaming; take the opportunity to mentally veg and let your mind wander. Or, if you're looking for more socially redeeming diversions, keep some interesting reading material in your pocket or purse whenever you go out. The reading material could be an amusing little paperback or articles in your tear file. (Turn to Book II, Chapter 3 to find out about creating a *tear file,* a collection of material you intend to read when you find time.) You can also turn to an iPod, BlackBerry, or e-book reader for solace.

Overcome SNS (Sunday night stress)

As the weekend winds to an end, many of you may find yourselves dreading Monday morning. The real culprit is Sunday night. In fact, after you get to the office and spent a couple of hours on the job, your stress level lowers. The trick is figuring out how to cope with the night before. Take in these tips:

- ✔ Get to bed a little bit earlier Sunday night. (Many people find that their Sunday night sleep is their worst of the week.)

- ✔ Avoid eating that late-night heartburn special, which is guaranteed to keep you up 'til Wednesday.

- ✔ Plan something relaxing and enjoyable that you can look forward to on Sunday evening — rent a movie, curl up with a good book, take a bubble bath.

- ✔ Try not to schedule something you dislike as the first thing to do on Monday.

- ✔ Plan something you can look forward to on Monday. (How about lunch with a friend?)

Generally, most people feel that Monday is the most stressful day of the week. Studies show that you're more likely to have a stroke or a heart attack on Monday morning than at any other time during the week.

De-Stressing during Your Workday

A day at work is usually a day filled with problems, pressures, and demands, with little time to think about your newfound relaxation skills. Your stress builds, and much of that stress takes the form of tension in your muscles. Drain that tension before it becomes more of a problem by using some of the techniques described in Chapters 2 and 3 of Book VI. This may include trying some relaxed breathing, meditation, imagery, or one of the many other relaxation techniques presented in these chapters.

One of the secrets of effective stress management at work is finding ways to incorporate a variety of stress-reduction techniques into your workday. By using these methods on a regular basis you can catch your stress early — before it has a chance to turn into something painful or worrisome. When can you incorporate these stress-busters? Some potential relaxation opportunities include the following:

- ✔ Every time you turn off your phone

- ✔ When someone leaves your office and closes the door

- ✔ Whenever you find yourself in a boring meeting that doesn't require your participation

Take a look at these surefire strategies to help you nip that stress in the bud.

Collect some mileage points

Get up and walk away from your desk — get some coffee or water, make copies. Walk around a lot, and at lunch be sure to get out of the office and take a quick stroll.

Stand up when you're on the phone — or, at least some of the time you're on the phone — and walk around. This gives your body a chance to use different sets of muscles and interrupts any buildup of tension.

Stretch and reach for the sky

For many of you, your days are characterized by long periods of sitting at a desk or stuck in a cramped work area, punctuated only by trips to the coffee or copy machine. Other folks are on their feet all day. In either case, stretching is a great way of releasing any tension that has accumulated in your muscles. Here are some of the most effective ways of stretching:

The cherry-picker

This stretch works well for shoulders, arms, and your back. Sit in your chair, with feet flat on the floor, or stand in place. Raise both your arms over your head and point your fingers directly toward the ceiling. Now, pretend to reach and pick a cherry on a branch that's just a little higher than your right hand. Stretch that hand an inch or so, and then make a fist. Squeeze for two or three seconds. Relax your hand. Do the same with your left hand. If cherries aren't your thing, consider apples.

The pec stretch and squeeze

This move is good for relieving tightness in your pectoral and deltoid muscles and upper back. Sitting at your desk, or standing up straight, put both of your hands behind your head with your fingers interlaced. Bring your elbows back as far as you can. (See Figure 1-1.) Hold that tension for five to ten seconds, release the tension, and then do it a second and third time. Find various times in your day when you can repeat this stretch.

The leg lift

This stretch relieves tension in your quadriceps (the thighs) and strengthens your abdominal muscles. Sitting in a chair, lift both of your legs straight in front of you. At the same time, flex your feet so that your toes point back toward you. (See Figure 1-2.) Hold that tension for five to ten seconds and then let your feet fall to the floor. Repeat two or three times, and at other points in your day.

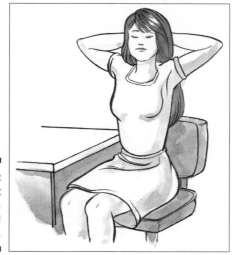

Figure 1-1:
Unwind a bit
with the pec
stretch and
squeeze.

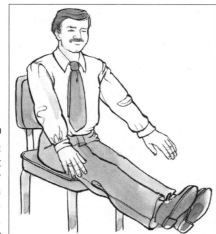

Figure 1-2:
The leg lift
works your
quadriceps
and abdomi-
nal muscles.

The upper-back stretch

This stretch is great for relieving any tension in your upper back. Put your
fingertips on your shoulders, with elbows out to the side. Raise your elbows
until they are in line with your shoulders (see Figure 1-3). Now bring your
elbows forward until they touch or almost touch each other. Hold that position for five to ten seconds, and then let your arms fall comfortably to your
side. Repeat two or three times, and also at different times in your day.

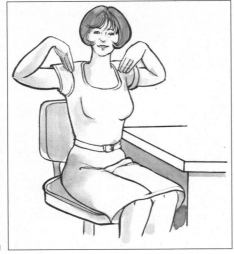

Figure 1-3:
Use some elbow grease to ease tension in your upper back.

If you'd like some more stretching ideas, take a look at *Stretching For Dummies,* by LaReine Chabut (Wiley). It has dozens of great ways you can stretch and release muscle tension.

Create a stress-resistant workspace

You may not be able to control every single aspect of your job, but you do have the power to control your personal work area. Your workspace can (literally) give you a pain in the neck, straining your muscles and tiring your body. The culprit may be an awkwardly placed computer monitor, uncomfortable seating, poor lighting, or simply a totally cluttered desk that's hiding that memo you remember writing and now urgently need. Your life is stressful enough as it is. You don't need your workspace adding to your daily dose of stress. This section shows you a few ways to make your workspace a lot more stress-resistant.

Lights! Sound! Action!

Here are a few ways to take some of the stress out of your workspace. *Note:* Your workplace may not be entirely supportive of all of your stress-reducing efforts. If you share a tiny cubicle with three others, it may be hard for you to burn incense, move in a couch, or install a multispeaker stereo system and personal video player. Nevertheless, see what you can do with some of the following ideas:

✔ **Soothe yourself with sound.** If you can orchestrate it, listening to calming music at your work site can unruffle your feathers. A radio or CD or MP3 player and some appropriate music can be very relaxing. Classical music, especially Bach and Mozart, works nicely. If these composers are too highbrow, try one of the "lite" radio stations. Just keep the volume down or use a headset. Go to Chapter 3, Book VI for some musical suggestions.

Recent studies at the University of California found that listening to Mozart, particularly the piano sonatas, can improve significantly a person's ability to reason abstractly. Not only do stress levels go down, but IQ goes up. On the other hand, listening to Philip Glass or Metallica didn't enhance anything.

Book VI

Managing Stress in Stressful Times

✔ **Lighten up.** Although a naked, 300-watt bulb dangling from your office ceiling can provide you with more than enough light, by the end of the work week you'll be searching for a stool and a rope. The right lighting in your workspace can reduce eyestrain and make your environment a more pleasant place to work. Go for soft and indirect lighting. Just make sure you have enough light.

✔ **Create visual resting spots.** Give your eyes — and your mind — a break. At regular intervals, look away from your computer screen or paperwork and focus on a distant object to "stretch" your eyes. You can also create visual relief to your office by adding a few interesting objects. For example:

  • Strategically place one or more photographs of people you care about to bring a warm glow to your heart. Better yet, have the picture include a scene — a vacation, a gathering — that reminds you of a happy experience.

  • Place a plant or flowers in your workspace to add an air of beauty and relaxation to your workday. Some plants (such as English ivy and spider plants) are even said to help clean the air of indoor pollutants — an added bonus!

  • Hang some artwork that you find calming and peaceful.

✔ **Be scent-sible.** Fill a bowl with green apples to add a relaxing scent to your office.

Here's quick (and inexpensive) suggestion: From time to time, sprinkle a little aftershave or other scent you like on top of the papers in your waste bin. See Chapter 3, Book VI for more tips on soothing away your stress with aromas.

✔ **Have more than one dumbbell in your office.** Keep a set of weights or mini-barbells in your office. In a spare moment or two you can rip through a set of reps and feel a bit more relaxed. Alternately, keep an elastic stretcher in your desk that you can use for both your arms and your legs.

✔ **Keep a toy chest.** What's an office without a few toys? (Balls that knock into each other . . . a game on your computer . . . that peg-jumping triangle game. . . .)

Such toys are great for an occasional diversion when you need a little downtime to distress. If you find that you're using these toys to avoid work, however, get rid of them. You don't need the temptation or distraction!

✔ **Don't get tied down.** A headset that attaches to your telephone, particularly a cordless model, can free you up to lift those weights, stretch, or move around your office.

De-stress your desk

Your desk can cause you stress. Yes, that polished piece of mahogany (laminated particleboard?) can be your enemy. Take this short true or false quiz to see if it's time to de-stress your desk.

1. When new company employees first see your desk, they ask if your office has been vandalized recently. True or false?

2. Your desk smells funny. You distinctly remember leaving half a tuna sandwich under some folders last month, but haven't seen it since. True or false?

3. If you had to find an important memo on your desk in the next hour and your job depended on it, you would be better off spending that time calling a headhunter. True or false?

Answering true to any of the above suggests that too much of your stress may be desk-induced.

Why can a neater desk reduce stress? Well, because the source of many types of stress comes from a feeling of being out of control, of being overwhelmed. When your work area looks like a battlefield, you feel the tension growing. And when you can't find that report you need, your stress level soars even higher. By organizing your files and piles, you get a sense (perhaps mistakenly) that there is some order in all the chaos.

Tennis (ball) anyone?

When you find that your bodily tension is over the top (better yet, try this before you get to that point), pick up a tennis ball or other soft ball, squeeze it for eight to ten seconds, and then slowly release all the tension in your fingers and hand. Let that feeling of relaxation spread out to the rest of your body. Repeat several times throughout the day.

At the end of your workday straighten things up. Doing so takes only a few minutes, but the rewards are large. Check out Book II, Chapters 3 and 6 for some ideas and direction that can help you to eliminate desk and office clutter and give your filing and organizing systems a tune-up.

Become EC (ergonomically correct)

Your desk or workspace can cause stress for other reasons besides disorganization. The problem is that your body was not designed to sit and work in one place for long periods of time. When you sit in a stationary position for long periods of time, your muscle groups contract. The blood flow to these muscles may become reduced, resulting in oxygen-deprived muscles. This can lead to pain, strain, muscle aches, and fatigue.

Book VI

Managing Stress in Stressful Times

Here are some suggestions that can help you avoid that ergonomic pain in the neck:

✔ If you spend long periods of time typing at your computer, where and how you sit becomes important. The height of your chair in relationship to your keyboard and monitor are important variables to consider in avoiding excessive muscle tension and fatigue in your shoulders, neck, and upper back. You don't want to be straining your neck while looking at your monitor. Adjustability is the key. If your chair or table is too high or too low, replace it. Better yet, find an adjustable chair and table. Seat heights should range from 15 to 22 inches, depending on what your body's dimensions look like.

A study carried out by AT&T on their telephone operators found that switching to easily adjustable tables and chairs resulted in a significant reduction of the reported discomfort, particularly in the back, shoulders, and legs. Operators could adjust the height of the table that held their monitors, their keyboards, and their chairs.

✔ Choose a chair that has some padded support for your lumbar (lower back) region. The backrest should be full-length, extending some 18–20 inches higher than the seat of your chair. If your lower back is not supported sufficiently, consider a *lumbar roll* — a cylindrical pillow that fits nicely in the small of your back.

✔ Keep your keyboard at elbow level when you're seated. When using your keyboard, make sure that your fingers are lower than your wrist. To avoid repetitive-stress injuries (such as carpal tunnel syndrome), you may want to consider an ergonomically designed keyboard that reduces the strain on your wrists. You should also consider a support for your wrist when you're using your mouse.

✔ Use a footrest to take some of the strain off your legs and back, especially if you're short.

✔ Find a pen that is particularly comfortable to work with. One with a good grip can help keep your fingers from becoming fatigued.

✔ If you spend a lot of time on your feet, finding the correct footwear becomes a necessity. If you find you have to trade some style for greater comfort, go for the comfort.

Listen to your mother: Sit up straight!

Sometimes your stress comes from the most unlikely of places — your posture, for example. Sitting improperly for long periods of time can result in bodily fatigue, tension, and, ultimately, pain. Sitting actually puts more pressure on your spinal discs than does standing. When you slump or hunch forward, the pressure is even greater.

Sit back in your chair with your spine straight. Your lungs now have room to expand, and you place less strain on your back. You may find that you have to invest in a more supportive chair. Spend the bucks — a good chair is well worth the money.

Delegate your stress away

When you have more than enough to do, doing it all yourself is a guaranteed recipe for stress. Most often, the greatest obstacle people face when deciding whether they should delegate or not is the fear that the job won't get done as well as it would if they did it themselves. The key with delegating is to hand off jobs that don't require your direct attention and that can be competently done by others. Doing so enables you to concentrate on your most important tasks.

Even if delegating to a co-worker or assistant results in a less than perfect outcome in terms of performance quality and effectiveness, that may not be such a disaster — the outcome may be quite satisfactory without being quite perfect. Sometimes setting realistic standards (rather than expecting perfection) can result in less stress.

If you can't find anyone who knows how to do what you need to have done, it may be worthwhile to make the investment in time and train someone. Yes, it will take longer in the short run, but you'll probably be way ahead in the long run. Flip to Book III, Chapter 3 to get the full scoop on delegating.

Nourish your body (and spirit)

What goes into your mouth from 9 to 5 (or from 8 to 7) can make a big difference in your stress level. Eating the wrong foods, or even eating the right foods but in the wrong amounts and/or at the wrong times, can make it harder for you to cope with the stress in your life. Also, when you eat poorly, your body doesn't work as efficiently as it should. This means that you're not in the best position to handle all the pressures and demands you must face at work. Here are some ideas and suggestions that can help make what you eat an ally in your battle against stress, not the enemy.

Do lunch (with a difference)

Although the days of the three-martini lunch are gone, you can still find the harried worker overloading his or her plate with the kinds of food that ensure a high stress level for the rest of the day. Some suggestions for powering up your body (and not creating a meltdown) for the afternoon:

- ✔ Never skip lunch — no matter how busy your day gets.

- ✔ Eat less at your midday meal — no seconds.

- ✔ Eat stress-reducing foods, like those described in the earlier section "Don't skip breakfast."

- ✔ Don't drink any alcohol.

- ✔ Skip dessert.

Lunchtime isn't only about eating; it's a great time to work on lowering your stress. Try to get out of your work environment at lunch. Even if the outing is as simple as going for a walk around the block, go. Better yet, find a park, library, waterfront — anything relaxing — that can put you (however temporarily) into a different frame of mind. Find your lunchtime oasis.

Work it out

If you can swing it, one of the better things to do on your lunch break is to hit a nearby gym or health club. A number of exercise facilities may even offer you a corporate discount for joining. Better yet, many companies and organizations have workout facilities right on their premises. Work up a sweat, take a shower, and then have a quick but nourishing bite to eat.

The coffee-free coffee break

The caffeine in two cups of coffee can increase your heart rate by as much as 15 beats per minute. It can also make you irritable and nervous. So forgo that third or fourth cup of coffee. Instead, eat something that adds to your body's ability to cope rather than weakens it, such as a:

- ✔ Cup of low-fat yogurt

- ✔ Cup of fruit salad

- ✔ Handful of mixed nuts

- ✔ Piece of chocolate (one piece!)

- ✔ Piece of fruit

- ✔ Cup of herbal tea

- ✔ Cup of unleaded (decaffeinated) coffee, if you absolutely must have it

Book VI

Managing Stress in Stressful Times

A staple in many offices and cubicles is the candy jar. While admittedly colorful, having gobs of candy at hand at work may not help you with your stress. A sugar fix energizes you in the short run but leaves you flagging later in the day. You're better off avoiding this and any other candy snack. If you need a pick-me-up, try to choose something from the preceding list.

Head home more relaxed (and stay that way)

You've had a long, long day. You're tired and dragging your tush. The last thing you want to do is take your work stress home with you. Consider these guidelines to make sure you arrive home in better shape than when you left work:

- **Create a to-do list for the next day.** Making lists is one of the simpler ways of getting control of your workday — and one of the easiest. All you have to do is make the list. You don't have to follow through, complete all the items on the list, or do any of them. Just having the list gives you a sense of personal control and provides you with a direction for your re-entry into work the next day. (Alternatively, you can make this list a part of a broader strategy to getting organized; Book II, Chapter 2 tells you how.)

- **After work, work out.** If early morning or lunch are impractical times to hit the gym or health club, consider exercising right after work. Take out your frustrations and worry on the stair climber or in a step class. Not only is this mode of venting healthy, you'll still have your job in the morning!

- **Leave your work at work.** One of the more common stress traps is to take your work-related stress and spread it around so that the other parts of your life now become stressful. You undoubtedly have enough stress at home without importing more stress from your work. If you find that you absolutely have to take work home, be very specific about what you want to accomplish and how much time you want to spend doing it. Never take work home routinely. And try not to go to work on the weekends unless it is absolutely necessary.

Ending Your Day with a De-Stress Plan

Ah, home sweet home! But is it? Even if your ride home has been relatively nonstressful, opening your front door can lead to a whole new set of challenges. Walking straight into these stressors can catch you off guard and put you into a foul mood. When you get home, be sure to build in a short period of relative quiet — say 15 or 20 minutes — that can help you make the transition into your second world.

One way to wind down after a long day at the office is to throw in the towel, literally speaking. Simply take one or two washcloths and immerse them in hot water. Squeeze out the excess water, lie back, close your eyes, and put them on your face. Ah, nirvana.

Following are some additional suggestions for low-stress segues:

- ✔ Take a relaxing bath or shower.
- ✔ Have a drink (one will do).
- ✔ Sit in your favorite chair and simply veg.
- ✔ Listen to some relaxing music.
- ✔ Read a chapter from a good book.
- ✔ Work out or do yoga.
- ✔ Take a relaxing walk.
- ✔ Have sex. Really, sex can be a marvelous way of unwinding and letting go of physical tension.

If, when you open your door, chaos descends, and it is clear that none of these activities are even remotely possible, you may want to consider implementing some of these relaxing segues *before* you reach home. Maybe sipping a latte and doing the crossword puzzle at the local coffee shop near your home will work for you. You can take that walk or spend a few minutes in a local park (with a good book?) before you open your door. You are now ready to cope with the chaos.

Book VI

Managing Stress in Stressful Times

Chapter 2

Letting Go of Tension

- -

In This Chapter

▶ Understanding the effects of tension

▶ Recognizing your tension

▶ Using a variety of stress-busting strategies

- -

For most people, their jobs and careers are the biggest source of stress in their lives. Killer hours, a long commute, unrealistic deadlines, a boss from hell, office politics, toxic co-workers, and testy clients are just a few of the many job-related stresses people experience. Workloads are heavier today than they were in the past, leaving less and less time for family and the rest of your life. An uncertain economy means that not having a job — or being fearful of losing a job — is a major source of stress for many people. Being out of work and finding yourself in an incredibly competitive job market can create a whole lot of anxiety. A new lexicon of work-related stresses exists: downsizing, organizational redeployment, early retirement. Whatever the word, the effect on the workforce is insecurity, uncertainty, and fear. People are experiencing more stress at work than ever before.

All that stress has a negative effect on your body. Muscle tension due to stress is nature's way of preparing you to cope with a potential threat — it's a part of the fight-or-flight response. Your body is now ready to fight, or run from, that tiger. Unfortunately, this once adaptive response — and the accompanying muscle tension — can be triggered by less than life-threatening situations (like when you sit across from your stern-faced boss at your yearly review). Muscle tension can result in a wide variety of stress-related conditions and disorders. Fortunately, you can eliminate your tension before it does its worst. All you need are the right stress-busting tools in your toolbox.

This chapter describes strategies and techniques that can help you let go of tension and relax your body in and out of the office. The next chapter in this book shows you how to relax your mind. Together, these tools provide you with an important set of stress management skills.

Stress Can Be a Pain in the Neck (And That's Just for Starters)

When you're under stress (and who isn't nowadays?), your muscles contract and become tense. Interestingly, as familiar as the symptoms of tensions are, many people don't recognize just how tense they are. The following section outlines what tension does to your body and provides an easy way to become aware that tension is building so that you can reduce it.

Recognizing stress's impact on your body

The following is a short — and only partial — list of some of the effects tension has on your body. Unfortunately, many of these symptoms are all too familiar:

- Neck pain
- Headaches
- Stomach cramps
- Lower-back pain
- Clenched, painful jaw
- Sore shoulders
- Muscle spasms
- Tremors or twitches

And that's just on the outside. Inside your body other tension-related changes are happening. Here is a sampling of what else is quietly going on in your body when you feel tense:

- Your blood pressure goes up
- Your stomach secretes more acid
- Your cholesterol goes up
- Your blood clots faster

All in all, knowing how to prevent and eliminate bodily tension seems like a pretty healthy idea.

Standing up straight

Your mother was right! When you're under stress, you have a tendency to hunch over, making your posture lousy and your breathing impaired. You then breathe less deeply, denying your system the proper supply of oxygen you need. As a result, your muscles get tense. When you stand or sit straight, you reverse this process. You don't need to stand like a West Point cadet to correct bad posture. Overdoing it probably produces as much tension as you felt before. Just keep your shoulders from slouching forward, whether you're sitting in front of a computer all day or standing behind a cash register. If you're unsure about what your posture looks like, ask your mother (or a good friend).

Funny, I don't feel tense: Tuning in with a body scan

The fact is, you may not know when your body is tense. You get so used to tension that you usually don't notice that you're feeling tense until you get a headache or feel the soreness in your neck and shoulders. It creeps up on you: Slowly and often imperceptibly your muscles tighten and, voilà, the tension sets in.

The trick is to become aware of any bodily tension before it builds up and does its damage. Tuning in to your body takes a bit of practice. One of the best ways to discover how to recognize bodily tension is to use a simple one-minute scanning exercise.

Here's how: Find a place where you can sit or lay down comfortably and be undisturbed for a minute (see Figure 2-1). Scan your body for any muscle tension. Start with the top of your head, and work your way down to your toes. Ask yourself:

- ✔ Am I furrowing my brow?
- ✔ Am I knitting my eyebrows?
- ✔ Am I clenching my jaw?
- ✔ Am I pursing my lips?
- ✔ Am I hunching my shoulders?
- ✔ Am I feeling tension in my arms?
- ✔ Am I feeling tightness in my thigh and calf muscles?
- ✔ Am I curling my toes?
- ✔ Do I notice any discomfort anywhere else in my body?

A yes answer indicates tension in that area. With a little practice, you can scan your body in less than a minute, finding your tension quickly. It's a great way to become aware of your stress. When you find your stress, of course, you want to do something about it. The following sections give you some options.

Try to do a body scan three or four times a day. Ideally you can take a few breaks during your workday and either sit in a comfy chair, lie on the floor, or lie on a yoga mat that you bring with you. If you can't take the time or find a place to do your body scans while at work, do a scan before you leave in the morning, another when you get home, and a third scan just before bed.

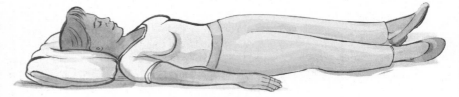

Figure 2-1:
A good position for body scanning.

Breathing Away Your Tension

Breathing properly is one of the simplest and best ways of draining your tension and relieving your stress. Simply by changing your breathing patterns, you can rapidly induce a state of greater relaxation. If you control the way you breathe, you have a powerful tool in reducing bodily tension — it can even help prevent your body from becoming tense in the first place, so maybe you can prevent that meltdown when the printer jams on you for the tenth time that day. This section shows you what you can do to incorporate a variety of stress-busting breathing techniques into your life.

Your breath is fine; it's your breathing that's bad

You probably take your breathing for granted. And why not? You've been breathing for years; you'd think by now you would have figured out how to do it right. No such luck. "Bad breathing" can take a number of forms:

- ✔ **Chest-and-shoulder breathing:** You bring air into your lungs by expanding your chest cavity and raising your shoulders. This description certainly fits if you have a touch of vanity and opt for never sticking out your tummy when you breathe.

- ✔ **Breath holding:** You stop breathing entirely when you're distracted or lost in thought.

Both types of breathing are inefficient and stress-producing. And when you're under stress, your breathing patterns deteriorate even more; making things worse, once your breathing goes awry, you feel even more stressed. Quite a nasty cycle.

When you feel stressed, your breathing becomes faster and shallower. When you breathe this way, your body reacts in the following ways:

- Less oxygen reaches your bloodstream.

- Your blood vessels constrict.

- Less oxygen reaches your brain.

- Your heart rate and your blood pressure go up.

- You feel lightheaded, shaky, and more tense.

Our primitive ancestors knew how to breathe. They didn't have to deal with ceaseless phone calls and e-mails, stacks of work with looming deadlines, or uncooperative co-workers. These days only opera singers, stage actors, musicians who play wind instruments, and a couple of dozen moonlighting yoga instructors actually breathe effectively. The rest of us mess it up. For a period of your life, however, you did get the whole breathing thing right. When was that? you wonder. It was as a baby lying in your crib, when your little belly rose and fell in the most relaxed way when you breathed. But then you grew up and blew it. Thankfully all is not lost. You can reteach yourself to breathe properly.

You probably think of breathing as a way of getting air into your lungs. However, in times past breathing was elevated to a more important status. Many religious groups and sects believed that a calming breath replenished the soul as well as soothed the body. In fact, the word *ruach* in Hebrew and the word *pneuma* in Greek have double meanings, connoting both breath and spirit.

Evaluating your breathing

You may be one of the few people who actually breathe properly. But before you skip this section, read a little further. To find out whether the way you breathe is stress-reducing, take this simple test.

1. **Lie on your back.**

2. **Put one of your hands on your belly and the other hand on your chest, as shown in Figure 2-2.**

3. Check to see whether your breathing is smooth, slow, and regular.

If you're breathing properly, the hand on your belly rises and falls rhythmically as you inhale and exhale. The hand on your chest should move very little, and if that hand does rise, it should follow the rise in your belly.

Figure 2-2: Evaluating your breathing.

Changing the way you breathe, changing the way you feel

Changing the way you breathe can make all the difference in how you feel. The following exercises present various ways to alter your breathing. Try them and discover whether all you need is one, simple change.

People who want to adopt new patterns of breathing typically want to get it perfectly right. They frequently get so lost in body parts or lung mechanics that they wind up more stressed out than they were before they started. Don't let this happen to you. There is no one exactly right way to breathe all the time. Give yourself lots of room to experiment with your breathing. And don't overdo it. If you've been breathing inefficiently for all these years, changing gears may take some time. Above all, you are not taking a test. Do not grade yourself on how deep your can breathe or how flat you can make your diaphragm. Remember, the goal is to reduce your stress, not add to it.

It's easier to learn and practice new techniques when someone reads them to you, rather than when you try to read them off the page — especially when the directions tell you to close your eyes or lie down. So buy a microphone for your computer or a handheld voice recorder and record these instructions so that you can listen to them as you practice the new techniques. Alternatively, find a friend with a soothing, mellifluous voice and have him or her be the reader. Of course, make sure the noise won't disturb your co-workers — close your door if you have an office or find an empty conference room or break room away from people who are working.

Looking under the hood

Breathing provides your body with oxygen and removes waste products — primarily carbon dioxide — from your blood. Your lungs carry out this gas exchange. Lungs, however, don't have their own muscles for breathing. Your *diaphragm* is the major muscle necessary for proper breathing. It's a dome-shaped muscle that separates your chest cavity from your abdominal cavity, and acts as a flexible floor for your lungs.

When you inhale, your diaphragm flattens downward, creating more space in the chest cavity, and permits the lungs to fill. When you exhale, your diaphragm returns to its dome shape. *Diaphragmatic* (also called *abdominal*)

breathing provides the most efficient way of exchanging oxygen and carbon dioxide. In diaphragmatic breathing, you let your diaphragm flatten completely so that your lungs can fill to capacity (and you can see your abdomen rise and fall with each breath, hence the name).

Your diaphragm works automatically, but you can override the process, especially when you're under stress. And that's where problems can arise. Too often you neglect to use your diaphragm properly when you breathe, and you interfere with the proper exchanges of gases in your system, which can result in greater tension, more fatigue, and more stress.

Breathing 101: Breathing for starters

Following is one of the best and simplest ways of introducing yourself to stress-effective breathing.

1. **Either lying or sitting comfortably, put one hand on your belly and your other hand on your chest.**

2. **Inhale through your nose, making sure that the hand on your belly rises and the hand on your chest moves hardly at all.**

3. **As you inhale slowly, count silently to yourself to three.**

4. **As you exhale, slowly count to four, feeling the hand on your belly falling gently.**

   Pause slightly before your next breath. Repeat for several minutes and whenever you get the chance.

Moving on to something more advanced: Taking a complete breath

Complete breaths (or *Zen breathing* as it is often called) help you breathe more deeply and more efficiently and maximize your lung capacity.

1. **Lie down comfortably on your back.**

   Keep your knees slightly apart and slightly bent. Close your eyes if you like.

2. **Put one hand on your abdomen near your belly-button, and the other hand on your chest so that you follow the motion of your breathing.**

   Try to relax. Let go of any tension you may feel in your body.

3. **Begin by slowly inhaling through your nose, first filling the lower part of your lungs, then the middle part of your chest, and then the upper part of your chest.**

   As you inhale, feel your diaphragm pushing down, gently extending your abdomen, making room for the newly inhaled air. Notice the hand on your abdomen rise slightly. The hand on your chest should move very little, and when it does, it should follow your abdomen. Do not use your shoulders to help you breathe.

4. **Exhale slowly through your mouth, emptying your lungs from top to bottom.**

   Make a whooshing sound as the air passes through your lips, and notice the hand on your abdomen fall.

5. **Pause slightly and take in another breath, repeating this cycle.**

   Continue breathing this way for ten minutes or so — certainly until you feel more relaxed and peaceful. Practice this technique daily if you can. Try this exercise while sitting and then while standing.

With a little practice, complete breathing comes more naturally and automatically. Over time, you may begin to breathe this way much more of the time. Stick with it.

Trying some "belly-button balloon" breathing

A simpler way of breathing more deeply and more evenly is to work with a visual image, in this case a balloon. Here's what you have to do:

1. **Imagine that a small balloon — about the size of a grapefruit — is replacing your stomach, just under your belly-button, as shown in Figure 2-3.**

2. **As you inhale through your nose, imagine that you're actually inhaling through your belly-button, inflating the balloon.**

   As the balloon gets larger, notice how your belly rises.

3. **Exhale slowly through your nose, again imagining that the air is leaving through your belly-button.**

   Your balloon is now slowly and easily returning to its deflated state.

4. **Pause slightly before the next breath in and then repeat, gently and smoothly inflating your balloon to a comfortable size.**

   Repeat this exercise, as often as you can, whenever you can.

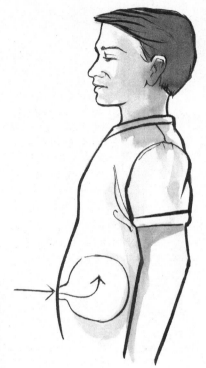

Figure 2-3:
Balloon
breathing.

Emergency breathing: How to breathe in the trenches

Breathing properly is no big deal when you're lying on your bed or vegging out in front of the TV. But what's your breathing like when you're caught in gridlock, when you're facing down a deadline, or when your boss criticizes your work? You are now in a crisis mode. You need another form of breathing. Here's what to do:

1. **Inhale slowly through your nostrils, taking in a very deep breath from the abdomen, filling your lungs and filling your cheeks.**

2. **Hold that breath for about six seconds.**

3. **Open your mouth slightly to exhale *slowly*, releasing *all* the air in your lungs.**

    Pause at the end of this exhalation. Now take a few normal breaths.

    Repeat Steps 1 through 3 two or three times and then return to what you were doing. This form of deep breathing should put you in a more relaxed state.

Refreshing yourself with a yawn

Yawning is usually associated with boredom. Business meetings you think will run well into the millennium or painful sales calls where the customer won't let you get in a word edgewise may trigger more than a few yawning gasps. However, your yawn may signal something more than boredom.

Yawning is another way Mother Nature tells you that your body is under stress. In fact, yawning helps relieve stress. When you yawn, more air — and therefore more oxygen — enters your lungs, revitalizing your bloodstream. Releasing that plaintive sound that comes with yawning is also tension reducing. Unfortunately, people have become a little oversocialized, making for polite, wimpy yawns. You need to recapture this lost art.

The next time you feel a yawn coming on, go with it. Open your mouth widely and inhale more fully than you normally might. Take that breath all the way down to your belly. Exhale fully through your mouth, completely emptying your lungs. What a feeling! Enjoy it. So what if your co-workers stare?

Tensing Your Way to Relaxation

One of the better relaxation techniques derives from a method called *progressive relaxation* or *deep muscle relaxation*. This method is based on the notion that you're not aware of what your muscles feel like when they're tensed. By purposely tensing your muscles, you are able to recognize what tension feels like and identify which muscles are creating that tension. This technique is highly effective, can be done while sitting at your desk, and has been proven to be a valuable tool for quickly reducing muscle tension and promoting relaxation.

Exploring how progressive relaxation works

You begin progressive relaxation by tensing a specific muscle or group of muscles (your arms, legs, shoulders, and so on). You notice the way the tension feels. You hold that tension and then let it go, replacing that tension with something much more pleasant — relaxation. By the time you tense and relax most of your major muscle groups, you'll feel relaxed, at peace, and much less stressed. The following general guidelines set the stage for more specific muscle-group and relaxation instructions that appear later in this chapter:

1. **Lie down or sit, as comfortably as you can, and close your eyes.**

   If you can, find a quiet, dimly lit place that gives you some privacy, at least for a while. If that's not possible, you can still do this exercise in your desk chair.

2. **Tense the muscles of a particular body part.**

   To practice, start by tensing your right hand and arm. Begin by simply making a fist. As you clench your fist, notice the tension and strain in your hand and forearm. Without releasing that tension, bend your right arm and flex your biceps, making a muscle the way you might to impress the kids in the schoolyard.

   Don't strain yourself in any of these muscle tensing maneuvers by over-doing it. When you tense a muscle group, don't tense as hard as you can. Tense about three-fourths of what you can do. If you feel pain or sore-ness, ease up on the tension, and if you still hurt, postpone your prac-tice till another time.

3. **Hold the tension in the body part for about seven seconds.**

4. **Let go of the tension fairly quickly, letting the muscles go limp.**

   Notice the difference in the way your hand and arm feels. Notice the dif-ference in feelings between the sensations of tension and those of relax-ation. Let these feeling of relaxation deepen for about 30 seconds or so.

5. **Repeat Steps 1 through 4, using the same muscle group.**

6. **Move to another muscle group.**

   Simply repeat Steps 1 through 4, substituting a different muscle group after two cycles. Continue with your left hand and arm and then work your way through the major muscle groups listed in the following sections.

Book VI

Managing
Stress in
Stressful
Times

Relaxing your face and head

Wrinkle your forehead (creating all those lines that everybody hates) by raising your eyebrows as high as you can. Hold this tension for about five seconds and then let go, releasing all of the tension in your forehead. Just let your forehead muscles become smooth. Notice the difference between the feelings of tension you felt and the more pleasant feelings of relaxation.

Now clench your jaw by biting down on your back teeth and at the same time force a smile. Hold this uncomfortable position for five seconds or so, and then relax your jaw, letting your mouth fall slightly ajar.

Finally, purse your lips, pushing them together firmly. Hold that tension for a bit, and then relax, letting your lips open slightly. Now notice how relaxed your face and head feels. Enjoy this sensation and let this feeling deepen by letting go of any remaining sources of tension around your mouth.

Relaxing your neck and shoulders

Bend your head forward as though you are going to touch your chest with your chin (you probably will). Feel the tension in the muscles of your neck. Hold that tension. Now tilt your head slightly, first to one side and then to another. Notice the tension at the side of your neck as you do so. Now relax, letting your head return to a more comfortable, natural position. Enjoy the relaxation for a moment or so.

Now scrunch up your shoulders as though you are trying to reach your ears. Hold it, feel the tension (again about five seconds), and let your shoulders fall to a comfortable, relaxed position. Notice the feelings of relaxation that are spreading through your shoulders and neck.

Relaxing your back

Arch your back, being careful not to overdo it. Hold that tension for several seconds, and then let your back and shoulders return to a more comfortable, relaxed position.

Relaxing your legs and feet

Either sitting or lying down, raise your right foot so that you feel some tension in your thigh and buttock. At the same time push your heel out and point your toes toward your head, as shown in Figure 2-4. Hold this tension, notice what it feels like and then let go, letting your leg fall to the floor, releasing any remaining tension. Let that relaxation deepen for a while. Repeat this sequence with your other leg and foot.

Figure 2-4:
Relaxing
your feet
and legs.

Relaxing your stomach

Take in a deep breath and hold that breath, tensing the muscles in your stomach. Imagine that you're preparing yourself for a punch in the stomach. Hold that tension. And relax, letting go of the tension.

After you finish this sequence, let your body sink into an even deeper state of relaxation. Let go more and more. Mentally go over the sensations you are feeling in your arms face, neck, shoulders, back, stomach, and legs. Feel your body becoming looser and more relaxed. Savor the feeling.

Scrunching up like a pretzel

Book VI

Managing Stress in Stressful Times

When pressed for time, you can use a quickie version of the progressive relaxation exercise explained in the preceding section. Simply, this technique compresses all the muscle-tensing and relaxing sequences into one. Think of it as one gigantic scrunch.

REMEMBER

In order to do this, you have to master the gradual version first. The success of this rapid form of relaxation depends on your ability to create and release muscle tension quickly, skills you master by slowly working through all of the muscle groups individually. Here's what to do:

If possible, sit or lie comfortably in a room that gives you some quiet and is relatively free of distractions. Now tense all of the muscle groups listed below, simultaneously:

- Clench both fists, bend both arms and tense your biceps.
- Lift both legs until you notice a moderate degree of tension and discomfort.
- Scrunch up your face, closing your eyes, furrowing your brow, clenching your jaws, and pursing your lips.
- Bring your shoulders as close as you can to your ears.
- Tense your stomach muscles.

Hold this total scrunch for about five seconds and then release, letting go of any and all tension. Let your legs fall to the floor, your arms to your sides, and let the rest of your body return to a relaxed position. Repeat this sequence at various points throughout your day.

Mind Over Body: Using the Power of Suggestion

Another important approach to bodily relaxation is called *autogenic training,* or *AT* for short. The word *autogenic* means *self-generation* or *self-regulation.* This method attempts to regulate your autonomic nervous functions (your heart rate, blood pressure, and breathing, among others) rather than by relaxing your muscles. With autogenic training, you use your mind to regulate your body's internal stress levels.

AT relies on the power of suggestion to induce physiological changes within you. These suggestions are mental images that your subconscious picks up and transmits to your body. Just thinking about certain changes in your body produces those kinds of changes. As a result, you experience deep feelings of relaxation. AT may sound very mysterious, but it isn't. After you master this technique, AT is a highly effective way of putting yourself in a more relaxed state. The following steps walk you through a more abbreviated form (better suited to a busy lifestyle) than the one originally devised. Here's what you do:

1. **Get comfy.**

   Find a suitably quiet, not-too-hot, and not-too-cold place. You can sit or lie down, but make sure that your body is well supported and as comfortable as possible. Try to breathe slowly and smoothly.

2. **Concentrate *passively*.**

   For this approach to be effective, you need to adopt a receptive, casual attitude of passive concentration. You want to be alert, not falling asleep, but you don't want your mind working too hard. You cannot force yourself to relax. Just let it happen. Be aware of your body and your mind but don't actively analyze everything or worry about how you're doing. Should a distracting thought come your way, notice it, and then let it go. If the relaxation doesn't come at first, don't worry. It comes with more practice.

3. **Allow various body parts to begin feeling warm and heavy.**

   Although autogenic training utilizes many suggestions and images, the two most effective images are warmth and heaviness. Start by focusing on your right arm.

4. **Slowly and softly say to yourself:**

   "I am calm . . . I am at peace . . . My right arm is warm . . . and heavy . . . I can feel the warmth and heaviness flowing into my right arm . . . I can feel my right arm becoming warmer . . . and heavier . . . I am at peace . . . I am calm. . . ."

   Take the time to become aware of the feelings in your arm and hand. Notice that your arm *is* becoming warmer and heavier. Repeat the phrases to yourself and don't rush this process. Enjoy the changes your body is now beginning to experience.

5. **After you complete the phrases, remain silent and calm for about 30 seconds, letting the relaxation deepen; then focus on your left arm.**

   Repeat the same phrases again, this time substituting *left arm* for right arm. (Hopefully, by now you have memorized these phrases and can close your eyes and not worry about a script.)

6. **Move to other parts of your body.**

   Focus on other areas, repeating the same phrases, but substituting other parts of your body. Here is the complete sequence:

   - Right arm
   - Left arm
   - Both arms
   - Right leg
   - Left leg
   - Both legs
   - Neck and shoulders
   - Chest and abdomen
   - Entire body

Book VI

Managing Stress in Stressful Times

Completing the entire sequence shouldn't take you more than a half hour or so. If you can fit in more than one autogenic session a day, all the better — you could do one during your lunch break and another when you get home from work. You may need some time to master this technique, but the results are well worth the effort.

Use your imagination? You're getting warmer!

With autogenic training, you may find that using the warm and heavy suggestions and images isn't effective for you. You may need a different image to release the tension in your body. Here are alternate suggestive images that can induce feelings of warmth and heaviness:

- ✔ Heat me up: Imagine that the body part in question (arm, leg, and so on) is wrapped in a heating pad. Slowly but surely the heat permeates your body, relaxing your muscles more and more.

- ✔ Get in hot water: Imagine that you're immersing your arm or leg in very soothing warm water.

- ✔ Sunny side up: Mentally direct a sun lamp to a particular part of your anatomy.

- ✔ Heavy metal: Visualize weights attached to your arm, leg, and so on.

- ✔ Get the lead in: Imagine that your limb is filled with lead.

Stretching Away Your Stress

Stretching is one of the ways that your body naturally discharges excess bodily tension. Waking up in the morning or just before retiring at night are the times you automatically feel the need for a stretch. But a good stretch can drain away much of your body's tension at other times, too. You may be desk-bound or sit for long periods of time during the day, causing your muscles to tense and tighten. Consider adopting one or more basic stretches and taking a stretch break at various points throughout the day. Cats do, dogs do, why not you?

Following are two tension-relieving stretches. They're simple and shouldn't evoke much comment or ridicule from friends or co-workers:

- **The twist.** This stretch is great for your upper body. Sitting or standing, put both your hands behind the back of your head, locking your fingers together. Move your elbows towards each other until you feel some moderate tension. Now twist your body slightly, first to the right for a few seconds, and then slowly to the left. When you finish, let your arms fall to your side.

- **The leg-lift.** This stretch is good for your lower body. Sitting in your chair, raise both your legs until you feel a comfortable level of tightness in them. Maintaining that tension, flex and point your toes toward your head. Hold that tension for about ten seconds or so and then let your legs fall to the floor. If doing this with both legs together is a wee bit uncomfortable, try it one leg at a time.

Stretch slowly and don't overdo it. You're trying to relax your muscles, not punish them.

Taking a Three-Minute Energy Burst

Any concentrated expenditure of energy produces more stress by tensing your muscles, speeding your heart-rate, and quickening your breathing. However, after you stop expending energy, you find that your muscles, heart, and breathing slow down to a level that's lower than when you started. This energy boost can come from walking very briskly, a short run, jumping jacks, rope jumping, sit-ups, push-ups, running up steps — anything that gets your body going.

Shaking off tension is another fun way to recharge. You can do this exercise either sitting or standing. Begin by holding your arms loosely in front of you and start shaking your hands at the wrist. Now let your arms and shoulders join in the fun. Continue for a short while, and taper off slowly, letting your arms fall comfortably to your sides. Now lift one leg and start shaking it.

Then shift to the other leg. (If you're sitting, you can do both legs at the same time). When you finish, notice the tingling sensations in your body and, more importantly, the feelings of relaxation. Admittedly, it looks a little strange, but it works.

Relaxing with a Massage? Ah, There's the Rub!

Massage and other touch and pressure therapies are among the most popular ways of relieving muscle tension. These days you can get a massage almost as easily as you can get your hair cut. The range and the popularity of touch and pressure disciplines and therapies has grown enormously in recent years.

Book VI

Managing Stress in Stressful Times

A partial list of available methods and techniques includes Swedish massage, reflexology, Shiatsu, chiropractic, and acupressure. All of these methods have their origins in early medicine and healing. Many claim spiritual as well as physical changes. Rather than go into each of these disciplines separately, the following sections discuss several of the simpler stress-relieving exercises that are particularly useful and easy to grasp.

You have several choices when it comes to massage. You can spend some bucks and get a professional to give you a massage. Or you can find someone who will give you a massage for free. Or you can give yourself a massage. The discussion starts with the last option, because it's often the cheapest and doesn't require friends.

Massaging yourself

You can go two ways: High-tech or low-tech. The high-tech route usually requires a wall-socket or lots of batteries. Many specialty stores stock loads of massage paraphernalia, from the mega-buck relaxation chair that transports you to relaxation heaven with the flick of a switch, to less expensive options like a handheld vibrating massager. Alternately, you can forego the batteries and the expense by letting your fingers do the work. Following are three simple ways to rub out your stress that you can do while sitting at your desk.

For your hands

Hold your left palm in front of you, fingers together. The fleshy spot between your thumb and index finger is a key acupressure point that should spread a sensation of relaxation when massaged. Using your right thumb, massage this spot in a circular motion for a slow count of 15. Switch hands, and repeat.

For stress-related fatigue, pinch just below the first joint of your pinkie with the thumb and index finger of the opposite hand. (Pressure should be firm but not painful). Increase the pressure slightly. Make small circular movements in a counterclockwise direction while maintaining pressure. Continue for 20 seconds. Release. Wait for 10 seconds and repeat up to five times.

For your feet

Try this sole-soothing exercise. Take off your socks and shoes and sit comfortably with one leg crossed over the other. (The sole of your foot should be almost facing you.) With both hands, grasp the arches of your foot and apply pressure, especially with your thumbs. Now kneading (like you would bread dough, using your thumbs and fingers) every part of your foot, work your way from your heel right up to your toes. Give each of your toes a squeeze. Now massage the other foot in a similar way.

If crossing your legs is more uncomfortable than it used to be, go to the kitchen and get your rolling pin. Sit in a chair and position the rolling pin next to your foot. Gently roll your bare foot back and forth slowly for two minutes or so. Then try it with the other foot. Now wash the pin. No rolling pin? Use a tennis ball. Put it under the arch of your bare foot, put some pressure on that foot, and move the ball backward and forward. Keep this rhythm going for about two minutes, and then switch to your other foot.

For your neck and shoulders

Stress most often finds its way to your neck and shoulders. To dissipate that tension, take your left hand and firmly massage your right shoulder and the right side of your neck. Start with some gentle circular motions, rubbing the muscle with your index and pointer fingers. Then finish with a firmer message, squeezing the shoulder and neck muscles between your thumb and other fingers. Now switch to the other side.

For your face

Start by placing both of your hands on your face with the tips of your fingers resting on your forehead and the heels of your palms resting just under your cheeks. Gently pull down the skin on your forehead with the tips of your fingers while pushing up the area under your palms. Rhythmically repeat this movement, contracting and releasing your fingers and palms. You can also try pulling on your ears in different directions.

Becoming the massage-er or massage-ee

Having someone else give you a massage certainly has its advantages. With someone else doing all the work, you can completely let go: Sit or lie back and totally relax. And another person can reach places on your body that you could never reach. Now, it isn't recommended that you give or receive massages (except from yourself) in the workplace. Your co-workers won't think you're very professional if you ask them to rub down your shoulders after a stressful meeting. Instead, visit a massage therapist or ask a friend to give you a massage after work. Of course, you may have to reciprocate. But even giving someone else a massage can relieve some of your tension. Here are some general hints and guidelines to get you started:

- ✔ Use some massage oil or body lotion to add a relaxing aroma and smooth the massage process.

- ✔ Lower the lights to provide a soothing, relaxing atmosphere. Calming music also adds a nice touch.

- ✔ Focus your massage on the lower back, neck, and shoulders — places stress tends to reside and cause the most discomfort.

- ✔ Start by applying pressure very lightly until the massage-ee is relaxed. Then increasing the pressure, using your palms to knead the muscles. Finish up with a lighter massage, and let the massage-ee linger for a while after the massage to extend the sense of relaxation.

- ✔ Don't overdo it. A good massage shouldn't have the massage-ee writhing in pain. A bad massage can cause more stress than it attempts to relieve.

Chapter 3

Quieting Your Mind

· ·

In This Chapter

▶ Slowing down your mind

▶ Using imagery to relax

▶ Stopping unwanted thoughts

▶ Investigating meditation

▶ Relaxing with hypnosis

· ·

*F*or many people, and you may be one of them, stress takes the form of psychological distress, and you find that your mind is filled with distressing thoughts that prevent you from feeling relaxed and at ease. It may be that your mind is racing a mile a minute. You may be worrying about your job, your relationships, your finances, or simply how you're going to juggle the hundred and one things on your plate. Whatever the source of your worry, you clearly aren't going to relax until you stop — or at least slow — this mental mayhem.

Here are some of the more common signs that your mind is working overtime:

✔ Your mind seems to be racing.

✔ You find controlling your thoughts difficult.

✔ You're worried, irritable, or upset.

✔ You're often preoccupied and find concentrating difficult.

✔ You find it difficult to fall asleep or to fall back asleep once awake.

If one or more of these describes you, you can benefit from learning to quiet your mind. One of the best ways to relax your mind is to relax your body. When your body relaxes, your mind slows. Check out Chapter 2, Book VI for some physical relaxation techniques. But there are other ways of taming your unruly thoughts and calming your restless mind, and this chapter shows you how.

Distract Yourself

The simplest way to calm your mind is to distract yourself. This idea may sound obvious, but you'd be surprised how often people overlook this option. Psychologists know that concentrating on two things at the same time is very difficult. Therefore, if your mind is flooded with distressing thoughts, change course and find something else to think about. Here are some pleasant diversions you may want to consider when you're at home:

- ✔ Watch some television.
- ✔ Go to a movie.
- ✔ Read a book, newspaper, or magazine.
- ✔ Talk to a friend.
- ✔ Work or play on your computer.
- ✔ Play a sport.
- ✔ Immerse yourself on some project or hobby.
- ✔ Listen to some favorite music.
- ✔ Think of something you're looking forward to.

If your stress comes from nonwork-related sources, you may find that being at work each day is a good distraction. However, if work is the source of your distress, you need other ways of distracting yourself, and your boss probably isn't going to let you watch TV.

 One of the best ways to distract yourself, calm your mind, and stop those unwanted, persistent worries is to use your imagination. The next section shows you how to imagine your way to relaxation, even if you're stuck at your desk.

Imagine This

If you can replace that stress-producing thought or image with one that's relaxing, the chances are that you'll feel much better. Here's how:

1. **Find a place where you won't be disturbed for a few minutes and get comfortable, either sitting in a favorite chair or lying down.**

2. **Think of an image — a place, a scene, or a memory — that relaxes you.**

   Use all your senses to bring that imagined scene to life. Ask yourself: What do I see? What can I hear? What can I smell? What can I feel?

3. **Let yourself become completely immersed in your image, allowing it to relax you completely.**

Finding a relaxing image

"Sounds good," you say, "but what is my relaxing image?" Try taking one these mental vacations (airfare included):

- ✔ **The Caribbean package:** Imagine that you're on the beach of a Caribbean isle. The weather is perfect. Lying on the cool sand, you feel the warm breeze caress your body. You hear the lapping of the ocean waves on the shore and the tropical birds chirping in the palms. You are slowly sipping a piña colada. You can smell your coconut-scented suntan lotion. You feel wonderful. You're relaxed. Your mind is totally at peace.

- ✔ **The pool package:** You are lying in a large inflatable raft, floating blissfully in an incredibly beautiful swimming pool. The day is perfect. The sky is a deep blue, the sun is warming your relaxed body. You feel the gentle rocking of the raft in the water. You can hear the soothing voice of a waiter announcing a buffet lunch in a half an hour. You are very content. You could lie here forever.

- ✔ **The winter wonderland package:** Picture yourself in a small cabin in Vermont (if your tastes lean to the more extravagant, switch the scene to Aspen or the Alps — the cost is the same no matter where you go). You're snowed in, but that's fine because you don't have to be anywhere and no one needs to contact you. Also, you're not alone — a favorite person is with you and you're both lying in front of a crackling fire. Soft music is playing in the background. You're sipping hot toddies, mulled wine, or champagne.

- ✔ **A pleasing memory:** Try to picture a memory, possibly when you were growing up, or one from more recent times that you find particularly happy and satisfying. It could be a vacation long ago, a birthday party you loved, or frolicking with a childhood pet.

None of these examples do it for you? Then come up with your own personal relaxation image. You might try one of these:

- ✔ Soaking in a hot, soapy bath . . . soft music . . . candlelight. . . .
- ✔ Walking in a quiet forest . . . birds chirping . . . leaves rustling. . . .
- ✔ Lying under a tree in the park . . . warm breezes . . . more chirping. . . .
- ✔ In your most comfortable chair . . . reading a great book . . . no chirping. . . .

What you see and hear usually dominates your imagination. But don't forget your senses of touch and smell. By adding these sensual dimensions you can enrich your images and make them more involving. Feel the sand between your toes; smell the freshly brewed coffee; taste the salt in the air.

Making things move

Your image need not be a static scene. It can change and move. You may, for example:

- Imagine a sports event that you enjoy. It could be a baseball game that you attended. Or make one up. Mentally follow the plays as you work your way through the innings. Not a baseball fan? Try imagining a tennis match.

- Try replaying favorite movies in your mind, visualizing different scenes and filling in bits of dialogue. Scenic movies work wonderfully.

- Remember the details of a trip you've taken in the past and retrace your journey from place to place.

Guided imagery, as it is called, can help keep you focused and interested in your image, and ensure that unwanted, intrusive thoughts stay out of the picture.

Stop Your Thoughts

Sometimes distracting yourself isn't enough to quiet your mind. Sometimes you need stronger measures to eliminate, or at least slow, those unwanted and stress-producing worries and concerns. Perhaps you have an upsetting worry that continually intrudes into your thinking and keeps you from focusing on an important project. Or maybe you're trying to fall asleep and the thoughts racing around in your head make sleeping impossible. You recognize that there is nothing you can do about your worry and that your worrying is only making things worse. You would be better off if you could somehow stop thinking about this. But how?

That's where a technique called *thought stopping* can be very useful. It's an effective way of not only keeping worries and upsets temporarily out of your mind, but also weakening those thoughts and making it less likely that they'll return. Here are the steps you need to take to get this technique to work for you:

1. **Notice your thoughts.**

   When a worrisome thought runs through your mind, mentally step back and recognize that it is an unwanted thought. It may be a worry, a nagging concern, or a regret — anything that you feel is not worth the stress at this particular time.

2. **Find a stop sign.**

   In your mind, picture a red and white octagonal stop sign — you know, the kind you see on the street corner. Make your sign large and vivid.

3. **Yell — in your head — "Stop!"**

   Silently shout the word *stop* to yourself.

4. **Do it again.**

   Every time the worrisome or unwanted thought reappears, notice that thought, imagine your stop sign, and yell *stop* to yourself.

5. **Find a replacement thought.**

   Find a thought or image that you can substitute for the distressing thought or image. It may be something taken from the list of relaxing images suggested in the preceding section or any other thought that's not the one you're trying to weaken.

Book VI

Managing Stress in Stressful Times

Imagining the image of the sign and hearing *stop* in your head disrupts your thought sequence and temporarily puts the unwanted thought out of mind. Be warned, however: The unwanted thought will probably return, and you may have to repeat this sequence again. If your stress-producing thought or image is very strong, it may take many repetitions of this technique to weaken or eliminate it. Stick with it.

One variation of thought stopping that has proven useful for many people is to use an elastic band to help interrupt the presence of a distressing thought. Simply take an ordinary elastic band and put it around your wrist. Now, whenever you notice an intrusive or unwanted thought crowding your thinking, pull the elastic and let it snap your wrist. This shouldn't be painful. Just a sharp reminder that you want this distressing thought to go. Use your mental stop sign and remember to replace your unwanted thought with something more pleasant.

What, Me Worry?

Worrying is one of the major ways your mind stays revved and keeps you stressed. You may find yourself worrying during your workday or at three in the morning when you'd rather be sleeping. You may find yourself fretting about the repercussions of that sarcastic comeback you gave your co-worker. Or maybe you're wondering how you're going to find the time to finish your big project on schedule. Whatever your worry, it may be keeping your mind running a mile a minute. Following are a few techniques that can help reduce and control those distressing worries.

Strike up the band (or better yet, a string quartet)

Music therapists know that listening to music can result in significant physiological changes in your body: Your heart rate drops, your breathing slows, and your blood pressure lowers. But not all music does the trick. Some music can upset you, making you more stressed. (Think of that Metallica groupie living upstairs.) Other music may delight you but still not have a calming effect.

Go for Baroque

Following is a short list of field-tested composers and compositions (Baroque and otherwise) that should slow your pulse.

- **Bach:** The slower second movements are particularly appropriate for relaxation. The Air on the G String is a real calmer.
- **Handel:** *Water Music.*
- **Chopin:** Nocturnes.
- **Schubert:** Symphony no. 8 in B Minor.
- **Pachelbel:** Canon in D.
- **Albinoni:** Adagio in G.
- **Mozart:** Piano Concerto no. 21.
- **Beethoven:** *Pastoral.*
- **Elgar:** "Salut d'Amour."

Not a fan of the classics?

Of course, relaxing music need not be all classical. Bach and Mozart probably aren't as effective as Charlie Mingus if you're a jazz fan. Other forms of music can be incredibly soothing. Many New Age recordings work nicely.

No single piece of music works for everyone. Experiment. Find what relaxes you. Listen in your car while commuting, in bed before going to sleep, in your favorite chair in your favorite room. Headphones and a personal music player allow you take your music — and a state of relaxation — wherever you go.

Some companies and organizations are okay with their employees using an iPod or other sound source. And even if you can't use it during prime time, you certainly can when you get a break or take your lunch break.

Visit the rain forest

These days, electronic sound machines can reproduce virtually any sound you can imagine. These machines cost dramatically less than they did just few years ago. So if you like the sounds of waves, no sweat. Or how about a tropical rain forest? Perhaps you like to be soothed by the sound of rain on a roof, the sound of a gurgling brook, or the sound of a beating heart. Your choice.

Use some common scents

Your ears are not the only road to mental relaxation. Your nose can work as well. People have been using scents to relieve stress and tension for centuries. An aroma can elicit feelings of calm and serenity. In fact, a school of therapy called *aromatherapy* is devoted to using your sense of smell as a vehicle for emotional change.

Studies carried out by Alan Hirsch, MD, neurological director of the Smell & Taste Treatment and Research Foundation in Chicago, suggest that there is a connection between smell and mood. He found that the part of the brain that registers smell may be biologically linked to the part of the brain that registers emotion. Certainly, the right scent can relax you and put you in a better mood. Here are some easy-to-find, soul-satisfying smells you may want to consider.

- ✔ Suntan lotion
- ✔ Vanilla extract
- ✔ Freshly baked just-about-anything
- ✔ Soaps, hand creams, bath oils and perfumes, and aftershave
- ✔ Freshly brewed coffee

Keep in mind that some people react very negatively (and may even have allergies) to certain scents. Unless you have a private office with a door that you keep closed all day, aromatherapy is not appropriate for the workplace and should be used to soothe your weary mind only when you're at home. Your cubicle neighbors won't thank you if you start each day by slathering on lotion with a strong, distracting scent (though they might not mind the smell of baked goods — if you share!).

Light up

Candles can be a wonderful addition to your repertoire of stress-reducing devices. A burning candle connotes romance, warmth, peace, and a sense of tranquility. The flickering of the flame can be hypnotic. Burning scented candles only adds to the effect. Which scent to use depends upon what you find most pleasant and appealing. Vanilla and floral fragrances tend to be most relaxing. Often these aromas recall pleasant memories of childhood. And just think of the money you can save on your electric bill. If your office doesn't allow candles, try a reed diffuser.

Mix your own aroma cocktail

If you have no time to bake bread or perk coffee, try concocting your own stress-reducing aroma by using commercially available oils. Some of the more common oils used to induce a relaxed, calming state include lavender, rose, jasmine, chamomile, orange blossom, vanilla, bergamot, geranium, and sandalwood. Often, you can combine oils to produce a new, relaxing aroma.

Essential oils and *natural oils* tend to produce better therapeutic benefits, but the synthetic oils are less costly. You can buy these pleasing fragrances from a number of shops or mail-order companies. Craft stores often carry essential oils at lower prices than more upscale boutiques or spas. If you're in a do-it-yourself mood, you can find books at your local library that show you how you can derive essential oils from flowers.

Get some knowledgeable advice before you begin experimenting with oils. Certain oils, for example, should be avoided during pregnancy, and others can act as irritants for some people. Some oils you can inhale directly; others should be diluted in bath water. Consult *Aromatherapy For Dummies* by Kathi Keville (Wiley) for more information on how to incorporate aromatherapy into your de-stressing regime. In addition, the National Association for Holistic Aromatherapy (www.naha.org) can help you with questions as to which oils to use and how to use them and how to find a professional aromatherapist in your area.

Eau de French fries?

You may think that sniffing food-related substances would send you immediately to your local fast-food chain. It seems that the opposite is the case. Dr. Alan Hirsch in Chicago studied some 3,000 people and found that smelling a banana, a green apple, or some peppermint whenever the person felt like eating resulted in weight loss. Dr. Hirsch speculated that maybe it was the induced relaxation that led to less eating.

Book VI

Managing Stress in Stressful Times

East comes West

People in the East — especially those who subscribe to certain religious or philosophical beliefs — have been practicing meditation for literally thousands of years. These practitioners use meditation as a means to search for and find inner peace, enlightenment, and harmony with the universe.

Meditation has not received such ready acceptance in the Western world, however. Westerners have tended to view meditation as foreign and remote, and sometimes as religious zealotry. In the '60s when the Maharishi — a then-popular guru — came along, westerners began to associate meditation with a somewhat wild fringe group of society.

But more recently, researchers started taking notice of the positive effects of meditation. Herbert Benson, MD, of the Benson-Henry Institute for Mind Body Medicine in Boston, was one of the first to adapt and introduce meditation to broader western audiences. Since then, the principles and practice of meditation have enjoyed widespread acceptance and enthusiasm in the West.

Do Nothing: Meditate

Of all of the methods available to help you relax, probably the one that evokes the most suspicion is meditation. When you think of meditation, chances are you conjure up images of bearded gents in saffron robes sitting in the lotus position. You feel that this is hardly an activity that would go over well at the office and you're leery about jumping in and joining the movement. Yet you likely have already meditated. You may not have been aware that you were doing so, but at those times when your mind becomes calm, uncluttered, and focused, and you're not processing your day, or thinking about a million things — you're doing something that closely resembles meditating.

The sections that follow present meditation as an important stress-reducing tool that fits nicely in your de-stress toolbox.

Finding out what meditation can do for you

The effects and benefits of meditation are wide and varied. Many of them you can notice immediately, while others are less obvious, affecting you in more subtle ways. Most importantly, meditation can help you relax your mind and body. It can help you turn off your inner thoughts. Meditating can help you feel less stressed; and your body will be less tense and your mind calmer. With some practice, after meditating you should feel rested, renewed, and recharged. Meditation allows you to develop greater control over your thoughts, worries, and anxieties. It is a skill that, once mastered, can serve you well throughout your life.

Simply amazing

Some meditators make claims that are, well, a bit over the top. It's highly unlikely that you will levitate or that your IQ will improve dramatically through meditation. However, some serious practitioners of meditation have had rather remarkable results. Some skilled meditators can

✔ Attain a state of deep relaxation relatively quickly, and some can tolerate extreme levels of pain and stress.

✔ Slow their heart rate to surprisingly low levels — their breathing slows and their rate of oxygen consumption is greatly reduced.

✔ Radically change their body temperatures.

In skilled meditators, brain-wave patterns associated with states of deep relaxation increase in intensity and frequency. Many enthusiasts claim the benefits of meditation go far beyond those of relaxation. They claim it helps you think more clearly, improves your relationships with others, improves self-esteem, and even offers enlightenment.

Enlightenment? Possibly. Levitation? Not likely.

Adopting the right mind-set

Meditating for a very short period of time (like a minute) is pretty doable. The challenge is being able to meditate for longer periods of time. Westerners in particular have some built-in resistances to meditating, such as the following traits:

✔ **Westerners like to be busy:** You probably like to be active and do things, rather than be passive and let things happen to you. Lengthy periods of immobility tend to elicit feelings of boredom and restlessness.

✔ **Westerners need scorecards:** You may find yourself with a need to evaluate yourself on how well you're doing. If, after a very brief period of practice, you find that you're doing well, you may rate yourself — and your performance — accordingly. One of the keys to meditation is not rating yourself — good or bad.

None of this should discourage you or deter you from practicing your meditative skills. No, you won't become an accomplished meditator in 12 minutes. However, you may be surprised at how quickly you begin to see positive results. Stick with it; the results are well worth it.

Preparing to meditate

Here is a step-by-step guide to preparing for meditation. Remember that there are many ways of meditating. These suggestions help you prepare for different types of meditation, especially the exercises featured later in this chapter.

1. **Find a quiet place where you won't be disturbed for a while.**

   No phones, no beeper, no computer, no TV — nothing. If your office offers a "quiet room," go there.

2. **Find a comfortable sitting position, like the one shown in Figure 3-1.**

   Contorting yourself in some yogi-like, snake-charmer squat (albeit impressive), may not be the best way to start meditating if you're a novice. Remember that you're going to remain in one position for 15 to 20 minutes.

Figure 3-1:
Sitting in a relaxed comfortable position.

3. **Focus on a sound, a word, a sensation, an image, an object, or a thought.**

4. **Maintain your focus and adopt a passive, accepting attitude.**

   When you are focusing in meditation, intrusive thoughts or images may enter your mind and distract you. When those thoughts occur, notice them, accept the fact that they are there, and then let them go: No getting upset, no annoyance, no self-rebuke.

After you have everything in place, you're ready to begin meditating. Although you have many forms of meditation to choose from, the most common ones are breath-counting meditation and meditation with a mantra. The following sections deal with each type.

Breath-counting meditation

Breath-counting meditation builds on the controlled breathing techniques and exercises discussed in Chapter 2 of Book VI. Breath-counting meditation is one of the basic and most commonly used forms of meditation. Here's what to do:

1. **Sit comfortably.**

   You can position yourself on the floor or in a chair. Keep your back straight and your head up. Dress comfortably as well — if no one at work will hassle you for it, remove your shoes, belt, and necktie if they constrict you.

2. **Close your eyes and scan for tension.**

   Scan your body for any tension by using the one-minute body scan technique described in Chapter 2, Book VI, and then let go of any tension that you find.

3. **Begin to breathe in a relaxed way.**

   Relax by taking some abdominal breaths (breathing using your diaphragm). Breathe slowly and deeply through your nose.

   To help you breathe in a relaxing manner, imagine a small balloon just under your belly button. As you inhale through your nostrils, imagine that balloon gently inflating and as you exhale through your nostrils, imagine the balloon slowly deflating.

4. **Focus on your breathing.**

   Your breathing now becomes the object of your focus. When you inhale, count this breath as *one.* The next time you inhale is *two,* and so forth until you reach ten. Then you start again at one.

   Count silently to yourself, and if you lose count, simply start back at one. If you lose count, don't worry — the number is merely something to focus on — there's no right or wrong number here.

5. **If you find a distracting thought or image intruding, let it go and return to your count.**

   Continue this exercise for about 20 minutes, and — if you can — do this exercise twice a day.

Psst, looking for a good mantra?

The word *mantra* comes from Sanskrit: *man* means *to think*, and *tra* means *to free*. Often mantras take the form of one or two syllables, such as *om* (meaning *I am*), or *so-ham* (*I am he*). Many teachers of meditation believe that your mantra should have personal meaning.

In his book *The Relaxation Response*, cardiologist and researcher Herbert Benson says that a personal mantra isn't necessary for successful meditation. In his teaching of meditative relaxation, he suggests using the word *one* as

a mantra. That word has very little meaning for most of us, and therefore isn't distracting. Your mantra can also be a soothing word such as *peace, love*, or *calm*. Whatever you come up with, choose a word or sound that has a relaxing feel for you. If you would like some additional information on mantras, and on meditation in general, take a look at *Meditation For Dummies*, 2nd Edition, by Stephan Bodian (Wiley).

Book VI

Managing Stress in Stressful Times

Probably the most common complaint among beginning meditators is that their minds keep wandering off, especially at the beginning of a meditation. Even on those days when you face no major pressure or pending deadline, your mind can still come up with a million things to think about. That's normal. Expect it, and don't beat yourself up when it happens. Don't make this exercise into a test of your ability to concentrate. Getting good at focusing without undue distractions may take some time. Hang in there.

Meditating with a mantra

Probably the best known and most popular form of meditation is meditation using a mantra. A *mantra* is a sound or a word that you repeat; it can help you focus your mind and avoid distractions. After you select your mantra (see the sidebar, "Psst, looking for a good mantra?"), you're ready to put it to use:

1. **Sit quietly, either in a chair or on the floor as you did for the breathing meditation detailed in the preceding section.**

    Eliminate any distractions. Close your eyes and relax as much as you can.

2. **Start with some deep breathing and try to clear your mind of the day's hassle and worry.**

    Remember not to breathe with your chest alone. Breathe until you notice that you feel much more relaxed. (About a dozen breaths should do it.)

3. **Do a body scan (described in Chapter 2, Book VI) to see where any residual tension may be hiding.**

4. **Focus on your breathing and begin to repeat your mantra to yourself, either silently or chanting it softly.**

As you say your mantra, see the word in your head. Repeat your mantra over and over. Find a timing and rhythm that is comfortable for you. As before, if you find your concentration slipping, simply become aware of that fact and gently guide your mind back to your mantra.

Do this exercise for about 20 minutes or so and try to squeeze in as many meditative sessions as you can in your week.

Squeezing in mini-meditations

Someone once asked a meditation teacher, "How long should I meditate?" "For about 20 minutes," the wise man answered, quickly adding, "But 5 minutes of meditation you do is better than the 20 minutes of meditation you plan on doing but don't."

You may not have 20 minutes twice a day to peacefully meditate in some quiet corner of your life. And even if you have the time, you may find that your boss — who is not nearly as enlightened as you are — frowns on your meditative sessions. Fortunately, you can practice abbreviated forms of meditation — they can be as long or as short as the time you have available. You can "mini-meditate" when you find a few extra minutes, for example, during the following opportunities:

✔ Sitting in traffic (only if you're a passenger)

✔ Waiting for your doctor or dentist to see you

✔ Standing (for what seems like forever) in line

✔ Sitting in a boring meeting (where you don't have to present anything and won't be asked questions)

✔ Riding the bus, subway, or a taxicab

There are plenty of opportunities in the work setting to steal a few moments to meditate. Those nonessential meetings, small work breaks, or a few minutes on your lunch hour can do it.

Hypnotize Yourself

When you think of hypnosis, two images probably come to mind. The first is from a B-movie where you see some evil doctor — usually deranged — dangling a pocket watch in the face of some innocent victim. The second image is of some hypnotist on a stage with a dozen or so audience volunteers who are either dancing with brooms or are clucking like chickens. Fortunately, neither image is accurate.

Actually, hypnosis is less mysterious and far more mundane than you may think. In fact, you may not realize it, but chances are you've been in a hypnotic trance many times before. We slip in and out of hypnotic states all the time. Remember those times when you were driving on the highway and it scarily dawns on you that you haven't been paying attention to the road or your driving for the last five minutes? Or remember those times when you left the movie theater and realized that your attention was so glued to the screen that you had no idea who was sitting next to you or what was going on around you? Or when you were daydreaming, or just lost in thought. In each case, you were in a hypnotic trance.

Book VI

Managing Stress in Stressful Times

Hypnosis is totally safe, but more importantly, it can be a very effective way of helping you relax and cope with stress. See if you can master the technique at home and then put it to use in your work setting. (It helps if you can close your door and keep out any noise.)

No, you will not be turned into a clucking chicken

Probably no other psychological technique for stress reduction is as misunderstood as hypnosis. Some things you need to know:

- ✔ You will not be asleep.
- ✔ You will not be unconscious.
- ✔ You will not lose control or be under someone's spell.
- ✔ You won't do anything that you don't want to do.

Hypnosis is simply a deeply focused state that makes you more acutely aware of suggestions and allows you to be more receptive to those suggestions. Some people are more susceptible to hypnotic suggestion.

For hypnosis to be as effective for you as possible, try to adopt a receptive, noncritical attitude. Don't fight the process. Just go with it. If you remain totally skeptical and resistant, not much is going to happen, so have an open mind.

Discovering the power of a trance

When you're in a trance, you're in a different mental state. You are still awake and in control, but your attention becomes narrow and incredibly focused. In this state, you're more receptive to any suggestions you may give yourself or that a hypnotherapist may offer. You basically give yourself a sort of shortcut to your subconscious. These suggestions can take many forms: cigarettes taste lousy, I'm growing taller day by day, I'm getting smarter, whatever. (Clearly some suggestions are more realistic than others.)

Some trances are deeper than others. In a light trance, you feel more relaxed and are able to respond to simple suggestions. In a heavier trance, you can learn how not to respond to pain and even to forget what occurred during hypnosis. The following sections show you how to induce a light trance, which is all you need to achieve a peaceful state of deep relaxation.

Inducing a light trance

You can induce a hypnotic trance in many ways (even the dangling watch can work). Here is one of the simpler induction techniques useful in reducing tension and stress:

1. **Find a comfortable position in a quiet, dimly lit room where you won't be interrupted.**

   Relax as much as possible. If you want, take off your shoes and loosen any tight clothing.

2. **Focus on an object across the room.**

   The object can be anything — a smudge on the wall, the corner of a picture, it really doesn't matter. Just choose an object that's above your normal line of sight so that you have to strain your eyeballs a wee bit looking up to see your spot.

3. **As you look at your spot, silently say to yourself,**

   "My eyelids are becoming heavier and heavier."

   "My eyelids feel as if heavy weights are pulling them down."

   "Soon they will be so heavy they will close."

   Repeat these sentences to yourself about every 30 seconds.

4. **Focus on your eyelids.**

   Soon you will notice that, indeed, your eyelids are beginning to feel heavier. Feel this heaviness deepen with time. Don't fight these sensations, just let them happen. Let your eyes close when you feel they want to close themselves.

5. **As your eyes begin to close, say to yourself:** *"Relax and let go."*

6. **When your eyes close, take in a deep breath through your nostrils and hold that breath for about ten seconds.**

7. **Slowly exhale through your slightly parted lips, making a swooshing sound.**

   At the same time, let your jaw drop and feel a wave of warmth and heaviness spread from the top of your head, down your body, all the way to your toes. Continue to breathe slowly and smoothly. As you exhale, silently say the word *calm* (or some other relaxing word) to yourself. As you breathe, let the feelings of relaxation deepen for another few moments.

Going a little deeper

After you induce a light trance, you're ready to move into a deeper state of hypnosis.

1. **Take a deep breath and hold it for about ten seconds.**

   Exhale slowly through your lips while saying the word *deeper* to yourself. Continue this process for several breaths more, saying the word *deeper* to yourself with every exhalation.

2. **Imagine that you're stepping onto a descending escalator, a long, slow escalator that will take you into a state of deeper relaxation.**

   As you begin your descent, silently say to yourself,

   > *"I am sinking slowly into a deeper state of relaxation."*

3. **As you descend, count backwards on each exhalation, from ten to one.**

   When you reach the bottom of the escalator, imagine that you are stepping off this escalator and onto a second descending escalator. As you imagine your descent, deepen your trance with each breath, again counting backwards from ten to one.

4. **Continue to deepen your trance until you feel you have reached a comfortable level of relaxation.**

   You may need only one escalator ride, or you may need several. With practice, a deeper trance will come more easily and more quickly.

Getting out of the trance

Alright, you are now in a trance. You're feeling quite relaxed, and your mind is totally at peace. You can choose to remain in this relaxed state and simply enjoy the benefits of relaxation and calm. You can also give yourself a suggestion that can extend this relaxation beyond the trance state. Here's what to do:

Simply count slowly backwards from five to one. Say to yourself beforehand,

"When I reach one, my eyes will open and I will feel totally awake and refreshed."

As you count, notice your eyes beginning to flutter and begin to partially open as you approach one.

Overcoming roadblocks when you practice self-hypnosis

Here are some suggestions that should help you overcome one or more of the possible roadblocks that may arise as you practice self-hypnosis:

- **Give yourself enough time to reach a trance state.** This process may take 15, 20, or even 25 minutes.
- **Don't ask yourself, *"Am I hypnotized yet?"*** This performance pressure only sets the process back. Don't force it or demand it; let it happen.
- **As you move into a trance, use the breathing and muscle relaxation skills that I discuss in Chapter 2, Book VI.** These techniques speed the hypnosis process and help you attain a greater level of relaxation.

Get Some Feedback with the High-Tech Route

Biofeedback is a fancy term that means letting you know (the *feedback* part) what your body is up to (the *bio* part). Of course, biofeedback is nothing new. Getting the results of a blood test, having your blood pressure taken, or getting an EKG at your doctor's office are all examples of medical biofeedback. However, these days, the term *biofeedback* is usually used for the electronic devices that measure your stress level, or more technically, your levels of physiological arousal.

Hard-wired to your own body

In the clinic or doctor's office, biofeedback is a wonderful tool that can tell you a lot about your stress and more importantly, help you learn ways of reducing that stress. Depending on the biofeedback device used, it may measure your heart rate, body temperature, your blood pressure, skin conductivity (sweating), levels of stomach acid, muscle tension, and even your brain activity (see Figure 3-2). Each of these can be controlled to some extent, and working with biofeedback can be useful in controlling each of these functions.

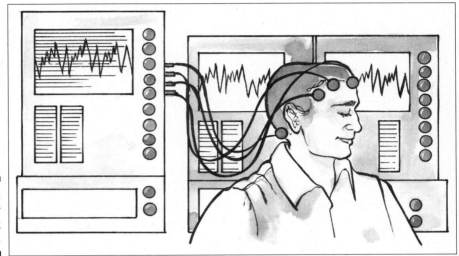

Figure 3-2:
Wired up for biofeedback readings.

Biofeedback is no substitute for learning the tools and techniques presented in Book VI. It can, however, help you use them more effectively. You may want to consult a certified biofeedback therapist who can work with you, showing you how biofeedback can help you learn to relax and reduce your levels of mental and physical stress.

Many companies now make inexpensive home biofeedback trainers that you can purchase and use by themselves or hook up to your computer. Again, a certified biofeedback therapist can tell you whom to contact.

Biofeedback without the wires

But what if you can't afford the time or money to use biofeedback equipment? Not to worry. You can come up with your own biofeedback tools. For example:

- ✔ **A watch with a second hand.** By taking your own pulse, you get a measure of your heart rate, which varies according to your level of relaxation. To feel your heartbeat, press your fingers to your neck, just under the corner of your jaw, or use a stethoscope.

Also, by counting the number of breaths you make in a fixed period of time, you have a measure of your rate of respiration. This should decrease as you become more relaxed.

✔ **A thermometer**. Holding the bulb of a thermometer between your fingers can give you a measure of your skin temperature. Relaxing your body should raise your skin temperature.

✔ **A pressure cuff.** These days, a home blood-pressure monitoring device is not all that expensive. Lowering your stress level and your levels of tension should result in lowered blood pressure readings.

✔ **A mirror.** The way you look can be a pretty good indicator of just how stressed you are. Furrowed brows, a clenched jaw, bags under your eyes — all can be signs of stress. Take a look!

Chapter 4

The Secrets of Stress-Resistant Thinking

*I*f someone cornered you at a cocktail party and asked you where most of your stress came from, chances are you'd tell them it was your job, or family pressures, or not having enough time or money. You probably wouldn't tell them that your thinking was creating much of your stress.

Yet your thinking plays a larger role in producing your stress than you may imagine. Fortunately, learning how to change your thinking is not all that difficult. This chapter shows you how to spot the specific ways your thinking makes your life more stressful than it has to be. More importantly, it shows you step by step how you can turn that stress-producing thinking into stress-resistant thinking.

Believe It or Not, Most of Your Stress Is Self-Created

Feeling stressed is, and always has been, a two-part process. First you need something "out there" to trigger your stress, and then you need to perceive that trigger as stressful. Then you feel stressed. You empower these external events and situations by the ways in which you view them. Look at something one way and you feel major stress; look at it another way and you feel less stress, maybe even no stress.

Your attitudes and beliefs about any potentially stressful situation or event determine how much stress you experience. By changing the way you look at a potentially stressful situation, you can change the way you emotionally react to that situation. In short, you can control the amount of stress you feel.

The concept of controlling the amount of stress you feel underlies a number of important approaches to psychotherapy and emotional change. An important secret of stress management is knowing how you create your stress and knowing how to change that thinking.

The notion that you play an active part in creating your own stress may not seem obvious. Consider, for example, some of these distressing scenarios:

- ✔ You feel stressed because you have to give a presentation at work tomorrow to win an important new client.

- ✔ You feel stressed at the supermarket because you got trapped in the slowest moving checkout line.

- ✔ You feel stressed because your picky Aunt Agnes is coming to stay with you for a whole week.

- ✔ You feel stressed because your neighbor is playing his music too loudly.

In each of these cases, the assumption is that the external situation or event produces the stress. That is, it's the presentation, the slow-moving line, the difficult relative, or the noisy neighbor causing you to feel stressed. And there is some truth in this. Let's face it, without those stress triggers you wouldn't be feeling stress. However, the reality is that presentations, slow lines, difficult relatives, and loud music do not, in themselves, have the power to make you stressed. For a situation or circumstance to trigger stress, *you* have to see that situation as stressful.

If *only* the external situation caused stress, then everyone would feel the same stress when placed in the same situation. Clearly, this is not the case. Whenever you take any group of people and expose all of them to the same stress or hassle, chances are you will get a range of reactions. Consider this scenario: You're sitting in your plane seat, white-knuckled, downing your third Scotch. You're thinking:

> *"Oh my gosh, I'm going to die! I know this plane is going down. We'll all be killed! That left engine sounds funny! This plane is in real trouble! Lord, just get me through this one and I promise. . . ."*

You're experiencing lots of stress. You notice your seat mate is smiling contentedly. She is experiencing absolutely no stress. She's thinking:

> *"This is the best! I love flying. Nobody can reach me up here. I'll just relax with my Grisham novel and nurse this Scotch. Ah, here comes dinner. This feels so good! I'll think I'll have the fish."*

In short, what is stressful for somebody else may be less stressful for you, or maybe not stressful at all. Consider these slightly modified scenarios:

- A few days before your presentation, you learn that you have been offered a better job at another company. You are delighted. Do you feel less stress about the presentation? Probably.

- You're in the slow-moving supermarket line but pick up a magazine with a story that intrigues you. Now you're pleased that the line is moving so slowly because you want to finish the article.

- You are reliably informed that your Aunt Agnes has rewritten her will and made you the sole beneficiary to her rather large estate. You're staying only one week, Aunt Agnes?

- Noisy neighbor? Who cares? Just that morning you signed the papers on a wonderful new place across town. Half the cost, twice the size. Knock yourself out, buddy!

Yes, these alternative scenarios aren't likely, but they do make the point. The triggering event alone doesn't cause the stress; your perceptions and expectations about that potentially stressful event determine how stressed you feel.

Book VI

Managing Stress in Stressful Times

Think Straight! Eliminating Thinking Errors

Want to feel less stressed? Think straighter! Whenever you feel stressed, there's a very good chance that you're distorting or misrepresenting the event or situation triggering your stress. Your thinking is a wee bit crooked. You're making too many thinking errors. To remedy this, it is important to understand what your thinking errors are and know how to correct them.

There are seven major thinking errors, all covered in the following sections.

Quit catastrophizing and awfulizing

Having a low-stress day? Why not catastrophize or awfulize? These forms of distortion guarantee that your day has at least some stress. Put most simply, *catastrophizing* and *awfulizing* make mountains out of molehills. With very little effort, you can turn an everyday hassle into a major tragedy. Here's what you do when you catastrophize and awfulize:

1. **You encounter a situation or event in your life with the potential to stress you in some way.**

   Suppose your boss makes you stay 20 minutes late tonight to finish up a last-minute project.

2. **Then you exaggerate the importance and meaning of this situation.**

   For example, you'd say to yourself something like:

   "Oh my gosh, this is the worst thing that could happen to me! I can't believe it! This is terrible! This is awful!"

   It adds to the effect if you can summon up a pained look on your face as you say these things to yourself.

By escalating a hassle to a catastrophe, you also elevate your stress levels. The reality is, unless you are about to be married in 20 minutes, having to work a little late, wait in a checkout line, or sit in traffic is just a small hassle or inconvenience and should be viewed as such. Even many of the bigger hassles can be emotionally exaggerated and blown out of proportion, creating more stress for yourself than is necessary.

Ask yourself these two questions to help reduce your catastrophizing or awfulizing:

- ✔ How important is this really?
- ✔ Will I remember this event in three years, three months, three weeks, or three days (or even in three hours!)?

By challenging and disputing your exaggerated thinking, you begin to look at the situation differently. And as a consequence, you feel less stress.

Minimize your can't-stand-it-itis

Can't-stand-it-itis, which may sound like some rare neurological condition, is just another form of emotional distortion designed to increase your stress level. Here's how this little number works:

1. **You find some hassle, situation, or circumstance that you don't like.**

2. **Then (and this is the important part) you turn that "I don't like it" into an "I can't stand it!"**

3. **Now, you utter with conviction:**

   - *"I can't stand it when this computer freezes!"*

   - *"I hate it when someone nearby talks on the phone while I'm working!"*

When you say and believe that you can't stand, hate, despise, or loathe something, your emotional temperature rises, and you become more upset — more stressed — than you would if you merely disliked that same something. Even though you may not like the hassles and frustrations you're confronted with, you don't have to go ballistic and explode with inflated rage.

When you really believe you can't stand something, you produce a great deal of internal stress, far more than is warranted by the situation or circumstance. You make yourself very upset, angry, and distraught. When you recognize that some can't-stand-it-itis is contributing to your emotional stress, step back, and challenge and dispute your thinking. Ask yourself:

✔ Can I really not stand it, or do I really mean I do not like it?

✔ Is my overreacting here helping me in any way? Or is it really making things worse?

✔ Couldn't I really stand it for quite a bit longer? And if someone were willing to fork over really big bucks, couldn't I stand this for even longer?

Cut out much of your what-if-ing

You may be a *what-if-er*. Whenever you what-if, you take a bad situation or event that could happen and make it into something that probably will happen. This way of thinking can and does add much unnecessary stress to your life. Here's how what-if-ing works: You're having a slow day and you stress yourself out about any of the following possible events:

✔ What if there's a transit strike!

✔ What if my company downsizes!

✔ What if my co-worker has a transmittable disease!

✔ What if there are terrorists on my plane!

✔ What if my new boss hates me!

✔ What if the stock market crashes!

✔ What if I get hit by a car!

✔ What if my office burns down and we lose everything!

✔ What if the mailroom clerk is a serial killer!

In life, many unpleasant things can happen. Can they happen to you? Yes. Will they happen to you? Unfortunately, some will. However, many, if not most of the things you worry about never happen. But this doesn't stop you from worrying about the possibility of their happening. What-if, what-if, what-if. . . .

To cut out your what-if-ing, ask yourself these thought-straightening questions:

✔ Realistically, what are the chances of this feared event really happening?

✔ Am I over-worrying about this?

✔ Is there something productive I could be turning my mind to instead of dwelling on this?

Book VI

Managing Stress in Stressful Times

Avoid overgeneralizing

If you *overgeneralize,* you cause yourself to be more stressed than you have to be. Take a look at the following overgeneralizations and see whether you recognize yourself:

- ✔ This company is run by idiots! (When you disagree with a corporate decision.)
- ✔ Nobody in this town knows how to drive! (When someone cuts you off in traffic.)
- ✔ I always have to do everything by myself! (When your request for someone to change the printer's ink toner goes unanswered.)
- ✔ You never listen! (When your project teammate isn't listening.)

Though there may be some truth in these statements, they are all clearly overgeneralizations. When you overgeneralize, you create a distorted image of what is really happening and create a reality that invites excessive and inappropriate anger and upset. By thinking in terms of all or nothing, good or bad, right or wrong, you make yourself more stressed than you have to be.

To help you curb any tendency to overgeneralize, here are some useful ideas:

- ✔ Ask yourself if you're seeing only one small part of a person's overall behavior and too quickly assuming that this sample truly characterizes that person as a whole.
- ✔ Try to think of individuals or situations that do *not* fit into your overgeneralization.
- ✔ Look out for language that reflects this all-or-nothing thinking — words like *always* and *never,* as in "People are *never* friendly," or "People *always* take advantage of you when they have the chance."

The reality is, the world and the people in it rarely fall into discrete, easily identified categories. Try to find the gray areas and spare yourself a lot of stress.

Stop mind reading and conclusion jumping

You *mind read* and *conclusion jump* whenever you believe that you know something as true, when in fact, it may not be true at all. Some examples of mind reading and conclusion jumping make this clear:

- ✔ Your boss writes notes throughout your presentation, and you conclude he's criticizing everything you say.

- ✔ You see a brown spot on the back of your hand and conclude it's a terminal disease.

- ✔ You do a complete personality evaluation on someone you just met, based largely on what she was wearing.

There are times when you simply don't have enough information or data to come to a conclusion with any degree of certainty. But that may not stop you from trying.

One method to determine whether you are mind reading or conclusion jumping is to do a Perry Mason. Simply ask yourself, "Do I really have enough evidence to support my beliefs? Would a jury of my peers agree with me?" If the answer is no, reconsider your case and hold off coming to any premature conclusions and reactions just yet. Who knows, you may be right. However, if you are like most people, you're also wrong much of the time. (By the way, if Perry Mason draws a blank, substitute Matlock.)

Curb your unrealistic expectations

Your expectations play an important role in determining just how stressed you feel in reacting to a potentially stressful situation. If your expectations are out of whack, there is a good chance you will overreact. The brief tongue-in-cheek reality test that follows can give you a better sense of how unrealistic expectations can increase your stress.

Take this short quiz to see just how realistic are your expectations are. Simply answer true or false to each of these items:

Your boss gives you an assignment just as you're about to take off early to enjoy the sunny day. You tell him that you really had your heart set on getting to the pool that afternoon. You expect he'll say, "In that case, you go on. I'll do the assignment myself."	T or F
You've been searching for a parking place for the last 45 minutes when you finally see a spot opening up. The guy in the car ahead of you also sees the spot and is closer to it than you are. You tell him how difficult it's been for you to find a parking place. You expect he will say: "Why don't you take this spot. I have lots of extra time today."	T or F
You arrive at your doctor's office at ten minutes to 3, ready for your 3 o'clock appointment. You expect that promptly at 3 a nurse will emerge and say, "Follow me please; the doctor is ready to see you."	T or F

You have an important report due early tomorrow morning. And because you plan to write it at home tonight, it is essential that your computer and printer not give you any trouble. You expect that your computer and printer will not give you any trouble.	T or F
Your two adolescent children have sworn that they will be totally responsible for taking care of a dog if you get them one. You expect that they will, in fact, honor their promise.	T or F

If you answered true to any of these items, good luck. Could any or all of the above expectations come about? Absolutely. However, the reality is, things often don't work out the way you'd like them to. Be realistic in what you expect.

The following sections offer advice about how to recognize unrealistic expectations (even when they're very subtle) and change the way you think.

Stop musterbating

Musterbation (with a *u!*) is what psychologist Albert Ellis dubbed the use of unrealistic *shoulds* and *shouldn'ts*. You make this error whenever you hear yourself saying, in a rather rigid, angry way, things like:

- ✔ People *shouldn't* be rude!
- ✔ People *shouldn't* cut you off in the parking lot!
- ✔ Life *should* be fair!

What's that you say? There's nothing wrong with these statements? People shouldn't be rude, insensitive, and unfair. You're right. There would be nothing wrong with these statements if they were merely preferences or a prescription for a better world.

However, when these *shoulds* and *shouldn'ts* take the form of rigid demands and inflexible expectations, you are going to be mighty upset and angry when they do not materialize. When others (even you, for that matter) violate one of these unrealistic demands, you find yourself morally judging them and becoming indignant and angry. And there will be lots to get stressed about, because people often don't and won't follow your rules and guidelines for correct living.

The antidote? Stop musterbating. Give up these rigid demands and replace them with healthier, more flexible preferences. Try saying to yourself:

- ✔ I would really like it if people were nicer.
- ✔ It certainly would be a better world if people were more considerate.
- ✔ It would be nice if life was fair.

Whenever you suspect you may be using an unrealistic *should* or *shouldn't,* challenge this thinking, and ask yourself the following two questions:

- Is my *should* really a disguised *must* or a *have-to?* Am I really making a demand in disguise?
- Why *must* other people act the way I want them to? They don't, and often won't.

By changing your unrealistic demands to healthy preferences, you'll feel much better. And certainly less stressed.

Watch out for "exclamation mark behavior"

One way of finding out whether your expectation is realistic or unrealistic is to look for *exclamation mark behavior.* Some examples of such behavior include saying any of the following things to yourself when you're faced with a situation that angers or upsets you:

- How can this be!
- I don't understand this!
- How could he do this!
- I don't believe this!
- Why would someone do this!

What characterizes this behavior is the tone of surprise and disbelief in your reaction.

Accompanying such exclamations of disbelief are tell-tale "I just can't believe this!" gestures. Commonly seen examples include:

- Excessive eye-rolling and eyebrow-lifting
- Excessive and loud sighing
- Head nodding with accompanying *tsk-tsks*
- Hands thrown into the air indicating total frustration

The importance of this behavior is that it indicates the presence of unrealistic expectations. Implicit in your disbelief is the unreasonable demand, "Other people should and must be more like me. I wouldn't act like that; therefore, neither should they." But they do, and you have to learn to accept it.

Stop self-rating

Whenever you equate your self-worth with your performance or the approval of others, you're *self-rating.* In either case, the end result is plenty of unnecessary stress.

The essence of this form of stress-producing thinking is that you believe you have worth, are a terrific person, and have a right to feel good about yourself because

- ✔ You have accomplished great things.
- ✔ You have marvelous traits (you're smart, good-looking, rich).
- ✔ Some important other person approves of you or what you have done.

Now you're probably asking, "What's the matter with that? Don't we all want the approval of others, want to do well, and want to have excellent traits?" Yes, we do. The problem arises when you feel you need to do well or absolutely must have success or the approval of others. The reality is, there are many times in life when you will not do as well as you would like, when your performance will be less than stellar, and you will not get approval from others. By making your worth contingent on any or all of these traits, you become vulnerable to unnecessary stress.

Frankly, giving up this self-rating tendency is not the easiest thing to do. It takes time and effort. To start, ask yourself the following questions:

- ✔ Do I really need to have others' approval to feel good about myself?
- ✔ Do I really have to be better than others to feel good about myself?
- ✔ I don't expect other people to be perfect, so why should I expect it from myself?
- ✔ Can I rate my total worth as an individual on the basis of one or two traits or abilities?

The answer to each of the above is, of course, no. None of these is truly necessary for you to be happy in life — or feel good about yourself.

Putting It All Together: Systematic Stress Analysis

After you have a better understanding about the ways in which your thinking can produce your stress, you're in a good position to do something about your stress-producing thinking. *Systematic stress analysis* is a structured technique that shows you, step by step, how to take any stressful situation and determine exactly how much of a role your thinking is contributing to your stress level. More importantly, it shows you how you can correct your stress-producing thinking and replace it with stress-resistant thinking.

To start, make several copies of the Stress-Analysis Worksheet that appears at the end of this chapter. If you are somewhere where you are unable to make copies (the base camp on Kilimanjaro, for example), grab a sheet of paper and copy down the headings and format.

Step 1: Write down what's stressing you

At the top of the page, beside *My stress trigger,* write down what is triggering your stress. Be brief.

For example, the following description . . .

> *I was so upset when my boss asked me late in the day for a detailed status report that she needed that afternoon. If she'd hadn't waited until the last minute to ask for the report, I could have worked it into my schedule and wouldn't have had to rearrange my other meetings or stay late.*

. . . can be shortened to:

> *Last-minute request for a report.*

Book VI

Managing Stress in Stressful Times

Step 2: Rate your level of stress

Rate your level of stress about that situation or event on a 10-point scale where 10 means major stress, being sure to consider the many forms of stress — frustration, aggravation, upset, annoyance, worry, anger, sadness, disappointment, and so on.

For the example situation, you might rate it a 5.

Step 3: Write down your response to the trigger

Beside *My stress response,* note your feelings — your reaction to that stress trigger. It could be any one or more of the stress indicators: irritation, anger, upset, anxiety, worry, headache, muscle tension, rapid breathing — or any of the many other stress-induced signs and symptoms.

Here, your stress response may be:

> *Got upset and angry.*

Step 4: Rate the importance of the stressful situation

On a 10-point scale (where 10 is a biggie), how important was the stressful situation?

Think of three major life stresses that could happen or have happened to you. These are your 9s and 10s, the major life-altering events that everyone fears, and some people dread: the death of a loved one, a major financial loss, a life-threatening illness, the loss of your job, chronic pain, and so on. Comparing your current situation to these, give it a rating from 0 to 10.

Here's what the example worksheet looks like at this point:

> **My stress trigger (stress-producing event or circumstance):** Last-minute request for a report.
>
> **My stress response level (0–10 scale):** 5
>
> **My stress response (how I reacted to the stress trigger):** Got upset and angry.
>
> **The importance of this stress trigger (0–10 scale):** 2

Assess your stress balance by asking yourself, "Does the level of my stress response match the importance of the situation?" If it doesn't, you are off balance. Your stress level is out of line. In the example situation, the stress reaction is three points higher than the importance of the situation, so you're experiencing too much stress relative to the importance of the situation.

Knowing you're off-balance tells you that you're overreacting to a situation that doesn't deserve that kind of emotional investment. Your stress button is bigger than it has to be, and you're causing yourself more stress than is necessary.

Step 5: Identify your stress-producing self-talk

Write down what you may be saying to yourself to create much of this stress. Remember that much of this self-talk is pretty automatic. You're probably not even aware of saying anything to yourself. But you are. To help you get in touch with this automatic self-talk, ask yourself, "What might I have been saying to myself about this stress trigger?"

In this example, you may write down on the worksheet something like this:

Oh my gosh! This is awful! It couldn't have happened at a worst time. My boss's poor planning is ruining my weekend! It's Friday afternoon, and now I have to work late. I just hate it when things like this happen! I'll never be happy again!

In his book *The Feeling Good Handbook* (Plume), psychiatrist David Burns suggests something called the *Vertical Arrow Technique* as a way of getting in touch with your less obvious or hidden thinking. Here's how it works. Suppose your automatic thought in the example above was:

If I can't leave work as I planned, I'll be late for my dinner date.

Ask yourself, "What would this mean?" Your response may be

That would be terrible! I would be devastated.

The value of this technique is that it takes you to another level of your thinking, and uncovers the more irrational parts of your self-talk, which may be hidden by fairly sensible descriptive statements. You may have to do it two or three times to uncover all the hidden self-talk.

Another example should make this clear. Suppose your child wanted to play roller-hockey. He's very distressed because it's raining out and he can't play. Using the arrow technique, you can see how a statement could lead to more hidden thoughts:

It's raining out.

Asking, "What does this mean?" leads to

Therefore, I can't play hockey.

Asking again, "What does this mean?" leads to

It's awful! My day is ruined!

You can use the vertical arrow technique to uncover layers of stress triggers, and then deal with them realistically.

Step 6: Find your thinking errors

From your self-talk, try to identify the thinking errors that seem to be relevant (refer to the earlier section "Think Straight! Eliminating Thinking Errors" for complete descriptions of these errors):

Book VI

Managing Stress in Stressful Times

✔ Catastrophizing and awfulizing

✔ Can't-stand-it-itis

✔ What-if-ing

✔ Overgeneralizing

✔ Mind reading and conclusion jumping

✔ Unrealistic expectations

✔ Self-rating

In the examples in the preceding section, you can see that there is more than a little catastrophizing and awfulizing going on, with a healthy dose of can't-stand-it-itis thrown in.

Step 7: Use your coping self-talk

You are now ready to respond to your stress-producing self-talk, correct any thinking errors, and come up with a more stress-resistant way of looking at your stress-triggers. Here's what your coping self-talk might look (and sound) like on your worksheet:

> *This isn't really a major tragedy. Yes, I am disappointed, but it's not any-thing I can't deal with. Don't blow it up. Calm down and see what you can do to fix this situation. Start breathing . . . You're doing fine. What to do? Call my date and tell her what happened. Maybe we can change our reservations.*

Or consider what your son's roller-hockey coping self-talk might sound like:

> *It's not the worst thing in the world. I can play tomorrow. Let me call Matt or Jenny and maybe we can go see a movie.*

Or consider your potential stress when you realize you've locked yourself out of the house (again!):

> *I'm an idiot! I've done it again. Calm down and try some relaxing breathing . . . and do it again. That feels better. Don't catastrophize or awfulize. Don't make this into a bigger deal than it is. On a scale of 1 to 10 this is still only a 2 or 3. Stay in balance. Just getting upset isn't going to help anything. Think. Who has another key? Nobody. Okay, Beth will be home in an hour. Go to the coffee shop, read the paper, and relax. I can handle this. I am handling this. Good for me. I may be a forgetful idiot, but at least I can cope with the consequences.*

Talk like an air-traffic controller

One way to help yourself use your coping self-talk is to think like an air-traffic controller. Consider this B-movie scenario:

> The weather at the airport is foggy. Very foggy. You are the air-traffic controller in charge. You learn that a novice pilot is having trouble landing and is panicking. He badly needs your help. You begin to talk him down. You say:
>
> *You're doing just fine, son. Hang in there . . . take a deep, slow breath . . . great!*
>
> *Now, remember what you learned in pilot school. Pull the throttle toward you. That's it. You can do this . . . let her steady out. Begin your decent. Good. Take another deep breath. Don't panic. Hold her steady . . . you're almost down . . . you're doin' great . . . you're on the ground. You made it!*

You get the idea. Talk to yourself in a way that helps you cope better with the stressful or potentially stressful situation.

What to say to yourself

If you're at a loss for words and can't seem to come up with what to say to yourself, use the following list as a reference. It includes most of the essential self-talk elements you need.

- ✔ Verbally correct your thinking errors by challenging and disputing their reasonableness. (Is this really so awful? Can I stand this for a little longer? Do I really need this person's approval? And so on.)

  If you're still a little shaky on how to do this, review the descriptions of the various thinking errors in the previous sections.

- ✔ Tell yourself to put the stress into perspective. Talk yourself into balance.

- ✔ Relax yourself. Include instructions to help you relax in your self-talk. Use the techniques and strategies described in Chapters 2 and 3.

- ✔ Problem solve. Give yourself some direction and instructions that help you cope with, and possibly remove, the source of your stress.

You can use the same approach whenever you find yourself in a stressful situation. Yes, you can talk yourself out of being stressed.

Your Stress Analysis Worksheet

My stress trigger (stress-producing event or circumstance):

_____

_____

My stress response level (0–10 scale): _____

My stress response (how I reacted to the stress trigger):

_____

_____

The importance of this stress trigger (0–10 scale): _____

My self-talk:

_____

_____

_____

_____

_____

My thinking errors:

_____

_____

My coping self-talk:

_____

_____

_____

_____

Book VII

Going Further to Get Ahead: Certifications and Courses to Enhance Your Value

The 5th Wave   By Rich Tennant

"Can you explain your online certification program again, this time without using the phrase 'yada, yada, yada?'"

In this book . . .

The ups and downs of the global economy have sent more learners back to school to retool or add credentials to their résumé. You could be one of them. Of course, balancing work, family, civic commitments, and school is an arduous task at best. Online education allows you to address your professional development needs at a time and in a manner that may be more flexible with your lifestyles. The chapters in this book help you figure out what online programs may be right for you.

Chapter 1

Discovering What's Available Online

*I*f your appetite for learning online has been whetted, where should you go to find the right course offering? You may be surprised at the variety of institutions that offer online courses and how these courses have been packaged together for degrees. This chapter walks you through the many places you can find different kinds of online courses and the various ways in which they are organized. Finally, it takes a look at accelerated courses and how they work online.

Examining Different Types of Online Programs and Courses

If you avoid school because it means hard work, don't feel bad — you're in the majority. However, there are good reasons to continue learning, including job promotions, higher earning potential, elevated status, and personal enrichment. The surprising thing is that school and learning are becoming synonymous with online education. This section discusses aspects you should consider when looking at online programs and courses.

How important is it to you to earn college credit for your work? Do you have the time and resources to take enough courses to complete a degree? Or do you only need a few courses for professional development or skill enhancement? Would a specific certification be the professional seal of approval you need? How you answer these questions determines the kinds of online programs that are best for you.

Earning traditional credit

If you've decided to take an online course, chances are good that you're looking to earn some sort of traditional credit for your work. This section describes the kinds of credit you can get for your efforts — specifically, credits toward undergraduate or graduate degrees and high school credits. You can earn traditional college credits at two-year and four-year higher education institutions (which are covered later in this chapter) if you have completed your high school education. If you're still working on high school, you can earn credits through accredited online programs that serve your unique needs.

Credits toward undergraduate and graduate degrees

Yes, you can earn an entire degree online! You can find programs that award associate's (two-year), bachelor's (four-year), master's, and even doctoral degrees online. You also can use online classes to supplement in-person coursework at a traditional institution. If you follow the suggestions for searching for a course at different institutions (which appear later in this chapter), you'll probably see this in the marketing information you find.

Schools package courses together for an online degree just like they do for a degree you would earn in a traditional fashion. The degree consists of required courses (classes you must take) and a handful of elective courses. Only when you earn the necessary number of credit hours in the right mix of required and elective courses do you get the degree conferred. How many hours depends on the type of degree you're seeking, the state you're studying in, and the individual institution. However, in general, these are the expectations:

- ✔ An associate's degree typically requires around 60 credit hours and may represent the first two years of a bachelor's degree.
- ✔ A bachelor's degree requires 124–128 credit hours.
- ✔ A master's degree requires 32–36 hours beyond a bachelor's degree. Some programs require as many as 44 credit hours.
- ✔ A doctorate requires around 60–75 credit hours beyond a bachelor's, plus successful completion of a comprehensive examination and a written dissertation of original research.

When you enroll in a college course, the number of credit hours you'll receive upon completing it should be evident in the course schedule or the marketing information. Schools are typically very good about stating how many credit hours they attach to a particular course, because this can make a difference in the total number of hours awarded that count toward a degree. A typical semester course awards three credit hours. By looking at the course number, you can tell whether those credits are undergraduate or graduate hours:

✔ Anything with a 100–400 number (for example, PSY101) indicates undergraduate credit, which is what you need for an associate's or bachelor's degree.

✔ Courses with numbers 500 and above grant graduate-level credit, suitable for master's degrees and doctorates.

You may have heard radio ads claiming you can finish your degree in as little as 18 months. These programs target adults who have previously earned some undergraduate credit and are now ready to complete a bachelor's degree. This newer twist in online education is actually a continuation of a former adult education model. These models started a couple of decades ago and established a night and weekend schedule for working adults. Some programs "accelerated" their courses by compressing a 16-week course into 8 weeks, but not all. The point was that you could go to work during the day and catch up on coursework on the weekend. Today's model of online education offers even more convenience in that you don't have to push it all off to Saturday or Sunday. Because you work from the comfort of your home or office, you can engage in learning throughout the week.

One factor you may experience in online degree programs is the use of *cohort groups*. Simply put, this means when you begin a series of courses toward the completion of a degree, you progress with the same group or cohort of students through the entire degree. If John is in your first class, John should be in your last class — and every class in between! Many people believe that the bonds formed among a cohort group of students are more supportive and therefore more likely to influence students to positively persist through programs. If John is your friend, he might talk you out of dropping out when times get tough. Plus, from an administrative perspective, cohorts are easier to track and often allow an institution to offer more start dates so that students don't have to wait several months to begin taking classes.

High school credits

High school credit functions a little like college credit in that you need to earn the right number of course credits and the right types. This varies from state to state in the United States, however. For example, in one state you may need four years of English, whereas you may be able to get by with only three in another state. Depending on what state you live in and whether you're homeschooled or attending a traditional school, you could earn all or part of your high school credits through online schools.

Make sure that any online high school courses you investigate will count toward graduation in your state. Start by checking your local school district's policies in accordance with the state requirements. A trip or phone call to the district office should get you the information you need, but you can also search your state's Department of Education Web site for policy statements concerning online education.

Obtaining certifications

Maybe you're interested in a career change or you want to branch into a new direction within your current field. A certification or endorsement may be just what you need, and you can earn many of these online.

Certificates are like miniature degrees that signify continuing education following a planned and purposeful curriculum. They offer only what you need for a specific professional field or task. For example, if you study for a certificate in Web site development, you don't have to take computer science courses in COBOL programming, but you do need graphics and multimedia instruction. If you're studying for a certificate as a dental assistant, you don't have to take an English composition course, but you need courses in radiology and diagnostics. Just the facts, ma'am.

Typically, a certificate is much shorter than a traditional degree. If you think of an associate's degree as a two-year degree (60 hours) and a bachelor's degree as a four-year degree (124–128 hours), the certification is a one-and-a-half-year degree. For example, you can earn a certificate in medical transcription for an average of 44 credit hours. Interested in private security? A certificate is available for as few as 50 credit hours.

Another point to keep in mind is that some certificates can lead to other degrees. For example, if you earn a certificate in e-learning, some of those courses may count toward a master's degree at the same institution. Ask the school officials about this if you think the certificate may take you further.

More and more institutions offer certification online, including traditional two- and four-year institutions. Quality programs are truly beneficial in that they allow students to extend their professional development while continuing to work full time. Every institution defines its own requirements for degrees and certificates. You need to compare carefully when looking at multiple programs. Drill down and see what courses are required and whether they hold your interest.

One of the best sources of information for a certification program is your professional association. Read professional newsletters and ask practitioners about the kinds of certificates and credentials valued in that field.

Continuing your education with a few classes for fun or profit

Online courses are not limited to degree or certificate programs. You can actually have fun online! For example, you could take a course in feng shui, an ancient Chinese practice of orienting objects to achieve desirable outcomes. You also can further your professional skills or ensure that you're meeting critical standards in your field by taking just a handful of classes. Whenever you enhance your professional skills, you stand to profit through promotions and salary boosts.

Personal interest

Ever wonder about your genealogy but don't know how to start researching and documenting your heritage? There's an online course for that. How about picking up a second language? Digital photography? These examples show the diversity of online courses.

What kinds of institutions offer such courses? To be honest, you may find a course for free or very little money by starting up your favorite search engine (such as Google or Yahoo!) and typing "online course + [name of topic]". Try it; you'll be surprised! These courses may not be supported by an institution, and you won't earn credit, but you will get the information you seek. For example, coauthor Kevin Johnson recently took an online photography course where he learned the nuances of digital photography. He paid a fee to the photography school and completed the work online.

If you're looking for an institution to back you, you may find that your local college (two- or four-year) offers quite a few online courses geared toward personal interests. Topics may include the ones listed earlier in addition to art history, nutrition, parenting, and much more. These courses are usually part of the institutions' "community development" catalog or noncredit courses.

Professional development

In many fields, professionals are encouraged or required to complete professional development courses on an annual basis. For example, in the state of Illinois, per state funding guidelines for grant-funded adult education programs, school faculty are required to complete six hours of professional development per fiscal year. So if you want to keep your teaching job, you have to get those six hours of training somehow! If you're a practicing medical or dental professional and want to maintain your licensure, you have to earn a prescribed number of continuing education credits per year. These kinds of courses may be found at institutions that award degrees in those fields. For example, if you need credits for teaching, a college that awards degrees in education would be a logical place to look.

Book VII

Going Further to Get Ahead

In addition, more and more professional associations offer professional development online. They know professionals appreciate the convenience of learning anytime, anywhere. You can find many opportunities by conducting a search for "[your field] + online courses." For example, the Young Adult Library Services Association offers its members online courses related to their professional needs. You can find these opportunities by searching for "[your association] + online courses" in your preferred search engine.

Make sure that any professional development course credits you earn will be accepted by the professional association that requires you to earn them. To find out, visit the association's Web site and search for statements concerning acceptance of online credit. For example, if you're a dentist, you can visit the American Dental Association's continuing education page to see a clear statement regarding states' limits on the number of hours that can be earned through self-paced online courses.

Compliance training

In business and industry, compliance training accounts for most course offerings. What kind of compliance? It could involve ethics training, safety and material data, or emergency preparedness. Other examples include what to do with forms, processes for requisitioning funds, or must-know policies. You may find all of these courses online. The most common provider is your company's human resources department.

Compliance training works very well as a self-paced course, so don't be surprised if you're in a course all by yourself. However, keep in mind that your participation, what pages or content you read, and how well you do in follow-up tests may be reported back to the company. Self-paced courses are discussed in more detail later in this chapter.

Finding Out Which Institutions Offer Online Programs and Courses

Whether you're interested in taking one or two online courses or completing an entire degree online, the process of searching for online education offerings isn't much different from researching traditional education options. First you need to determine what kind of institution best meets your needs. Are you seeking a bachelor's degree or higher? Then you need at least a four-year school. This section walks you through your choices according to the type of institution so you know what to look for.

Four-year colleges

Many four-year colleges and universities, both public and private, offer bachelor's degrees and graduate degrees online. They may also offer certificates and personal enrichment courses. Some are traditional schools with real brick-and-mortar campuses; others are completely virtual with no physical place to go. The following sections discuss how to get course information from both of these types of schools.

Hold on there! Before you go randomly searching, considering the following recommendations may save you time:

- ✔ **If you're completing a degree you previously started at a traditional school:** Go back to the institution where you were a student and talk to them about what may be available online. Jump to the section "Brick-and-mortar schools."

- ✔ **If you're starting an entire degree from scratch:** You have to decide which of the two types of institutions you want to earn it from: brick and mortar or wholly online. Read both of the following sections to find out how to get necessary information.

- ✔ **If you simply need a course or two for personal interest or professional development:** Look at your local state institutions. Not only do you keep your money in-state, but you're closer if you need to drive to the campus for any reason.

Brick-and-mortar schools

If you type "online courses" into a search engine, some of the schools in the resulting list will be traditional institutions with physical campuses. For example, you may find Colorado Technical University or DeVry University, which offer their programs and classes both on traditional campuses and through online counterparts.

Traditional brick-and-mortar schools, such as your local state university, don't seem to pop to the top of the search results. They're competing against the online giants and their marketing dollars aren't going as far. However, these are still worthy of consideration — you just have to follow a different process to get the information you need:

1. **Rather than conduct an open search, go directly to the local school's Web site.**

   Once there, look for links to online learning, online education, online courses, distance learning, or distance education on the home page. If they aren't obvious, look for a link to academics or future students and see whether online courses are mentioned there.

2. **Know what kind of degree you're looking for and the school, college, or academic department it typically falls under.**

   For example, if you want to become a teacher, look in the College of Education or something similar. If you want a degree in business, look for the College of Business or something to that effect.

3. **Once you find your way to the correct department, begin sorting through the course listings.**

   Look for links to course schedules rather than the course catalog.

   A school's catalog tells you what courses you need to put together for an entire degree, but it may not tell you whether the entire degree is available online.

4. **See whether the school gives you the opportunity to sort through the ways in which a given class is offered.**

   The best schools state clearly and unquestionably when a class is offered online or in a blended format. (Blended learning — a combination of online and traditional teaching methods — is explored a little later in this chapter.)

5. **When you have an idea that the school offers online courses or a degree in which you're interested, follow up.**

   Send an e-mail or make a telephone call to the department you're interested in. Ask for more information.

Wholly online schools

When you do a search for "online courses" online, other names besides those of traditional institutions pop up. Schools like University of Phoenix, Kaplan University, Capella University and other entirely online four-year schools have grown in popularity, and are now mainstream in the media and online search worlds.

Listings from the major players will come up in a general search for "online courses" plus the field you're interested in, as well as agencies that market online programs for a variety of schools. An example of an agency is EarnMyDegree (www.earnmydegree.com). This particular Web site represents universities you may recognize as well as some that may be unfamiliar.

In most cases, you're asked to complete an online form with your name, e-mail address, and some other basic information such as the type of program you are considering. You will then receive more information by e-mail.

College: One word, two meanings

College of Lake County and College of Education both use the word *college,* but in different contexts. Here's the lowdown:

✔ **The word *college* can be part of the name of the institution.** In North America, smaller schools, two-year schools, and schools that focus on undergraduate education are often named as colleges.

✔ **The word *college* can also describe a group of departments or programs that offer degrees with the same foundations but distinct expertise.** This is often the case at larger institutions where degrees are more highly differentiated. An example would be a large university that's divided into multiple colleges, including a College of Business that offers degrees in entrepreneurship, administration, marketing, and accounting.

This is a direct method of finding out what's available, but it has the following drawbacks:

✔ You're put on everyone's mailing list, and your e-mail inbox grows exponentially.

✔ You begin receiving phone calls during the dinner hour.

✔ You may hear from institutions that are not accredited (see the next chapter for the importance of accreditation).

✔ You may have so many choices that it becomes overwhelming!

Book VII

Going Further to Get Ahead

Two-year colleges

If you're looking for a two-year (associate's) degree, you'll have an easier time with your search process than you will with other types of institutions. Why is this? The short answer is that two-year brick-and-mortar colleges (also known as community colleges or junior colleges) have had the most experience with online courses. In fact, according to the researchers at the Sloan Consortium, a professional group of institutions and individuals focused on quality online education, almost half of the students enrolled in online courses in 2007 were studying at two-year colleges.

The search process for online courses at a two-year college is very similar to what you would experience for a four-year school, but you're more likely to be able to go directly to course listings that specify online delivery. In short, you might see a glowing icon that says *Online Courses Here!* on the community college's home page. That means you won't have as much difficulty finding information about what online courses are available.

If you don't see an obvious link to online learning, online education, online courses, distance education, or distance learning, follow the same steps that you would for a four-year brick-and-mortar school (listed earlier in this chapter).

Other institutions for certificates, professional development, and training

Finding an online certification program is very similar to searching for online courses through two-year or four-year institutions. Again, you have to know what you're looking for, and you have to know what kind of institution will serve you best.

Suppose you want to earn a certificate in a new career field. Using your standard search engine, you find that you can earn such a certificate through two- and four-year schools, some with brick-and-mortar operations, and others that are wholly online. (You even find programs that are sold by companies and don't offer traditional credit, but those aren't recommended.)

Here are a few pointers to help you decide:

- ✔ **Is your area of study mostly introductory and associated with a two-year degree, such as medical transcription or allied health?** If so, look to a two-year school.

- ✔ **Is your area of study more closely aligned with a field requiring a bachelor's degree?** This would include fields like computer science or education, where certificates and endorsements often mean job promotions. In this case, look to a school that can offer graduate degrees.

- ✔ **Do you need to earn Continuing Education Units (CEUs) to maintain a license or for employment?** Maybe a professional association in your field has recommended schools. Start with the association's Web site.

- ✔ **Has your employer recommended specific skills training (for instance, database management)?** Your human resources department may already have a subscription to a provider that delivers such training online. This is big business!

When you search for any individual course, read the prerequisite information carefully so you know whether that course is available to you independently or whether you can only take it if you're enrolled in a specific degree or certificate program.

Checking Out Different Structures of Online Courses

After you know that you can find a class you need at your institution of choice, your next consideration should be the structure of the class. Structure refers to whether the course is completely online or a blend of online and face-to-face time, instructor led or self-paced, and real-time or asynchronous. If you have recently searched for a college course, you may already recognize that quite a variety of structures is available. This section helps you sort through some of the differences.

Before getting to the different course structures, it's worthwhile to establish a baseline for classes in general. Every course typically has two components:

- **Content:** The guts of the course, or what you are to learn. The content of an accounting course is accounting. The content of a history course is the history of whatever you are studying, and so on.

- **Evaluation:** A nice word for figuring out what grade you earn. In many cases, testing determines your grade, but it may also be determined by a final paper or project.

Ideal courses also include a third component: practice. In other words, somewhere between content and evaluation, the student gets to practice what is being learned, either through homework assignments, short papers, or other activities.

Just you and the monitor (fully online) versus blended courses (partly online)

One big consideration for courses should be whether they're completely online or a blend of online and traditional class time.

- A *completely online course* means just that. You complete all the work online. You could enroll in a course at a school that's physically located across the globe because you won't need to travel. Because of the popularity of online courses, institutions readily identify which classes are online.

Book VII

Going Further to Get Ahead

✔ *Blended courses* are a combination of online screen time and traditional *seat time* (the amount of time a student sits in a seat in a classroom). Faculty appreciate blended formats because they can move portions of instruction online, thus freeing up class time for other activities. For example, the instructor may ask you to read articles, complete quizzes, or watch prerecorded lectures online. In the class time on campus, she may have groups work on projects, conduct a lab, or host a class discussion.

The major advantages of blended courses are human contact and accountability. Students aren't likely to slip through the cracks or procrastinate when a teacher has real face time with them every week. And yet, the student can work on other available course materials when it's convenient for them and may benefit from the independence and reflective thinking that often accompanies online courses.

An obvious disadvantage of the blended format is that you need to live close enough to drive to campus for the regularly scheduled meetings. If you enroll in a course at a college that is three hours from home, this could be a significant nuisance, not to mention an undue expense.

Some colleges fail to advertise the blended requirements of traditional classes appropriately. For example, you could enroll in a business management course that meets Mondays and Wednesdays, only to learn during the first week that you're also required to log in twice a week and complete activities online. For this reason, be sure to ask about the structure of a course before enrolling and putting your money down. If the academic advisor or registrar can't answer your question, go directly to the instructor.

Instructor-led courses versus self-paced courses

Online education is about connecting the student to educational materials by way of the Internet. As shown throughout this chapter, online education can happen in a variety of forms and fashions, but the underlying use of the Internet and its technologies are fundamental. Lessons, communication, and assessment (grading) all happen by way of the World Wide Web. The following sections describe the two major models for this communication and assessment: instructor-led and self-paced.

Instructor-led courses

An instructor-led course is just what you think it is; an instructor determines what happens with the content, pace of instruction, and evaluation. Here are a few distinguishing traits of this type of course, which is the most common type out there:

- ✔ **In an instructor-led course, there is a distinct schedule, and the whole class works through the content at the same time.** While you are reading and completing activities for module two, so is the rest of the class. Typically, you find the schedule posted as a calendar or within the class syllabus. If you're a procrastinator, an instructor-led course can keep you on task.

- ✔ **Not only do you interact with your peers, but you have regular communication with the instructor.** The instructor is present and virtually "visible" through regular announcements and interaction in public discussions.

    Be sure to read the regular announcements posted by the instructor. Doing so not only keeps you on task and on time, but also helps you avoid looking silly by asking a question she has already addressed.

    You also see the instructor through private communication. As you complete assignments and turn them in, the instructor communicates with you and provides feedback. This may come via private e-mail or by way of the electronic grade book. This communication reminds you that the virtual classroom has a live instructor and you're not alone.

- ✔ **You don't see the whole course at once.** This fact may be one of the most distinctive features of an instructor-led course. Many instructors prefer to time-release the content according to when the students need it. In other words, if you're in the fourth week of an eight-week course, you may not be able to see the content for weeks five and beyond. You only see the week you're working on. This strategy keeps all the students in the same place and prevents discussions from becoming disjointed and confusing.

    If you find yourself in a course that uses the time-release method and you know in advance that you'll be traveling, let your instructor know the dates you'll be on the road. Ask whether it's possible for you to view some of the content in advance so that you won't fall behind if you experience technological difficulties getting connected to the Internet.

Three basic components of an online course are mentioned earlier in this chapter: content, evaluation, and practice. An instructor-led course is more likely to have the practice component than a self-paced course because someone is available to check your homework and smaller assignments. Your learning can be evaluated through means other than traditional testing. It takes the capacity of a real human to read someone's essay and determine whether it makes sense. A computer can't possibly evaluate that kind of assignment as well as an instructor. If practicing what you're learning is important to you, an instructor-led class is right for you.

Self-paced courses

In a self-paced course, you're on your own to determine your schedule, so if you're a self-starter, you may find this type of course to your liking. The content, or what you're going to learn, is predetermined. When you access the course, you usually find that it has been divided up into modules or units. You click on the first unit, read the content, and move through the course at your own pace. You can spend more time in the challenging areas and breeze through those that are easier for you.

In a business setting, self-paced courses are often prepackaged with very simple software interfaces.

These courses have navigational tools to help you move through the content. You'll probably see arrows at the bottom to help you advance and a menu on the left. You use these tools to help you move through the content at your own pace.

Just because a course is self-paced doesn't mean there isn't an instructor standing by in the wings to help you with questions or concerns. Consider the case of Carrie. Wanting to learn better keyboarding skills, she enrolled in an online course through her local community college. The introductory information came from an instructor who guided Carrie through the process of downloading and installing special software for working through the lessons. All the lessons were made available when the course started, and they could be completed any time during the eight-week period. There were no scheduled meetings, and Carrie could work at her leisure.

Even self-paced courses often have instructors assigned to monitor what's happening, but before enrolling, find out what that person does. Will you have regular contact throughout the course or just at the beginning or end? Can you call with questions? When you identify a potential self-paced course, see whether the instructor has an e-mail address available and ask! If no instructor is assigned to the course, be wary.

What about evaluation? How does the person in charge know that you learned the content? In the business world, most often this comes through traditional testing. After you read or listen to a portion of the content, you take a short quiz that's embedded in the program. These quizzes test your ability to recall or apply what you learned.

Determining whether the course you want is instructor-led or self-paced

How do you know the difference between an instructor-led course and a self-paced course when you're doing the research described earlier in this chapter? This is where you need to drill down to course descriptions. See whether they include terms like *instructor-led*. If nothing is mentioned but the name of the instructor is listed, e-mail that person and ask whether the course is self-paced. This information helps you succeed because you know what to expect. It also makes you look very savvy in the instructor's eyes!

Sometimes schools don't mention that the courses are instructor-led, and a lot of students sign up thinking they'll be taking independent-study courses. It's worth asking about before you register so you don't waste time or money.

Asynchronous (on your schedule) courses versus synchronous (real-time) courses

Most online courses are *asynchronous* in nature, meaning you do the work when it's convenient for you. As long as you meet the deadlines for assignments, all is good. However, instructors may also have *synchronous components* to their courses, such as weekly meetings, and some instructors require attendance or participation. For example, an instructor may host a weekly office hour during which he reviews assignments and introduces extra material.

This information should be available in the course description. However, be sure to ask an academic advisor about this possibility if you don't see any reference to synchronous sessions. Better safe than sorry!

Book VII

Going Further to Get Ahead

Finishing Your Schooling Faster with Accelerated Programs and Courses

Teachers would love for you to believe that learning is fun, but the truth is that it can be a major headache and very disruptive to real life! For that reason, you may really appreciate the speed at which you can finish schooling online.

Now that colleges and universities have discovered a ready market of busy students who want to learn on their own time, they want to enroll and keep those customers. A great way to achieve this is to make sure the courses hold the students' interest and move quickly. With this in mind, many institutions offer *accelerated courses,* which are traditional 16-week semester courses that have been condensed into half the time. Eight weeks is a common length for an online course.

Do course catalogs and descriptions specify which courses are accelerated? Nope, not necessarily. It's up to you, smart reader, to do the math. If you see a three-credit-hour course with start/end dates indicating that it runs 8 weeks, it's accelerated. A traditional course would extend a semester, or 16 weeks.

Also, if you see marketing materials that recommend only taking one course at a time, it's probably because the courses are accelerated and very demanding. After all, you're fitting 16 weeks' worth of content into less time.

This section describes the pros and cons of accelerated online education and provides a few pointers for surviving such programs and courses.

The benefits and challenges of accelerated programs

The good news is that accelerated courses generally teach you information you can apply right away. Have you ever heard the phrase "use it or lose it"? That's the mantra of instructional design for accelerated courses. Courses require students to apply the content right away through ongoing assignments. The more you use the information, the more likely you are to learn and retain it.

Obviously, if a course is accelerated, you get more information in less time. In theory, you can complete a degree in half the time. However, the reality is that how much information you take in depends on your own capacity to absorb information. In other words, if your jug (brain) is full of holes (distracted or disorganized), it won't matter how much water (knowledge) you pour in. You'll never hold it all!

So yes, with accelerated courses you receive more information in less time, but you have to be sure you have the time and the study strategies to process this information.

Tips for successfully completing accelerated classes

So how do you succeed in an accelerated course? Here are a few handy guidelines:

- **Enroll in only one course at a time until you know what you can handle.** You may even find degree programs that limit the number of courses you can take simultaneously at first for this very reason.

✔ **Establish a definite schedule for study.** Procrastination doesn't work well online, even for self-paced courses. Log in daily.

✔ **Set reasonable goals for participation.** You don't have to answer every post. Check your course requirements and exceed them slightly, but not extremely!

✔ **If you're really crunched for time and have discussions to read, hit the first posts from the original authors.** Unless your instructor says "you must read every post," you can get by skipping a few responses here and there.

✔ **Develop a method for saving links and resources that you want to go back to later.** For some people, this means keeping a running document where they paste links and URLs. For others, it means opening an account on a social bookmarking tool like delicious (`www.delicious.com`). The point is that you don't have to read everything immediately.

✔ **Save projects from one course to the next.** This isn't necessarily so you can repurpose them, but so you can draw on the resources, methods, and so on that you've previously utilized.

✔ **Work ahead if you can.** Take advantage of a slow week to get a head start on the next one.

✔ **Keep in mind the intensity will only last eight weeks!** There's great comfort in knowing that it won't go on forever, even if you love the class.

✔ **If you're working on a degree that involves a thesis, try to connect all your assignments to your thesis.** Pick a topic early in your studies, and investigate different angles throughout the various courses.

✔ **Set time aside at the beginning of the course for the basics.** Read your syllabus, become familiar with the course navigation, and begin reading the text.

✔ **Take advantage of synchronous tools.** When you're conducting group work, using the phone and Web conferencing tools is more productive than writing e-mails, especially during the organizing process.

Chapter 2

Debunking Myths about Online Education

....

In This Chapter

▶ Exposing the common myths of online education

▶ Revealing the truth about learning online

....

Despite the growing popularity of online courses, a number of myths related to online learning persist. People don't know what to make of studying and learning online. This chapter busts the most common myths about online education and gives you plenty of information about what really goes on in online education so you're prepared to make the right choices for your professional development.

Online Education Is Anytime, Anywhere

One of the best features of online education is that you get to work when it's convenient for you. Suppose you're a supervisor assigned to the third shift, and you work from 11 p.m. to 7 a.m. You may be able to squeeze in a morning class, but chances are that your biorhythms put you in a groggy state after work. You could sleep a little and then wake up and take a night class before your shift, but then when are you going to do your homework? And, what about tomorrow night when your son has a Little League game? Online education is great because it works around your schedule — anytime and anywhere you want, right? Well, it's not quite that simple.

Online courses come in two flavors: synchronous and asynchronous. In a *synchronous* (real-time) course, you meet at a prescribed time using Web conferencing software. Like in a regular classroom, you need to be available at the right time in order to participate in the class. In an *asynchronous* course, you don't have a set time to meet; in effect, you can show up to class whenever you want. This setup is especially convenient if you're the third-shift supervisor mentioned in the earlier example or if you just like to work on your own schedule. That said, students sometimes struggle because they fail to recognize that even an asynchronous course maintains its own kind of schedule.

Make sure you know what kind of course you're taking before you run into problems. The following sections provide more detail about the distinction between synchronous and asynchronous classes.

The other area in which the myth "Online education is anytime, anywhere" breaks down is the *anywhere* part. In theory, you should be able to travel and do your work as long as you have a decent Internet connection. However, experience shows that online education and travel don't always mix! If you must take a two-week business trip in the midst of an eight-week course, consider postponing enrollment. Even if your hotel has free Internet, do you really want to come back after a long day of traveling, introductions, meetings, and business dinners and do homework? The reality is that you probably won't.

Asynchronous learning

When a class is *asynchronous,* it doesn't meet at an appointed time. This type of online education is the most flexible because there is no synchronization of schedules. However, that's not to say that there isn't any schedule at all. Your asynchronous class may have a very definite schedule of due dates for assignments and activities. For instance, every week an assignment may be due on Monday at midnight. When you work on that assignment, however, is entirely up to you. If working at 5 a.m. before you head off to work is good for you, then that's when you go to class! On the other hand, if you prefer to study after the 11 p.m. news, you can go to class then. By not having synchronized schedules, students can attend to coursework when it's convenient.

You can see that asynchronous learning represents a big difference between online education and traditional education. While you may complete homework on your own schedule, very few traditional schools allow you to show up when it's convenient! On the other hand, most online schools assume you will work when it's convenient, while submitting assignments according to the prescribed schedule.

Synchronous (real-time) learning

Some online education requires a coordinated or synchronized schedule, hence the term *synchronous* learning. In this situation, you're provided a schedule of times to be available and explicit instructions concerning the software you need to connect with others.

Real-time learning most closely approximates traditional education; the meeting time is specific. Courses use synchronous time a few different ways:

✔ Some instructors require classes to meet so that they can lecture in real time. This also allows them to interact with students and determine whether students are following along in class.

✔ Other instructors host online office hours or informal times when they're available to answer student questions. These instructors may not have a specific agenda for that time but are open to whatever the student needs.

✔ You may be involved in a group project. Synchronous meetings provide an excellent method to get a lot of work done in short order.

Keep in mind these synchronous or scheduled meetings don't require you to be in the same *physical* place. While you may have to get online at a certain time, you can do so from the comfort of your home, office, or hotel room. And if you want to wear your pajamas, no one will be the wiser!

The business world loves synchronous meetings. Companies have been saving time and money by offering part of their employee education through synchronous Webinars and online conference meetings. Although staff may be in different cities, everyone shows up at the same time online. Common Web conferencing software includes

✔ Adobe Connect (www.adobe.com/products/acrobatconnectpro)

✔ Elluminate (www.elluminate.com)

✔ GoToMeeting (www.gotomeeting.com)

✔ WebEx (www.webex.com)

Book VII

Going Further to Get Ahead

Online Education Is Easier Than Traditional Education

Contrary to popular belief, online education isn't easier than traditional education, it doesn't require less work, and it's not a watered-down version of a traditional course. Although you may have the opportunity to choose when and where you study, you don't get to choose the content. If you're taking an online history course, you're going to study the same material that you would if you sat in a traditional classroom. However, there are significant differences in the way you get the information and what you do with it, as the following sections explain.

Although online education is not easier, you may find that you do better when you can do the work when it suits your lifestyle and schedule (as long as you still meet required deadlines set forth by the instructor). For instance, you may struggle to stay alert if you have to go to class at 7 a.m., but you may find yourself more attentive and interested if you can "go to class" online at 8 p.m.

Doing the same amount of work, often in less time

In an accredited educational program, the amount of work expected of a student is the same whether the course is delivered in a traditional classroom or online. If you attend a course offered once a week in a regular classroom, for example, the instructor may lecture or guide activities for three hours and expect you to work on your own completing readings or assignments for another six hours, resulting in a total of nine hours of active involvement in learning. The same course transferred online may deliver the lecture or activities by way of technology tools, but the assignments and the outcomes are the same. And most importantly, you're expected to be engaged for approximately nine hours total.

However, many online programs are accelerated, which has the potential of doubling your workload per course. For example, an on-campus course might take 16 weeks, whereas online, the same course covering the same amount of material may be only 8 to 12 weeks. That's not any easier, especially since you may be working full time as well. (Chapter 1 of Book VII has more details on accelerated courses and programs.)

If you're considering enrolling in an online course because you think it will be an easy, independent study, think twice! Read the course materials very carefully before enrolling. Chances are good that your course will require a substantial amount of dedicated time and that you will have to adhere to definite deadlines.

Taking responsibility for your own learning

Because online education requires students to take more responsibility for their own learning, it can be *more* challenging than traditional education! You may have to work a little harder to understand the concepts, and chances are you'll be asked to do more than read a chapter and take a test. You're required to use critical thinking, to share your ideas in writing (not just by talking), and to demonstrate that you understand the material in ways other than by taking tests.

In addition, online education is more challenging for those who struggle with time management and study skills. Some students find it easier to attend a face-to-face class because the teacher's physical presence motivates them to complete assignments. If that describes you, you may struggle with an online course. Hopefully, if you're motivated enough to enroll in courses for your professional development, you're motivated enough to see them through whether or not a teacher is looking over your shoulder.

Trying new learning methods and technologies

Online education stretches most learners. In addition to a full workload, you have the added difficulty of learning online procedures and processes that feel awkward at first, and you have to become comfortable with any new technology tools the instructor may throw in. How well you adapt to these additional challenges can make a difference in your overall survival online. Following is a short list of some of the tools or methods you may face online:

- ✔ **Group work:** Very common online. Instructors pair up students or assign them to small discussion groups to work out a problem.

- ✔ **Wiki:** A Web page that different people can edit. It's a simple tool that is used in group work. If you can edit a Word document, you can handle a wiki.

- ✔ **Blog:** A Web page that you may use two ways. You may just be asked to go to a blog and read the entries. Or you may be asked to keep a blog — kind of like a public journal — of what you experience in the class.

- ✔ **Webinar:** A live session where you can hear a presenter and see images. Instructors who have live office hours often use a similar tool.

- ✔ **Chat or IM:** Instant communication used for asking a question or working in real time with another person or a group.

- ✔ **Podcasts:** Audio files that you can download and play on your computer or on your portable MP3 device.

Book VII

Going Further to Get Ahead

Online Education Is Lower in Quality Than Traditional Education

In the early days of online education, some courses were little more than technology-enhanced correspondence courses with hardly any accountability as to how well the students learned. Online education has come a long way since then, and today's online courses offer the same standards and outcomes as traditional courses. Not only does research fail to reveal a statistically significant difference between online and traditional delivery methods, but it also fails to show that online courses are of lower quality. In fact, reputable institutions routinely review their courses using accepted standards of quality. Online programs are also beginning to participate in separate accreditation processes from agencies such as the United States Distance Learning Association.

Look for an accredited program or institution. Accreditation status is important for both you and the institution. From the institution's perspective, it provides credibility and status within the academic community, and becomes an important marketing tool. Accredited schools also have the ability to attract more highly-qualified students, like you.

The benefits from your perspective as a student include the following:

- ✔ You know that quality standards have been reviewed and met.

- ✔ You can market yourself to prospective employers who look for applicants from accredited schools and programs.

- ✔ You enhance your chances for graduate school. Having an existing undergraduate degree from an accredited institution is often a minimum requirement when applying for graduate school. Although it doesn't guarantee that your credits will transfer, it definitely helps.

- ✔ You have an increased likelihood of receiving financial aid. Students attending nonaccredited institutions may be ineligible for student assistance such as federal/state aid and tuition reimbursement programs.

The following sections explain the two types of accreditation and how to determine the accreditation status of the school or program you're considering.

Recognizing the two types of accreditation

Schools themselves can be accredited, and programs within schools can be accredited. (And yes, an accredited school can have accredited programs!):

- ✔ **Institutional accreditation:** This means that all the parts of the institution work well together to meet its overall mission. There are both national and regional accreditation-granting organizations. Though national accreditation may sound like a higher level of accreditation, regional accreditation tends to be more credible.

- ✔ **Specialized or programmatic accreditation:** This means that a specific program within the school has successfully completed the accreditation process relevant to its field. For example, if you look at Eastern Illinois University's education program, you will find that it is accredited through the specialist level by the Commission on Institutions of the North Central Association of Colleges and Schools and by the National Council for Accreditation of Teacher Education for the preparation of elementary and secondary teachers and school service personnel. This means that this college meets general academic quality standards, plus standards specific to the education of future teachers. Most specialized accreditors only confer the accreditation status to programs within a regionally accredited institution. However, this isn't always the case. A few will accredit institutions that are not regionally accredited.

When looking at colleges and universities, investigate whether the institution is accredited and, if so, at what level. Don't be surprised if you find that community colleges are accredited at the institution level but not at the program level. It simply depends on the programs the institution offers and the level of program completion they provide. For example, most community colleges provide enough math courses to fulfill general studies prerequisites, but do not offer a degree in mathematics. Therefore, they're not likely to have an accredited math program.

Determining whether an online program is accredited

Most institutions are proud of their accreditation status and want to show it off. Therefore, determining whether an institution is accredited usually isn't difficult. In most cases, you can find out by visiting the institution's Web site and clicking on the About Us or Academics link. If you can't find it on the Web site, your academic advisor will definitely be able to share this information with you.

The demand for alternative education delivery methods to meet the needs of busy adults has increased dramatically over the last decade. Unfortunately, as a result, several institutions have tried to quickly capitalize on this by creating *diploma mills,* which are nonaccredited institutions offering quick, online degrees without quality standards or properly trained faculty. Here are few things to look for that may identify an organization as a diploma mill:

- ✔ The institution has a name very similar to a more well-known university.
- ✔ The institution is not accredited by an agency approved by the U.S. Department of Education.
- ✔ Students can earn degrees in very little time compared to other institutions. No one can get a degree in 30 days!
- ✔ There are no admissions criteria. For example, if you're researching a Bachelor of Nursing program that doesn't require a RN degree or any clinical experience, be careful.
- ✔ The cost to attend the institution is much less than any other college or university offering the same program.

In response, an equally aggressive movement has arisen to establish quality standards for online courses. Organizations such as Quality Matters (www. qualitymatters.org) provide schools with benchmarks and a process they can use to assure quality in the way they offer online courses. Schools may conduct other internal reviews. Be sure to ask every school you're interested in about how they monitor the quality of their online programs.

Book VII

Going Further to Get Ahead

Other factors that contribute to an institution's credibility

As you conduct your research regarding an institution's accreditation status, also look for other signs that the institution is a credible one. Following are some additional criteria for evaluating online programs and courses. These include the awards and recognition they've received, as well as the research conducted at the school. In most cases, institutions highlight this information on their Web sites as a way of enhancing their marketing efforts.

- ✔ **National awards and recognition:** Look for awards that are bestowed specifically to online academic programs or individual courses. Other awards that you may want to keep an eye out for are those bestowed on faculty. Faculty awards for work within the field or excellence in teaching are both indicators of quality.

- ✔ **Leading research efforts in the field of distance education:** Another indicator of quality is whether the faculty study the impact of online education. For example, the University of Wisconsin in Madison, Nova Southeastern University in Fort Lauderdale, and Indiana University in Bloomington are all well-known for their research in online education.

- ✔ **Consortium membership:** By joining a consortium (a group of like-minded institutions), schools have access to training, research in the field, and cutting edge practices that help ensure quality.

Online Education Is Less Personal Than Traditional Education

An amusing video on the Internet shows a professor refusing to accept a late exam from a student. The student asks, "Do you know who I am?" to which the professor replies that he doesn't. The student jams his paper into the middle of the stack of exams, smirks, and walks away. That's impersonal!

You can't hide in an online course. Your instructor will get to know you and your ideas possibly better than he would have had you sat in a traditional classroom and said nothing. This is because the majority of online classes, like the workplace, require participation; you can't log in and lurk and not do the work. In fact, if you try to approach your course that way, you're going to have a few intimate conversations with your instructor! Your boss wouldn't let you get away with shirking, and neither will your instructor.

Do you need a Webcam for an online class?

No one needs to see you sitting in your pajamas at the computer. While Webcams have real advantages for communication, they're rarely required in online courses. For starters, you only use a Webcam if you have a synchronous component that accommodates video; for example, an office hour in a Web-conferencing tool. Even then, because Webcams require greater bandwidth, instructors may ask you to turn them off. However, it doesn't hurt to go ahead and purchase a headset with a microphone for those occasional synchronous sessions.

Most of the communication in an online course occurs on the discussion boards or via e-mail. These are not communication tools that require a real-time connection or video. If classmates are curious about what you look like, a photo works just as well.

Online education can actually be much more personal than traditional courses. Have you ever noticed that some people feel free to disclose information about themselves to strangers? Some instructors report similar occurrences with online students, indicating that students are freer to share insights and personal details that support course concepts than they would if they had to face a classroom full of live people.

In a robust online course, you can expect to see communication occurring on several different levels. Messages are directed toward the class as a whole from the instructor, individually from the instructor to single students (and from students to the instructor), and from student to student. If you were to visually plot that network of messages, a good course would look messy because there would be so many connections between learners. This section examines some of the primary ways people communicate in an online course.

Book VII

Going
Further to
Get Ahead

Instructor-to-class communication in news and announcements

Think about the first day of school at a traditional college. Assuming security remembers to unlock the classroom door, the instructor stands at the front of the class and welcomes students. Entering the virtual classroom isn't much different. Typically a welcome message or some kind of greeting from the instructor awaits you. This communication is intended to be read by every member of the class. It may be posted on the course's home page in a "News and announcements" area, or within a specially designated discussion forum (discussions are described later in this chapter). This kind of introductory message lets you know that you're in the right place. It may also tell you what to do next. After that initial announcement, your instructor may use the same public method for several different purposes. She may use announcements to

- ✓ **Keep everyone on task.** For example, if you're three days into the course and no one has been brave enough to post the first assignment, the instructor may post an announcement to reinforce the procedures and help students feel more comfortable trying the assignment. Again, this announcement may appear on the course's home page or in a discussion forum.

- ✓ **Post transitional information.** She may summarize what the class examined in the previous unit and preview what's to come in the next unit. Read these kinds of summaries with the idea of mentally testing yourself. Do you know what the instructor is talking about? If not, go back and review!

- ✓ **Reinforce news that you should know from the institution.** For example, occasionally the school needs to shut down its servers for maintenance. They may e-mail you and post a message on the portal or first page you log in to, but chances are good your instructor will remind you again.

Read *all* the messages posted by your instructor, even if you're tempted to bypass lengthy messages in favor of getting to your next task. Instructors include pertinent information in their messages. Plus, you spare yourself the embarrassment of asking a question that was already addressed in an announcement.

Student-to-student communication in discussions

A course in which students actively discuss and debate is a course where the learners are interested! It's also a course that demonstrates active, engaged learning at its best. Hopefully, this is the kind of communication you find most common within your course.

Many online courses follow a *social-constructivist* format of presenting information and then asking students to discuss and add to the concept. By writing about how the materials fit into the world or one's profession, everyone in the class gets a clearer picture of the subject matter. Collectively, they construct their understanding. For that reason, instructors ask students to engage in discussions with one another.

One-on-one communication via private e-mail or messaging

Private, one-on-one communication is meant for your eyes only and may come through your e-mail or an internal messaging feature if your course management system supports this.

Whenever possible, use the tools that are available within the course management system to communicate. For example, your system may have built-in instant messenger type tools that you can use when the other person is online. If the person isn't online when you send the message, she receives it when she next logs in. Your system may also have an internal e-mail that doesn't require you to give out your personal e-mail address. The advantage of sending and receiving messages within the system is that your academic work is all recorded in one place. You don't have to sort through your Aunt Tilda's forwarded jokes to find the instructor's note.

The following sections describe several types of private communication: instructor-to-student, student-to-instructor, and student-to-student.

Instructor-to-student communication

Instructors communicate with students privately for several reasons.

- ✔ **They send feedback.** Many instructors like to follow longer assignments, such as papers, with comments. While these can be posted in an electronic grade book, there usually isn't sufficient space. Therefore, instructors e-mail comments and feedback.

- ✔ **They nudge**. Occasionally, you may have a really nice instructor who notices you're not making the deadlines. She may send you a little note to remind you to stay on task.

- ✔ **They praise and send additional resources.** Sometimes an instructor wants to acknowledge excellent work from a student and perhaps provide additional resources that the rest of the class wouldn't be interested in. This may be a case for private communication.

- ✔ **They communicate grades to you.** Thank goodness! Actually, your instructor must communicate grades privately by law. Your grades and feedback can't be posted publicly.

Student-to-instructor communication

Not only can instructors send students private communication, but students may also need to communicate privately with instructors. Why would you want to communicate with your instructor privately? Here are some reasons:

Book VII

Going Further to Get Ahead

✔ **You're in distress.** Something is going on in your life that requires your attention and is preventing you from focusing on school or completing your assignments. The whole class doesn't need to know about this, but your instructor does. This is a case for private e-mail.

✔ **You're experiencing technological difficulties**. Whenever you have a problem with your computer, the software, or the system and need to work with technical support, it's a good idea to also inform your instructor. He may not be able to remedy the situation, but at least this alerts him to the problem.

✔ **You want to ask a question specifically about your academic work.** Instructors cannot discuss your work publicly; it's against the law! Therefore, if you ask a question in a public forum about your performance, your instructor can't answer it. On the other hand, you can discreetly e-mail the instructor to ask about your work.

When it comes to communicating with your instructor, diplomacy is the best policy. In other words, try not to push the instructor beyond reasonable expectations. Most institutions have faculty guidelines related to how quickly instructors should respond to e-mails — usually within 24 to 48 hours. If you send an SOS at midnight, don't expect a response right away!

Student-to-student communication

Students can privately communicate with one another, too. For example:

✔ **E-mail is a way to continue conversations that may be of interest to only you and one other person.** For example, if you read that your classmate Sarah has an interest in the culture-based health issues specific to the Polish community and you're a Polish immigrant, you may want to e-mail her privately to share some family stories. Having the opportunity to continue a conversation with one of your peers keeps you from overposting on discussions as well.

✔ **Students may work through group projects via e-mail.** E-mail allows you to exchange files, send updates, and establish meetings. Plus, it's easy to copy your instructor on the e-mail so she knows your group's progress.

✔ **Sometimes students exchange instant message (IM) screen names.** IMs may be another way of communicating some of the same student-to-student information, but that assumes you're lucky enough to catch each other online at the same time.

Other Myths You May Have Heard

So far this chapter has hit the most common misconceptions, but there are still more crazy notions about online education. The next set of myths addresses some of the beliefs that keep people from trying online courses. On the one hand, some people believe online courses are only for kids or people who don't want the kind of human interaction you'd expect in a traditional course. Or they swing to the other side of the pendulum thinking that taking an online course would be the perfect mechanism for learning how to use the computer. That needs to happen before you become an online student! Finally and sadly, many believe that since no one is watching directly, it's okay to cheat your way through online courses. This next section dispels these ideas.

Only kids take online courses

Check the statistics for some of the larger online programs, and you'll find the average online learner is middle-aged. The convenience of studying while balancing work and family attracts slightly older students to online courses. Younger, traditional-age college students are also online, but they're more likely to be blending Web-based and traditional courses at a land-based college.

In fact, adults beyond traditional college age make up a significant portion of online students, and many of these are professionals who want to enhance their careers. Earning an advanced degree or picking up courses that directly relate to your job can help you do so. Not only do you acquire the knowledge and skills you need, but you also appear to be much more motivated to employers. Furthermore, very few people these days retire from the same profession and company they started out at. Online courses can enable you to completely change career tracks without having to attend school full time for four years. Consider these examples:

- Sandra's boss wanted to move company sales online, but no one in the office understood how to manage Web pages and Internet sales. Sandra enrolled in a series of online courses at the local community college and became a very valued asset in her office.

- Karl worked as a train engineer. His job took him all over the continent and made it difficult to enroll in a traditional class. Wanting to move into a managerial role, online classes fit his lifestyle perfectly. He was able to complete a degree and stay on track!

Book VII

Going Further to Get Ahead

✔ Caryn earned a master's in nursing online while working as a surgical nurse at a local hospital. Her additional degree made it possible for her to teach nursing courses and supervise others. That meant more money!

✔ Michael was a successful mortgage seller but wanted to branch into human resources. Although he had taken college courses, he hadn't yet earned his bachelor's degree. Finishing his degree online allowed him to look for work in his field of interest as competitively as any other graduate.

If you're looking for career advancement and think that taking an online course might benefit you from a time-management perspective, look for a program that caters to working adults. Take advantage of the opportunity to talk to a live representative either via the phone or online chat and ask how many students complete the course. That will give you a good idea of how many students are satisfied as well as how attentive the school and faculty are to making sure their offerings work for students. See Book VII, Chapter 1 for more information on researching different schools.

The notion that young kids know how to use computers to their advantage and slightly older students do not is an erroneous assumption. Don't overlook the computer skills of working professionals. Few of us get through our workday without e-mail, shared projects, and collaboration. These are the same skills needed in online education!

Online education is always independent

While you may do a considerable amount of work independently, such as reading or writing assignments, most online courses require students to interact with each other in a manner that is far from independent. Following are two examples:

✔ **Discussion forums:** In discussion forums, students read one another's submissions and comment on or reply to them. This becomes a rich exchange of ideas and extends everyone's understanding of the concepts. This manner of learning is hardly independent! In fact, it can't happen without participation from multiple voices, including the instructor's.

✔ **Group projects:** Group projects are carried out online, too. Often students collaborate with peers to create a final product. These situations may require even more time and commitment specific to communicating with others than traditional classroom projects.

People working in the 21st century must be able to participate productively in teams and groups (both across distances and with others just over the cubicle walls), and teamwork rather than independence seems to rule in online courses as well.

An online course is a great way to learn how to use your computer

This statement may be true if you're enrolled in a personal development course on using a computer. However, for the kinds of courses that are discussed in this book, taking an online course to learn how to use your computer is a very bad idea. People who do this spend so much time focusing on learning to use their computer that they waste money by not learning anything about the content area of the course. Why pay $300 for a geology course and not learn about rocks?

Additionally, the instructor may not have the time or patience to walk you through every little course-related task. Even if you have 24/7 technical support, their job is to help you with software related to your course, not tell you how to use your computer.

In fairness to the other students and your instructor, learn how to use your computer well before you enroll in an online course. Here is a short list of skills that you should have before you enroll. You should be able to

✔ Turn on your computer and start a Web browser (the software application that connects to the Internet).

✔ Navigate the Web including opening links in new tabs or windows.

✔ Create a folder on your hard drive to store course-related information and know how to locate that information for later access.

✔ Open and answer e-mail with and without attachments.

✔ Download and install applications and application plug-ins.

Book VII

Going Further to Get Ahead

You do need to understand the basics of how your computer works and how to find files (see the preceding section), but you don't need to be a full-fledged geek to survive in an online course! If even the basics of using a computer elude you, contact your local two-year college or continuing education department and see what kinds of basic computer courses they offer. Chances are very good that they have an introductory course that would be perfect for you.

Everyone cheats online

There is no evidence of greater cheating online than in a traditional classroom. Unfortunately, too much cheating takes place everywhere! However, smart online instructors now design their courses to minimize the possibility of cheating and use tools to help them detect plagiarism. Cheating online simply doesn't pay because the technology is on the instructor's side. For example:

- ✔ Instructors ask for major projects to be submitted in pieces, showing prior drafts and revisions. Or they ask for projects that are based on personal or professional circumstances knowing that no one else could possibly write about your life the way you can.

- ✔ Some institutions use very sophisticated software that checks written submissions for plagiarism.

- ✔ Finally, some instructors actually have one-on-one conversations with students where they ask questions to see whether students are able to properly articulate course materials.

Chapter 3

Using ePortfolio to Track and Tout Your Accomplishments

. . . .

In This Chapter

▶ Creating an ePortfolio of your work

▶ Using your ePortfolio to propel yourself towards promotion

. . . .

C hapter 1 of Book VII explains how to find a program and institution that meet your needs. Why are pursuing additional education or certification? The vision of your goal should be a constant driving force throughout your academic career. Keeping your main objective in mind helps motivate you to complete courses and stay on track,

If you plan to look for the perfect job after you finish your online education, or wish to demonstrate progress in your existing job, collecting a few artifacts throughout your journey can help you when it comes time to prepare for job interviews, performance appraisal meetings, or promotional interviews. Artifacts are like souvenirs of your trip. They should demonstrate your skills and abilities within the field. This chapter introduces some ideas on how to find and prepare for that dream interview through the creation of an electronic portfolio or *ePortfolio*.

Developing an ePortfolio

A portfolio is a physical document that outlines a person's past work, both academic and professional. It demonstrates skills and abilities by providing sample work created in various work and school settings.

An ePortfolio does the same thing, but instead of sharing a physical document with prospective employers, you simply provide them with the URL to a Web site where the same information is stored digitally, available either for public viewing or by private invitation only. Figure 3-1 illustrates what a public ePortfolio may look like (specifically, this figure is the public view of the Desire2Learn ePortfolio 2.0). The illustration displays a single project a student documented on his ePortfolio site. On this particular student's site, he allows visitors to interact with him by providing the ability to leave comments specific to the information being displayed.

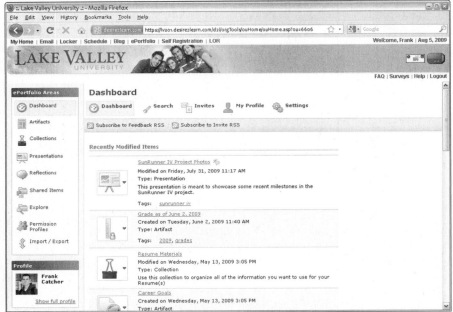

Figure 3-1: The public view of the Desire2Learn ePortfolio 2.0.

Courtesy of Desire2Learn Incorporated

This section provides a general explanation of how you can use an ePortfolio to your advantage and describes its components. The information here can help you choose a method for building an ePortfolio, provide pointers for successful design, and tell you how to include items that aren't a part of your online coursework. Be sure to refer to your institution's ePortfolio creation system for more specific details.

Understanding how to use an ePortfolio

You can use an ePortfolio in three important ways:

✔ **To satisfy educational requirements:** Many degree programs now require students to build and maintain an ePortfolio throughout their academic career as a way of documenting growth and highlighting their academic accomplishments. In this situation, students are often asked to also reflect on the experience of creating the artifacts added to the ePortfolio as a way of assessing their understanding of the project overall (see the later section "Creating reflection statements" for more information). As a degree program requirement, graduating is dependent upon the completion of the ePortfolio. Some institutions even require a formal presentation to accompany the project.

✔ **To land a job:** ePortfolios can also be used for promoting your knowledge, skills, and abilities to prospective employers. When applying for a new job or promotion, you can share your ePortfolio's Web site address (URL) with the hiring manager. The hiring manager can visit your site and get a clearer picture of your academic and work experiences to facilitate the hiring decision.

✔ **To document progress or land a promotion:** For those of you who already have a great job and wish to demonstrate improved skills and possibly be promoted within your organization, an ePortfolio is a great way to illustrate and share your progress. An ePortfolio should document professional development workshops and conferences that you have attended and/or describe on-the-job projects you have successfully completed. When appropriate, you can even share the actual product with visitors to your ePortfolio site.

Book VII

Going Further to Get Ahead

Be sure not to share private information or end products that your organization may not wish for you to share publically. If you have to question whether or not you can share something, ask for permission first. For example, if you build a database to track important client information, your organization may allow you to share the database as long as you share a blank copy of it that has no client information. This way visitors to your ePortfolio can see your skills at building a database without infringing on the privacy of your organization's clients.

Checking out typical components of an ePortfolio

You can choose several items from your online coursework to add to your ePortfolio. Choose the pieces carefully and organize your site in a manner that's logical and easy to navigate. This section reviews different types of items and provides some examples of specific information to include.

Attaching artifacts such as papers and projects

Artifacts are objects created by you that can be added to your ePortfolio as attachments. When adding artifacts to your ePortfolio, you want to be sure your audience understands why you included them. Therefore, for each artifact be sure to include a title, description, and the context in which the artifact was created.

When adding artifacts to your site, keep in mind that visitors will be downloading your work directly to their computer. Therefore, consider protecting files by converting them to PDF files before uploading and linking them to your ePortfolio. This allows visitors to open and view your documents, but not edit them.

Here are a few examples of the different types of artifacts you may want to consider adding to your ePortfolio (Figure 3-2 shows the administration page for uploading and organizing different types of artifacts in the Desire2Learn ePortfolio 2.0):

✔ **A document:** For example, an essay on the connection between Bloom's Taxonomy and ePortfolios as it relates to education. Consider using text to briefly summarize the essay's contents with a link to click on to download the document in its entirety.

✔ **Images:** Perhaps a series of digital images that you took and modified for an online photography course. Consider using text to describe the images and the purpose for taking them.

✔ **An audio file:** For instance, an audio interview you conducted with a professional in your field. Consider adding a written transcript and general description of the assignment when attaching an audio file to your ePortfolio.

✔ **A PowerPoint presentation:** Say, a group presentation on the benefits and challenges of creating and maintaining a Web site for your Web development course. Consider describing your contributions to the project and the tools you used to collaborate with your group in a reflection statement (see the next section).

✔ **A video file:** For example, a video illustrating your ability to take, edit, and encode video for your Introduction to Video Editing course. Consider adding a written transcript and general description of the assignment when attaching a video file to your ePortfolio.

If your institution doesn't require you to use an ePortfolio system, be sure to acquire your instructors' permission before posting graded work with their comments on it. Instructors may ask you not to display their comments or grades publically. The reason for this isn't that they treated you differently than other students; it's because it has the potential to stir up other classmates who may not have done as well as you.

Creating reflection statements

Reflection statements are used in the academic world as a way of helping the instructor assess your process as well as your final product. These statements can be very helpful to both instructors and employers reviewing your ePortfolio for either academic or professional reasons. For example, by seeing your reflections on a project you completed in school, an employer can see how you organize and process information in order to obtain a goal.

The length of a reflection statement can range from one paragraph to multiple pages, depending on the context. A good rule of thumb is to briefly describe the project, the educational objectives it meets, how the project can be applied, and what you learned from completing the project. For example, following is a reflection on an assignment requiring the creation of an ePortfolio Web site:

> *By requiring me to organize and document all of my academic, professional, and volunteer experiences, I have been able to better understand where I have been, where I am currently, and where I am going. As a part of this project, I was required to learn about the resources and services available to create an online portfolio. The design process required me to develop a site that organizes my information into manageable chunks while maintaining an easy navigation structure for my visitors. This project also forced me to reflect on each assignment and how lessons learned could be applied in my life outside of the classroom. As a living document, my ePortfolio will continue to be updated and therefore require me to continuously reflect and grow with my field.*

Book VII

Going Further to Get Ahead

Figure 3-2:
An artifact in the Desire2Learn ePortfolio 2.0.

Courtesy of Desire2Learn Incorporated

Providing informal transcripts of courses

Posting transcripts on your ePortfolio Web site lets your visitors see your level of dedication and provides a general sense of the quality of your work. You can let your visitors know what grade you earned for each course or your cumulative grade point average (GPA) for a program in a couple ways:

✔ **You can simply provide your cumulative grade point average (for example, 4.8/5.0) on the program description page and the actual grade earned (A, B, and so on) next to the title of each course.** In this case, the reader has to believe you.

✔ **You can scan your official transcript, adding it to your ePortfolio as an artifact and linking to it from your program's description page.** Of course, scanning your transcript, even an official transcript, takes away its official status. Prospective employers may still require you to send them an official transcript directly from the institution in a sealed envelope.

If for any reason you had a bad semester (and many people do), consider not adding this information to your ePortfolio. Most employers don't require this information, and if they do, you can supply them with official transcripts upon request. Being consistent in presentation and supplying this information for all courses and programs is better than posting it only for those courses you did well in.

Including recommendations from faculty

There are no better people to serve as your advocates than your instructors. They know the quality of work you produce and the level of dedication you put forth to complete your assignments. Therefore, be sure to build a professional relationship with them and don't be afraid to ask them for letters of recommendation. Here are some guidelines to follow:

✔ **Be selective about which instructors you ask for a recommendation.** You don't need a recommendation from every instructor. One way of filtering is to ask only those instructors who teach subjects that most resemble the type of work you're doing or hope to be doing in the future.

✔ **Don't wait until you've completed your program to ask for a recommendation.** Timing is everything. Think ahead and ask each instructor at the end of the course, when your participation and the quality of your work are fresh in the teacher's memory.

✔ **Provide instructors with an overview of your professional goals and a link to your ePortfolio.** Doing so helps them write a letter that matches your career goals. You can also send them your résumé if your ePortfolio is still in progress.

> ✔ **Provide instructors with two or three weeks to complete the letter.** Extending this courtesy gives them time to turn in grades and review your information more before writing.

> ✔ **Be sure to explain to your instructors exactly what you're looking for and the fact that you would like to publicly display the recommendation on your ePortfolio Web site.** Many institutions house instructor recommendations in the student's file, but these recommendations are anonymous to the student, making them unsuitable for your purpose.

Incorporating your résumé and work history

The nice thing about having an ePortfolio is that it gives you the ability to expand on things you can't fit on a two-page résumé.

Though this is a great feature, don't forget to spread chunks of information across multiple pages so that everything isn't on the same page — you don't want to overwhelm the reader. Arrange chunks of information by dates of service and organization. Following is a list of components to add when including work history in your ePortfolio:

> ✔ **Organization profile:** Provide the organization's name, geographic location, and mission.

> ✔ **Position title:** Include the title of the position(s) you held within the organization and a brief description of the position's overall purpose.

> ✔ **Dates of service:** Sequence your position titles within each organization by dates of services, in descending order. This puts your most recent experience at the top of the list.

> ✔ **Accomplishments:** Provide a bulleted list of the accomplishments by stating the tasks you handled, how you accomplished each task, and the end result in quantifiable terms when possible. For example, you may write: *Created a database that analyzed recoverable charges to the organization, which led to the company's recovery of 1.5 million dollars.*

> ✔ **Project artifacts:** Provide artifacts for the accomplishments listed when possible. For example, you could provide an empty copy of the database that was created to recover the 1.5 million dollars noted in the preceding bullet.

Don't forget to remove private information that could violate the law or have negative repercussions. For example, in the preceding database example, you'd want to share the database with either no data or fictitious data in it so that viewers could see what you developed without seeing the private information used by the organization, such as names, addresses, dollar amounts, and so forth.

Sharing favorite resource links

Providing your visitors with a list of resources proves that you're aware of what's going on within your field. Plus, it provides you with a single location to return to when you need to find information yourself. Resources can include links to professional blogs, podcasts, journal articles, associations, conferences, citation style resources, career help, and other academic resources.

This is not the place to link to your favorite satire blog, cartoon site, or daily word puzzle; stick to professional links.

Choosing a method for creating an ePortfolio

You can go about creating an ePortfolio in three different ways: You can use institutional resources, subscribe to a service, or create your own from scratch.

Using institutional resources

Your institution may incorporate the use of an ePortfolio system in its program curriculum, which you are subsequently required to use. This system may be either built-in or external:

- ✔ Some institutions build ePortfolio programs into their course management systems and tie them directly to each major assignment's rubric. This allows the student to upload the assignment and import the instructor's assessment with comments to the ePortfolio system.

- ✔ Some institutions alternatively use an external service in a similar fashion, but it requires the student to log in to a separate Web site using a different username and password. The system may also have the capability of allowing instructors to create rubrics to attach to artifacts. However, in this situation, the instructor is required to also log in to a separate system and copy/paste rubric elements and assessment comments to that system.

To find out whether or not your institution provides an ePortfolio system, first ask your academic advisor. If he is unable to help, you can either contact your instructor or career services staff. Some institutions provide a career-oriented ePortfolio product, which is often available after graduation for a yearly or monthly fee.

Either way, this type of ePortfolio system allows the institution to dictate some of the artifacts to be added, along with their respective grades and instructor comments. Required artifacts could include course essays, final projects, or reflection assignments. By having all this information in one place, program faculty and deans can see each student's growth throughout the program as a way of assessing student performance and program effectiveness.

One benefit to using your institution's required ePortfolio system is that you're already paying for it through program fees, so you won't have an external cost to use it while you're a student. However, the possible downside is the fact that you may be required to subscribe to that service upon graduation in order to maintain your site and its contents. In some situations, you get to continue using the service for one year after graduation before having to decide whether to subscribe to that service or re-create your site by building it yourself or subscribing to a different service.

Subscribing to a service

You can subscribe to a service if your school doesn't have a required ePortfolio system or you prefer to exercise more control over its contents. Several subscription-based services offer Web space for you to house and display your ePortfolio. These services offer templates for adding content and disk storage for uploading documents and other artifacts. Following are a few such services:

- ✓ **Live Text:** https://college.livetext.com/college/
- ✓ **Pupil Pages:** www.os4e.com/pupilpages/pupilpages.htm
- ✓ **TaskStream:** www.taskstream.com

Book VII

Going Further to Get Ahead

One advantage to subscribing to a service is that it provides online templates for you to complete, requiring only Web navigation skills and your portfolio content. Another advantage is the ability to lock down your site so that only invited guests can view it.

Of course, these sites cost money, so prepare to pay for the convenience and keep paying the bill. Imagine the embarrassment of sending a potential employer to your site and finding out that it's not available because you forgot to make a payment!

Creating your own ePortfolio from the ground up

The third method of building an ePortfolio is to create your own from scratch. The biggest advantage to creating your own ePortfolio is the ability to customize the design and navigation of the site to reflect your individuality. When you subscribe to a service, you're limited to the number of templates available from the service provider, which means your portfolio may physically look like those of other students who subscribe to the same service.

The biggest drawback to creating your own ePortfolio is that you're limited to your own programming skills. Programming your own site also requires more time because you have to create the design of the site as well as the content that will be placed within the site.

If you want to create your own site, you need the following:

- ✔ **A Web hosting service:** A service where you can store your site so that it's available to others with an Internet connection. One example is `http://dreamhost.com`.

- ✔ **A registered domain name:** Domain names are used as the Web site address for navigating to your site, for example, `http://kevin johnsonresume.info`. Most Web hosting services have a process that includes registering and paying for your domain.

- ✔ **Programming knowledge:** You need to be able to program using HTML or other Web programming languages, such as PHP. If your online education has focused on these languages, you're set! But if you don't have this knowledge and want to learn, consider picking up *Creating Web Pages For Dummies,* 9th Edition, by Bud E. Smith (Wiley) to help you get started. You can also consider using an HTML editing program such as Dreamweaver, which uses a more visual approach to programming, allowing the user to enter information on the screen while it writes the code in the background. And, of course there's a resource for that too if needed: *Dreamweaver CS4 All-in-One For Dummies* by Sue Jenkins and Richard Wagner, also from Wiley.

Some students have found creative ways to use free Web 2.0 tools, such as blogs and wikis, to create ePortfolios for free. These tools often require less programming skills and don't cost you a dime!

Designing a successful ePortfolio

Think about all the things you've accomplished as an employee, a volunteer, and/or a student. You probably have quite a list. The most helpful tip you can heed is to find a way to organize your information into chunks so that visitors can quickly access data without being overwhelmed. Here are a few more tips for designing a successful ePortfolio site:

- ✔ **Create a welcome page:** The first thing a visitor to your ePortfolio site should see is a welcoming screen with basic information such as your name, current position, contact information, and possibly a picture. Think of this page as a digital business card.

✔ **Create an overview page:** The overview page should include a brief overview of who you are academically/professionally, what you've learned from your school/work experience, and how your education has been applied in different situations. Think of this page as your digital cover letter, preparing visitors to view your digital résumé.

✔ **Create a top-level navigation based on categories:** Organize information into logical sections and create a Web menu and navigation system around that structure. For example, consider organizing your information using the following categories: Home, Overview, Education, Work Experience, and Community Involvement.

✔ **Create a sublevel navigation within your top-level categories:** Arrange and sequence the information in each of the top-level categories based on dates, organizations, job titles, and so on. For example, when a visitor clicks on Education, she should see a list of institutions you've attended, the dates you attended, a brief description of the programs you were enrolled in, and links that give her the option of seeing a list of specific courses, course syllabi, and course-specific projects. When a user clicks on Work Experience, a page should appear with a list of job titles, organizations, brief job descriptions, dates of employment, and links to specific job responsibilities and projects for each job. Figure 3-3 illustrates what sublevel navigation in an ePortfolio may look like (specifically, this figure shows sublevel navigation in the Desire2Learn ePortfolio 2.0).

✔ **Know your audience:** Understanding why you are creating your ePortfolio can help you design for and write to your audience. For example, you may write differently for your instructors than you would for future employers. Because your ePortfolio may be shown to multiple audiences, be sure that the description of each component reflects the intended context. For example, when writing for instructors, provide an overview of each assignment along with what you learned specific to the objectives of the course. When writing for a more general audience, again provide an overview of each assignment, along with how you scored, what you learned from the project, and how what you learned can be applied to other situations such as a work environment.

✔ **Be authentic and cite sources when necessary:** Displaying work that's authentic in nature and providing sources when you share nonoriginal ideas are important. Remember, this site is a reflection of you, including your ethical standards.

✔ **Keep your information up to date:** A portfolio is always a work in progress. However, unlike your physical portfolio, viewers may have access to your ePortfolio at any time. Therefore, it's important to keep your information current. You can also add the "last updated" date on your ePortfolio to inform readers that the information is up to date.

Book VII

Going Further to Get Ahead

Courtesy of Desire2Learn Incorporated

Figure 3-3:
Sublevel
navigation
in the
Desire2Learn
ePortfolio 2.0.

Transferring your existing portfolio to the Web

You may have previous work from volunteer, education, or workplace experiences from an existing portfolio that you want to include in an ePortfolio. Great! The next step is to prepare that material for the Web. Here is a list of the different artifact types and considerations to make when transferring them to the Web:

- ✔ **Word processing documents:** Consider converting short (one page or less) word processing documents to HTML so that visitors don't have to download them. Save longer documents as one of the more common file types so that visitors can view your work in multiple applications. Some of the more popular document types include .pdf, .rtf, and .doc. Each of these formats can be opened with either a free document viewer or a basic word-processing program that comes installed on most computers.

- ✔ **Images/photographs:** Unless you're in the field of marketing or photography, consider reducing image size and resolution to a Web-friendly configuration. Web files should be set at 72 dpi (dots per inch) and around 20 to 50k (kilobytes) in size. A great free program has been created for both Windows and Mac machines that can help you do this quickly: Gimp (`www.gimp.org`). Reducing image size and resolution allows for quick loading. Common image file types include .png, .gif, and .jpg.

Try not to place multiple images on one page when possible. The fewer the photos, the faster the page loads for your visitors.

✔ **Audio files:** Audio files are larger files and can take longer to download. Consider using a compressed audio file type such as .mp3 for adding audio to your ePortfolio. For the more advanced programmer or more up-to-date service providers, embedding streaming audio is better for longer pieces.

Streaming refers to how media such as audio and video files are delivered to a user over the Internet. Audio and video files are often large in size. If visitors are required to wait for the entire file to download to their computer before listening to or viewing the file, they may get bored and navigate to another site. Streaming audio and video files are stored on a Web server and begin to play for the visitor immediately, while slowly continuing to load in the background, so that visitors have less wait time.

✔ **Video files:** Video files are large files that can take a long time for visitors to download. Consider streaming these files as well. Common video file types include .avi and .mpg.

If large video files are needed, consider providing visitors with a clip of the video online and contact information on how to request a full-length video on CD or DVD via snail mail.

No matter what type of artifact you choose to add to your ePortfolio, make sure that each element has some introductory content that allows your visitors to quickly look at your work and choose which elements they want to explore in greater detail.

Book VII

Going Further to Get Ahead

Documenting Progress and Preparing for Promotion

Even the most dedicated employees want to challenge themselves to learn new skills and grow within an organization. Whether you have your eye on a specific promotion or simply want to improve your skills, it's always a good idea to document your progress and be prepared when a promotional opportunity presents itself. This section provides you with some ideas of what you should be tracking along with other resources to cross-reference when building an ePortfolio.

Utilizing organizational resources

Many companies can provide you with information and services that can help you plan and achieve your advancement in the company, including the following. By accessing this information (see your supervisor or your company's human resources department), you can find out about potential job openings, availability of training, and more:

- ✔ **Job descriptions:** Most employers require that all positions be described in details using a job description and task list. This information can be used to help describe your current job, required skills, and daily tasks. You can also speak to your human resources department to get the job descriptions of those positions you may wish to consider for promotional purposes. This provides you with a list of knowledge, skills, and abilities that you may need to obtain in order to be promoted. Knowing this can help you choose courses, workshops, and other resources needed to gain the necessary knowledge, skills, and abilities.

- ✔ **Internal training:** Many organizations offer in-house training. Be sure to document this training in your ePortfolio. Include the date, time, title, and description of every training session you attend. This provides your visitors with the knowledge that you are a dedicated employee open to being a lifelong learner.

- ✔ **External training funds:** Many organizations budget monies allocated for employees to attend professional development workshops and conferences. When possible, take advantage of these opportunities and document them in your ePortfolio. Also consider adding a section that describes how you plan to or currently apply information learned to your existing position.

- ✔ **Education reimbursement:** Some employers offer a reimbursement program for those wishing to go back to school and increase knowledge, skills, and abilities that would benefit both the employee and the organization. If your organization offers such benefits, take advantage of this opportunity to take additional courses in your field. Be sure to document your coursework in your ePortfolio.

Participating in professional networks

As you attend workshops, conferences, and/or classes, be cognizant of all the networking possibilities you run into. These could lead to future project collaboration, which only increases your marketability when you're ready to move up in your career. Here are a few networking opportunities to keep an eye out for:

✔ **Peer introductions:** Pay close attention to the introduction of your peers. You'll probably find that they come from a variety of backgrounds and experiences. Befriend those who currently work in your field of interest and/or have a lot of experience.

✔ **Partner and group work:** Much like the student introductions, you'll also want to network with group-work partners. Take time to introduce yourself to your partner or group, and share your goals and your current situation.

✔ **Volunteer opportunities:** Look for opportunities to volunteer within the field you're studying. By doing this, you connect with professionals in the field, demonstrate the quality of your work, and get experience to add to your résumé and ePortfolio.

✔ **Guest lecturers:** If your online course has a guest lecturer come and interact with the class, be sure to document the guest's name and contact information. One way to get on that person's radar for future interactions is to send the guest a private thank-you letter with your contact information.

✔ **Associations:** Professional fields are often defined by their associations. Though they cost to join, most associations have a student rate if you're currently taking classes. Take advantage of this while you can and join the professional organizations associated with your profession. Doing this provides you access to professionals within the field, job bulletins, and conference discounts. You may want to see if your current organization will help pay for your membership if you can prove that being a member would benefit both you and the organization. Be sure to post any professional association memberships on your ePortfolio.

✔ **Conferences:** Look for and attend conferences within your field. If none are offered locally, consider traveling and asking peers within your academic program or co-workers to split travel costs such as gas and hotel. Attending conferences is a great way to hear presentations on trends and issues within your field. Again, see if your organization can help with costs when appropriate and add your experiences to your ePortfolio.

✔ **Social networking Web sites:** You may want to take advantage of social networking applications available on the Web, such as Facebook (www.facebook.com), LinkedIn (www.linkedin.com), and MySpace (www.myspace.com). These sites provide networking opportunities on both social and professional levels. However, we recommend that you try to create separate profiles for your professional networking versus your social interactions. These sites often post updates from your friends on your profile page, and you may not want prospective employers to view that material. Keep the two separate to save any possible embarrassment.

Book VII

Going Further to Get Ahead

Index

Notes

Business/Accounting & Bookkeeping

Bookkeeping For Dummies
978-0-7645-9848-7

eBay Business
All-in-One For Dummies,
2nd Edition
978-0-470-38536-4

Job Interviews
For Dummies,
3rd Edition
978-0-470-17748-8

Resumes For Dummies,
5th Edition
978-0-470-08037-5

Stock Investing
For Dummies,
3rd Edition
978-0-470-40114-9

Successful Time
Management
For Dummies
978-0-470-29034-7

Computer Hardware

BlackBerry For Dummies,
3rd Edition
978-0-470-45762-7

Computers For Seniors
For Dummies
978-0-470-24055-7

iPhone For Dummies,
2nd Edition
978-0-470-42342-4

Laptops For Dummies,
3rd Edition
978-0-470-27759-1

Macs For Dummies,
10th Edition
978-0-470-27817-8

Cooking & Entertaining

Cooking Basics
For Dummies,
3rd Edition
978-0-7645-7206-7

Wine For Dummies,
4th Edition
978-0-470-04579-4

Diet & Nutrition

Dieting For Dummies,
2nd Edition
978-0-7645-4149-0

Nutrition For Dummies,
4th Edition
978-0-471-79868-2

Weight Training
For Dummies,
3rd Edition
978-0-471-76845-6

Digital Photography

Digital Photography
For Dummies,
6th Edition
978-0-470-25074-7

Photoshop Elements 7
For Dummies
978-0-470-39700-8

Gardening

Gardening Basics
For Dummies
978-0-470-03749-2

Organic Gardening
For Dummies,
2nd Edition
978-0-470-43067-5

Green/Sustainable

Green Building
& Remodeling
For Dummies
978-0-470-17559-0

Green Cleaning
For Dummies
978-0-470-39106-8

Green IT For Dummies
978-0-470-38688-0

Health

Diabetes For Dummies,
3rd Edition
978-0-470-27086-8

Food Allergies
For Dummies
978-0-470-09584-3

Living Gluten-Free
For Dummies
978-0-471-77383-2

Hobbies/General

Chess For Dummies,
2nd Edition
978-0-7645-8404-6

Drawing For Dummies
978-0-7645-5476-6

Knitting For Dummies,
2nd Edition
978-0-470-28747-7

Organizing For Dummies
978-0-7645-5300-4

SuDoku For Dummies
978-0-470-01892-7

Home Improvement

Energy Efficient Homes
For Dummies
978-0-470-37602-7

Home Theater
For Dummies,
3rd Edition
978-0-470-41189-6

Living the Country Lifestyle
All-in-One For Dummies
978-0-470-43061-3

Solar Power Your Home
For Dummies
978-0-470-17569-9

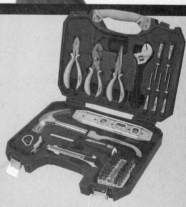